SOS– Calling All Black People

A Black Arts Movement Reader

EDITED BY John H. Bracey Jr., Sonia Sanchez, and James Smethurst

University of Massachusetts Press AMHERST AND BOSTON

ISBN 978-1-62534-031-3 (paper); 030-6 (hardcover)

Designed by Dennis Anderson
Set in Minion Pro and Gill Sans
Printed and bound by Sheridan Books, Inc.

Library of Congress Cataloging-in-Publication Data

SOS/Calling All Black People : a Black Arts Movement Reader / edited by John H. Bracey Jr.,
Sonia Sanchez, and James Smethurst.
     pages   cm
   Includes bibliographical references.
   ISBN 978-1-62534-031-3 (pbk. : alk. paper) — ISBN 978-1-62534-030-6 (hardcover : alk. paper)
   1. American literature—African American authors. 2. African Americans—Intellectual life—
20th century. 3. Black Arts movement. 4. Black nationalism—United States—History—20th century.
5. African Americans in literature. I. Bracey, John H., editor of compilation. II. Sanchez, Sonia, 1934–
editor of compilation. III. Smethurst, James Edward, editor of compilation.
   PS508.N3S66 2014
   810.8'0896073—dc23

                                                                                      2014007781

British Library Cataloguing-in-Publication Data
A catalogue record for this book is available from the British Library.

Publication of this volume and other titles in the series In the Spirit of W. E. B. Du Bois,
edited by John H. Bracey Jr., is supported by the Office of the Dean, College of Humanities
and Fine Arts, University of Massachusetts Amherst.

A Note from the Volume Editors:
We wish to acknowledge the support of our colleagues in the W.E.B. Du Bois Department of
Afro-American Studies at the University of Massachusetts Amherst. We are deeply grateful to
Chancellor Kumble Subbaswamy, Vice Chancellor for Research and Engagement Michael Malone,
and College of Humanities and Fine Arts Dean Julie Hayes for their financial support of this volume.
We wish to acknowledge also the cooperation of many of the artists who appear in this anthology.
A particular thanks is due Nelson Stevens for providing the cover art for the volume. We owe a
special debt of gratitude to Flávia Santos de Araújo for helping obtain permissions and documents
for this volume. Many thanks also to Tricia Loveland for her usual help in making all our efforts
go more smoothly.
    In the rush to get into print we neglected to mention the monumental efforts of Bruce Wilcox,
former Director of UMass Press. Bruce retired during the final stages of production, but his support
from our original conception to the final published work was steadfast and essential. Thanks Bruce,
your leadership over the years has led the Press to the forefront of academic publishing. Your rest is
well earned. Have a happy retirement.

To the Memory of

Amiri Baraka (1934–2014)

Poet. Playwright. Essayist. Novelist. Short story writer.
Critic. Educator. Steadfast warrior in the struggle for justice
for all human beings. Rest in peace, our dear brother.
A luta continua.

SOS

Calling black people
Calling all black people, man woman child
Wherever you are, calling you, urgent, come in
Black People, come in, wherever you are, urgent, calling
you, calling all black people
calling all black people, come in, black people, come
on in.

Amiri Baraka (1969)

For My People

For my people everywhere singing their slave songs
    repeatedly: their dirges and their ditties and their blues
    and jubilees, praying their prayers nightly to an
    unknown god, bending their knees humbly to an
    unseen power;

For my people lending their strength to the years, to the
    gone years and the now years and the maybe years,
    washing ironing cooking scrubbing sewing mending
    hoeing plowing digging planting pruning patching
    dragging along never gaining never reaping never
    knowing and never understanding;

For my playmates in the clay and dust and sand of Alabama
    backyards playing baptizing and preaching and doctor
    and jail and soldier and school and mama and cooking
    and playhouse and concert and store and hair and Miss
    Choomby and company;

For the cramped bewildered years we went to school to learn
    to know the reasons why and the answers to and the
    people who and the places where and the days when, in
    memory of the bitter hours when we discovered we
    were black and poor and small and different and nobody
    cared and nobody wondered and nobody understood;

For the boys and girls who grew in spite of these things to
    be man and woman, to laugh and dance and sing and
    play and drink their wine and religion and success, to
    marry their playmates and bear children and then die
    of consumption and anemia and lynching;

For the people thronging 47th Street in Chicago and Lenox
　　Avenue in New York and Rampart Street in New
　　Orleans, lost disinherited dispossessed and happy
　　people filling the cabarets and taverns and other
　　people's pockets needing bread and shoes and milk and
　　land and money and something—something all our own;

For my people walking blindly spreading joy, losing time
　　being lazy, sleeping when hungry, shouting when
　　burdened, drinking when hopeless, tied, and shackled
　　and tangled among ourselves by the unseen creatures
　　who tower over us omnisciently and laugh;

For my people blundering and groping and floundering in
　　the dark of churches and schools and clubs and
　　societies, associations and councils and committees and
　　conventions, distressed and disturbed and deceived and
　　devoured by money-hungry glory-craving leeches,
　　preyed on by facile force of state and fad and novelty, by
　　false prophet and holy believer;

For my people standing staring trying to fashion a better way
　　from confusion, from hypocrisy and misunderstanding,
　　trying to fashion a world that will hold all the people,
　　all the faces, all the adams and eves and their countless
　　generations;

Let a new earth rise. Let another world be born. Let a
　　bloody peace be written in the sky. Let a second
　　generation full of courage issue forth; let a people
　　loving freedom come to growth. Let a beauty full of
　　healing and a strength of final clenching be the pulsing
　　in our spirits and our blood. Let the martial songs be
　　written, let the dirges disappear. Let a race of men now
　　rise and take control.

Margaret Walker (1942)

CONTENTS

SECTION II. STATEMENTS OF PURPOSE: GROUPS AND JOURNALS

SECTION III. POETRY

1. Consciousness

2. Malcolm

5. Women

6. Heritage

7. Songs

SECTION IV. DRAMA

SECTION V. FICTION / NARRATIVE

AFTERWORDS

SOS–
Calling
All
Black
People

JOHN H. BRACEY JR.,
SONIA SANCHEZ, AND
JAMES SMETHURST

Editors' Introduction

The term "Black Arts Movement" (BAM) was coined by the poet, playwright, critic, and political activist Larry Neal for the outpouring of politically engaged African American art from the mid-1960s to the late 1970s, which Neal described as the "sister of the Black Power concept." BAM encompassed a wide range of ideological and aesthetic stances. Nonetheless, like the Black Power Movement, all strains of BAM were generally united by a belief in the need for personal and social transformation of African Americans to determine their own political and cultural destiny and by a sense that the movement was part of an international struggle against colonialism, neocolonialism, and racism.

One of the ironies in tracing the origins of the Black Arts Movement of the late 1960s is that two of its most important catalysts, Malcolm X and John Coltrane, died before it came to fruition. Reflected in their significant presence in the literary and visual works that were to follow, it would be difficult to overestimate the two men's role in setting both the political and the cultural agendas that made BAM such a potent force in the Black Power and Black Liberation Movements.

Rising to prominence during the years between the *Brown v. Board of Education* decision and the onset of the urban rebellions, Malcolm and Coltrane came to be seen as the twin pillars of the new outlook and attitude that gained full expression in the Black Arts Movement. Coltrane's dismantling the foundations of western music while simultaneously producing beautiful and moving works outside of its constraints demonstrated that a new world was possible. Malcolm's words made explicit the critique implicit in Coltrane's music: Do you want to integrate in a burning house? Do you want human rights or civil rights? He constantly reminded his listeners that Europeans and people of European descent were a small minority of the global population.

The broader context in which Malcolm and Coltrane evolved was the reality of the Cold War and the rapid development of the anticolonial movements stimulated by the impact of World War II on the European colonial powers. In the 1940s and early 1950s, the rise of dynamic independence movements that ultimately led to the emergence of independent states in Africa in the late 1950s and early 1960s stimulated a new engagement with traditional African arts and cultures. A number of influential Black musicians, including Art Blakey, Randy Weston, Dizzy Gillespie, Yusef Lateef, Dakota Staton, and Ahmad Jamal, traveled to Africa or incorporated African elements in their music, especially from the cultures of Nigeria. Some even converted to Ahmadiyya Islam (one of the smaller branches of Islam, which, although originating in South Asia, is particularly influential in

West Africa). At the time, despite the growing turmoil among Black artists and the prominence of some leading figures in the more radical sectors of the Civil Rights Movement, there was not a clear or coherent view of exactly what the role of culture was in the broader struggle against racial injustice. Most early assessments of the transition from civil rights to Black liberation do not mention the term "Black Arts Movement." Many of the artists involved during the period were viewed according to their politics and not necessarily in terms of their cultural work.

Malcolm X had performed the magic that turned "Negroes" into Black people, but the exact social, political, and cultural content of this new self-designation was not self-evident. John Coltrane and the other adherents of what was then called "free Jazz" demonstrated that one could transgress the boundaries of "western music" and yet create work of great power and beauty. However, as popular as some of the younger artists were among a college-educated audience, their art was not so accessible to many Black people whose cultural tastes were anchored in their traditions of blues, R&B, gospel, and Motown. Askia Touré's prescient essay "Keep on Pushin': Rhythm & Blues as a Weapon" is an indication of what was needed and the connections that would have to be made to generate a culture in tune with a new Black awareness and consciousness. Malcolm's Organization of Afro American Unity had as one of its goals a "cultural revolution." Frantz Fanon's *The Wretched of the Earth* was just being translated, putting into English his harsh critique of the culture of colonization and the need to break both with it and with traditional African cultural forms that did not function to advance the liberation of the colonized.

What validated Malcolm's importance to the incipient Black Arts Movement was his endorsement by older cultural figures such as Ossie Davis, Gwendolyn Brooks, Margaret Burroughs, and Margaret Walker. It was Davis who gave the eulogy at Malcolm's funeral, and it was older poets who produced the first and still most influential responses to what it meant that Malcolm was no longer on this earth—as seen in many of the poems in the early Broadside Press anthology *For Malcolm,* edited by Margaret Burroughs and Dudley Randall. It is at this critical juncture in the immediate aftermath of Malcolm's assassination that Amiri Baraka moved from the East Village to Harlem to begin to lay out a program for the "Black Arts."

In its early days, the Black Arts Movement was relatively gender-egalitarian. Given the deep sexism running through U.S. society, it was actually much more open in this regard than the vast majority of cultural and political institutions and formations. Sonia Sanchez, Nikki Giovanni, Margaret Burroughs, Margaret Danner, Johari Amini (Jewel Lattimore), Carolyn Rodgers, Jayne Cortez, Sarah Webster Fabio, Aishah Rahman, Barbara Ann Teer, Val Gray Ward, and Elma Lewis played leading and very visible roles as artists and as creators of new Black cultural institutions. In the late 1960s, however, Maulana Karenga proposed a clear and influential cultural nationalist model based on neo-Africanist principles that posited women as "complementary, not equal." As Karenga's Kawaida ideology circulated throughout the Black Power and Black Arts movements, patriarchal notions of art and culture gained increasing currency, although these views never characterized BAM as a whole. Women continued to hold leadership positions in the movement and remained among the most popular artists within the Black community. Both men and women also contested expressions of male chauvinism in BAM. In fact, one result of Kawaidism and other patriarchal ideologies within the movement was the rise of an explicit Black Power and Black Arts feminism, exemplified by Toni Cade Bambara's landmark 1970 anthology *The Black Woman* and by the actions of women artists who literally fought their way onto stages with men.

BAM and Its Predecessors

BAM activists sought a usable past not simply in the idea of a general Black artistic tradition but more specifically in antecedent African American cultural movements. By far the most important was the Harlem, or New Negro, Renaissance of the 1920s. Like BAM, the Renaissance was a multidisciplinary and multi-genre arts movement that gave Black artists a national and even international status. Yet, in many respects, BAM artists treated the Harlem Renaissance as a cautionary tale as much as a beloved parent. They judged the artists of the Renaissance to be insufficiently political, not actively enough engaged with the concerns of working-class African Americans, too dependent on the support of jaded white patrons, and (with the exception of a relative few such as Langston Hughes, Sterling Brown, and Zora Neale Hurston) distant from the culture of the Black masses. Nevertheless, despite the charges they leveled against the Renaissance, BAM critics like Neal and Addison Gayle Jr. were among the first to take its writers, such as Countee Cullen, Jean Toomer, Zora Neale Hurston, Sterling Brown, and Claude McKay, seriously. In fact, the rise of Harlem Renaissance studies can be traced to the work of Neal and BAM critics and early Black studies scholars of the 1960s and 1970s.

Also important to BAM activists as both antecedents to their movement and examples of what Harold Cruse would make famous as "the crisis of the Negro intellectual" were the radical political and cultural circles of the 1930s, 1940s, and early 1950s, especially those associated with the Communist Party. These circles provided audiences and venues for African American artists, some of whom, like Sterling Brown, Margaret Burroughs, Langston Hughes, John O. Killens, Jacob Lawrence, and Margaret Walker, provided critical support and mentoring for the nascent BAM. Quite a few of the young BAM activists themselves had participated in study groups, lecture series, educational organizations, and the like connected to the Old Left. At the same time, many of the young artists and activists criticized the Old Left (at least its members of the Communist Party) for an undue attachment to the Soviet Union, a romantic fetishizing of white workers and their revolutionary potential, a lack of understanding of the importance and appeal of Black nationalism, an underestimation of the Third World as the leading force for social liberation, and a lack of appreciation of the spiritual dimension of life.

BAM activists and Black Power militants as well were keenly aware of the political and cultural developments in the Third World, especially the debates between the adherents of Négritude, notably Senegal's Leopold Senghor, and what might be thought of as the revolutionary nationalist Africanism of such independence leaders as Guinea's Sekou Touré and Ghana's Kwame Nkrumah. In general, BAM writers and artists, whether they considered themselves revolutionary nationalists or cultural nationalists, sided with the revolutionary activism of Touré and Nkrumah against what they saw as the depoliticized culturalism of Senghor and Négritude. They were also inspired by non-aligned movements that arose out of the 1955 Bandung Conference of newly independent African and Asian nations and from the often violent independence struggles against colonialism and neocolonialism. Of particular importance was the Cuban Revolution, which actively sought the support of Black artists and intellectuals, sponsoring tours for Black radicals, and having Fidel Castro stay at the Hotel Theresa in Harlem when he came to speak at the United Nations in 1960, for example. Proto-Black Power and Black Arts activists advanced the idea of a "Bandung World," in which Black radicals were part of a worldwide revolutionary movement encompassing the vast majority of the world's people, rather than seeing themselves as a minority within a minority in the United States.

An immediate antecedent to BAM was the bohemian counterculture of the 1950s and early 1960s. Although such literary groups as the Beats, the New York School, and the Black Mountain School are often still characterized as "white," they were actually among the most interracial intellectual circles in the United States at the time, especially in New York, Chicago, Detroit, Washington, D.C., and the San Francisco Bay Area. Such African American writers as Amiri Baraka, Bob Kaufman, Ed Bullins, Ted Joan, A. B. Spellman, and the seminal Umbra Poets Workshop were intimately tied to the literary counterculture. In fact, Baraka as writer, editor, and publisher was a key figure in creating the idea of a "New American Poetry" in the 1950s and 1960s. The institutionalization of the public reading as a central means of disseminating poetry and the engagement of literature with music and other forms of popular culture, especially Black popular culture, in BAM owed much to the Beats and other bohemian "schools." In the end, though, many important African American cultural activists like Baraka publicly broke with the counterculture as a way of asserting the independence of Black artists.

Not to be overlooked is the continuing presence of older Black artists, writers, and intellectuals, such as Samuel Allen, Romare Bearden, Gwendolyn Brooks, Sterling Brown, Margaret Burroughs, Elizabeth Catlett, Alice Childress, Charles Davis, Owen Dodson, Margaret Danner, Robert Hayden, Langston Hughes, John O. Killens, Jacob Lawrence, Melvin Tolson, Darwin Turner, Margaret Walker, and Theodore Ward. While only a few of these artists can be said to have truly been a part of BAM—most notably Gwendolyn Brooks—many were mentors and critical supporters of younger BAM members, encouraging their work and reminding them of earlier moments of Black political and cultural radicalism.

The Black Arts Movement and Black Nationalism

BAM cannot be comprehended outside the context of the rise of Black nationalism in the 1960s. Of course, Black nationalism has a long history in the United States reaching back to the eighteenth century. However, with the mass circulation of the ideas of Malcolm X, first within and then outside the Nation of Islam, and the explosion of the uprisings of the 1960s, especially after the Watts Rebellion of 1965, nationalism exerted a new influence on Black artists and on the African American community in general to an extent unseen since the heyday of Marcus Garvey's Universal Negro Improvement Association (UNIA) in the 1920s. And even Marcus Garvey never directly affected most Black artists during the Harlem Renaissance in the way Malcolm X moved those whose who would start BAM in the 1960s. However, Malcolm X's analysis of white supremacy in the United

States and its relationship to imperialism around the world and his call for Black cultural and political independence were taken in different directions after his assassination in 1965 left many key questions unanswered. Artists were extremely important in framing the discussion of what it would mean to be liberated, of what it did mean to be Black, of what the content of Blackness was.

Debates among nationalists turned not only on how liberation might be achieved but also on what a liberated nation would look like and how it should function. Some envisioned a socialist society run on Marxist- Leninist principles. Others imagined communal societies rooted in a vision of African traditional culture. Still others promoted a notion of Black entrepreneurship or Black capitalism. Some insisted that a large, unified state would be necessary to ensure Black independence and national development. Others saw a linked federation of city-states as the natural territory of the Black community in the second half of the twentieth century.

More often than not, African American artists and activists combined many or all of these visions, or considered the answers to the essential questions of liberation to be a process rather than a set of settled alternatives. As a result, the still-too-common practice of dividing 1960s–70s Black nationalism into separate cultural and revolutionary strands has to be approached carefully, since in many ways that divide owes more to organizational disputes between the Black Panthers and proponents of Maulana Karenga's vision than to ideological distinctions that might be useful now in understanding Black Arts and Black Power. Virtually all the dominant forms of nationalism during the 1960s and 1970s supported the idea of a fundamental transformation of the existing social order as a cornerstone of Black liberation, and all nationalist groups saw culture as an essential arena of political struggle. Similarly, BAM artists saw their cultural work as fundamental contributions to Black liberation. In fact, one of things that most distinguished Black Arts and Black Power from earlier movements is that political organizations were frequently headed by artists, such as Amiri Baraka and the Congress of African People (CAP), or by activists with a deep background in the arts, such as Muhammad Ahmad (Max Stanford) and the Revolutionary Action Movement (RAM) and Bobby Seale and the Black Panther Party for Self-Defense.

Black Aesthetics

There was never a consensus on a "Black Aesthetic," although there was wide agreement in BAM that the characteristics and content of Black art should define itself from and against "Western" art. There was also a general sense that the development of some aesthetic system for the evaluation, analysis, and creation of revolutionary Black art was necessary, since the dominant aesthetic norms and artistic canons were irrelevant at best and oppressive at worst for Black artists and their African American audience. BAM members vigorously objected to notions of aesthetic universalism promoted by the academy and the intellectual establishment in the United States, seeing those notions as white supremacist particularism. These objections brought BAM into conflict not only with white critics, scholars, and artists but also with some Black artists and intellectuals who continued to subscribe to "mainstream" universalist aesthetic values, leading to sharp debates, for example, on the legacy of the Harlem Renaissance as well of more contemporary writers like Ralph Ellison and Robert Hayden. Of course, even within the movement there was considerable disagreement over the worth of the work of Ellison and Hayden—though the arguments turned more on the degree to which those writers engaged African American expressive culture rather than on any universalist ideas of art and aesthetic value.

One aspect of the political mission of BAM which had a profound impact on aesthetics was the emphasis on the performative and on artistic genres that lent themselves to public performance and potentially reach masses of people. As a result, the most popular genres of the movement were poetry and theater, since it was comparatively easy to present poems or plays at a political rally, on a street corner, or in a public housing project court-yard or community room. Poetry, too, was particularly important because it could be eas-ily circulated in Black-run journals, newspapers, broadsides, and small-press chapbooks in a way that was not possible with longer fiction. Likewise, the public mural became the best-known form of Black visual art during the period, with such landmarks as the *Wall of Respect* on Chicago's South Side becoming sites of political rallies as well as of other artistic events. There was also a stress on art as a process of personal and social liberation rather than as a product or artifact to be sold or appreciated in an abstract way.

One area of considerable debate within BAM was the relation of revolutionary art to Black popular culture, both traditional and contemporary. What, for example, was the value of the blues tradition, both lyrically and formally, to Black art, especially Black music, drama, and literature? How were R&B, doo-wop, soul, soul jazz, and so on, to be assessed in terms of the new Black art? Some BAM members, notably among proponents of Karenga's Kawaidaism, essentially rejected the blues tradition and modern Black popu-lar culture, positing instead the jazz avant-garde, especially John Coltrane, and a neo-Africanist construct of precolonial African culture as the basis of a new Black countercul-ture. Others, following an anti-colonial Left position in large measure derived from Frantz Fanon, argued for a vanguard art that rejected both popular culture and traditional Afri-can culture, echoing perhaps Marx's famous pronouncement in *The Eighteenth Brumaire of Louis Bonaparte* that the "social revolution of the nineteenth century cannot draw its poetry from the past, but only from the future." Still others, even some others closely tied for a time to Karenga, such as Amiri Baraka, argued for a cultural continuum stretching from Africa through the blues, free jazz, and such contemporary R&B musicians as James Brown, Curtis Mayfield, Marvin Gaye, and Stevie Wonder.

Another characteristic of BAM artistic practice, especially of those BAM members who drew on Black popular culture, was the blurring of the boundaries of artistic genre and medium. Black Arts performances frequently mixed poetry, drama, music, dance, and even visual arts. Similarly, mural painting often entailed multidisciplinary, multi-genre performances at the mural sites. In addition, murals such as the *Wall of Respect* incorporated photographs, literary texts, and works from other artistic mediums. Even in works that were printed, for example, Sonia Sanchez's "A Coltrane Poem" and Haki Madhubuti's "Don't Cry, Scream," writers often tried recreate aspects of non-literary per-formance through lineation, typography, spacing, and so on. Finally, many Black artists worked in multiple genres: in addition to being jazz musicians Archie Shepp was an accomplished playwright, Sun Ra and Cecil Taylor wrote poetry, and Marion Brown was a painter; poet Jay Wright played bass with jazz musician Pharoah Sanders; and poet Jayne Cortez worked in theater and dance.

BAM artists valued jazz musicians such as Max Roach and Charles Mingus who were fairly traditional in formal terms but whose work was often politically radical as much as they valued those musicians—especially John Coltrane, Ornette Coleman, Albert Ayler, and Cecil Taylor—who created relatively few overtly political pieces but whose formal experimentation was seen as analogous to the search for social liberation. Randy Weston, in many respects, too, a more traditional jazz pianist, was valued for his early incorporation of African music in his work. In short, Coltrane's "My Favorite Things," Weston's *Uhuru Afrika*, Mingus's *Fables of Fabus,* and Roach's *Freedom Now Suite: We Insist* were all admired, if for different reasons. However, it was unquestionably Coltrane's relentless search for a new musical vocabulary and syntax not tied to "Western" values and aesthetics that was most influential.

Circuits of Transmission

The growth of the Black Arts Movement was enabled through the emergence of a new radical African American arts infrastructure run and largely supported by Black people in the early and mid-1960s. The creation of such magazines as *Freedomways, Liberator, Soulbook, Black Dialogue,* and *Umbra* and editor Hoyt Fuller's transformation of *Negro Digest* (later *Black World*) from a Black *Reader's Digest* into the most widely circulating journal of radical Black politics and culture helped create networks of younger (and not so young) African American artists and intellectuals that would form the basis of the Black Arts Movement. Similarly, such institutions as the Ebony Museum (later the Du Sable Museum) in Chicago, the International Afro-American Museum (later the Charles Wright Museum of African American History), the Free Southern Theater in New Orleans, and Boone House in Detroit, the Umbra Poets Workshop in New York, and the Freedom Singers of the Student Non-Violent Coordinating Committee (SNCC) provided local examples inspired Black Arts activists in their later institution-building efforts combining art and politics.

In part, these proto–Black Arts and Black Power institutions were the result of the Civil Rights upsurge, especially the more militant wing of the movement manifested in the sit-ins of 1960 and the creation of the SNCC. It was also motivated by a conscious desire to avoid the sort of white patronage that many Black Arts participants came to feel had undermined the Harlem Renaissance. Although the ideological cast of the newly established journals, festivals, conferences, presses, schools, groups, museums, and so on was increasingly nationalist, this impulse toward institution-building was also encouraged by the examples of the older Black Left in the 1930s, 1940s, and 1950s, such as Paul Robeson's *Freedom* newspaper, *Negro Quarterly, Negro Story,* the Southside Writers Group, the Harlem Arts Center, *Harlem Quarterly,* the Harlem Writers Club, and the American Negro Theater. In fact, veterans of these older Left efforts, including Margaret Burroughs, John Henrik Clarke, John O. Killens, Carlton Goodlet Jr., Margaret Walker, and Elizabeth Catlett, played important roles in the creation of this new framework.

The watershed moment in the development of a Black Arts infrastructure was the establishment of Detroit's Broadside Press by Dudley Randall in 1965. Randall, an active member of the "Detroit Group" of Black writers that coalesced around such institutions as Boone House and Concept East Theater, initiated the press by publishing broadsides written by him and older Black authors such as Langston Hughes, Robert Hayden, Gwendolyn Brooks, Melvin Tolson, and Sterling Brown. Within a relatively short period of time, however, the press concentrated on chapbooks and broadsides by Sonia Sanchez, Carolyn Rodgers, Haki Madhubuti, Sterling Plumpp, Johari Amini, and literally dozens of other young Black writers. Between 1966 and 1975 Broadside published a half million volumes, a huge number for a small poetry press—and according to Melba Joyce Boyd more than twice as many books by African American poets than had been issued by the entire U.S. publishing industry in the two decades between 1945 and 1965. Broadside not only made the new Black poetry and criticism available to a national audience, it also inspired the creation of other African American literary publishing ventures, such as Third World Press, the Journal of Black Poetry Press, Lotus Press, and Jihad Productions.

Broadside Press soon became a integral part of a midwestern network of Black artists' groups and institutions that included *Negro Digest,* Concept East, the Organization for Black American Culture (OBAC) with its writers and visual arts workshops, the Affro Arts Theater, Africobra, the Kuumba Theater, and the Association for the Advancement of Creative Music (AACM), which joined with like-minded groups and institutions across the nation. When Gwendolyn Brooks moved from Harper & Row, one of the largest trade publishers, to Broadside Press in the late 1960s, it was an event of enormous symbolic and practical significance, which led African American writers to publish with Black-run presses (or at least justify why they did not).

To understand the ways in which Black Arts built a national community among artists and found an audience, it is crucial to remember that the Black Liberation Movement did not simply exert an ideological influence over Black Arts; it also aided the cultural movement in material ways. What might be thought of as fundamentally political events, such as the 1970 founding convention of the Congress of African People (CAP) in Atlanta, were also showcases for Black visual art, literature, dance, music, and dramatic performance as well as venues for the discussion of Black aesthetics and the role of culture in political struggle. Very often important local and national political leaders, Amiri Baraka and Haki Madhubuti, for example, were major artists. Frequently, such Black liberation advocates would promote radical Black art as a central part of their organizing efforts. Of course, the reverse was also true: Black artists would help build political organizations like CAP and the African Liberation Support Committee on tours of poetry readings, theater performances, and other cultural events.

Legacies

BAM was arguably the most influential U.S. arts movement ever. Certainly no other radical cultural movement reached such a large American audience. Black Arts cultural groups, writers' and artists' workshops, theaters, bookstores, study circles, dance companies, schools, journals, small presses, reading series, galleries, museums, public art spaces sprouted up wherever there was a Black community, large or small. Most big cities had multiple Black Arts institutions. Black Arts, too, for a time became a staple of popular culture media aimed primarily at Black audiences, the magazines *Ebony* and *Jet,* for example, the television programs *Soul!* and *Like It Is,* and even such "Blaxploitation" films as *Sweet Sweetback's Baadasssss Song* and *Super Fly.* In short, the movement directly reached a grassroots audience of millions—an amazing achievement for such a politically and aesthetically radical cultural movement.

Many of BAM's members remained artistically active to a degree that few of their living contemporaries from the 1960s could match. Many well-known post–Black Arts artists—the novelist Toni Morrison, the novelist and playwright Pearl Cleage, the playwright August Wilson, the poet and playwright Ntozake Shange, filmmaker Spike Lee, musicians Chaka Khan and Earth, Wind, and Fire (not too mention a huge proportion of the jazz avant-garde), the actors Avery Brooks, Samuel L. Jackson, Denise Nichols, and Danny Glover—were molded by the movement. The movement served as a catalyst for Asian American, Chicana/o, Puerto Rican, and Native American cultural movements. It provided an important template for the literature, theory, and criticism coming from the second-wave feminist movement. The more radical "Third World" wing of early multiculturalism, too, largely emerged out of Black Arts and Black Power. Finally, it remains almost impossible to discuss work by African American artists without reference to the criteria suggested by the movement, especially with respect to issues of authenticity and the relationship of art to an idea of Black community.

Black Arts also did much to demolish the distinction between popular culture and "high art." It was a major force in introducing the idea that "high" art can be popular in form and content and popular culture can be socially and artistically serious. Today this is an unremarkable notion, but it was revolutionary in the 1960s and 1970s. This change is perhaps most clearly exemplified in hip hop, where the more "conscious" artists publicly associate themselves with Amiri Baraka, Askia Touré, Sonia Sanchez, and other leading Black Arts poets and vice versa in ways that one could not imagine happening between serious poets and popular musicians to that degree before the 1960s—Langston Hughes and Sterling Brown notwithstanding. This breakdown of genre distinctions and the changed conceptions of audience have also enabled artists like Pearl Cleage to mix popular fiction genres (such as urban romance and detective) with Black nationalist ideology and reach mass Black audiences largely outside "mainstream" channels of publicity, marketing, and critical review. The Black Arts practice of creating a socially engaged mixture of poetry, music, dance, visual arts, and other media performed for a popular audience laid the groundwork for the growth of performance poetry as a popular art form.

Further, Black Arts dramatically altered the landscape of public funding for the arts, and it stimulated the discussion about what kind of work publicly funded art should do. The efforts and model of the Black Arts Movement led to an efflorescence of publicly supported murals, arts centers, workshops, performance groups, and the like within Black communities as well as in many other sorts of communities. In addition, the art-for-the-people efforts of BAM catalyzed the growth of institutions that reached millions of Americans generally, such as the Public Broadcasting System and National Public Radio, both founded in the late 1960s. For better or worse, many of the current debates about culture and public funding that arise perennially over the National Endowment for the Arts, the

National Endowment for the Humanities, National Public Radio, and public cultural institutions, are significantly rooted in the Black Arts Movement.

The Mission of *SOS—Calling All Black People*

As happened with Black Power, a new scholarship examining the Black Arts Movement has emerged and gained wide academic attention over the last decade. There is also dramatically increased interest in Black Arts and Black Power outside the academy, especially, but not exclusively, among young African Americans. However, a major problem in teaching courses on the Black Arts Movement is the lack of an anthology that can be used as the primary textbook. Certainly none of the existing anthologies of African American literature adequately capture the ideological, aesthetic, and geographical breadth of BAM. Even the recently reprinted edition of Amiri Baraka and Larry Neal's seminal BAM anthology *Black Fire* comprises only the early days of the movement. Further, so many of the essential documents are inaccessible that anyone without access to a major research library would find it very difficult to get a real sense of BAM. And, of course, access does not of itself identify the documents or provide contextualization.

This collection is intended to remedy those problems. It presents a representative sample of five BAM genres: theory / criticism, statements of purpose, poetry, drama, and short fiction / narrative. This sample demonstrates the ideological, geographical, and aesthetic scope of the movement. We include works that were considered essential at the time as well as others that seem to us significant in retrospect.

In addition to the editors' introduction, the volume includes a foreword and three concluding essays discussing the significance and legacy of the movement. Most sections feature a short introduction as well as a reminiscence by a major practitioner of the genre to give a tangible sense of the moment and the lived feeling of BAM. The volume also includes a selected bibliography of primary and secondary texts.

The Black Arts Movement

By the late 50's the U.S. Civil Rights movement had reached a new height of intensity with the victory of the Montgomery Bus Boycott, the emergence of Dr. King and the formation of the S.C.L.C. The Cuban Revolution brought the 50's to a roaring climax with yet another popular democratic victory. By 1960 the Black Student Movement had formed out of the Greensboro black student "sit-ins" and soon S.N.C.C. would step onto the stage of Black peoples' struggle. And now at the beginning of the 60's we welcomed the move into the leadership of Malcolm X.

Clearly, this was the era when, as Mao Tse Tung said, "Countries want Independence, Nations want Liberation and The People want Revolution!" And as we used to quote him often, "Revolution Is The Main Trend In the World Today!"

The African Liberation Movements, from the earlier Mau Mau insurrection in Kenya, were likewise gaining worldwide recognition. And the names Kenyatta, Azikiwe, Toure, Nyerere, Nasser were becoming familiar. In 1961, I 1st met Askia Toure, along with other life long comrades, in front of the U.S. Mission to the U.N. where we were gathered with hundreds of other people, including Aishah Rahman and Mae Mallory and Calvin Hicks to protest the murder of Patrice Lumumba by the U.S., Belgium and the traitorous scum who still sits in the seat of power of Zaire, Joe Mobutu.

For many of us who lived in the "village" in New York, the political dimensions of the times were always muted by the petty bourgeois anarchy of the largely white soi-disant arts community we lived in. But as the whole society heated up with struggle and rebellion and revolution, I suppose the most politically sensitive of us began to pull away from the bourgeois rubric that art and politics were separate and exclusive entities.

So that by the beginning of the 60's not only had I already gone to Cuba to witness the beginnings of the revolution Fidel Castro and the people of Cuba had brought into the world, but when I returned I became quickly involved in helping put together political organizations like *Organization of Young Men,* a political newspaper, *In/Formation,* and became a member of the left organization *On Guard,* headed by Calvin Hicks, along with Archie Shepp.

In a few months I had also become the New York chairman of the Fair Play for Cuba organization. I had gone to Cuba with Harold Cruse, Sarah Wright, Julian Mayfield, Ed Clark, among others, and there had met the great Robert Williams, of Monroe, North Carolina, who had most recently been excommunicated from the NAACP for not only stating openly that Black people had the right to self defense against the attacks of the Klan, Williams even led his unique branch of the NAACP to ambush the Klan and remove their hoods and guns.

I'm saying all this to set the stage for the coming together of the young Black people who would put forth the concept and the organization called *The Black Arts Repertory Theater/School.*

Not only was the struggle for democracy raging at higher and higher levels, but when Malcolm X stepped into center stage, there came also a wave of Black nationalist agitation and propaganda unlike many of us had ever heard before. Many of us were not familiar with the Nation of Islam, especially if we were living outside Black communities. Elijah Muhammad was unknown, but Malcolm X put words to the volcanic torrent of anger and frustration many of us felt with the Civil Rights Movement.

The "turn the other cheek," "non-violent" approach to the struggle for democracy we rejected. We did not understand why we must continue to let crazed ignorant hooligans attack us to show we were noble or that we deserved to be citizens. The endless television horror shows of Black people being water hosed, beaten, dogged by two and four legged dogs, lynched, jailed, got our jaws tight not only at the sum who did this but the negroes who accepted it.

That's why the Cuban revolution was so heavy in our sensibility. That's why Robert Williams was our hero. That's why we demonstrated for Lumumba and wrestled in those streets with the police despite Ralph Bunche telling us he was embarrassed that we were in public acting like niggaz.

So when Malcolm stepped forward and began to teach Self Determination, Self Respect and Self Defense, it struck a chord deep within the soul of a wide spectrum of Black people, particularly Black youth. And for those of us living outside the community, his impact was deeply profound and life changing.

In some respects it was like Fanon says about the native intellectuals in colonial societies who have become so integrated into the petty bourgeois superstructure and even marginal social life of the oppressor nation that when we first receive that degree of self consciousness that makes us aware of how deeply we have joined with our own oppressors even to taking up the philosophies of our own inferiorization we are deeply mortified.

Fanon says such intellectuals next become blacker than Black or Super African to cover and dismiss their double consciousness, as Du Bois calls it. I think there is very obviously some of this over compensation in some of the interior and public manifestations of the Black Arts Movement. Fanon also said that if such an intellectual continues to struggle in the day to day practical revolutionary movement then there is a chance that they might become authentic revolutionaries rather than compensating poseurs.

We were a group of Black intellectuals living mostly downtown New York, Greenwich Village, or the Lower East Side. Our day to day social life was, for the most part, joined directly, or marginally, with the petty bourgeois arts and intellectual community or at least that was their and our presumption. Except that whatever else the most sensitive of us was doing, what remained is what was the deepest hunger in our souls, the urge to democracy to self determination, the understanding that no matter how much we might be "recognized" or "accepted" or even lionized as artists, we were still somehow burdened with the disorienting realization of alienation.

On the surface, as we grew more conscious we knew that as we demanded an art of struggle, an art that related to the reality of our history and the real life of the world, particularly of the Afro American people, it became clearer and clearer that the standard bourgeois aesthetic of separation of arts and politics was stupid and becoming more and more openly bankrupt.

In a deep sense the music, jazz, blues, new music, these were sustaining elements of our lives. We could feel ourselves, we could become truly self conscious inside it. And as the 60's moved on, a significant sector of Black artists downtown became more and more isolated from that so called "mainstream" by the growing need to fully express our soul and mind connection with Black struggle in our art and in the street. When I met Askia, I didn't even know he was a poet. Ditto Larry Neal, Max Stanford. We were in the struggle to liberate Black people, to liberate ourselves.

We began to come together to discuss the movement. We were in different organizations. *On Guard, RAM, Umbra,* some even in the *CP* and *SWP.* Black intellectuals and artists seeking true self consciousness. We hit upon the idea of circulating propaganda and agitation among the downtown Blacks to involve ourselves directly in the liberation struggle. When Robert Williams was struggling with the Klan we even discussed sending him guns. One of our group was even busted in a set up by the FBI where he was framed for trying to blow up the statue of liberty, just like the Muslims framed by the FBI and Mossad today for the World Trade Center Reichstag explosion.

We spent much time now traveling back and forth between the Village and Harlem. Working politically in Harlem, that became the badge of our sincerity. No matter we still lived downtown for the most part, some in integrated marriages or what have you.

The explosive transformation of our quantitative frustration, built and genuine desire for liberation into the qualitative persona who must be wholly militant activist in the liberation struggle was Malcolm's murder. His murder by the FBI, the federal government through native agents, Spike Lee, not by the Nation of Islam, was what sent us hurtling out of those various downtowns across the country seeking our "Blackness" like Faust trying to reclaim his soul.

The month after Malcolm's assassination, a group of us arrived in Harlem, this time to seek permanent residence and to avenge Malcolm's murder. We had held fundraisers downtown. Just before we left, we had a fundraiser at the old St. Marks Theater, where my plays, *The Toilet,* and *Experimental Death Unit #1,* featuring Barbara Ann Teer, Charles Patterson's *Black Ice* and *The Black Tramp* by Nat White (who we never heard from again) were performed to raise money to go uptown.

We rented a brownstone on W. 130th St. near Lenox, tore down the 1st floor walls and began our work. The announcement of our arrival in Harlem was a parade, with the small group of young Black artists, led by the great genius Sun Ra and his then Myth Science Arkestra. We still have photos of that. What the people of Harlem thought of that we would find out in various ways as we travailed. But that was the opening. The weird, the interplanetary, the heliocentric world of Sun Ra, our syncopated point and I carried a brand new flag, designed by painter William White, the tragic/comic (like the earth, the south the smile of joy, the north the frown of sadness, dig it) dialectical mask of drama, fashioned into an African shield in black and gold. We walked all the way determined to make a revolution.

The name Black Arts had come in one of our meetings downtown where we gave each other military rank and made a commitment to any means, even armed revolution. We said what should we call this, then, secret Black organization of artists and intellectuals. I remember Larry Neal, Max Stanford, Cornelius Suares, Clarence Franklin, Askia Toure, William White, Charles and William Patterson (the last two from *Umbra,* our in-house trouble makers). And it came to me out of the black hole, I said, the Black Arts!

Part 2

But whatever our vision and theory, it could be nothing but speculation and argument unless we could make them real with the objective "proof" of practice. At best, we were a loose united front, joined most securely around the "new" idea of "Blackness." But what was that? was the relentless question that defined our confusion.

We had put out a manifesto of sorts, as we prepared to go uptown, which said we wanted to draw the most serious and committed Black artists and intellectuals from everywhere in the world to help us create the *Black Arts Repertory Theater School* [BARTS]. We linked the common Eurocentric distortion of Black Arts as an evil magic, as a mystic pursuit. A power used to transform reality. We had long before understood the twisted racism of Europe and America when referring to Black. That everything Black was bad. But we was Bad, in fact we was trying to get Badder dan Nat. We was trying to get outright "terrible." Understanding, in various degrees, that "to turn their Evil backward, is to Live!"

We set up classes on history, politics, drama. Sun Ra even taught "Myth Science" as part of "the Blacker Arts." We began to put on plays in the small downstairs space. We had forums, some of which became near violent ideological shootouts. But one thing was clear, we were not merely subjective in our registration of the tenor of the times, or the motion of history. People came, not only from the larger community of Harlem, but young Black artists began to make the trek to the brownstone on W. 130th St. with the Black & Gold flag hung outside, to find out what was going on—to support this new movement and to participate.

Not only that, but as we began to function, to do our programs, the plays, poetry readings, new music concerts and stalk through the community preaching "Blackness (which differed depending on who you were talking to) the world spread in all directions. And, indeed, talk began to come back to us of a Black Arts Movement!

One escalating program with this united front of Black artists and intellectuals was that among a small group of us, on the inside, we began to struggle each day with more and more intensity. About what? About Blackness. Who was, and who wasn't. What was and what wasn't.

We had made a line of demarcation (we felt) between the artists we'd left downtown and ourselves. We could put them down too easily as "whited out" or as unserious negroes committed only to hedonism and individualism. With serving white people. But certainly that could not be factual in many cases.

We *were* arrogant and often the Super Black neophytes that Fanon spoke of. But at the same time there was real resistance from many of our erstwhile friends and fellow Afro American artists downtown. There was a common dismissal of our efforts that were crazy and even violent.

Some said we weren't really artists. "How could you be an artist when all you wanted to talk about is Black and Hating White people . . . specially since some of yall just left their company a few minutes ago."

But there was, no matter how crazy and wild and even violent and non-artistic we might have seemed to our one time friends (many of whom now openly denounced us) or to various white folks and negroes, there was a developing line of truth to our ideas and our practice, that part of them not wholly distorted by our continuing ideological confusion. For one thing, in that broad but small united front, there were mainly the petty bourgeois. Certainly most of the leadership was. Which meant that we were given to extremes and occasional fanaticism. It meant we would vacillate from this to that, which was exacerbated by the disciplineless environments many of us had come out of. Yet in spite of these impediments to ideological clarity, plus constant internal conflicts, some manifest as disruptive undermining, others as straight out physical violence, we did accomplish some things of value, both in theory (as we later summed it up) and in actual practice.

For instance, that summer of 1965, we did bring an advanced Black Art to Harlem! But the effort became, even at our most successful and expansive, wrought and torn with ongoing problems. First of all the BARTS was a small group of artist-intellectual-activists who formed the formal organization. All of whom had paramilitary rank and responsibility in the organization. Many of our strongest supporters refused to join the actual organization because they felt some of us were just too crazy and hard to get along with. And there is no disputing that—a couple of those dudes I couldn't even get along with. Ironically, two brothers, who had split from the *Umbra* organization who I did not know well at the outset of our attempt to build an independent institution of Afro American artists and intellectuals, were the sickest, most disruptive negroes in militant clothing I have ever met.

There were brand new Elijah Muslims (at least that was the rhetoric and even the dress and style. I dont know if any of these were ever actually in The Nation. Then there were brand new Sunni Muslims and even a few brand new Hanafi Mussulmen, at least one of whom was related to Brother Khalis whose D.C. HQ was left full of dead brothers and sisters by some crazed hitmen. Some later went to jail when Khalis occupied a building owned by or somehow associated with Jews for making a film about the prophet Muhammad.

Most of us maintained an alienation from the NOI because of Malcolm, but we knew it was the Devil that had him murdered. Baba Oserjeman's Yoruba temple also influenced us. It was, for some of us, the essence of Blackness. The authentic historical presence of our African history and culture. It is not unimportant that all of these groups had distinct and ultimately oppressive roles for women. Particularly their adherents. Whether the veils and segregation of the various Muslims or the polygamy of their tradition and the common practice of the Yoruba. And we were also influenced by these ideas and practices as legitimate forms of *Blackness.*

There were cultural nationalists of all persuasions. Left Right & Centrist. Some as radicals some as progressives some as revolutionaries, some as political Black, some as mystical-spiritual Black. Some as Pick-Up-The-Gun Blacks, most as Hate Whitey Blacks. We had the most unity on that, that being Black meant despising as openly as possible All White People, Groucho or Karl. So that since methodology and ideology are connected, doing anything involved sharp struggle and even violence.

But that one glorious summer of 1965, we did, even with all that internal warfare, bring advanced Black Art to Harlem. We organized, as part of HARYOU ACT, the nation's 1st anti poverty program, a summer arts program called Operation Boot Strap (under the overall direction of Adam Clayton Powell's point cadre, Judge Livingston Wingate). For eight weeks, we brought Drama, Poetry, Painting, Music, Dance, night after night all across Harlem. We had a fleet of five trucks and stages created with banquet tables. And each night our five units would go out in playgrounds, street corners, vacant lots, play streets, parks, bringing Black Art directly to the people.

Young Steve Young was the most trustworthy coordinator. He and my sister, Kimako (who was constantly attacked by certain negroes because she was an independent creative woman). She dealt with drama and dance. Andrew Hill was music coordinator, Joe Gregory coordinated the painters, assisted by Joe Overstreet and William White who came to help us but refused to leave the Village.

One of my closest poet friends, in fact, pulled a pistol on me to emphasize his determination to stay downtown! It was that wild! But Sun Ra and Archie Shepp and Pharoah Sanders and Milford Graves and Don Pullen and Albert Ayler and at our benefits downtown, John Coltrane, Grachan Moncur, Bobby Hutcherson, and more. And uptown Larry Neal, Askia Toure, Bobb Hamilton, Sonia Sanchez, Ted Wilson, so many poets and black actors, directors, Jim Campbell, Rob Jackson, Kimako (who directed and did the lead role in *Dutchman*), Frank Adu, Barbara Montgomery, Yusef Iman (our stalwart classic Black Arts warrior artist) and his whole family.

That was an important, ideologically impacting and exciting time. Black artists came by constantly to talk, to argue, to join, to support, to learn, to teach. Harold Cruse taught politics, with two agents in his class. One night even Sammy Davis Jr. came uptown and did a benefit on 125th St. And from inside Harlem, artist like poets Clarence Reed and Clarence Franklin, Ojijiko, the Weusi Sanaa artists, Ademola, Rahman, Babatunde added strength to strength, Valerie Maynard, and so many others.

We had evolved through our practice a growing rationale for what we felt and did. We wanted Black Art. We felt it could move our people, the Afro American people, to revolutionary positions (see essay, "The Revolutionary Theater," *Liberator,* July 1965). We wanted Black Art that was 1. *Identifiably Afro American.* As Black as Bessie Smith or Billie Holiday or Duke Ellington or John Coltrane. That is, we wanted it to express our lives and history, our needs and desires. Our will and our passion. Our self determination, self respect and self defense. 2. We wanted it to be a *Mass Art.* We wanted it to Boogaloo (like them Deacons for Self Defense down in Boogaloosa, La., when they routed the Klan). Yeh, Boogaloo out the class rooms and elitist dens of iniquitous obliquity and speak and sing and scream abroad among Black people! We wanted a mass popular art, distinct from the tedious abstractions our oppressors and their negroes bamboozled the "few" as Art. We thought it was Ain't! White Ain't. And we wanted Black Art.

That's why Rap delighted me so and still does (even though now its been widely coopted by Uncle Bubba and the Mind Bandits) because I could see that some of what came out of us had taken root. An open popular mass based poetry. It arrived, that's why the corporations moved so swiftly top "cover" and co-opt. Why they disappeared Grand Master Flash and Africa Bambataa, accused Prof Griff of the big A-S and brought in flesh rap like Two Live Crew; middle class negro rap such as Jazzy Jeff and Fresh Prince and finally the straight out Americans like Vanilla Ice and "Young Black Teen Agers" (white). Gangsta Rap was also brought in to exchange political agitation with ignorant braggadocio and thuggish imbecility, justifying the state nigger-youth annihilation program.

The last part of our eventual summation of the Black Arts Movement was that 3. We wanted an art that was revolutionary. We wanted a Malcolm art, a by-any-means-necessary poetry. A Ballot or Bullet verse. We wanted ultimately, to create a poetry, a literature, a dance, a theater, a painting, that would help bring revolution!

That was what it *all* was about. That's what the whole movement and essence of The Black Arts was raised and forwarded by, the desire by Black youth to make revolution in the U.S. To resist and finally destroy the slave system of racism and national oppression.

The Black Arts Repertory Theater School lasted formally a little more than a year, but by the end of 1965, there were similar efforts rising all over the country. There was a Black Arts Midwest (Woodie King and Ron Milner), a Black Arts West (Ed Bullins, Marvin X, Furaha Broadus) in San Francisco/Oakland/Berkeley. Both Emery Douglas the Black Panther revolutionary artist and Danny Glover came out of the Black Communications Project that we put together during that period at San Francisco State, and in the then Black Fillmore community. Black Arts South emerged in New Orleans with Val Ferdinand (Kalamu ya Salaam).

At one point Black Arts theaters and poetry organizations sprung up ubiquitously across the country, usually in the larger cities where there were Afro American pluralities or majorities. It was clear there was a torrent of inspiration that lifted the Black artists communities across the country, and the evidence is coming in.

What seemed most important about the BARTS was that it was a living paradigm of what many people had come to feel was the direction Afro American artists and the art with which they expressed the particular culture they reflected had to go. Fundamentally we must pursue what Du Bois called True Self Consciousness and defeat its reverse the Double Consciousness. The Black Arts Movement raised this antagonistic contradiction once again, as part of the cultural revolution still necessary to raise and unite the consciousness of the oppressed Afro American people, so that they better understand themselves as well as better resist their enemies.

We felt (and I still do feel) that the Afro American people were and are still involved in a war. A war for Self Determination, Self Respect and Self Defense. It is a war for equal rights and democracy. But how can we press this struggle to victory if we suffer for a Double consciousness, i.e., if we see ourselves, like Spike Lee and the other new wave Fechits, through the eyes of people that hate us? (Even in Living Color!) If we look at ourselves in that grim mixture of amusement and contempt? As artists we felt that that was our chief function, to reshape the minds of the people. To move them to revolutionary positions.

The dicta we arrived at 1. To create a true Afro American Art 2. To create a mass art. 3. To create a revolutionary art, were simply three of the most important and positive aspects of our methodology, our ideological practice, such as we understood it. This was the broad spearhead of Blackness that emerged and that I feel has lasted yet still to be further summed up.

But this broad credo came under attack fundamentally because we had initially cloaked our call to battle in the starkest terms of cultural nationalism and Hate Whitey language. Yet the essence of our call and our work was to try to unite the Afro American people, by raising their consciousness by attempting to raise our own consciousness and that of the Afro American artists and intellectuals.

We were new nationalists, older nationalists and others and that was the center of our loose front. But by the middle 70's, many of us still held the general credo of The Black Arts but no longer upheld nationalism. Even so, the three points remain strong and essentially correct. But we received opposition because we called for Black Art to define itself and speak for itself from the security of its own institutions. We were opposed because we withdrew from white people and for many of our downtown contemporaries this was unthinkable or impossible. But at the root of our most profound feeling was that it was the social context and practice of petty bourgeois Liberalism that we wanted to flee.

The Afro American people are an oppressed nation, objectively, with the right of Self Determination. This remains the valid issue of our struggle. But even broadening the take on our opposition, for many of our contemporaries the idea that somehow Black people could express themselves through institutions of their own creation and with ideas whose validity was confirmed by their own interests and measure was absurd.

Certainly in the hot 60's when "Revolution was the main trend in the world . . ." and many people felt they had to give lip service to "Blackness" much opposition was more covert, sub rosa or unable to find broad circulation in the Black community. Opposition was quickly identified as from the "whited out," the bourgeois negroes, the backward—though that was not necessarily always true. There were some people on the Left who occasionally tried to point out the excess and errors of our cultural nationalism. But since that time until the fullest unfolding of the Black Arts concept in the 70's until the eventual reaction that paralleled the shape and direction and dynamic of the overall political movement itself, with its Sisyphus-like historic pattern, evidence of the validity and continued existence of the Black Arts stance remains. Even though today, and for several years now, it is also obvious that the rock we rolled to the top of the mountain in the 60's and early 70's has been rolled back down on our heads. And now the essence of the opposition to what the Black Arts stood for and symbolizes has come "full out"—it is even empowered.

The Black Liberation Movement and even the Civil Rights Movement are held up each day to either public ridicule as backward and passé or the most valid ideas of our struggle are replaced with the ideas of the sickest and the most backward of our contemporaries, by Hanging Judges from the Caucasian Chalk Circle. And because of the continuous stream of distorted anti-democratic and anti Black and counter revolutionary images in all media have been used to try to "reverse correct verdicts" reached through struggle, to character assassinate the Black Liberation Movement and its chief combatants.

Spike Lee trashed Malcolm X and Martin Luther King, The Nation of Islam and Elijah Muhammad in the same movie. We hear from Bruce Perry that Malcolm was white and psychosexual. From various ex-revolutionaries we are told of the bankruptcy of the Panthers and every day people tell me that the BARTS movement tried to tell people what to write. No, it tried to unite the best of us to fight our oppressors!

And now in the midst of the starkest period of reaction we have ever seen, a new generation of the backward, the Buppies, the little neo negro greed balls bloated with the arrogant ignorance of abject submission to imperialism. The various Fly Boys in The Butter Milk and Affirmative Action Babies, Colored People whose mission like the Spikes and Skips, just like the Tom Ass Clarences and Colon Powells is to attack and give lie to the idea and movement for Black Self Determination. To make it seem that, Hey! we are all Americans and you all that ain't skipping the light fantastic of celebration by the imperialist super-structure are simply cursed by the Gods for trying to push that Black Shit—when we know it is America, America the Beautiful, that gives our salaries, our prizes, our note, hey, even our ideas.

Yet the deepest problem, aside from our history being covered, and gains won by our struggles being reversed being claimed by our enemies, conscious or un, is that we still have not built organizations and institutions to struggle for Self Determination, Self Respect, Self Defense. If we had built those institutions, those journals (like *Journal of Black Poetry, Black Nation, The Cricket, BARTS, The Spirit House, The Black House, The New School of Afro American Thought*), we would not have to worry about the distortions of the terminally backward, Black or White. We would define ourselves and speak for ourselves and carve up our enemies with the graceful ease of our high art. Duke and Trane and Billie them to death! But our enemies have created our spokespersons, and they speak for us every day, covering and distorting reality and this is the state in which we exist today.

The very people who even denied the existence of Black Art were immediately given grants to claim it. Even in this festival the Neals, Dumases, Sanchezes, Toures, Madhabutis are packed into single readings while opposition forces (remember the name of the festival itself) are given full range now to claim what we painfully struggled to bring into existence! The Lesson, where are our institutions and organizations of the Black Arts? Where are our theaters and newspapers and journals and truly independent films (not skin black but speaking from the essence of the most advanced consciousness of the Afro American people)? That no one has the right to rule our lives for a *second,* the true self consciousness, who we are, who we were and who we would become!

That is the continuing task we face, as revolutionary Black artists and intellectuals, to make Cultural Revolution. To fight in the super structure, in the realm of ideas, philosophies, the arts, academia, the class struggle between oppressed and oppressor. To recreate and maintain our voice as a truly self conscious, self determining entity, to interpret and focus our whole lives and history. And create those organizations and institutions that will finally educate, employ, entertain and liberate us!

AB Atlanta 8/94

I

Theory/Criticism

Introduction to Theory/Criticism

The Black Arts Movement (BAM) was not like a school of European modernism in art: it was not promulgated with a manifesto that codified its purpose, aesthetic, method, and the academy that it sought to overthrow. To be sure there were some bits of all of those things, as will be seen in the texts that follow. But despite the towering primacy of such a founding intellectual as Amiri Baraka, there was no grumpy old scroll-wielding high priest who certified artists for membership and expelled apostates as André Breton did for Surrealism. The result was a heterodoxical and aesthetically plural array of art that ranged from abstraction to social realism, revolutionary screed to diasporan idealism, historical reflection to projection of possible worlds, with all of the stops in between.

The times did impose a measure of consensus; some words of power did recur: artists aspired to be "relevant," as in "relevant to the struggle," as the ineluctable and inspirational force of African-American political activism was breaking and making history in undeniable ways, and the great majority of black artists wanted their work to be a part of that. "Community" weighed a great deal, as the projectile momentum of the movements that filled the street required that one had a place to stand, and our history, as fouled as it was in the United States, did offer a communal bond among African-Americans who would accept it, no matter how diverse we were regionally, socially and economically. Thus, elusive "unity" was a goal and a purpose. And then there was "blackness," as platonic ideal for adherents and as litmus for art and artists of dubious "relevance."

Combine these definitive elements with the imperative of *ars gratis populis* (art for the people) as opposed to the art-for-art's-sake orientation under which the founding artists of the BAM matured, and the making of black art was almost a new discipline. Artists wanted to communicate with African-Americans who were criminally mis- and under-educated, whose schools had not trained them to parse two-dimensional nuances of measure and metaphor, of irony and symbolism. Marry this concern with the fact that the wealth of African-American culture was to be found in its peasantry, proletariat, and petit-bourgeoisie and not in the middle class into which most of the BAM artists were born. The BAM artists desired more than anything to mine this lode at the radical, or foundation, of their culture at the same time that they wanted to speak to the source elements of their community, so it was no surprise that many artists had to reconsider the way that they worked as well as the material that their work was made of.

Thus, the visual artists of the Chicago-based collective Africobra talked of "Kool Ade colors" to reflect the pastels that were commonly seen in those days in the apparel of urban

African-American men. Poets applied the black vernacular as frequently as possible and composed for the stage as much as the page. Playwrights explored dilemmas that were beyond the situation of the black middle class. This is not to say that all of the artists of the BAM employed those particular concerns and devices all of the time, but they were frequently expressed, along with Pan-African imagery, designs that derived from ancient Egypt and sub-Saharan Africa, and clothing and hairstyles that bridged the continents. New critical tools had to be forged to discuss and present these developments.

It is arguable that the most formally aggressive artists were the jazz musicians, whom the editors have wisely included in this discussion, for they are too often omitted in treatments of the BAM. From the free blowing of the New York soloists to the modality of John Coltrane to the new systems of Cecil Taylor, Ornette Coleman & others to the theatricality of many of the artists of the Association for the Advancement of Creative Musicians, jazz practitioners broke out of the song form that had given structure to the first half century of jazz music and the diatonic-chromatic progressions that had governed jazz improvisation.

How to make sense of all this, indeed of all of the trends that the editors have outlined in their astute introduction? There was discussion of a "new mimesis" that would describe how black artists represented the real world; yet, as often as not, BAM artists made new worlds of imagination or of the ideal, and thus their art could be more accurately described as anti-mimetic. The numerous other attempts at a unified theory similarly captured the BAM in parts; none illuminated the whole, and that is as much an indication of the power, diversity, and beauty of the BAM as it is of African-American people. Furthermore, the universalism that governed the critical aesthetic models in which most Western writers were trained had to be refuted as did the assumed standards of beauty. The issue was raised: in a plural world, must there be plural conceptions of excellence and beauty? Clearly, the answer from the BAM perspective was yes, for they would not submit to the judgments of the establishment.

The texts that follow are exemplary of the kinds of critical, descriptive, and motivational writing that accompanied the art. If, in sum, they do not confect into a singular thesis, that does not diminish their importance, for each sermon that is included here enjoyed a congregation, and each congregation enriched and broadened the BAM.

Poetry and Black Liberation: Freedom's Furious Passions

Great art comes not from thought, but from ecstasy. And ecstasy always co-exists with pain.
—William Butler Yeats, 1913–14

Throughout the earth
let dead lips congregate,
out of the depths spin this long night to me
as if I rode at anchor here with you.
—Pablo Neruda, "The Summits of Macchu Picchu"

This is not a poem, but a Way into things, not a poem, but a prayer.
—Larry Neal, 1965

I

I am the representative of a generation of dreamers, warriors, and visionaries, who sought to forge a new direction for the African-American Nation, the Blues people, inventors of Soul Food and Soul Music, creators / innovators of that great, modern music popularly known as "Jazz." Laboring under the vicious bondage of official United States–sanctioned Apartheid in the 1950s and '60s, known as "Jim Crow" segregation, we sought not only to free ourselves from modern 20th Century Slavery, but to create Another Reality, where our entire people would not only be free—but *powerful;* an emerging, sovereign force in a Post-Colonial World, consisting of, to quote Dr. W. E. B. Du Bois, "mainly colored people." *In fact, four-fifths of the human population being Peoples of Color.*

Well, being *bards* as well as *activists,* we began the awesome task of *imagining a New Reality for African-America.* A Reality where Black women and men would actually have, and wield, *power.* Hence, our call for "Black *Power*" which seemed to really upset our friends, and "fellow Americans," the dominant Anglo-Saxon Majority. If we had, like our betters, the Black Middle-class Civil Rights elite, called for merely "Civil Rights" and Integration / Assimilation, then our liberal, Protestant masters would've been quite satisfied, even reassured. But we were poets and visionaries who kept asking questions about *who really controls* America? And why were "*They*" rich and the majority of "*us*" poor? And what was white skin privilege, and White Supremacy? and why did the poorest white feel superior to Dr. King and Mrs. Rosa Parks? And why did the Anglo Majority, for the most part, live in well-groomed suburbs, while the majority of us lived in modern *Bantustans* known as Black Inner City ghettoes? . . .

Meanwhile, in our drama, like "Day of Absence," or "Dutchman," or "The Slave," we imagined what it would be like if Black people "called the shots," were in power, or if the poor, working masses held power in the land. Then, of course, Africa had recently over-thrown centuries of European colonialism, and was busily engaged in "Wars of Libera-tion" against the invader Portuguese, and the Boers in Southern Africa. Then, ninety miles from Florida, the workers and farmers, the poor of tiny Cuba, seized power and threw out the local dictator, Batista, along with the Mafia gangsters who ran Cuba's gambling casi-nos. They declared Socialism, a workers and farmers revolution—and invited hundreds of young "Americans," including Black students, scholars, and artists: among whom were Prof. Harold Cruse, poet, LeRoi Jones / Amiri Baraka, and boxing champion Joe Louis. Concurrently, President Kwame Nkrumah of Ghana invited many African-Americans, including John H. Clarke, Maya Angelou, and Tom Feelings, to Ghana. From there Black people visited Nigeria and other countries; witnessed the North Africans of Algeria throw out the French colonialists, and declare Algeria free! In Asia, the Vietnamese defeated the French, then had to fight a second war against U.S. invaders; and ended up defeating the U.S. military machine . . . And so, we witnessed the *Dark Majority* fighting for freedom— and *winning,* in many cases!

As a young, oppressed Generation, our poetry imagined a World where no one was priv-ileged while millions were starving, or homeless, or preyed upon by drugs, or murderous, vicious killer-cops, invading armies, or arrogantly labeled "culturally deprived," or "Third World," or "savages" or "terrorists" merely for wanting Freedom and Self-Determination. As we began to mature and become more politically aware, ***we began to echo the voices of our greatest poets—our Prophets: young Dr. King, and the fiery Minister Malcolm X— both viciously assassinated by our Masters because they dared to dream, and work, for the liberation of African-Americans, and all of oppressed Humanity.*** More and more our vision grew wings—and flew throughout uptight, white, racist " Amurica," as we poets, artists and visionaries met each other demonstrating on picket lines, conducting boy-cotts, and marching at the United Nations, protesting the murder of Prime Minister of the Congo, the freedom-fighter, and poet, Patrice Lumumba. As we grew, through struggle, our poems began to reflect our Advanced Vision:

> *We want a Black Poem and a Black World.*
> *Let the World be a Black Poem,*
> *And let all Black people speak this Poem*
> *Silently or LOUD!*
> **—LeRoi Jones / Amiri Baraka**
>
> *I'm not an Invisible Man. My song, like rain,*
> *is universal. I'm not an Invisible Man,*
> *my anger stalks on ghetto-legs*

and illuminates the Nordic night,
like Roman candles, or Roman bombs,
over Ethiopia . . .
—Rolland Snellings / Askia Touré

We are unfair and unfair.
We are black magicians, Black Arts
we make in black labs of the heart.
The fair are fair and deathly white.
The day will not save them,
and we own the night.
—LeRoi Jones / Amiri Baraka

Say it loud, I'm Black and I'm proud.
—James Brown

We Insist, Freedom Now!
—Max Roach & Abby Lincoln

We must become stone-cold killers,
panther-spirits, invisible men,
night specters: your uncle tom teeth brightly grin
or you scratch your stepin' fetchit head,
while thrusting the blade into the beast-heart,
and still grinning with your uncle tom grin,
say: "you de boss, boss, heh, heh, heh, heh,
        now try this for size, motherfucker!"
—Larry Neal

The time
cracks into furious flower. Lifts its face
all unashamed. And sways with wicked grace . . .

It is lonesome, yes. For we are the last of the loud.
Nevertheless, live.

Conduct your blooming in the noise and whip of the whirlwind.
—Gwendolyn Brooks

[Malcolm X]
He was the sun that tagged
the western sky and
melted tiger scholars
while they searched for stripes.
He said, "fuck you white

man. We have been
curled too long. Nothing
is sacred now. Not your
white face nor any
land that separates
until some voices
squat with spasms.
—Sonia Sanchez / Laila Manan

The enemies polishing their penises between
oil wells at the pentagon
the bulldozers leaping into demolition dances
the old folks dying of starvation
the informers wearing out shoes looking for crumbs
the lifeblood of the earth almost dead in
the greedy mouth of imperialism
and my friend
they don't care
if you're an individualist
a leftist a rightest
a shithead or a snake . . .
—Jayne Cortez

II

The specter of a storm is haunting the Western world . . . The Great Storm, the coming
Black Revolution, is rolling like a tornado, roaring from the East; shaking the moor-
ing of the earth as it passes through countries ruled by oppressive regimes; toppling the
walls of mighty institutions; filling the well-paved, colonial streets with crimson rivers
of blood. Yes, all over this sullen planet, the multi-colored "hordes" of undernourished
millions are on the move like never before in human history. They are moving to the
rhythms of a New Song, a New Sound; dancing in the streets to a Universal Dream
that haunts their wretched nights: they dream of Freedom! Their minds are fueled and
refueled by the fires of that dream.
—Rolland Snellings / Askia Touré

In our manifestos and critiques, we vigorously questioned, and challenged, white supremacy and the Eurocentric World-view, and literary "canon." We called for, and sought to
create "a Cultural Revolution in art and ideas." Why was the narrow, parochial Eurocentric
World-view defined as "Universal," while the radical views of Pan Africanists and Peoples
of Color worldwide defined as "primitive," "backwards," or "childlike and naïve" (usually
when we called for revolutionary Socialism and the sharing of the World's extensive wealth
and resources between the Dark Majority and the wealthy European / White Minority)?

*The Black Arts Movement is radically opposed to any concept of the artist that alien-
ates him from his community. The movement is the aesthetic and spiritual sister of the
Black Power concept . . . The Black Arts Movement proposes a radical reordering of the
Western cultural aesthetic. It proposes a separate symbolism, mythology, critique, and
iconology . . . both concepts are nationalistic. One is concerned with the relationship
between art and politics; the other with the art of politics.*
—Larry Neal, "The Black Arts Movement"/Visions of a Liberated Future

As developing young poets and writers, we moved to create our own radical journals
and institutions, such as *Black America, Soulbook, Black Dialogue, The Black Scholar, The
Journal of Black Poetry, Black News, Nkombo, Black Theatre, Black World,* and *Liberator*
magazine; in other words, we created a Black, radical press in order to inspire, organize,
and coordinate the thinking of an entire Generation, a Movement of artists, intellectuals, and political and cultural theorists toward the goals of Black power, Black liberation
and sovereignty, with, or without, white allies or "liberals." As we said in SNCC (Student
Nonviolent Coordinating Committee), during Its Black Power phase, Blacks were moving toward mass uprisings nationally; our Movement needed organization, guidance and
direction. White people, allies, had the duty to wake up and also organize their own down-
trodden and poor communities. Other oppressed peoples, Native Americans, Latina/os,
and Asians understood this and began also organizing their specific cultural and political
movements, following our example. Young white students, and women, moved leftward,
following our spirited example; they became peace activists/war resisters: organized themselves by the hundreds of thousands, standing up, en masse, for Freedom, Justice, Human
Rights, and Women's Liberation. A new American Revolution was under way, sparked by
the poets and visionaries, female and male, leading the Black Arts Cultural Revolution,
which took the lead in imagining a New World, free from injustice, exploitation, racism,
sexism, and imperial greed . . .

Our close comrades, the Great Black Musicians, reached similar conclusions, influencing us, and also being influenced by us. The masters Max Roach and Abby Lincoln called
for "Freedom Now" on their best-selling album, *We Insist: Freedom Now!* It seems that
"Freedom" was in the air, and airwaves, across the repressive American landscape. The
great songstress Nina Simone recorded her best-selling album, *Mississippi, Goddamn!,* and
her sister-diva, Aretha Franklin, called for "Respect." R & B griot Curtis Mayfield and
the Impressions urged us to "Keep On Pushin'" and declared that "We're A Winner," and
Martha Reeves & the Vandellas sang "Dancin' in the Streets," which fearful racists labeled
the "riot song," which mirrored the yearly Urban Rebellions of the "Long, Hot, Summers,"
as our Natural hair grew long & untamed, as we wore geles, bubas, dashikis & agbadas,
reclaimed Mother Africa and our unchained souls . . . The great musical Master, John
Coltrane Onedaruth, envisioned, wrote, and performed "Naima," "A Love Supreme," "Alabama," "Africa Brass," "Ascension" and other Cosmic Music masterpieces, as he, Pharoah
Sanders, Andrew Hill, Archie Shepp, Marion Brown, Sunny Murray, Albert and Don
Ayler, and others raised funds for our Black Arts Repertory Theatre / School in Harlem. In
the summer of 1965, we took the Freedom poetry / New Music Rebellion to the legendary
Harlem streets, where the hip, politically aware Black masses welcomed us—musicians,
poets, actors, dancers, performing troupes—with open arms. A newly awakened, visionary,

politically conscious African-America [New Afrika] was on the National Scene; and the progressive '70s would be the creative Fruit which grew from this, *the largest Cultural Renaissance of the Twentieth Century.*

How the White Protestant Majority responded to this Cultural Revolution—soon joined by Native Americans, Asian-Americans, Latinas / os, and white women and youths—would determine the birth of *a Progressive, Democratic American Dream, as envisioned by Dr. Martin Luther King, Jr. at the March on Washington in 1963, or a vicious, racist, sexist, imperialist, war-mongering, neo-fascist World Terrorist: an "American Nightmare," as envisioned by our other Prophet, the equally brilliant Brother Malcolm X, in 1964. What has America become: Dream or Nightmare? My fellow Americans, you define this current Reality.*

DA-DUM-DUN: A BAM Triumvirate of Conch/Us/Nest: Miles Davis, Henry Dumas & Katherine Dunham in East St. Louis, Illinois

I

Surroundsounddrums

We learned by leading

Surroundsoundmusic

Led by learning

Surroundsoundpoetry

Led & Learned by Yearning

Surroundviewblackness

Spinning & spun by webs of conch-us-nests, hugely & brightly & bluesaically loded with Arkansippi consciousness, upriver driving wheels choo-chooing & checking in at points along 'Sippi's Corridor. Arrivants & dispersants: Until within the nearly limitless number of concentric circles of art & activism in Metro-East St. Louis (Illinois) *cum* Midwest, Miles Dewey Davis III came to occupy the center ring of the dawn, peak & afterglow of the Black Arts & Black Power Movements. Yes, we established common cause & comradeship with other regional centers & stars—Chicago, Detroit, Gary, Indianapolis, Kansas City, Omaha, Minneapolis–St. Paul—but Davis' expressivity, visibility, audibility & (self-styled) breeding/breathless originality, dominated & led other enveloping rings in East Saint's Soular System. To wit, the briefly lit Henry Lee Dumas (1934–1968), writer & poet who came to us via Sweet Home (Arkansas), Harlem, the Arabian Peninsula, Texas, Rutgers U. & Hiram College; & Katherine Dunham (1909–2006), who'd spent 30 years in 60 countries—as a dancer, choreographer, activist, anthropologist, filmmaker, author & educator—when she landed to found the Performing Arts Training Center (PATC), followed in the 70's & 80's by her namesake Dynamic Museum & Children's Workshop. Arriving in 1967, both Hank & KD taught at Southern Illinois University's Experiment in Higher Education (EHE), a local star in the national constellation of the Great Society's War on Poverty—& the umbrella for PATC, Upward Bound & other critical new planets in the Soular System. Saxophonist Julius Hemphill of St. Louis' Black Artists Group (BAG). Painter & Pan African Theorist Oliver Jackson, later of Oberlin College & California State

University–Sacramento. Sociologist Joyce Ladner, later of the Institute of the Black World, Hunter College & Howard U. Author Shelby Steele, later of California State University–San Jose. Fiction Writer Jerry Herman of American Friends Service & a Traverser of Africa. All taught at EHE where poet & Dumas protégé Sherman Fowler (then/later of *Negro Digest/Sides of the River/Black American Literature Forum* & *Drumvoices Revue*), actor Ron Tibbs (later w/Danny Glover of San Francisco's American Conservatory Theater's Black Actors Workshop) & filmmaker Warrington Hudlin III (*House Party*/Black Filmmaker Foundation) were students.

An inventory of circles of influence—& how they rippled & resonated across neo- & sub-centers of BAM—would require reams of paper & several semesters because the interconnecting & interdisciplinary struggles in East St. Love, like those elsewhere, included native & imported artists, activists & institutions. East Saint felt the direct & vicarious presences/influences of local, national & Third World artists, warriors & warrior-artists like "Leaping" Leon Thomas, Angela Davis, Motown's posse, Malcolm X, Black Panthers, Frantz Fanon, James Brown, John Coltrane, Che Guevara, Stokely Carmichael & H. Rap Brown (the latter two frequent visitors to Arkansippi), LeRoi Jones/Amiri Baraka (Lincoln Park circa 1969 w/Simbas) & Sister Sonia, as in Sanchez (who would accompany homeboy Leon on a voyage home in 1972), Fidel Castro—& Cuba!, Kwame Nkrumah, Sekou Toure & Mao Tse Tung.

Miles was a luminous soldier, too, but he was also *ours*: Native Prince, Star (who gigged with marquee names: think Bird, Billy, Billie, Monk, Dizzy), Rebel & Paragon in the ozone of jazz. Blowin' through town in the 60's/70's with wife Frances Taylor, former Dunham Company dancer. And later with actress Cicely Tyson ('82) for the naming of Miles Dewey Davis III Elementary School ("Home of the Blue Notes!"). Concurrently, we empathized with his wars, scars, phases, cycles, shifts & permutations. Wore tikis & gris gris fashioned from *Kind of Blue*'s "All Blues," "Blue and Green," "So What" & "Flamenco Sketches." Adorned ourselves in 1960's jewels like *ESP, Miles Smiles, Sorcerer, Nefertiti, Miles in the Sky, Filles de Kilimanjaro* & the uneclipseable *Bitches Brew*. Devoured & aped (his favorite) writers James Baldwin & Marc Crawford. Then, crisscrossed the US—NYC to East Boogie to Los Angeles—with him. Even 1974's *On the Corner*—with its so-real/surreal cover drawings—conjured up real life corners in the city of homeboy's upbringing. 15th Street at Broadway (site of the 1967 Rebellion where, earlier, Dr. Miles Dewey Davis Sr. planted his dental office & domicile). 15th at Bond Avenue where Miles & siblings attended John Robinson Elementary School (namesake of city's Black patriarch, where Nat Turner's granddaughters—Lucy & Fannie—taught) & St. Paul Baptist Church (where Fannie was organist). 15th at Piggott Avenue where he saw movies at the Lincoln Theater & hung out in Lincoln Park. These features completed the socialization arena that Dumas—in *Jonoah & the Green Stone* (1976)—would refer to as the three-ring concentric circles of home, church & school.

II

The great god Shango in the African Sea
reached down with palm and oozed out me.
HD (in *Knees of a Natural Man*)

When Henry Lee Dumas & East St. Louis interpenetrated presences in 1967—an act remi-niscent of Conrad Kent Rivers' lines, "Wandering through . . . France / As France wan-dered through me"—it was a rare moment in the Soular System. It was also the final such mutual immersion for Dumas after his birth & early childhood in Sweet Home, Arkansas, and additional youth years in Harlem, New York, before flirting with college, joining the Air Force, marrying & fathering two sons, returning to college & working briefly at Hiram College's Upward Bound Program in Ohio. African- & bible-centered, musicographic & choreographic, Hank's Sun Ra–inspired planet had already witnessed a succession of self-inventions at a time when the term "identity" was exhaled as naturally as air—& almost as frequently. Nearly 40 years later, in a kwansaba titled "Dumas' Rebirth in Word-Deed," I catalogued some of his favorite personal & family re-inventions during the Black Arts Movement:

> Awake as a quake, dreamin' Henry wrought
> Hank into "Ankh," Dumas into "Samud": Named
> his poems "sabas" & "ikefs," his friends
> "Headeye" & "Jonoah," his settings "Sweetwater" &
> "Harlem," his vessels "afro-horn" & "soul-
> boat," his heroes "Probe" & "Sun Ra"
> & his brothers "Fon" & "cosmic arrows."

In Sweet Home, Harlem & elsewhere Hank became a culturally "stored" & multi-storied boy-man who bonded richly with "villagers," something he accomplished almost instantly with EHE colleagues & students in East Saint Love. (You did that during Civil Rights & BAM despite the omnipresent paranoia—we called it "healthy" paranoia—stoked in part by the infiltration of agent provocateurs.) Hank's homework on East St. Louis yielded the city's backdrop via the Great Migration—& 1917 Race Riot; nurturing of Miles Davis, Ike & Tina Turner (at the Manhattan Club), Chuck Berry (at the Cosmo Club), Barbara Ann Teer & Leon Thomas (at Lincoln High School, also Miles' alma mater); hosting of Katherine Dunham, his new colleague; & its front-drop of poverty, gangs, high unemploy-ment & other hand-me-downs from slavery, Jim Crow & Midwestern apartheid. Riffin' in poems like "East Saint Hell" & "Our King is Dead" (an elegy for MLK), he merged BAM themes—"healthy" paranoia, the scourge of racism, art as self-defense, nationalism, & songification of struggle—with localized/East Boogie history & causes. Meanwhile, our self-studies of Hank included imbibing litmags in which he appeared—*Trace, Umbra, Hiram Poetry Review* & *Negro Digest*—along with his infectious love for knowledge, espe-cially Black folklore & music.

Students & faculty—of EHE & PATC—represented a range of socioeconomic & ideo-logical derivations & conditions. But nationalism, thanks to Black Arts/Black Power &

Elijah's "Nation," took deepest hold. We slept with one eye open but Hank slept fully awake, as noted by all who knew him, including friend/poet Jay Wright & his wife Loretta Dumas. (At Dumas' funeral in May 1968, a childhood friend said, "Henry thought too deep for the average person.") In December of 1967—in a mixture of real & surreal, mystical & mythical, cosmic & funkadelic—Hank described himself:

> Even the dust of the earth and the gravel and the twigs like fingers grappling, even the shadows, even these sleepy children of the sun yonder, even the family of trees, all these watch me run, hear my passage, see me, my phantom style racing across their vision, pulsing through their dialogues, and they rejoice, and they turn over inside themselves and they say, There he goes and there he goes. Look at him.

Attesting to the fecundity & productivity that paralleled such speed are numerous posthumously published collections of his writings from *Poetry for My People* to *Ark of Bones* to *Jonoah & the Green Stone* to *Knees of a Natural Man* to *Echo Tree.* Nobel Laureate Toni Morrison who, along with Amiri Baraka, has been a primary director of the Dumas "cult" cum "movement," called HD "A genius, an absolute genius."

III

> Taylor Jones said, "When I die / I don't want my brothers to cry. / When I go out old death to meet, / I want fire and dancing in the street!"

BAM! Daring lights & sets, interwoven with dance, music, song, drums, dialogue, monologue & oratory, ushered from the creative genius of Katherine Dunham, exploding on local & national stages less than a year after her arrival in East St. Louis. The words were part of an "ode" inspired by the death of Taylor Jones III, activist & leader of the Midwestern Region of the Congress of Racial Equality (CORE). Dunham's mettle had already been tested a few days after the July '67 Rebellion, when she was arrested after going to the aid of a young Black Power spokesman on one of East St. Louis' war-torn corners. The Rebellion & Jones' death/funeral fueled the writing & staging of "The Ode to Taylor Jones III."

Beginning with the "Ode," Dunham inserted EHE students, local organizers, activists & orators into skits, ballets, or full-length plays; wrote playlets around specific issues & causes; & incorporated works & words of East St. Louis artists/writers into PATC's fluid & flexible stage events. PATC's recruitment, curriculum & programmatic schedules included bringing the most influential organizers & gang leaders into consciousness & using them to attract theater, drum & dance initiates, many of whom at first sneered at the idea of men dancing on stage & disparaged leotards as "pantyhose." Charles "Swede" Jeffries' Imperial War Lords, Frank Smith's Black Egyptians & Charles Koen's Black Liberators were among gangs &/or organizations that Dunham & EHE helped politicize, enlist in new ideological-intellectual armies of activism, & place on stages of education & cultural arts. Hyman Frankel, Donald Henderson & Edward Crosby, EHE's triumvirate of brilliant leaders, frequently conferenced with Dunham & "street" leaders—resulting in an effective threefold forum of EHE, PATC & residential communities.

Meanwhile, international artists, scholars, activists—including South Africans in exile—statespeople & revolutionaries streamed through our offices, classrooms, workshops & hangouts. Visitors/consultants included Harry Belafonte & wife Julie, a former Dunham Company member; Eartha Kitt, also a former Company member; Oscar Brown Jr.; D.C. architect Topper Carew; psychologist Erich Fromm (whom we visited in the Apple, thanks to KD); Mille. Suzanne Diop of the Senegalese Supreme Court; renaissance man R. Buckminster Fuller; Nina Simone; H. Rap Brown & Stokely Carmichael; Gordon Parks & artist Charles White (from Dunham's Chicago days of leading a Works Project Administration [WPA] writer's unit); drummers Rene Calvin (Haitian) & Mor Thiam (Senegalese); St. Clair Drake; Hattie McDaniel & Brock Peters; & numerous other former Dunham Company members like Lucille Ellis & Tommy Gomez, based in nearby Chicago.

Performing, workshopping & lecturing throughout metropolitan East St. Louis, PATC & EHE also did tours of the Midwest, US & world; hosted student-faculty exchange programs with Nigeria, France & Haiti; & gave classes, workshops & forums in schools, prisons, neighborhood centers, churches, bars, restaurants. All of these offerings were, for the most part, extracurricular. But there were of course the main courses: While EHE restructured & renamed those in the General Education curriculum (for example, Joyce Ladner & I co-taught "Socialization of the Black Child," which qualified as "Introduction to Sociology" on the main/Edwardsville campus of SIU), PATC reprised the curriculum of the Dunham School of Dance from 1940's New York. Course offerings, beyond the obvious ones in drumming, dance & acting, included French, Wolof & Haitian Creole languages; African-Diaspora History; textiles, weaving, cooking & sewing; martial arts, including capoeira; poetry & playwriting. From enrollees, Dunham drew members of her newly developing company. When combined, EHE, PATC & St. Louis organizations like BAG helped form the nation's most comprehensive/inclusive Black Arts Collective during the BAM era. "We must create a theater-going audience," KD said time & time again: "We have to have cultural, literary, consciousness-raising, activist-oriented & performing arts—& audiences for them!" And there was no doubt that Miles "So What" Davis & Henry "Ankh" Dumas were in soul-sync with her.

I

Politics and Culture

The Harlem Black Arts Theater—New Dialogue with the Lost Black Generation

Thus ends my critique, yet this long analysis does not end the inquiry, nor does the inquiry treat every possible aspect of the problem. It is my conviction, though, that enough has been revealed of the antecedents to indicate the "clear and present" danger, in several of its many facets. Although I began by saying that this unraveling of ideas would relate to eighteen years of my own personal experiences and observations, it was not to deny that these, too, were not historically determined, but rather that when I began to have such experiences I did not realize that they were determined by what had happened before.

It seems that every generation has the illusion that what they discover in life as personal problems had never previously existed. Often there are grounds for this attitude inasmuch as old problems simply recur in new forms, with new qualities. The catch is that, with old problems in new guises further and further removed from their origins, the new generation often fails to see the historical connections. And if the new generation happens to be uninterested in history—and this is characteristic of the American existential mood—we have on our hands yet another Lost Generation who, unlike the Hemingways, find the contemporary world offering fewer and fewer paradises for exile that are not either swamped, or threatened by, revolutions. However, the first Lost Generation was white—notwithstanding those Negro intellectual emigrés to Europe who were the black parallel to that 1920's phenomenon.

But today we do have a Lost Black Generation—very young and very historically conditioned. They are lost within the deep canyons of the Northern urban cities, aliens to white western culture of the American style, whose exile is within themselves. Their alienation is reflected in many ways—in delinquency, crime, sex, drugs, hatred of whites, hatred of the United States, sometimes in hatred of themselves, and sometimes even in poetry and other art forms. These outlets become *their* manner of self-exile within a social system from which there is no longer any easy escape. Yet, if earlier Lost Generations escaped to Europe for inspiration, many of the contemporary black generation, without exiling themselves bodily, find their inspiration not in Europe, but in Africa. In this sense I find today's mercurial young black generation quite unprecedented, radically surprising, and beyond the conventional scope of politics. Although I find them exasperatingly anti-historical, many are extremely mature in their thinking—especially in a situation that many say offers no

From *The Crisis of the Negro Intellectual* (New York: Morrow, 1967).

future for black people (or for anyone else, for that matter). These are the qualities that distinguish this young black generation from the one that was emerging when I first ventured into that Harlem YMCA amateur drama group just prior to America's entry into World War II. As I said at the outset of this study, "One of my first acts in the pursuit of becoming a more 'social being' was joining that theater group."

I and my generation thought that we were the "greatest," the most "hep," with our garrulous, undigested knowledge of pseudo-radical-Left social wisdom. We were planning and plotting to do great things as we dissected Marx, Shaw, Ibsen, O'Neill, Du Bois (and Hitler). Little did we know that we were being groomed to be "wasted" in the Pacific, Africa, Asia and Europe despite the fact that the moving finger was visibly writing its message on the wall. And even afterwards, when we emerged as the "war generation," we still considered ourselves the chosen people of contemporary history. We, the Veterans, were the most important, the most pampered of any segment of the population. However, the *Negro* veteran, a misplaced, outlandish product of the second international world war among the imperialists, was ironically, a man of history who was being pushed further and further adrift from the consciousness of his own particular history in America, not to speak of his African beginnings. I have felt for a long time that World War II severed the American Negro not only from his prewar American provincialism, but from whatever tenuous moorings he might have had with his own historical past. Practically every able-bodied Negro either had made more money than he ever had in his life, or else had gone through the psychological trauma of being purged by the American military machine. Most of us Negro soldiers who survived this ordeal were, like myself, never quite the same again, *inside.* Those, especially, who had served in the European, Mediterranean theaters and who had known Ireland, Scotland, England, North Africa, Italy, France, Belgium, etc., became very "internationalist" in outlook after the war. This mood served to enhance the feeling that we were still the Chosen Generation, the generation of accomplishments, of experiences, whose demands would and must be met. But time has shown that we were in fact the Wasted Generation, destined to be used up in the war years as a means of dealing with that sole historical emergency. I say this in order to account for a personal sense of rootlessness that has never left me since the end of the war. In retrospect, I can see now that this rootlessness was my own personal form of alienation, but the word was not then in vogue. I also see, from a distance, that this rootlessness was related to that qualitative difference between "purpose" in war and "purpose" in peace. The war was forced on many of us, whether we liked it or not. The Negroes in the army swore, cursed, bitched and "snafued"—but they carried out army orders. Yet none of us realized that the war would banish forever our prewar way of life and obliterate our former social frame of reference so completely as to make it seem the vicarious experience derived from a book describing America of 1940. Hence, the period from 1946 to the 1950's was a new era, a new frame of reference, but what new purpose had we found? Were we actually as crucial a generation as we thought? The fact is, we had no purpose. We did not know that our "purpose" had already been served. As a result, quite a number of us were led into the radical leftwing, where we were "wasted" again. Through all those years of rather blind, intuitive and frenetic searching, many of us did not realize that another generation would have to emerge on the scene before a purpose could be divined in all its many ramifications. That new generation was being born into the world as we boarded the troop ships.

As it turned out, it was in the new Harlem Black Arts Repertory Theater and School in May, 1965, that I realized the full potential of the new young black generation. There, at a round-table discussion on Negro playwrights and the black theater, a young man, in his early twenties, discussed his views on the theater. He said, in effect, that *a black theater should be about black people, with black people, for black people, and only black people.* Immediately, there are startled objections to this radical idea, from both the panelists and the audience: "This is impossible, impractical and anti-humanistic EXTREMISM!" . . . "Black people cannot close themselves off in a compartment separate from whites" . . . "Art is universal" . . . "Art is for everybody" . . . and so on. Then came the question: "*Suppose the Black Arts Theater wanted to put on a play with Negro and white characters?*" "You see," said the opponent with a smug smile, "you would have to eliminate such a play. You would limit the repertory of the Black Arts Theater. You would limit the range of your playwrights to writing only about black people." But the young man, the ranting extremist, said: "Oh no, it won't be that way—you dig? We have black actors who can play white roles—you dig? *They can be made up to play white people.*" In other words, this young man was intent on having a truly *black* theater, come what may. And the whole historical truth is, that this young man was absolutely right. Even *I,* who have been castigated and refuted for eighteen years by the theatrical integrationists for my views on the need for a purely ethnic Negro theater, could not have put the question so clearly. *I* would have made room for the mixed-cast play in a black theater repertory by having white people play white roles, whenever demanded. Beyond that, my own standards for a black theater would be one where Negroes themselves would finance the institution and man all the technical and administrative posts.

But Negro theatrical history has demonstrated time and time again the inexorability of that unique Negro-white aesthetic, that culturally false symbiosis that undermines and negates the black theater idea. First off, the Negro creative intellectual, as writer, artist and critic has no cultural philosophy, no cultural methodology, no literary and cultural critique on himself, his people, or on America. Hence he cannot create, establish, and maintain a code of cultural ethics, an artistic standard, a critical yardstick or any kind of cogent and meaningful critique on society that might enable him to fashion viable and lasting institutions in the cultural spheres that motivate progressive movements.

If any group of Negroes were to start a black theater in a black community without a well-thought-out rule of thumb on administration, Negro playwrights, white playwrights, Negro actors, white actors, Negro technicians, white technicians, Negro directors, white directors, Negro audience, white audience, Negro plays, mixed-cast plays, etc.—such a theater venture would soon collapse. Even if this theater group started with the hopes of becoming "for, or, about, and by" black people, *without a code,* it would soon be integrated out of existence. Somewhere down the line the first white integration breach would be made, probably the first breach would be the drama about Negroes by a white playwright *negating the Negro writer,* but accepted by the Negro actors, eager for roles. Next would come the drama about whites with a Negro cast (for instance Shakespeare, Shaw, Ibsen, Williams or Miller). The Negro actors would suggest this gambit in the interest of perpetuating the classics, further ignoring the Negro writer. In the meantime, there would be a "name" Negro writer off somewhere peeping at the "signs" in white people's "windows" in search of themes; all the Negroes in the theater, from avowed integrationists to vocal but pseudo-nationalists, would stop and applaud his achievement. Next would come the white "name" directors and the Negro group would forget about the necessity of training a corps of black ones. Then would come the white technicians who, downtown, had gained the invaluable experience backstage in several off-Broadway groups where they often grant token administrative and technical posts to favored fair-haired Negroes in the interests of integration. Last would come the exhilarated white liberal or Communist leftwinger with the final message: "How wonderful! Let us all broaden this great theatrical beginning by integrating it into an institution of humanistic universality for the whole wide world to see and enjoy!" The Negroes would agree, and that would be the beginning of the end of the group. It has happened time and time again in the annals of the Negro in the theater.

For these reasons, and more, the young extremist at the Black Arts Repertory Theater was historically accurate. For at the *outset* it will require precisely such uncompromising hard-line cultural philosophy to maintain and sustain the kind of black ethnic theater he wants to see. Give the Negro integrationists one foot in the door of that theater and it is dead. It does not matter whether or not, in the long run, this young extremist will relent on white casting, in the interests of stage realism. Maybe he will, maybe he won't, but no damage will be done because by then, he will have *established a theater*. After that, local public opinion will head this theater group in its proper direction. For, after all, if such a black theater seeks to educate a black audience, it will be the audience who has the final say about the intrinsic value of a Black Arts Repertory Theater in the black community. When this young extremist said "We will have black people, made up as white people to play white roles," the symbolic cycle in the history of the American theater had made, in my view, a complete revolution. Back in the nineteenth century, in the years following the Civil War, white theatrical companies did not even allow Negro performers to play Negro roles in their productions. They used white actors in blackface, and it was considered standard procedure in the American theater. James Weldon Johnson tells the story of what a startling revelation it was to the theatrical producers of 1876 when it was decided to permit a real Negro performer to play the lead in the stage version of *Uncle Tom's Cabin*. "Why not have a real Negro play Uncle Tom?" someone said.[1]

The Black Arts Repertory Theater and School was started by LeRoi Jones and others, and hence my reticence in this book in discussing much of Jones' work. Jones has come so far and so fast since 1961, and in the meantime been so contradictory, that it is difficult to place him. In 1961, after my own personal ideological tussle with the Jones-Shepp-Hicks contingent in Harlem, no one could have made me believe that in 1965 LeRoi Jones would start a Black Arts Repertory Theater and School in Harlem. But he did—in itself amazing, because Jones is not a ghetto product. Any of my personal early misgivings about Jones grew out of my critical responses to his different poses and postures. As it turns out these Jonesian posturings have not been all upstage antics, but rather the ambivalence of the supreme actor brazenly in search of just the right "role" that would best suit the purposes in life of the real man inside Jones. Nevertheless, it is my belief that his play, *The Slave*, stamps Jones as the most original dramatist Negroes have produced since Oliver Pitcher (who still remains unheard of by the general public). Nonetheless, the Black Arts Theater and School, after an auspicious beginning, lasted about seven months and collapsed. It

---

1. James Weldon Johnson, *Black Manhattan* (New York: Knopf, 1930), 91.

had a very short, stormy, creative career that has left an indelible impression on the minds of both its supporters and detractors. The causes of this collapse deserve examination because they relate graphically to the general theme of this critique—the social role of the Negro creative intellectual. The Black Arts was not a failure in achievement, so much as a failure in its inability to deal with what had been achieved. When Jones, the radical, avant-garde, literary integrationist, turned nationalist, he did not go far enough in his understanding of nationalism. Moreover, he had too much to overcome—forty-five years of leadership mismanagement on this question. As a result, the Black Arts Theater began without the foundation of a tradition of cultural nationalism. Lacking this tradition, the role of the Negro creative intellectual as nationalist is not understood even by the nationalists themselves. Even Garveyism, for example, was not cultural nationalism in Afro-American terms. Note this description of a Garvey meeting in New York during the 1920's.

> Garvey held a mass meeting at Carnegie Hall, in downtown New York City. It was packed to overflowing; white people attended too, as it was well advertised in white newspapers. . . . Items on the musical part of the programme were: Ethel Clarke, Soprano, singing Eckert's Swiss song, and Cavello's Chanson Mimi; The Black Star Line Band, in smart uniforms, rendering Overtures from "Rigoletto" and "Mirello"; New York Local Choir, fully robed, singing The Bridal Chorus from "The Rose Maiden" and "Gloria" from Mozart's 12th Mass; the "Perfect Harmony Four" in Sextette from "Lucia"; Basso Packer Ramsay sang Handel's "Hear me ye Winds and Waves." The second half of the programme were speeches by the Officers and [Garvey]. Subjects were: "The future of the black and white races, and the building of the Negro nation."[2]

It is very likely that all these singers were West Indians, which accounts for their Anglicized or Europeanized musical tastes. Not a note of the American Negro musical heritage was sounded on this occasion (and this was typical), not even a spiritual, not to mention jazz or a classical melody by an Africanized composer such as J. Rosamond Johnson or Samuel Coleridge Taylor. This nationalist blindspot on cultural affairs is characteristic, and the general lack of rapport between nationalistic trends and the creative intellectuals no one-sided affair.

However, when the creative intellectual moves toward the nationalist wing, he must understand the implications of what he is tackling—a trend without a cultural school of thought. The Negro writer must be firm in his role because the nationalist trend will not respect it, and will attempt to force the writer into the mold of being a political, rather than a cultural, leader. The Negro writer will be negated as creator if his cultural role is not paramount. On a larger scope, and in a different way, that is what happened to Paul Robeson.

LeRoi Jones, after establishing the Black Arts Theater, tried then to play the role of political spokesman on nationhood, in the absence of any official organization established to back up his political pronouncements about "destroying the system." Although again Jones was advised that these steps would have to be taken if the Black Arts was to be

---

2. Amy Jacques Garvey, *Garvey and Garveyism* (self-published, 1963), 103.

sustained, he failed to pay adequate attention. He made no attempt to link up a cultural institution with political and economic organization; without it, the Black Arts could not win the broader community support it needed to survive. Instead Jones attempted the triple-threat role of writer, cultural leader, and political spokesman, and consequently, all three roles were inadequately filled.

LeRoi Jones considered that to have established the Black Arts Theater was enough, but even so he did not pursue this cultural trend to its full potential. For example, his successful book, *Blues People,* suggested that much greater effort be mounted in the jazz field. Indeed, as jazz is his specialty, Jones' next step should have been to found a critical Negro jazz publication. Beyond that, Harlem could well use a jazz institute, a type of foundation that has never existed, to further the creative, economic, research and educational interests of the jazz musician. The problem here is that despite *Blues People,* the white jazz critics are still deciding the status and fortunes of Negro jazzmen. Cultural nationalism must be expressed by all possible organizational and educational means that might further and equalize the status of the Negro artist as creator, interpreter, or critic. Such an aim is certainly in consonance with the cultural development of the Negro community.

It is not the role of the Negro creative intellectual or writer to play the Big Leader Spokesman. His role as spokesman is to see what has to be done, point to it, and then explain why. He must be able to instruct others in what he cannot (or should not) do himself. Jones' failure to implement this kind of leadership in the Black Arts inevitably forced him into the position of being told by his "opposition" what to do—within the very institution he had founded. These oppositional elements in the Black Arts were dangerously irrational, misguided, negative, and disoriented. They represented the terrorist fringe of the nationalist wing—an alienated and psychotic separatism that has developed as a result of the long-standing cultural neglect and leadership default endemic to Harlem. This nihilistic fringe has its counterparts, no doubt, in all the great urban ghettoes, especially in the North. This trend is anti-middle class, anti-intellectual, anti-anything that resembles the establishment—from a college education to pressed-suit manners, whether Negro or white. Mainly it is anti-bourgeois—covering a rather broad spectrum of class "sins." This trend carries its separatism and black irrationality to such extremes that it bans Negro spokesmen from television, radio, and panel programs involving whites, among other things. In the absence of their own viable and positive program, the Afro-American Nationalists will have severe difficulties with this trend. Unless many more representatives of the Negro middle classes and the intelligentsia become increasingly committed to basic political, economic and cultural issues in the ghettoes, aggravated class conflict is in store for the Negro movement as a whole.

The experiences of LeRoi Jones in the Black Arts Theater reveal several hard truths about the nationalist wing. In dealing with Afro-American Nationalist trends, Negro writers and other creative elements must maintain their own autonomy absolutely; they must not permit themselves to come under the domination of activists and politicians who do not favor cultural front activities. The political activists will attempt to either suppress or control the creative elements, and especially the writers. This is, of course, a problem of long standing for all radical or revolutionary movements, especially those of the Marxist Left. The Negro writer, who is nationalistically oriented, must, at all times, fight within movements to maintain his creative and critical independence within a reasonable context of the general aims of the movement. The American system, unlike the Soviet, Chinese or African, has had its full flowering of the industrial revolution on the economic front; thus the Negro movement as a whole has no need for the politics of suppression and control of criticism and creativity. As a matter of fact, the precise cultural aim of the Negro movement *has* to be for the enhancement of criticism and creativity, not the other way around.

In this regard, Jones' defeat in the Black Arts Theater is attributable to the fact that the Afro-American Nationalists do not understand the functions of criticism on the cultural front. For example, *Liberator* magazine carried Jones on its masthead as a contributor to this publication. It also hailed the establishment of the Black Arts and ran a two-part series interpreting LeRoi Jones as creative artist and spokesman.[3] Yet not a single problem relating to the internal conflicts within the Black Arts Theater program was ever aired, debated, or criticized in the pages of this magazine. What was the validity of the experimental plays performed in the Black Arts? What value was there in the plays that expressed Jones' revolutionary theater concept? What was the value of the courses taught at the Black Arts? Where did the Black Arts get its money? Was it or was it not "politically" appropriate for the Black Arts to obtain funds from Federal sources? Why was it not possible to get financial assistance for the Black Arts from Negro middle-class sources? Why did so many Harlem nationalist groupings of the separatist variety, who had been condemning every Negro reform leader for begging for Federal assistance, rush in to obtain a share of the Black Arts program's Federal assistance funds? Why was the "opposition" within the Black Arts permitted license to drive young representatives of the middle class out of the institution? Why did not Jones himself prevent this, since he is from the Negro lower-middle class? These are a sample of issues that should have been aired in *Liberator*. But this magazine, like its predecessors, was unable to achieve any organic or functional journalistic relationship to any Harlem community issue or institutional movement.

The history of the Negro intelligentsia indicates that the role of the Negro creative intellectual is an interim role at best, insofar as leadership is concerned. This role is necessary, in the absence of other willing, or able, spokesmen, in order to bring the cultural front (as differentiated from the political and economic fronts) into its proper focus. Negro creative intellectuals must not become political leaders or mere civil rights spokesmen in the traditional sense. To do so, means that intellectuals who are creative will be forced to subordinate their potential to the narrow demands of the politics of nationalism and civil rights. The only real politics for the creative intellectual should be the politics of culture. The activists of race, nationalism, and civil rights will never understand this, hence this dilemma becomes another ramification of the manifold crisis of the Negro intellectual.

---

3. L. P. Neal, "Development of LeRoi Jones," *Liberator*, January–February 1966.

CAROLYN GERALD

Symposium: The Measure and the Meaning of the Sixties

Janheinz Jahn, in the Appendix of his book, *Neo-African Literature, A History of Black Writing,* stated that, as of January 1967, there existed no magazine in the United States concerned 'exclusively' with African-American literature. The statement is rather remarkable, when we consider that Soulbook, Black Dialogue and the Journal of Black Poetry were all publishing by then. The statement thus submerges a whole literary movement. The emergence of these journals and others similar to them was the literary enactment of the crisis of the Sixties: the Break With The West. Through them, black literature reorganizes itself, serving the cause of blackness by analyzing its suppression and recreating its images and its myths. Their role is thus revolutionary, and since the building of a black national consciousness is conceived of as urgent by those who write in the revolutionary journal, it must be accomplished on many levels. The immediate outer realities call for a reporting of the facts of oppression, for a mobilization of forces, for socio-political analysis. The soul within and the fragmented community require an image-making, myth-building symbolization of that reality. Political activism and poetry can thus complement each other. It is not the subject matter which distinguishes socio-political literature from esthetic literature here. The subject matter is really always the same: black survival through identity and strength. But the fiction or poetry of survival is rendered through imagery, through symbols, through experimentation with different rhythms, with different syntactical forms, with a different vocabulary, through the indirectness of its statement about our condition. The revolutionary journals thus attest to an all-inclusive view of the black experience and it would be a mistake to pass them by in the vain search for evidences of the literary expression of a people neatly fractured off from life, as is too often the case in old, tired societies with nothing left to fight for; it would be a misreading of the times.

All the journals with which we are concerned have certain things in common: in addition to their double development (political and literary), all of them show a non-commercial orientation. They have operated on limited funds and a missed edition has not been infrequent. They are distributed principally through black dealers and by subscription. They thus are written by black people for black people and it is rare that a white writer appears in their pages (as did Ted Vincent in Soulbook 2, with many editorial reservations. And a letter to the editor of Black Dialogue from a rather pompous white reader of the first issue

From *Negro Digest* 19.1 (November 1969).

states in part "i cannot find one word in this Black Dialogue which comes from one of You to me, one of Us."). The advertising is limited to black bookstores, black publishing companies, the other black journals (except the first two issues of Black Dialogue had some advertising from radical white groups). The editorial boards tend to have overlapping membership. A number of the poets and writers publish in all of the journals; most of them do not publish in white journals or anthologies.

We can isolate the following aspects as typical of the literature appearing in these journals: 1) the black community of brothers, those who share our condition and with whom we work for the common liberation may be perceived as national, Western Hemispheric, international, or the community may be perceived as Bandung—the whole of the non-white world; 2) the existing black culture may be glorified in a conscious effort to build a sense of identity from the immediate past, or it may be rejected as the heirloom of slavery, and a new or modified cultural image projected which incorporates Bandung elements and/or draws on the pre-Western past; 3) a gap may exist, particularly in the early phases, between the political and the esthetic consciousness, i.e., one writer may single out certain aspects of reality as having immediate relevance in practical life, yet another may be symbolically working through other aspects in his art; 4) similarly, either the socio-political or the artistic-literary thrust may have greater emphasis, or there may be a shift in emphasis; 5) there is a sustained myth-building process which creates new gods and renovates the universe, and which provides the black community with black or Bandung heroes or restores those heroes to it which white society has sullied and submerged behind negative terms and concepts.

Among the revolutionary journals, several types can be isolated: those which have local contributorship and readership, and deal with local issues; those produced on college campuses by black student organizations; those which have, or are seeking, wide representation and wide readership in the black community. It is impossible to discuss all the journals here. I could list perhaps thirty, some of which are now defunct, which to my knowledge have appeared in the past four years or so and which share all the characteristics listed above.* However, Soulbook, Black Dialogue and the Journal of Black Poetry are the most important ones in terms of age and consistency of publication, circulation and how well-known the contributors are. Through these three, we can analyze some of the developments which characterize the 'genre' as a whole.

Black Dialogue provides a good study in the growth and development of the revolutionary journal. The first issue (1965) resulted from efforts by a group of San Francisco State College students. Much of this first issue is local in tone, but succeeding issues come more and more to reflect Black America generally. The editorial board expands; at present, the board has regional representatives from New York (headquarters), San Francisco/West

---

*NEGRO DIGEST itself may be considered with this group, as it began considering the nationalist alternative long before the others existed (see for example, the August 1963 issue, article "Integration or Black Nationalism?" by Richard Thorne). Many of the contributors to the revolutionary journals are regular contributors to NEGRO DIGEST. Still, in addition to its much longer history of publication, it has a much wider readership, contributorship, circulation and scope. It is, if you will, an "exception." Black Theatre is important enough to be mentioned here. It is one year old, but written by people who were involved from the beginning with the black revolutionary journal movement, and indeed, with the black theater movement, which began really to take shape at about the same time as the first revolutionary black journals emerged.—The Author

Coast, the Mid-West, Southern United States, Africa. In terms of content, Black Dialogue has come to include art forms (particularly graphic) other than literary. There are issues in which political writing dominates (Winter 67–68), in which political and artistic content is almost equally divided (July-August 65), and the latest issue (Spring 69) contains no political articles (although political concerns are evident in other ways, e.g., the full-page announcement "Don't let them destroy Harlem. Stop the State Building," with an illustration showing angry blacks pelting a corralled, grinning Lindsay and cohorts). This is by no means the essential criterion by which to judge the magazine's maturity. The growing evenness of tone, which was not there in the first issues, is a surer indication. The political articles of the first issue show an acute awareness of the international character of black literary expression, and of the right of a society of people to non-annihilation (i.e., non-absorption by the West) and to nationhood, whether that society is African or African-American. But the intellectual analysis has not yet been internalized, and the fiction and poetry show us still to be in the painful Break With White Society, still tormenting ourselves with the moribund integrationist experience. The literature shows us still on the lonely quest which preludes the discovery of peoplehood as a lived experience. This attitude is replaced—you can see the process from issues to issue—by a growth, a hope, a conscious creation. The personal poems now acquire an archetypal sense which the earlier ones lack: the poet is not a black man, he is the Black Man. Negative images of black society tend now to have behind them a missionary message ("we know / the trickery that exiles us . . . / and still we dance," Ed Spriggs, Autumn, 66); black images are now projected on the cosmos as we now begin to perceive ourselves as universal beings ("our souls are open skies and children / zooming across green places." Larry Neal, Autumn, '66).

Soulbook, more militant than Black Dialogue (it is "the quarterly journal of revolutionary afro-america") and more consistent in tone and format, appeared shortly before Black Dialogue and also on the West Coast (Berkeley, "racist u.s.a."). Soulbook publishes a proportionately large amount of political analysis, but its short stories and poetry are an important part of its format. Frantz Fanon on the political front, Aimé Césaire on the cultural, are frequently featured, written about and translated. Articles and communiqués keep us posted on liberation movements everywhere. Soulbook thus embraces as brothers all the Bandung world ("We black people realize that we have something in common with the majority of the world's peoples: we are all non-white and we are all oppressed by white," Cedric Little, Soulbook 6). The theme of throwing off the shackles and the call to arms of the revolutionary writings is transmuted, in the poetry, into various motifs, and that of castration is one of the most prevalent. By ritual reenactment of the death of virility, the poet gives himself and/or his audience a chance to be reborn into manhood. ("Black Soldier / Marched home . . . / Hung up his balls," Patricia Bullins, Soulbook 4; "when deranged vipers/ sliced through your black / genitals my body was one / huge bleeding ball," K. Willy Kgositsile, Soulbook 5; "Black bourgeois man / . . . / He got no nuts; / Left one in desk drawer, / Wife got other one in pouch 'tween her legs.," Bobb Hamilton, Soulbook 6).

The Journal of Black Poetry, unlike Black Dialogue or Soulbook, is mainly concerned with one phase of literature. But the Journal also expresses activist concerns within its literary format, and yet maintains a consistent tone and approach. To do this, it relies heavily on pictorial expression. The center spread, for instance, of the Fall '67 issue shows an outline map of the United States cut into two jagged halves. One half of the map bears part of a photograph of young black men behind bars. The caption directly over them reads "U.S.A." and above that, the label "Others." In the other half of the map, black hands clasp each other in brotherhood, and above the heads of a family unit (black man, woman and child), a raised black arm clasps a rifle. The caption above reads "Afro-America" and above that, "Self-Rule." Also the Journal often includes essays which, in discussing black art or culture, look inevitably to the political aspects ("when Black people talk about 'Black Consciousness or Power,' they are speaking indirectly of Nationalism—whether cultural, political or economic. . . . We are cultural slaves! Dig it! Victims of what Bro. Harold Cruise calls 'Cultural Imperialism,'" Askia Muhammad Touré (Rolland Snellings, Spring 68). Black culture and black survival are, after all, one and the same thing.

If we compare chronologically the issues of all three journals, we discover that the literature which glorifies the 'sub-culture' (works in dialect, works which describe the black woman in very sensual terms, works which accept or glorify cohabitation) occur most clearly in the earlier issues of Soulbook and of Black Dialogue, and that the embracing of African and Eastern symbols and images, some experimentation with the forms within these cultures, is most clearly illustrated in later issues of the Journal of Black Poetry. Clearly, there is a widening of the potentials here for a renovated literature, and a forsaking of chauvinism as too confining.

In the work of the poets to give us back our heroes and to provide us with new ones, two types of black men are always sung: Jazz and blues musicians (Otis Redding, Ornette Coleman, Charlie Parker, and above all, John Coltrane) and political activists (Chaka, Nat Turner, Marcus Garvey, Patrice Lumumba and, more than any man any time anywhere, Malcolm). Photographs and drawings of Malcolm as well as poetry abound in these journals. (Of course, poetry about Malcolm is not confined to those writing in the journals; so much of it exists that it has been anthologized: *For Malcolm: Poems on the Life and Death of Malcolm X,* Broadside Press). It is a sign of Malcolm's growing status as the source at which to renew our faith in our destiny that his example is invoked in a Black Dialogue editorial to help two groups within the black community see the way clear to settling their differences. His actions in life have become symbolic of the destiny of African Americans (". . . the statements and comments made by Brother LeRoi represent a step Eastwards in African American culture that was prophesied by the epic journeys of El Hajj Malik El Shabazz (Malcolm X) to Mother Africa, the Holy City Mecca, and the Middle East," Askia Muhammad Touré, Journal of Black Poetry Fall '68). The choice of adjective *epic* is indicative. Malcolm is the epic hero of our struggle, of our journey toward a new consciousness, toward a new nation. His significance, far more than historical, is mythological.

These three journals with which we have dealt did not exist more than five years ago. Yet their writers and thinkers, many of whom are now in their thirties, existed long before then, as writers and thinkers, somewhere in the black communities. The journals emerged to fill the need for that "meeting place for members of the black community wherever that community may exist" (to quote Black Dialogue). Through these journals, and the many others which have sprung up since, current black literature is being grouped and diffused, digested and, in a sense, even created. The revolutionary black journal made its appearance at that moment in our history, somewhere in the mid-Sixties, when black people began to forsake civil rights and integration, and began to seek out a sense of self. They exist as one manifestation of that intense looking inward to see what we really wanted. The direction and developing quality of black literature can be but imperfectly seen if these journals are ignored. The revolutionary black journals attest to a growth toward nation-hood in an ever-expanding harmony with the non-white universe. They are an important index of the measure and meaning of the sixties.

Black Cultural Nationalism

Black art, like everything else in the black community, must respond positively to the reality of revolution.

It must become and remain a part of the revolutionary machinery that moves us to change quickly and creatively. We have always said, and continue to say, that the battle we are waging now is the battle for the minds of Black people, and that if we lose this battle, we cannot win the violent one. It becomes very important then, that art plays the role it should play in Black survival and not bog itself down in the meaningless madness of the Western world wasted. In order to avoid this madness, black artists and those who wish to be artists must accept the fact that what is needed is an aesthetic, a black aesthetic, that is a criteria for judging the validity and/or the beauty of a work of art.

Pursuing this further, we discover that all art can be judged on two levels—on the social level and on the artistic level. In terms of the artistic level, we will be brief in talking about this, because the artistic level involves a consideration of form and feeling, two things which obviously involve more technical consideration and terminology than we have space, time or will to develop adequately here. Let it be enough to say that the artistic consideration, although a necessary part, is not sufficient. What completes the picture is that social criteria for judging art. And it is this criteria that is the most important criteria. For all art must reflect and support the Black Revolution, and any art that does not discuss and contribute to the revolution is invalid, no matter how many lines and spaces are produced in proportion and symmetry and no matter how many sounds are boxed in or blown out and called music.

All we do and create, then, is based on tradition and reason, that is to say, on foundation and movement. For we begin to build on traditional foundation, but it is out of movement, that is experience, that we complete our creation. Tradition teaches us, Leopold Senghor tells us, that all African art has at least three characteristics: that is, it is functional, collective and committing or committed. Since this is traditionally valid, it stands to reason that we should attempt to use it as the foundation for a rational construction to meet our present day needs. And by no mere coincidence we find that the criteria is not only valid, but inspiring. That is why we say that all Black art, irregardless of any technical requirements, must have three basic characteristics which make it revolutionary. In brief, it must be functional, collective and committing. It must be functional, that is *useful,* as

From *The Black Aesthetic,* ed. Addison Gayle Jr. (Garden City, N.Y.: Doubleday, 1971).

we cannot accept the false doctrine of "art for art's sake." For, in fact, there is no such thing as "art for art's sake." All art reflects the value system from which it comes. For if the artist created only for himself and not for others, he would lock himself up somewhere and paint or write or play just for himself. But he does not do that. On the contrary, he invites us over, even *insists* that we come to hear him or to see his work; in a word, he expresses a need for our evaluation and/or appreciation and our evaluation cannot be a favorable one if the work of art is not first functional, that is, useful.

So what, then, is the use of art—our art, Black art? Black art must expose the enemy, praise the people and support the revolution. It must be like LeRoi Jones' poems that are assassins' poems, poems that kill and shoot guns and "wrassle cops into alleys taking their weapons, leaving them dead with tongues pulled out and sent to Ireland." It must be functional like the poem of another revolutionary poet from "US," Clyde Halisi, who described the Master's words as "Sun Genies, dancing through the crowd snatching crosses and St. Christopher's from around niggers' necks and passing the white gapped legs in their minds to Simbas[1] to be disposed of."

Or, in terms of painting, we do not need pictures of oranges in a bowl or trees standing innocently in the midst of a wasteland. If we must paint oranges and trees, let our guerrillas be eating those oranges for strength and using those trees for cover. We need new images, and oranges in a bowl or fat white women smiling lewdly cannot be those images. All material is mute until the artist gives it a message, and that message must be a message of revolution. Then we have destroyed "art for art's sake," which is of no use anyhow, and have developed art for all our sake, art for Mose the miner, Sammy the shoeshine boy, T.C. the truck driver and K.P. the unwilling soldier.

In conclusion, the real function of art is to make revolution, using its own medium.

The second characteristic of Black art is that it must be collective. In a word, it must be from the people and must be returned to the people in a form more beautiful and colorful than it was in real life. For that is what art is: everyday life given more form and color. And in relationship to that, the Black artist can find no better subject than Black People themselves, and the Black artist who does not choose or develop this subject will find himself unproductive. For no one is any more than the context to which he owes his existence, and if an artist owes his existence to the Afroamerican context, then he also owes his art to that context and therefore must be held accountable to the people of that context. To say that art must be collective, however, raises four questions. Number one, the question of popularization versus elevation; two, personality versus individuality; three, diversity in unity; and four, freedom *to* versus freedom *from*.

The question of popularization versus elevation is an old one; what it really seeks to do is to ask and to answer the question whether or not art should be lowered to the level of the people or the people raised to the level of art. Our contention is that if art is from the people, and for the people, there is no question of raising people to art or lowering art to the people, for they are one and the same thing. As we said previously—art is everyday life given more form and color. And what one seeks to do then is to use art as a means of educating the people, and being educated by them, so that it is a mutual exchange rather

---

1. Swahili for Young Lions, the Youth Movement in US Organization.

than a one-way communication. Art and people must develop at the same time and for the same reason. It must move with the masses and be moved by the masses.

For we should not demand that our people go to school to learn to appreciate art, but that an artist go to school formally or informally to learn new and better techniques of expressing his appreciation for the people and all they represent and his disdain for anything and everything that threatens or hinders their existence. Then and only then can both the artist and the people move forward with a positive pace rooted to the reality of revolution.

The second question raised is the question of personality versus individuality. Now this question is one of how much the emphasis on collective art destroys the individuality of the artist. We say that individualism is a luxury that we cannot afford, moreover, individualism is, in effect, non-existent. For since no one is any more than the context to which he owes his existence, he has no individuality, only personality. Individuality by definition is "me" in spite of everyone, and personality is "me" in relation to everyone. The one, a useless isolation and the other an important involvement. We have heard it even said that the individual is like an atom, that which can no longer be reduced, or the essence of humanity. However, aside from this being a rather strained analogy, it does not prove that a man who wants to be an individual can stand alone. For the atom itself is a part of a molecule and cannot exist without interdependence, and even then, it is at best a simple theoretical construction for the convenience of conversation. We say that there is no virtue in a false independence, but there is value in a real interdependence.

The third question raised with regard to collective art is an extension of the second one, and that is, does unity preclude diversity? Our answer to that is an emphatic, "NO," for there can be and is unity in diversity, even as there can be diversity in unity. What one seeks, however, is not a standardization of every move or creation, but a framework in which one can create and avoid the European gift of trial and error. One can seek the reality of the concept of diversity in unity or unity in diversity in listening to a Trippin ensemble.[2] In a Trippin ensemble, the "leader" sets the pace and others come in, or go out, as it pleases them, but in the end they all come to a very dynamic and overwhelmingly harmonious conclusion. So it is with our dance—two partners dance together the same dance and yet they provide us with a demonstration of that which is unique in each of them. But that is not individuality—that is personality. For it is an expression of uniqueness, not isolation from, but in relation to, each other and the collective experience that they both have shared.

The last question is one of freedom *to* versus freedom *from*. This is really a political question, or social one, and is one that raises contradiction for the artist who rejects the social interpretation of art. However, when he demands freedom to do something or freedom from the restriction that prohibits his doing something, he is asking for a sociopolitical right, and that, as we said, makes art social first and aesthetic second. Art does not exist in the abstract just like freedom does not exist in the abstract. It is not an independent living thing; it lives through us and through the meaning and message we give it.

---

2. Trippin is our word for what white boys and others call jazz. In line with our obsession with self-determination which demands new definitions and nomenclature, we reject the word jazz, for jazz is taken from the white word, jazzy, i.e., sexy, because that is what he thought our music was. We call it Trippin because that is what we do when we play it or listen to it.

And an artist may have any freedom to do what he wishes as long as it does not take the freedom from the people to be protected from those images, words and sounds that are negative to their life and development. The people give us the freedom from isolation and alienation and random searching for subject matter and artists, in view of this, must not ask for freedom to deny this, but on the contrary must praise the people for this. In conclusion, the concept of collective art can best be expressed in the African proverb showing the interdependence of all by saying, "One hand washes the other."

The final thing that is characteristic of Black art is that it must be committing. It must commit us to revolution and change. It must commit us to a future that is ours. In a word, it must commit us to all that is US-yesterday, today and the sunrise of tomorrow. It must tell us like Halisi's poem, "Maulana and Word Magic," that we must give up the past or be found out and exposed, "as the notes of a new day come tripping through searching each one's heart for any traces of Peyton Place." It must commit us to the fact that the earth is ours and the fullness thereof. As LeRoi Jones says, "You can't steal nothing from the white man. He's already stole it, he owes you anything you want, even his life." So, "Black People take the shit you want, take their lives if need, but get what you want, what you need. Dance up and down the street, turn all the music up." This is commitment to the struggle, a commitment that includes the artist and the observer. We cannot let each other rest; there is so much to do, and we all know we have done so little. Art will revive us, inspire us, give us enough courage to face another disappointing day. It must not teach us resignation. For all our art must contribute to revolutionary change and if it does not, it is invalid.

Therefore, we say the blues are invalid; for they teach resignation, in a word acceptance of reality—and we have come to change reality. We will not submit to the resignation of our fathers who lost their money, their women, and their lives and sat around wondering "what did they do to be so black and blue." We will say again with Brother LeRoi, "We are lovers and the sons of lovers, and warriors and the sons of warriors." Therefore, we will love—and unwillingly though necessarily, make war, revolutionary war. We will not cry for those things that are gone, but find meaning in those things that remain with us. Perhaps people will object violently to the idea that the blues are invalid, but one should understand that they are not invalid historically. They will always represent a very beautiful, musical and psychological achievement of our people; but today they are not functional because they do not commit us to the struggle of today and tomorrow, but keep us in the past. And whatever we do, we cannot remain in the past, for we have too much at stake in the present. And we find our future much too much rewarding to be rejected.

Let our art remind us of our distaste for the enemy, our love for each other, and our commitment to the revolutionary struggle that will be fought with the rhythmic reality of a permanent revolution.

The Black Arts Movement

I.

The Black Arts Movement is radically opposed to any concept of the artist that alienates him from his community. Black Art is the aesthetic and spiritual sister of the Black Power concept. As such, it envisions an art that speaks directly to the needs and aspirations of Black America. In order to perform this task, the Black Arts Movement proposes a radical reordering of the western cultural aesthetic. It proposes a separate symbolism, mythology, critique, and iconology. The Black Arts and the Black Power concept both relate broadly to the Afro-American's desire for self-determination and nationhood. Both concepts are nationalistic. One is concerned with the relationship between art and politics; the other with the art of politics.

Recently, these two movements have begun to merge: the political values inherent in the Black Power concept are now finding concrete expression in the aesthetics of Afro-American dramatists, poets, choreographers, musicians, and novelists. A main tenet of Black Power is the necessity for Black people to define the world in their own terms. The Black artist has made the same point in the context of aesthetics. The two movements postulate that there are in fact and in spirit two Americas—one black, one white. The Black artist takes this to mean that his primary duty is to speak to the spiritual and cultural needs of Black people. Therefore, the main thrust of this new breed of contemporary writers is to confront the contradictions arising out of the Black man's experience in the racist West. Currently, these writers are re-evaluating western aesthetics, the traditional role of the writer, and the social function of art. Implicit in this re-evaluation is the need to develop a "black aesthetic." It is the opinion of many Black writers, I among them, that the Western aesthetic has run its course: it is impossible to construct anything meaningful within its decaying structure. We advocate a cultural revolution in art and ideas. The cultural values inherent in western history must either be radicalized or destroyed, and we will probably find that even radicalization is impossible. In fact, what is needed is a whole new system of ideas. Poet Don L. Lee expresses it:

> . . . We must destroy Faulkner, dick, jane, and other perpetuators of evil. It's time for Du Bois, Nat Turner, and Kwame Nkrumah. As Frantz Fanon points out: destroy the

From *TDR: The Drama Review* 12.4, Black Theatre Issue (Summer 1968).

culture and you destroy the people. This must not happen. Black artists are culture stabilizers; bringing back old values, and introducing new ones. Black Art will talk to the people and with the will of the people stop impending "protective custody."

The Black Arts Movement eschews "protest" literature. It speaks directly to Black people. Implicit in the concept of "protest" literature, as Brother Knight has made clear, is an appeal to white morality:

> Now any Black man who masters the technique of his particular art form, who adheres to the white aesthetic, and who directs his work toward a white audience is, in one sense, protesting. And implicit in the act of protest is the belief that a change will be forthcoming once the masters are aware of the protestor's "grievance" (the very word connotes begging, supplications to the gods). Only when that belief has faded and protestings end, will Black art begin.

Brother Knight also has some interesting statements about the development of a "Black aesthetic":

> Unless the Black artist establishes a "Black aesthetic" he will have no future at all. To accept the white aesthetic is to accept and validate a society that will not allow him to live. The Black artist must create new forms and new values, sing new songs (or purify old ones); and along with other Black authorities, he must create a new history, new symbols, myths and legends (and purify old ones by fire). And the Black artist, in creating his own aesthetic, must be accountable for it only to the Black people. Further, he must hasten his own dissolution as an individual (in the Western sense)—painful though the process may be, having been breast-fed the poison of "individual experience."

When we speak of a "Black aesthetic" several things are meant. First, we assume that there is already in existence the basis for such an aesthetic. Essentially, it consists of an African-American cultural tradition. But this aesthetic is finally, by implication, broader than that tradition. It encompasses most of the useable elements of Third World culture. The motive behind the Black aesthetic is the destruction of the white thing, the destruction of white ideas, and white ways of looking at the world. The new aesthetic is mostly predicated on an Ethics which asks the question: whose vision of the world is finally more meaningful, ours or the white oppressors'? What is truth? Or more precisely, whose truth shall we express, that of the oppressed or of the oppressors? These are basic questions. Black intellectuals of previous decades failed to ask them. Further, national and international affairs demand that we appraise the world in terms of our own interests. It is clear that the question of human survival is at the core of contemporary experience. The Black artist must address himself to this reality in the strongest terms possible. In a context of world upheaval, ethics and aesthetics must interact positively and be consistent with the demands for a more spiritual world. Consequently, the Black Arts Movement is an ethical movement. Ethical, that is, from the viewpoint of the oppressed. And much of the oppression confronting the Third World and Black America is directly traceable to the Euro-American cultural sensibility. This sensibility, anti-human in nature, has, until recently, dominated the psyches of most Black artists and intellectuals; it must be destroyed before the Black creative artist can have a meaningful role in the transformation of society.

It is this natural reaction to an alien sensibility that informs the cultural attitudes of the Black Arts and the Black Power movement. It is a profound ethical sense that makes a Black artist question a society in which art is one thing and the actions of men another. The Black Arts Movement believes that your ethics and your aesthetics are one. That the contradictions between ethics and aesthetics in western society is symptomatic of a dying culture.

The term "Black Arts" is of ancient origin, but it was first used in a positive sense by LeRoi Jones:

> We are unfair
> And unfair
> We are black magicians
> Black arts we make
> in black labs of the heart
>
> The fair are fair
> and deathly white
>
> The day will not save them
> And we own the night

There is also a section of the poem "Black Dada Nihilismus" that carries the same motif. But a fuller amplification of the nature of the new aesthetics appears in the poem "Black Art":

> Poems are bullshit unless they are
> teeth or trees or lemons piled
> on a step. Or black ladies dying
> of men leaving nickel hearts
> beating them down. Fuck poems
> and they are useful, would they shoot
> come at you, love what you are,
> breathe like wrestlers, or shudder
> strangely after peeing. We want live
> words of the hip world, live flesh &
> coursing blood. Hearts and Brains
> Souls splintering fire. We want poems
> like fists beating niggers out of Jocks
> or dagger poems in the slimy bellies
> of the owner-jews . . .

Poetry is a concrete function, an action. No more abstractions. Poems are physical entities: fists, daggers, airplane poems, and poems that shoot guns. Poems are transformed from physical objects into personal forces:

> . . . Put it on him poem. Strip him naked
> to the world. Another bad poem cracking
> steel knuckles in a jewlady's mouth
> Poem scream poison gas on breasts in green berets . . .

Then the poem affirms the integral relationship between Black Art and Black people:

> . . . Let Black people understand
> that they are the lovers and the sons
> of lovers and warriors and sons
> of warriors Are poems & poets &
> all the loveliness here in the world

It ends with the following lines, a central assertion in both the Black Arts Movement and the philosophy of Black Power:

> We want a black poem. And a
> Black World.
> Let the world be a Black Poem
> And let All Black People Speak This Poem
> Silently
> Or LOUD

The poem comes to stand for the collective conscious and unconscious of Black America—the real impulse in back of the Black Power movement, which is the will toward self-determination and nationhood, a radical reordering of the nature and function of both art and the artist.

2.

In the spring of 1964, LeRoi Jones, Charles Patterson, William Patterson, Clarence Reed, Johnny Moore, and a number of other Black artists opened the Black Arts Repertoire Theatre School. They produced a number of plays including Jones' *Experimental Death Unit # One, Black Mass, Jello,* and *Dutchman.* They also initiated a series of poetry readings and concerts. These activities represented the most advanced tendencies in the movement and were of excellent artistic quality. The Black Arts School came under immediate attack by the New York power structure. The Establishment, fearing Black creativity, did exactly what it was expected to do—it attacked the theatre and all of its values. In the meantime, the school was granted funds by OEO through HARYOU-ACT. Lacking a cultural program itself, HARYOU turned to the only organization which addressed itself to the needs of the community. In keeping with its "revolutionary" cultural ideas, the Black Arts Theatre took its programs into the streets of Harlem. For three months, the theatre presented plays, concerts, and poetry readings to the people of the community. Plays that shattered the illusions of the American body politic, and awakened Black people to the meaning of their lives.

Then the hawks from the OEO moved in and chopped off the funds. Again, this should have been expected. The Black Arts Theatre stood in radical opposition to the feeble attitudes about culture of the "War on Poverty" bureaucrats. And later, because of internal problems, the theatre was forced to close. But the Black Arts group proved that the community could be served by a valid and dynamic art. It also proved that there was a definite need for a cultural revolution in the Black community.

With the closing of the Black Arts Theatre, the implications of what Brother Jones and his colleagues were trying to do took on even more significance. Black Art groups sprang up on the West Coast and the idea spread to Detroit, Philadelphia, Jersey City, New Orleans, and Washington, D.C. Black Arts movements began on the campuses of San Francisco State College, Fisk University, Lincoln University, Hunter College in the Bronx, Columbia University, and Oberlin College. In Watts, after the rebellion, Maulana Karenga welded the Blacks Arts Movement into a cohesive cultural ideology, which owed much to the work of LeRoi Jones. Karenga sees culture as the most important element in the struggle for self-determination:

> Culture is the basis of all ideas, images and actions. To move is to move culturally, i.e., by a set of values given to you by your culture.
>
> Without a culture Negroes are only a set of reactions to white people.
>
> The seven criteria for culture are:
>   1. Mythology
>   2. History
>   3. Social Organization
>   4. Political Organization
>   5. Economic Organization
>   6. Creative Motif
>   7. Ethos

In drama, LeRoi Jones represents the most advanced aspects of the movement. He is its prime mover and chief designer. In a poetic essay entitled "The Revolutionary Theatre," he outlines the iconology of the movement:

> The Revolutionary Theatre should force change: it should be change. (All their faces turned into the lights and you work on them black nigger magic, and cleanse them at having seen the ugliness. And if the beautiful see themselves, they will love themselves.) We are preaching virtue again, but by that to mean NOW, toward what seems the most constructive use of the word.

The theatre that Jones proposes is inextricably linked to the Afro-American political dynamic. And such a link is perfectly consistent with Black America's contemporary demands. For theatre is potentially the most social of all of the arts. It is an integral part of the socializing process. It exists in direct relationship to the audience it claims to serve. The decadence and inanity of the contemporary American theatre is an accurate reflection of the state of American society. Albee's *Who's Afraid of Virginia Woolf?* is very American: sick white lives in a homosexual hell hole. The theatre of white America is escapist, refusing to confront concrete reality. Into this cultural emptiness come the musicals, an up-tempo version of the same stale lives. And the use of Negroes in such plays as *Hello Dolly* and *Hallelujah Baby* does not alert their nature; it compounds the problem. These plays are simply hipper versions of the minstrel show. They present Negroes acting out the hang-ups of middle-class white America. Consequently, the American theatre is a palliative prescribed to bourgeois patients who refuse to see the world as it is. Or, more crucially, as the world sees them. It is no accident, therefore, that the most "important" plays come from Europe—Brecht, Weiss, and Ghelderode. And even these have begun to run dry.

The Black Arts theatre, the theatre of LeRoi Jones, is a radical alternative to the sterility of the American theatre. It is primarily a theatre of the Spirit, confronting the Black man in his interaction with his brothers and with the white thing.

> Our theatre will show victims so that their brothers in the audience will be better able to understand that they are the brothers of victims, and that they themselves are blood brothers. And what we show must cause the blood to rush, so that prerevolutionary temperaments will be bathed in this blood, and it will cause their deepest souls to move, and they will find themselves tensed and clenched, even ready to die, at what the soul has been taught. We will scream and cry, murder, run through the streets in agony, if it means some soul will be moved, moved to actual life understanding of what the world is, and what it ought to be. We are preaching virtue and feeling, and a natural sense of the self in the world. All men live in the world, and the world ought to be a place for them to live.

The victims in the world of Jones' early plays are Clay, murdered by the white bitch-goddess in *Dutchman,* and Walker Vessels, the revolutionary in *The Slave.* Both of these plays present Black men in transition. Clay, the middle-class Negro trying to get himself a little action from Lula, digs himself and his own truth only to get murdered after telling her like it really is:

> Just let me bleed you, you loud whore, and one poem vanished. A whole people neurotics, struggling to keep from being sane. And the only thing that would cure the neurosis would be your murder. Simple as that. I mean if I murdered you, then other white people would understand me. You understand? No. I guess not. If Bessie Smith had killed some white people she wouldn't needed that music. She could have talked very straight and plain about the world. Just straight two and two are four. Money. Power. Luxury. Like that. All of them. Crazy niggers turning their back on sanity. When all it needs is that simple act. Just murder. Would make us all sane.

But Lula understands, and she kills Clay first. In a perverse way it is Clay's nascent knowledge of himself that threatens the existence of Lula's idea of the world. Symbolically, and in fact, the relationship between Clay (Black America) and Lula (white America) is rooted in the historical castration of black manhood. And in the twisted psyche of white America, the Black man is both an object of love and hate. Analogous attitudes exist in most Black Americans, but for decidedly different reasons. Clay is doomed when he allows himself to participate in Lula's "fantasy" in the first place. It is the fantasy to which Frantz Fanon alludes in *The Wretched Of The Earth* and *Black Skins, White Mask:* the native's belief that he can acquire the oppressor's power by acquiring his symbols, one of which is the white woman. When Clay finally digs himself it is too late.

Walker Vessels, in *The Slave,* is Clay reincarnated as the revolutionary confronting problems inherited from his contact with white culture. He returns to the home of his ex-wife, a white woman, and her husband, a literary critic. The play is essentially about Walker's attempt to destroy his white past. For it is the past, with all of its painful memories, that is really the enemy of the revolutionary. It is impossible to move until history is either recreated or comprehended. Unlike Todd, in Ralph Ellison's *Invisible Man,* Walker cannot fall outside history. Instead, Walker demands a confrontation with history, a final shattering of bullshit illusions. His only salvation lies in confronting the physical and psychological forces that have made him and his people powerless. Therefore, he comes to understand that the world must be restructured along spiritual imperatives. But in the interim it is basically a question of *who* has power:

> Easley: You're so wrong about everything. So terribly, sickeningly wrong. What can you change? What do you hope to change? Do you think Negroes are better people than whites . . . that they can govern a society *better* than whites? That they'll be more judicious or more tolerant? Do you think they'll make fewer mistakes? I mean really, if the Western white man has proved one thing . . . it's the futility of modern society. So the have-not peoples become the haves. Even so, will that change the essential functions of the world? Will there be more love or beauty in the world . . . more knowledge . . . because of it?
>
> Walker: Probably. Probably there will be more . . . if more people have a chance to understand what it is. But that's not even the point. It comes down to baser human endeavor than any social-political thinking. What does it matter if there's more love or beauty? Who the fuck cares? Is that what the Western ofay thought while he was ruling . . . that his rule somehow brought more love and beauty into the world? Oh, he might have thought that concomitantly, while sipping a gin rickey and scratching his ass . . . but that was not ever the point. Not even on the Crusades. The point is that you had your chance, darling, now these other folks have theirs. *Quietly.* Now they have theirs.
>
> Easley: God, what an ugly idea.

This confrontation between the black radical and the white liberal is symbolic of larger confrontations occurring between the Third World and Western society. It is a confrontation between the colonizer and the colonized, the slavemaster and the slave. Implicit in Easley's remarks is the belief that the white man is culturally and politically superior to the Black Man. Even though Western society has been traditionally violent in its relation with the Third World, it sanctimoniously deplores violence or self assertion on the part of the enslaved. And the Western mind, with clever rationalizations, equates the violence of the oppressed with the violence of the oppressor. So that when the native preaches self-determination, the Western white man cleverly misconstrues it to mean hate of *all* white men. When the Black political radical warns his people not to trust white politicians of the left and the right, but instead to organize separately on the basis of power, the white man cries: "racism in reverse." Or he will say, as many of them do today: "We deplore both white and black racism." As if the two could be equated.

There is a minor element in *The Slave* which assumes great importance in a later play entitled *Jello*. Here I refer to the emblem of Walker's army: a red-mouthed grinning field slave. The revolutionary army has taken one of the most hated symbols of the Afro-American past and radically altered its meaning.* This is the supreme act of freedom, available only to those who have liberated themselves psychically. Jones amplifies this inversion of emblem and symbol in *Jello* by making Rochester (Ratfester) of the old Jack Benny (Penny) program into a revolutionary nationalist. Ratfester, ordinarily the supreme embodiment of the Uncle Tom Clown, surprises Jack Penny by turning on the other side of the nature of the Black man. He skillfully, and with an evasive black humor, robs Penny of all of his money. But Ratfester's actions are "moral." That is to say, Ratfester is getting his back pay; payment of a long over-due debt to the Black man. Ratfester's sensibilities are different from Walker's. He is *blues people* smiling and shuffling while trying to figure out how to destroy the white thing. And like the blues man, he is the master of the understatement. Or in the Afro-American folk tradition, he is the Signifying Monkey, Shine, and Stagolee all rolled into one. There are no stereotypes any more. History has killed Uncle Tom. Because even Uncle Tom has a breaking point beyond which he will not be pushed. Cut deeply enough into the most docile Negro, and you will find a conscious murderer. Behind the lyrics of the blues and the shuffling porter loom visions of white throats being cut and cities burning.

Jones' particular power as a playwright does not rest solely on his revolutionary vision, but is instead derived from his deep lyricism and spiritual outlook. In many ways, he is fundamentally more a poet than a playwright. And it is his lyricism that gives body to his plays. Two important plays in this regard are *Black Mass* and *Slave Ship*. *Black Mass* is based on the Muslim myth of Yacub. According to this myth, Yacub, a Black scientist, developed the means of grafting different colors of the Original Black Nation until a White Devil was created. In *Black Mass,* Yacub's experiments produce a raving White Beast who is condemned to the coldest regions of the North. The other magicians implore Yacub to cease his experiments. But he insists on claiming the primacy of scientific knowledge over spiritual knowledge. The sensibility of the White Devil is alien, informed by lust and sensuality. The Beast is the consummate embodiment of evil, the beginning of the historical subjugation of the spiritual world.

---

*In Jones' study of Afro-American music, *Blues People,* we find the following observation: ". . . Even the adjective *funky,* which once meant to many Negroes merely a stink (usually associated with sex), was used to qualify the music as meaningful (the word became fashionable and is now almost useless). The social implication, then, was that even the old stereotype of a distinctive Negro smell that white America subscribed to could be turned against white America. For this smell now, real or not, was made a valuable characteristic of 'Negro-ness.' And 'Negro-ness' by the fifties, for many Negroes (and whites) was the only strength left to American culture."

Black Mass takes place in some pre-historical time. In fact, the concept of time, we learn, is the creation of an alien sensibility, that of the Beast. This is a deeply weighted play, a colloquy on the nature of man, and the relationship between legitimate spiritual knowledge and scientific knowledge. It is LeRoi Jones' most important play mainly because it is informed by a mythology that is wholly the creation of the Afro-American sensibility.

Further, Yacub's creation is not merely a scientific exercise. More fundamentally, it is the aesthetic impulse gone astray. The Beast is created merely for the sake of creation. Some artists assert a similar claim about the nature of art. They argue that art need not have a function. It is against this decadent attitude toward art—ramified throughout most of Western society—that the play militates. Yacub's real crime, therefore, is the introduction of a meaningless evil into a harmonious universe. The evil of the Beast is pervasive, corrupting everything and everyone it touches. What was beautiful is twisted into an ugly screaming thing. The play ends with destruction of the holy place of the Black Magicians. Now the Beast and his descendants roam the earth. An off-stage voice chants a call for the Jihad to begin. It is then that myth merges into legitimate history, and we, the audience, come to understand that all history is merely someone's version of mythology.

Slave Ship presents a more immediate confrontation with history. In a series of expressionistic tableaux it depicts the horrors and the madness of the Middle Passage. It then moves through the period of slavery, early attempts at revolt, tendencies toward Uncle Tom-like reconciliation and betrayal, and the final act of liberation. There is no definite plot (LeRoi calls it a pageant), just a continuous rush of sound, groans, screams, and souls wailing for freedom and relief from suffering. This work has special affinities with the New Music of Sun Ra, John Coltrane, Albert Ayler, and Ornette Coleman. Events are blurred, rising and falling in a stream of sound. Almost cinematically, the images flicker and fade against a heavy back-drop of rhythm. The language is spare, stripped to the essential. It is a play which almost totally eliminates the need for a text. It functions on the basis of movement and energy—the dramatic equivalent of the New Music.

3.

LeRoi Jones is the best known and the most advanced playwright of the movement, but he is not alone. There are other excellent playwrights who express the general mood of the Black Arts ideology. Among them are Ron Milner, Ed Bullins, Ben Caldwell, Jimmy Stewart, Joe White, Charles Patterson, Charles Fuller, Aisha Hughes, Carol Freeman, and Jimmy Garrett.

Ron Milner's *Who's Got His Own* is of particular importance. It strips bare the clashing attitudes of a contemporary Afro-American family. Milner's concern is with legitimate manhood and morality. The family in *Who's Got His Own* is in search of its conscience, or more precisely its own definition of life. On the day of his father's death, Tim and his family are forced to examine the inner fabric of their lives: the lies, self-deceits, and sense of powerlessness in a white world. The basic conflict, however, is internal. It is rooted in the historical search for black manhood. Tim's mother is representative of a generation of Christian Black women who have implicitly understood the brooding violence lurking in their men. And with this understanding, they have interposed themselves between their men and the object of that violence—the white man. Thus unable to direct his violence against the oppressor, the Black man becomes more frustrated and the sense of powerlessness deepens. Lacking the strength to be a man in the white world, he turns against his family. So the oppressed, as Fanon explains, constantly dreams violence against his oppressor, while killing his brother on fast weekends.

Tim's sister represents the Negro woman's attempt to acquire what Eldridge Cleaver calls "ultrafemininity." That is, the attributes of her white upper-class counterpart. Involved here is a rejection of the body-oriented life of the working class Black man, symbolized by the mother's traditional religion. The sister has an affair with a white upper-class liberal, ending in abortion. There are hints of lesbianism, i.e., a further rejection of the body. The sister's life is a pivotal factor in the play. Much of the stripping away of falsehood initiated by Tim is directed at her life, which they have carefully kept hidden from the mother.

Tim is the product of the new Afro-American sensibility, informed by the psychological revolution now operative within Black America. He is a combination ghetto soul brother and militant intellectual, very hip and slightly flawed himself. He would change the world, but without comprehending the particular history that produced his "tyrannical" father. And he cannot be the man his father was—not until he truly understands his father. He must understand why his father allowed himself to be insulted daily by the "honky" types on the job; why he took a demeaning job in the "shit-house"; and why he spent on his family the violence that he should have directed against the white man. In short, Tim must confront the history of his family. And that is exactly what happens. Each character tells his story, exposing his falsehood to the other until a balance is reached.

Who's Got His Own is not the work of an alienated mind. Milner's main thrust is directed toward unifying the family around basic moral principles, toward bridging the "generation gap." Other Black playwrights, Jimmy Garrett for example, see the gap as unbridgeable.

Garrett's *We Own the Night* (see this issue of TDR, pp. 62–69) takes place during an armed insurrection. As the play opens we see the central characters defending a section of the city against attacks by white police. Johnny, the protagonist, is wounded. Some of his Brothers intermittently fire at attacking forces, while others look for medical help. A doctor arrives, forced at gun point. The wounded boy's mother also comes. She is a female Uncle Tom who berates the Brothers and their cause. She tries to get Johnny to leave. She is hysterical. The whole idea of Black people fighting white people is totally outside of her orientation. Johnny begins a vicious attack on his mother, accusing her of emasculating his father—a recurring theme in the sociology of the Black community. In Afro-American literature of previous decades the strong Black mother was the object of awe and respect. But in the new literature, her status is ambivalent and laced with tension. Historically, Afro-American woman have had to be the economic mainstays of the family. The oppressor allowed them to have jobs while at the same time limiting the economic mobility of the Black man. Very often, therefore, the woman's aspirations and values are closely tied to those of the white power structure and not to those of her man. Since he cannot provide for his family the way white men do, she despises his weakness, tearing into him at every opportunity until, very often, there is nothing left but a shell.

The only way out of this dilemma is through revolution. It either must be an actual blood revolution, or one that psychically redirects the energy of the oppressed. Milner is fundamentally concerned with the latter and Garrett with the former. Communication between Johnny and his mother breaks down. The revolutionary imperative demands that men step outside the legal framework. It is a question of erecting *another* morality. The old constructs do not hold up, because adhering to them means consigning oneself to the oppressive reality. Johnny's mother is involved in the old constructs. Manliness is equated with white morality. And even though she claims to love her family (her men), the overall design of her ideas are against black manhood. In Garrett's play the mother's morality manifests itself in a deep-seated hatred of Black men; while in Milner's work the mother understands, but holds her men back.

The mothers that Garrett and Milner see represent the Old Spirituality—the Faith of the Fathers of which Du Bois spoke. Johnny and Tim represent the New Spirituality. They appear to be a type produced by the upheavals of the colonial world of which Black America is a part. Johnny's assertion that he is a criminal is remarkably similar to the rebel's comments in Aimé Césaire's play, *Les Armes Miraculeuses* (*The Miraculous Weapons*). In that play the rebel, speaking to his mother, proclaims: "My name—an offense; my Christian name—humiliation; my status—a rebel; my age—the stone age." To which the mother replies: "My race—the human race. My religion—brotherhood." The Old Spirituality is generalized. It seeks to recognize Universal Humanity. The New Spirituality is specific. It begins by seeing the world from the concise point-of-view of the colonialized. Where the Old Spirituality would live with oppression while ascribing to the oppressors an innate goodness, the New Spirituality demands a radical shift in point-of-view. The colonialized native, the oppressed must, of necessity, subscribe to a *separate* morality. One that will liberate him and his people.

The assault against the Old Spirituality can sometimes be humorous. In Ben Caldwell's play, *The Militant Preacher,* a burglar is seen slipping into the home of a wealthy minister. The preacher comes in and the burglar ducks behind a large chair. The preacher, acting out the role of the supplicant minister begins to moan, praying to De Lawd for understanding.

In the context of today's politics, the minister is an Uncle Tom, mouthing platitudes against self-defense. The preacher drones in a self-pitying monologue about the folly of protecting oneself against brutal policeman. Then the burglar begins to speak. The preacher is startled, taking the burglar's voice for the voice of God. The burglar begins to play on the preacher's old time religion. He *becomes* the voice of God insulting and goading the preacher on until the preacher's attitudes about protective violence change. The next day the preacher emerges militant, gun in hand, sounding like Reverend Cleage in Detroit. He now preaches a new gospel—the gospel of the gun, an eye for an eye. The gospel is preached in the rhythmic cadences of the old Black church. But the content is radical. Just as Jones inverted the symbols in *Jello,* Caldwell twists the rhythms of the Uncle Tom preacher into the language of the new militancy.

These plays are directed at problems within Black America. They begin with the premise that there is a well defined Afro-American audience. An audience that must see itself and the world in terms of its own interests. These plays, along with many others, constitute the basis for a viable movement in the theatre—a movement which takes as its task a profound re-evaluation of the Black man's presence in America. The Black Arts Movement represents the flowering of a cultural nationalism that has been suppressed since the 1920's. I mean the "Harlem Renaissance"—which was essentially a failure. It did not address itself to the mythology and the life-styles of the Black community. It failed to take roots, to link itself concretely to the struggles of that community, to become its voice and spirit. Implicit in the Black Arts Movement is the idea that Black people, however, dispersed, constitute a *nation* within the belly of white America. This is not a new idea. Garvey said it and the Honorable Elijah Muhammad says it now. And it is on this idea that the concept of Black Power is predicated.

Afro-American life and history is full of creative possibilities, and the movement is just beginning to perceive them. Just beginning to understand that the most meaningful statements about the nature of Western society must come from the Third World of which Black America is a part. The thematic material is broad, ranging from folk heroes like Shine and Stagolee to historical figures like Marcus Garvey and Malcolm X. And then there is the struggle for Black survival, the coming confrontation between white America and Black America. If art is the harbinger of future possibilities, what does the future of Black America portend?

Broadside Press: A Personal Chronicle

Broadside Press did not grow from a blueprint. I did not, like Joe Goncalves when he planned the *Journal of Black Poetry,* save money in advance to finance the press. Broadside Press began without capital, from the twelve dollars I took out of my paycheck to pay for the first Broadside, and has grown by hunches, intuitions, trial and error.

Our first publication was the Broadside "Ballad of Birmingham." Folk singer Jerry Moore of New York had it set to music, and I wanted to protect the rights to the poem by getting it copyrighted. Learning that leaflet could be copyrighted, I published it as a Broadside in 1965. Jerry Moore also set the ballad "Dressed All in Pink" to music, and in order to copyright it I printed this poem also as a Broadside. Being a librarian, accustomed to organizing and classifying material, I grouped the two poems into a *Broadside Series,* and called them Broadsides number one and number two. Since Broadsides, at that time, were the company's sole product, I gave it the name Broadside Press.

In May 1966 I attended the first Writers' Conference at Fisk University, and obtained permission from Robert Hayden, Melvin B. Tolson, and Margaret Walker, who were there, to use their poems in the *Broadside Series.* I wrote to Gwendolyn Brooks and obtained her permission to use "We Real Cool." This first group of six Broadsides, called "Poems of the Negro Revolt," is, I think, one of the most distinguished groups in the *Broadside Series,* containing outstanding poems by some of our finest poets.

At that time my intention was to publish famous familiar poems in an attractive format so that people could buy their favorite poems in a form worth treasuring. A reviewer in *Small Press Review,* however, suggested that I could serve contemporary poetry better by publishing previously unpublished poems. Beginning with Broadside twenty-five, I have attempted to do this. I try to make the format of the Broadside harmonize with the poem in paper, color, and typography, and often employ artists to design or illustrate the Broadsides. Some Broadsides outstanding for their appearance are number four ("The Sea Turtle and the Shark," by Melvin B. Tolson), designed in blue by sculptor-painter Cledie Taylor; number six ("We Real Cool," by Gwendolyn Brooks), lettered white on black by Cledie Taylor to simulate scrawls on a blackboard; and number eighteen ("Black Madonna," by Harold Lawrence), gold on white with an illustration by painter Leroy Foster.

The first book planned (but not the first published) by Broadside Press was *For Malcolm: Poems on the Life and the Death of Malcolm X.* This book had its genesis at the first Fisk

From *The Black Seventies,* ed. Floyd B. Barbour (Boston: Porter Sargent, 1970).

University Writers' Conference. As I was walking to one of the sessions, I saw Margaret Walker, the poet, and Margaret Burroughs, the painter, sitting in front of their dormitory. Mrs. Burroughs was sketching, and Miss Walker was rehearsing her reading, for she was to read her poems that afternoon. I sat down to watch and to listen, and when Miss Walker read a poem on Malcolm X, I said, "Everybody's writing about Malcolm X. I know several people who've written poems about him."

"That's right," Margaret Burroughs said. "Why don't you collect the poems and put out a book on Malcolm?"

I thought it over for a few seconds, snapped my fingers, and said, "I'll do it. And you can be my co-editor."

Thus the anthology *For Malcolm* was born.

Most conferences have much talk, but little action. Mrs. Burroughs and I decided to inject some action into this conference by announcing our book at the final session, and offering the writers there a concrete vehicle for their poems. David Llorens promised to announce it in *Negro Digest* (now *Black World*) and in a few days I received the first poem. This anthology is notable not only for the many fine poems it includes, but also because it brings mature poets such as Robert Hayden, Margaret Walker, and Gwendolyn Brooks together with younger poets such as LeRoi Jones, Larry Neal, Bobb Hamilton, Sonia Sanchez, Julia Fields, Etheridge Knight, David Llorens, and others. My editorship of the book acquainted me with many of the younger poets and with the periodicals *Soulbook* and *Black Dialogue,* and led to rewarding friendships with some of the poets.

Although this anthology was the first book planned by Broadside Press, it was not the first one published. Because of printer's delays, it was not published until June 1967. In the meantime, *Poem Counterpoem,* by Margaret Danner and myself, was published in December 1966; it is the first book published by Broadside Press. It has a unique format, as its title suggests. The poems are arranged in pairs, a poem by each author on facing pages, and each pair of poems is on the same or a similar subject. The most obvious example of this pairing is the last pair of poems, each of which bears the title "Belle Isle."

The first edition, limited to five hundred numbered, autographed copies, had a four-by-five inch format like that of the Russian poetry series "The Young Guard," which sold for ten or twelve kopeks (eight or ten cents), and which favorably impressed me when I visited Russia in 1966. The American public, however, buys books like cabbages, by weight not by content, and it did not sell well in this format. The second printing was enlarged to the regular book size of eight by five inches, and although it contained the same poems and the same number of pages, it sold better. The book is now in its second, revised edition and its third printing. I suppose a few copies of the original printing are still available at a few bookstores.

The next book to be published by Broadside Press was one of our best selling books, *Black Pride,* by the popular young poet, Don L. Lee. I had met Mr. Lee when the copies of *For Malcolm* arrived at Mrs. Burroughs' Museum of African American History. Don Lee, at that time an assistant at the Museum, whose quiet manner belied the fires underneath, helped us as we autographed and mailed authors' copies. Later, he sent me some poems for comments, and then sent me a copy of his first book, *Think Black,* which he had had privately printed in an edition of 700, which sold out in one week. I wrote him a note thanking him for his book and commented on it.

When his second book, *Black Pride,* was ready, he asked that Broadside Press publish it, and that I write the introduction. We published *Black Pride* in 1968, and took over *Think Black.* In 1969, we published his *Don't Cry, Scream,* in both paperbound and cloth editions. The cloth edition of *Don't Cry, Scream* was a first with Broadside Press, but shortly afterward we put out our second hardcover book, the second edition of *For Malcolm.*

At this writing, *Think Black* has had twelve printings, and there are twenty-five thousand copies in print. *Black Pride* is in its seventh printing, and *Don't Cry, Scream,* just out in March 1969, had its third printing (5000 copies) the following September. It is only lack of money which prevents these printings from being 10,000 instead of 5000, as they sell rapidly and it is hard to keep bookstores in supply. All together, there are about 55,000 copies of Don Lee's books in print at this time. This has occurred without book reviews in the mass media. The only reviews of Lee's books have appeared in small black and underground magazines. In March 1969 there was an article on Lee by David Llorens in *Ebony,* a widely circulated black magazine, but the article appeared after, not before, Lee had attained his popularity.

Another poet who has been warmly praised is Etheridge Knight. He contributed three poems to *For Malcolm,* and I corresponded with him in Indiana State Prison. I asked him to do a book for Broadside Press, and we published his *Poems from Prison* in 1968, which is now in its third printing. Mr. Knight is now living in Indianapolis, and is working on his second book of poetry.

James Emanuel's first book of poetry, *The Treehouse and Other Poems* was also published in 1968, as was my second book of verse, *Cities Burning.* The same year we became distributors for Nikki Giovanni's second book, *Black Judgment,* and published Margaret Danner's *Impressions of African Art Forms.* This book, which is a facsimile of the original edition privately printed in 1960, has the distinction of being the only volume of poetry completely devoted to the vivid, varied, sophisticated arts of Black Africa. In 1969, books by Jon Eckels, Beatrice Murphy and Nancy Arnez, Sonia Sanchez, Marvin X, Keorapetse Kgositsile, and Stephany were published.

Our list has expanded considerably from the two Broadsides with which we began in 1965. Now, in 1970, we have sixteen books and thirty-two Broadsides. Scheduled to be published are books by Lance Jeffers, Doughtry Long, and John Raven. Among books promised to us are two by Pulitzer Prize winner Gwendolyn Brooks and Margaret Walker, winner of the Yale University Younger Poets Award.

In 1969 we published our second anthology, *Black Poetry: A Supplement to Anthologies Which Exclude Black Poets.* Robert Hayden and I, both of whom have taught at the University of Michigan, were asked by the chairman of the Department of English to compile a small collection of black poetry, as students had pointed out that the anthologies used in the introduction-to-poetry courses contained no black poets. Because of pressures of time in moving to different teaching posts, Mr. Hayden had to withdraw from the project, but I completed it, and the new anthology can be used both by students and by the general reader. We are also distributing an anthology of poetry and prose, *Black Arts: An Anthology of Black Creations,* edited by Ahmed Alhamisi and Harun Kofi Wangara, and published in 1969 by Alhamisi's Black Arts Publications.

In a different dimension is *Broadside Voices,* which is a series of poets reading their own books on tape. So far, James Emanuel, Dudley Randall, Etheridge Knight, Sonia Sanchez,

Jon Eckels, Beatrice Murphy and Nancy Arnez, Marvin X, Willie Kgositsile, Don Lee, and Stephany have taped their books. James Emanuel was the first to complete a tape, and he read so well that Etheridge Knight, to whom I sent Emanuel's tape as a model, said that Emanuel gave him an inferiority complex in regard to his own reading. Knight made four tapes before he produced one which was satisfactory.

There are interesting sound effects in some of the tapes. An explosive sound which occurs at a dramatic moment in Emanuel's tape near the end of "A View from the White Helmet" is the sound of an automobile backfiring. The percussive sounds at the beginning of Sonia Sanchez's tape, which she recorded in my home, are the tapping of her shoes as she walked back and forth while reading. When I played back the first few poems, I detected the noise, and asked her to pull off her shoes.

In 1968 Broadside Press began United States distribution of Paul Breman's *Heritage Series,* imported from England, which includes Conrad Kent Rivers' posthumous *The Still Voice of Harlem* and Russell Atkin's *Heretofore.* Eventually the series will include books by Lloyd Addison, Ray Durem, Owen Dodson, Audrey Lorde, Dudley Randall, Ishmael Reed, and other poets.

Up to now, Broadside Press has published poetry only. A new departure will be the series *Broadside Critics,* which will be pamphlets of criticism of black poetry by black critics. James Emanuel has consented to be editor of the series. Pamphlets for which tentative commitments have been made are: Don L. Lee on poets emerging during the 1960's, Arna Bontemps on Jean Toomer, Robert Hayden on Countee Cullen, James Emanuel on Langston Hughes, and Dudley Randall on Gwendolyn Brooks. It is hoped that these pamphlets will be enlightening and influential.

I have not locked myself in any rigid ideology in managing Broadside Press, but I suppose certain inclinations or directions appear in my actual activities. As clearly as I can see by looking at myself (which is not very clearly, because of the closeness) I restrict the publications to poetry (which I think I understand and can judge not too badly). An exception is the new *Broadside Critics,* which, even though prose, will be concerned with poetry. I reserve the press for black poets (except in *For Malcolm*), as I think the vigor and beauty of our black poets should be better known and should have an outlet. I try to publish a wide variety of poetry, including all viewpoints and styles (viewpoints as opposed as Marvin's X's and Beatrice Murphy's, styles as diverse as James Emanuel's and Don L. Lee's). I deplore incestuous little cliques where poets of a narrow school or ideology band together, cry themselves up, and deride all others. I believe that in the house of poetry there are many mansions, and that we can enjoy different poets for the variety and uniqueness of their poetry, not because they are all of a sameness.

Broadside Press has not been subsidized or funded by any individual, organization, foundation, or government agency. It is, has been, and always will be, free and independent. It is a free, black institution. Support for the Press has come from the grass-roots, from poets who donated their poems to the anthology *For Malcolm,* in honor of Malcolm; from the poets in the first group of the *Broadside Series,* who steadfastly refused payment for their poems; from the many persons who subscribed in advance for the *Broadside Series* and the anthologies, so that they could be printed; and from others who donated sums above their subscriptions. It is the poets and the people who have supported Broadside Press.

I've declined partnerships, mergers, and incorporations, as I want freedom and flexibility of action; want to devote the press to poetry; and am afraid that stockholders in a corporation would demand profits and would lower quality or go into prose in order to obtain profits. Income from the press goes into publishing new books in an attractive and inexpensive format. I pay royalties to other poets, but royalties on my own books go back into the press. I'm not against royalties for myself, or profits for the company, if they ever come, but I'm more interested in publishing good poetry.

Once Gwendolyn Brooks asked me what title to call me by. I replied that since I, in my spare time and in my spare bedroom, do all the work, from sweeping floors, washing windows, licking stamps and envelopes, and packing books, to reading manuscripts, writing ads, and planning and designing books, that she just say that Dudley Randall equals Broadside Press.

In a broader sense, though, Broadside Press is, in embryo, one of the institutions that black people are creating by trial and error and out of necessity in our reaching for self-determination and independence. I don't think it's necessary to belabor the importance of poetry. Poetry has always been with us. It has always been a sustenance, a teacher, an inspiration, and a joy. In the present circumstances it helps in the search for black identity, reinforces black pride and black unity, and is helping to create the soul, the consciousness, and the conscience of black folk.

Instead of trying to justify poetry and the necessity of our own presses such as Broadside and the others like it—Don L. Lee's Third World Press, Tom Dent's Free Southern Theatre, Eugene Perkins' Free Black Press, LeRoi Jones' Jihad Productions, Ed Spriggs' and Nikki Giovanni's Black Dialogue Press, Joe Goncalves' Journal of Black Poetry Press, Casper Jordan's and Russell Atkins' Free Lance Press, and Norman Jordan's new Vibration Press—it would be more fruitful to look toward the future and plan how to turn these small beginnings into viable and permanent institutions. One must recognize, however, their lack of capital in a capitalistic society where a large proportion of small businesses fail every year.

I admit that I am not well qualified to operate in a capitalistic society. I came of age during the Great Depression, and my attitude toward business is one of dislike and suspicion. Writers who send me manuscripts and speak of "making a buck" turn me off.

Capitalistic writers praise the profit motive as a powerful incentive. I think they're liars. I have to confess that I seldom think of profits. My strongest motivations have been to get good black poets published, to produce beautiful books, help create and define the soul of black folk, and to know the joy of discovering new poets. I guess you could call it production for use instead of for profit.

Nevertheless, I think we should remember the lesson of the Negro Renaissance, and try to stay solvent in this jungle society. Negro writers who were a fad during the twenties were dropped by white publishers and readers when the Depression came in the thirties. Black publishers should try to build a stable base in their own communities. It is the black bookstores which are most genuinely interested in their books. In my own home town, Detroit, neither of the large department stores (in a black neighborhood, incidentally) and almost none of the white book stores stock Broadside books. Vaughn's Book Store (black) alone carries all of them. There is an interdependence between black booksellers and black publishers. One Chicago bookseller, who had just opened a store, told me, "Only Broadside and Free Black Press would give me credit. The white companies wouldn't do it."

Publishers should foster the closest and most helpful relations with these small bookstores, should visit them, furnish them with advertisement and information, and help them with ordering. They should encourage their authors to give readings in the bookstores and to meet their readers. They should encourage sound business practices among them by such means as giving extra discounts for early payment. Black book jobbers should be developed, as the white book jobbers are singularly uninterested in the small black publisher. Baker & Taylor, Campbell and Hall, and other large white jobbers, for instance, do not stock Broadside Press books, but only order single copies when they receive an order. We need black distributors who'll buy large quantities of books from black publishers and furnish them promptly to the trade.

We need more small publishers who will specialize in other genres besides poetry. We have always had good actors, but we have not had black playwrights to furnish them material. Today, however, we have a flowering of dramatists in LeRoi Jones, James Baldwin, Ed Bullins, Douglas Turner Ward, Owen Dodson, Sonia Sanchez, Marvin X, and others. Black publishers, like the French and the Baker Companies, could publish their plays in inexpensive pamphlets like poetry, and could supply mimeographed copies of parts to the many schools, colleges, churches, and grass-roots theatres springing up over the country which are clamoring for meaningful material.

We have produced many fine essayists, of eloquence and moral urgency, from Frederick Douglass through Du Bois, Wright, Ellison, Baldwin, and Jones to Addison Gayle and Larry Neal. Essays, like poetry and the drama, are another genre which could be published in inexpensive pamphlets, singly or in collections.

Reference librarians, like myself, have often been frustrated by the gaps in reference materials on the Negro. Ira Aldridge, for instance, one of the greatest Shakespearean actors, has only in the last few years been included in biographical or theatrical reference works. Teachers, librarians, professors, and scholars could compile bibliographies, handbooks, directories, indexes, and biographical works to supplement inadequate reference works like *Who's Who in America, Encyclopedia Americana, Contemporary Authors,* and others. These would find a ready market in libraries, schools, colleges, businesses, and homes. A forthcoming example of such a work is Charles Evans' *Index to Black Anthologies,* which will index anthologies likely to be left out of *Grainger's Index to Poetry.* Another example, although not a reference work, is my own *Black Poetry: A Supplement to Anthologies Which Exclude Black Poets,* the title of which is self-explanatory.

Large works such as novels, biographies, and non-fiction books, which are more costly to produce and market, will have to be left to more affluent publishers, like the Johnson Publishing Company, which has already published several novels and non-fiction books.

There is a growing market for black books, not only among the young black high school and college students, but also among older, less educated persons. A neighbor told me that he saw a worker on the production line of an automobile factory with a copy of the anthology *For Malcolm* in his hip pocket. I often get orders for poetry books which are scrawled and misspelled on paper torn from notebooks, and once received an order scrawled on part of a brown paper bag. I am more pleased to receive such individual orders than to receive a large order from a bookstore or a jobber, for they show that black people are reading poetry and are finding it a meaningful, not an esoteric, art.

We are a nation of twenty-two million souls, larger than Athens in the Age of Pericles or England in the Age of Elizabeth. There is no reason why we should not create and support a literature which will be to our own nation, and to the world, what those literatures were to theirs.

On the Boycott

*black writers/white publishers: an alliance that boycotts black publishers**

I come in low—like a dust cropper pilot flying over the heads of fruit trees—because cats want to know about the "boycott." I come in this low because I know abt our own ugliness. I think you shld know about it too. dig the split making our eyes protrude from what rests whitely betwn them. because we can close the split is why the boycott.

Cold-blooded. the dirt of whitey's hell beneath our fingernails. why? dead light bulb. zombie calisthenics. powerless to sanctify our hell. yesterday's ashes on today's ebony ambers. frosty faustian fraud. plain bad feet.

but what shld we smell as we stand in the world? our own body before the calla lily. burning in the sun. a different masturbation on our fingernails? historical tragedy. repeat. repeat. but not for me. as in the song. talk to me baby. whisper in my ear. like in that song too.

what I want understood is this boycott thing, and it is necessary to deal with this, is that this did not come about due to a personal clash with Clarence Major. I mean it is not about C. Major the man, the poet, but the ideological stance that is him, a lot of other Black writers and until recently, myself. and another thing that needs clarification is that it aint about International Publishers per se, yeah, we dig where they at. along with a lot of other publishers in that same direction and Praeger, say, in the opposite.

the ideological stance: where we at? writers. Black. seeking new dimensions of power. the orientation is BLACK POWER. generally, that's the stance. the image most of us present. the assumption. the writer that embraces Black Power uses that Power in a fashion that will directly (concretely) be of benefit to us all.

listen to us. theoretical raps. work and talk abt art *collectively benefiting black people.* we are artists working out of a still too nebulous ideology. something Black we have a feeling for. something Black we have to take responsibility for. something Black we say is art and then we let it go at that. why for?

broken paned window. kaleidoscopic beings. mishappenings in thot constructions. all of that, but I have another challenge to deal with here. the boycott. it implies, according

---

*In the spring issue (1968) of the Journal of Black Poetry we announced that Ed Spriggs intended to "boycott" an anthology to be published by International Publishers and edited by bro Clarence Major. We asked bro Ed for a statement. This is it.

From *Journal of Black Poetry,* Black Art / Black Culture Issue (1970): 11–14.

to current acceptance, an active campaign against something. not exactly where I'm at. I did threaten that initially tho. but later a better notion was just to throw the idea out there. see where the brothers wld go with it without an immediate explanation, so i threw it out there. The Journal of Black Poetry picked up on it. the word came that a number of brothers across this arcadia had "joined" in. what their reasons are I cannot tell you. i know where a few went with it. seems some thot it was abt International Publishers being CP apparatus. but no. the issue is heavier than that. it is about *us*. and that's heavy. it's abt *Black-Arts-Power*. and that's even heavier if we can get to it.

enough has been written about the all-encompassing notion of Black Power so there is a basis—a contemporary relevance—that is available to all the cats who be writers and claim our particular stance. cats that function in our social and policial milieu shld be putting the theory to work. it's that simple. yeah, but, the absolute end, plotted as some wld have it, is a compromise. contemporary relevance? Black cats are writing great books. but many seem to deal in or out of their personal Black ideology. what they rake in is also their personal black ideology. dig it? low blow? naw, their take is peanut power and I don't mean the kind G. W. Carver was dealing with either. mickey mouse stuff. percentages designed to provide creature comforts to Black writers while the heavy percentages *fortify the status quo*.

iced reality we thot to be dead in the volcanism of our heads. back stabs in time. pus running down our faces like long winter snot. too long to suck back. bitter-sweet. taste it. then fatten up. busting out at the seams white publishers expand, become more and more entrenched in the imperialism of the west. the juices of our servitude. wld maggots squirm out of our village minds if the ice melted there? some minds keep turning up cameoed. still tricking for downtown merchants. not for uptown lovers of laugh. you dig. a clock losing time. and we say BLACK POWER. published history of the sixties is all you have to dig. white publishers and black writers. Black publishers ignored constantly by our favorite sons. yesterdays ashes on today's ebony ambers. frosty faustian fraud. plain bad feet.

why? disunity? the age. irrelevant. EGO. baby, ego. individual power. you dig? IN DIVID(E) (YO)U AL(L). so yeah, disunity also. ham mercy Malcolm. what cld possibly be behind the hip brother artist's inability to see how his powers can function for the total community? for the power the community is flirting with? a pivoting soul out of vortex of soul. cold blooded.

Dig how much mileage has been gotten out of the Malcolm legacy by Merit, et al. whose fault it is is slightly off my point. but leRoi the terrible, baldwin the goodie gum drop, malcolm the irreplaceable, and all the rest of us git compromised just because we want to git our things out there. it's weird. black publishers and the would be ones stand in the shadows subsisting on broadsides, throwaways, rubberstamps and other trivia because black writers won't give them a decent play. but we scream "*Black Power.*"

the change up wld mean that desired monies would have to be sacrificed. but the chosen few could give the black publishers one of their manuscripts a year as a start. how in the hell are the black publishers ever going to get off into it if not by the assistance of the writers. how are distributorships ever going to mature with the publishers if the highly marketable works of a wm kelly, j. killens, ja wms, l neal, e bullins, leroi j, or the like never comes their way? does the concept of black power and black arts extend *that* far? i say yea. i say yea, yea. review the lit and you'll say yea, yea, too. what abt these writers? am i just shooting at them because, maybe, i aint among their number? all you got to do, i say, is review the lit. these writers, with the possible exception of a ja wms have repeatedly stated the need for establishment of black of black institutions, e.g., black publishers, distributors, etc. and when you review the lit. see what definitions you come up with re what black art is. pull it together. put it out there some more. growth is still a potential. but sacrifices are still the order of the day. sacrifices. deferred gratifications is what sacrifices is. do you dig it?

I took a stand. boycott. it's time for that. it grew out of telephone conversation with c major. while we talked the necessity to take the stand crystallized. repeat: black writers are being exploited even when they're talking abt black power thru the white press. i mean some cat's total economics and prestige depend upon the white publishers—not that they want it that way. we can break that up if we want to. our publishers will never be able to break out of this system if the boost doesn't come from the black writers. swamp our publishers with the level of material that we turn over to the white publishers and domestic and international distributorships will be a reality *before* the present system crumbles. there are many levels of power. let's move on up a little higher.

We already have black publishers (no matter how minor some are) who consistently work with us. are we ready for that? c major wasn't. even tho he had been published in dudley r's Broadside press anthology (*For Malcolm X*) and in the *Journal of Black Poetry. Journal of Black Poetry* is printed and published by black people entirely. Jamerson printing company does the job for the *Journal.* julian richardson, owner of Success Printing company does the job for *Black Dialogue.* Richardson and Associates are publishing a reprint of the *Philosophy and Opinions of Marcus Garvey* in paper and hard covers. san francisco could become the black publishing capital of afro-america if we had our souls where our mouths are. a lot more could be said abt the way we could support black publishers and what kind of changes we wld have to go thru to initiate that support. but we need to think, talk and act on this right away quick. we can take up the challenge now. we need to. unless some of us are already too revolutionary to entertain this kind of thing. it's still possible for us to get our cookies and help the black publishers get theirs too.

repeat. it's abt discontinuing the freeze we have dealt out to black publishers by ignoring their existence. me? i'm nuttin on every thing directed to the mother country's houses that shat shld and cld be published black. so i wont get a poem here or a piece there. my life could never depend on it anyway. of course there are a couple of things due to come out that i let go of before i saw the necessity for this stance. no matter. we've got to stop the contradiction at the point that we become aware of them. black publishers are laying in the cut waiting for the righteous black writers. black writers can bail them out.

There are institutions to be built. we're young and strong enough to build but we've gotta have the vision. we have the power. if you don't believe it just ask dial, harpers, wm morrow, grove, merit, marzani and munsell or even international publishers. couldn't julian richardson, dudley randall and lafayette jamerson get into some very heavy drama if they could get just a little play from our co-opted black writers? you know they could. holes in yr front because you choose not to. fatten up. writers. black. seeking new dimensions of power. talk to me baby. we been laying back too long.

The Development of the Black Revolutionary Artist

Cosmology is that branch of physics that studies the universe. It then proceeds to make certain assumptions, and from these, construct "models." If the model corresponds to reality, and certain factors are predictable, then it can be presumed to substantiate the observable phenomena in the universe. This essay is an attempt to construct a model; a particular way of looking at the world. This is necessary because existing white paradigms or models do not correspond to the realities of black existence. It is imperative that we construct models with different basic assumptions.

The dilemma of the "negro" artist is that he makes assumptions based on the wrong models. He makes assumptions based on white models. These assumptions are not only wrong, they are even antithetical to his existence. The black artist must construct models which correspond to his own reality. The models must be non-white. Our models must be consistent with a black style, our natural aesthetic styles, and our moral and spiritual styles. In doing so, we will be merely following the natural demands of our culture. These demands are suppressed in the larger (white) culture, but, nonetheless, are found in our music and in our spiritual and moral philosophy. Particularly in music, which happens to be the purest expression of the black man in America.

In Jahn Janheinz's *Muntu,* he tells us about temples made of mud that vanish in the rainy seasons and are erected elsewhere. They are never made of much sturdier material. The buildings and the statues in them are always made of mud. And when the rains come the buildings and the statues are washed away. Likewise, most of the great Japanese artists of the eighteenth and nineteenth centuries did their exquisite drawings on rice paper with black ink and spit. These were then reproduced by master engravers on fragile newssheets that were distributed to the people for next to nothing. These sheets were often used for wrapping fish. They were a people's newssheet. Very much like the sheets circulated in our bars today.

My point is this: that in both of the examples just given, there is little concept of fixity. The work is fragile, destructible; in other words, there is a total disregard for the perpetuation of the product, the picture, the statue, and the temple. Is this ignorance? According to Western culture evaluations, we are led to believe so. The white researcher, the white scholar, would have us believe that he "rescues" these "valuable" pieces. He "saves" them

From *Black Fire: An Anthology of Afro-American Writing,* ed. LeRoi Jones (Amiri Baraka) and Larry Neal (New York: Morrow, 1968).

from their creators, those "ignorant" colored peoples who would merely destroy them. Those people who do not know their value. What an audacious presumption!

The fact is that *these* people did know their value. But the premises and values of their creation are of another order, of another cosmology, constructed in terms agreeing with their own particular models of existence. Perpetuation, as the white culture understands it, simply does not exist in the black culture. We know, all non-whites know, that man can not create *a* forever; but he can create forever. But he can only create if he creates as change. Creation is itself perpetuation and change is being.

In this dialectical apprehension of reality it is the act of creation of a work as it comes into existence that is its only being. The operation of art is dialectical. Art goes. Art is not fixed. Art can not be fixed. Art is change, like music, poetry and writing are, when conceived. They must move (swing). Not necessarily as physical properties, as music and poetry do; but intrinsically, by their very nature. But they must go spiritually, noumenally. This is what makes those mud temples in Nigeria go. Those prints in Japan. This is what makes black culture go.

All white Western art forms, up to and including those of this century, were matrixed. They all had a womb, the germinative idea out of which the work evolved, or as in the tactile forms (sculpture and painting, for instance), unifying factors that welded the work together, e.g. the plot of a play, the theme of a musical composition, and the figure. The trend in contemporary white forms is toward the elimination of the matrix, in the play "happenings," and in music, aleatory or random techniques. All of these are influenced by Eastern traditions. It is curious and sometimes amusing to see the directions that these forms take.

The music that black people in this country created was matrixed to some degree; but it was largely improvisational also, and that aspect of it was non-matrixed. And the most meaningful music being created today is non-matrixed. The music of Ornette Coleman.

The sense in which "revolutionary" is understood is that a revolutionary is against the established order, regime, or culture. The bourgeoisie calls him a revolutionary because he threatens the established way of life—things as they are. They can not accept change, though change is inevitable. The revolutionary understands change. Change is what it is all about. He is not a revolutionary to his people, to his compatriots, to his comrades. He is, instead, a brother. He is a son. She is a sister, a daughter.

The dialectical method is the best instrument we have for comprehending physical and spiritual phenomena. It is the essential nature of being, existence; it is the property of being and the "feel" of being; it is the implicit *sense* of it. This sense, black people have. And the revolutionary artist must understand this sense of reality, this philosophy of reality which exists in all non-white cultures. We need our own conventions, a convention of procedural elements, a kind of stylization, a sort of insistency which leads inevitably to a certain kind of methodology—a methodology affirmed by the spirit.

That spirit is black.

That spirit is non-white.

That spirit is patois.

That spirit is Samba.

Voodoo.

The black Baptist church in the South.

We are, in essence, the ingredients that will create the future. For this reason, we are misfits, estranged from the white cultural present. This is our position as black artists in these times. Historically and sociologically we are the rejected. Therefore, we must know that we are the building stones for the New Era. In our movement toward the future, "ineptitude" and "unfitness" will be an aspect of what we do. These are the words of the established order—the middle-class value judgments. We must turn these values in on themselves. Turn them inside out and make ineptitude and unfitness desirable, even mandatory. We must even, ultimately, be estranged from the dominant culture. This estrangement must be nurtured in order to generate and energize our black artists. This means that he can not be "successful" in any sense that has meaning in white critical evaluations. Nor can his work ever be called "good" in any context or meaning that could make sense to that traditional critique.

Revolution is fluidity. What are the criteria in times of social change? Whose criteria are they, in the first place? Are they ours or the oppressors'? If being is change, and the sense of change is the time of change—and what is, is about to end, or is over—where are the criteria?

History qualifies us to have this view. Not as some philosophical concept acting out of matter and movement—but as being. So, though the word "dialectic" is used, the meaning and sense of it more than the word, or what the word means, stand as postulated experience. Nothing can be postulated without fixing it in time—standing it still, so to speak. It can not be done. The white Westerner was on his way toward understanding this when he rejected the postulated systems of his philosophies; when he discarded methodology in favor of what has come to be called existentialism. But inevitably, he postulated existence; or at least, it was attempted. Therefore, existentialism got hung up in just the same way as the philosophical systems from which it has extricated itself.

But we need not be bothered with that. We need merely to see how it fits; how the word dialectic fits; what change means; and what fluidity, movement and revolution mean. The purpose of writing is to enforce the sense we have of the future. The purpose of writing is to enforce the sense we have of responsibility—the responsibility of understanding our roles in the shaping of a new world. After all, experience is development; and development is destruction. The great Indian thinkers had this figured out centuries ago. That is why, in the Hindu religion, the god Siva appears—Siva, the god of destruction.

All history is "tailored" to fit the needs of the particular people who write it. Thus, one of our "negro" writers failed to understand the historicity of the Nation of Islam. He failed to understand. This was because his assumptions were based on white models and on a self-conscious "objectivity." This is the plight of the "negro" man of letters, the negro intellectual who needs to demonstrate a so-called academic impartiality to the white establishment.

Now, on the other hand, a dialectical interpretation of revolutionary black development rooted in the *Western* dialectic also will not do. However, inherent in the Western dialectical approach is the idea of imperceptible and gradual quantitative change; changes which give rise to a new state. This approach has also illustrated that there are no immutable social systems or eternal principles; and that there is only the inherency in things of contradictions—of opposing tendencies. It has also illustrated that the role of the "science of history" is to help bring about a fruition of new aggregates. These were all good and canonical to the kind of dialectics that came out of Europe in the nineteenth century.

But contemporary art is rooted in a European convention. The standards whereby its products are judged are European. However, this is merely *one* convention. Black culture implies, indeed engenders, for the black artist another order, another way of looking at things. It is apparent in the music of Giuseppe Logan, for example, that the references are not white or European. But it is jazz and it is firmly rooted in the experiences of black individuals in this country. These references are found also in the work of John Coltrane, Ornette Coleman, Grachan Moncur and Milford Graves.

A revolutionary art is being expressed today. The anguish and aimlessness that attended our great artists of the 'forties and 'fifties and which drove most of them to early graves, to dissipation and dissolution, is over. Misguided by white cultural references (the models the culture set for its individuals), and the incongruity of these models with black reality, men like Bird were driven to willful self-destruction. There was no program. And the reality-model was incongruous. It was a white reality-model. If Bird had had a black reality-model, it might have been different. But though Parker knew of the new development in the black culture, even helped to ferment it, he was hung up in an incompatible situation. They were contradictions both monstrous and unbelievable. They were contradictions about the nature of black and white culture, and what that had to mean to the black individual in this society. In Bird's case, there was a dichotomy between his genius and the society. But, that he couldn't find the adequate model of being was the tragic part of the whole thing. Otherwise, things could have been more meaningful and worthwhile.

The most persistent feature of all existence is change. In other words, it is this property which is a part of everything which exists in the world. As being, the world is change. And it is this very property that the white West denies. The West denies change, defies change . . . resists change. But change is the basic nature of everything that is. Society is. Culture is. Everything that is—in society—its people and their manner of being, and the way in which they make a living. But mainly the modes of what is material, and how the material is produced. What it looks like and what it means to those who produce it and those who accept it. And this is how philosophy, art, morality and certain other things are established. But all established things are temporary, and the nature of being is, like music, changing.

Art can not apologize out of existence the philosophical ethical position of the artist. After all, the artist is a man in society, and his social attitudes are just as relevant to his art as his aesthetic position. However, the white Western aesthetics is predicated on the idea of separating one from the other—a man's art from his actions. It is this duality that is the most distinguishable feature of Western values.

Music is a social activity. Jazz music, in particular, is a social activity, participated in by artists collectively. Within a formal context or procedure, jazz affords the participants a collective form for individual group development in a way white musical forms never did. The symphony, for instance, is a dictatorship. There is a rigidity of form and craft-practice—a virtual enslavement of the individual to the autocratic conductor. Music is a social activity in a sense that writing, painting and other arts can never be. Music is made with another. It is indulged in with others. It is the most social of the art forms except, say, architecture. But music possesses, in its essence, a property none of the other forms possesses. This property of music is its ontological procedures—the nature of which is dialectical. In other words, music possesses properties of being that come closest to the condition of life, of existence. And, in that sense, I say its procedures are ontological—which doesn't mean a thing, but that music comes closest to being. This is why music teaches. This is what music teaches.

The point of the whole thing is that we must emancipate our minds from Western values and standards. We must rid our minds of these values. Saying so will not be enough. We must try to shape the thinking of our people. We must goad our people by every means, remembering as Ossie Davis stated: that the task of the Negro (*sic,* black) writer is revolutionary by definition. He must view his role *vis-à-vis* white Western civilization, and from this starting point in his estrangement begin to make new definitions founded on his own culture—on definite black values.

Needed: A New Image

While the questions of the black woman and the exposure of her one dimensional roles portrayed in the theatre are important, they are relatively minor in the larger scheme of things. There are issues in the theatre far more basic and fundamental. The black woman's existence in the theatre or the lack of her existence is associated and related to issues of much greater magnitude. Yes, it is necessary to correct and clarify her image! Yes, she is more than a domestic, matriarch and/or sex symbol! However, it is far more important to establish a positive relationship between black men and black women in the theatre and all other mass media. It is vital that black artists project an image of love, respect, and solidarity for one another. It seems almost ludicrous to think that without this unity and understanding there can be fed into or sustained in any of the communicative arts anything of lasting and significant value for the race. Black people are spiritually very loving, and it is imperative that we begin to have stable romantic interests projected. America has never seen a Negro couple make love in any mass media. Does this not seem strange? The black artist must begin to recognize the necessity for and the many social ramifications involved in portraying this kind of unity.

The black writers and playwrights have a great responsibility here. They must become the spokesmen, the forerunners. They must pave the way with new thought patterns. They must set the pace and feed society a new image. This is a basic problem the black artist must contend with. However, before he can yet deal with this problem, he must first solve one even more fundamental—that of his individual racial consciousness.

The problem of racial equality which confronts the Negro performer in Show Business is no different from that which he faces in any other field of endeavor. What he is doing to alleviate this problem, however, is quite different. He is desperately lagging behind in social consciousness in this new struggle for black identity and racial solidarity. He is at the end of the totem pole mainly because he is struggling to be a part of or integrated into Show Business. The name itself is self-explanatory. It is a trade, owned, operated, and formulated by white people for the purpose of making money. In order for a black performer to become successful and/or accepted in this business, it is mandatory that he adapt to the values of that white system physically, spiritually, and morally. The compromises and sacrifices involved in making these adjustments are extremely dangerous. In order for the

From *The Black Power Revolt: A Collection of Essays,* ed. Floyd B. Barbour (Boston: Peter Sargent, 1968).

black performer to become successful in the dominant society which in this case is white, puritanically Anglo-Saxon, he must think in accordance with these values which necessarily dictate that he become the same as his white counterpart. Consequently, he begins to act out of their set of values and to pattern his life and personality after their way of life. The fact that he has allowed this to happen to him is indeed a misfortune. The American public, both black and white, can see the results of this compromise daily on television, in the theatre and on the screen.

Providing more jobs for black performers was one of the major solutions to this problem less than three years ago. A program of action was designed. As in most cases, we headed for the streets carrying picket signs, passing out pamphlets and chanting slogans such as "Last to be hired, first to be fired," "Don't exclude us," "We exist," "The image of the American Negro must be changed," "Employ us in roles that more realistically depict us as we really exist in America today," "We want to see more Negroes on television."

So now in 1967, the American viewer sees several handsome, virile Negro men fighting international spies, outwitting German prison camp commanders, capturing white hoods and facing down fast-drawing western sheriffs in dusty little western towns, and even telecasting the news.

While the problem of depicting the Negro male in roles natural to any actor has not been fully solved, it has been attacked with several dramatic and highly noticeable thrusts. He has dropped the broom, taken off the butler and porter uniforms and now clenches a Colt .45, a cocktail glass, a detective's badge, a computer, or a Geiger counter in his strong black hands.

Well, now we have accomplished the first phase of our program of action. We have been given a few more jobs by the white man. This was to be the beginning of an overall reform.

Television and movies, being mass media which influence millions of minds daily, are now establishing for the black man new patterns of behavior. The black performer should stop and appraise this situation. Is this the image that he wants portrayed? Is this the image that will further his racial identity or is it in fact simply reproducing more whiteness? Look around you. The proof is in the pudding. The few directors, choreographers, television and movie actors we have are doing in fact the same thing as the white man and not even as effectively.

Therefore, the answer to the problem of racial equality is far more complex certainly than simply "Employing more Negroes in roles that more realistically depict them as they really exist in America today." If this means that in order to "make it" we must deny our blackness—the very thing that makes us uniquely individualistic; if it means that we must blend into and become the same as whites, we should in fact refuse to perpetuate this image any longer. No one should or can dictate to us what our true cultural roots are.

It is true that the black performer has a dual cultural heritage. He is American with an African ancestry. (What an exciting theatrical combination!) However, he is often completely confused as to which of these images he should project.

It should be his duty as a public figure to reflect an image which his people cannot only identify with, but can emulate. More often than not he sacrifices his African heritage in order to become more commercial. If he is more commercial, which means more white, it therefore follows that he will become more successful financially. And if those performers who are at present more commercially successful could begin to change this image, it would certainly help those young performers, who are trying to make it now, have a much easier road to climb.

There is nothing wrong with being financially successful, or with being accepted by or in the white world. There is nothing wrong with living in comfort but there is something wrong with the attitudes which produce this success and the way in which one sets out to achieve acceptance. For instance, the height of accomplishment for a Negro performer is reached when he is bestowed with the signal honor of such catchy phrases as: "The fact that Joe Blow happens to be Negro is literally unimportant" or "Joe Blow is not Negro, he is universal, a first rate performer." Very few Negro performers have reached the level of achievement where this catchy phrase can be applied to them, but thousands are striving for it. You never see "The fact that Joe Blow happens to be white is literally unimportant," or "Joe Blow is not white, he is universal, a first rate performer." Why the double standard? This is a clear and open admission that the Negro must lose his unique identity and become molded in the image of the white man before he can be recognized as a human being in this country.

The black masses, i.e., the man in the street, do not have this problem of racial identity. The man in the street just by his very nature *Is*. With the exception of Rhythm and Blues singers, jazz musicians and performers of the magnitude of Nina Simone, very few black entertainers are clear as to what cultural image they should reflect. Culture is a way of life or the sum total of a way of living built up by a group of human beings which is transmitted from one generation to another, and this culture for theatrical purposes should be enhanced and enlightened. That means, the way we talk (the rhythms of our speech which naturally fit our impulses), the way we walk, sing, dance, pray, laugh, eat, make love, and finally, most important, the way we look, make up our cultural heritage. There is nothing like it or equal to it, it stands alone in comparison to other cultures. It is uniquely, beautifully and personally ours and no one can emulate it. It is the cultural responsibility of those before the public eye to wear our heritage like a badge of honor and project it whenever and wherever the opportunity arises. It is our responsibility as black artists not to assimilate another set of cultural values but to create and establish more realistic ones. This must be done before the black performer can truly progress. This double consciousness must be removed and replaced by a stronger black one. We must begin thinking and using more energy toward developing and sustaining our own cultural identity. Too much time, energy, pain and frustration is being utilized trying to maintain a dual personality. It is impossible for us to merge and identify at the same time.

An ideal situation would be to have black television stations, film companies and theatres. But, at this time, we do not have this kind of economic power. However, at this point in our growth, if we did have economic solidarity, we must just as easily fall into the same traps and pitfalls as whites. Essentially, there is no difference between the psyche of a white businessman and a black one. In this country, their sole concern is to make money. They stick to what has been tried and proven: the safe way; the easy follow-the-leader way. These narrow concepts have apparently, until now, been the code of ethics of the American businessman.

So in planning his own businesses, the black performer must be very careful to analyse his thought patterns so that he will not make the same errors. The seeds that the Negro performer plants in the mind of America and eventually of the world must reflect more positive attitudes concerning his blackness. The white businessman does not have the time, knowledge, nor inclination to do our research for us. Furthermore, it is not his responsibility. The black artist must solve this problem by himself and for his own salvation. The time has come to break down and destroy these antiquated stereotypes and concepts. The black youth of America needs a new image, and it should be the responsibility of the black artist to provide it for them.

ROLLAND SNELLINGS (ASKIA TOURÉ)

Keep on Pushin': Rhythm & Blues as a Weapon

In the Lash Years when we wore the chains of our dishonor, we were a defiant, spirited people. So much so, that there occurred a slave revolt on the average of once every three weeks. The slave revolts were the outward PHYSICAL manifestations of the inner SPIRIT of the captive people. The inner SPIRIT was also manifested in what were to become the rudiments or foundations of African-american culture: the spirituals, hollers, field-chants, etc.

The African-american spiritual was an ingenius instrument molded in the fires of oppression—disguised as mere "sacred songs," the spiritual was a vessel which carried the message of resistance, escape, or revolt. Resistance, escape, or revolt, the message of the spiritual, has been handed down through the years, in the collective memory of our people, in the "double-talk" of the parables, folk-tales, folksongs, etc. of the Black Man.

Given the primary powerlessness of our people to Whitey's brute force, we had to create a subtle instrument which would increase our "value" to the Beast while "taking care of business" for ourselves. "Boy, those niggers sure can sing; gather 'em up at the big house tonight from all over the plantation, so they can serenade us." So, the "get togethers" were very instrumental in providing many coded messages, details, etc. to the Underground Railroad and networks developing throughout the South.

From the period of "Reconstruction," where the neo-colonialism of White America was exposed for what it was, down to the outright betrayal and institution of color seg-regation, our people shifted their emphasis to the painful irony of the Blues (or Country Blues) to describe or "run down" our philosophy, attitudes, and outlooks. It is recorded that when Gertrude "Ma" Rainey gave a show in the Southern "back country," the Black farmers and sharecroppers (landless peasants) came from miles around, from neighbor-ing districts and counties, to view the scene.

Such songs as "Backwater Blues" (describing the tragedy of the floods), "Yellow Dog Blues," and others were the crystallized philosophies, hopes, and aspirations voice FOR our people by their PRIEST-PHILOSOPHERS: the Black singers and musicians. (This attitude of the Black musician and poet as priest-philosopher goes back to the indigenous African civilizations, where the artist-priest had a functional role as the keeper or guard-ian of the spirit of the nation—as well as the ancestors.) This attitude, curiously enough, has remained among us despite the dehumanization of chattel slavery and the "white-

From *Liberator* 5.10 (October 1965).

washing" of the Western Missionary Educational System. It has, of course been either ignored or by-passed by bourgeois "negro" sociologists, either through ignorance of heritage or fear of being classified "alien" to American cultural standards.

ONCE MORE: We are a defiant, spirited people who have a history of over three hundred years of constant slave revolts, in which our music played a vital role. Our main philosophical and cultural attitudes are displayed through our MUSIC, which serves as the ROOT of our culture; from which springs our art, poetry, literature, etc. Our creative artists—especially singers and musicians—function as PRIESTS, as PHILOSOPHERS of our captive nation; a holdover from our ancient past.

> "I got to keep on pushin', can't stop now. Move up a little higher, some way,
>   some how.
> 'Cause I got my strength, don't make sense: Keep on pushin'!"

In the smoldering epoch of our times, eruptions of the Captive Nation are once again reflected in the songs of Black Folks. In the period of the early Fifties, JAZZ, which had been a vital part of Black people's music, was taken over by the racketeers and moved downtown into the clubs and bars of the middle-class pleasure-seekers, away from the roots, away from the Heart, the Womb, away from the home of the people: uptown-ghetto!

With JAZZ—Bird, Diz, Miles, Max, Lady Day, Lester Young—JAZZ all gone away: Rhythm and Blues was the only music left to sing out the aspirations and soul stirrings of Blacks folks uptown N.Y. and "uptown-ghetto" across the face of the land. This was, at first, a blow to the Soul Folks: What would they possibly DO without BIRD, DIZ, MILES or LADY DAY or LESTER YOUNG to make them "feel alright" deep down in the nitty-gritty of their hearts? But, being a people raised on change, raised with the insecurities of change throbbing in the nerve-ends of their lives, they ADAPTED themselves to expression with their only cultural weapon or potential weapon: Rhythm and Blues.

Yes, JAZZ, fine JAZZ, great JAZZ was gone away, gone away, away into the Ofay night, away from the warm earth smell of their rhythms and soul vibrations, to make the cash registers clang and sing, ring and pile up green capital for the "negroes' 'FRIEND'" and sponsor "downtown" in the air-conditioned nightmares of the West.

The Fifties, the early Fifties, the later Fifties of suicidal Johnny Ace, Big Mabel, Chuck Willis, Chuck Jackson: all legendary Blues People, scorched with the pain reflected in bleary red-eyed heartbreak sweat-stained songs and tears flooding into the "Ebb-tide" of Roy Hamiltons or the Moonglows; Clyde McPhatter and the Drifters blown to the "White Cliffs of Dover" on the "Wind" of the Diablos; "Crying in the Chapels" of the Orioles; or shot down, cut and beaten up in "Smokey Joe's Cafe."

These were OUR songs, OUR lives reflected in a thousand blue notes, notes of hopelessness marked with thicker callouses on black hands, more muscle cramps in mama's knees, more heartache and unemployment for our fathers and brothers, as Korea loomed distantly and we went away to slaughter up the Yellow race for Whitey's cause.

My people, YES, a million lonely eyes burning to touch Happiness, to touch Human Sympathy, Brotherhood, Justice: all those BIG words that BIG white learned men invited to taunt us into dissatisfaction with eight kids to a room, bedside roach crawl and rats gnawing at the eight kids to a room on gloom street, on your street, my street: Ghetto-uptown U.S.A.!

My people, YES, my love, my Fifties of Martin Luther King, minister of youth: Large liquid eyes then searching for the Gandhi-secret Freedom-message looming huge and idealistic from Southern horizons bleeding in the sun of a thousand lynch-fires; echoing whitely in the poison-voice of Eastland, Talmadge, Russell, Earl Long and other Favorite Sons of the "Land of the Tree." (In those years of Martin Luther King, bus boycotts and other evidence of our growing struggle, we grew up, developed, expanded our souls, our minds churning to the beat of our people's only music, Rhythm and Blues. We lived it; sang it in vocal groups, in cabarets, on street corners: junkies nodding in the rain. We didn't call it "culture," didn't call it "negro art," it was just OUR music, OUR soul, like OUR girl-friends, OUR comrades, OUR families who didn't understand. It, again, was OUR voice, OUR ritual, OUR understanding of those deep things far too complicated to put into words—except those of Fats Domino, Little Richard, Ray Charles, Dinah Washington, Faye Addams, Ruth Brown, Lloyd Price and many more.)

> "Look, a 'look a 'yonder: what's that I see?
> Great big stone wall standing straight ahead of me.
> But I've got my pride, move the wall aside:
> Keep on pushin'!"

The Sixties, roaring in like a rocket, roaring through the Southland with freedom riders, more boycotts, sit-ins, wade-ins, stand-ins, kneel-ins; Black Muslims rising in the Northland new angry voice, young copper-skinned Malcolm X shaking up the psyche of the nations—Black and White. Lumumba, the U.N. Congo demonstrations, Robert Williams defends a Southern town against the Klan. WE are on the move, WE are moving to a New Tempo, to a New Dynamism—like Coltrane blowing SCREAMING in the downtown nightclubs: "Afro-Blue," "Blue Trane," "Africa," "Out of This World;" and we hear in his screams the bloody Whiplash moans and screams of our great-grandfathers and grandmothers bending low; eyes ablaze with terror at castration, rape, mutilation, SCREAMING into the Raven Universe, SCREAMING into the coming generations, SCREAMING into the Womb of Mother Africa violated and crushed by the Roman Prophylactic: AAAAAAAIIIIIIEEEEEEE! AAAAAAAIIIIIIEEEEEEE!

We sing in our young hearts, we sing in our angry Black Souls: WE ARE COMING UP! WE ARE COMING UP! And it's reflected in the Riot-song that symbolized Harlem, Philly, Brooklyn, Rochester, Patterson, Elizabeth; this song, of course, "Dancing in the Streets"—making Martha and the Vandellas legendary. Then FLASH! It surges up again: "We Gonna' Make It" (to the tune of Medgar Evers gunned down in Mississippi: POW! POW! POW! POW!) "Keep On Trying" (to the tune of James Powell gunned down in Harlem: POW! POW! POW! POW!) "Nowhere to Run, Nowhere to Hide," "Change Is Gonna' Come" (to the tune of Brother Malcolm shot down in the Audobon: POW! POW! POW! POW! POW! POW! POW! POW!)

THIS is, once again, a people's music, THIS is the reflection of their rising aspirations, THESE are the Truths sung by their modern PRIESTS and PHILOSOPHERS: We are on the move and our music is MOVING with us. WE are expressing our heartfelt anger, conjuring up strong Black Armies marching to the tune of "The Same Old Song" while gas bombs and myths explode in Watts, Los Angeles, explode into the putrid white heart of the racist hell that has us STILL IN CHAINS! YES, IN CHAINS! Look at our Rhythm and Blues singers! Look at the musicians! WHO own their contracts? WHO are their agents, managers; WHO speaks for them? CHAINS! CHAINS! MORE CHAINS! WHITE CHAINS CLANKING IN OUR SOULS! But we are coming out, we are coming up (WHITE AMERICA: DO YOU HEAR?), we are coming out from the chains that bind us: whether culture, economics, politics, military chains: WE ARE COMING OUT! FORGET about his computers, jetplanes, rocketships, blue-eyed troops; FORGET about atomic bombs, police-dogs, cattle-prods and dynamite. OUR songs are turning from "love," turning from being "songs," turning into WAYS, into WAYS, into "THINGS." We are making BLACK magic, BLACK NIGGER magic with our SONGS, with our LIVES: this is our BOMB, our BLACK BOMB, our TIME BOMB, our TIME BOMB which will bring on the "DESTRUCTION OF AMERICA," A PLAY BY LEROI JONES. The Social Voice of Rhythm and Blues is only the beginning of the end. Somewhere along the line, the "Keep on Pushin'" in song, in Rhythm and Blues is merging with the Revolutionary Dynamism of COLTRANE of ERIC DOLPHY of BROTHER MALCOLM of YOUNG BLACK GUERRILLAS STRIKING DEEP INTO THE HEARTLAND OF THE WESTERN EMPIRE. The Fire is spreading, the Fire is spreading, the Fire made from the merging of dynamic Black Music (Rhythm and Blues, Jazz), with politics (GUERRILLA WARFARE) is spreading like black oil flaming in Atlantic shipwrecks spreading like Black Fire: the Black Plague spreads across Europe in the Middle Ages—raining death. WORK your magic, BLACK magic, NIGGER magic across the Empire to the beat, to the dynamism of Social-conscious RHYTHM AND BLUES, NEW JAZZ, BLACK POETRY: WORK your NIGGER MAGIC in the sweaty smile of the Boston Monkey, "SUGAR PIE, HONEY-BUNCH:" twist and shimmy frug monkey down the Empire with thick ruby lips grinning like MAD like BLAZING RED EYES LURKING IN THE MOON.

EACH TIME a Black song is born, EACH TIME a Black Sister has another child, EACH TIME Black Youth says NO! to the racist draft boards, EACH TIME someone remembers Brother Malcolm's smile, EACH TIME we write a poem an essay as a Way into "Things," EACH TIME we love each other a little more: THIS THING QUAKES! WE are moving forward, WE are on the move, WE record it all in Rhythm and Blues, New Jazz, Black Poetry, WE—the Captive Nation listening to its priests and wisemen; growing stronger; donning Black Armor to get the job done so Rhythm and Blues can once again sing about "Love," "mellow" black women, and happy children: after it sings this Empire to the grave, after it sings the Sun of the Spirit back into the lonely heart of man. (For Dinah Washington, Sam Cooke, Nat Cole, Eric Dolphy, James Chaney, James Powell, Medgar Evers, Brother Malcolm, Leon Ameer, Walter Bowe, Khaleel Sayyed, Robert Collier: Many Thousand Gone!)

> Maybe someday, I'll reach that higher goal.
> I know I can make it with just a little bit of soul.
> 'Cause I've got my strength, don't make sense:
> Keep on Pushin'!
> Ha-al-lelujah! Ha-al-lelujah!:
> Keep on Pushin'!
> Keep on Pushin'!

2

Gender

Preface

We are involved in a struggle for liberation: liberation from the exploitive and dehumanizing system of racism, from the manipulative control of a corporate society; liberation from the constrictive norms of "mainstream" culture, from the synthetic myths that encourage us to fashion ourselves rashly from without (reaction) rather than from within (creation). What characterizes the current movement of the 60's is a turning away from the larger society and a turning toward each other. Our art, protest, dialogue no longer spring from the impulse to entertain, or to indulge or enlighten the conscience of the enemy; white people, whiteness, or racism; men, maleness, or chauvinism; America or imperialism . . . depending on your viewpoint and your terror. Our energies now seem to be invested in and are in turn derived from a determination to touch and to unify. What typifies the current spirit is an embrace, an embrace of the community and a hardheaded attempt to get basic with each other.

If we women are to get basic, then surely the first job is to find out what liberation for ourselves means, what work it entails, what benefits it will yield. To do that, we might turn to various fields of studies to extract material, data necessary to define that term in respect to ourselves. We note, however, all too quickly the lack of relevant material.

Psychiatrists and the like, while compiling data on personality traits and behavioral patterns, tend to reinforce rather than challenge social expectations on the subject of woman; they tell us in paper after paper that first and foremost the woman wishes to be the attractive, cared-for companion of a man, that she desires above all else motherhood, that her sense of self is nourished by her ability to create a comfortable home. Hollywood and other dream factories delight in this notion and reinforce it, and it becomes the social expectation. The woman who would demand more is "immature," "anti-social," or "masculine."

And on the subject of her liberation, when it is considered at all, the experts (white, male) tell us that ohh yes she must be free to enjoy orgasm. And that is that.

When the experts (white or Black, male) turn their attention to the Black woman, the reports get murky, for they usually clump the men and women together and focus so heavily on what white people have done to the psyches of Blacks, that what Blacks have done to and for themselves is overlooked, and what distinguishes the men from the women forgotten.

From *The Black Woman: An Anthology,* ed. Toni Cade Bambara (New York: New American Library, 1970).

Commercial psychologists, market researchers, applied psychologists (by any other name are still white, male) further say, on the subject of women and their liberation, that she must feel free to buy new products, to explore the new commodities, to change brands. So thousands of dollars are spent each year to offer her a wide range of clothes, cosmetics, home furnishings, baby products so that she can realize herself and nourish her sense of identity.

The biologists are no help either. Either they are busily assisting the psychologist in his paper on the Sex Life of the Swan or they are busily observing some primate group or other and concluding, on the basis of two or three weeks, acting as voyeurs to captive monkeys, that the female of the species is "basically" submissive, dependent, frivolous; all she wants to do is be cared for and be played with. It seems not to occur to these scientists (white, male) that the behavioral traits they label "basic" and upon which the psychologists breezily build their theories of masculine/feminine are not so "basic" at all; they do not exist, after all, in a context-free ether. They may very well be not inherent traits but merely at-the-moment traits. What would happen to the neat rows of notes if alterations were made in the cage, if the situation were modified, if the laboratory were rearranged. Add another monkey or two; introduce a water wheel or a water buffalo. Would other traits then be in evidence? Would the "basic" traits change or disappear? People, after all, are not only not rhesus monkeys, they also do not live in a static environment.

The biochemists have been having their day on the podium too. They, too, have much to say on the subject of woman. Chemical agents, sex hormones or enzymes, are the base of it all. They do make an excellent case for sex hormones' influencing physiological differences. But when it comes to explaining the role of either the hormones or the physiological differences in the building of personality, the fashioning of the personality that will or will not adapt to social expectations—all the objective, step-by-step training is out the window. As for woman and the whole question of her role, they seem to agree with Freud: anatomy is destiny.

History, of course, offers us much more data . . . and much more difficulty. For the very movements that could provide us with insights are those movements not traditionally taught in the schools or made available without glamorized distortions by show business: the movement against the slave trade, the abolitionist movement, the feminist movement, the labor movement. But even our skimpy knowledge of these phenomena show us something: the need for unified effort and the value of a vision of a society substantially better than the existing one.

I don't know that literature enlightens us too much. The "experts" are still men, Black or white. And the images of the woman are still derived from their needs, their fantasies, their second-hand knowledge, their agreement with the other "experts." But of course there have been women who have been able to think better than they've been trained and have produced the canon of literature fondly referred to as "feminist literature": Anais Nin, Simone de Beauvoir, Doris Lessing, Betty Friedan, etc. And the question for us arises: how relevant are the truths, the experiences, the findings of white women to Black women? Are women after all simply women? I don't know that our priorities are the same, that our concerns and methods are the same, or even similar enough so that we can afford to depend on this new field of experts (white, female).

It is rather obvious that we do not. It is obvious that we are turning to each other.

Throughout the country in recent years, Black women have been forming work-study groups, discussion clubs, cooperative nurseries, cooperative businesses, consumer education groups, women's workshops on the campuses, women's caucuses within existing organizations, Afro-American women's magazines. From time to time they have organized seminars on the Role of the Black Woman, conferences on the Crisis Facing the Black Woman, have provided tapes on the Attitude of European Men Toward Black Women, working papers on the Position of the Black Women in America; they have begun correspondence with sisters in Vietnam, Guatemala, Algeria, Ghana on the Liberation Struggle and the Woman, formed alliances on a Third World Women plank. They are women who have not, it would seem, been duped by the prevailing notions of "woman," but who have maintained a critical stance.

Unlike the traditional sororities and business clubs, they seem to use the Black Liberation struggle rather than the American Dream as their yardstick, their gauge, their vantage point. And while few have produced, or are interested in producing at this time, papers for publication, many do use working papers as part of their discipline, part of their effort to be clear, analytical, personal, basic; part of their efforts to piece together an "overview," an overview of ourselves too long lost among the bills of sale and letters of transit; part of their effort to deal with the reality of being Black and living in twentieth-century America—a country that has more respect for the value of property than the quality of life, a country that has never valued Black life as dear, a country that regards its women as its monsters, celebrating wherever possible the predatory coquette and the carnivorous mother.

Some of the papers representing groups and individuals are presented here along with poems, stories, and essays by writers of various viewpoints. What is immediately noticeable are the distinct placements of stress, for some women are not so much concerned with demanding rights as they are in clarifying issues; some demand rights as Blacks first, women second. Oddly enough, it is necessary to point out what should be obvious—Black women are individuals too.

For the most part, the work grew out of impatience: an impatience with the all too few and too soon defunct Afro-American women's magazines that were rarely seen outside of the immediate circle of the staff's and contributors' friends. It grew out of an impatience with the half-hearted go-along attempts of Black women caught up in the white women's liberation groups around the country. Especially out of an impatience with all the "experts" zealously hustling us folks for their doctoral theses or government appointments. And out of an impatience with the fact that in the whole bibliography of feminist literature, literature immediately and directly relevant to us wouldn't fill a page. And perhaps that impatience has not allowed me to do all that needs to be done in this volume.

I had thought, in the overly ambitious beginnings, that what we had to do straightaway was (1) set up a comparative study of the woman's role as she saw it in all the Third World Nations; (2) examine the public school system and blueprint some viable alternatives; (3) explore ourselves and set the record straight on the matriarch and the evil Black bitch; (4) delve into history and pay tribute to all our warriors from the ancient times to the slave trade to Harriet Tubman to Fannie Lou Hamer to the woman of this morning; (5) present the working papers of the various groups around the country; (6) interview the migrant workers, the quilting-bee mothers, the grandmothers of the UNIA; (7) analyze the Freedom Budget and design ways to implement it; (8) outline the work that has been done and remains to be done in the area of consumer education and cooperative economics; (9) thoroughly discuss the whole push for Black studies programs and a Black university; (10) provide a forum of opinion from the YWCA to the Black Women Enraged; (11) get into the whole area of sensuality, sex; (12) chart the steps necessary for forming a working alliance with all non-white women of the world for the formation of, among other things, a clearing house for the exchange of information . . .

And the list grew and grew. A lifetime's work, to be sure. But I am comforted by the fact that several of the contributors here have begun books; several women contacted have begun books; several magazines are in the making; several groups are talking about doing documentary films. So in the next few months, there will be appearing books dealing exclusively with the relationships between Black men and women, with the revolutionary Black women of the current period, with the Black abolitionists, with the whole question of Black schools.

This then is a beginning—a collection of poems, stories, essays, formal, informal, reminiscent, that seem best to reflect the preoccupations of the contemporary Black woman in this country. Some items were written especially for the collection. Some were discovered tucked away in notebooks. Many of the contributors are professional writers. Some have never before put pen to paper with publication in mind. Some are mothers. Others are students. Some are both. All are alive, are Black, are women. And that, I should think, is credentials enough to address themselves to issues that seem to be relevant to the sisterhood.

I should like to thank Marvin Gettleman; my agent, Cyrilly Abels; my editor, Nina Finkelstein; my typists, Jean Powell of City College and Nat White of the Lower East Side. And especial thanks to my man Gene.

The book is dedicated to the uptown mammas who nudged me to "just set it down in print so it gets to be a habit to write letters to each other, so maybe that way we don't keep treadmilling the same ole ground."

The Negro Woman in American Literature

Paule Marshall, Alice Childress, and Sarah Wright spoke at the conference "The Negro Writer's Visions of America" held at the New School for Social Research in New York City in 1965. The women on this panel were pioneers in criticizing the degrading and stereotypical portrayals of women in American literature. Alice Childress was the author of the novel A Hero Ain't Nothin But a Sandwich *and the play* A Wedding Band. *Sarah Wright is a poet and novelist. Her classic* This Child's Gonna Live *has recently been reissued. Paule Marshall is author of the award-winning novel* Brown Girl, Brownstones *and a collection of short stories,* Soul Clap Hands and Sing, *among other works.*

Sarah E. Wright

I am convinced that most American men, and unhappily, far, far too many of our Afro-American men, are walking around begging for a popular recognition of what is fictitiously called "manhood," a beginning which takes the form of attacks on women launched from many different directions.

It is for this reason (since men are the most prolific producers of literature) that we have so much slop concerning women in the popular literature and advertisements of our day.

One can hardly pick up a book which does not advertise naked, or suggestively naked women on the cover. Now women for the most part do not slink around naked or in flimsy negligees unless they are adolescent and uninformed about what makes the world go around.

One can hardly pick up a book and read anything about the thoughts of women regarding the conditions of the world unless there are sexual innuendoes and overtones coming through first and foremost. As most of the authors with whom I am acquainted would have it, a woman does not have non-sexual preoccupations. She has been reduced, according to one of the most commercially successful films of recent times, into being, and I quote, "Pussy Galore."

The popular musical literature of our time is in a supreme state of chaos. The reduction of women in song to mere sexual animals is at the point beyond which it can go no further.

From *Freedomways,* no. 1 (1966).

A virtual wilderness of the human mind exists with respect to what it is to be a woman, a mother, a responsible-minded citizen, a creator of significant and humanly meaningful work, a thoughtful person.

Mothers are treated as stranglers; as people who eternally refuse to "cut the navel cord" even if the child grows up to be one hundred. It is no news to any women of my acquaintance that this is not so. A mother's womb and the intelligence which guides the womb is utterly glad when the child is freed from it. For almost every minute that she carries a child, feels that child nursing on the foods that she has eaten, the nights and days of life which transpired before, feeling that child nudging and kicking for life, she is in a state of anxiety for her own safety, as well as that of the baby's. Most mothers do not refuse to cut the navel cord. They are happy to be freed of the child and, I am sure, from the signs of pre-delivery kicking, the child is glad to be freed of the mother. And this is true in the years of childhood and adolescence as well. So much for the "strangling mother" scene.

The stern and fearsome grandmother is another "way out" scene which ought to be abandoned. The grandmothers whom I know are for the most part kind and sometimes overly indulgent. They forgive easily, they talk far more kindly than most people I know, they love graciously and with good judgment. They love with experience in the ways of loving. They are most susceptible to learning. They are people who have achieved humanity. They are usually not "wits" or jokers, as I understand much of our popular literature to say. They are life understood, life lived through many a trial and many an error and many, many successes in the ways of being human beings. They are lovers, not correctors. They are at peace because of the conditioning given by the sense of loving.

If you look at the way most women, and I give particular stress to Afro-American women, being as they are in our society generally on the lowest rung of the ladder, if you look at the way women are treated in literature (most produced by men), you can begin to wonder why they are readers at all, and why particularly, they are producers of literature.

However, there are some of us who come through as producers, as well as readers. I for one have a very limited reading experience, but I am a writer. There are women among us who in spite of economic enslavement in various forms, in spite of being in the condition of Afro-American enslavement, are both readers and writers. Some of these women you will meet today. . . .

Alice Childress

I agree that the Negro woman has almost been omitted as important subject matter in the general popular American drama, television, motion pictures and radio, except for the constant, but empty and decharacterized faithful servant. And her finest virtues have been drawn in terms of long suffering, with humility and patience.

Today, the Negro woman's faults are sometimes pointed out, that she is too militant, so domineering, so aggressive, with son, husband and brother, that it is one of the chief reasons for any unexpressed manhood on the part of the Negro man in America.

There must be some truth in this charge. The mother in James Baldwin's *Amen Corner* attempts to restrict her son and husband to her passive and withdrawn way of life, but fails. The husband abandons her and seeks to find himself in music. He returns home to die, then advises the son she has raised to break free of her gentle domination. The son leaves home.

In Lorraine Hansberry's *A Raisin in the Sun,* the strong, loving mother so dominates the home that she restricts her children and infringes upon the rights of her son as a man.

In Louis Peterson's *Take a Giant Step,* a Negro mother tries to separate her son from his black heritage in order to shield him from the realities of life.

All Negro writers have written, first, about that strong, matriarchal figure. I did in a one-act play, *Florence,* and in *Trouble in Mind.*

But now we frequently hear that strength has taken femininity away from her with the end result that she is the main culprit in any lack of expressed black manhood, and that she has been masculinized in the process.

Certainly this is too easy and too misleading a conclusion. We know that most alien visitors are guaranteed rights and courtesies not extended to at least one-fifth of America's citizens. They are entitled to travel, without restriction, reside in hotels, eat at restaurants and enter public and private places closed to Americans who have built up the country under bondage and defended it under a limited and restricted liberty.

But the American Negro woman has been *particularly* and deliberately oppressed, in slavery and up to and including the present moment, above and beyond the general knowledge of the average American citizen.

After the Emancipation, the white South was faced with a dilemma. How could it protect itself against the legal claims of slaveowners' half-Black children? Some of them were the only offspring of a white master. Many Black women had been purchased to fulfill the role of wives, but most were used as sexual outlets under degrading circumstances and none had the privileges of consent or refusal concerning the use of her body. She was forced to bear children and her offspring belonged legally, not to her, but to her owner-master.

There were many Black men who were resentful of being named father to the white slave-owners' children and eager to escape the additional bondage of an enforced family set-up.

There were also some cases of whites who wished to acknowledge their colored children and leave property to them. Laws were passed declaring what percentage of "Black blood" made a human being all Black, and thus no responsibility to their white parents.

To spare white men the responsibility of support claims, and to avoid Black men challenging in court the paternity of some fair-complexioned child, the white South took action against the Negro woman.

State after state passed legislation declaring that all children born to Black women during slavery shall be known as the legitimate children of *their mothers only.*

In the first generation of "freedom," the Black woman was abandoned, not only by the white father-owner, but by any Black man faced with acknowledging children bred by the slave-master, or by other Black men, since women were mated by the owners with various men, to bring forth various kind of offspring. Mated for strength, endurance, size, color, and even docility.

With one stroke of the pen, she was told that no man, Black or white, owed her anything, and her children were disinherited of all property rights. Her brothers, her father, male cousins, all family ties had been sold, resold, scattered, and so lost that she was, in the majority of cases, without family of any kind.

In so-called freedom, she could now seek a Negro husband. A man who, like herself, was jobless, without education, and doomed to petition for basic human rights and needs for the next century, and God knows how many more years past that century mark of 1963.

The white South and much of the North destroyed reconstruction efforts and passed laws designed to subjugate and keep the ex-slave in a state of ignorance. He was not allowed to attend schools, churches, parks, libraries, and most certainly, not the concert halls or theatres.

Two hundred years of outlawing the use of African languages has divorced Africans from their folk stories, songs, ritual ceremonies, even the ability to pass on crafts and handiwork.

The Negro was ridiculed; he was emancipated in rags and tatters. Cartoonists lampooned his appearance; vaudeville performers blackened their faces and made mocking, comic characters of "Mandy" and "Sambo."

The mainstay of television and movies has ever been the first fight scene; the hero fights the villain for mistreating or manhandling a defenseless woman. How many times have you seen these men fighting for the honor of a Negro woman? How many guns have been fired for *her* protection? How many detectives have rescued *her* in the nick of time?

She came out of bondage with the burden of the white and the black man's child. Her former master passed laws absolving him of all moral and financial obligation to his children, and she has to feed, raise and educate them by her own effort.

And today, the slave owners' acknowledged children fight to keep their own, as well as ours, out of the school and out of the voting booth.

Writers be wary of those who tell you to leave the past alone and confine yourselves to the present moment. Our story has not been told in any moment.

Have you seen us in any portrayal of the Civil War? *Gone with the Wind* is not our story. And our history is not gone with the wind; it is still with us. . . .

Facing the world alone makes a woman strong. The emancipated Negro woman of America did the only thing she could do. She earned a pittance by washing, ironing, cooking, cleaning, and picking cotton. She helped her man, and if she often stood in the front line, it was to shield him from a mob of men organized and dedicated to bring about his total destruction.

The Negro mother has had the bitter job of teaching her children the difference between the White and Colored signs before they are old enough to attend school. She had to train her sons and daughters to say "sir" and "ma'am" to those who were their sworn enemies.

She couldn't tell her husband "a white man whistled at me, or insulted me, or touched me," not unless she wanted him to lay down his life before organized killers who strike only in anonymous numbers. Or worse, perhaps to see him helpless and ashamed before her.

Because he could offer no protection or security, the Negro woman has worked with and for her family. She built churches, schools, homes, temples and college educations out of soapsuds and muscle.

It seems a contradiction for a woman to be degraded by law, and by popular opinion which was shaped and formed by that law, and yet also take her rightful place as the most heroic figure to emerge on the American scene, with more stamina than that shown by any pioneer.

Finally, I would like to say, today we hear so much about the *new Negro*. As though we never breathed a protest until a few years ago.

But the story of the old Negro has not been told.

Denmark Vesey, Francis Watkins Harper, Monroe Trotter—if their true stories were told, there would not be so many school drop-outs.

Who wants to sit in a classroom and be taught that he is nobody?

The Negro woman will attain her rightful place in American literature when those of us who care about truth, justice and a better life tell her story, with the full knowledge and appreciation of her constant, unrelenting struggle against racism and for human rights.

Paule Marshall

As I see it, and it is a very subjective view on my part, the person we are talking about, the Negro woman, has been until recent times almost non-existent in the prose literature of the country.

This is not to say that some creature which has been passed off as the Negro woman hasn't appeared in stories and novels written by both white and Negro writers since the earliest beginnings of the country's literary history; but I contend that, by and large, the figure which emerges even upon the most cursory examination of these works, is a myth, a stereotype, a fantasy figure, which has very little to do with the Negro woman in reality.

In other words, the black woman as portrayed, has suffered the same unhappy fate as the black man. She has in a sense been strung up on two poles and left hanging. At one end of the pole, there is the "nigger wench"—sensual, primitive, pleasure seeking, immoral, the siren, the sinner. Her type was perhaps best summed up by Gertrude Stein in her description of Rose in the story "Melanctha." "Rose," Miss Stein wrote, "a real black, well-built, sullen, stupid, child-like, good-looking Negress," who had, in Miss Stein's words, "the simple, promiscuous immorality of the black people."

At the other end of the pole, we find that larger than life figure, the Negro matriarch, who dominates so much of fiction—strong, but humble, devoted, devoutly religious, patient—a paragon of patience, if you will—wise beyond all wisdom, the saint, the mammy, the great wet nurse of the society, and the country deep within the recesses of its psyche longs to return to her ample breasts.

We see her in the early novels of Thomas Nelson Page, in *Gone with the Wind*. She is Berenice out in the kitchen in *Member of the Wedding* and William Faulkner's Delsey trudging up the stairs with the hot water bag for Mrs. Compson. She has become an almost legendary figure. She endures.

Now, I am not saying that there is anything wrong in writing about sinners or saints, matriarchs or wenches, black or white. All is grist for the novelist's mill. But what is wrong, glaringly and inexcusably wrong, is that the Negro woman as a character in the fiction, has been confined largely to these two categories. Moreover, to compound the crime, she is seldom realized as a valid character in these two categories; by this I mean she is denied the complexities, the contradictions, the ambiguities that make for a truly rich and credible character in fiction. The reason for this is simple and yet complex and it has to do with the history of this country, a history grounded in slavery. The purpose . . . was to deny the

Negro woman her humanity. For if she was less than human, all sorts of crimes could be committed against her and go unpunished. She could be exploited in the fields and kitchens, her body freely used, her children taken from her, her men castrated before her eyes, and yet in the mind of white America, this abuse, this outrage, was somehow not serious.

The use of the Negro woman as an embodiment of myths and fantasies that have . . . much to do with the troubled and repressed conscience has over the years reached so far down in the national psyche that not even the best of the white writers have escaped it.

Lorraine Hansberry: On Time!

John Oliver Killens wrote the novels Youngblood *and* And Then We Heard the Thunder *and* The Great Black Russian, *a novel based on the life and times of the Afro-Russian poet Alexander Pushkin. Killens was a founding member of the* Freedomways *collective. This essay appeared in the* Freedomways *special issue "Lorraine Hansberry: Art of Thunder, Vision of Light."*

At a writers conference at Howard University sponsored by the Institute for the Arts and the Humanities in April of 1976, Sister Toni Cade Bambara said, "The responsibility of a writer representing an oppressed people is to make revolution irresistible." Several decades before, the great Paul Robeson had said, "An artist must elect to fight for freedom or for slavery. . . . I have made my choice. I had no alternative." To immodestly quote myself from a book of essays entitled *Black Man's Burden,* I wrote: "Every time I sit down to the typewriter, every line I put on paper, I'm out to change the world, to capture reality, to melt it down and forge it into something entirely different."

How does one evaluate the life of the late Lorraine Hansberry, as a Black person, as a Black woman, as a human being? How is she to be evaluated literarily, politically, historically?

Did Lorraine Hansberry take upon herself the responsibility "to make revolution irresistible"? Did she recognize the battle lines, freedom or slavery? Did she choose sides?

To me, Lorraine Hansberry was a one-woman literary warrior for change—qualitative and fundamental change. She was, moreover, a Pan-Africanist. In her plays *A Raisin in the Sun* and *Les Blancs,* she expressed, through character development and dramatic situations, a oneness with the African peoples and their struggles for liberation. This is certainly the meaning of Asagai, the young, articulate African student in *Raisin.* And it is the entire meaning of *Les Blancs,* which endorses change *and* revolution. Lest there be any misunderstanding, however, it should be emphasized that Lorraine was a consummate artist. Her writing is not agit-prop. Her characters are flesh and blood people who possess all the flaws and fears and foibles and aspirations and courage that lie restive in human beings. The situations she placed them in are believable and recognizable. She knew that the Western notion of "art for art's sake" is an unadulterated myth, and that art can be a weapon to liberate the people.

I remember Lorraine Hansberry, when she first came to New York from her native Chicago. I remember her as a brilliant young woman when she worked with Louis Burnham

From *Freedomways,* no. 4 (1979).

for Paul Robeson's newspaper, *Freedom*. We engaged in many dialogues and shared many concerns about the world, about its movement in the direction of fundamental change and how the change would affect Black people. The question that would always come up was what role should the artist play in bringing this change about? Those days were a profound learning experience for all of us *Youngbloods,* a time when I was working with Dr. Alphaeus Hunton and Mr. Robeson and Dr. W. E. B. Du Bois in an organization known as the Council on African Affairs. Our offices were in the same building the *Freedom* office was in on 125th Street in Harlem.

We had many lively discussions about the state of the world and the nation, and especially about the condition of the Afro-American people. It was a time of great excitement, when we took our convictions into the streets, a time of boycotts, of demonstrations and mass meetings at Rockland Palace and the Golden Gate Ballroom, of street meetings on the corner of 125th Street and Seventh Avenue in front of Michaux's book store which boasted of containing "A Hundred Thousand Facts About the Negro." We were part of all that along with Paul Robeson, Adam Powell, Benjamin Davis! It was a time when so many of us young warriors matriculated in the University of the Streets. Robeson was an inspiration to us all. By his example, he taught us the true meaning of manhood and womanhood and, especially, of commitment. In the arts, he was our patron saint. Who was Lorraine Hansberry?

One could safely say, in retrospect, that Lorraine Hansberry was a Pan-Africanist with a socialist perspective. Let me be even bolder. In my view, Lorraine was a Black nationalist with a socialist perspective. Her world view combined a commitment to Black liberation with an equally fierce commitment to the demise of capitalism. I think she knew that the contradiction was more apparent than real. As an artist, she saw the paradox and irony of every human being's sojourn on this earth, especially where Black Americans are concerned. The ancestors of most Americans came to these shores seeking freedom, while most of our ancestors came in chains. There is the terrible paradox, the national contradiction. I think she saw contradictions as the very spice of life, and dialectics as the method one uses to go about resolving the contradictions.

A Black nationalist with a socialist perspective? Have not all the revolutions of the 20th century been about national liberation? And haven't they all been socialist revolutions— Russia, China, Cuba, Vietnam?

Her double commitment was explicit and implicit in everything she wrote, in every lecture and every statement. As with Robeson and Malcolm, her nationalism had an internationalist context that is reflected in a statement by one of her African characters in *Les Blancs.* Tshembe tells the white man, Charlie Morris:

> I shall be honest with you, Mr. Morris. I do not "hate" all white men—but I desperately wish I did. It would make everything infinitely easier! But I am afraid that, among other things, I have *seen* the slums of Liverpool and Dublin and the caves of Naples. I have *seen* Dachau and Anne Frank's attic in Amsterdam. I have seen too many raw-knuckled Frenchmen coming out of the Metro at dawn and too many pop-eyed Italian children to believe that those who raided Africa for three centuries ever "loved" the white race either.[1]

---

1. *Les Blancs: The Collected Last Plays of Lorraine Hansberry,* Random House, pp. 102–103.

Lorraine believed that the road to socialism is through national liberation, just as the literary road to universality is through local identity. Many critics said of *Raisin* that it is "universal," that it isn't specifically about Blacks. "It is about people. It could be about anybody." But a play that could be about anybody would most probably be about nobody at all. Lorraine was very clear on this point when she said in an interview

> One of the most sound ideas in dramatic writing is that in order to create the universal, you must pay very great attention to the specific. . . . In other words, I have told people that not only is this a Negro family. . . . It is specifically South Side Chicago. . . . So I would say it is definitely a Negro play before it is anything else.[2]

One of the most important qualities of Lorraine Hansberry was that she cared. She cared about the whole damn human race. Her caring is expressed eloquently in *The Sign in Sidney Brustein's Window,* when her protagonist says:

> Is that all you can ever say? Who cares, who cares? Let the damn bomb fall, if somebody wants to drop it, 'tis the last days of Rome, so rejoice ye Romans and swill ye these last sick hours away! Well, I admit it. I *care!* I care about it all. It takes too much energy *not* to care. Yesterday I counted twenty-six grey hairs in the top of my head—all from trying *not* to care.[3]

Lorraine unquestionably identified herself with the aspirations of the people of the so-called Third World (which I prefer to call the First World, since even racist anthropologists grudgingly concede that civilization first began in Africa and Asia). She was always there with Fanon's "wretched of the earth," her anti-fascist vision of liberation embracing all of the oppressed regardless of race, color or ethnicity. Ahead of her time? I think not. As Sister Betty Shabazz once said of her husband, Malcolm, Lorraine was not ahead of her time—she as *on* time. Too many of us were lagging far behind the times.

In a historic Town Hall forum entitled "The Black Liberation Movement and the White Backlash," she called for "a basic change of society" and called upon the white liberal to "stop being a liberal and become an American radical." She also said she'd never heard of Negroes booing the name of John Brown and noted that "the vantage point of Negroes is entirely different [from the rest of the nation]."[4]

Lorraine Hansberry was an extraordinarily articulate young Black woman, committed to the struggle and very fast on the draw. Indeed, literarily and intellectually, she was one of the fastest guns in the East—and her gun was for revolution and for change. She was a humanist; she was anti-slavery (meaning she was anti-capitalist). The pity of it, and the loss to us, is that she was with us for so terribly short a period. Who knows to what heights this courageous falcon might have soared!

---

2. *To Be Young, Gifted and Black,* New American Library, p. 128.

3. *A Raisin in the Sun / The Sign in Sidney Brustein's Window,* New American Library, p. 247.

4. *To Be Young, Gifted and Black,* op cit., pp. 247–249. (Speech on *Lorraine Hansberry Speaks Out: Arts and the Black Revolution,* Caedmon Records.)

Who Will Revere the Black Woman?

Mark Twain said, in effect, that when a country enslaves a people, the first necessary job is to make the world feel that the people to be enslaved are sub-human. The next job is to make his fellow-countrymen believe that man is inferior and, then, the unkindest cut of all is to make that man believe himself inferior.

A good job has been done on the black people in this country, as far as convincing them of their inferiority is concerned. The general white community has told us in a million different ways and in no uncertain terms that "God" and "nature" made a mistake when it came to fashioning of us and ours. The whole society, having been thoroughly convinced of the stained, threatening, and evil nature of anything unfortunate enough to be, or referred to as, black, as an intended matter of courtesy refers to those of African extraction as "colored" or "Negro."

The fact that "negro" is the Spanish word for black is hardly understood, it would seem; or it would seem that the word "black" may be intimated or suggested, but never simply stated in good English.

Too many Negroes, if described or referred to as "black," take it as an affront; and I was once told by a Canadian Irishman that I'd insulted *him* by referring to *my* person as a black woman. He insisted that, in actuality, I was brown, not black; and I felt obliged to tell him he described himself as "white," and that he wasn't white either.

The fact that white people readily and proudly call themselves "white," glorify all that is white, and whitewash all that is glorified, becomes unnatural and bigoted in its intent *only* when these same whites deny persons of African heritage who are black the natural and inalienable right to readily and proudly call themselves "black," glorify all that is black, and blackwash all that is glorified.

Yet, one is forced to conclude that this is not the case at all, that an astonishing proportion of the white population finds it discomforting that blacks should dare to feel so much glory in being beautifully black. In the face of this kind of "reasoning," the only conclusion one can logically come to is that there is something wrong with this society and its leadership. "The Man's" opinion of God is sorry, to put it nicely, and his opinion of himself is simply vague and hazy. Consider:

Swearing his love and devotion to the Omnipotent One on the one hand, yet defying and cursing him with rank impudence on the other; using the crutch of his "inherently"

From *Negro Digest,* September 1966.

base and callow nature on the one hand, and claiming his godhood on the other; worshipping a Jew as the Son of God on the one hand, yet persecuting all other Jews as enemies of God on the other; historically placing this same Jew on the African continent on the one hand, and describing him as a European in physical appearance on the other; (still, one would suppose that it's tacitly understood by all that "God" couldn't be anything other than "white," no matter where He was born) advocating that the black man is made of inferior stuff on the one hand, yet defying him not to prove his superiority on the other; naming hurricanes for women on the one hand, yet H is for the heart as pure as gold on the other; giving her pet names such as "whore," "slut," "bitch," etc., on the one hand, yet put them all together and they spell mother, the *word* "that means the world to me" on the other.

No wonder the slogan "White is right," could take a whole nation by storm. One could never accuse this society of being rational.

Still, instead of this irrational society warping my delicate little psyche, it only drove me, ultimately, to the conclusion that any black human being able to survive the horrendous and evil circumstances in which one inevitably finds oneself trapped must be some kind of a giant with great and peculiar abilities, with an armor as resistant as steel yet made of purest gold.

My mother is one of the most courageous people I have ever known, with an uncanny will to survive. When she was a young woman, the white folks were much further in the lead than they are now, and their racist rules gave her every disadvantage; yet, she proved herself a queen among women *any* women, and as a result will always be one of the great legends for me.

But strange as it is, I've heard it echoed by too many black full-grown males that black womanhood is the downfall of the black man in that she (the black woman) is "evil," "hard to get along with," "domineering," "suspicious," and "narrowminded." In short, a "black, ugly, evil" you know what.

As time progresses I've learned that this description of my mothers, sisters, and partners in crime is used as the basis and excuse for the further shoving, by the black man, of his own head into the sand of oblivion. Hence, the black mother, housewife and all-around girl Thursday is called upon to suffer both physically and emotionally every humiliation a woman can suffer and still function.

Her head is more regularly beaten than any other woman's, and by her own man; she's the scape-goat for Mr. Charlie; she is forced to stark realism and chided if caught dreaming; her aspirations for her and hers are, for sanity's sake, stunted; her physical image has been criminally maligned, assaulted, and negated; she's the first to be called ugly and never yet beautiful, and as a consequence is forced to see her man (an exact copy of her, emotionally and physically), brainwashed and wallowing in self-loathing, pick for his own the physical antithesis of her (the white woman and incubator of his heretofore arch enemy, the white man). Then, to add guilt to insult and injury, she (the black woman) stands accused as the emasculator of the only thing she has ever cared for, her black man; accused by her black man. She is the scape-goat for what white America has made of the "Negro personality."

Raped and denied the right to cry out in her pain, she has been named the culprit and called "loose," "hot-blooded," "wanton," "sultry," and "amoral." She has been used as the white man's sexual outhouse, and shamefully encouraged by her own ego-less man to persist in this function. Wanting, too, to be carried away by her "Prince Charming," she must, in all honesty, admit that he has been robbed of his crown by the very assaulter and assassin who has raped her. Still, she looks upon her man as God's gift to black womanhood and is further diminished and humiliated and outraged when the feeling is not mutual.

When a white man "likes colored girls," his woman (the white woman) is the last one he wants to know about it. Yet, seemingly, when a Negro "likes white girls," his woman (the black woman) is the first he wants to know about it. White female rejects and social misfits are flagrantly flaunted in our faces as the ultimate in feminine pulchritude. Our women are encouraged by our own men to strive to look and act as much like the white female image as possible, and only those who approach that "goal" in physical appearance and social behavior are acceptable. At best, we are made to feel that we are poor imitations and excuses for white women.

Evil? Evil, you say? The black woman is hurt, confused, frustrated, angry, resentful, frightened *and* evil! Who in this hell dares suggest that she should be otherwise? These attitudes only point up her perception of the situation and her healthy rejection of same.

Maybe if our women get evil enough and angry enough, they'll be moved to some action that will bring our men to their senses. There is one unalterable fact that too many of our men cannot seem to face. And that is, we "black, evil, ugly" women are a perfect and accurate reflection of you "black, evil, ugly" men. Play hide and seek as long as you can and will, but your every rejection and abandonment of us is only a sorry testament of how thoroughly and carefully you have been blinded and brainwashed. And let it further understood that when *we* refer to *you* we mean, ultimately, *us. For you are us, and vice versa.*

We are the women who were kidnapped and brought to this continent as slaves. We are the women who were raped, are still being raped, and our bastard children snatched from our breasts and scattered to the winds to be lynched, castrated, de-egoed, robbed, burned and deceived.

We are the women whose strong and beautiful black bodies were—and are—still being used as a cheap labor force for Miss Anne's kitchen and Mr. Charlie's bed, whose rich, black and warm milk nurtured—and still nurtures—the heir to the racist and evil slavemaster.

We are the women who dwell in the hell-hole ghettos all over this land. We are the women whose bodies are sacrificed, as living cadavers, to experimental surgery in the white man's hospitals for the sake of white medicine. We are the women who are invisible on the television and movie screens, on the Broadway stage. We are the women who are lusted after, sneered at, leered at, hissed at, yelled at, grabbed at, tracked down by white degenerates in our own pitiable, poverty-stricken and prideless neighborhoods.

We are the women whose hair is compulsively fried, whose skin is bleached, whose nose is "too big," whose mouth is "too big and loud," whose behind is "too big and broad," whose feet are "too big and flat," whose face is "too black and shiny," and whose suffering and patience is too long and enduring to be believed.

Who's just too damned much for everybody.

We are the women whose bars and recreation halls are invaded by flagrantly disrespectful, bigoted, simpering, amoral, emotionally unstable, outcast, maladjusted, nymphomaniacal, condescending, white women . . . in desperate and untiring search of the "exceedingly outsized black penis, that will be attached to the animalistic, frothing-at-the-mouth-for-a-white-woman, strongbacked, sixty-minute hot black." Our men.

We are the women who, upon protesting this invasion of our privacy and sanctity and sanity, are called "jealous," and "evil," and "small-minded," and "prejudiced." We are the women whose husbands and fathers and brothers and sons have been plagiarized, imitated, denied, and robbed of the fruits of their genius, and who consequently we see emasculated, jailed, lynched, driven mad, deprived, enraged and made suicidal. We are the women who nobody, seemingly, cares about, who are made to feel inadequate, stupid and backward, and who inevitably have the most colossal inferiority complexes to be found.

And who is spreading the propaganda that "the only free people in the country are the white man and the black woman"? If this be freedom, then Heaven is hell, right is wrong, and cold is hot.

Who will revere the black woman? Who will keep our neighborhoods safe for black innocent womanhood? Black womanhood is outraged and humiliated. Black womanhood cries for dignity and restitution and salvation. Black womanhood wants and needs protection, and keeping, and holding. Who will assuage her indignation? Who will keep her precious and pure? Who will glorify and proclaim her beautiful image? To whom will *she* cry rape?

LOUISE MOORE

Black Men vs. Black Women

As a Black woman I am being forced to realize that I must kill a Black man before I die if I and my Black sisters all over the world are ever to be free. Killing never fazed me because even as a small child I knew whitey was killing us with lynchings and shootings. I knew how brutal the white man was. Naturally, it was my duty to eliminate some whites, maybe about a dozen. Sartre in his introduction to Fanon's book, *The Damned,* states our case: "First the only violence is the settler's; but soon they (the oppressed) make it their own."

Just recently I was forced to realize who my immediate oppressor really was; it was men—Black men. I can truly say I was shocked and sickened, for I have loved my Black man, my race, my people. Then I learned that this was not my personal experience. Every Black sister to whom I have confided my agony has agreed with the solution, that the answer to our problem must be revolutionary and that means armed struggle—killing the Black man who oppresses us. What gave me the real courage to write this article, was the many Black men who agreed with us Black women.

I am not a true revolutionary Black woman and neither are most of my Black sisters. We overlook too much, accept too little for what is our human right as women, wives and mothers. We make excuses for our men when they lie to us, refuse to pay the bills, abandon us and our children and give us nothing but half-ass excuses about why they can not take their place as men in this changing world. Our men mistake our kindness and love for weakness. In our search for love and affection, we have created a situation between the Black man and the Black woman that has become intolerable. No Black sister can afford to remain blind to the true character of our so-called Black men. We are the last screen between the Black man and his white oppressor. We get killed, beat up, left, insulted as if we were the oppressors. Black men we are refusing the honor. We are tired of being cheated of our womanhood by Black men, white men, white women and a whole capitalist-military system.

Black women everything depends on you. We must become familiar with guerrilla warfare as our sisters in Africa, South America and Vietnam have had to do. We must have a Mau Mau here and now. Malcolm advised us of this many times, that we must begin to clean up within our own ranks first, then in the areas where we live, and then we will branch out and take on whitey . . . cool, discreetly and without advance publication. Just as the village chiefs in Vietnam who continue to cooperate with the South Vietnamese

From *Liberator* 6.8 (August 1966).

puppets and the U.S. against their own villagers are killed by the Vietcong, we will have to dispose of negro male leaders and their puppet followers that betray us.

I want to try to explain how we Black women got into this bind. The man's society is a masculine one that builds itself around the male and *his* masculine organ. His penis is played *up* at every opportunity. We see it in the skyscrapers of the cities, the military missiles, the church steeples. He even has one God, one sex, in fact a whole holy trinity of one sex. Poor Mary was given the business. Here's a woman who has a child and can't explain how she got it. She took a screwing from the "get-go."

This society is anti-woman. That's why it has been so hard to see who the real oppressors were because women are oppressed at all levels. In the twenties white women marched for equality like ignorant negroes march for equality today. Equality means to be like the oppressor. How are negroes going to get *white* and how did those white women expect to get a penis? That's what equality with men really means—to be like them. I would like to be just a woman. I don't want to be equal to men.

In the homes in which I have worked (over 300), I have found very little happiness. The white women can't seem to get the necessary loving from their husbands and this makes them bitter and hard. I remember one white woman saying, she had often been whored but never loved. To replace their lack of sex satisfaction, they take to tennis, golfing, drinking and milltowns or a so-called lover. Many times this is a very poor investment because *he* like most men is anti-woman and on the make. On top of all this "Cracker Johnson" insists on taking the young men to fight his wars. If 30,000 men are killed, wouldn't you figure that 30,000 women are doomed to sleep alone. American women are known to be the "Great Pretenders" and they live the great "Romantic Illusion."

In Russia, China, Africa, the Socialist and under-developed countries, women still do hard manual labor. Have you ever noticed their faces . . . the sadness that is there? Even in Socialist countries women are still slaves and oppressed. We must alert our sisters to their oppressors whether they be in socialist capitalist or have-not countries.

I do domestic work along with 7 million women here in the United States and no one gives a damn about our conditions in which we must work . . . not any of those big mouth simple-ass preachers, or organizations for we are not supposed to be heard. Most of our big negroes today hide the fact that their mothers or grandmothers worked in somebody's kitchen. How often we women have taken food from Miss Ann to feed our families. Many of us will not work in a household that isn't generously supplied in groceries and the like because we couldn't make *it* without taking. We have a tacit understanding with Miss Ann, for she knows she owes our ancestors plenty.

Early this spring Miss Connie Carr put on a big act, saying that William Booth of the Human Rights Commission was interested in domestic workers. It was all a bunch of lies. Everyone lies to women and the poor because we let them get away with it. A woman must work in a laundry, be a presser, hospital or restaurant worker, day worker or sleep-in on those damn jobs, should unite into a strong body for our own protection against our oppressors. In every city we got work to do. As women we are going to improve this world and put women and all she stands for, love and life, in their (our) rightful place.

New Fashions for Afro-American Women

The social, art, fashion and political orientation of a country is indicative of the people of the country. From an artistic and fashion point of view one could justifiably say that Africans are a spiritual free flowing people. As Afro-Americans, we too, have an inherited sense of fashion. After all, it was the Black nanny that dressed *miss ann,* told her how to use her cosmetics, where to and not to put those delicate dabs of perfume.

The nouveau patterned fabric worned today by so-called women of high fashion, is a copy of the very early Nubian fabric worned by our African sisters centuries ago. However, Lord and Taylor's would have you believe that they are the innovators of this design.

The other day, I wondered into a fashionable 57th Street store, one of the fashions on display, was a large Buba sleeve dress, the sleeve of course was a direct copy of the Bubas worned by the Yoruba women of Nigeria.

Recently I was married in the Yoruba Temple on 116th Street, New York City. The wedding was one of the most colorful occasions I have ever seen. The bold printed fabric of the men and women, the African wraps and Bubas, the galies, the colorful agbodas worned by the men and the beautifully dressed children is something only a people of spiritual and soulful orientation could enhance.

As Afro-Americans we have had painful experiences in racist america, which we have assimilated into our lives along with our already inherited sense of *rhythm* from Africa. Indeed, our fashions should compliment our cultural consciousness and political awareness.

The most popular fashion today, *uptown,* is natural hair, African wraps and Bubas, with the head attire. Some of the sisters have mixed the two cultures, they wear the Buba sleeve in a sort of shift like dress with the head attire. Most of the dresses are loose fitting made in bold colorful print, the length of the dresses vary (but *never* two inches above the knee). Pants are very seldom seen on the sisters.

Never in a million years could the clientele of Lord and Taylor, Saks Fifth Avenue, and the other "high fashion" and high priced stores matched the beauty of the sisters on 125th Street; *uptown!*

From *Liberator* 6.8 (August 1966).

Her body is like new brown bread
Under the Woolworth mignonette.
Her body is a honey bowl
Whose waiting honey is deep and hot,
Her body is like summer earth,
Receptive, soft, and absolute . . .

Gwendolyn Brooks, "The Sundays of Satin-Legs Smith"

SONIA SANCHEZ

Introduction (Queens of the Universe)

We Black/woooomen have been called many
things: foxes, matriarchs, whores,
bougies, sweet mommas, gals,
sapphires, sisters and recently Queens.
i would say that Black/woooomen have been
a combination of all these words because
if we examine our past/history, at
one time or another we've had to be like
those words be saying.
                    but today, in spite
of much vulgarity splattering us, there are
many roles we can discard.
                   there are many we
must discard for our own survival for our
own sanity for the contributions we must
make to our emerging Black nation.
                  and what/how
we must mooooOOOVE to as the only QUEENS
OF THE UNIVERSE to sustain/keep our sanity
in this insane messed up/diet/conscious/
pill taking/faggotty/masochistic/miss anne/
orientated/society has got to be dealt with
because that's us. You hear me? US.
                 Black/woooomen.
the only QUEENS OF THE UNIVERSE, even though
we be stepping unqueenly sometimes. like it ain't
easy being a queen in this unrighteous world
full of miss annes and mr. annes.
but we steady trying.
             for the thing that

From *A Blues Book for Blue Black Magical Women* (Detroit: Broadside Press, 1974).

Black/woooomen of today must understand
is that loooove/
                    peace/
                              contentment will never
be ours for this crackerized country has dealt
on us and colonized us body and soul and
the job of Black/woooomen is to deal with this
under the direction of Black men. We mussssST
absorb/mooovVVE on pass the waylaying whiteness
of our minds while never letting it keep us
from our men, children, naturrrals, long dresses,
morals and our humanity.
                              for Black/woooomen
are the key. and our reward will be
seeing our warrior sons and beautiful young
sisters moving in human/nationalistic/
revolutionary/ways toward each other. &
the enemy.
              Black/woooomen must embrace
Blackness as a religion/husband. Blackness
mussssST sustain us through all these coming
hard years for sisters they are coming. & we
have to be strooong, strooonNGER
                                        than our
yesteryears. our
                    tomorrows. we must be prepared for all:
gaming, rhetoric. poverty. empty beds.
death. sisters calling in the nite screeeeamen
        an arethasong.
                          save me. somebody saaaAVVE
me. yeh. we be crying together from coast to
coast saying
              somebody savvvvVVVE me.
yeh, save us.
              savvvVVVE us all.
                                  did you hear us?
yeh. us. sisters.
              your sisters. we be steady
calling each other and Black/woooomen
must organize/reorganize their groups to meet
answer these needs/screeeeeams of living.
i mean. sisters must be prepared to go out
to sisters homes to keep them out of bars,
off of quick relationships that will
eventually destroy them and their families.

& our nation.

we must preserve. prolong our
lives. we have to stop eating unhealthy foods/
smoking/drinking/leaning over bars elbowing
away our lives because we blue over some maaaAANN.
sisters. we beautifully Black. not blue.
ain't no time for tears shed for one/single
maaaAAN.

yeh. life's somethingelse. but our
children's lives can't

won't/mussSN'T be like
ours. & their lives will be like ours if we don't
mooooVVVE awaaaAAY from slave actions.
slave mentalities. the only tears to be shed
must be for our nation as we fight a
lonnng fight for freedom. sisters. some
of us Black woooomen who have to move in
the nation without men can have looooOOVE.
it can be the love of/for freedom. we can get
high off the knowledge that one day our
children will moooVVE like free menNNN/woooomen.
can't you see them, sisters? there they be.
walking. moving in freedom. strutting a
high/walk of freedom. runnnnNNING in their
Black air. holding their free/land/nation
up with their laughter. listen to em.
watch em. yeh. do it young brothers.
sisters. dooooooo it.
we Black/wooomen

are the first teachers.
nurses, givers of life. teachers of all
human things.

we must be about building
a strong nation since we are a nation.
loooven. teaching our children. looooven.
teaching our brothers. sisters. loooven.
teaching them so they will be able to
looovve/livvvVVE when their time comes
generations removed from whiteness. we
have to be the guerilla/

fighters for our
children's minds. we musssSSST begin
basement schools in our homes or support
existing Black schools.

white schools teach

Black children to hate themselves, each other
and their parents.
                              white schools teach our
children tomish ways.
                                   white schools bring
our children in contact with unholy people
who contaminate not only their minds but
their bodies as well.
                                   & if we are committed &
not jiving then our children's minds must be
upmost in OUR minds. are we brothers. sisters
gonna change the world then later on find
out because we didn't educate our children
in our ideology that we have children who are
only part/time/Black children. or would
be hippies? we need young Black minds.
and public schools/catholic schools do
not turn out what we need. & those of us
moving in a warrior's
                              strength must support.
loooVVVE our warrior/Kings/Gods.
mussSST bear children.
                                   musssSST teach them
their fathers are warriors
                              among white
faggotry. that we are his core his base
for him to move out against the white men
who plot & connive our destruction each &
every day.
                    for we must return to Black men
his children full of our women/love/tenderness/
sweet/Blackness full of pride/so they can
shape the male children into young warriors
who will stand alongside them.
                                   so that young
sisters will know the strength. majesty of
Black fathers and smile.
                                   feel warmed by this
strength and mooooVVE
                                   on to their husbands
with these feelings. It has be done.
sisters. because Black men and Black
wooomen have a history of alienation in
this country. the devil has superimposed
on our minds myths about ourselves.

we are busy calling each other matriarchs
or no good bums
                           because the devil has
identified us as such. listen, sisters. i'm not
saying that some of that might not be. we know
it exists. & requires work. new ideas. new thoughts
but it's an easy way out too.
                           i mean there are
reasons for brothers not able to support their
families. like no gigs. There are reasons for
ago brothers living their lives in bars.
or riding majestic/white
                           horses in a machine
age. they couldn't see a win nohow.
                           or there are reasons
for wooomen being the head of families.
like brothers cutting out because this
was the coooooollLLL thing to do or because
the sisters made more money than the
brothers and put them out.
                           we must looook
at our past. not be angered at it. nor upset.
nor reinstigating a hate/name/calling/contest.
we must loooOK.
                    learnNNN.
                           moove on passSST. because
waiting for us all if we begin to deal
honestly with each other.
                           in love ways. in trust.
there's waiting for us.
                           a Nation. a place for our
BLACKNESS.
                    if we are about freedom then we must
start talking. moving. towards
                           an organization
that will sustain us & mooooooVVE us
awaaay from white values & a hollywood/
directed/revolutionary change.
                           if we are about
just rapping/jiving/gaming
                           then our life
styles will continue as they are now.
& that means our destruction.
                           a continuation

of our slave/culture.
                        sisters.
                                like that song
be saying. it ain't easy.
              it won't be easy a-tall.
because since we are the moral keepers/
teachers/nurses/civilizers/
we must move always in loving ways
toward each other & our brothers.
                            there must be no
competition between us. no hatred.
                                    & that will
be hard because some sisters are still
moving in negative.
                        peculiar ways toward
themselves and others. they still believe
what the devil has told them about
themselves.
                so we must, those who are wise
enough to belong to an organization
                                MOOOVVE toward
these sisters and run down their white ways
that define them, make them move as
whores and not as QUEENS.
that's what they are if they could only see
their beauty.
                & know that Black/mennNNN
must be left alone to TCB for the nation
for our children for our people.
                                but after
many talks if they don't listen
                            then they must be expelled
from the nation/builders
                        & turned loose
to runNNNN with all the other white/cavish
whores running/polluting the land.
                        because we are about
              keeping to our morals
about building an everlasting nation.
              we are about education our children.
moving in non/competitive/ways.
                                loving each
other.
      we are about WORK. CONSTANT. TCBING

the kind of movement that is in
the NATION OF ISLAM.
                             i have seen
Warrior/Gods. moving. TCBing.
i have seen sister Queens moving in
sun wrapped beauty
and for those of us who do not move in an
organization yet. know that you will.
if you are serious about building a nation.
you'll move to ELIJAH MUHAMMAD.
where Black/MennNNN are steady moving.
where Black/Woooomen are loooVVVING/
teaching Blackness. wherever the desire for
freedom is.
               until you reclaim your own,
perhaps this oath/poem to be said everyday
will help you sisters:
                      i am a Black/woooOOOOMAN
                  my face.
                  my brown
              bamboo/colored
black/berry/face
will spread itself over
this western hemisphere and
be remembered.
                      be sunnnNNGG.
for I will be called
                   QUEEN. &
 walk/move in
              black/queenly/ways
and the world
                 shaken by
my Blackness
                 will channnNNGGEE
colors. & be
            reborn.
                  BLACK. Again.

3

Aesthetics / Poetics

The Changing Same (R&B and New Black Music)

The blues impulse transferred . . . containing a race, and its expression. *Primal* (mixtures . . . transfers and imitations). Through its many changes, it remained the exact replication of The Black Man In The West.

An expression of the culture at its most un-self- (therefore showing the larger consciousness of a *one self,* immune to bullshit) conscious. The direct expression of a place . . . jazz seeks another place as it weakens, a middle-class place. Except the consciously separate from those aspirations. Hence the so-called avant-garde or new music, the new Black Music, is separate because it seeks to be equally separate, equally unself-conscious . . . meaning more conscious of the real weights of existence as the straightest R&B. There are simply more temptations for the middle-class Negro because he can make believe in American more, cop out easier, become whiter and slighter with less trouble, than most R&B people. Simply because he is closer to begin with.

Jazz, too often, becomes a music of special, not necessarily emotional, occasion. But R&B now, with the same help from white America in its exploitation of energy for profit, the same as if it was a gold mine, strings that music out along a similar weakening line. Beginning with their own vacuous "understanding" of what Black music is, or how it acts upon you, they believe, from the Beatles on down, that it is about white life.

The Blues, its "kinds" and diversity, its identifying parent styles. The phenomenon of jazz is another way of specifying cultural influences. The jazz that is most European, popular or avant, or the jazz that is Blackest, still makes reference to a central body of cultural experience. The impulse, the force that pushes you to sing . . . all up in there . . . is one thing . . . what it produces is another. It can be expressive of the entire force, or make it the occasion of some special pleading. Or it is all equal . . . we simply identify the part of the world in which we are most responsive. It is all there. We are exact (even in our lies). The elements that turn our singing into direction reflections of our selves are heavy and palpable as weather.

We are moved and directed by our total response to the possibility of all effects.

We are bodies responding differently, a (total) force, like against you. You react to push it, re-create it, resist it. It is the opposite pressure producing (in this case) the sound, the music.

From *The Black Aesthetic,* ed. Addison Gayle Jr. (Garden City, N.Y.: Doubleday, 1971).

The City Blues tradition is called that by me only to recognize different elements active in its creation. The slick city people we become after the exodus, the unleashing of an energy into the Northern urban situation. Wholesale.

The line we could trace, as musical "tradition," is what we as a people dig and pass on, as best we can. The call and response form of Africa (lead and chorus) has never left us, as a mode of (musical) expression. It has come down both as vocal and instrumental form.

The rhythm quartet of the last thirty years is a very obvious continuation of Black vocal tradition, and a condensation in the form from the larger tribal singing units . . . through the form of the large religious choirs (chorus) which were initially *dancers and singers,* of religious and/or ritual purpose.

Indeed, to go back in any historical (or emotional) line of ascent in Black music leads us inevitably to religion, i.e., spirit worship. This phenomenon is always at the root in Black art, the worship of spirit—or at least the summoning of or by such force. As even the music itself was that, a reflection of, or the no thing itself.

The slave ship destroyed a great many formal art traditions of the Black man. The white man enforced such cultural rape. A "cultureless" people is a people without a memory. No history. This is the best state for slaves; to be objects, just like the rest of massa's possessions.

The breakdown of Black cultural tradition meant finally the destruction of most formal art and social tradition. Including the breakdown of the Black pre-American religious forms. Forcibly so. Christianity replaced African religions as the outlet for spirit worship. And Christian forms were traded, consciously and unconsciously, for their own. Christian forms were emphasized under threat of death. What resulted were Afro-Christian forms. These are forms which persist today.

The stripping away, gradual erosion, of the pure African form as means of expression by Black people, and the gradual embracing of mixed Afro-Christian, Afro-American forms is an initial reference to the cultural philosophy of Black People, Black Art.

Another such reference, or such stripping, is an American phenomenon, i.e., it is something that affected all of America, in fact the entire West. This, of course, is the loss of religiosity in the West, in general.

Black Music is African in origin, African-American in its totality, and its various forms (especially the vocal) show just how the African impulses were redistributed in its expression, and the expression itself became Christianized and post-Christianized.

Even today a great many of the best known R&B groups, quartets, etc., have church backgrounds, and the music itself is as churchified as it has ever been . . . in varying degrees of its complete emotional identification with the Black African-American culture (Sam and Dave, etc. at one end . . . Dionne Warwick in the middle . . . Leslie Uggams, the other end . . . and fading).

The church continues, but not the devotion (at no level of its existence is it as large, though in the poorest, most abstractly altruistic levels of churchgoing, the emotion is the devotion, and the God, the God of that feeling and movement, remains as powerful though "redistributed" somewhat).

But the kind of church Black people belonged to usually connected them with the society as a whole . . . identified them, their aspirations, their culture: because the church was one of the few places complete fullness of expression by the Black was not constantly censored by the white man. Even the asking of freedom, though in terms veiled with the biblical references of "The Jews," went down in church.

It was only those arts and cultural practices that were less obviously capable of "alien" social statement that could survive during slavery. (And even today in contemporary America, it is much the same . . . though instead of out and out murder there are hardly more merciful ways of limiting Black protest or simple statement . . . in the arts just as in any other aspect of American life.)

Blues (Lyric) its song quality is, it seems, the deepest expression of memory. Experience re/feeling. It is the racial memory. It is the "abstract" design of racial character that is evident, would be evident, in creation carrying the force of that racial memory.

Just as the God spoken about in the Black songs is not the same one in the white songs. Though the words might look the same. (They are not even pronounced alike.) But it is a different quality of energy they summon. It is the simple tone of varying evolution by which we distinguish the races. The peoples. The body is directly figured in it. "The life of the organs."

But evolution is not merely physical: yet if you can understand what the physical alludes to, is reflect of, then it will be understood that each process in "life" is duplicated at all levels.

The Blues (impulse) lyric (song) is even descriptive of a plane of evolution, a direction . . . coming and going . . . through whatever worlds. Environment, as the social workers say . . . but Total Environment (including at all levels, the spiritual).

Identification is Sound Identification is Sight Identification is Touch, Feeling, Smell, Movement. (For instance, I can tell, even in the shadows, halfway across the field, whether it is a white man or Black man running. Though Whitney Young would like to see us all run the same.)

For instance, a white man could box like Muhammad Ali, only *after* seeing Muhammad Ali box. He could not initiate that style. It is no description, it *is* the culture. (AD 1966)

The Spirituals . . . The Camp Meeting Songs at backwoods churches . . . or Slave Songs talking about deliverance.

The God the slaves worshipped (for the most part, except maybe the "pure white" God of the toms) had to be willing to free them, somehow, someway . . . one sweet day.

The God, the perfection of what the spiritual delivery and world are said to be, is what the worshippers sang. That perfect Black land. The land changed with the God in charge. The churches the slaves and freedmen went to identified these Gods, and their will in heaven, as well as earth.

The closer the church was to Africa, the Blacker the God. (The Blacker the spirit.) The closer to the will (and meaning) of the West, the whiter the God, the whiter the spirit worshipped. The whiter the worshippers. This is still so. And the hard Black core of America is African.

From the different churches, the different Gods, the different versions of Earth. The different weights and "classic" versions of reality. And the different singing. Different expressions (of a whole). A whole people . . . a nation, in captivity.

Rhythm and Blues is part of "the national genius," of the Black man, of the Black nation. It is the direct, no monkey business expression of urban and rural (in its various stylistic variations) Black America.

The hard, driving shouting of James Brown identifies a place and image in America. A people and an energy, harnessed and not harnessed by America. JB is straight out, open, and speaking from the most deeply religious people on this continent.

The energy is harnessed because what JB does has to go down in a system governed by "aliens," and he will probably never become, say, as wealthy, etc., that is he will never reap the *material* benefits that several bunches of white folks will, from his own efforts. But the will of the expression transcends the physical-mental "material," finally alien system-world it has to go through to allow any "benefits" in it. Because the will of the expression is spiritual, and as such it must transcend its mineral, vegetable, animal, environment.

Form and content are both mutually expressive of the whole. And they are both equally expressive . . . each have an identifying motif and function. In Black music, both identify place and direction. We want different contents and different forms because we have different feelings. We are different peoples.

James Brown's form and content identify an entire group of people in America. However these may be transmuted and reused, reappear in other areas, in other musics for different purposes in the society, the initial energy and image are about a specific grouping of people, Black People.

Music makes an image. What image? What environment (in that word's most extended meaning, i.e., total, external and internal, environment)? I mean there is a world powered by that image. The world James Brown's images power is the lowest placement (the most alien) in the white American social order. Therefore, it is the Blackest and potentially the strongest.

It is not simply "the strongest" because of the transmutation and harnessing I spoke of earlier. This is social, but it is total. The world is a total. (And in this sense, the total function of "free music" can be understood. See, especially, H. Dumas' story in *Negro Digest* "Will the Circle Be Unbroken?" and understand the implications of music as an autonomous *judge* of civilizations, etc. Wow!)

By image, I mean that music (art for that matter . . . or any thing else if analyzed) summons and describes where its energies were gotten. The blinking lights and shiny heads, or the gray concrete and endless dreams. But the description is of a total environment. The content speaks of this environment, as does the form.

The "whitened" Negro and white man want a different content from the people James Brown "describes." They are different peoples. The softness and so-called "well being" of the white man's environment is described in his music (art) . . . in all expressions of his self. All people's are.

If you play James Brown (say, "Money Won't Change You . . . but time will take you out") in a bank, the total environment is changed. Not only the sardonic comment of the lyrics, but the total emotional placement of the rhythm, instrumentation and sound. An energy is released in the bank, a summoning of images that take the bank, and everybody in it, on a trip. That is, they visit another place. A place where Black People live.

But dig, not only is it a place where Black People live, it is a place, in the spiritual precincts of its emotional telling, where Black People move in almost absolute openness and strength. (For instance, what is a white person who walks into a James Brown or Sam and

Dave song? How would he function? What would be the social metaphor for his existence in that world? What would he be doing?)

This is as true, finally, with the John Coltrane world or the Sun-Ra world. In the Albert Ayler world, or Ornette Coleman world, you would say, "well, they might just be playing away furiously at some stringed instrument." You understand?

In the Leslie Uggams world? They would be marrying a half-white singer and directing the show . . . maybe even whispering lyrics and stuff from the wings. You understand? *The song and the people is the same.*

The reaction to any expression moves the deepest part of the psyche and makes its identifications throughout. The middle-class Negro wants a different content (image) from James Brown, because he has come from a different place, and wants a different thing (he thinks). The something you want to hear is the thing you already are or move toward.

We feel, Where is the expression going? What will it lead to? What does it characterize? What does it make us feel like? What is its image? Jazz content, of course, is as pregnant.

The implications of content.

The form content of much of what is called New Thing or Avant-Garde or New Music differs (or seems to differ) from Rhythm and Blues, R&B oriented jazz, or what the cat on the block digs. (And here I'm talking about what is essentially *Black Music.* Although, to be sure, too often the "unswingingness" of much of the "new" is because of its association, derivation and even straight-out imitation of certain aspects of contemporary European and white Euro-American music . . . whether they are making believe they are Bach or Webern.) Avant-garde, finally, is a bad term because it also means a lot of quacks and quackers, too.

But the significant difference is, again, direction, intent, sense of identification . . . "kind" of consciousness. And that's what it's about; consciousness. What are you *with* (the word Con-With/Scio-Know). The "new" musicians are self-conscious. Just as the boppers were. Extremely conscious of self. They are more conscious of a total self (or *want* to be) than the R&B people who, for the most part, are all-expression. Emotional expression. Many times self-consciousness turns out to be just what it is as a common figure of speech. It produces world-weariness, cynicism, corniness. Even in the name of Art. Or what have you . . . social uplift, "Now we can play good as white folks," or "I went to Juilliard, and this piece exhibits a Bach-like contrapuntal line," and so forth right on out to lunch.

But at its best and most expressive, the New Black Music is expression, and expression of reflection as well. What is presented is a consciously proposed learning experience. (See "The New Wave.") It is no wonder that many of the new Black musicians are or say they want to be "Spiritual Men" (Some of the boppers embraced Islam), or else they are interested in the Wisdom Religion itself, i.e., the rise to spirit. It is expanding the consciousness of the given that they are interested in, not merely expressing what is already there, or alluded to. They are interested in the *unknown.* The mystical.

But it is interpretation. The Miracles are spiritual. They sing (and sing about) feeling. Their content is about feeling . . . the form is to make feeling, etc. The self-conscious (reflective, long-form, New Thing, bop, etc.) Art Musicians cultivate consciousness that wants more feeling, to rise . . . up a scale one measures with one's life. It is about thought, but thought can kill it. Life is complex in the same simplicity.

R&B is about emotion, issues purely out of emotion. New Black Music is also about emotion, but from a different place, and, finally, towards a different end. What these musicians feel is a more complete existence. That is, the digging of everything. What the wisdom religion preaches.

(But the actual New Black Music will be a larger expression. It will include the pretension of The New Music, as actuality, as summoner of Black Spirit, the evolved music of the then evolved people.)

The differences between rhythm and blues and the so-called new music or art jazz, the different places, are artificial, or they are merely indicative of the different placements of spirit. (Even "purely" social, like what the musicians want, etc.)

For instance, use of Indian music, old spirituals, even heavily rhythmic blues licks (and soon electronic devices) by new music musicians point toward the final close in the spectrum of the sound that will come. A really new, really all inclusive music. The whole people.

Any analysis of the content of R&B, the lyrics, or the total musical will and direction, will give a placement in contrast to analysis of new jazz content. (Even to the analysis of the implied vocalism of the new music: what are its intent and direction, what place it makes, etc., are concerned.) Again even the purely social, as analyzing reference, will give the sense of difference, what directions, what needs are present in the performers, and then, why the music naturally flows out of this.

The songs of R&B, for instance, what are they about? What are the people, for the most part, singing about? Their lives. That's what the New Musicians are playing about, and the projection of forms for those lives. (And I think any analysis will immediately show, as I pointed out in *Blues People,* that the songs, the music, changed, as the people did.) Mainly, I think the songs are about what is known as "love," requited and un. But the most popular songs are always a little sad, in tune with the temper of the people's lives. The extremes. Wild Joy—Deep Hurt.

The songs about unrequited, incompleted, obstructed, etc., love probably outnumber the others very easily. Thinking very quickly of just the songs that come readily to my mind, generally current, and favorites of mine (and on that other *top ten,* which is, you bet, the indication of where the minds, the people, are). "Walk On By" "Where Did Our Love Go?" "What Becomes of the Broken Hearted?" "The Tracks of My Tears," high poetry in the final character of their delivery . . . but to a very large extent, the songs are about love affairs which do not, did not, come off. For God knows how many reasons. Infidelity, not enough dough, incredibly "secret" reasons where the loved and the lover or the lovers are already separated and longing one for the other, according to who's singing, male or female. And all more precise and specific than the Moynihan Report, e.g., listen to Jr. Walker's "Road Runner." And this missed love that runs through these songs is exactly reflect of what is the term of love and loving in the Black world of America Twentieth Century.

The miss-understanding, nay, gap . . . abyss, that separates Black man and Black woman is always, over and over, again and again, told about and cried about. And it's old, in this country, to us. "Come back baby, Baby, please don't go . . . Cause the way I love you, Baby, you will never know . . . So come back, Baby, let's talk it over . . . one more time." A blues which bees older than Ray Charles or Lightnin' Hopkins, for that matter. "I got to laugh to keep from cryin'," which The Miracles make, "I got to dance to keep from cryin'," is not only a song but the culture itself. It is finally the same cry, the same people. You really got a hold on me. As old as our breath here.

But there are many songs about love triumphant. "I feel good . . . I got you . . . Hey!" the score, the together self, at one and in love and swinging, flying God-like. But a differently realized life-triumph than in the older more formally religious songs. The Jordans, the Promised Lands, now be cars and women-flesh, and especially dough. (Like, *power*.) There are many many songs about Money, e.g., Barrett Deems "Money," J.B.'s "I Got Money . . . now all I need is love," among so many others. But the songs are dealing with the everyday, and how to get through it and to the other side (or maybe not) which for the most part still bees that world, but on top of it, power full, and beauty full.

The older religiosity falls away from the music, but the deepest feel of spirit worship always remains, as the music's emotional patterns continue to make reference to. The new jazz people are usually much more self-consciously concerned about "God" than the R&B folks. But most of the R&B people were *really* in the church at one time, and sang there first, only to drift or rush away later.

Even the poorest, Blackest, Black people drifted away from the church. Away from a church, usually corrupted, Europeanized, or both, that could no longer provide for their complete vision of what this world ought to be, or the next. The refuge the church had provided during the early days of the Black man's captivity in America, when it was really the one place he could completely unleash his emotions and hear words of encouragement for his life here on earth. Now the world had opened up, and the church had not. But the emotionalism the church contained, and the spirit it signified, would always demand the animating life of the Black man, and as Frazier says, "The masses of Negroes may increasingly criticize their church and their ministers, but they cannot escape from their heritage. They may develop a more secular outlook on life and complain that the church and the ministers are not sufficiently concerned with the problems of the Negro race, yet they find in their religious heritage an opportunity to satisfy their deepest emotional yearnings." (*The Negro Church in America,* E. Franklin Frazier, Shocken, 1963, p. 73.)

It was the more emotional Blacker churches that the blues people were members of, rather than the usually whiter, more middle-class churches the jazz people went to. The church, as I said, carries directly over into the secular music, which is really not secular at all. It's an old cliché that if you just change the lyrics of the spirituals they are R&B songs. That's true by and large, though there are more brazen, even whiter, strings and echo effects the blues people use that most of the spiritual and gospel people don't use. But that's changed and changing, too, and in the straight city jamup gospel, echo chambers, strings, electric guitars, all are in evidence, and Jesus is jamup contemporary, with a process and silk suit too, my man.

But the gospel singers have always had a more direct connection with the blues than the other religious singers. In fact, gospel singing is a city blues phenomenon, and Professor Thomas Dorsey, who is generally credited with popularizing the gospel form back in Chicago in the late twenties and thirties was once a blues singer-piano player named Georgia

Tom, and even worked with Ma Rainey. (He was last known to be arranging for Mahalia Jackson, who with Ray Charles at another much more legitimate and powerful level, were the popularizers of Black church sound in "popular" music during the 50's.) But then so many of them, from G.T., and even before that to J.B., have all come that way.

The meeting of the practical God (i.e., of the existent American idiom) and the mystical (abstract) God is also the meeting of the tones, of the moods, of the knowledge, the different musics and the emergence of the new music, the really new music, the all-inclusive whole. The emergence also of the new people, the Black people conscious of all their strength, in a unified portrait of strength, beauty and contemplation.

The new music began by calling itself "free," and this is social and is in direct commentary on the scene it appears in. Once free, it is spiritual. But it is soulful before, after, any time, anyway. And the spiritual and free and soulful must mingle with the practical, as practical, as existent, anywhere.

The R&B people left the practical God behind to slide into the slicker scene, where the dough was, and the swift folks congregated. The new jazz people never had that practical God, as practical, and seek the mystical God both emotionally and intellectually.

John Coltrane, Albert Ayler, Sun Ra, Pharaoh Sanders, come to mind immediately as God-seekers. In the name of energy sometimes, as with Ayler and drummer Sunny Murray. Since God is, indeed, energy. To play strong forever would be the cry and the worshipful purpose of life.

The titles of Trane's tunes, "A Love Supreme," "Mediations," "Ascension," imply a strong religious will, conscious of the religious evolution the pure mind seeks. The music is a way into God. The absolute open expression of everything.

Albert Ayler uses the older practical religion as key and description of his own quest. *Spirits. Ghosts. Spiritual Unity, Angels,* etc. And his music shows a graphic connection with an older sense of the self. The music sounds like old timey religious tunes and some kind of spiritual march music, or probably the combination as a religious marching song if you can get to that. (New crusades, so to speak. A recent interview article, with Albert Ayler and his brother, trumpet player Donald Ayler, was titled "The Truth Is Marching In," and this is an excellent metaphor of where Albert and his brother Donald want to move.)

Albert's music, which he characterizes as "spiritual," has much in common with older Black-American religious forms. An openness that characterizes the "shouts" and "hollers." But having the instruments shout and holler, say a saxophone, which was made by a German, and played, as white folks call it, "legitimately" sounds like dead Lily Pons at a funeral, is changed by Ayler, or by members of any Sanctified or Holy Roller church (the blacker churches) into howling spirit summoner tied around the "mad" Black man's neck. The Daddy Grace band on 125th Street and 8th Avenue in Harlem, in the Grace Temple, is a brass band, with somewhat the same instrumentation as a European brass choir, but at the lips of Daddy's summoners, the band is "free" and makes sounds to tear down the walls of anywhere. The instruments shout and holler just like the folks. It is their lives being projected then, and they are different from the lives Telemann, or Vivaldi sought to reanimate with their music.

But James Brown still shouts, and he is as secular as the old shouters, and the new ones. With the instruments, however, many people would like them to be more securely European oriented, playing notes of the European tempered scale. While the Eastern Colored peoples' music demands, at least, that many many half, quarter, etc. tones be sounded, implied, hummed, slurred, that the whole sound of a life get in . . . no matter the "precision" the Europeans claim with their "reasonable" scale which will get only the sounds of an order and reason that patently deny most colored peoples the right to exist. To play their music is to be them and to act out their lives, as if you were them. There is then, a whole world of most intimacy and most expression, which is yours, colored man, but which you will lose playing melancholy baby in B-flat, or the *Emperor Concerto,* for that matter. Music lessons of a dying people.

If Black English Isn't a Language, Then Tell Me, What Is?

ST. PAUL DE VENCE, France—The argument concerning the use, or the status, or the reality, of black English is rooted in American history and has absolutely nothing to do with the question the argument supposes itself to be posing. The argument has nothing to do with language itself but with the role of language. Language, incontestably, reveals the speaker. Language, also, far more dubiously, is meant to define the other—and, is this case, the other is refusing to be defined by a language that has never been able to recognize him.

People evolve a language in order to describe and thus control their circumstances, or in order not to be submerged by a reality that they cannot articulate. (And, if they cannot articulate it, they are submerged.) A Frenchman living in Paris speaks a subtly and crucially different language from that of the man living in Marseilles; neither sounds very much like a man living in Quebec; and they would all have great difficulty in apprehending what the man from Guadeloupe, or Martinique, is saying, to say nothing of the man from Senegal—although the "common" language of all these areas is French. But each has paid, and is paying, a different price for this "common" language, in which, as it turns out, they are not saying, and cannot be saying, the same things: They each have very different realities to articulate, or control.

What joins all languages, and all men, is the necessity to confront life, in order, not inconceivably, to outwit death: The price for this is the acceptance, and achievement, of one's temporal identity. So that, for example, though it is not taught in the schools (and this has the potential of becoming a political issue) the south of France still clings to its ancient and musical Provençal, which resists being described as a "dialect." And much of the tension in the Basque countries, and in Wales, is due to the Basque and Welsh determination not to allow their languages to be destroyed. This determination also feeds the flames in Ireland for among the many indignities the Irish have been forced to undergo at English hands is the English contempt for their language.

It goes without saying, then, that language is also a political instrument, means, and proof of power. It is the most vivid and crucial key to identity: It reveals the private identity, and connects one with, or divorces one from, the larger, public, or communal identity. There have been, and are, times, and places, when to speak a certain language could be dangerous, even fatal. Or, one may speak the same language, but in such a way that one's

From *New York Times,* July 29, 1979.

antecedents are revealed, or (one hopes) hidden. This is true in France, and is absolutely true in England: The range (and reign) of accents on that damp little island make England coherent for the English and totally incomprehensible for everyone else. To open your mouth in England is (if I may use black English) to "put your business in the street": You have confessed your parents, your youth, your school, your salary, your self-esteem, and alas, your future.

Now, I do not know what white Americans would sound like if there had never been any black people in the United States, but they would not sound the way they sound. Jazz, for example, is a very specific sexual term, as in *jazz me, baby,* but white people purified it into the Jazz Age. *Sock it to me,* which means, roughly, the same thing, has been adopted by Nathaniel Hawthorne's descendants with no qualms or hesitations at all, along with *let it all hang out* and *right on! Beat to his socks,* which was once the black's most total and despairing image of poverty, was transformed into a thing called the Beat Generation, which phenomenon was, largely, composed of *uptight,* middle-class white people, imitating poverty, trying to *get down,* to get *with it,* doing their *thing,* doing their despairing best to be *funky,* which we, the blacks, never dreamed of doing—we *were* funky, baby, like *funk* was going out of style.

Now, no one can eat his cake, and have it, too, and it is late in the day to attempt to penalize black people for having created a language that permits the nation its only glimpse of reality, a language without which the nation would be even more *whipped* than it is.

I say that this present skirmish is rooted in American history, and it is. Black English is the creation of the black diaspora. Blacks came to the United States chained to each other, but from different tribes: Neither could speak the other's language. If two black people, at that bitter hour of the world's history, had been able to speak to each other, the institution of chattel slavery could never have lasted as long as it did. Subsequently, the slave was given, under the eye, and the gun, of his master, Congo Square, and the Bible—or, in other words, and under these conditions, the slave began the formation of the black church, and it is within this unprecedented tabernacle that black English began to be formed. This was not, merely, as in the European example, the adoption of a foreign tongue, but an alchemy that transformed ancient elements into a new language: *A language comes into existence by means of brutal necessity, and the rules of the language are dictated by what the language must convey.*

There was a moment, in time, and in this place, when my brother, or my mother, or my father, or my sister, had to convey to me, for example, the danger in which I was standing from the white standing just behind me, and to convey this with a speed, and in a language, that the white man could not possibly understand, and that, indeed, he cannot understand, until today. He cannot afford to understand it. This understanding would reveal to him too much about himself, and smash that mirror before which he has been frozen for so long.

Now, if this passion, this skill, this (to quote Toni Morrison) "sheer intelligence," this incredible music, the mighty achievement of having brought a people utterly unknown to, or despised by "history"—to have brought this people to their present, troubled, troubling, and unassailable and unanswerable place—if this absolutely unprecedented journey does not indicate that black English is a language, I am curious to know what definition of language is to be trusted.

A people at the center of the Western world, and in the midst of so hostile a population, has not endured and transcended by means of what is patronizingly called a "dialect." We, the blacks, are in trouble, certainly, but we are not doomed, and we are not inarticulate because we are not compelled to defend a morality that we know to be a lie.

The brutal truth is that the bulk of the white people in America never had any interest in educating black people, except as this could serve white purposes. It is not the black child's language that is in question, it is not his language that is despised: It is his experience. A child cannot be taught by anyone who despises him, and a child cannot afford to be fooled. A child cannot be taught by anyone whose demand, essentially, is that the child repudiate his experience, and all that gives him sustenance, and enter a limbo in which he will no longer be black, and in which he knows that he can never become white. Black people have lost too many black children that way.

And, after all, finally, in a country with standards so untrustworthy, a country that makes heroes of so many criminal mediocrities, a country unable to face why so many of the non-white are in prison, or on the needle, or standing, futureless, in the streets—it may very well be that both the child, and his elder, have concluded that they have nothing whatever to learn from the people of a country that has managed to learn so little.

L. ELDRIDGE CLEAVER

As Crinkly as Yours

In every society, in every historical period, it is demonstrable that human beings have always made some type of judgment as to what is beautiful and what is not beautiful. The things, or aspects of things, esteemed as beautiful have changed; but always men have looked upon some things as beautiful and others as unbeautiful or, condemnatorily, as ugly. Indeed, an entire branch of philosophy—Esthetics—has this phenomenon as its subject-matter.

As time goes by, these judgments seep into, and become deeply entrenched in, the culture of a people, and are looked upon as standards by which value judgments are made. To each cultural group, the acceptance of these traditional standards is as natural and unquestioned as is the acceptance by the group of any other aspect of its culture.

It seems that, from time immemorial, mankind has passed judgment on the human body, pronouncing these characteristics and traits beautiful and these un-beautiful—or ugly. As the judgments are reiterated over the years, they become objectified into standards by which the merits and demerits of individual human beings are determined. This practice can be observed amongst all people, be they so-called civilized or so-called primitive. They all ornament themselves in various ways—in conformity to an accepted standard of beauty; and failure to do so marks one as an oddity, an eccentric, or one type of freak or another.

This phenomenon would not be the subject of remark outside the bounds of the discipline which embraces it, were it not for the fact that the traditional judgments which Western Man has made, and still tenaciously clings to, are now (and, indeed, have been) the cause of very serious maladjustments in our society and, much more seriously, in the world at large. In this essay, the attempt will be made to show that the continued application of these judgments is the cause of an untold amount of mental illness and frustration.

In our culture, the recognized standard of beauty—one could just as well say, "the official standard of beauty"—is that of the Caucasian peoples; and since the Caucasian has possessed hegemony over the world for the duration of the epoch which is now drawing to a close, along with other values of Western culture, he has also exported *his* standard of beauty. In a profound sense, the Caucasian standard of beauty has been—and is now—one of the corner-stones of the doctrine of "White Supremacy." We have only to observe in order to see the destructive psychological impact of this standard of beauty on the people

From *Negro History Bulletin* 25 (March 1962).

around the world who have unknowingly fallen under its subtle influence. In this essay, the discussion will be confined chiefly to the situation as it relates to the American Negro; but by extension, most of what is said here can be applied in a general way.

It is generally held that the first incidence of Africans being seized and abducted from their native soil and brought to America and enslaved, occurred in the year 1619; if that is so, then that is the date on which the traditional standard of beauty of the transplanted African was first undermined and the corroding process of subversion began. Certainly, up until that time, the Africans had their own standards of beauty, and they accepted them just as naturally, proudly, and unquestioningly as all other people accepted their own.

But after being crushed down into a position of slavery, degradation, poverty and general wretchedness—but most important, after the arbitrary and more or less total disruption of his cultural continuity, due largely to the indiscriminate and unceremonious mixing of different tribes and cultural groups by the Slavers, who cared not a tack for the cultures of their prey—the black slave began to identify everything that fell to his lot with the conditions under which he suffered. The lodging that was forced upon him; the food that was parceled out to him; the crude work-a-day clothing that he was obliged to wear— all of these items became in his eyes, badges of bondage; and therefore he passionately hated them.

Under the harsh physical brutality, the taunts, castigations and deprecatory harassments of his slavemasters, who looked upon the black man as a sub-human beast of burden, after generation on top of generation of slaves, born into slavery and knowing nothing but the miseries of their state and the constant brain-washing of their every-day life, totally stripped of their own culture—under that pressure the slaves began to identify everything that is good and desirable with the Caucasians for who they toiled. It was the Caucasians whom they saw dressed in the finest garments and attire that the fabulous profits of slavery could command; it was the Caucasians whom they saw inhabiting the palatial mansions of the plantations in the "great white world beyond . . ."—consequently the slaves came to regard the surroundings of the "whites" as a veritable heaven on earth; something to dream of, yet never attain. The pomp and show of the ostentatious Southern Aristocracy served to hammer the black man down, dwarfing his pride and extirpating his self-esteem by shackling to his neck the huge, iron collar of the inferiority complex. This went on for some 240 years, and after this blanket annihilation of his traditional way of life, the black man was set free in a "white" oriented society. With the advent of freedom, the adverse effects of the Caucasian standard of beauty on the black men upon whom it had been imposed became more apparent.

Following the Civil War, the great mass of "Freedmen," now designated as "Negro," were able, in a quasi-free way, to determine their own destiny. For the first time in the history of the race, black men found themselves 'free' en masse in the midst of Western culture and civilization. And if Negroes, while in slavery, identified the fabled 'Good Life' with the standards of the Caucasians, after freedom was achieved the desires and dreams of attaining this 'Good Life' mushroomed and took on new tantalizing proportions in their minds by virtue of the fact that the actual conditions to which they aspired were everpresent and all around them, as it were "so near and yet so far."

Negroes migrated to the big cities, to the fashion capitals of the nation, there to be fascinated and dazzled by, what must have seemed to them, splendor and finery fit for kings—treasures unparalleled in their most inspired dreams. And who possessed the objects of these dreams? The Caucasians. (It is important to remember that the ideals and values which were born in slavery were carried over and persisted into the new era.)

There were deeply imbedded in the thinking and folklore of the race such adages and beliefs as: "If you're white you're all right; if you're brown stick around; but if you're black—GET BACK!" And some of these same old sayings are still current in the Negro community.

Think on it: this was the era of the camera. Negroes saw photographs, paintings and portraits in which the beauty of the Caucasian was extolled saturatingly throughout the land. Negroes witnessed beauty contests in which Caucasian men and women were held up and proclaimed the most beautiful creatures that God had fashioned and placed upon the face of the earth (it never dawning on the Negroes that it was the Caucasians themselves who were pinning roses on their own lapels). Great numbers of Negroes were learning to read and write; and in the books which they read, the process took on a sweeping new dimension. When a Negro retired in solitude to relax and enjoy a *great* book, it was the Caucasian standard of beauty which was flaunted before him and held up for him to praise—and praise it he did, unable to resist or dispute, having no criterion by which to refute. In the novels, he met heroines with *creamy white skin, sparking blue eyes, and long flowing blonde tresses;* and heroes with *rugged Roman noses, wavy black hair* and perhaps a *gentle* sun-tan. And then the motion-picture industry sprang into being, and with it, a constant deluge reiterating and indisputably establishing the Caucasian standard of beauty.

At this point let it be recalled that *physical appearance,* i.e., skin color and texture of hair, is what primarily distinguishes the great majority of Negroes from other Americans. It is this salient factor—physical appearance—which points out the Negro and makes him readily available as a target of abuse and a more vulnerable mark for exploitation. Significantly, the historical fact is that the other despised minority groups which America has known were able, after a comparatively brief time, to disappear into the main-stream of our national life and take active parts in the social, political and economic affairs of the country. Unlike the Negro, the other minority groups could not be identified as such merely on the basis of physical appearance. For those minorities, assimilation was an accomplished fact simply by learning to speak English and smoothing out the family name from Schmidt to Smith.

To an excruciatingly painful degree, Negroes were very much aware of their "burden of color and bad hair."

How can the effects of the Caucasian standard of beauty be identified in the thinking and actions of Negroes? Why, observe the great vogue of hair-straighteners, wigs, and skin-bleaches that sprang into being! Great geniuses were at work! One such savant, after much pondering and tedious toil, emerged and created a revolution amongst Negro women when he introduced that Magic Wand—the Straightening Comb:

"After one preparation, Madam, you too can have *silky-straight* flowing tresses, just as *beautiful* and *lovely* as your pale sister. Or perhaps you *require* a hank of this *flattering* Store Bought Hair? Just come as you are and when we are finished with you—well just come in to see us—then you be the judge!"

Another great benefactor was at work, but due to the fact that the Negro male would run the risk of burning out his brains if he took to the Hot Comb, this Einstein had a more difficult, arduous and exacting quest. But not to be daunted, he experimented, researched and concocted: and then one fateful day he returned victorious and announced to the world that, at long last, the Negro male, too, could have *silky-straight* locks, wavy and curly which, if you master the technique, you can even toss around a bit; it will even fall down in front of your eyes, just like the movie stars—that is, if you are prudent and do not overdo it.

"All you have to do, Sammy, my boy, is go see your barber, or go to the Beauty Parlor (oh, it's all right); just tell them to 'tighten' your mop for you, man, and when they get through applying their Lye Solutions, their Caustic Soda Preparations, their Miracle Acids and Combinations of Acids—after that, you will be just like Boss Charlie! You will have such Beautiful Straight Hair!"

Ah! Love that scientific spirit.

"After Madam and Monsieur have finished their coiffure, why go right around the corner to the Drug Store and buy a big fat bottle of Skin Bleach! Get the six-month economy size! Oh, don't worry about which brand, all of them are medically tested, proven, and guaranteed to bleach your dull skin Pretty-Pink and White!"

According to Ebony's Hall of Fame, Madame C. J. Walker, the "founder of the world's oldest and biggest Negro cosmetics company," became the first Negro woman millionaire, after starting business with $2 and an original formula for "refining the scalp and straightening hair," (as if the Negro's head was an unfinished product!). Madame Walker is acclaimed as a "pioneer in the field of Negro beauty culture," and was elected to the Hall of Fame for her "contributions to the progress of the Negro and the American way of life." Incidentally, Madame Walker mixed her first batch of hair straightener in a washtub; and her last prayer went thus:

"Not for me, O Lord, but for my race."

Apparently she felt that her "formula" had delivered the Negro from all evil.

Now it is not surprising that the Negro reacted so. That is the logical outcome of his historical experience. But it is time that he checked himself. That he should continue to react in this way is not only surprising—it is beginning to be something of a scandal. Do not think that the reasons for such behavior have disappeared: on the contrary, they have gathered force and broadened. All of the mass media are constantly busy publicizing the Caucasian standard of beauty: the motion pictures, magazines, newspapers, television, literature, illustrated wall posters and bill boards—an unthinking (or money-hungry) Negro press—and most obvious and telling of all, the beauty contests.

What reaction do you think a young Negro girl has when a blonde haired, blue eyed 'white' girl is held up and proclaimed as Miss America, or Miss Universe? When this is done, implicitly they are saying:

"This type of female is the ideal, the most beautiful female on earth, and the more closely you approximate her characteristics the more beautiful you will be, otherwise, my dear little black girl, you are just plain ugly!"

What unspoken and unspeakable wretchedness must scorch and flame in the heart of the young black girl when she witnesses this type of thing! especially when the values of her friends, the Negro press—and in many cases—her own values, seem to acquiesce in applauding the Caucasian standard of beauty.

What Negro is there who has not felt an inarticulate questioning—deep down inside— upon being confronted with the Caucasian standard of beauty, especially if he has to make a decision, in his own mind, as to whether or not this is really beauty upon which he is looking? What rationalizations he is forced to make! And, oh! what frustration and feelings of inferiority result! How much pathological, insane, peculiar behavior, do you think, is a direct result of this frustration caused by the standard of beauty which Negroes have accepted? Undoubtedly the proportion would prove alarming. With all the mass media disseminating this doctrine, it would be difficult, if not impossible, to find a Negro who has not been influenced by it.

Implicit in the very acceptance of the Caucasian standard of beauty is the negation of typical Negroid traits. If it is believed that blue eyes, long straight blonde hair, and non-colored skin are the component parts of beauty—then it logically follows that since Negroes generally do not share this particular variety of attributes, Negroes generally are not beautiful. To be sure, Negroes have eyes, and hair, and skins; but if you will just think about the words which Negroes employ to describe themselves, you will see that the words reflect degrees and gradations *away* from the Caucasian ideal of beauty.

Eye color does not present much a problem, but notice that a Negro who possesses blue eyes, grey eyes, hazel eyes, light-brown eyes—a Negro with eyes of either of these colors is generally looked upon as being fortunate, whereas the majority of Negroes have eyes of a dark hue. It is axiomatic of the eye that when we look at it in search of beauty, we look for such things as the clearness—the sparkle, as it were—of the eyeball; the length and density of the eye-lashes and eye-brows, and the general contour of the eye. And it does not matter too much what the type of face is in which a beautiful eye is set. But still, when we consider the eye, we take our cue from the Caucasian standard of beauty.

But what happens when we consider skin color and hair texture? The very words that we use indicate that we have set a premium on the Caucasian ideal of beauty. When discussing inter-racial relations, we speak of "white people" and "non-white people." We will refer to people all over the world as "white" and "non-white." Notice that that particular choice of words gives precedence to "white people" by making them a center—a standard—to which "non-white" bears a negative relation. Notice the different connotations when we turn it around and say "colored" and "non-colored," or "black" and "non-black." Our thinking is so foggy on this issue that we describe our complexions as if they are qualities strewn along a yard-stick, the opposite ends of which are painted black and white respectively—black being the negative end. In this type of thinking, to be black is extremely unfortunate, and the higher up towards the white end of the yard-stick your complexion is located, the better off you are. We have a host of terms to fit the ascending graduations of the yard-stick: passing for white, high-yellow, real-light, light, high-brown, dark-brown, dark, black, blue-black, jet-black. In a sense these descriptive terms are accurate, because the complexions of those designated as 'Negro' run the gamut of the spectrum from 'jet-black' to 'passing for white.' However, it is our thinking—the relative value which we set on these various hues: and the fact that we do set *values* on them—that is what we are concerned with herein.

Now, when we consider the hair, we reach a topic on which we are extremely sensitive. This is because of the obvious variation between the texture of the typical Negro's hair and that of the typical Caucasian. But if Negroes are going to adhere to the Caucasian standard of beauty, must they not also pass judgment on the hair? Of course we must, and we have: we look upon our texture of hair as an affliction, a fiendish mockery of us by Mother

Nature. Consequently we have another yard-stick for *evaluating* the relative *quality* of our hair. This one progresses from "bad hair" to "good hair." The straighter the hair—that is to say, the more one's hair resembles that of the Caucasian—the "better" it is. Good hair, bad hair, nappy hair, kinky hair and so on. And *short-haired women*? Good Gravy! (God bless the soul to whom we must forever be humble for inventing the "Boyish Bob") Short hair is looked upon as an especial abomination. We do not have even any flattering words with which to describe our hair: but this is not surprising since we do not look upon our hair as being particularly flattering.

In her brilliant play, *A Raisin in the Sun,* Lorraine Hansberry focuses the spot light squarely on this problem. But as it turned out, the lady Hansberry filed charges against the American Negro woman, and then refused to prosecute. In Act One, Scene Two, she has Asagai, the young Nigerian student who symbolizes the rebirth of Africa, tell Beneatha, an American Negro girl who is looking for her *identity*, that she has "mutilated" her hair, and this is what follows:

> Beneatha A (Turning suddenly): My hair—what's wrong with my hair?
> Asagai (Shrugging): Were you born with it like that?
> Beneatha (Reaching up to touch it): No . . . of course not. (She looks back to the mirror, disturbed)
> Asagai (Smiling): How then?
> Beneatha: You know perfectly well how . . . as crinkly as yours . . . that's how.
> Asagai: And it is ugly to you that way?
> Beneatha (Quickly): Oh, no—not ugly . . . (More slowly, apologetically) But it's so hard to manage when it's well—raw.
> Asagai: And so to accommodate that—you mutilate it every week?
> Beneatha: It's not mutilation!
> Asagai (Laughing aloud at her seriousness): Oh . . . please! I am only teasing you because you are so very serious about these things. (He stands back from her and folds his arms across his chest as he watches her pulling at her hair and frowning in the mirror)

How much worry, frustration—and wasted money—is a direct result of our attempts to run away from ourselves! We can pick up any issue of probably any Negro newspaper, and we will see a report of some opportunistic itinerant witch doctor, or perhaps an entire troup of witch doctors, touring the country, hitting the big "progressive" cities, teaching the eager populace the latest methods of becoming carbon copies of the Caucasian via the "last word" in beauty culture.

That the Negro press is a primary sower of these seeds of inferiority complexes, feelings of rejection and self-rejection, can be seen at a glance. Open almost any one of the Negro publications which carry advertisements of skin bleaches and skin lighteners, hair straighteners, false hair and wigs, etc., all with an emotion-charged indictment such as "Why should you *suffer* with hard to manage kinky ugly hair? Use Dr. Flop's Hair Straightener and become a big hit!" "Do you suffer from dull ugly skin? Get Hosana Bleaching Cream and have a fair, beautiful complexion!" This type of advertising is usually accompanied by one of those convincing "Before and After" illustrations of some wretched, despondent young Negro girl or boy who, immediately after applying the product advertised, is suddenly transformed into a sparkling young center of attraction.

Ebony Magazine, which is probably the most widely read Negro magazine, periodically runs a feature which is presumptuously entitles, "The World's Most Beautiful Negro Women" or something to that effect.

And what are the contents of this feature? Why the Caucasian standard of beauty, of course! Invariably, they will crown Lena Horne, Dorothy Dandridge, or someone else whose appearance would nominate them to compete rather for the title of Miss Scandinavia, Miss Greater Europe, or Miss Anything—other than that which is indicated by the title of the feature. And what emotions do you think the typical Negro girl experiences when she reads this feature? Why obviously, exactly the ones that are evoked when she sees the results of the Miss America or Miss Universe contests!

Thus, it is obvious that while on one hand, through no fault of his own, the Negro is a victim of a set of cultural values—on the other hand it is equally true that the Negro's response to this vicious situation has been to adjust to the environment through the dubious process of "mutilating" his natural ethnic characteristics in order to conform as best he could, to the Caucasian standard of beauty.

Of course, it would be facetious of us to campaign for a law to ban the Caucasian standard of beauty; but it is of paramount importance that we realize that there is absolutely no such thing as a universal standard of beauty for all people—black, brown, red, yellow, white—measuring up to which they stand or fall. The standards of beauty which exist in the world today are nothing but manifestations of ethnocentrism. Our concepts of beauty enter our minds through social indoctrination. We think a person with a certain complexion, a certain type of hair, a certain shape of nose, a certain color of eyes—we think that person possessed of beauty, not because he is beautiful per se, but rather because we have been culturally conditioned to look upon the particular traits of which he is possessed as being the most desirable, the most becoming: the beautiful. Let it be remembered that, historically, each ethnic group has looked upon its own characteristic traits as being beautiful.

If Negroes continue to respond blindly and unthinkingly to this indoctrination, then they as surely will continue to be plagued by the divisive self-hatreds, feelings of inferiority, etc., which are vestiges of the bygone days of the unchallenged sway of the odious doctrine of "White Supremacy." When we judge ourselves by the Caucasian standard of beauty and find that it does not fit us, if we have accepted that standard as absolute, then our reaction is not merely that we think our own individual selves ugly, it extends much farther than that: it touches every facet of our existence, it influences the very value which we set on ourselves as individuals, it colors our thinking and our opinion of the race as a whole—in short—it has a disastrous effect. This confusion pursues many of us all through life, "like the Furies in a Greek play," driving us deeper into a private hell.

To be sure, it is a hyper-ethnocentric act—but one consonant with the doctrine of "White Supremacy"—for the Caucasian to hold up one of his members and crown him or her Mister or Miss Universe; but it is *something* else when the Negro accepts this standard, and then proceeds with a host of contrivances to warp his natural characteristics in a vain effort to measure up to that alien standard. Until the social values of human beings evolve to the point where we no longer feel the need to aggrandize ourselves above our fellow men on the quicksand ground of ethnic superiority, until that time, we will have with us the spectacle of the Eskimos in Alaska saying that they are the most beautiful people in creation; the Chinese in China saying that they alone are beautiful; the Japanese, the Arabs, the Australian Aborigines, all in their own lands saying the same thing, while the Caucasian proclaims it to the entire world. But let us hope that the Negro will not still be running along behind in the "white shadows" with his Hot Combs and Bleaching Creams in an orgy of self-destroying mimicry.

It is superficially absurd for a given ethnic group to judge itself by the standard of some other group. If we were to take a Caucasian man and woman and judge their beauty by a people's standard other than their own, that Caucasian man and woman would be judged as ugly. The same will be the result when we judge others by the Caucasian standard of beauty, or when we judge a member of one ethnic group by the prevailing standard of another ethnic group.

Would it not be superfluous for the Pygmys to take for their standard of beauty that of the Watusi? The average height of the Watusi is about 7 feet, while that of the Pygmy is about 4½ feet! In addition, the Watusi are rather large of body while the Pygmys are rather small. Would it not be a fallacy for the Pygmy to set about inventing contrivances with which to eradicate their natural physical endowments in order to measure up to the Watusi ideal of beauty? They could invent stretching machines to elongate their diminutive bodies; and they could inflate their torsos with helium and become Watusi-like! And wouldn't the Watusi seem ridiculous to try to approximate the ideal of the Pygmy? They would have quite a shrinking job on their hands! But should either of them consider himself inferior because of their differences? This is analogous to the Negro's present position.

Let it be remembered that the purpose of this essay is to call attention to certain unhealthy concepts and ideals which currently are held by all to many Negroes. Essentially, the problem is a psychological one. It concerns unexamined ideals and practices which are an integral part of our social heritage, and which are fostered and inculcated by the white oriented culture of which we are members. By becoming aware of the nature and origin of our beliefs and ideals, we are better able to understand and manipulate them if it becomes apparent that they need readjustment. When a group of ideals and beliefs become the authors of as much evil as the ones under discussion, then it is obvious that they require examination and readjustment. If there is a general stigma attached to the Negro because of his previous condition of servitude, and if the Negro does have something of an inferiority complex, it is composed of elements such as the ones isolated in this essay. We try to escape this stigma and complex by becoming 'passively Negro,' i.e., we accept our status as Negroes only because we can not escape it. The danger lies in the fact that there are only three main positions from which one must choose on the issue of belonging to a particular ethnic group: there is a positive, a neutral, and a negative position. The ethnocentric bigot will take the positive; he who realizes that all men are brothers and that they are all of the same moral value must, in order to be consistent, take the neutral position; the negative is owned by those who despise what they are, consciously or subconsciously, their vociferations to the contrary not withstanding.

Psychologically, a Negro of the negative position, i.e., a Negative Negro, attempts to purge himself of any and all traits which identify him as Negro. This brings us to a very important point, one which goes hand in hand with the Caucasian standard of beauty, and yet runs deeper and cuts deeper than any other facet of the entire affair.

The Polarized Western Mind

What we term as *The Polarized Western Mind* derives from the symbolism attached to the two colors, black and white, in the mind of Western man. These two colors are highly charged and the symbolization is deeply ingrained in the thinking and culture of the West. Everything that is good, desirable, beautiful, morally elevated, pure—in short, the highest abstractions of the Western mind are denoted by the celestial hue of white. And at the opposite end of the pole lies the degrading shade of black. Everything that is debased, corrupt, feared, evil, and ugly, is identified with the color black.

Even in those activities which touch us deepest, such as religion, we find manifestations of this polarization. For an instance, when persons are united in the *sacred* rites of matrimony the traditional garments worn by the bridge to symbolize her virtue and chastity are of the color white. While at the other end of the pole, at the time of deaths, or rather the funeral following death, the traditional attire of those in mourning is of the *dreary* hue of black. Instances of this polarization could be cited from now until dooms-day: there is an old Negro Spiritual which calls upon Jesus to "wash my sins away and make me white as snow." We speak of black cats causing bad luck, and black magic, and individuals with malignant black hearts.

This polarization affects the mind in very subtle ways. We are not conscious of it, as such, when it is in motion, but it colors our thinking just the same. An obvious and striking example of polarized thinking came to our attention recently. It concerned an illustrated cartoon satirizing the fallacious stupidity of the non-policy of segregation. The artist presents Jesus Chris hanging sufferingly from his cross; there ran a barbed wire fence through the center of Jesus and the cross, bisecting them; on one side of the fence kneeled a black man, and on the other side kneeled a white man; everything on the black man's side was painted black to symbolize the separation, and everything on the other side was painted white to further emphasize the separation; the cross, too, was painted black and white on the respective sides—but Jesus himself was pure white! If the artist had been logically consistent, he would have painted Jesus one-half black and one-half white. But the artist's polarized mind would not allow him to represent the Savior in the infamous hue of despised black.

And just as the Negro lives in the shadows cast by the connotations of the terms Negro and black, the Caucasian is living in the reflected glory of the term white. By describing himself as white, the Caucasian associates himself with the highest ideals and values in our culture.

Have you ever seen such a thing as a *white* man? Wow, what a sight that would be! Actually, if the Caucasian were forced to describe his hue realistically, he would be hard pressed to discover a hue in the spectrum that would plausibly coincide with his own. But, having labeled himself *white,* whenever he hears that name called, a flattering process of association goes on in his mind. And whenever a non-Caucasian with a polarized mind utilizes the term white in referring to the Caucasian, the same associations are made.

When the term *black* is applied to the Negro (Negro being the Latin for *black*), the process is reversed. Along with all of the unsavory connotations of the word *black,* in the polarized mind, the Negro is subconsciously condemned and degraded. Not that the term *black* is, in itself, derogatory, but rather that it is incumbent upon the polarized mind to make the associations that the connotations of the term carry, and through those associations, the imperative condemnation follows.

A Negro with a polarized mind is daily committing a type of mental suicide on the installment plan. The component parts of his polarization are constantly gnawing away at his sanity. He has to make myriad rationalizations; but there are times when the mind is unable to come up with the appropriate rationalization; these are the times when the conscious mental aberrations occur, the crushing of the personality under the leaden weight of the inferiority complex, the slow burn of suppressed rage; and these are the times when the black hand will reach for the bottle of whiskey, narcotics, or what have you, to blot out the insupportable reality which hovers above one in a stultifying cloud of condemnation, and one is further crushed when this occurs because one will describe the burdensome reality as: "Ah, the *black* clouds!"

It is manifest, then, that for the sake of the people who are the victims of this polarization, they must shatter these antiquated clichés of thought and, as it were, de-polarize their minds. It is not to be supposed that values so deeply rooted in our culture can be refashioned overnight; but, by realizing that the problem exists the job is half-done.

What we must do is to stop associating the Caucasian with these exalted connotations of the word *white* when we think or speak of him. At the same time, we must cease associating ourselves with the unsavory connotations of the word *black*. "A house divided against itself cannot stand," how much truer this must be for the mind! We can talk, preach, and write about race pride and self-respect interminably, but in the last analysis, if we are indeed to have any pride, we must root-out from our thinking and folklore those elements which have robbed us of our pride.

When a black President Kwame Nkrumah of Ghana, arrayed majestically in colorful tribal robes, can stride in towering dignity and pride onto the highest rostrum of the United Nations General Assembly, and deliver a rousing, epoch-making speech—without first pausing to either 'straighten' his hair or 'bleach' his skin, the unspoken message to his brethren is unmistakable: Black is Coming Back! The rebirth of Africa, black dignity and black power, is destined to raise the black end of the yard-stick from the depths to which it was crushed by the oppressive weight of the doctrine of "White Supremacy"—raise it back into proper equilibrium. And then when Africa asks the American Negro with what type of hair was he born, he will answer loud and clear, with dignity and pride: "As crinkly as yours."

Tripping with Black Writing

The move toward liberation from slave to serf to self, for Black folk, has meant a long, arduous trip. The history of this development, which we might call "The Black Experience," has been chronicled in the annals of Black Literature. Always the movement has had to be bilateral—that is, both external and internal; language has played an important part in communicating the experience from within and without. And while Blacks have had to define and validate Black reality, they, concurrently, have had to protest and protect themselves from exploitation and dehumanization. They had to not only devise ways of speaking in tongues so that "the man" could not always understand everything, but also had to speak out of both sides of their mouths—hurrahing Black; badmouthing White.

Original hoodoo, badmouthing the man, forerunners of the "Stomp Me, O Lord" slave accounts and protests Black-perspective accounts of what was really going down with the wind, start with Lucy Terry, digging the scene of an Indian Massacre, 1746:

> And had not her petticoats stopt her
> The awful creatures had not cotched her
> And tommyhawked her on the head
> And left her on the ground for dead.

Or Jupiter Hammon on *An Evening Thought, Salvation by Christ, with Penitential Cries,"* turning hearts and souls away from an unbearable reality to spiritualism:

> Lord turn our dark benighted Souls;
> Give us a true Motion,
> And let the Hearts of all the World,
> Make Christ their Salvation.

Early turnings; trying to turn these bedeviled mothers around, shame them in their human trafficking; these wrenchings of conscience from those short on conscience but long on bread and black gold—earliest forms of Black power. Image-making from early

---

From *The Black Aesthetic,* ed. Addison Gayle Jr. (Garden City, N.Y.: Doubleday, 1971).

days from pure spirit and communion with nature. Nation-building from the ground. Loss of king-of-the-jungle images, lion-and-panther form. Beaten to the ground; gagged and shackled, but singing free:

> Keep a-inching along
> Like a poor inch worm
> JESUS IS COMING BY AND BY.

Or George Moses Horton transcending that hell-bound scene in *On Liberty and Slavery*, rapping on "the man," calling on the ancestors' spirit world:

> Say unto foul oppression, Cease:
> Ye tyrants rage no more,
> And let the joyful trump of peace,
> Now bid the vassal soar.
> Soar on the pinions of that dove
> Which long as cooed for thee,
> And breathed her notes from Afric's grove,
> The Sound of liberty. . . .

And with *The Life of Olantudah Equiano* or *Gustavus Vassa, The African, Written by Himself,* the beginning of the Black gift to American Mainstream Literature, a new genre— the slave narrative. "For-real" world literature. Gustavus Vassa running it down how he was run across the world, making giant steps, building civilization. Born in Benin, slaved in Virginia and Pennsylvania, farmed-out on a Caribbean plantation, working out as an abolitionist in England—as a self-made man. Bootstrap pulling; defying laws of gravity and gravitation. Gaming for self, the bootstrap-yanking for brother boots.

Getting that soul together in times of dehumanization and desecration of the souls of Black men. *Life and Times,* Frederick Douglass, a put-down as early as 1845; altogether in 1881. Whipping it to the original outhouse ruler of the "Harry Sam" vintage, Abe Lincoln; running down such a heavy game that runaway slave turns presidential adviser and Consul General to Haiti. Shades of Papa Doc! Wearing two faces. Seer. Invoking spirits, calling for an exorcism of the spirit and body of racism manifested by *Dred Scott* decision and the act of nullifying the Fourteenth Amendment in 1883. Instances of bad Supreme Court decisions which made him cry out:

> But when a deed is done for slavery, caste, and oppression and a blow is struck at human progress, whether so intended or not, the heart of humanity sickens in sorrow and writhes in pain. It makes us feel as if some one were stamping upon the graves of our mothers, or desecrating our sacred temples. Only base men and oppressors can rejoice in a triumph of injustice over the weak and defenseless, for weakness ought itself to protect from assaults of pride, prejudice, and power. . . . (pp. 541–47)
> No man can put a chain about the ankle of his fellow-man, without at last finding the other end of it about his own neck.

The lesson of all the ages upon this point is, that a wrong done to one man is a wrong done to all men. It may not be felt at the moment, and the evil may be long delayed, but so sure as there is a moral government of the universe, so sure will the harvest of evil come.

Stomp us, O Lord! Getting into the power of speaking in tongues. W. E. B. Du Bois. *The Souls of Black Folk.* Those of the double consciousness, born with veils over their eyes . . . From *Darkwater,* "A Litany at Atlanta, Done at Atlanta, in the Day of Death, 1906":

. . . Wherefore do we pray? Is not the God of the fathers dead? Have not seers seen in Heaven's halls Thine hearsed and lifeless form stark amidst the black and rolling smoke of sin, where all along bow bitter forms of endless dead? . . .
Thou art still the God of our black fathers, and in Thy soul's soul sit some soft darkenings of the evening, some shadowings of the velvet night.

Stomp us, O Lord! James Weldon Johnson raising *God's Trombones,* giving a new folk "Creation," rhapsodizing about Africa's prodigal son's return home. Setting the beat of marching feet on the road to victory in "Life Every Voice and Sing":

. . . Stony the road we trod,
Bitter the chastening rod,
Felt in the days when hope unborn had died;
Yet with a steady beat,
Have not our weary feet
Come to the place for which our fathers sighed?

Speaking in tongues. Uncle Julius, in "The Goophered Grapevine," describes one of Sycorax's daughters, Aun' Peggy, who has goophered, cunju'd, bewitched the scuppernon' vineyard:

She sa'ntered 'roun' mongs' de vimes, en tuk a leaf fum dis one, en a grape-hull fum dat one, en a grape-seed fum annuder one; en den a little twig fum here, en a little pinch er dirt fum dere,—en put it all in a big black bottle, wid a snake's toof en a speckle' hen's gall en some ha'rs fum a black cat's tail, en den fill' de bottle wid scuppernon' wine.

Speaking in tongues and running his games. Charles Chesnutt. And Paul Laurence Dunbar running it down how "We wear the Mask / That grins and lies." An African orientation . . .

Alain Locke—that necessary critic for *The New Negro;* a special critic for a special time. Harlem Renaissance. Fathering Negritude. Giving the possibility of showing forth a triumph of spirit and mind. A decolonized mind shining through colonial language. Locke sees Caliban's early move:

. . . Then eventually came the time when the hectic rhetoric and dogged moralism had to fall back in sheer exhaustion on the original basis of cultural supply. Through

Dunbar,—part of whose poetry, nevertheless, reflects the last stand of this rhetorical advance, Negro poetry came penitently back to the folk-tradition, and humbled itself to dialect for fresh spiritual food and raiment.

William Stanley Braithwaite, who gave America the possibility of an American poetry, speaks of Dunbar as closing one age in Black poetry and beginning another. Check out the Sesqui-Centennial Edition of *Braithwaite's Anthology of Magazine Verse for 1926, Yearbook of American Poetry.* Black poetry—a main tributary of mainstream American poetry. A Black man willing to bring an indigenous, non-derivative poetry into being. He got lost in the shuffle after 1929. But he'd done his thing. Sterling Brown, one of the most capable writers using Black form chronicling the literary movement in *Negro Caravan.* Sterling Brown in his *Negro Poetry and Drama* said this:

"Dialect, or the speech of the people, is capable of expressing whatever the people are. And the folk Negro is a great deal more than a buffoon or a plaintive minstrel. Poets more intent upon learning the ways of the folk, their speech, and their character, that is to say better poets, could have smashed the mold. But first they would have had to believe in what they were doing. And this was difficult in a period of conciliation and middle class striving for recognition and respectability."

Early there was a self-consciousness and a mold which a deriding white America put on Black folk speech. This meant that many feigned representing folk speech, according to Brown, by:

"A few pat phrases, a few stock situations and characteristics, some misspelling: these were the chief things necessary. The wit and beauty possible to folk speech, the folk-shrewdness, the humanity, the stoicism of these people they seldom say."

The Harlem Renaissance period closed the credibility gap between the Black man, his articulation of his experience, and his selfhood. Zora Neal Hurston, anthropologist, throwing light on language. Open the way for today's freedom-wigged freaks. Stone-cold, bad-blood revolutionaries. Escapees from prisons of Anglo rhetoric. Frontiersmen in the lumbering netherlands of Black language. Medicine men schooled in witchcraft, black magic, the voodoo of words. Immortalized, subterranean, out-of-this-world travelers. Dutchmen. LeRois. LeRoi Joneses. Quick-change sleight-of-hand magicians. Dons. Don Lees. Changing. "Change your enemy change your change change change your enemy change change . . . change your mind nigger." Killens. Killens' chilluns. On their jobs. Taking care of business. "De-niggerizing the world." Voodoo cowboys. Loop Garoo Kids. Riding loose—cool ones—into the whirlwind of change; who, as they gallop into town, have a "posse of spells phone in sick." Ishmaels. Ishmael Reeds. Yeah. Yellow Back Radio Done Show Good Broke-Down. Up against the wall, Prospero.

Calibans all. Exploding Prospero's premises with extraordinary, for-real, supernatural departures. Trips. More benevolent despotism, spelled Tyranny. Any way you look at it. And his gift of language—his "prison in which Caliban's achievements will be realized and restricted"—is a boomerang. New-breed Blacks, those desperadoes who "Take the Money and Run," leave "the man" behind bound and bankrupt; marooned on a barren island of derivative Anglo-Saxon, European-like culture. Walled in by the "law and order" of his own restrictive rhetoric. And those newly free? They are on their jobs making jujus, working their mojos, peeping Chuck's hold cards. Understanding the real meaning of his excessive articulation of so much nonsense. Seers and sages. Reporters such as Eldridge Cleaver sending back messages about the "technologically gifted moon men": "I heard what he said; he said 'oink.'" LeRoi Jones-created criminals intent on robbing the family of its jewels in *Home on the Range*. Mystified, momentarily, with the father's talk; "Crillilly bagfest. Gobble Gobble. Gobble." But understand their task is to give these robots the gift of soul, of language of the real world. Once more, Mr. Tooful: "I was born in Kansas City in 1920. My father was the vice-president of a fertilizer company. Before that we were phantoms. . . ." Which explains all that shit. Packaged under the brand name of "Standard English," mainstream American literature. Or Sister Carolyn Rodgers taking a look at the spineless, flat imitation in "Portrait of a White Nigger"! who "talks like/a biscuit that will/ not rise . . . got a jelly mind/and shimmy thighs"; whose purpose in life is reduced to an endless search trying "to find the MAGIC that/will/PRESTO"/Black/off/ . . ."

No mere children of nature these. They are indeed, Sycorax-the-Sorceress' offspring. With magic potions to tame the beasts of nature. With so many thumping, twangling instruments giving the beat. Informing William Melvin Kelley and his likes that he moves to the rhythms of *A Different Drummer*. Dere's Us'ns and dere's *Dem*. Magic knowledge. Source of power found rooted in the residue of a wellspring of aged and ageless African native culture—soul. Spooky Stuff. Sins of the father's revisited! Great balls of fire!!! Brother, brush off your Br'er Rabbit's foot. Shine up your John-The-Conqueror root. Whip up your own brand gris-gris. It's Voodoo time again.

LeRoi Jones, dramatizing the dilemma. Don Lee, chronicling the changes. Ishmael Reed, S-p-e-l-l-i-n-g it out. Nikki Giovanni, recording "Records": "a negro needs to kill/something/trying to record/that this country must be/destroyed/if we are to live/must be destroyed if we are to live/must be destroyed if we are to live." Jimmy Garret, bucking the whitewashed system. White power—the same which done got his mama—challenged to a duel. By a deathly game of dozens, in the one-act *And We Own the Night*. Cracker-walled prisons of rhetoric crumbled before the double-whammied eyes of crumb-snatching blues logic, Semple-fied by Langston Hughes, passed on as sacrament to Stanley Crouch and Dante. Stone walls of marital law and bad conditions failing to imprison the spirit of Blacks. Etheridge Knight, breaking through in *Cell Song,* answering the call to "take/your words and scrape/the sky, shake rain/on the desert, sprinkle/salt on the tail/of a girl . . ." And Sonia Sanchez preparing for *Homecoming:* "Leaving behind me/all those hide and/ seek faces . . . I have learned it/ain't like they say/ in the newspapers." Soul talk for soul folk. *Boss Soul,* by Sarah Fabio: ". . . gut bucket, gospel spiritual, jazz/touching cords of Feeling any live person/has to tune into or turn on to that/special deepdown/inside you thing."

New Day. Dawn. Light of Broken Night. Night breaks. Night trippers. Check out the Bad, Bold scene of the Mojo workers. Dig the star-crossed bones uncovered by Ishmael Reed in *15 Nigromancers From Now.* If you dare. Any day or night—or séance in between—get on down to what's really there. Clean-picked bones. The skulls of ones who talked too much. Get to that. Another necessary trip: *Amistad,* with Charles Harris and John Williams piloting.

Black writers, finding themselves up a tree with "the man's" rhetoric and aesthetic, which hangs them up, lynching their black visions, cut it loose. All the way—swinging free. Flying home. Wings flapping, raucously, in the breeze. So many unnatural demands from the establishment, the tradition, beamed into a subject people from a hostile, alien culture, shined off as irrelevant, self-defeating. Needing to respond as integral beings not having to compromise integrity. Bringing black perspective, black aesthetic, black rhetoric, black language to add authenticity to the felt reality. Knowing America has no rhetoric matching its racist reality; no reality matching its "universal" and "democratic" idealistic state of existence. Knowing the simple-minded, fascist, pseudo-Europeanized mandate of "universality" to be a funky issue in any aesthetic consideration. A hustle to make wall-eyed, white-eyed America the all-seeing Cyclops of our age.

Giving the finger to blind justice. Peeping the loosened blindfold. Peeping her peeping; favoring the apples of her eye—rotten though they may be. Playing the game of dozens with her. Combating her status-quo games. Knowing the truth about this society. One that devaluates the lives of a people for the duration of its existence. One that dehumanizes them for fun and profit. A mere matter of pragmatism and utilitarianism. Knowing that society to be guilty of: emasculating manhood; deflowering womanhood; exploiting spirit and soul; blinding vision; binding motion; dulling sensitivity; gagging speech.

Black Writing-repressed, suppressed, ignored, denounced. Black writers having rained upon them not respect, riches, rewards, but disrespect, discouragement, non-recognition, deculturation, assimilation, isolation, starvation, expatriation, derangement, criminal indictment. LeRoi Jones's case but a recent and flagrant example of a system's way of dealing with creative, liberated black minds. The same brutal white backlash that cut the cord of David Walker's life after his writing of his "Appeal" in the early nineteenth century still tears at the flesh of articulate Blacks of the recent past and the present—men such as Malcolm X, Martin Luther King, Eldridge Cleaver, Bobby Seale.

No turning back, though. This is the day of Biggers and ghosts of Biggers. Black writers—most of them poets plus—have always been barometers, even when America kept bell jars on them. Have always been/still are/will be. Always traveling with ears to the ground; attuned to the drumbeats of the age. Check out the Harlem Renaissance poets, such as Langston Hughes, Claude McKay, Sterling Brown. Check out the post depression poets of the thirties, including Richard Wright. Check out Margaret Walker's words to her people in the early forties. Check out the poets in *Beyond the Blues,* a time when Black poetry was so far underground it had to travel to England for publication. Check out Black poets publishing with Broadside Press, Third World Press, Success Press. Check out Black periodicals—*Journal of Black Poetry, Black Dialogue, Negro Digest, Liberator.*

Take the A-Train to Black liberation. Black writing of the seventies will be the Sweet Chariots of our time: swinging low / swinging high / swinging free. Communicant. Continuum. Change. Consummation.

Towards a Black Aesthetic

The black revolt is as palpable in letters as it is in the streets, and if it has not yet made its impact upon the Literary Establishment, then the nature of the revolt itself is the reason. For the break between the revolutionary black writers and the "literary mainstream" is, perhaps of necessity, cleaner and more decisive than the noisier and more dramatic break between the black militants and traditional political and institutional structures. Just as black intellectuals have rejected the NAACP, on the one hand, and the two major political parties, on the other, and gone off in search of new and more effective means and methods of seizing power, so revolutionary black writers have turned their backs on the old "certainties" and struck out in new, if uncharted, directions. They have begun the journey toward a black aesthetic.

The road to that place—if it exists at all—cannot, by definition, lead through the literary mainstreams. Which is to say that few critics will look upon the new movement with sympathy, even if a number of publishers might be daring enough to publish the works which its adherents produce. The movement will be reviled as "racism-in-reverse," and its writers labeled "racists," opprobrious terms which are flung lightly at black people now that the piper is being paid for all the long years of rejection and abuse which black people have experienced at the hands of white people—with few voices raised in objection.

Is this too harsh and sweeping a generalization? White people might think so; black people will not; which is a way of stating the problem and the prospect before us. Black people are being called "violent" these days, as if violence is a new invention out of the ghetto. But violence against the black minority is in-built in the established American society. There is no need for the white majority to take to the streets to clobber the blacks, although there certainly is *enough* of that; brutalization is inherent in all the customs and practices which bestow privileges on the whites and relegate the blacks to the status of pariahs.

These are old and well-worn truths which hardly need repeating. What is new is the reaction to them. Rapidly now, black people are turning onto that uncertain road, and they are doing so with the approval of all kinds of fellow-travellers who ordinarily are considered "safe" for the other side. In the fall 1967 issue of the *Journal of the National Medical Association* (all-black), for example, Dr. Charles A. De Leon of Cleveland, Ohio, explained why the new turn is necessary: "If young Negroes are to avoid the unnecessary burden of

From *The Black Aesthetic,* ed. Addison Gayle Jr. (Garden City, N.Y.: Doubleday, 1971).

self-hatred (via identification with the aggressor) they will have to develop a keen faculty for identifying, fractionating out, and rejecting the absurdities of the conscious as well as the unconscious white racism in American society from what is worthwhile in it."

Conscious and unconscious white racism is everywhere, infecting all the vital areas of national life. But the revolutionary black writer, like the new breed of militant activist, has decided that white racism will no longer exercise its insidious control over his work. If the tag of "racist" is one the white critic will hang on him in dismissing him, then he is more than willing to bear that. He is not going to separate literature from life.

But just how widespread is white racism—conscious and unconscious—in the realm of letters? In a review of Gwendolyn Brooks's *Selected Poems* in the old *New York Herald Tribune Book Week* back in October 1963, poet Louis Simpson began by writing that the Chicago poet's book of poems "contains some lively pictures of Negro life," an ambiguous enough opener which did not necessarily suggest a literary putdown. But Mr. Simpson's next sentence dispelled all ambiguity. "I am not sure it is possible for a Negro to write well without making us aware he is a Negro," he wrote. "On the other hand, if being a Negro is the only subject, the writing is not important."

All the history of American race relations is contained in that appraisal, despite its disingenuousness. It is civilized, urbane, gentle and elegant; and it is arrogant, condescending, presumptuous and racist. To most white readers, no doubt, Mr. Simpson's words, if not his assessment, seemed eminently sensible; but it is all but impossible to imagine a black reader not reacting to the words with unalloyed fury.

Both black and white readers are likely to go to the core of Mr. Simpson's statement, which is: "if being a Negro is the only subject, the writing is not important." The white reader will, in all probability, find that clear and acceptable enough; indeed, he is used to hearing it. "Certainly," the argument might proceed, "to be important, writing must have *universal values, universal implications;* it cannot deal exclusively with Negro problems." The plain but unstated assumption being, of course, that there are no "universal values" and no "universal implications" in Negro life.

Mr. Simpson is a greatly respected American poet, a winner of the Pulitzer Prize for poetry, as is Miss Brooks, and it will be considered the depth of irresponsibility to accuse him of the viciousness of racism. He is probably the gentlest and most compassionate of men. Miss Brooks, who met Mr. Simpson at the University of California not many months after the review was published, reported that the gentleman was most kind and courteous to her. There is no reason to doubt it. The essential point here is not the presence of overt hostility; it is the absence of clarity of vision. The glass through which black life is viewed by white Americans is, inescapably (it is a matter of extent), befogged by the hot breath of history. True "objectivity" where race is concerned is as rare as a necklace of Hope diamonds.

In October 1967, a young man named Jonathan Kozol published a book called *Death at an Early Age,* which is an account of his experiences as a teacher in a predominantly Negro elementary school in Boston. Mr. Kozol broke with convention in his approach to teaching and incurred the displeasure of a great many people, including the vigilant policeman father of one of his few white pupils. The issue around which the young teacher's opponents seemed to rally was his use of a Langston Hughes poem in his classroom. Now the late Langston Hughes was a favorite target of some of the more aggressive right-wing pressure groups during his lifetime, but it remained for an official of the Boston School Committee to come to the heart of the argument against the poet. Explaining the opposition to the poem used by Mr. Kozol, the school official said that "no poem by any Negro author can be considered permissible if it involves suffering."

There is a direct connecting line between the school official's rejection of Negro poetry which deals with suffering and Mr. Simpson's facile dismissal of writing about Negroes "only." Negro life, which is characterized by suffering imposed by the maintenance of white privilege in America, must be denied validity and banished beyond the pale. The facts of Negro life accuse white people. In order to look at Negro life unflinchingly, the white viewer either must relegate it to the realm of the subhuman, thereby justifying an attitude of indifference, or else the white viewer must confront the imputation of guilt against him. And no man who considers himself humane wishes to admit complicity in crimes against the human spirit.

There is a myth abroad in American literary criticism that Negro writing has been favored by a "double standard" which judges it less stringently. The opposite is true. No one will seriously dispute that, on occasions, critics have been generous to Negro writers, for a variety of reasons; but there is no evidence that generosity has been the rule. Indeed, why should it be assumed that literary critics are more sympathetic to blacks than are other white people? During any year, hundreds of mediocre volumes of prose and poetry by white writers are published, little noted, and forgotten. At the same time, the few creative works by black writers are seized and dissected and, if not deemed of the "highest" literary quality, condemned as still more examples of the failure of black writers to scale the rare heights of literature. And the condemnation is especially strong for those black works which have not screened their themes of suffering, redemption and triumph behind frail façades of obscurity and conscious "universality."

Central to the problem of the irreconcilable conflict between the black writer and the white critic is the failure of recognition of a fundamental and obvious truth of American life—that the two races are residents of two separate and naturally antagonistic worlds. No manner of well-meaning rhetoric about "one country" and "one people," and even about the two races' long joint-occupancy of this troubled land, can obliterate the high, thick dividing walls which hate and history have erected—and maintain—between them. The breaking down of those barriers might be a goal, worthy or unworthy (depending on viewpoint), but the reality remains. The world of the black outsider, however much it approximates and parallels and imitates the world of the white insider, by its very nature is inheritor and generator of values and viewpoints which threaten the insiders. The outsiders' world, feeding on its own sources, fecundates and vibrates, stamping its progeny with its very special ethos, its insuperably logical bias.

The black writer, like the black artist generally, has wasted much time and talent denying a propensity every rule of human dignity demands that he possess, seeking an identity that can only do violence to his sense of self. Black Americans are, for all practical purposes, colonized in their native land, and it can be argued that those who would submit to subjection without struggle deserve to be enslaved. It is one thing to accept the guiding principles on which the American republic ostensibly was founded; it is quite another thing to accept the prevailing practices which violate those principles.

The rebellion in the streets is the black ghetto's response to the vast distance between the nation's principles and its practices. But that rebellion has roots which are deeper than most white people know; it is many-veined, and its blood has been sent pulsating to the very heart of black life. Across this country, young black men and women have been infected with a fever of affirmation. They are saying, "We are black and beautiful," and the ghetto is reacting with a liberating shock of realization which transcends mere chauvinism. They are rediscovering their heritage and their history, seeing it with newly focused eyes, struck with the wonder of that strength which has enabled them to endure and, in spirit, to defeat the power of prolonged and calculated oppression. After centuries of being told, in a million different ways, that they were not beautiful, and that whiteness of skin, straightness of hair, and aquilineness of features constituted the only measures of beauty, black people have revolted. The trend has not yet reached the point of avalanche, but the future can be clearly seen in the growing number of black people who are snapping off the shackles of imitation and are wearing their skin, their hair, and their features "natural" and with pride. In a poem called "Nittygritty," which is dedicated to poet LeRoi Jones, Joseph Bevans Bush put the new credo this way:

> . . . We all gonna come from behind
>   those
> Wigs and start to stop using those
> Standards of beauty which can never
> Be a frame for our reference; wash
> That excess grease out of our hair,
> Come out of that bleach bag and get
> Into something meaningful to us as
> Nonwhite people—Black people . . .

If the poem lacks the resonances of William Shakespeare, that is intentional. The "great bard of Avon" has only limited relevance to the revolutionary spirit raging in the ghetto. Which is not to say that the black revolutionaries reject the "universal" statements inherent in Shakespeare's works; what they do reject, however, is the literary assumption that the style and language and the concerns of Shakespeare establish the appropriate limits and "frame of reference" for black poetry and people. This is above and beyond the doctrine of revolution to which so many of the brighter black intellectuals are committed, that philosophy articulated by the late Frantz Fanon which holds that, in the time of revolutionary struggle, the traditional Western liberal ideals are not merely irrelevant but they must be assiduously opposed. The young writers of the black ghetto have set out in search of a black aesthetic, a system of isolating and evaluating the artistic works of black people which reflect the special character and imperatives of black experience.

That was the meaning and intent of poet-playwright LeRoi Jones' aborted Black Arts Theater in Harlem in 1965, and it is the generative idea behind such later groups and institutions as Spirit House in Newark, the Black House in San Francisco, the New School of Afro-American Thought in Washington, D.C., the Institute for Black Studies in Los Angeles, Forum '66 in Detroit, and the Organization of Black American Culture in Chicago. It is a serious quest, and the black writers themselves are well aware of the possibility that what they seek is, after all, beyond codifying. They are fully aware of the dual nature of their heritage, and of the subtleties and complexities; but they are even more aware of the terrible reality of their outsideness, of their political and economic powerlessness, and of the desperate racial need for unity. And they have been convinced, over and over again, by the irrefutable facts of history and by the cold intransigence of the privileged white majority that the road to solidarity and strength leads inevitably through reclamation and indoctrination of black art and culture.

In Chicago, the Organization of Black American Culture has moved boldly toward a definition of a black aesthetic. In the writers' workshop sponsored by the group, the writers are deliberately striving to invest their work with the distinctive styles and rhythms and colors of the ghetto, with those peculiar qualities which, for example, characterize the music of a John Coltrane or a Charlie Parker or a Ray Charles. Aiming toward the publication of an anthology which will manifest this aesthetic, they have established criteria by which they measure their own work and eliminate from consideration those poems, short stories, plays, essays and sketches which do not adequately reflect the black experience. What the sponsors of the workshop most hope for in this delicate and dangerous experiment is the emergence of new black critics who will be able to articulate and expound the new aesthetic and eventually set in motion the long overdue assault against the restrictive assumptions of the white critics.

It is not that the writers of OBAC have nothing to start with. That there exists already a mystique of blackness even some white critics will agree. In the November 1967 issue of *Esquire* magazine, for instance, George Frazier, a white writer who is not in the least sympathetic with the likes of LeRoi Jones, nevertheless did a commendable job of identifying elements of the black mystique. Discussing "the Negro's immense style, a style so seductive that it's little wonder that black men are, as Shakespeare put it in *The Two Gentlemen of Verona,* 'pearls in beauteous ladies' eyes,'" Mr. Frazier singled out the following examples;

"The formal daytime attire (black sack coats and striped trousers) the Modern Jazz Quartet wore when appearing in concert; the lazy amble with which Jimmy Brown used to return to the huddle; the delight the late "Big Daddy" Lipscomb took in making sideline tackles in full view of the crowd and the way, after crushing a ball carrier to the ground, he would chivalrously assist him to his feet; the constant cool of 'Satchel' Paige; the chic of Bobby Short; the incomparable grace of John Bubbles—things like that are style and they have nothing whatsoever to do with ability (although the ability, God wot, is there, too). It is not that there are no white men with style, for there is Fred Astaire, for one, and Cary Grant, for another, but that there are so very, very few of them. Even in the dock, the black man has an air about him—Adam Clayton Powell, so blithe, so self-possessed, so casual, as contrasted with Tom Dodd, sanctimonious, whining, an absolute disgrace. What it is that made Miles Davis and Cassius Clay, Sugar Ray Robinson and Archie Moore and Ralph Ellison and Sammy Davis, Jr. seem so special was their style. . . .

"And then, of course, there is our speech.

"For what nuances, what plays of light and shade, what little sharpnesses our speech has are almost all of them, out of the black world—the talk of Negro musicians and whores and hoodlums and whatnot. 'Cool' and all the other words in common currency came out of the mouths of Negroes.

"'We love you madly,' said Duke Ellington, and now the phrase is almost a cliché. But it is a quality of the Negro's style—that he is forever creative, forever more stylish. There was a night when, as I stood with Duke Ellington outside the Hickory House, I looked up at the sky and said, 'I hope it's a good day tomorrow. I want to wake up early.'

"'Any day I wake up,' said Ellington, 'is a good day.'

"And that was style."

Well, yes. . . .

Black critics have the responsibility of approaching the works of black writers assuming these qualities to be present, and with the knowledge that white readers—and white critics—cannot be expected to recognize and to emphathize with the subtleties and significance of black style and technique. They have the responsibility of rebutting the white critics and of putting things in the proper perspective. Within the past few years, for example, Chicago's white critics have given the backs of their hands to worthy works by black playwrights, part of their criticism directly attributable to their ignorance of the intricacies of black style and black life. Oscar Brown, Jr.'s rockingly soulful *Kicks and Company* was panned for many of the wrong reasons; and Douglas Turner Ward's two plays, *Day of Absence* and *Happy Ending,* were tolerated as labored and a bit tasteless. Both Brown and Ward had dealt satirically with race relations, and there were not many black people in the audiences who found themselves in agreement with the critics. It is the way things are—but not the way things will continue to be if the OBAC writers and those similarly concerned elsewhere in America have anything to say about it.

Cultural Strangulation: Black Literature
and the White Aesthetic

This assumption that of all the hues of God, whiteness is inherently and obviously better than
brownness or tan leads to curious acts.
W. E. B. Du Bois

The expected opposition to the concept of a "Black Aesthetic" was not long in coming. In separate reviews of *Black Fire,* an anthology edited by LeRoi Jones and Larry Neal, critics from the Saturday Review and the New York Review of Books presented the expected rebuttal. Agreeing with Ralph Ellison that sociology and art are incompatible mates, these critics, nevertheless, invoked the clichés of the social ideology of the "we shall overcome" years in their attempt to steer Blacks from "the path of literary fantasy and folly."

Their major thesis is simple: There is no Black aesthetic because there is no white aesthetic. The Kerner Commission Report to the contrary, America is not two societies but one. Therefore, Americans of all races, colors and creeds share a common cultural heredity. This is to say that there is one predominant culture—the American culture—with tributary national and ethnic streams flowing into the larger river. Literature, the most important by-product of this cultural monolith, knows no parochial boundaries. To speak of a Black literature, a Black aesthetic, or a Black state, is to engage in racial chauvinism, separatist bias, and Black fantasy.

The question of a white aesthetic, however, is academic. One has neither to talk about it nor define it. Most Americans, black and white, accept the existence of a "White Aesthetic" as naturally as they accept April 15th as the deadline for paying their income tax—with far less animosity towards the former than the latter. The white aesthetic, despite the academic critics, has always been with us: for long before Diotima pointed out the way to heavenly beauty to Socrates, the poets of biblical times were discussing beauty in terms of light and dark—the essential characteristics of a white and black aesthetic—and establishing the dichotomy of superior *vs.* inferior which would assume body and form in the 18th century. Therefore, more serious than a definition, is the problem of tracing the white aesthetic from its early origins and afterwards, outlining the various changes in the basic formula from culture to culture and from nation to nation. Such an undertaking would be more germane to a book than an essay; nevertheless, one may take a certain starting point

From *The Black Aesthetic,* ed. Addison Gayle Jr. (Garden City, N.Y.: Doubleday, 1971).

and, using selective nations and cultures, make the critical point, while calling attention to the necessity of a more comprehensive study encompassing all of the nations and cultures of the world.

Let us propose Greece as the logical starting point, bearing in mind Will Durant's observation that "all of Western Civilization is but a footnote to Plato," and take Plato as the first writer to attempt a systematic aesthetic. Two documents by Plato, *The Symposium* and *The Republic,* reveal the twin components of Plato's aesthetic system.

In *The Symposium,* Plato divides the universe into spheres. In one sphere, the lower, one finds the forms of beauty; in the other, the higher, beauty, as Diotima tells Socrates, is absolute and supreme. In *The Republic,* Plato defines the poet as an imitator (a third-rate imitator—a point which modern critics have long since forgotten) who reflects the heavenly beauty in the earthly mirror. In other words, the poet recreates beauty as it exists in heaven; thus the poet, as Neo-Platonists from Aquinas to Coleridge have told us, is the custodian of beauty on earth.

However, Plato defines beauty only in ambiguous, mystical terms; leaving the problem of a more circumscribed, secular definition to philosophers, poets, and critics. During most of the history of the Western world, these aestheticians have been white; therefore, it is not surprising that, symbolically and literally, they have defined beauty in terms of whiteness. (An early contradiction to this tendency is the Marquis DeSade who inverted the symbols, making black beautiful, but demonic, and white pure, but sterile—the Marquis is considered by modern criticism to have been mentally deranged.)

The distinction between whiteness as beautiful (good) and blackness as ugly (evil) appears early in the literature of the middle ages—in the Morality Plays of England. Heavily influenced by both Platonism and Christianity, these plays set forth the distinctions which exist today. To be white was to be pure, good, universal, and beautiful; to be black was to be impure, evil, parochial, and ugly.

The characters and the plots of these plays followed this basic format. The villain is always evil, in most cases the devil; the protagonist, or hero, is always good, in most cases, angels or disciples. The plot then is simple; good (light) triumphs over the forces of evil (dark). As English literature became more sophisticated, the symbols were made to cover wider areas of the human and literary experience. To love was divine; to hate, evil. The fancied mistress of Petrarch was the purest of the pure; Grendel's mother, a creature from the "lower regions and marshes," is, like her son, a monster; the "bad" characters in Chaucer's *Canterbury Tales* tell dark stories; and the Satan of *Paradise Lost* must be vanquished by Gabriel, the angel of purity.

These ancients, as Swift might have called them, established their dichotomies as a result of the influences of Neo-Platonism and Christianity. Later, the symbols became internationalized. Robert Burton, in *The Anatomy of Melancholy,* writes of "dark despair" in the seventeenth century, and James Boswell describes melancholia, that state of mind common to intellectuals of the 17th and 18th centuries, as a dark, dreaded affliction which robbed men of their creative energies. This condition—dark despair or melancholia—was later popularized in what is referred to in English literature as its "dark period"—the period of the Grave Yard School of poets and the Gothic novels.

The symbols thus far were largely applied to conditions, although characters who symbolized evil influences were also dark. In the early stages of English literature, these characters were mythological and fictitious and not representative of people of specific racial or ethnic groups. In the 18th century English novel, however, the symbolism becomes ethnic and racial.

There were forerunners. As early as 1621, Shakespeare has Iago refer to Othello as that "old Black ewe," attaching the mystical sexual characteristic to blackness which would become the motive for centuries of oppressive acts by white Americans. In *The Tempest,* Shakespeare's last play, Caliban, though not ostensibly black, is nevertheless a distant cousin of the colonial Friday in Daniel Defoe's *Robinson Crusoe.*

Robinson Crusoe was published at a historically significant time. In the year 1719, the English had all but completed their colonization of Africa. The slave trade in America was on its way to becoming a booming industry; in Africa, Black people were enslaved mentally as well as physically by such strange bedfellows as criminals, businessmen, and Christians. In the social and political spheres, a rationale was needed, and help came from the artist—in this case, the novelist—in the form of *Robinson Crusoe.* In the novel, Defoe brings together both Christian and Platonic symbolism, sharpening the dichotomy between light and dark on the one hand, while on the other establishing a criterion for the inferiority of Black people as opposed to the superiority of white.

One need only compare Crusoe with Friday to validate both of these statements. Crusoe is majestic, wise, white and a colonialist; Friday is savage, ignorant, black and a colonial. Therefore, Crusoe, the colonialist, has a double task. On the one hand he must transform the island (Africa—unproductive, barren, dead) into a little England (prosperous, life-giving, fertile), and he must recreate Friday in his own image, thus bringing him as close to being an Englishman as possible. At the end of the novel, Crusoe has accomplished both undertakings; the island is a replica of "mother England"; and Friday has been transformed into a white man, now capable of immigrating to the land of the gods.

From such mystical artifacts has the literature and criticism of the Western world sprung; and based upon such narrow prejudices as those of Defoe, the art of Black people throughout the world has been described as parochial and inferior. Friday was parochial and inferior until, having denounced his own culture, he assimilated another. Once this was done, symbolically, Friday underwent a change. To deal with him after the conversion was to deal with him in terms of a character who have been civilized and therefore had moved beyond racial parochialism.

However, Defoe was merely a hack novelist, not a thinker. It was left to shrewder minds than his to apply the rules of the white aesthetic to the practical areas of the Black literary and social worlds, and no shrewder minds were at work on this problem than those of writers and critics in America. In America, the rationale for both slavery and the inferiority of Black art and culture was supplied boldly, without the trappings of 18th century symbolism.

In 1867, in a book entitled *Nojoque: A Question for a Continent,* Hinton Helper provided the vehicle for the cultural and social symbols of inferiority under which Blacks have labored in this country. Helper intended, as he states frankly in his preface, "to write the negro out of America." In the headings of the two major chapters of the book, the whole symbolic apparatus of the white aesthetic handed down from Plato to America is graphically revealed: the heading of one chapter reads: "Black: A Thing of Ugliness, Disease"; another heading reads: "White: A Thing of Life, Health, and Beauty."

Under the first heading, Helper argues that the color black "has always been associated with sinister things such as mourning, the devil, the darkness of night." Under the second, "White has always been associated with the light of day, divine transfiguration, the beneficient moon and stars . . . the fair complexion of romantic ladies, the costumes of Romans and angels, and the white of the American flag so beautifully combined with blue and red without ever a touch of the black that has been for the flag of pirates."

Such is the American critical ethic based upon centuries of distortion of the Platonic ideal. By not adequately defining beauty, and implying at least that this was the job of the poet, Plato laid the foundation for the white aesthetic as defined by Daniel Defoe and Hinton Helper. However, the uses of that aesthetic to stifle and strangle the cultures of other nations is not to be attributed to Plato but, instead, to his hereditary brothers far from the Aegean. For Plato knew his poets. They were not, he surmised, a very trusting lot and, therefore, by adopting an ambiguous position on symbols, he limited their power in the realm of aesthetics. For Plato, there were two kinds of symbols: natural and proscriptive. Natural symbols corresponded to absolute beauty as created by God; proscriptive symbols, on the other hand, were symbols of beauty as proscribed by man, which is to say that certain symbols are said to mean such and such by man himself.

The irony of the trap in which the Black artist has found himself throughout history is apparent. Those symbols which govern his life and art are proscriptive ones, set down by minds as diseased as Hinton Helper's. In other words, beauty has been in the eyes of an earthly beholder who has stipulated that beauty conforms to such and such a definition. To return to Friday, Defoe stipulated that civilized man was what Friday had to become, proscribed certain characteristics to the term "civilized," and presto, Friday, in order not to be regarded as a "savage under Western eyes," was forced to conform to this ideal. How well have the same stipulative definitions worked in the artistic sphere! Masterpieces are made at will by each new critic who argues that the subject of his doctoral dissertation is immortal. At one period of history, John Donne, according to the critic Samuel Johnson, is a second rate poet; at another period, according to the critic T. S. Eliot, he is one of the finest poets in the language. Dickens, argues Professor Ada Nisbet, is one of England's most representative novelists, while for F. R. Leavis, Dickens' work does not warrant him a place in *The Great Tradition.*

When Black literature is the subject, the verbiage reaches the height of the ridiculous. The good "Negro Novel," we are told by Robert Bone and Herbert Hill, is that novel in which the subject matter moves beyond the limitations of narrow parochialism. Form is the most important criterion of the work of art when Black literature is evaluated, whereas form, almost non-existent in Dostoyevsky's *Crime and Punishment,* and totally chaotic in Kafka's *The Trial,* must take second place to the supremacy of thought and message.

Richard Wright, says Theodore Gross, is not a major American novelist; while Ralph Ellison, on the strength of one novel, is. LeRoi Jones is not a major poet, Ed Bullins not a major playwright, Baldwin incapable of handling the novel form—all because white critics have said so.

Behind the symbol is the object or vehicle, and behind the vehicle is the definition. It is the definition with which we are concerned, for the extent of the cultural strangulation of Black literature by white critics has been the extent to which they have been allowed to define the terms in which the Black artist will deal with his own experience. The career of Paul Laurence Dunbar is the most striking example. Having internalized the definitions handed him by the American society, Dunbar would rather not have written about the Black experience at all, and three of his novels and most of his poetry support this argument. However, when forced to do so by his white liberal mentors, among them was the powerful critic, William Dean Howells, Dunbar deals with Blacks in terms of buffoonery, idiocy and comedy.

Like so many Black writers, past and present, Dunbar was trapped by the definitions of other men, never capable of realizing until near the end of his life, that those definitions were not god-given, but man-given; and so circumscribed by tradition and culture that they were irrelevant to an evaluation of either his life or his art.

In a literary conflict involving Christianity, Zarathustra, Friedrich Nietzsche's iconoclast, calls for "a new table of the laws." In similar iconoclastic fashion, the proponents of a Black Aesthetic, the idol smashers of America, call for a set of rules by which Black literature and art is to be judged and evaluated. For the historic practice of bowing to other men's gods and definitions has produced a crisis of the highest magnitude, and brought us, culturally, to the limits of racial armageddon. The trend must be reversed.

The acceptance of the phrase "Black is Beautiful" is the first step in the destruction of the old table of the laws and the construction of new ones, for the phrase flies in the face of the whole ethos of the white aesthetic. This step must be followed by serious scholarship and hard work; and Black critics must dig beneath the phrase and unearth the treasure of beauty lying deep in the untoured regions of the Black experience—regions where others, due to historical conditioning and cultural deprivation, cannot go.

STEPHEN E. HENDERSON

The Question of Form and Judgement in Contemporary Black American Poetry: 1962–1977

For one reason or another, the question of how to judge a Black poem has been fudged, blurred, evaded, or ignored. Now that the spectacular Black Arts Movement seems to have run its course, the question of evaluation takes on crucial importance. Among the signs that the movement is over, or is entering a new phase, are the demise of *Black World* magazine, the most important cultural periodical of the Black Consciousness Movement: the intensified sniping by scholars, Black and white, who disagreed with the idea of a Black Aesthetic; the systematic efforts by white scholars either to blunt, appropriate, or discredit the artistic achievements of the sixties, and their attendant critical justifications; and the defection of important writers to other camps, both aesthetic and political.

Although sniping at the Black Aesthetic is not new, its critics have not relented. In some instances, the concern is largely scholarly, as in the case of Arthur P. Davis, for example. In others, it is essentially polemical. Whether scholarly or not, reactions to the Black Aesthetic rest overtly or implicitly on a political base. At any rate, no one can accuse Prof. Davis of inconsistency, for throughout his long and distinguished career he has made plain his views on integration, on American literature, and the role which Black writers have played in shaping that literature. Yet the achievement of *From the Dark Tower,* 1974, his recent admirable history, is marred by his failure to grapple with the hard issues raised by the Black Aesthetic. He lumps all of the critics together, calls them honorable men, but asserts that to date they have failed either to destroy the white aesthetic or to erect another in its place. So, then, the question remains a matter of ranking authors according to their craftsmanship, their thematic concerns, in historical and social context, or the size of their output. Prof. Davis solves the problem of judgment by avoidance or oversimplication.

Another example of scholarly fudging is found in Robert Rosenblatt's recent book *Black Fiction.* He disposes of the problem of judgment by a retreat into formalism. The social issues are not important—technique is technique and pattern is pattern. Although he discusses fiction, not poetry, many of the issues are the same. Professor Rosenblatt solves the problem of judgment by ignoring it.

From *A Dark and Sudden Beauty: Two Essays in Black American Poetry* by George Kent and Stephen Henderson, ed. Houston A. Baker Jr. (Philadelphia: Afro-American Studies Program, University of Pennsylvania, 1977).

In Helen Vendler's review of a series of Broadside books for the *New York Times Book Review,* September 29, 1974, liberal sympathy is tempered by unconscious liberal condescension which reveals an essential ignorance of the issues involved in the Black Aesthetic in general and in the evaluation of Black poetry in particular. After praising the range and variety of Black "verse" and the pioneering role of Dudley Randall, she expresses the fond hope that in the future some single giant Black poet will unite all of those varied threads and themes in one single giant voice—as Whitman did, for example, for the American nation. What she fails to realize is that the Black epic voice is collective and communal, and it has already achieved what she speaks of, though in forms, perhaps, which she doesn't understand or recognize—in the tales and the spirituals especially, but also in the worksongs and the blues. Prof. Vendler also solves the problem of judgment by oversimplification.

Not so the editors of the *Saturday Review.* They solve it by overkill. In their infamous issue of November 15, 1975, devoted to "The Arts in Black America," the intent is clearly political, clearly designed to give a *coup de grace* to the Black Arts Movement. The article, written by Robert F. Moss, describes the state of the arts in Black America in pathological and racist terms. It links the political problems of FESTAC and the Nigerian government with the author's views on Black art in general. Of the Black Aesthetic, he predicts that it seems "destined to produce more heat than light." But one important by-product, he asserts, has been the building of Black audiences, presumably for legitimate art, that by whites or based on white models. Matters of "form and style" in Black art, he states, "have not really been ignored so much as they have been translated into ethnic terms, and in some cases thoroughly politicized. Black verse is perhaps the most obvious example." (p. 15) He continues: "The elder statesmen among black poets—notably Robert Hayden, Melvin B. Tolson, and Gwendolyn Brooks—achieved recognition from the literary establishment by adjusting their timbre and rhythms, their style and vocabulary, to the requirements of mainstream verse, although their subject matter was sometimes racial. Perhaps the last important 'accommodationist' was Baraka, a competent beat poet who was beached by the receding currents of that short-lived movement in the early sixties. Taking the techniques of Ginsberg & Company—a declamatory voice, deliberate formlessness, street language— and fusing them to virulent outbursts of racial protest, Baraka was able to found a new school of black poetry." (pp. 15, 16.)

It should be apparent that Moss would not think very highly of that poetry. Speaking of technical matters, Moss states:

> Baraka-ites such as Don L. Lee, Nikki Giovanni, Sonia Sanchez, and David Anderson profess to have tossed every scrap of whitey's *ars poetica*—along with his "diseased civilization"—onto the cultural bonfire. In its place they have introduced black consciousness, carefully equipped with a black literary technique to articulate it correctly. In practice this usually means a free use of obscenities (especially the omnipresent m-f), ghetto slang, phonetic spellings, typographical hijinks *a la* Cummings, a striving after oral effects, and a tone of voice pitched at megaphone level. (p 16)

After examining examples of "verse" that he disagrees with from Carolyn Rodgers, Don Lee and Baraka, Moss concludes his observations on Black literary technique with the following:

> Beyond this, there is a taste for black word games like "playing the Dozens" and "Signifying." Such is the route favored by Ishmael Reed, though he is better known as a novelist than as a poet. A devout follower of William Burroughs' comic surrealism with generous helpings of black folklore, pop culture, and ghetto sociology. Despite its imitativeness, his writing has a creative energy and a stylistic reach that is beyond most black writers today. (p. 17)

An analysis of these views and others will be made later in this essay. Suffice it to say at present that Prof. Moss repeats most of the cliches which critics of Black art, especially of the poetry, have made for some time. He adds a special virulence couched in the self-satisfaction of one who feels that he has done his homework and who knows, in addition, that his views have the editorial support of a powerful and influential periodical. That does not, of course, make them either accurate or important.

A further sign of reaction to the Black Consciousness Movement can be seen in another recent book by a white scholar—*Folklore in Nigerian Literature,* 1973, by Bernth Lindfors. Lindfors' book is relevant to our discussion for several reasons: (a) the aggressive, defensive tone of the introduction; (b) the rejection of white critics of their literature by both African and Afro-American critics; and (c) the theoretical implications of some of the chapters, especially the two listed under "Critical Perspectives" (p. 6, p. 23) and the one under "Rhetoric," entitled "Characteristics of Yoruba and Ibo Prose Styles in English." (p. 153).

Like numerous other white critics of "black" literature, Lindfors is concerned about the "territorial imperative" which Black critics asserted during the sixties. Lindfors quotes a statement which I made in *The Militant Black Writer,* 1969, that "despite the proliferation of 'experts,' whites are unable to evaluate the Black Experience, and, consequently, any work of art derived from it or addressed to those who live it." He adds: "Whites should therefore abandon the field to blacks, who are innately better qualified to understand and appreciate their own literature." (p. 1)

Lindfors calls attention to a similar rejection of white critics by African writers. Then he proceeds to some tacky logic and linguistic sleight of hand. "While these statements condemning the incompetence of white critics are not as extreme as those heard in America today, they do point in the same racial direction: black critics are acclaimed as the best possible interpreters of their own literature." (p. 1) And Prof. Lindfors gives what he calls the "standard reply" to these views.

> A favorite tactic is to reverse the argument by asking "Should all the black critics—and this includes Africans as well as Afro-Americans and teachers and professors of literature throughout the world—be given a similar 'hands off' ultimatum on non-black writing?"

"An affirmative answer to this question," Lindfors concludes, "would be very hard to justify." And, one might add, hardly worth the time.

The reactions cited above have one important common factor: They substitute for the question "How does one judge a Black poem?" the related, question "*Who* is to judge a Black poem?" While the substitution reveals a great deal about those who make it, it nonetheless leaves the prior question unanswered. To repeat, then, How does one judge a Black poem?

Curiously, very few answers were given to that question during the sixties. The responses among Blacks tended to be mystical, ideological, defensive, or hostile. Among whites, they tended and still tend to be condescending, defensive or preemptive, when not narrowly or naively academic. At any rate, there has been poor and uninformed criticism written by Blacks and whites alike. And, conversely, there has been on occasion, some useful criticism by Blacks, less frequently by whites. (A major exception is the important study of Baraka, *The Renegade and the Mask,* 1976, by Kimberly Benston.) Older Black poets and poets who are not Nationalists have stated that they would rather be reviewed by a good white critic than by a poor Black one. And writers as diverse as Frank Marshall Davis, Robert Hayden, and Clarence Major have said that they were not especially writing for a Black audience.

To begin with, the question of judgment is tied up with the question of definition. What is a Black poem? What is Black poetry. In *Understanding the New Black Poetry,* Morrow, 1973, I made an approach to that question in a series of statements, which I repeat below. These statements may be approached in an historical or empirical manner. In either case, one could say with varying degrees of validity that Black poetry is chiefly:

> Any poetry by any person or group of persons of known Black African ancestry, whether the poetry is designated Black or not.
>
> Poetry which is somehow *structurally* Black, irrespective of authorship.
>
> Poetry by any person or group of known Black African ancestry, which is *also identifiably* Black, in terms of structure, theme or other characteristics.
>
> Poetry by any identifiably Black person who can be classed as a "poet" by Black people. Judgment may or may not coincide with judgments of whites.
>
> Poetry by any identifiably Black person whose ideological stance vis-a-vis history and the aspirations of his people since slavery is adjudged by them to be "correct." (p. 7)

Since an empirical approach has the advantage of historical anchorage and verifiability, let us place that perspective on the foregoing statements. Again, since I have discussed the implications of these statements in *Understanding the New Black Poetry,* I shall not pursue them here. Nevertheless, when the statements are examined from this perspective one must consider the following items: (a) *What the record or canon says,* (b) *What the poets say,* (c) *What the reader/audience/critic says,* and (d) *The notion of standards and evaluation.* In the following pages, I shall address each of these items in some detail.

a. *What the record reveals* is a rich tradition of both oral and written poetry which is usefully designated the folk and the formal. In the United States the oral traditions go back to the emergence of distinctive Afro-American verbal expression—the field cries and hollers, work songs, ballads, spirituals, sermons and blues. The size of this literature though not so complex as that of the West Indies or Africa is enormous. John Lovell, Jr. estimates the number of spirituals alone at over 10,000, with no way of knowing how many were not recorded. The tradition continues today in children's songs, in rapping, the dozens and its contemporary descendants, in the sermon, and in gospel and pop songs at their best. But gospel and pop songs are individually composed and written down, so here the oral tradition merges with that of the formal literary tradition. The literary tradition itself dates back to Lucy Terry's *Bars Fight,* 1746, a long ballad of historical rather than literary merit, and to Jupiter Hammon and Phillis Wheatley.

The nineteenth century produced dozens of published poets, some of significant talent. Notable among them were George Moses Horton, Charles L. Reason, Frances E. W. Harper, and Alberry A. Whitman. An introduction to these writers can be obtained from Benjamin Brawley's *Early American Negro Writers;* William H. Robinson's *Early Black American Poets;* Sterling A. Brown's *Negro Poetry and Drama,* and *The Negro Caravan* edited with Arthur P. Davis and Ulysses Lee. An important work in this area is Joan Sherman's recent book *The Invisible Poets.* In addition, there are individual volumes which are listed in Sherman's bibliographies and in checklists by Arthur Schomburg and Dorothy L. Porter.

Paul Laurence Dunbar, W. E. B. Du Bois, and James Weldon Johnson open the twentieth century. Their work was followed by Langston Hughes, Claude McKay, Jean Toomer, Sterling Brown, Countee Cullen, and the various poets of the New Negro Movement. The next generation produced Margaret Walker, Owen Dodson, Gwendolyn Brooks, Robert Hayden, and others. Some of these poets were active in the fifties and the sixties. And, of course, the 1960's produced a veritable explosion of Black poetry, with such notable names as Amiri Baraka, Larry Neal, Sonia Sanchez, Nikki Giovanni, Don L. Lee (Haki Madhubuti) and others. Much of the work of this period has probably never been published so no one has a complete picture of the phenomenon. Notwithstanding, one can easily acquaint himself with this poetry by reading the individual volumes published by Broadside Press, Paul Bremen Press, and by major publications such as *The Journal of Black Poetry; Liberator; Negro Digest/Black World; Soul Book; Black Creations,* and *Umbra.* Some journals had limited, regional circulation, such as college publications like *Ex Umbra.* Some poets printed their works themselves. Many of these are listed in *Negro Digest/Black World.* Other sources include useful anthologies such as *Soul Script,* June Jordan; *Dices and Black Bones,* Adam David Miller; *Natural Process,* Tom Weatherly and Ted Willenz; *Understanding the New Black Poetry,* S. E. Henderson; *The Black Poets,* Dudley Randall; *The New Black Poetry,* Clarence Major. Current publishers of Black poetry include *First World, Essence, Black Arts South, Yardbird Reader, Black Books Bulletin,* etc. In addition, Black poetry is being published at workshops, on campuses, etc., as well as by white publishers. At any rate, this brief account merely hints at the corpus of poetry produced by Black Americans. To this (if one were talking about the entire range of modern Black poetry) could be added the poetry published in English by Caribbean and African poets living in the United States. Less tenable, but logical, would be the addition of all poetry in English by Africans on the continent and in the Dispersion. While that could be done and, eventually, must be done, the problem of focus would thereby be greatly increased. Thus for the purpose of this study, Black poetry must be studied in historical context—with Black people in the United States as the focus. The justification for this is simple. Modern Black formal poetry has existed longer in the United States than it has in Africa or the West Indies (Cf. Jahn, *Neo-African Literature,* p. 50, Table 1). In addition, the poetry of the Harlem Renaissance helped stimulate the flowering of modern Black Poetry in Africa, Europe and the West Indies, during the Negritude Movement. With that in mind, one could still benefit from studying work produced in Africa and the West Indies, not only in English, but in Portuguese, French, Dutch, Spanish as well as the various African languages. Conversely, any serious and extended study of the oral tradition of Afro-American poetry must recognize the vast resources of that tradition in Africa and the West Indies. This includes not only traditional materials but popular contemporary expression as well.

b. *What the poets say.* Historically, the question of what constitutes a Black poem or how to judge one does not really come to a head until the 1960's and the promulgation of the Black Aesthetic in literature and the other arts. In a special sense, then, "Black" poetry was invented in the 1960's along with the radicalization of the word "Black" and the emergence of the Black Power philosophy. From the beginning, however, there were problems of definition, contradiction, ideology, and taste, resulting from differences in personal background and in political and cultural orientation. In the January, 1968 issue of *Negro Digest,* Hoyt Fuller, the Executive Editor, conducted a survey of the opinions of 38 Black writers on some 25 questions which included the following:

> Do you see any future at all for the school of black writers which seeks to establish 'a black aesthetic'?

> Do you believe that the black writer's journey toward 'Art' should lead consciously and deliberately through exploitation of 'the black experience'?

> Should black writers direct their work toward black audiences?

Some older writers, like Robert Hayden, felt that a writer's chief concern should be with the truth of all people everywhere. Others stressed craftsmanship and felt that writers should write to be read. Others felt enthusiastically that they should write about what they knew best, themselves and their people. There was, in effect, no simple consensus as to what Black writing was, could be, or should be, though there was fairly general agreement that Black writers should write about Black people, for Black people, and sometimes for sympathetic whites. Some younger writers were immersed in the self-consciousness of other "modern" writers; others still were rigidly nationalistic. The split among the younger writers was best exemplified in an exchange between Ron Karenga, of US and James Cunningham, of OBAC. Their views were polar. Karenga set forth his famous and influential dicta that literature must be functional, collective, and committing, and must support the Revolution. Cunningham felt that the writer should be free to express himself.

Perhaps the most insightful statement in the *Negro Digest* survey was made by Larry Neal. On the question of the Black Aesthetic, he said:

> There is no need to establish a "black aesthetic." Rather, it is important to understand that one already exists. The question is: where does it exist? And what do we

do with it. Further, there is something distasteful about a formalized aesthetic. This is what the so-called New Critics never understood. Essentially, art is relevant when it makes you stronger. (p. 35).

In that opening statement Neal not only demonstrated an understanding of the aesthetic questions under discussion but also an extensive grasp of the roots of Afro-American art, thereby linking up with a tradition of "criticism" which includes James Weldon Johnson, W. E. B. Du Bois, Alain Locke, and Sterling Brown. That was an important linkage, for it not only insured historical continuity but kept the field of discussion open to a wide range of approaches. At the same time that it claimed for the poet much of the personal freedom which Cunningham advocated, it insisted on the wider dedication advocated by Ron Karenga. But this was done with a greater degree of subtlety, as, for example in his sensitive understanding of the blues and the central importance of the Black Church.

c. *The Reader/Critic/Audience.* Specifically, the question of the poet's audience was crucial to the sixties. It was encapsulated in the *Negro Digest* survey. The response ranged from Karenga's paraphrase of Senghor that art is "functional, collective and committing or committed," to Gwendolyn Brooks' shrewd comment that Black writers "should concern themselves with TRUTH." Truth should be put upon paper. That phrase, 'direct their work,' she said in reference to the questionnaire, "suggests a secret contempt for the intelligence of the black audience" (p. 29). Some other writers hedged their bets, writing for ideal audiences, or for anyone who would buy their books. But the question was not altogether new, nor the consciousness. Langston Hughes had said to a similar question posed in 1927 by *Crisis* magazine, "We younger Negro artists who create now intend to express our individual dark-skinned selves without fear or shame. If white people are pleased we are glad. If they are not, it doesn't matter. We know we are beautiful. And ugly too. The tom-tom cries and the tom-tom laughs. If colored people are pleased we are glad. If they are not, their displeasure doesn't matter either. We build our temples for tomorrow, strong as we know how, and we stand on top of the mountain, free within ourselves" ("The Negro Artist and the Racial Mountain"). What is often overlooked in this passage is an individualism that borders on "Art for Art's sake."

But Langston Hughes also pioneered some of the techniques of direct audience communication which were to become popular in the sixties. His readings with jazz accompaniment, his strong sense of the aural tradition, of the preacher and the musician, of the oral tradition of the raconteur and the rapper, provided a strong model. So that Larry Neal was to say in the sixties:

To explore the black experience means that we do not deny the reality and the power of the slave culture; the culture that produced the blues, spirituals, folk songs, work songs, and "jazz." It means that Afro-American life and its myriad of styles are expressed and examined in the fullest, most truthful manner possible. The models for what Black literature should be are found primarily in our folk culture, especially in the blues and jazz. Further models exist in the word-magic of James Brown, Wilson Pickett, Stevie Wonder, Sam Cooke, and Aretha Franklin. Have you ever heard a Black poet scream like James Brown? I mean, we should want to have that kind of energy in our work. The kind of energy that informs the music of John Coltrane,

Cecil Taylor, Albert Ayler, and Sun Ra—the modern equivalent of the ancient ritual energy. An energy that demands to be heard, and which no one can ignore. Energy to shake us out of our lethargy and free our bodies and minds, opening us to unrealized possibilities. (*Negro Digest,* p. 81)

Again at this point one sees Neal's understanding of and linkage to the tradition of W. E. B. Du Bois, James Weldon Johnson, Langston Hughes, Sterling Brown, and Richard Wright. He adds two dimensions: popular music and African ritual. The crucial insight is the realization of Black oral expression as a continuum—in fact, oral expression as part of the larger global continuum of Black expressive culture.

Central to that continuum are music and dance. Small wonder then that when Black poets described what they were trying to do they used the language of these arts. Small wonder still that readers who conceived of poetry in Euro-American terms were unable to come to grips with the new Black poetry. This was true of some older Blacks as well as many white professional critics. Again, that should have surprised no one, for the history of the criticism of Black music and dance is a systematic attempt to deny the originality, the power, and the ultimate worth of those forms also. Thus Robert Moss and the others have their tradition too, of denial, presumption, subversion, and neglect.

The beauty and power of Black American poetry, notwithstanding these negative views, have long been recognized. Among the first to bring the oral tradition to national attention was Colonel Thomas Wentworth Higginson, in an article which appeared in the *Atlantic Monthly,* June, 1867, entitled "Negro Spirituals." He points out the verbal as well as the musical beauty of the songs. His reaction to one of the songs has been quoted by W. E. B. Du Bois, James Weldon Johnson, Sterling Brown and John Lovell, Jr. It is worth quoting again. He stated:

But of all the "spirituals" that which surprised me the most, I think—perhaps because it was that in which external nature furnished the images most directly—was this. With all my experience of their ideal ways of speech, I was startled when first I came on such a flower of poetry in that dark soil:

XVII. I KNOW MOON-RISE

I know moon-rise, I know star-rise,
    Lay dis body down.
I walk in de moonlight, I walk in de starlight,
    To lay dis body down.
I'll walk in de graveyard, I'll walk through de graveyard,
    To lay dis body down.
I'll lie in de grave and stretch out my arms;
    Lay dis body down.
I go to de judgment in de evenin' of de day,
    When I lay dis body down:
And my soul and your soul will meet in de day
    When I lay dis body down.

"I'll lie in de grave and stretch out my arms." Never, it seems to me, since man first lived and suffered, was his infinite longing for peace uttered more plaintively than in that line.

Note Higginson's expression—"their ideal ways of speech." It not only furnishes a corrective to the stereotypes created by the minstrel tradition, but provides an important literary insight. For speech is a chief element of anybody's poetry. And here the manner of the speech is noted in a useful way. We shall return later to this point.

Frequently the words of these songs are referred to as poems, as they are in this study. Their composers are also referred to as poets, by Blacks and whites alike. This practice is found not only in Higginson and others who appreciated the slaves' "ideal ways of speech," but by those who satirized the songs on the minstrel stage, and even, as John Lovell brings to our attention, on the concert stage.

At any rate, the language posed a challenge to the serious collector and the casual listener alike. There were problems of intelligibility and of transcription. Regarding the latter, V. S. Nathanson recounts his difficulty in transcribing a refrain which imitates a wild turkey's gobble. He concludes that "I am aware that no words can express the rich, unctuous, guttural flow of the line, when uttered in perfect time by a full gang at their corn-shucking task."

In "Song of the Slaves," John Mason Brown observes:

> To convey a correct idea of negro pronunciation by ordinary rules of orthography is almost impossible. Combinations that would satisfy the ear would be grotesquely absurd to the eye. The habits of the negro in his pronunciation of English words are not such as minstrelsy would indicate. Just as the French and German characters in our comedies have passed into a conventional form of mispronunciation which the bulk of playgoers firmly believe to be lifelike and true, so have minstrels given permanency to very great mistakes in reproducing negro pronunciation. (*Lippincott's Magazine,* II, Philadelphia, December, 1868, 617–623).

The problem confronted Black scholars and poets also, just as it was to confront poets of the 1960's and the present decade. Paul Laurence Dunbar, for example, wrote in a dialect tradition popularized by whites, although his orthography was more idealized than satirical or fanciful. James Weldon Johnson wrote "coon songs" in the white manner of his time, but later turned to a serious confrontation of the problem of rendering the sounds of Black speech and song. In his two collections of Negro spirituals, *The Book of American Negro Spirituals,* 1925, and *The Second Book of Negro Spirituals,* 1926, he indicated the importance of preserving the original pronunciation of the words, and in the preface to the first volume, he discussed serious questions of dialect, voice timbre, and poetry, with informed sensitivity. Like John Mason Brown before him, he attacks visual grotesqueries masquerading as speech.

> Negro dialect is for many people made unintelligible on the printed page by the absurd practice of devising a clumsy, outlandish, so-called phonetic spelling for words in a dialect story or poem when the regular English spelling represents the very

same sound. Paul Laurance Dunbar did a great deal to reform the writing down of dialect, but since it is more a matter of ear than of rules those who are not intimately familiar with the sounds continue to make the same blunders. (*The Books of American Negro Spirituals,* James Weldon Johnson and J. Rosamond Johnson. Viking Press, 1940, p. 38.)

Later, Johnson spoke thus of his intent and method in his volume *God's Trombones,* 1927. These poems were sermons in the folk manner. He wanted to go beyond the limitations of dialect with its twin stops of pathos and humor. What he wanted was "a form that will express the racial spirit by symbols from within rather than by symbols from without, such as the mere mutilation of English spelling and pronunciation." The form would be "freer and larger than dialect, but which will still hold the racial flavor; a form expressing the imagery, the idioms, the peculiar turns of thought, and the distinctive humor and pathos, too, of the Negro, but which will also be capable of voicing the deepest and highest emotions and aspirations, and allow of the widest range of subjects and the widest scope of treatment." (*The Book of American Negro Poetry,* pp. 41, 42).

But Johnson, like others, was acutely aware of the difficulties involved in developing this form. Earlier, he had said of the spirituals:

What can be said about the poetry of the texts of the Spirituals? Naturally, not so much as can be said about the music. In the use of the English language both the bards and the group worked under limitations that might appear to be hopeless. Many of the lines are less than trite, and irrelevant repetition often becomes tiresome. They are often saved alone by their naivete. And yet there is poetry, and a surprising deal of it in the Spirituals. There is more than ought to be reasonably expected from a forcedly ignorant people working in an absolutely alien language. (*The Book of American Negro Spirituals,* p. 38)

And Thomas W. Talley makes the point with a Black anecdote. Speaking of the secular rhymes, he observes:

When critically measured by the laws and usages governing the best English poetry, Negro Folk Rhymes will probably remind readers of the story of the good brother, who arose solemnly in a Christian praise meeting, and thanked God that he had broken all of the Commandments, but had kept his religion. (*Negro Folk Rhymes,* p. 228.)

Note Johnson's use of the terms "racial spirit" and "racial flavor" as well as the more explicit reference to "imagery," "idioms," and "peculiar turns of thought." Note, too, the humorous but meaningful use of the term "religion" by Talley. To this one might add a remark by an experienced preacher from the folk tradition. When his language was questioned by his self-consciously academic brothers in the seminary, he stated: "A verb is like a nut. You got to crack it to get the goodie out of it." And Sterling Brown reports an encounter with a young minister at Virginia Seminary, in 1923, when he took his first job, teaching English. He was so exacting in his grading that the students called him a "red ink man." The exasperated seminarian said to him one day, "Prof., you run them verbs, and I'll drive the thought." And Brown concedes, "He could drive the thought."

And a few years later James Weldon Johnson wrote the preface to Sterling Brown's masterly first volume of poems *Southern Road*. He said:

> He infused his poetry with genuine characteristic flavor by adopting as his medium the common, racy, living speech of the Negro in certain phases of *real* life. For his raw material he dug down into the deep mine of Negro folk poetry. He found the unfailing sources from which sprang the Negro folk epics and ballads such as "Stagolee," "John Henry," "Casey Jones," "Long Gone John" and others.
>
> But as I said in commenting on his work in *The Book of American Negro Poetry*: he has made more than mere transcriptions of folk poetry, and he has done more than bring to it mere artistry; he has deepened its meanings and multiplied its implications. He has actually absorbed the spirit of his material, made it his own; and without diluting its primitive frankness and raciness, truly re-expressed it with artistry and magnified power. In a word, he has taken this raw material and worked it into original authentic poetry.

In other words, Sterling Brown had achieved the kind of form that Johnson himself had spoken of and had experimented with in *God's Trombones*.

Johnson had singled out other young poets for special mention. Among them were Claude McKay, Jean Toomer, Countee Cullen, and Langston Hughes. Even a cursory examination of their work would reveal a wide range of styles, technique, subject matter, and tone, from the Romantic sonorities of Cullen to the jazzy rhythms of Hughes. Yet they had something in common, their concern with "race" and their response to it. Johnson states, "In their approach to 'race' they are less direct and obvious, less didactic or imploratory; and, too, they are less regardful of the approval or disapprobation of their white environment." ("Preface" to *SR*, xxxvi.)

These statements of Johnson's, taken together with other observations of his, pose most of the larger critical questions of Black poetry, questions of *range, theme, form* and *structure*, and *judgment*. As far as the theme is concerned, that which makes it Black is "race," in his words, "the principal motive of poetry written by Negroes . . ." (xxvi). As for form and structure, they are found in "the deep mine of Negro folk poetry" (xxxvi). Yet he includes the sonnets of Claude McKay and Countee Cullen and the free verse odes of Jean Toomer, all written in "standard English." And we may recall some of the difficulty which Johnson experienced with the language of the spirituals, a difficulty not really unlike that encountered by the white collector John Mason Brown. Not merely the problem of orthography, but of poetic expression. Notwithstanding the beauty of the music, the difficulty of working in an unfamiliar language caused the slaves to produce many lines which "are less than trite, and irrelevant repetition often becomes tiresome. They are often saved alone by their naivete." Yet Johnson makes critical judgments, both of the spirituals, and, as we have seen, of the formal poets, of whom the "Younger Group" received his special blessings.

On what basis was Johnson able to distinguish the excellent from the trite in this vastly varied body of material? Obviously he had some means, some measure, some touchstone that would allow him to accept both the Keatsean lushness of Cullen, the sonorous language of the sermons, and the transcendent simplicity of the spirituals. Johnson himself suggests something of his mechanism, his method, and his consideration in several places, among them the two works previously cited and in his *Autobiography of an Ex-Coloured Man.* The mechanism included a reliance upon the ear rather than the eye, for example, and he states:

> Paul Laurence Dunbar did a great deal to reform the writing down of dialect, but since it is more a matter of ear than of rules those who are not intimately familiar with the sounds continue to make the same blunders.

This reliance upon the ear includes a deep and sympathetic and sensitive knowledge and love of music, not only that of his own people but of other cultures as well. He could thus say with complete assurance of the motif of the spiritual "Go Down Moses" ("Preface," *The Book of American Negro Spirituals,* 13):

> I have termed this music noble, and I do so without qualifications. Take, for example, *Go Down Moses:* there is not a nobler theme in the whole musical literature of the world. If the Negro had voiced himself in only that one song, it would have been evidence of his nobility of soul.

And his knowledge of Black music ran the gamut, from the worksongs and the spirituals to ragtime and the newly emergent jazz. Black music, he says in effect, is the touchstone of Black art. And the touchstone can be applied also to the creative work of other cultures. This is implicit in the statement above. It is more explicit in his poetic statement in "O Black and Unknown Bards."

But Johnson certainly did not slight the verbal component of the songs. He recognized the poetry in their very titles. Although later scholarship has demonstrated that he overstated his case for the originality of the spirituals, it is still essentially correct.

> The white people among whom the slaves lived did not originate anything comparable even to the mere titles of the Spirituals. In truth, the power to frame the poetic phrases that make the titles of so many of the Spirituals betokens the power to create the songs. Consider the sheer magic of:

> Swing Low Sweet Chariot
> I've Got to Walk my Lonesome Valley
> Steal Away to Jesus
> Singing With a Sword in My Hand
> Rule Death in His Arms
> Ride on King Jesus
> We Shall Walk Through the Valley in Peace
> The Blood Came Twinklin' Down
> Deep River
> Death's Goin' to Lay His Cold, Icy Hand on Me

And confess that none but an artistically endowed people could have evoked it.

No one has even expressed a doubt that the poetry of the titles and text of the Spirituals is Negro in character and origin, no one else has dared to lay claim to it; why then doubt the music? ("Preface," pp. 15, 16.)

Of course, even the texts were later disputed by George Pullen Jackson. And Johnson's protege, the young Sterling Brown, was to make the final point with his characteristic wit:

> In bringing forth proof that in words and melody many Negro spirituals are traceable to white songs, southern white scholars have succeeded in disproving the romantic theory of completely African origin for the spirituals. All of those who assiduously collect evidence grant, however, that now the Negro song is definitely the Negro's regardless of ultimate origin, and one of them writes as follows: 'The words of the best White Spirituals cannot compare as poetry with the words of the best Negro spirituals.' It remains to be said that for the best Negro spirituals, camp-meeting models remain to be discovered. (*Negro Poetry & Drama,* 17.)

   d.   *The notion of standards and evaluation.* I have taken thus long to suggest the outlines of this argument on the originality and the power of Black folk poetry for two reasons: (1) the poets of the sixties claim a kinship with this poetry and music; and (2) the questions raised cast some light on the latter body of poetry, some of the disputes, some of the achievement, and some of the promise.

   Some of the dispute over recent Black poetry is traceable to the experimental nature of much of it, and it follows that this dispute is not necessarily racial in character. For example, Robert F. Moss's reference to the "typographical hijinks" of e. e. cummings, or W. E. Farrison's peevish dismissal of similar experimentation in his review of Beatrice Murphy's anthology of young Negro poets. White critics, of course, have dismissed white writers in much the same manner. And, of course, one remembers the furor raised over Alan Ginsberg's "Howl" and, earlier, over Walt Whitman's *Leaves of Grass,* to name two works at random.

   But the reaction goes deeper than mere resistance to change and experimentation. It seems rooted in white America's perception of the lives and culture of Black Americans, which has been marked by distortion, and by a continuing and systematic attempt to ridicule, to deny, to absorb, or to appropriate that culture. Specifically, both traditions of Afro-American poetry have long been under siege, and just to mention Black poetry is to evoke a history of white critical condescension and snobbery, and more recently, outright pathological ignorance and fear. The roots of this reaction are deep and pervasive. They are entwined in nineteenth-century attempts to justify slavery by proving the innate inferiority of the African slave. They are entwined in the African's supposed inability to master the "difficult" European languages. They are entwined in the questioning of the African's very humanity. (cf. Thomas Jefferson on the African and Greek verb, or on Benjamin Banneker.) They are likewise entwined in European conceptions of the poet and poetry— the poet as maker, or prophet, or divine madman; the poetry as sacred text or as edifying verbal diversion, producing pleasure.

   Since a poem is made of words and since the slave was incapable of mastering the "difficult" English tongue, how could one take seriously the idea of a Black American poet? Most did not. A few did, as the history of the early poets, Jupiter Hammond, Phillis Wheatley, and George Moses Horton attests. But essentially they were curiosities. Phillis Wheatley was a successful experiment to test the strength of nurture vs. nature; and Hammond and Horton were sports of nature (which was, indeed, one eighteenth century definition of genius).

Other early poets took as their central aim the vindication of their race from calumny and, indeed, the larger task of Liberation through appealing to the conscience of the ruling whites. This appeal ranged from direct protest to demonstrations of worthiness as evinced by learning and by mastery of the craft of poetry. Thus Alberry A. Whitman justifies his use of the difficult Spenserian stanza, the " 'stately verse,' mastered only by Spenser, Byron, and a very few other great poets," because, "Some negro is sure to do everything that anyone else has ever done, and as none of that race have ever executed a poem in the 'stately verse,' I simply venture in" (quoted by J. Sherman, p. 12).

This emphasis on craftsmanship is historically quite important. It shows the Black poet reflecting the same kind of concerns as other gifted Black individuals. It also shows a continuing need to test oneself according to white standards, and sometimes to receive white praise. Whitman treasured the praise he received from Bryant, just as Phillis Wheatley had treasured the praise of the literati of her day. And decades later, W. D. Howells was to praise Paul Laurence Dunbar in the same liberal manner. Later still Gwendolyn Brooks was awarded a Pulitzer prize for her technical mastery of the forms of Modernist poetry, and Karl Shapiro and Allen Tate were to praise Melvin B. Tolson for having assimilated the language of the Anglo-Saxon poetic tradition and for writing in "Negro" at the same time.

All of this was the recognition of individuals, not of a tradition. Indeed, the attempt has been from the outset to ignore, absorb, or to destroy the tradition in both its folk and formal dimensions. Despite this, however, the beauty and power of the tradition have been recognized by many, even though grudgingly at times.

As I have suggested, a good deal of the confusion comes from the variety of the poetry itself. Some comes from the desire of certain poets to be free from racial identification which implied inferiority of achievement or judgment by less rigorous standards. Some too comes from certain poets' unwillingness to be limited to writing on racial themes. One certainly thinks of Cullen, Hayden, Oden, Major and others.

The central concern seems to be the assumption that poetry which can be identified as Black is "racist" or inferior or un-American, so that one pretends that race is unimportant or that Black poetry is merely a fad or a bad imitation of experimental white poetry (as the Robert Moss analysis states). All of this, of course, is nonsense. Black poetry can and should be judged by the same standards that any other poetry is judged by—by those standards which validly arise out of the culture. Some of it is good, some excellent, and some downright bad. Much of this awareness has been expressed by the poets themselves, some of whom are excellent critics, like Lance Jeffers, Ethelbert Miller, Sarah Fabio, June Jordan, Margaret Walker, and Carolyn Rodgers to name but a few.

At any rate, scattered throughout their interviews, their essays, and their conversations, there are many critical pronouncements by Black poets themselves. Similarly, there are the pronouncements and preferences of their readers and their audiences, including professional scholars and critics, white, Black and other. Whether the poets approve or not is now certainly irrelevant since their work has become part of the general consciousness.

And that consciousness has been formed by the media, both the national institutions and myths, and by the educational system, both public and private. That, of course, is obvious. What is less obvious is the extent to which the Black reader/audience/poet has been shaped by these forces and, further still, and more important, how they have created and synthesized a special consciousness out of their special history and experience.

Thus we have the phenomenon of Tolson out-Pounding Pound and critics and scholars employing constructs derived from English, European, or American literature to evaluate Black literature. There is nothing necessarily wrong with this. Intellectually, we are to a large extent what we read. And we certainly need not ignore non-Black writing and criticism. Indeed, we do so at our own risk.

Nevertheless, the question, in a practical sense is whether Black poetry can most effectively be understood, experienced, explicated and encouraged by complete or even major reliance upon methodologies and standards that have evolved out of the larger Euro-American Society. To the extent that we share those values and concerns, then perhaps it should be, for the sake of efficiency and simplicity, especially for those readers who are university trained. Yet we all know that even those of us who are so trained and are accustomed to think in certain academic patterns also react in complex ways to the cultural referents and forms which arise from our Black Experience. Since the poetry often consciously or unconsciously draws upon this dual heritage one would expect a useful critical method to do likewise. Accordingly, if one were to approach the work of the past fifteen years one could begin at whatever intellectual locus he may inhabit and push toward the central experience of the poem. Easily a good deal of the work is approachable in this way, much of early Baraka, for example.

Notwithstanding, we are soon confronted with the ambiguities and densities which make up a wide range of the poems, which make up, in effect, the *blackness* of the poems. Some of these elements can be explicated through historical and cultural study. Others have to be experienced because they are "saturated" in Black Experience and these may include some which are written in so-called "Standard English."

Let us recall that there are two large categories of Black poetry of this period: (a) the political poetry of Black Power, and (b) the cultural poetry of the Black Experience. Although these categories overlap, they are by no means congruent, and writers shift from one to the other, sometimes without much clarify.

At any rate, purpose is important. The object of a Black Power poem is to raise Black people's consciousness. The classic statement is given by Ron Karenga in his paraphrase of Leopold Senghor and in Baraka's "Black Art." These poems were often frankly propagandistic and, technically speaking, quite often not very interesting. They were meant to be "throw-away" poems. Perhaps then, they should be examined in this light—they were raps for the occasion, and the occasion was the Revolution.

But all of these were not raps, and certainly not deficient either in execution or in delivery. Excellent examples can be found in Touré, Baraka, Neal, Lee, Sanchez, the Last Poets, Ahmed A. Alhamisi and elsewhere. And one needs to observe that many great poems of the West were highly political in their time, among them the *Divine Comedy* and *Paradise Lost.* So it does not follow that Black Power poems had to be shoddy or trite. In fact, there is a "revolutionary obligation" to make the poem as good as one can. Too, many of these poems were written by non-poets, by ordinary people in a state of excitement and fervor which they felt compelled to express. This was not a function of education or class necessarily, though many were obviously written by college students. In a word, then, one should judge these poems in historical context, even that of specific readings and performances where records are available. Did the poet "get over"? That was the criterion. That was all he was trying to do.

The other category of poems was generally more sophisticated and ambitious. They not only wanted to raise consciousness, they also wanted to do it with style, to celebrate Black life and culture, to seek a larger cosmic consciousness, which, at any rate, was black, the Original Blackness.

And they wanted to do this with the energy and subtlety and precision of a John Coltrane or with the people-reaching power of a James Brown. In this regard they were certainly following in a long tradition extending formally back to Dunbar and James Weldon Johnson on one hand and to the spirituals and blues on the other. And behind that to Mother Africa.

The more astute among those poets realized that they were seeking interior models, not archeological revivals of older musical/poetic forms. But what were those forms to be like? How were they to be transmitted, created? They spoke by necessity in metaphoric terms, as Neal's mention of "the modern equivalent of the ancient ritual energy" or "word-magic" or Stanley Crouch's "The Big Feeling." And the object of all of this is, again in Neal's words, "to shake us out of our lethargy and free our bodies and minds, opening us to unrealized possibilities." These "unrealized possibilities," as suggested by the work of Baraka, Dumas, June Jordan, Alhamisi and many others, go far beyond the narrow political concerns of Black Power to a concern (no less rooted in history) with ultimate philosophical and spiritual questions.

How did the poets approach these problems in terms of craft? How successful have they been? As I have stated in this essay, and at considerable length in others, they employed a wide variety of language, at times drawn from Black speech patterns, at times not. They also through a variety of means—some clever, some clumsy—sought to tap the resources latent in Black music. These are structural considerations, and when they are successful, they form the most striking features of the recent Black poetry.

But again, how successful have these works been? And how do we judge? Essentially on the terms posed by the individual poem. If a love poem is written in blues style, it can be judged against thousands of such poems—from the urban and folk traditions, as well as from the literary versions of Hughes and Sterling Brown. There are individual blues poems which stand up under any critical examination—such as Son House's "Death Letter." For drama, for lyrical intensity and sensual precision it competes favorably with many literary poems. Blues lovers, Black, white and Japanese, know the traditionally great blues songs—the masterpieces, the legendary sessions, the mind melting lines. Any love poem written in the blues manner has to be measured against the bitter humor of: "I asked her for water and she gave me gasoline." Or the pathos of "I folded by arms, I slowly walked away/She's a good old girl—gotta lay there till judgment day." And the self destructive despair of Tommy Johnson's lines—"Canned heat, canned heat, sure, Lord, killin' me." And the poet's *Angst* has be measured against "the blues ain't nothin' but a low-down shakey chill." Henry Dumas measured against this standard is successful.

But just as jazz musicians have explored and extended the blues experience through technical means, one must ask whether in an analogous way the poets of the sixties were able to extend the achievement of Langston Hughes and Sterling Brown; or better still, whether they have been able to build on the stylistic dynamics of Black language styles (in speech and song) to create the "word-magic" that they aspired to. Intuitively, I know that some like June Jordan, like Baraka, like Neal, like Jayne Cortez, like Carolyn Rodgers, like Sonia—intuitively, I know that they have. However, in criticism intuition, though vital, is not enough. The canons, the categories, the dynamics must be as clear and as reasoned as possible. These must rest on a sound empirical base. Beneath Larry Neal's "word-magic" lie many subtle and useful linguistic patterns which merit some critical description and organization, not to restrict the poet's freedom to invent and to discover, but to serve as a guide, a framework against which these discoveries may be understood and appreciated. And in the final analysis, the issue is still the problem of definition and the problem of control, not only in literature, but in the life which it refracts and reflects.

What Good the Word without the Wisdom? or "English Ain't Relevant"

What could be more unseemly than to speak of *wisdom* at this late date on the continent of North America? It is rather like arriving at a ten-cent pay toilet with a solid quarter in hand. One has more than enough to pay the price but one's coin simply will not fit in the slot. It is in going for change that one is struck by the full weight of the travesty, the sense that something is unspeakably out of order and that one, moreover, is a part of that something. What does one do? Indeed, what can one do? Most of us settle for change for the quarter because we have neither the faith nor the energy that a more meaningful change would require. We make peace with what has on occasion been spoken of as the American way-of-life. Which is to say that we surrender all claim to wisdom in order that we may— make no mistake—properly relieve ourselves.

Educators, and especially educators who have a particular and very special relationship to words and the national language, ought to consider quite literally the question: What good is the word without the wisdom?

It is a way of asking if there is any value to all of these exercises in the name of education lest they help somebody to see? Finally it suggests that teachers cannot measure their value outside of the collective wisdom of the society in which they work, for it is precisely the collective wisdom of that society that is in fact the ultimate measure of their value as teachers.

By what act of presumption, or madness, does one come upon such impolite questions and suggestions? I am a Black man living in this time and place who happens to be a teacher of Black American literature, and I speak and write the English language. On several occasions I have heard Black students protest against the traditional academic assumptions pertaining to English as a subject of study or as an element essential to the educational process. No doubt most teachers of English have either had this same experience or at least heard of its occurrence.

"English ain't relevant," say the Black students, and those of us whose very lives are charged with that special relationship to the language of which I spoke are made to shudder, even though we may be sympathetic to the students' outcries. We know, of course, that the students, taken literally, could not be further from the truth in this expressed attitude toward English. Try as we may we cannot help but be just a bit defensive, English being, as

From *College Composition and Communication,* October 1971.

it most certainly is, so crucial to our own sense of who we are and who or what we might someday be.

We might, as we so often do, reply that the student had damn well better change his attitude toward English if he expects to function in this society. And while there may be more than a modicum of truth in such a reply, it is finally irresponsible in that it is a refusal to investigate the symbolic possibilities in the students' outcry. "English ain't relevant" is, I think, the Black students' way of giving voice to a whole set of outrages that might otherwise go unspoken. When the Black student says "English ain't relevant," it is not merely a commentary on the language (which is, in itself, hostile to Blackness) but is as well, and more importantly I think, a commentary on the users of the language—especially including those persons who might be described as the custodians of the language.

I am suggesting that while the remark "English ain't relevant" may appear, on the surface, to be without substance, or maybe even crude, it actually is a remark which upon investigation raises fundamental questions about American society. To dismiss such a remark as wrongheaded is to ignore the likelihood that the makers of the remark know something about this America that is yet incomprehensible to others of us. In denying the validity and the importance of their experience, one denies, in effect, their experience—and in this country the particular experience of Black people has been denied with an Olympian ease which gives rise to the assumption that those who are less clever also are quite naturally without wisdom.

I am reminded of Albert Murray's perceptive observation in a rather curious volume called *The Omni-Americans*. "In spite of all the substandard test scores," wrote Murray, "anybody who assumes that the average white U.S. schoolboy is really closer to the classics, for instance, than the average U.S. Negro schoolboy is either talking about the relative percentage of literary snobs or is simply kidding himself. A white schoolboy *may* be persuaded to bone up and pass a formal exam on, say, metaphysical poetry, but that doesn't actually mean that he gives a damn about it. A Negro boy, on the other hand, might well have a genuine feeling for the blues, which certainly represent an indigenous 'substitute' for certified high-culture poetry."

What Murray strikes upon is, of course, that disassociation of feeling from intelligence which is so peculiar to education, and life, in the Western world and which, quite obviously, lies not only at the heart of the racial conflict in America but is equally at work in the war of the generations now being fought in the suburbs. Black art in America has in large part remained faithful to its deepest emotional source, Africa, in its refusal to disassociate feeling from intelligence. It is of some note, however, that this same concern has occupied, for example, the poetry of Allen Ginsberg and the song of Janis Joplin. Like her or no, anyone who listened closely to Joplin should have known that she, too, in her own way, was saying "English ain't relevant." It is altogether understandable that her very personal and tortured quest for *wisdom* should have led her not to the academies—where one becomes trained and, now and then, smart—but instead to the blues.

"The blues," wrote Ralph Ellison, "is an impulse to keep the painful details and episodes of a brutal experience alive in one's aching consciousness, to finger its jagged grain, and to transcend it."

We know to be sure that the two-and-a-half centuries of slavery on which this country was built was as brutal an experience as mankind has recorded, and we should know, lest we know next to nothing about the complexity of being human, that it was an experience finally as brutal in its effect upon white men as upon Black men. Perhaps if white men had sought to keep alive in their consciousness those painful details and episodes, if, in short, they had learned to sing the blues, they might better have transcended that tragic experience and would not today so closely resemble the slavemasters of their heritage. Unfortunately, the story of White America informs us *not* of the effort to keep that experience alive in the consciousness but instead of the tremendous attempt to falsify experience and to bury actual experience deep in the unconscious from where it would be unknowingly passed from generation to generation.

As James Baldwin must be tired of repeating, if one does not really know what happened in this country 200 years ago, one cannot really know what is happening before one's own eyes in this country today. The key here is *really know,* for it suggests not merely, or even primarily, that body of information that one receives from history books and the like, but more importantly that knowledge which lives, as it were, in the bones of a people. In failing to find a way to the blues, White America failed to find a way to feel. In denying that they as much as Blacks had cause to sing the blues, they in fact denied feeling, thereby paving the way for the ongoing denial of Black experience, which is in truth Black-white or American experience, the acceptance of which is the price of any wisdom this republic can hope to possess.

The typical kid who grows up Black in America, though he may never even utter the word *wisdom,* or even suspect that the word has meaning, does nonetheless know in his bones that he is wiser than the typical white kid (a fact which has a shocking but usually quite remarkable impact on the best white students in Black Literature classes) and he assumes, rightly I think, that his parents who work those mundane, poor-paying jobs in most cases know more about life than does the average white university teacher. He cannot really afford to respect the "intelligence" of a people whose inability to dance is so apparently related to their inability to live in peace with people whose culture differs from their own.

"English ain't relevant" becomes, then, a calling into question of the world that has been built on the words of white people, containing at its core a judgment on those for whom English *is* relevant. Academicians, so involved in making judgments (albeit under the guise of objectivity and universality more often than not) do not of course take too well to being judged by anyone outside of the academy. But the Black students would do well to persist in their judgment, and they deserve the encouragement of all who recognize that making teachers accountable is as difficult as it is necessary.

At the heart of the teacher's frustration in this matter, assuming he is sincere, might be a genuine concern over his having acquired some tool or skill (such as the ability to write) that the protesting student does, after all, need. Presumably one does have the word if not the wisdom. Doesn't the student, notwithstanding everything I have suggested, need the word? It is a legitimate question. On one level the question can easily be answered in the affirmative, but to my mind it raises other, possibly more crucial, questions. What price did the well-meaning teacher actually pay for the word? Must the student, in acquiring the skill or tool one offers, pay that same price? It is true that we do pay, in some way, for everything that we receive. And the best protection against cynicism in the face of that law is the power to estimate, in advance, the worth of the promised goods and to measure that against the price that one is expected to pay.

It is not, I think, permitting the imagination to roam too freely to suggest that the student sitting before the teacher senses that the teacher is always and everywhere, even when he has not admitted it to himself, teaching the student to be at least a little bit like the teacher. What if the student does not particularly want to be like the teacher? He usually rebels in some manner. And what if the student definitely does not want to be like the teacher; if he actually despises, with some passion, the kind of person that he perceives the teacher to be? Unless he is a quite willing slave—happily most young people are not— he does indeed rebel.

As I recall my own formal educational ordeal, which was rather brief and extraordinary only for the confusion created for all concerned, it occurs to me that there was but one teacher, in search of whom I must go all the way back to the fourth grade, who embodied human qualities that I should have truly liked to imitate. The great majority of my teachers, all of whom were white, simply did not, for me, come alive—save for the several who of course came alive as tyrants.

This places us in touch with something that is, I think, at work on the college level in the relationship between Black students and faculty, including almost all white faculty and, I fear, a great many academy trained Black faculty as well. Again I am alluding to that subterranean message which is implicit in the remark "English ain't relevant." The teacher is saying that he has something of real value to pass on to the student—and one who cannot say as much would make a more honorable bus driver than teacher—and I hear the Black student asking if he can learn that which one is trying to teach him without becoming like the teacher. The evidence that would support the possibility is indeed scarce, and the student does have eyes. While this may be a simplification that does not begin to account for the complexity of the teacher-student relationship, it does nevertheless suggest something of the apprehension which is at the center of the Black student–white teacher conflict.

Most Black youngsters, do not, God forbid, want to be the way white people are. (This is a classic case where the exception, on either side, proves the rule.) The intention in saying that is not to put down but simply to make a point of fact, one that is not without profound reason. By way of explanation I offer the following example.

The Black student knows that until quite recently the word *motherfucker* would have frightened most white teachers out of the classroom, and one suspects that it still holds the power to make a sizable majority uncomfortable. It happens, however, to be a word that in Black possession can be an obscene curse or the most splendid of praises. When, for instance, Lew Alcindor floats with the grace of a Nureyev over three other giants and stuffs that pill through the net, he would not expect that the "brothers" who are cheering him on should call him anything less than "a bad muthafucka." And all the white folks in the world saying "Isn't he terrific" or "Gee whiz, he's great" simply do not—if you can dig it—measure up. Lest this appear to be a peculiar kind of racial chauvinism, I am reminded that I've heard Black folk, myself included, speak of Joe Namath and Jerry West as bad muthafuckas.

What is appropriately at question here is the flexibility of language, and where other than to Black people has the English language as spoken in America looked for its flexibility? (Nobody familiar with TV commercials can possibly deny that.) Those who would teach the Black student how to use the language "properly" had better first learn to use it with his style or, in the least, equip oneself to coexist with his style and his vitality. The particular word selected to make the above point did not, as used, have any sexual connotations, still less was it insulting to anybody's mother. But the fact that this understanding, so obvious to Blacks, is a little difficult for most whites suggests the working of two radically different imaginations. All of which returns us once more to our respective roles in this republic's history.

It is, make no mistake, the very mess that white people have made of sex and sexuality (not to mention sensuality) which places them at such a distance from the ingenious use that Black people have made of so taboo a word. The pertinence of such a truth is not lost on the Black student. The pathetic condition of American sexuality—from the Pilgrims to Andy Warhol—is something about which he is aware (and must protect himself against) though he has not read Updike or Mailer or O'Hara or Roth—or, for that matter, Suzanne or Robbins. He is aware because he has been told about it all of his life, and ironically enough he has been told about it not by Black people but by white people themselves. Actions, someone said, speak louder than words.

So it is perfectly logical that the Black student should say, "Well, if you can't deal with sex, what in hell can I learn from you?" His charge is that the people who would teach him the *word* cannot deal with *life,* and he has every reason to view such a people as a collective danger, surely more dangerous than bank robbers and other assorted so-called criminals!

The Black student says "English ain't relevant" because he does not trust the language or the people for whom it works, who are the people whose work it does. The language works, does it not, for those who have found in it some degree of personal power. To be certain, all such individuals are by no means white. It cannot be said, however, that the language works for any community in this country that is not white. There is yet no evidence with which to believe that the language will be translated into Black Power so handily as it was translated into White Power. And so the Black student voices a condemnation of the American republic, and he trusts no one who does not join him in that condemnation. He is, in his distrust, wise, for anyone who lives in this place and cannot condemn her is either naive, without courage, or corrupt.

It is not easy to condemn the country where one was born, where one lives, where live the people that one loves. It is all the more difficult when one has outlived one's own innocence, which so quickly, and so painfully, happens to each of us. There was a time, say in my first youth, when condemning America came easy, but that, paradoxically, was before I had truly imagined the depth of either her sins or my own. Youthful rebellion gives way, quietly, to an unnameable anguish as one recognizes oneself to be an occupant on a runaway train that nobody claims to be driving and nobody knows how to stop. But one cannot describe such a train as driverless for in so doing one has made it not less but more ominous, for it suggests that everyone is driving it and that the madness is, alas, complete, and that we are completely without hope.

America's shortsightedness has long reached the point of epidemic. In his essay called "Americanism," Santayana wrote: "The greatest external success may easily involve an essential failure. The success, being physical, might go on indefinitely; but what if the moral failure should pervade the experiment." Santayana, as we know, was a philosopher, but America, shamefaced in its capitulation to the canons of anti-intellectualism, has never had time for the philosophical question. She has never readied herself for testing the moral quality of that power which passes for greatness against the sacred laws of the human spirit.

Santayana further observed that the American, whom he called simple and fearless, admires and trusts the vast momentum of modern business because his soul shares that momentum and is divorced from the life of the spirit. He observed the spiritual life to be "the seat and judge of all values I take to be an axiom" and concluded that "every maxim, every institution, and the whole universe itself, must be tested morally by its effect on the spirit."

The Negro, said Richard Wright, is America's metaphor, and it is the Black presence on these shores that has provided this country with the great moral test that de Tocqueville anticipated a century before the writings of Santayana. Black people have survived in America—indeed survived America—at great and terrible risk. White America's childish expectation that this society can somehow survive without their risking anything is perhaps our best example of a people's sense of themselves as some sort of elevated beings, not merely human beings. Life has a term, and to understand life's term is to understand that White Americans must risk precisely that which Black people have had to risk in this place. Everything!

When that has been achieved, the rightful content will have been returned to the words, and once again Black students will listen. But not until. Words like *dignity* and *integrity* and *honor* and *humility* and *courage* and, above all, *love* ("Love is the only wisdom," says Baldwin) must once more have meaning—or else! In the meantime, lest teachers unwisely assume that this train cannot crash, they might listen. After all, that whites yet require surveys in a half-hearted attempt to learn what Blacks know by their scars is no mean metaphor for the tragic divide.

Blacks, for all the suffering, know the essential truth of the American experience . . . the painful details and episodes. "That's why I sing the blues," says B. B. King. For the blues the white man has found no real or meaningful counterpart, and for his salvation he has placed faith in a system of education that in the light of reality is pure disgrace. One cannot honor a tradition save by making use of it in such manner as to achieve a set of guidelines that will serve the quest for a more decent life. That *is* the way of the wise. To insist upon tradition at the expense of imagination is the way of the fool. America is incredibly foolish, and Black people, who have lived where in Lerone Bennett's words the darkness is light enough, have always been wiser than America. Perhaps that is something white people have long known in their bones, for in the face of what have they been passionate if not Blackness?

University of Washington

Self-Determination and the Black Aesthetic:
An Interview with Max Roach

Black World: What can Black scholars and critics contribute to the development of Black music, as well as to helping gain more control over it?

Max Roach: I feel like this: of course, criticism and clarifying the history of the development of the music—along the lines of saying what our musical heritage is or who are the true innovators, the data from a historical sense—I think that's extremely important. Analyzing the music is especially important if you are going to be involved as a musician. It's important, say, for a potential John Coltrane or Charlie Parker. But the way to go about that is very personal to each musician. It must be done in a way to preserve each person's individuality. You see, our music isn't one that demands, "Okay, we're going to turn out a group of Charlie Parkers or a group of Duke Ellingtons." We allow each other the luxury of being an individual and we accept him as an individual. In fact, he receives the highest praise if he does break through; we then say, "Oh, we have another Charlie Parker," but in the sense that he's an *individual* like Parker, not that he *sounds* like him. That, I think, is a major difference between our music and Western music, which, as I've said, happens to be distilled at this point, with the conservatories most of the time turning out people who sound and do pretty much the same thing musically.

As far as control is concerned, this is where I think the Black people outside of music—the organizers, the economists, those in business administration, the technocrats—they're the ones we need in order to control what is produced by Black artists today, people who know how to organize and package and sell, on the same level that anybody else in the world is doing, only more so. In fact, I believe that those people would be more important at this juncture than the historian, analyst or critic. Control is the matter. Take the people in gospel music. They produce their own records and they take them around with them and do the selling themselves. So, therefore, they're writing, performing, criticizing themselves, analyzing different phases of, say, the operations of giants like James Cleveland and Mahalia. Nevertheless, they are competing in the market without the real skills, whereas people who were trained in these areas could perhaps do a much better job. The creators, I think, should be left to analyze and criticize ourselves and people involved with our work, and leave the other areas to our

---

From *Black World,* November 1973.

brothers and sisters whom we can trust and who are going to treat us fairly. . . . I think these are the folks who are sorely needed out here today.

. . .

Black World: What is it about "jazz" that has made people view it as such a "radical" form of music?

Max Roach: For one thing, it's the high level of sophistication that is involved. Ortiz notes in his book that, beginning with "bop," for once [the focus was on the music itself and the complex improvisatory feats of the soloists] . . . He says it takes thousands of manhours put into developing yourself to be that skillful on an instrument. So when you get to that level, and people just try to take it up and imitate it, you'll find that it's not possible to imitate a John Coltrane, Charlie Parker or Art Blakey. There's a sense of achievement there too. You see the kind of *intellect* that comes out of the Black experience when you hear Ellington, Coltrane, Fats Waller, Art Tatum—a level of accomplishment that artistically would diminish anything else around it. You understand what I'm trying to say? Unless you're willing to have the kind of commitment that these people have, then you're not going to be able to sit on the same bandstand, so to speak.

Black World: There's a little more to it than "I got rhythm."

Max Roach: Right. When you look at people like that and talk to Imamu or Archie Shepp, you find out that not only are they fine musicians and writers, but they also are able to articulate and just about slaughter anybody intellectually who's not up to what's happening, because they are committed, hard workers. It's a science.

But I think culture politically is a very powerful weapon. When they brought us over to these shores, the first thing that they did was try to take away our culture and impose theirs on us, which has kept us looking up to them. And so culture—especially European culture—is used as part of the whole colonial psyche, that whole thing they drop on us—that the greatest music that was ever written was by Europeans, who were also the greatest thinkers, the greatest writers, *etc.* Now, I will submit that they are great, but when you say the *greatest,* I just have to disagree with that, because I believe there's greater and greater and greater. And this is why I say our culture is fluid, that each generation . . . we just keep growing and growing and we grow out of each other, just like chapter, after chapter, after chapter. It's an endless book. Whereas European cultures are static, in the sense that they stop and say the greatest happens to be Shakespeare or Bach or Michelangelo. They stop around the 15th, 16th, 17th or 18th century, and only once in awhile will somebody [more recent] sneak in. But they do use their culture politically, and it's racist; that whole attitude is racist. But it's deeper than that; it's part of that whole colonial thing to me.

Black World: Yes, people almost everywhere else, except in the United States—when you say "American" music, the first thing they think of, of course, is Black music. In Duke Ellington's autobiography, he mentions that he was honored with having his portrait put in a series of stamps, that also included, I think, two or three European composers.*

---

*"In 1967 the Republic of Togoland released a set of four postage stamps dedicated to the Twentieth Anniversary of UNESCO. Each stamp bore the likeness of a musician, the four chosen being Bach, Beethoven, Debussy, and myself. . . ."—from *Music Is My Mistress,* which will be published this month (November) by Doubleday and Co., Inc.

So, in other words, the only *American* composer included was Duke. And yet this country would never say that Duke Ellington was its greatest composer. Just recently, a series of reviews in the New York Times on books about George Gershwin [whose fame rests a great deal on his use of Black music] intimated that *he* should be among those considered for that title. Do you, too, feel that Black music is the true American music?

Max Roach: Yes, I certainly do. I see it a little bit differently from that, though, as far as the terminology is concerned. I think that Black music is really *African*-American music, and this is the reason that our music is not fully recognized, nor won't be until we as a people are recognized. They don't even recognize that we really exist in this country. . . . Our culture is tied into our position politically, sociologically, economically. It's all on the same level. And it's difficult for those folks to say, "Yes, that ['American music'] is Black music," because that's admitting that Black people are a great people who have something to offer. They still look at us as a people who were brought over here for something else—to be their servants, inferior people—and they really believe that. . . .

I really think we must be about the business of redefining everything about us as Black people, and we should be about the business of looking hard at all the things that the media fling at us. I mean, we should be listening to the music and figuring out, "What does it mean to my own development; what does it mean to the struggle?" I think we should be looking at the film industry; we should be looking at our literary people and our scholars, and asking ourselves the very same questions. And I think our young people should take a hard look at all these things—at all this garbage that comes into our communities by way of television, motion pictures, radio, *etc.*—and see just what it means to our whole development, to preserving and protecting our cultural heritage—what's left of it, that is.

CAROLYN M. RODGERS

Black Poetry—Where It's At

In the last few years, we have seen a significant increase in the amount of Black Poetry being published. We have also seen a change in style and subject matter. At this point, it is possible to see distinctions in the various types of poetry being written. That is to say, all Black poets don't write the same KIND of poetry, or all Black poems ain't the same kind. They differ. Just as white poems differ and just as white poems come in sonnets, ballads or whatever.

   I have attempted to place all Black poetry in several broad categories, all of which have variations on the main form. Very few poems are all one type or another. It is possible and probable that a poem will be three or four different types of poetry at one time. That is, a signifying poem will be a *teachin, spaced, pyramid* poem. Here are the main headings:

1. *signifying*
   a. open
   b. sly
   c. with or about
2. *teachin/rappin*
3. *coversoff*
   a. rundown
   b. hipto
   c. digup
   d. coatpull
4. *spaced* (spiritual)
   a. mindblower (fantasy)
   b. coolout
5. *bein* (self/reflective)
   a. upinself
   b. uptight
   c. dealin/swingin
6. *love*
   a. skin

From *Negro Digest,* September 1969.

     b. space (spiritual)

     c. cosmic (ancestral)

7. *shoutin* (angry/cathartic)

     a. badmouth

     b. facetoface (warning/confrontation)

     c. two faced (irony)

8. *jazz*

     a. riffin

     b. cosmic ('Trane)

     c. grounded (Lewis)

9. *du-wah*

     a. dittybop

     b. bebop

10. *pyramid* (getting us together/building/nationhood)

Some of these categories are self-explanatory and familiar. Most poems, as previously stated, fall into more than one category which, to my way of thinking, attests to the flexibility of Black writers. Unconsciously, I think, poets fall into their bag—or bags—and it is no discredit to a writer if he chooses to deal with only one form—or two, or three. . . . However, a Black writer will be classifiable in at least ONE of these categories, although it is conceivable to me that Black writers are creative enough to uncover forms which are yet to be acknowledged. We will know if the writing is Black.

Briefly, I am going to give examples of several of the headings, and then devote a large amount of discussion to signifying poetry since it has reached an exciting unprecedented level of sophistication in the written word.

The *teachin* poem is a poem which seeks to define and give direction to Black people. The two examples chosen and quoted in part here are Ronda Davis's "Towards A Black Aesthetic" and Barbara Mahone's "What Color Is Black."

> if tomorrow's black poetry will
> not EXPLAIN what is
> but BE it
> then pens will be electric with feeling
> igniting
> and the paper shall become the poet
> and the poets shall be earth-clouds . . .
> —Ronda Davis

and Mahone:

> Black is the color of
> my little brother's mind,
> the grey streaks
> in my mother's hair.
> Black is the color of

my yellow cousin's smile,
the scars upon my neighbor's wrinkled face . . .

The *coversoff, rundown, hipto, digup or coatpull* are basically the same type of poem, so the terms can be used interchangeably. There are many, many examples of this kind of poem today. For example, Cleveland Webber's poem, from his recently released book of poetry, *Africa Africa Africa,* "In America"—

the people are in all the areas
we occupy little parts of air,
telling little lies, taking little trips,
at least 5 days a week . . .
. . . ghetto streets get empty while the pig is
internalized in a suffering too old to be.

Or Don L. Lee's poem on "Nigerian Unity"—

little niggers
killing
little niggers
the weak against the weak
the ugly against the ugly . . .

These poets hip you to something, pull the covers off of something, or run it down to you, or ask you to just dig it—your coat is being pulled.

The *spaced* poem is very beautiful and many Black poets, after writing a lot of *signifying, coversoff* or *shoutin* poems, find that an inner calm, becomes, and inherent in that, a mystical and positive way of looking at the Black man's relationship to the universe. Amiri Baraka (LeRoi Jones) has a poem called "Black People: This Is Our Destiny," and I quote from it here:

. . . we got to meet the realization of makers knowing who we are
. . . knowing how to live, and what life is . . .
. . . we must spin through in our seventh adventures in the endlessness
of all existing feeling, all existing forms of life, the gasses, the plants, the
ghosts minerals the spirits the souls the light in the stillness where the
storm the glow the nothing in God is complete except there is nothing to
be incomplete the pulse and change of rhythm, blown flight to be anything
at all . . . vibration holy nuance beating against itself, a rhythm a playing
re-understood now by one of the 1st race the primitives the first men who
evolve again to civilize the world . . .

The *spaced* poem returns to the spiritual wisdom of our Egyptian/African forefathers. Returns to the natural laws, the natural state of man before subhuman massacres. Spaced poems say that our ancestors are in the air and will communicate with us. As is the case in Jones' "No Matter, No Matter, The World Is The World"—

> A broke dead genius
> moved on to dust
> will touch you one night . . .
> . . . and the stacked dust of a gone brother will
> hunch you
> some father you needed who left you . . .

We speak of the vibrations, positive and negative, and we believe again in what we have never truly denied; the power of NOMMO, JU-JU and the collective force of the positive spirits, moving in time with the universe. In our poetry, we sing of Sun-Ra and Coltrane, and their life-motion which is sound. The new Black poets believe that we are the seventh dimension (as the seventh sun/son). They further believe in the over-all importance of the astrological signs of people (the writer is Sagittarius—No. 5). The dream is to utilize our beginning to conceptualize and direct a Black end that is as beautiful as our beginning.

The *mindblower* poem may seem similar to the *spaced* poem, but the two are not be confused. There are basic differences. *Mindblower* poems seek to expand our minds, to break the chains that strangle them, so that we can begin to imagine alternatives for Black people. They seek to ridicule and mutilate that which may have formerly been esteemed. Often these poems predict an awful or glorious future and are gorier than the *spaced* poem. Sometimes the awful predictions are for Black people, oftener, for subhumans.

Larry Neal in his book *Black Boogaloo,* in an untitled poem says:

> We gathered in the open place
> Piled their symbols one on top of the other,
> Their flags and their death books; took their holidays rolled
> their platitudes into nice burnable heaps,
> Gathered and piled this stuff from the stink
> pots of the earth which they have made so.
> In the distance their cities burn . . .
>   We piled their histories skyward with destruction
> acknowledgement to our ancestors and gods,
> then we light it.
>   Singing.

By contrast is Jewel Lattimore's "Folk Fable"—

> . . . but the niggas wadn't hip & wadn't hipped
> until they was copped.
> too.
> to work in the mines on the moon
> . . . & the ships had promises had names

that all the niggas knew names
like JESUS & HEAVEN & FREEDOM
to take the niggas to a new world . . .
. . . & when they was shipped to the moon
mainland sold
to companies who
was bidden
while the chasemanhattan bank
supervised the auctions . . .

Or Ebon's poem, "The Statue of Liberty Has Her Back to Harlem" (two other alternate titles excluded)—

I saw them bayonet
her spine
and pin her 16th birthday
to a cross
where it hung.
dank and slimey
it hung,
like stagnant death
in shallow pools,
vomiting blood
on poets
and mothers
and flower children . . .

Surely, he was talking about "them," and he is a master of the gory.

Every poet has written a *bein* poem. In fact, most poets start off writing them. Just writing about the way they be, they friends be, they lovers be, the world be . . . An example presented here is one of my own, from my book *Songs of A Blackbird*—

it's me
bathed and ashy
smellin down with
                    (revlons aquamarine)
me with my hair black
and nappy good and rough
as the ground
me sitting in my panties
. . . it's me in the sky
where pharaoh and coltrane playing
. . . and it's me screammmmmmmming into the box
and the box is screammmmmmmming back
. . . in kulu se & karma . . .

And all praise is due ALLAH; we are now getting more, more & more love poems from/ about Black men and women. Such is this fragile jewel of Barbara Mahone's. The poem, "With Your Permission," combines *skin & space* (spiritual) aspects, as they should be—

> smooth surfaces are easy
> . . . i would rather deal with
>   what moves you
> explore the fire and texture
>   of your soul
>   with your permission
> i would chart a course
>   across your skin
>   and travel all day
>   all night
> up and down that rocky road.

And one Black warrior, William Wandick, writes spears of honey:

> my eyes took your slender fingers & dreamed on them,
> they thinned imagination to a queen called sheba/nefertiti
> deeming you royalness/making a fetish of your hand . . .

And there are love poems for all Black people, such as Ronda Davis's poem about the "Wine Dipped Woman." And we need more. And more. More . . .

The *shoutin* poem is perhaps at this time the most familiar to us all. For awhile, it seemed to be the only kind of poem being written. It usually tells the subhuman off. Or offs him with word bullets. An example of the *facetoface poem,* which is an aspect of the *shoutin* type, is one written by Sonia Sanchez in her hard-hitting book of poetry, *Homecoming*—

> git the word out
> now to the man/boy
> taking a holiday
> from murder tell him
> we hip to his shit and that
> the next time he kills one
> of our
>   blk/princes
>   some of his faggots
> gonna die
>   a stone/cold/death.
>   yeah.

The last category with which I will deal briefly is the *two-faced* poem. As kids, we used to call a person two-faced if they grinned in our faces and talked about us behind our backs. In poetry, this concept takes on similar, but broader, meanings. For example, I will use my poem, "You Name It"—

> I will write about things that are universal!
> So that hundreds, maybe even thousands of
> years from now, White critics and readers
> will say of me, Here is a good Black writer,
> who wrote about truth and universal topics.
> > I will write about people who eat,
> > > as it was in the beginning
> > I will write about people who sleep,
> > > is now
> > I will write about people who fuck,
> > > and ever shall
> > I will write about babies being born,
> > > world without end
> > I will write about Black people
> > > re-po-sses-sing this earth,
> > > > ah-men.

I would hope that everyone who reads the poem catches the two facededness (irony), implicit in the theme.

Signifying poetry holds a special fascination for me. Probably because I could not/can not signify and have always admired those who can. From a literary point of view, it is a significant, exciting aspect of today's poetry. I know, and you know, that we have always signified. On the corners, in the poolrooms, the playgrounds, anywhere and everywhere we have had the opportunity. "We sig" with somebody, about somebody, and if we can't be open about it, we "sig" on the sly! Langston Hughes' character, Simple, signified: with his landlady, his partners, his girlfriend, everybody . . . And Richard Wright deals it in *Black Boy*. However, to my knowledge, no *group* of Black writers has ever used it as a poetic technique as much as today's writers. It is done with polish. And the audiences love it! Too much *signifying* can be negative, I think; however, most of today's poets are very conscious of how important positive vibrations are, and few have carried signification to an extreme. In the main, it is being used, for constructive destruction.

A quick, or lengthy, look at the poetry of Don L. Lee, Nikki Giovanni or Sonia Sanchez shows that these three poets *signify* with their readers and the objects of their poems. *Signify*—fuh days . . .

> "wallace for president
> his mamma for vice-president"
> —Don L. Lee

and—

> Memorial. The supremes—cuz they dead
> —Sonia Sanchez

or Nikki Giovanni—

> ever notice how its only the ugly
> honkies
> who hate . . .

And of course the master of it all, Amiri Baraka (LeRoi Jones), on wigs—

> . . . why don't you take that thing
> off yo haid
> you look like Miss Muffet in a
> runaway ugly machine. I mean,
> like that."

Signifying is a way of saying the truth that hurts with a laugh, a way of capping on (shutting up) someone. Getting even talking bout people's mammas & such. It's a love/hate exercise in exorcising one's hostilities. It's a funny way of saying something negative that is obviously untrue like:

> "you look like you been whupped wid uh ugly stick"

or saying something that is negative as:

> . . . nigger: standing on the corner, thought him was
> cool. him still
> standing there. it's winter time, him cool

Signifying is very often a bloody knife job, with a vocal touch. It moves in progressions sometimes and it is both general and specific. In *Black Boy,* by Richard Wright, we are taken through a dozens scene or *signifying* scene (to me they are the same), and each phrase is labeled in terms of its significance.

> "You eat yet? [uneasily trying to make conversation]
> "Yeah, man I done really fed my face." [casually]
> "I had cabbage & potatoes." [confidently]
> "I had buttermilk & blackeye peas." [meekly informational]
> "Hell, I ain't gonna stand near you, nigger!" [pronouncement]
> "How come?" [feigned innocence]
> "Cause you gonna smell up this air in a minute!" [a shouted accusation]
> "Nigger your mind's in a ditch." [amusingly moralistic]
> "Ditch, nothing! Nigger, you going to break wind any minute now!" [triumphant pronouncement creating suspense]
> "Yeah, when them black-eyed peas tell that buttermilk to move over, that buttermilk ain't gonna wanna move and there's gonna be war in your guts and your stomach's gonna swell up and bust!" [climax]

As you see, every line leads up to the cap, the final one. And the last statement is based on a reality that all Blacks know. Peas, buttermilk, cabbage & potatoes will cause you to fart! It is a four-to-four balanced way of making love to—while poking hurt/fun at—one's self and one's life-styles.

A great deal of what today's poets do is hit & run *signifying*—or, another way of saying it: spot-*signifying*. That is, they do not usually sustain the length of a standard *signifying* circle. But they are traveling too fast. They hit—

yo mamma!

and keep on moving to the next point—

your daddy too!

or

if dracula came to town now
he'd look like daley
booing senator ribicoff
no pretty man himself
but at least out of the beast
category
—Nikki Giovanni

The poets *signify* with/about a whole lot of people in one poem, hitting one, then another, and usually, though not always, one theme holds the poem together.

When two people *signify* with each other, one feeds the other for progression, dramatic buildup to impact, but the object of ridicule doesn't have to be around or vocal. Responses can be imagined or drawn from the poet's own experiences—

you followed him niggers
all of you—
                yes you did,
i saw ya. [implied response—no, I didn't]
—Don L. Lee

Now, because *signifying* often contains such a broad base of truth, it has been known to cause—in fact, it is famous for causing—a fight or a death. It can get too down, too real, so true and personal it uncovers too much. If the signifier can REALLY get down (and in grammar school the last word was "yo mama is uh man . . .") the second party who cannot move his tongue to balance the scale may use his fists to do so—or his knife, or both. And it is a matter of pride. No Black person wants to be "sigged" about or capped all over . . .

No Black person can listen to some *signifying* without responding in some way. It pulls us in and we identify with the bad "signifer." Obviously, this style of poetry has the power to involve Black people and to MOVE them. It is a familiar mover, and is probably the most dynamic type of poetry I have mentioned up to now.

I trust that I have initiated here a rather complete incomplete picture of where Black poetry is at. Some may quibble with the actual attempt to label what Black writers are doing. Others may take issue with the labels.

We do not (it cannot be said too often) want subhumans defining what we be doing. There is no human reference point. And objectivity does not REALLY exist in criticism. There is, perhaps, reason, tempered by a good strong sense of what is reasonable, what is fair. Ultimately, one's life-style is his point of view.

Black Poetry is becoming what it has always been but has not quite *beed*. And we have love and the spirit of our ancestors to guide us.

II

Statements of Purpose: Groups and Journals

The following documents represent a sampling of organizations and institutions that stimulated and were stimulated in turn by the Black Arts initiatives. Some of these organizations and institutions were primarily cultural in orientation, but with a strong social and political engagement; others were basically political but with a deep sense of the importance of art and culture to the development of a liberated Black nation; still others tied politics and culture together so closely that it is not possible to classify them as distinctly cultural or political in nature.

Final Communique of the Asian-African Conference

The Asian-African Conference, convened upon the invitation of the Prime Ministers of Burma, Ceylon, India, Indonesia and Pakistan met in Bandung from the 18th to the 24th April, 1955. In addition to the sponsoring countries the following 24 countries participated in the conference:

1. Afghanistan	13. Liberia
2. Cambodia	14. Libya
3. People's Republic of China	15. Nepal
4. Egypt	16. Philippines
5. Ethiopia	17. Saudi Arabia
6. Gold Coast	18. Sudan
7. Iran	19. Syria
8. Iraq	20. Thailand
9. Japan	21. Turkey
10. Jordan	22. Democratic Republic of Vietnam
11. Laos	23. State of Vietnam
12. Lebanon	24. Yemen

The Asian-African Conference considered problems of common interest and concern to countries of Asia and Africa and discussed ways and means by which their people could achieve fuller economic, cultural and political cooperation. . . .

B. *Cultural Cooperation*

1. The Asian-African Conference was convinced that among the most powerful means of promoting understanding among nations is the development of cultural cooperation. Asia and Africa have been the cradle of great religions and civilizations which have enriched other cultures and civilizations while themselves being enriched in the process. Thus the cultures of Asia and Africa are based on spiritual and universal foundations. Unfortunately contacts among Asian and African countries were interrupted during the past centuries. The peoples of Asia and Africa are now animated by a keen and sincere desire to renew their old cultural contacts and develop new ones in the context of the modern

world. All participating Governments at the Conference reiterated their determination to work for closer cultural cooperation.

2. The Asian-African Conference took note of the fact that the existence of colonialism in many parts of Asia and Africa in whatever form it may be not only prevents cultural cooperation but also suppresses the national cultures of the people. Some colonial powers have denied to their dependent peoples basic rights in the sphere of education and culture which hampers the development of their personality and also prevents cultural intercourse with other Asian and African peoples. This is particularly true in the case of Tunisia, Algeria and Morocco, where the basic right of the people to study their own language and culture has been suppressed. Similar discrimination has been practiced against African and coloured people in some parts of the Continent of Africa. The Conference felt that these policies amount to a denial of the fundamental rights of man, impede cultural advancement in this region and also hamper cultural cooperation on the wider international plane. The Conference condemned such a denial of fundamental rights in the sphere of education and culture in some parts of Asia and Africa by this and other forms of cultural suppression.

In particular, the Conference condemned racialism as a means of cultural suppression.

3. It was not from any sense of exclusiveness or rivalry with other groups of nations and other civilisations and cultures that the Conference viewed the development of cultural cooperation among Asian and African countries. True to the age-old tradition of tolerance and universality, the Conference believed that Asian and African cultural cooperation should be developed in the larger context of world cooperation.

Side by side with the development of Asian-African cultural cooperation the countries of Asia and Africa desire to develop cultural contacts with others. This would enrich their own culture and would also help in the promotion of world peace and understanding.

4. There are many countries in Asia and Africa which have not yet been able to develop their educational, scientific and technical institutions. The Conference recommended that countries in Asia and Africa which are more fortunately placed in this respect should give facilities for the admission of students and trainees from such countries to their institutions. Such facilities should also be made available to the Asian and African people in Africa to whom opportunities for acquiring higher education are at present denied.

5. The Asian-African Conference felt that the promotion of cultural cooperation among countries of Asia and Africa should be directed towards:

(I) the acquisition of knowledge of each other's country;
(II) mutual cultural exchange, and
(III) exchange of information.

6. The Asian-African Conference was of the opinion that at this stage the best results in cultural cooperation would be achieved by pursuing bilateral arrangements to implement its recommendations and by each country taking action on its own, wherever possible and feasible.

October 1966 Black Panther Party Platform and Program

What We Want, What We Believe

1. *We want freedom. We want power to determine the destiny of our Black Community.* We believe that black people will not be free until we are able to determine our destiny.
2. *We want full employment for our people.* We believe that the federal government is responsible and obligated to give every man employment or a guaranteed income. We believe that if the white American businessmen will not give full employment, then the means of production should be taken from the businessmen and placed in the community so that the people of the community can organize and employ all of its people and give a high standard of living.
3. *We want an end to the robbery by the white man of our Black Community.* We believe that this racist government has robbed us and now we are demanding the overdue debt of forty acres and two mules. Forty acres and two mules was promised 100 years ago as restitution for slave labor and mass murder of black people. We will accept the payment in currency which will be distributed to our many communities. The Germans are now aiding Jews in Israel for the genocide of the Jewish people. The Germans murdered six million Jews. The American racist has taken part in the slaughter of over fifty million black people; therefore, we feel that this is a modest demand that we make.
4. *We want decent housing, fit for shelter of human beings.* We believe that if the white landlords will not give decent housing to our black community, then the housing and the land should be made into cooperatives so that our community, with government aid, can build and make decent housing for its people.
5. *We want education for our people that exposes the true nature of this decadent American society. We want education that teaches us our true history and our role in the present-day society.* We believe in an educational system that will give to our people a knowledge of self. If a man does not have knowledge of himself and his position in society and the world, then he has little chance to relate to anything else.
6. *We want all black men to be exempt from military service.* We believe that Black people should not be forced to fight in the military service to defend a racist government that does not protect us. We will not fight and kill other people of color in the world who, like black people, are being victimized by the white racist government of America. We

will protect ourselves from the force and violence of the racist police and the racist military, by whatever means necessary.

7. *We want an immediate end to POLICE BRUTALITY and MURDER of black people.* We believe we can end police brutality in our black community by organizing black self-defense groups that are dedicated to defending our black community from racist police oppression and brutality. The Second Amendment to the Constitution of the United States gives a right to bear arms. We therefore believe that all black people should arm themselves for self-defense.

8. *We want freedom for all black men held in federal, state, county and city prisons and jails.* We believe that all black people should be released from the many jails and prisons because they have not received a fair and impartial trial.

9. *We want all black people when brought to trial to be tried in court by a jury of their peer group or people from their black communities, as defined by the Constitution of the United States.* We believe that the courts should follow the United States Constitution so that black people will receive fair trials. The 14th Amendment to the U.S. Constitution gives a man a right to be tried by his peer group. A peer is a person from a similar economic, social, religious, geographical, environmental, historical and racial background. To do this the court will be forced to select a jury from the black community from which the black defendant came. We have been, and are being tried by all-white juries that have no understanding of the "average reasoning man" of the black community.

10. *We want land, bread, housing, education, clothing, justice and peace. And as our major political objective, a United Nations-supervised plebiscite to be held throughout the black colony in which only black colonial subjects will be allowed to participate, for the purpose of determining the will of black people as to their national destiny.* When, in the course of human events, it becomes necessary for one people to dissolve the political bands which have connected them with another, and to assume, among the powers of the earth, the separate and equal station to which the laws of nature and nature's God entitle them, a decent respect to the opinions of mankind requires that they should declare the causes which impel them to the separation.

We hold these truths to be self-evident, that all men are created equal; that they are endowed by their Creator with certain unalienable rights; that among these are life, liberty, and the pursuit of happiness. *That, to secure these rights, governments are instituted among men, deriving their just powers from the consent of the governed; that, whenever any form of government becomes destructive of these ends, it is the right of the people to alter or to abolish it, and to institute a new government, laying its foundation to such principles, and organizing its powers in such form, as to them shall seem most likely to effect their safety and happiness.* Prudence, indeed, will dictate that governments long established should not be changed for light and transient causes; and accordingly, all experience hath shown, that mankind are more disposed to suffer, while evils are sufferable, than to right themselves by abolishing the forms to which they are accustomed. *But, when a long train of abuses and usurpations, pursuing invariably the same object, evinces a design to reduce them under absolute despotism, it is their right, it is their duty, to throw off such government, and to provide new guards for their future security.*

Editor's Notes

In its premiere issue, *Black World* magazine focuses, appropriately, on the two principal centers of Black population in the world, the African continent and the United States of America. The writers of the eight articles, the short story and the poems all make it abundantly clear that Black people on both continents have very grave and very similar problems, and that these problems have a common source: the experience of colonialism and enslavement. It is the hope of the editors of *Black World* magazine that Black people everywhere—in Brazil, Venezuela, Colombia and the islands of the Caribbean, as well as in Africa, Europe and North America—have reached a level of political maturity where they understand that the empowerment of the Black people of Harlem is not possible until Black men in the Congo are in full control of the vast mineral wealth of that country, that the millions of Black people who grovel under the boot of the white minority in Zimbabwe (Rhodesia) will remain debased until Nigeria evolves into the economic and military giant which is her potential, and that the *favelas* of Rio will continue to house a disproportionate number of Blacks until Black men control the governments of Angola and Mozambique. *Black World* will routinely publish articles which will probe and report the condition of peoples and their struggles throughout the Black World.

At the same time, the magazine also will continue in the old tradition of *Negro Digest,* publishing the thoughtful essays, the fiction and the poetry of both known and unknown writers, reporting on the arts, educational movements and innovations, and guarding against the opportunists and charlatans who would exploit Black Art and Literature for their own gain and for the spiritual and artistic colonization of Black people. As in the past, the magazine will publish a number of Special Issues during the year, including the Fiction Issue (June) and the Poetry Issue (September). Special Issues this year will focus on the Harlem Renaissance and on the life and work of novelist Ralph Ellison.

Hoyt W. Fuller
Managing Editor

From *Black World,* May 1970.

the history of SUDAN (in Texas?)

During the heat of a Texas summer night in early 1968, brothers Cornell Linson, Thomas Melonson, Harvey King, Sidney Wilson, and Bill Milligan stood in a parking lot and agreed that the time had come for them to move to develop and maintain a community based on the cultural and political program. A program designed to educate and redirect young brothers and sisters toward engaging in positive actions that would strengthen and develop the Houston Black community as one for and of the Black Nation.

The program was named the Progressive Youth Movement, and the Fourth Ward community was chosen as a base of operations. For nine months these five brothers, along with several other brothers and sisters exhausted their energies in experiences that did more to educate them than those for whom the program was intended.

In early October of 1969, Free Southern Theater presented a program at H.O.P.E. Development Incorporated, which made a profound impact on all brothers and sisters who were in attendance, including those brothers and sisters who were exhausting their energies in the Progressive Youth Movement effort.

Brother Rashaan (Linson), and brother Muntu (Meloncon) talked at length with brother Val Ferdinand of F.S.T., about culture F.S.T.'s history, and what he viewed as priority work needed to be done in our black communities.

Shortly after F.S.T. left Houston, members of the Progressive Movement reassessed their efforts. It was discovered that most of the brothers and sisters involved were gifted in the arts, and that everyone agreed that a cultural program based on tradition, reason, justice and honesty, was a priority need. As a result program changes and alterations were made. After an additional four months The Progressive Youth Movement had completely changed in scope, and had begun to shape into the embryo of what is now SUDAN Arts South West Inc.

During the earlier days, SUDAN was directed by Rashann Linson, who has since gone on to build and direct the Black Arts Center (B.A.C). The poetry ensemble, the African dance troupe, and the drama group, were the principal components of the SUDAN effort. The brothers and sisters involved in each component contributed to the development of what is now Black Cultural Institution, designed to research, develop and promote a Black lifestyle that in fact complements the needs and objectives of the Black Nation.

Presently SUDAN is directed by Brother Bill Milligan, a protégé of Brother Rashaan, Brother Bill's house and field experiences, and his literary talents have blended into a sound steering wheel for the movement of SUDAN in a positive direction.

SUDAN functions on the basic premise that Black people have been corrupted by European cultural indoctrination, and that a Black Nation cannot exist on the cultural values of the enemy.

There are three levels on which SUDAN operates:

A. Performances and Production
B. Education and Instruction
C. Everyday Lifestyle.

A. There are at present two performing groups: the Sudan Poets, an ensemble of five poets: Sister Margie, and Brothers Muntu, Orowo, the Prophet, and Bill Milligan. The SUDAN Poets teach in performances, on streets, in schools in homes and churches and in joints in the community, wherever Blacks are to be found so do you find the Sudan Poets. The SUDAN Dancers make up the other performing group; both a children and adult troupe, each of which are as mobile and as active as the poetry ensemble. (The SUDAN Dancers are co-directed by Sisters Gwendolyn Jones, and Rose Davis).

B. Presently there is a standard poetry workshop headed by Brother Muntu (Thomas Meloncon) often referred to as the philosopher, poet and also known as a singer. (Brother Meloncon is nationally known as a Black Folk Singer; he has recorded the relevant sellers, "400 Years" and "Waiting On Your Mind").

C. All SUDAN members attempt to practice what they believe to be life ways based on tradition, reason, and honesty. The Seven Principles (The Nguzo Saba) serves as the overall guideline for all actions.

SUDAN is a young institution in an old struggle whose maturity will come as a result of hard work and efforts toward our victory in the struggle, and the building and maintaining of the Black Nation there after.

This is the symbol of SUDAN:
It simply means: SUDAN seeks to promote the unity of all Black people for the immortality of our race.

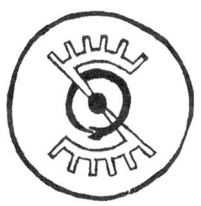

even in texas brothers and sisters are on the case.

THE INSTITUTE OF THE BLACK WORLD
MARTIN LUTHER KING, JR.
MEMORIAL CENTER
ATLANTA, GEORGIA
STATEMENT OF PURPOSE AND PROGRAM
FALL, 1969

Introduction

The Institute of the Black World is a community of black scholars, artists, teachers and organizers who are coming together in Atlanta under the aegis of the Martin Luther King, Jr. Memorial Center. (It is also a group of several dozen "Associates of the Institute" who are located in various parts of the hemisphere.)

The Institute of the Black World is a gathering of black intellectuals who are convinced that the gifts of their minds are meant to be fully used in the service of the black community. It is therefore an experiment with scholarship in the context of struggle.

Among our basic concerns and commitments is the determination to set our skills to a new understanding of the past, present and future condition of the peoples of African descent, wherever they may be found, with an initial emphasis on the American experience. This seems the least that history, or the present—to say nothing of our children— would demand of those persons who have lived the black experience and have developed certain gifts of analysis, creativity and communication.

Program of Work

In cooperating with several institutions of higher education, the Institute of the Black World has set itself to the following specific tasks in the years ahead:

1. *The definition and refining of the field now loosely called "Black Studies."* After having taken the lead in calling for a new encounter the staff of the Institute has now begun a long-range, careful analysis of the content and direction of Black Studies programs

---

From *The Massachusetts Review,* Autumn 1969.

across the nation. A recently-ended summer workshop and a series of seminars with Black Studies directors over the next academic year (1969–70) will eventually produce a set of documents which will analyze existing programs, review and respond to the major criticisms of Black Studies, put forth a set of ideological positions concerning the field and offer certain suggestions about its future directions.

2. *The development of a new Consortium for Black Education.* This consortium will involve the Institute and a group of colleges and universities drawn primarily from the historically black institutions of higher education. During the 1969–70 academic year the Institute of the Black World will definitely share its staff, personnel and Associates with Fisk, Howard, Shaw and Wesleyan Universities and probably with Tuskegee Institute and several of the Atlanta University Center schools. IBW staff and Associates will lecture, offer seminars, engage in workshops and generally consult with students, faculty and administrators on these campuses. Students from at least one of these schools will work in Atlanta with Institute personnel in seminars and individual research.

   In the course of this year our staff will also be developing new, black-saturated curriculum and course models in several areas of the Humanities and the Social Sciences. The Consortium schools will experiment with and evaluate these materials over a period of several years, beginning with the 1970–71 academic year.

3. *The encouragement of basic academic research in the experiences of the peoples of African descent.* All of the research staff will be engaged in individual projects, such as "Education and Decolonization"; "The Poetry of the Blues"; "The Self-Concepts of Black Women"; "Black American Attitudes Towards Africa in the 19th Century"; "Black Radicalism and Black Religion." Each senior staff person will offer at the Institute one seminar per semester related to his research area. (See the attached list of research staff persons.) In addition, several persons will be encouraged to relate to the Institute on a part-time basis so that their research can add to our mutual strengthening.

4. *The encouragement of black artists, especially those who are searching for an aesthetic which will contribute to the struggle for the minds and hearts of our people.* Such artists will be invited to enter the dialogue and search of the Institute, to create out of their own vision and materials, and to share their creativity with the black community off campus.

5. *The development of new materials and methods for the teaching of black children.* Several members of the Institute staff are responsible for our work with two independent, black community schools in Atlanta, the H. Rapp Brown Community School and the Martin Luther King Jr. Community School. These institutions will serve as laboratories for new content and approaches, especially related to the black experience. (Some relationships to the Atlanta Public School system are also being developed.) In turn, the results of this experimentation will be fed back into the teacher training programs of the colleges and universities associated with the Institute, through workshops, seminars and new curriculum.

6. *The development of a Black Policy Studies Center.* An attempt will be made to develop solid tools of social analysis focused on the contemporary situation of the black community in America and committed totally to the struggle of that community for

self-determination. Persons and organizations representing the full spectrum of ideological thought in the black community will be brought together periodically for unpublicized encounters outside of the polemical arena. It is expected that this Center will make it possible for persons who need it to find a place of creative withdrawal from the day-to-day activity of the struggle and to enter into significant dialogue with a committed community of black artists, scholars and organizers from other parts of the nation and the world. A variety of policy papers and guidelines will likely develop out of this section of the IBW. Eventually, the Institute will move to the training of community organizers whose work flows out of a rigorous and non-romantic analysis of the situation of the black community (which includes, of course, a realistic assessment of the state of the white community and its leaders). We are certain that no significant movement for justice and self-determination can continue without this level of analysis and organization.

7. *The establishment of creative links with our counterparts in other areas of the Black World.* In Latin America, the Caribbean, Africa and elsewhere black scholars, artists, educators and organizers are grappling with many issues very similar to those which engage us in North America. The Institute will continue its attempt to carry on significant dialogue and mutually agreed upon work with such persons, through individual visits, seminars, conferences and many types of exchanges.

8. *The preparation of a new cadre of men and women who are at once precisely trained in the scholarship of the black experience and fully committed to the struggles of the black world.* Through affiliation with graduate and undergraduate schools, the Institute expects eventually to be of service to persons who wish both to relate to its work and to seek degrees. (However, the IBW has no immediate plans of its own for becoming a degree-granting institution. It prefers to serve those institutions which already have this capacity.) At the same time, the Institute will experiment with new ways to prepare non-degree educators for their role in the instruction of the black community.

9. *The sponsoring of short-term seminars and of vacation and summer workshops and conferences, both independently and in concert with one or more of the cooperative institutions.* In each of the areas of concern mentioned above, the Institute will be seeking to share its findings and to expand its own competence by meeting regularly with others who are engaged in similar concerns and commitments. Among the first of these will be a seminar for selected Black Studies Directors (November 7–9) and a Conference on "Black Studies and the Future of Negro Colleges" (December 27–29 or January 2–4).

10. *The development of a publishing program.* Such a program will make available to a broader audience much of the work and concern of the Institute and other groups and individuals working at the same tasks. Its output would include basic academic research on the black experience, policy study papers, curriculum materials and the creative productions of black artists. A newsletter of Black Studies will be one of its first periodicals. A *Dictionary of Black American Biography* is a long-range task.

LIBERATION COMMITTEE FOR AFRICA

P.O. Box 303, Cathedral Station   •   New York 25, N.Y.   •   UN 6-1256

Daniel H. Watts
Chairman

STATEMENT OF AIMS

The Liberation Committee for Africa has been founded in the belief that freedom and equality for Americans of African descent is inextricably linked with freedom for Africans in their own home lands. The aims of this Committee have been developed in accordance with this belief.

> TO WORK FOR AND SUPPORT THE IMMEDIATE LIBERATION OF ALL COLONIAL PEOPLES
>
> TO PROVIDE A PUBLIC FORUM FOR AFRICAN FREEDOM FIGHTERS
>
> TO PROVIDE CONCRETE AID TO AFRICAN FREEDOM FIGHTERS
>
> TO RE-ESTABLISH AWARENESS OF THE COMMON CULTURAL HERITAGE OF AFRO-AMERICANS WITH THEIR AFRICAN BROTHERS

What Africa Means to Americans

FOR 20 MILLION AMERICANS of African descent, Africa means the homeland of their ancestors, a rediscovered cultural heritage, a renewed pride in their history and a new sense of dignity as black men who see Africa's struggle for freedom as part of their own struggle for freedom and equality in the United States.

FOR MANY OTHER AMERICANS, Africa is the crucial test for the United States, which will determine whether the ideals of independence and freedom which this country has long proclaimed are to be concrete in our foreign policy, and indeed even within our own borders.

Although 20 African countries have won their independence from colonial rule in less than a decade, elsewhere in Africa millions of African freedom fighters are being murdered, tortured and imprisoned. It is the duty of all men who care for liberty to give all possible aid to these freedom fighters in

Algeria	**Rhodesia and Nyasaland**
Angola	**Ruanda-Urundi**
Congo	**South West Africa**
Mozambique	**South Africa**

On February 15th, 1961, following Premier Lumumba's foul murder, some 60 Afro-Americans demonstrated their passionate concern for Africa's freedom in the U.N. Security Council. They were bodily ejected from the Security Council chambers, but continued their demonstration for several days before the U.N. Building, where their ranks were swollen by hundreds of Americans of all races.

The Liberation Committee for Africa, organized in June 1960, includes Americans of all races, took part in that demonstration and now seeks to make permanent that unity of purpose and effort. The Committee seeks to give Africans a voice here in the United States, it tries to give concrete aid and assistance to those who are battling overwhelming odds in Africa, it seeks to inform all Americans of Africa's proud heritage, long obscured by racist myths. It calls on all Americans to join it in making real the ideals of freedom, justice and equality, which have long been proclaimed in this country but not yet made tangible to many millions of Americans of African descent.

THE LIBERATION COMMITTEE FOR AFRICA NEEDS YOUR SUPPORT

Would you like to help? Fill out the form below.

Daniel H. Watts, Chairman   Richard Gibson, Executive Secretary

Lowell P. Beveridge, Research Secretary

FOOD FOR THOUGHT

We are now into the seventies and we all agree that the number one issue for black people in the seventies is survival. And in a beautiful and crazy complimentary sense the number one issue for <u>NKOMBO</u> is survival. The future of <u>NKOMBO</u> is directly tied to the collective destiny of black people. So as long as black people are breathing <u>NKOMBO</u> will survive because it and black people are one. <u>NKOMBO</u>, just as all black people, caught hell trying to stay together. Many people don't realize the behind the lines shuffling that must go down in order to keep a black magazine coming out issue after issue. The human side of the revolution is often forgotten amid the thunderous roars of rhetoric rapping so-called revolutionaries put down instead of doing the work of nation building. The human, black humanistic touch of love/sacrifice that is so, so necessary is too often overlooked. If the whiteboys are talking about they have to try harder, just think what <u>we</u>, all of us, must have to do. Money is scarce. Ask any black organization out there trying to get something done about the money situation. But we're gonna survive, we gonna make it. <u>NKOMBO</u> is going to keep on coming, miss the rent a month, skip a car note, dig some ditches, whatever it takes to keep it coming we're going to do it. We have received many encouraging letters from readers, writers and well-wishers. Asante brothers and sisters, your words are appreciated.

The writers, artists, etc. who comprise BLKARTSOUTH are no different from black people everywhere when it comes to being victims of this sick white west. The writers eat and shit too. Poets may not act like it but they have rent bills that are due each month. And we all know that the oppressive system we live under makes no distinctions. And so since the very beginning we have been talking about us black people, our relation to America, our problems, and our common struggle to liberate ourselves. We are all well aware that a poem will not stop a bullet and that black people cannot eat books. When the baby cries for milk a new poem will not fill his stomach. When the pigs push us up against the wall a hip short story ain't gonna make magic and let us walk away. We can't off pigs with plays! We know this. But what we hope to do with our writing is reflect where black people are at, to show how we as black people are dealing with common problems that we all face. We hope to somehow connect all of us up. We hope to be able to bring black people closer together and at the same time push us farther on down that road that leads to the <u>nation</u>. It is very easy to see that we do not all agree on methods, ideologies, and systems of thot. Our influences that we have absorbed are many and various. Some of us are pan-africanists, some are muslims, some are black nationalists and some of us don't know what we are, but we are all trying. All of us are striving to make things happen for our people. Good things.

As our readers have probably noticed we are still experimenting with format. This is something that will continue to happen as it is a legitimate reflection of the different tactics and techniques that our people are applying in this struggle with the devil. There are some problems that we are faced with that only time coupled with an honest assessment of ourselves will solve. We have only to be honest in our assessments of what we are doing; we can solve the problems. We of NKOMBO invite your criticisms, suggestions, advice or what have you. We need it. We need to see ourselves from as many different black views as possible.

Our main criticism of ourselves would be our laxity in living up to what we write and say we are. The beginning of the seventies find us deeply examining ourselves trying to cast out the shortcomings of our characters and reinforcing the natural goodness of our black spiritualities. And to this end we are much more religious/spiritual in our outlooks than we were last year. We are much more aware of ourselves as black people and the images that we present to black people. We have a lot of growing to do. We are not asking you to bear with us as we attempt this black growth, but rather we insist that you grow with us, we insist that we be our black selves.

Speak/BE

the poets should
remember
that the people
have eyes
as well as ears

for surely
no book one
could write
can teach a child
to dance
and just as important
the words of the
poets should be
descriptions
of the poets'
being/actions

the male child/female child
learns the ways
of manhood/womanhood
from the actions
of men/women
speak the words
of a man/ woman
and the people
will expect
to see the actions of
a man/ woman
so that when you
speak
of manhood/womanhood
you will
be
a righteous poet

a poet is a poem
and his life is
the greatest book
he will ever write

when people seek the poets
let them find the men and women
whose voices they hear
for a poet must do more than
write

do not call
yourself a poet
unless you are
prepared
to live
your poems

as salaam alaikum
PEACE & LIBERATION

(Kalamu ya Salaam signature)

Kalamu ya Salaam
(val Ferdinand)

ELIJAH MUHAMMAD

"WHAT DO THE MUSLIMS WANT?"

What do the Muslims want?

This is the question asked most frequently by both the whites and the blacks. The answers to this question I shall state as simply as possible.

Since we cannot get along with them in peace and equality, after giving them 400 years of our sweat and blood and receiving in return some of the worst treatment human beings have ever experienced, we believe our contributions to this land and the suffering forced upon us by white America, justifies our demand for complete separation in a state or territory of our own.

1. We want freedom. We want a full and complete freedom.

2. We want justice. Equal justice under the law. We want justice applied equally to all, regardless of creed or class or color.

3. We want equality of opportunity. We want equal membership in society with the best in civilized society.

4. We want our people in America whose parents or grandparents were descendants from slaves, to be allowed to establish a separate state or territory of their own—either on this continent or elsewhere. We believe that our former slave masters are obligated to provide such land and that the area must be fertile and minerally rich. We believe that our former slave masters are obligated to maintain and supply our needs in this separate territory for the next 20 to 25 years—until we are able to produce and supply our own needs.

5. We want freedom for all Believers of Islam now held in federal prisons. We want freedom for all black men and women now under death sentence in innumerable prisons in the North as well as the South.

We want every black man and woman to have the freedom to accept or reject being separated from the slave master's children and establish a land of their own.

We know that the above plan for the solution of the black and white conflict is the best and only answer to the problem between two people.

6. We want an immediate end to the police brutality and mob attacks against the so-called Negro throughout the United States.

From Elijah Muhammad, "The Muslim Program," *Muhammad Speaks,* July 31, 1962.

We believe that the Federal government should intercede to see that black men and women tried in white courts receive justice in accordance with the laws of the land—or allow us to build a new nation for ourselves, dedicated to justice, freedom and liberty.

7. As long as we are not allowed to establish a state or territory of our own, we demand not only equal justice under the laws of the United States, but equal employment opportunities—NOW!

We do not believe that after 400 years of free or nearly free labor, sweat and blood, which has helped America become rich and powerful, that so many thousands of black people should have to subsist on relief, charity or live in poor houses.

8. We want the government of the United States to exempt our people from ALL taxation as long as we are deprived of equal justice under the laws of the land.

9. We want equal education—but separate schools up to 16 for boys and 18 for girls on the condition that the girls be sent to women's colleges and universities. We want all black children educated, taught and trained by their own teachers.

Under such schooling system we believe we will make a better nation of people. The United States government should provide, free, all necessary text books and equipment, schools and college buildings. The Muslim teachers shall be left free to teach and train their people in the way of righteousness, decency and self-respect.

10. We believe that intermarriage or race mixing should be prohibited. We want the religion of Islam taught without hinderance, or suppression.

These are some of the things that we, the Muslims, want for our people in North America.

Statement of Basic Aims and Objectives
June 28, 1964

VI—Culture

"A race of people is like an individual man; until it uses its own talent, takes pride in its own history, expresses its own culture, affirms its own selfhood, it can never fulfill itself."

Our history and our culture were completely destroyed when we were forcibly brought to America in chains. And now it is important for us to know that our history did not begin with slavery's scars. We come from Africa, a great continent and a proud and varied people, a land which is the new world and was the cradle of civilization. Our culture and our history are as old as man himself and yet we know almost nothing of it. We must recapture our heritage and our identity if we are ever to liberate ourselves from the bonds of white supremacy. We must launch a cultural revolution to unbrainwash an entire people.

Our cultural revolution must be the means of bringing us closer to our African brothers and sisters. It must begin in the community and be based on community participation. Afro-Americans will be free to create only when they can depend on the Afro-American community for support and Afro-American artists must realize that they depend on the Afro-American for inspiration. We must work toward the establishment of a culture center in Harlem, which will include people of all ages, and will conduct workshops in all the arts, such as film, creative writing, painting, theater, music, Afro-American history, etc.

This cultural revolution will be the journey to our rediscovery of ourselves. History is a people's memory, and without a memory man is demoted to the lower animals.

Armed with the knowledge of the past, we can with confidence charter a course for our future. Culture is an indispensable weapon in the freedom struggle. We must take hold of it and forge the future with the past.

OBAC [Organization of Black American Culture]

Editor's Note: The following Statement of Purpose and commentary by Abdul Alkalimat, Haki Madhubuti, Hoyt Fuller, Sterling Plumpp, and Angela Jackson were originally published in OBAC's periodicals, NOMMO and Cumbaya. They provide a brief overview of the organization's philosophy, founding and development.

Statement of Purposes

To work toward the development and definition of a Black Aesthetic

To encourage the highest quality of literary expression reflecting the Black Experience

To establish and define the standards by which that creative writing which reflects the Black Experience is to be judged and evaluated

To encourage the growth and development of Black critics who are fully qualified to evaluate and judge Black literature on its own merits while, at the same time, cognizant of the traditional values and standards of Western literature and fully able to articulate the differences between the two literatures

To encourage an atmosphere of brotherhood and tolerance within the workshop, so that criticism can be both given and accepted as being constructive in intent

To work toward the establishment of a regular publication—in the form of newsletter, journal or newspaper, or in whatever form the workshop members choose—which will make available to the Black community the creative products from the workshop, ideas relative to Black Experientialism and OBAC, and news and announcements

To work toward the periodical publication of books and anthologies containing the literary work of workshop members, plus, if desirable, creative work from other OBAC workshops

To provide a forum and a community of hospitality for local and visiting writers

STATEMENT OF PURPOSE

Rhythm is a component of the Atlanta Center for Black Art. Like the Center, Rhythm is committed to Revolutionary Pan-African Nationalism, which we broadly define as the recognition that people of African origin did not cease to be Africans because they were enslaved; that we are citizens of Africa, responsible to work with other African people, wherever they are, to build liberated zones which ultimately can merge into the new Africa of the 21st century. Rhythm sees African people as having no moral or legal responsibility to the west except to oversee its destruction.

Rhythm is based in the southern u. s. and will focus on southern readers, writers and realities. However, we will publish any and all materials made available to us which clarify in a relevant way the present, future and the past of African peoples.

From *Rhythm* 1.1 (1970).

To the Peoples of Afroamerica, Africa, and to all the Peoples of the World

We the Editors of SOULBOOK subscribe to the view expressed by the great Black martyr Patrice Lumumba that ". . . without dignity there is no liberty, without justice there is no dignity, and without independence there are no free men." Furthermore, we adhere to the view that it will take a radical socio-economic transformation within the United States before the freedom of the Black man in the U.S., the Congo, and anywhere else the victims of racial discrimination have been maimed by this gorgonesque practice can be won and guaranteed for all time.

Thus to further the cause of the liberation of Black peoples we feel that this Journal and all ensuing issues of it must be produced, controlled, published and edited by people who are sons and daughters of Africa.

By this control we feel we can more freely present to the world the widest scope and the highest quality of thoughts, ideas and works that will most accurately describe racial oppression and how best it is being and/or how it can be fought against and destroyed.

We feel by having Black control of SOULBOOK we can be sure that the poetry and prose presented in this Journal will give the most meaningful understanding of what Blackness is, and be sure that it is expressed, as much as possible, as a natural fact of experience. We are certain that the necessary prerequisite to achieve these two ends is that the authors of this literature be Black.

Black American literature has tended to be parochial simply because most Black writers did not actually believe that their experience and understanding of the world was valuable merely because it was theirs (and real), but rather because they were Black or half-Black or "passing" or even because they could pretend not to be any of these, and by such set make a display of "culture" in the White man's hopeless world.

The Blackness of the best Black writing is not only in the fact of its creating myth and emotion that has legitimately been got by translating into art the peculiar emotional life of the Black man, but as world gesture that should be understood by any human being.

Lastly, to be sure that no one misunderstands where our commitment lies, we publicly dedicate our publication to Felix Moumie, Medgar Evers, Reuben Um Nyobo, the six

---

From *Soulbook* 1 (Winter 1964).

child-martyrs of the Birmingham bombings of 1963, Patrice Lumumba, Ronald Stokes, Antonio Maceo, the dead Freedom Fighters of Kenya and Algeria, and the endless number of other known and unknown Black Freedom Fighters who have been gunned down by the imperialist oppressors in Afroamerica, Africa, Latin America and Asia.

the editors

BY-LAWS, SOUTHERN BLACK CULTURAL ALLIANCE

Article I – Name

The name of this organization is and shall be
THE SOUTHERN BLACK CULTURAL ALLIANCE INC.,
chartered under the laws of the state of Florida as a non-profit corporation, hereinafter known as the Alliance.

The principal office of the Company shall be located in the City of Miami, Florida.

Article II – Objectives

The objectives of the Alliance shall be:

(1) To produce, exhibit and promote cultural attractions of our members; including drama, musical performances, intellectual, instructive, and educational entertainment to all parts of the country. The bulk of the attractions shall be concerned with an emphasis on those aspects of history and human culture that have heretofore been neglected.

(2) To conduct all such activities as may be appropriate to carry out the objectives of the corporation. Because the corporation is being organized and will be operated exclusively for literary, educational and/or cultural purposes, no substantial part of the corporation shall be to influence legislation or intervene in any political campaign on behalf of any candidate for public offices.

(3) To provide a structured intra-state organization for persons involved in the kinds of activities identified in subparagraph (1) above, whereby, directors, actors, writers, technicians, business managers, artists, communications specialist, etc., may better learn their crafts and apply their acquired skills.

(4) To make the community more aware of the history and culture of those segments of the community whose history and culture have heretofore been neglected.

(5) Publish a newsletter at least 4 times a year.

(6) To use our creative talents as a vehicle for positive social change in our communications.

(7) To document the creative work produced by the member persons and organizations.

(8) To develop and encourage communication among the Black Cultural institutions in the South.

Article III – Memberships

Membership in the Alliance shall be schools, individuals, community theatres, professional theatres, dance troupes, and other interested organizations.

Section A. The member organizations shall be:
Any college, university, or community organization interested in the dramatic and communications arts.
Section B. The individual membership shall consist of:
Any person interested in either visual, performing arts, or communications arts.

Article IV – Regional Units

There shall be 3 geographical regional units of the organization for the purpose of administering regional activities. They are as follows:

Southeastern Region: North Carolina, South Carolina, Florida, Virginia, and West Virginia.
South Central Region: Alabama, Mississippi, Kentucky, Tennessee.
Southwestern Region: Arkansas, Oklahoma, Louisiana, and Texas.

Article V – Meetings

Section A. The Annual conference of the association shall be held each year on Memorial Day at a place designated 1½ years prior to that conference.
Section B. The chairperson may call a meeting of the Executive Committee at any time between conferences to act in an emergency.

THIRD WORLD PRESS,
A STATEMENT OF PURPOSE

The third world is a liberating concept for people of color, non-europeans—for Black people. That world has an ethos—a black aesthetic if u will—and it is the intent of Third World Press to capture that ethos, that black energy. We attempt to give an initial exposure to black writers. We publish black (poetry, historical notes, essays, short stories, and hopefully novellas) for Africans here (most often referred to as "negroes") and Africans abroad. And because we publish black—profit is not our thing/not our thing.

—The Editors

MAX STANFORD (MUHAMMAD AHMAD)

TOWARDS REVOLUTIONARY ACTION
MOVEMENT MANIFESTO

RAM was officially organized in the winter of 1963 by Afro-Americans who favored Robert F. Williams and the concept of organized violence. Through a series of workshop discussions, the group decided there was a need for a "Third Force" or movement that would be somewhere between the Nation of Islam (Black Muslims) and SNCC (Student Non-Violent Coordinating Committee.)

Objectives

1. To give black people a sense of racial pride, dignity, unity and solidarity in struggle.
2. To give black people a new image of manhood and womanhood.
3. To free black people from colonial and imperialist bondage everywhere and to take whatever steps necessary to achieve that goal.
4. To give black people a sense of purpose.

The motto was "One Purpose, One Aim, One Destiny," meaning:

ONE PURPOSE—To free black people from the universal slavemaster (slang for capitalist oppression).

ONE AIM—To develop black people through struggle to the highest attainment possible.

ONE DESTINY—To follow in the spirit of black revolutionaries such as Gabriel Prosser, Toussant L'Overture, Denmark Vesey, Nat Turner, Sojourner Truth, Harriet Tubman, Frederick Douglass, Marcus Garvey, Dr. Du Bois, Robert F. Williams, and to create a new world free of colonialism, racism, imperialism, exploitation, and national oppression.

Thus RAM was officially organized as a movement. With rotating chairmen to develop leadership, RAM immediately plunged into action. It helped organize one of Philadelphia's largest black mass rallies for the NAACP over the issue of a "research project" designed by white liberals for the black community.

We felt a need for "fresh, young and new ideas" to be discussed in the black community, so we began publishing a bi-monthly *Black America*. RAM then organized several street

From Max Stanford, "Towards Revolutionary Action Movement Manifesto," *Correspondence* (March 1964): 3, 5.

meetings in the heart of the black ghetto to bring its program to our people, obtained an office, and began to hold free weekly African and Afro-American history classes. Through a free weekly publication, *Ram Speaks,* RAM attempted to raise the consciousness of the black community by the discussion of political issues.

RAM found, through its active involvement and living with the black masses, that one of the main reasons that we (black people) are unorganized is because we (black people) are politically unaware. RAM then reorganized its program to education in political revolution. We soon saw that the key to the black man's plight is his lack of revolutionary organization. We felt that this could best be brought about by the organization of a black political party. But we also felt that this black political party must have revolutionary objectives and not that of peaceful co-existence with the oppressor. In other words, we felt the need for a black revolution that could and would seize power.

In spreading revolutionary concepts throughout the community and especially among youth, RAM became a target for the power structure. When RAM demonstrated, along with many other groups over the racist-fascist police tactics used against unarmed women, children and men in Birmingham, the NAACP tried to oust RAM from a "united" picket line because of its sign stating, "We do not advocate non-violence in a police state." The more RAM pushed, the more the reformist leadership had to sound aggressive. When the NAACP decided to organize demonstrations over union discrimination on a school construction site, RAM played a major role. The racist-fascist police seized the opportunity to attack some RAM organizers and frame them on trumped-up charges of assault and battery, cutting, disorderly conduct, disturbing the peace, and conspiracy.

It soon became apparent that the NAACP and CORE were fighting to get headlines, so RAM ceased its public program and began to develop its members and those around them. RAM felt this was necessary since, in order to make our black revolt into a successful black revolution, we would have to train people in what real revolution means and what it is going to take.

To answer some question raised by "orthodox black nationalists" and charges that RAM is an integrationist group, I will explain why we participated in the school construction site struggle.

As revolutionary black nationalists, we do not believe that standing on the street corners alone will liberate our people. Revolutionary black nationalists must act as a vanguard to show our people how to seize power so that they may gain some control over their lives. The main reason they are treated the way they are is that they are powerless. In the school construction site demonstration, our people saw the system denying them opportunity. As our struggle developed, they saw that the police who represent the state or state power were not on our side but on the side of those who uphold racism. This brought in the concept of government, protection of the community by a black people's police force, and the concept that we are at war with white America. Thus by our action, our people gained a vital lesson in the need for a revolutionary organization that has power by physical example and involvement.

RAM soon found that just being out in the streets was not enough and that national revolutionary organization was the key to victory of our revolution. RAM also shifted its program to an accent on youth. After careful analysis through action and study, RAM feels that black youth are the key to our revolution. We see youth all over the world leading the revolutions of our people. In the Angolan liberation army the soldiers' age range is 17–20; in the Congo's guerilla force called "Youth" the age range is 14–20; in the Viet Cong the age range is 14–19; in Kenya the Mau Mau was started by roving bands of youth. In Cuba Castro's forces were very young.

During the summer of 1963 RAM reorganized and sent field organizers throughout the North to help local groups organize demonstrations. Through our experience we have developed an organization on three levels of involvement: 1) *Field Organizers,* who are full-time organizers with a period of orientation and training in the movement; 2) *Active Members,* who cannot be full-time but actively support RAM by physical, financial and other help, and have also been through a period of orientation; 3) *Associate Members,* who have been through a period of orientation but, for reasons approved by the movement, cannot give physical support but do pledge financial support. During the fall of 1963, RAM field organizers helped groups throughout the South develop a perspective beyond the limits of the integrationist movement. Also in Philadelphia, RAM's home base, RAM in 1962 and 1963 fought several cases of police brutality and in one case achieved unity among the young black militant groups for a brief period. RAM has recently been active in organizing demonstrations around the frame-up of Mae Mallory and the other Monroe defendants.

RAM philosophy

RAM philosophy may be described as revolutionary nationalism, black nationalism or just plain blackism. It is that black people of the world (darker races, black, yellow, brown, red, oppressed peoples) are all enslaved by the same forces. RAM's philosophy is one of the world black revolution or world revolution of oppressed peoples rising up against their former slave-masters. Our movement is a movement of black people who are coordinating their efforts to create a "new world" free from exploitation and oppression of man to man.

In the world today there is a struggle for world power between two camps, the haves (Western or white capitalist nations) and the have-nots (Eastern or newly independent nations struggling for independence, socialist nations). There are two types of nationalism. One type suppresses or oppresses, that is, a nation or particular group reaps profits or advances materially at the expense, exploitation, slavery or torture of another group or nation. In this nation and in the world today, this nationalism is considered "white nationalism" or the cooperation of the white Western nations to keep the new emerging oppressed world in bondage. This is capitalist or reactionary nationalism. The other type of nationalism is to liberate or free from exploitation. That is the binding force of a nation or particular group to free itself from a group or nation that is suppressing or oppressing it. In this country and in the world, this is considered black nationalism or revolutionary nationalism.

We can see that black nationalism is the opposite of white nationalism; black nationalism being revolutionary and white being reactionary. We see also that nationalism is really internationalism today.

While defining nationalism as a force towards black liberation, we define nationalism as black patriotism.

Nationalism is an identification and consciousness of our own kind and self. Knowledge of self is an integral part of nationalism. Knowledge of our own history of struggle is an essential part of nationalism. Love for our own people and not for the enemy is nationalism.

RAM feels that with the rise of fascism, the black man must not only think of armed self-defense but must also think aggressively.

Our black nation is still in captivity. RAM feels that the road to freedom is self-government, national liberation and black power. Our slogan is "Unite or perish." Our definition of revolution is one group's determination to take power away from another.

In ending this manifesto, we (RAM) say, "Think what you wish, but we shall accomplish what we will."

FOREWORD

UMBRA is not another haphazard 'little literary' publication. UMBRA has a definite orientation: 1) the experience of being Negro, especially in America; and 2) that quality of human awareness often termed 'social consciousness.'

We do not exist for those seemingly selected perennial 'best sellers' and literary 'spokesmen of the race situation' who are currently popular in the commercial press and slick ingroup journals. There are unpublished and infrequently published ethnic writers whose works are excellent, important and often far superior to those adopted few with which the standard press habitually and expediently affronts the public.

UMBRA exists to provide a vehicle for those outspoken and youthful writers who present aspects of social and racial reality which may be called 'uncommercial', 'unpalatable', unpopular', 'unwanted'—but cannot with any honesty be considered nonessential to a whole and healthy society. Because UMBRA is not preoccupied with monetary or prestige considerations it can afford to offer a platform to writers who are young, unknown or <u>too hard</u> on society. The subject matter of accepted journals is too often dictated by the fears of backers, and the views of readers whom those journals fear to lose.

We maintain no iron-fisted, bigoted policy of preference or exclusion of material. UMBRA will not be a propagandistic, psychopathic or ideological axe-grinder. We will not print trash, no matter how relevantly it deals with race, social issues, or anything else. We are not a self-deemed radical publication; we are as radical as society demands the truth to be. We declare an unequivocal commitment to material of literary integrity and artistic excellence.

UMBRA is a group project. The magazine grew out of Friday night workshops, meetings and readings on Manhattan's Lower East Side last summer—and out of the need expressed for it at those meetings.

We will finance ourselves by contributions, sales of the magazine and fund-raising parties. A writer whose material we use will receive two (2) copies of the issue in which his

---

From *Umbra* 1.1 (Winter 1963)

work appears. We hope your support will enable us to eventually reward our contributors in cash.

A self-addressed, stamped envelope must accompany each unsolicited submission.

Send us your material: poetry, short stories, articles and essays. If you believe UMBRA deserves to survive and grow, a subscription would help. UMBRA exists for you.

The Editors

Resolutions

Creativity is the soul of the nation. It influences and shapes the mind and direction of the struggle for national self-determination. It is concerned with the collective ethos of the people. Without it, the whole of whatever we want to be cannot be realized. For when we speak of creativity, we are, in fact speaking about the spiritual manifestations of the people, of their will to survive beyond the merely physical. We are speaking of ways of thinking, ways of styling the struggle, and ways of insuring that the victories gained in areas of politics, economics, education, religion, etc., will not be lost in the battle for the soul. We therefore must be concerned with establishing our own cultural institutions devoted to cultural analysis and cultural education.

Contrary to popular belief, an institution is not merely brick and mortar. It may be thought of as a set pattern of social action and interaction. It concerns a value system. It concerns the manner in which people should relate to one another. One of the most positive examples of institution-building is the Congress of African Peoples itself. This is an institution committed to the creation, recreation and circulation of the positive ideals of nation building.

Art for art's sake is an invalid concept; art reflects the value system from which it comes. It is the charge of the artist to create, preserve, promote and perpetuate these values through art. Art must speak to and inspire Black people.

INSTITUTION-BUILDING PROPOSAL

We the members of the committee for institution-building understand the necessity of building and stabilizing Black institutions that are relevant and elevate the ongoing struggle for self-liberation. We propose to initiate through the C.A.P. a major effort to build new institutions and make relevant and consequently stabilize existing ones. It is further understood that these institutions must be founded and sustained using the principles of self-determination, eventually self-sufficiency and self-respect at all times.

The Committee for Black Institution-Building recommends the following schedule for

---

From *African Congress; A Documentary of the First Modern Pan-African Congress,* ed. LeRoi Jones (Amiri Baraka) (New York: Morrow, 1972).

local members of the Congress of African Peoples and the national creative workshop of the Congress of African Peoples.

Schedule of activities for local members of
the Congress of African Peoples

A. Get a legal charter prepared and submitted within two weeks after the adjournment of the congress.
B. Upon receipt of a charter (estimated time November 5, 1970), immediately apply for a tax-exempt status.*

Note: The percentage you are granted determines the percentage of income a donor can give. Apply for the highest percentage initially, since applications for changes in percentage are not easily obtained.*

C. Upon receipt of the tax exemption (estimated ninety days), local members should notify the congress of their tax-exempt status.

Note: Miss Elma Lewis of the National Center of Afro-American Artists stated the center would assist *all* creative member organizations upon receipt of tax exemptions. The notification should be done by letter and should include the conceptual view of operations and the needs of the local member's organization.

Duties of the congress with regard to building and
sustaining creative institutions

A. Creation of a component to deal with the problem of funding for member organization.
   1. The congress should have on file a proposal from each member organization.
   2. The congress should have on file all foundations, companies and individuals who *can* contribute to cultural groups.
   3. In an effort to concentrate larger amounts of monies, the congress should attempt to obtain bulk grants for all member groups. This could be done by the congress submitting the proposal in the name of *all* member groups. Upon receipt of funds the congress would act as the distributing agency.
B. The congress should establish an international pool of groups and personalities immediately. A list can be started by members of the congress having international contacts. This list should be made available to all members of the congress.
C. The Congress of African Peoples should immediately begin to collect all available data (slides, poems, short stories, etc.), to begin the establishment of a cultural repository. This could be done by each member group submitting a copy of its works to the congress. Within sub-groups (regional and other) a repository should be set up for the same purpose. This should be coordinated with the existing Atlanta University effort. Also, members should submit the works of non-members who are desirous of cooperating with the venture.
D. Sub-groups of the national congress should be established regionally to carry out the area program. This should be done upon issuance of the list of members.

---

*Costs vary from $25 to $100 according to the state.

E. An endowment should be established for the purpose of putting congress monies into investments. Each member should be taxed 10 percent of his income reporting on a monthly basis. The exact use of the endowment should be determined by the creative council; some suggestions are needed about how to purchase equipment, buildings and how to hire essential personnel. Since an endowment is not money received from a foundation, it can be used for outright purchases.

F. A tour bureau should be established for the purpose of coordinating and expanding the range of touring members. This could be achieved initially by the present touring groups submitting schedules to the congress for study. This effort would permit the exchange of sub-groups and personalities between members of the congress without undue strain on either member.

In summary, the Institution-Building Committee of the Creativity Workshop of the Congress of African Peoples took under consideration the twin problems of institution-building and stabilizing. The suggestions made should by no means be considered complete, but rather a step in the right Black direction.

THEATER:

1. The New Lafayette Theater Workshop's facilities were donated to the Creativity Workshop of the Congress of African Peoples, which should be used collectively, functionally and committedly for:

   A. Co-opting groups around the country who would contribute money and in return guarantee time to perform, insuring enough money for administration and maintenance.

   B. This would involve Black Arts groups, music groups, big-time performers to perform and contribute money. The Spirit House Movers volunteer to help and offer programs and money.

   C. The Congress of African Peoples' theater should be used as a model for setting up new theaters.

   D. The building should be a physical statement of National Liberation.

2. Theater groups should submit a list of their personnel and materials available to their regional representatives so that we can pool our resources and skills. Theater groups are requested to allow slots within their yearly schedule for visiting groups to perform. This will insure collective and operational unity within theater movement.

3. The Negro Ensemble Company has donated its theater from June 13 through September 1 to the Creativity Workshop of the Congress of African Peoples, which should be used for cooperative economics mainly to build and maintain the C.A.P. Theater and to profit together from it.

4. It was proposed that a semiannual journal would come out of and be supported by the Creativity Workshop, which would be involved with the arts. It would:

   A. Rotate editorially.

   B. Aid in strengthening publications already existing, i.e., *Cricket, Journal of Black Poetry.*

   C. Committee would operate with Poor Peoples Corp. in Jackson, Mississippi, which would house an office for operations, and Free Southern Theatre would be the copy office.

5. It was proposed that a clearing house organization and periodical be implemented through the Pan-African Artists' Alliance, an established organization for exposure and sales, and that a permanent council of Black literature and press within the Congress of African Peoples be established. This council will involve itself in:

   A. A periodic bulletin listing of all books produced by Black companies which will be published by them.

   B. It was proposed that a list of books be selected to be included in a special Christmas newsletter. This newsletter will be a part of the abovementioned campaign to advertise, promote, and sell books for raising the level of Black consciousness.

   C. A C.A.P. negotiating committee should be established to induce Negro publishers to place aware Black editors on their editorial boards and protect presently employed journalists from arbitrary dismissal by their Negro press employers.

   D. A Creativity Chest Fund will be established with cash donations coming from (1) affluent writers, (2) fund-raising activities. The creativity section of C.A.P. should initiate and carry out the work involved in making this proposal work.

   E. There should be a Congress of African Peoples' library and Research Center for all Black publications, papers on the movement, works for Black artists, etc.

Revolutionary art must be collective, functional, and committing, i.e., from whole people to a whole people, it must speak to and inspire Black people, it must commit you to revolution (change).

MUSIC:

1. A Black Music Center should be set up to collect and gather information on, and knowledge of, the various musical concepts of Black music.

2. Black musicologists are to be trained to produce a creative cadre of qualified persons who would be able to synthesize, conceptualize, and actually describe our music from a correct perspective, i.e., a Black frame of reference (cultural ideology).

3. Formation of a National Black Music Orchestra. The purpose of this orchestra unit would be to contain, develop, and preserve all of the elements of our musical forms, African traditional music, folk, blues, bebop, new music, etc. It would seek to collect all of the music, so as to break down the differences that now divide us. It would propose by its very form and feeling an alternative to bars and nightclubs.

4. The maintenance and distributions of a Black Music Journal—i.e., strengthening of *Cricket.*

5. Establish a recording studio and a publishing firm. Also, this institute would maintain the following: a worldwide library on the music of peoples of African descent; a legal counseling service, and services for economic and business consultation.

Within the next three months, we will be preparing, submitting, and publicizing proposals among various influential persons and institutions for funding, grants, loans, concerts, and fund-raising banquets.

Special Proposal Passed by Creativity Workshop

The Creativity Workshop agreed to set up an apparatus for the purpose of having a Pan-African Festival of the World African Arts, during the year 1971; preferably it would be held in Africa. This idea was proposed by artist Dana Chandler and passed unanimously by our workshop.

VISUAL ARTS PROPOSAL

1. *The Problem*
    A. Institutions and individuals are not taking advantage of knowledge now available for dealing with individual and institutional problems, due to inadequate channels of communication. Some of the things neglected and/or omitted are:
        1. processes which acquaint African peoples with African art, artists and institutions.
        2. the promotion of a concept of nationhood through unity, developed by a communications/information/resource exchange.
        3. a vehicle whereby African peoples and African arts can be brought together.
        4. helping individuals and institutions to get around problems by helping them to profit from each other's mistakes and successes.
        5. overcoming the "Ebony Fashion Fair" syndrome that high-priced Black visual art has created. We emphasize that this statement is not intended to isolate *Ebony,* but is being used as a symbolic, rather than a specific qualitative reference.
    B. PAAA
    Our discussions led us to the idea of a clearing-house type organization and a periodical to meet the problems mentioned in an expeditious manner.
        The Pan-African Artists' Alliance (PAAA) is the nonprofit organization instituted to meet this need.
2. *Implementation*
    A. A catalog of work; and a sales system, for exposure and sale of work by the PAAA.
        1. Proceeds from items in the catalog will pay for the first publication costs of our periodical.
        2. Subsequent finances will be acquired from sustainer/supporter membership fees and from individuals and groups such as: African peoples, Black student unions, art departments at high schools and colleges, art clubs, libraries and Black businesses, whether small or large.
        3. These individuals and organizations would be required to pay an annual membership fee which entitles them to:
            a. Access to PAAA art works and audio-visual material
            b. PAAA journal,
                articles on African artists, traveling shows, historical information, socio-aesthetic dialogue, reviews and criticism, consulting service on printing and reproductions; techniques and educational resources. In addition, funds will come from donated works, from artists not in attendance at the congress, and through the sale of work-consigned to PAAA. These procedures will eliminate the need for public advertising in the journal.
            c. As of today, PAAA has sustainer/support commitments from Howard University, The National Center of Afro-American Artists (Boston), Pride, Inc.,

Atlanta University Center, Wayne County Community College (Detroit), Anton Studios (New York), Eugene E. White Gallery (San Francisco), and Arthur Britt (Savannah). Tentative commitments have come from the Nairobi Cultural Center and the Mid-Block Art Gallery (New Jersey).

3. *Task Assignments*

The following *ad hoc* assignments have been made:

A. PAAA's mailing address is: Pan-African Artists' Alliance,
c/o Jeff Donaldson, Chairman,
Art Department,
Howard University,
Washington, D.C. 20001

B. The *ad hoc* council will consist of: Jeff Donaldson, Barry Gaither, Terry Hamilton, Floyd Coleman, Harold Neal and Eugene White. The council will maintain close communications and administrate the above program until a permanent mechanism is established, at our second meeting, which is to be held in Boston, January 22, 23, 24, 1971.

4. *The Time Schedule*

Bank account established:	September 10, 1970
Sustainer/support invitations extended:	September 20, 1970
Initial sustainer/support fees due:	October 5, 1970
Catalog—"Images of Independence":	November 5, 1970
Sales of works:	December–February, 1971
Publication—PAAA Review,	
Vol. 1, Issue No. 1:	March 15, 1971

Poetry

The Poetry of the BAM: Meditation, Critique, Praise

Part I: Meditation

Frantz Fanon said: ". . . what is needed is to hold oneself, like a sliver, to the heart of the world, to interrupt if necessary the rhythm of the world, to upset, if necessary, the chain of command . . . but to stand up to the world. I do battle for the creation of a human world, that is, a world of reciprocal recognition."

Jose Marti wrote: "In the world there must be a certain degree of honour just as there must be a certain degree of light. When there are many men/women without honour, there are always others who bear in themselves the honour of many men and women."

How to tell you of peace? Change? Hope? Of racial and sexual and economic injustice? Of an America rising up out of an aristocracy of death. An aristocracy of slavery. Racism. An aristocracy of color. An aristocracy of corporate greed? An America that made Langston Hughes write: "We the people must redeem our land and make America, America again."

How to tell you about lives running on hairpins? Of a country needing parts from people to live? Step right up. I say step right up a good sale on legs today. Eyes today. Hands today. Kidneys today. Hearts today. History/herstory today. Integrity today. Truth today. Families today.

How to tell you of a country that will not recognize the two most important revolutions that were rooted in a cultural base: Cuba and Haiti. These two countries symbolize a regional process of struggle and liberation of the mind which must be an essential part of our journey towards the fulfillment of the western integrity.

How to tell you of progress so we move beyond a politician saying Cuba and Haiti and everyone has the automatic voice of Washington shouting communism. Continue the blockade. Boat people. AIDS. Poverty. But never the eloquent and graceful poetic voice of Marti, the spiritual father of the Cuban Revolution who said as he observed the conduct of the U.S. delegation in 1889 at the monetary congress of the American Republic: They believe in need, in the barbarous right as the only right: "This will be ours because we need it." Almost 100 years late, after the invasion of Grenada by 6,000 U.S. soldiers, the U.S. Secretary of State, George Schultz arrived and his first observation was complete: He said, "This is a delicious piece of real estate."

How to tell you of walking, climbing the Citadel in Haiti and hearing the footsteps of a people, a country crying out for liberty. Economic justice. Equality. And change.

How to really make you understand that it's the poets as prophets. As teachers. As visionaries. As activists. As writers who, sing of peace, racial and social and sexual and economic justice.

How to make you remember Baraka in his 1965 poem "Black Art" declaring "we want poems that kill . . . we want a black poem of a black world! Or Larry Neal's . . . "and there there is jail. America is the world's greatest jails, and we are all in jails, black spirits contained little magnificent birds of wonder."

How to make you remember James Baldwin, a man Baraka called "Gods Black revolutionary mouth" who said in 1979 in a NY Times article, "If Black English isn't a language, then tell me, what is?" Baldwin said, it goes without saying that language is the most novel and crucial key to identity. It reveals the private identity and connects one with or divorces one from the larger public or communal identity.

How to make you hear your hearts sounding, pounding out what W. E. B. Du Bois wrote. This is a beautiful world, this is a wonderful America which the founding fathers dreamed until their sons (and daughters) drowned it in the blood of slavery and devoured it in greed.

How to make you remember the sister poets singing of the workers with words that had the scent of the earth and the genius of the stars. How to make you store in your blood the memory of Black women's voices: Jordan, Fields, Cortez, Clifton, Evans, Fabio, Angelou, Lorde, Giovanni, Rodgers, Sanchez linking continents making the country and the world abandon closed minds, spreading themselves rainbow-like across seas. Their voices stalking the morning stars as they helped a generation of young people begin to question their silence, their poverty. Their scarcity. Their greed. They helped us all ask the most important question we can ask ourselves: What does it mean to be human in the 20th and 21st century?

How to make you continue to lift your eyes off the ground into a higher ground of living. Of Being. Loving?

How to make you remember the poets coming behind us in 1989, Public Enemy? 1989, the number, another summer (get down), sound of the funky drummer, music hitting your heart cuz I know you got soul, gotta give us what we want (uh!), gotta give us what we need (hey), our freedom of speech is freedom or death, we got to fight the power that be, lemme hear you say, Fight The Power. Fight The Power.

As James Stewart the Black critic wrote: Man/woman cannot create a forever. But she/he can only create forever. But she/he can only create if he/she creates as *change*. Creation is itself perpetuation. Change is being! The question of art is dialectical. Art goes. Art is not fixed. Art cannot be fixed. Art is change, like music, poetry and writing are, when concerned.

They must move, sway, not necessarily as physical properties, but by their nature. But they must go spiritually–as we people, lovers and workers of change must go out into this world spiritually and if we do, ebe yiye, ebe yiye, ebe yiye (it'll get better, it'll get better, it'll get better).

Part II: Critique

THE POET AS A CREATOR OF SOCIAL VALUES

I. The Development of Social Values and the Birth of the Poet

Social values spring from human interaction with the environment and are the resultant perception of that experience. The environment of man is all the suggestions which surround the mind and impact it as it pursues human survival, awareness, understanding of itself, its place in society and the universe. Environmental suggestions include nature and its creatures, climate, habitat, the ideas and words of people. Environmental suggestions around the mind create impressions within the mind from which the social personality is formed.

The collective experience of people who interact with the same environment form a worldview, i.e., a version of life by which the significance of all thought and action by members of the society are weighed.

This worldview emerges first in the language and symbol and then in all of society's institutions. But with the birth of symbol, the *birth of the poet* is presaged.

A symbol, for our purposes, is an arbitrary representative of reality, visual or spoken, emanating from a group experience by which that reality is cloaked as well as revealed.

The symbol cloaks reality from those outside the experience and reveals reality on different levels of intensity to those within the experience. For example, the sun is a universal symbol; the three-leaf clover a more parochial one.

Language itself, in a broad sense, is a symbol of the thought interaction and experiences of a people, although it is designed primarily to communicate experiences in fundamental ways. Poetry on the other hand, is the *symbol* or *essence* of *language* designed to sensitize meaning, motivate, create or re-create experience and bestow a state of perception not ordinarily experienced or not experienced in an ordinary way.

The poet then, even though he/she speaks plainly, is a manipulator of symbols and language—images which have been planted by experience in the collective subconscious of a people. Through this manipulation, he/she creates new or intensified meaning and experience whether to the benefit or detriment of his/her audience. Thus poetry is *subconscious conversation:* it is as much the work of those who understand it and those who make it.

The power that the poet has to create, preserve or destroy social values depends greatly on the quality of his/her social visibility and the functionary opportunity available to poetry to impact lives. Like the priest and the prophet (with whom she/he was often synonymous), the poet in some societies has had infinite powers to interpret life; in others his/her voice has been drowned out by the winds of mundane pursuits.

II. The First Poets in Ancient Society and the Crystallization of Symbols

Art, no matter what its intention, reacts to or reflects the culture it springs from. But from the very beginning two types of poetry developed. One can be called the Poetry of Ethos because it was meant to convey personal experience: feelings of love, despair, joy, frustration arising from very private encounter; the other, Functionary Poetry, dealt with themes in the social domain: religion, God, country, work, social institutions, social problems, war, family, marriage and death in the distinct context of that society's perception.

The Poetry of God, The River and The Sun

Poetry's oldest formal ties were with religion. Man's first civilizations, it must be remembered, were theocratic and therefore religiously inspired. Thus were the ancient Black civilizations of the Nile, Mesopotamia, the Indus River and Meso-America societies in which religion as a social vector, not as ritual, exerted a prime force that motivated human action consciously and unconsciously.

The moral and materialistic were not antagonists, science and religion not incongruous. Thus the pyramid as a fitting symbol of the social charter embodied science and of religion as two eyes seeing one vision. A man developing sight into insight, taste into discrimination, feeling into awareness, could become a god and in becoming godlike became a greater servant of God.

The poet-priests of ancient society (Egypt, India, Mesopotamia) are examples of men/women who had the power to interpret life for the society. The poet and priest were synonymous. The priest as poet devoted him/herself to developing symbols of collective experience into teaching tools that inculcated the social values and wisdom of the culture and conveyed the nature of being and the interrelationship between man, God and the universe.

III. Origins of Black and White Poetic Symbol

But nowhere is the power of the poet as a creator of social values so presaged as in the evolution of the dialectics surrounding the colors black and white. These dialectics which were originally used to inculcate metaphysical truth were later manipulated as a weapon of political and racial hegemony. Again, however, the black and white poetic symbology arose from universal environmental experience.

The fact that men/women early in history associated progress with the sun (light), danger and evil with darkness and the night, stemmed from universal primitive experience. During the day man/woman was given a gift of visibility and therefore the ability to pursue survival, enhancement and greater understanding of him/herself and the world. With night came immobility, fear of predators, and the unknown afforded by non-visibility, weakness of limbs, and sleep—the unavoidable simulation of death. Thus the sun or light was associated with good, divinity, knowledge, moral and intellectual development, wealth, prosperity and power. The night was associated with death, evil, immorality, weakness and mystery. Carried to color symbolism extremes, God and purity were associated with white; evil and defeat with black.

Pyramid poems of the oldest origin exuded the light-dark white-black motif pervasively and are found in five pyramids dating from before 2180 B.C. African proverbs likewise and Indie texts also are filled with this symbolism but nowhere is it applied to skin color before 1500 B.C., the advent of the Indo-European (Aryan) invasion of India.

Prior to 1500 B.C. in India, and 587 B.C. in Babylonia, Black and White were purely metaphysical terms. From Egypt a pyramid poem excerpt reads, "Praise to thee, Thou Eye of Horus (the sun), White and great, over whose beauty the Ennead of Gods rejoice, when thou riseth in the Eastern horizon. They that are in what Shu (the atmosphere) upholdeth adore thee . . . men fear thee; the foreign peoples bow down before thee upon their faces and the Nine Bows, bow their heads to thee." From East Africa a proverb: "The friendship between two wives of the same husband is like dye water, always black."

It is truly amazing that after such an intense period of indoctrination, 4,000 years for Western whites and 400 years for African Blacks (regarding the myth of superiority and inferiority) that the Black poets in a short decade of the 60s could convince anyone that "Black is beautiful." Their success however was closely tied to parallel religious movements with which they were contemporary—specifically, the diametrically positioned Martin Luther King and Elijah Muhammad movements on which the era was focused.

The fall of Black civilization to the sword of Alexander, the Aryans (and other representatives of Europe) and its subsequent replacement by Greece, Rome, Christian mercantilism and Calvinistic imperialism respectively, led to the replacement of a whole venue of social values by a new version of man's/woman's life on earth.

In this transformation, the poet played no small part. Black civilizations: Egypt, India, etc., had defined man/woman as in the world journeying toward godhood and toward life in the hereafter. Human excellence and devotion, moral and intellectual were the currency of transformation and final reckoning.

In the sub-saharan civilization of West and East Africa, life was a quest for unity with nature and tradition. Traditional African poetry then was distinguished by its affinity with nature and the African's relationship to his/her folklore, mythology and culture. It was and is poetry best exemplified through oral expression which incorporates the rituals, songs and lifestyles indigenous to the African's way of life.

IV. African and African-American Poetic Resistance to Imperialistic Social Values

African and African-American resistance to the imposition of imperialistic social values were different but equally intense. African-American Blacks—enslaved and disarmed of African culture—wrestled relentlessly to identify themselves. Given only the worldview of slave masters as reality, they sometimes accommodated that reality with the hope of being treated fairly; or they protested or revolted against it demanding the blessing of equal rights and positive self-definition or they sought to escape it in folktales, songs and poems of fantasy which depicted the master-type being outwitted by the slave-type.

Accommodational poems such as those of Phillis Wheatley and Paul Laurence Dunbar emphasized survival as a social value for African Americans. Survival often meant pretended or affected agreement with reality as written by the master, but it also meant the exploitation of that agreement for the benefit of the slave.

"Twas mercy brought me from my pagan land, taught my benighted soul to understand—Remember, Christians, Negroes, Black as Cain, may be refined and join the angelic train," wrote Phillis Wheatley.

Protest poems, though often angry, appealed to some sense of assumed decency in the logos of the master. It sought to shame him or threaten him with the moral consequences of his oppression. Protest poems upheld and instilled social values of moral courage in the

Black cause. Frances Harper's poem "Bury Me in a Free Land" and George Moses Horton's poem "On Liberty in Slavery" are representative of this theme.

Escape poems were poems that projected themes of freedom, within slavery afforded by wit and manipulation; stealing away to Jesus or waiting on religious deliverance. The Brer Rabbit tales and the poetic lyrics in hymns like "Go Down Moses" are examples of escape poetry which sought to instill the social values of wit and patience in Afro-Americans, during antebellum slavery.

During the 1920s and 1960s, the role of the poet as a creator of social values was dramatically demonstrated. The themes of accommodation, protest and escape were changed to themes of self-acceptance and love, self-confirmation and self-determination, the theme of redemption through the historical awareness of past African glory; the theme of ethnic pride based on Black lifestyle and echoes of Marcus Garvey, formed the poetry of the New Negro 1920–1933.

The poetry of Langston Hughes, Anne Spencer and Georgia Douglas Johnson glorified what Blacks had hitherto been ashamed of. Ironically, however, the Black poetic visibility that allowed them to be impactful was financed by white money; the depression knocked out that money, that visibility and to a certain extent, that awareness.

In the 1960s, the question of Black identity was addressed head on by Elijah Muhammad and his spokesman Malcolm X. The turning of Black to beautiful was due to the theology of Elijah Muhammad's version of Islam which came into prominence in 1959. Black replaced white in that cosmology as the origin of good in the world and white replaced Black as the source of all evil. Thus Allah replaced Jesus or God, Black replaced Negro, self-sufficiency replaced dependency as the labels of reality. Through the charisma and intellect of Malcolm X and the overwhelming prophetic significance of the King movement, Black pride emerged as a social value on the lips of poets, in the lyrics of musicians, in the environmental trappings of Black life from hairdos to sandals, from jazz or Black classical music to Kwanzaa.

A Black Aesthetic emerged which took identity from the Black Nationalist movement of E. Muhammad and others. A chief characteristic of this new awareness was the changing of names to African and Islamic ones, e.g., LeRoi Jones became Amiri Baraka, Don L. Lee became Haki Madhubuti, Roland Snellings became Askia M. Touré, and Jewel Lattimore became Johari Amini, etc. Perhaps characteristic as any of the poetic process of instilling Black social value in the 60s is the poem by Bobb Hamilton: "*Poem to a Nigger Cop.*"

The 70s was a decade of decision and dismantling of rhetoric and a search for tangible values. To a certain extent, Black consciousness of the 60s was eroded in the 70s. This would be good if that consciousness became, instead of rhetoric, a subconsciousness motivating behavior and part of the natural rhythm of Black life. To the extent that it has become subconscious it has benefited Blacks as well as Whites.

Part III: Praise

The Black Arts Poets

The birth of your poem
The essentiality of your poem

The elasticity of your poem
The complicity of your poem
The past splendor of your poem
The death swellings of your poem
The apartments of your poem
The fears of your poem
The bouquet of your poem
The chemical black of your poem
The frenetic faith of your poem
The privileged eyes of your poem
The cathedrals of your poem
The middle passage of your poem
The thumb prints of your poem
The latitude/longitude of your poem
The hand shake of your poem
The pelvic sound of your poem
The collarbone laughter of your poem
The membrane of your poem
The golden nipples of your poem
The mouth prints of your poem
The lotus moon of your poem
The squats of your poem
The guaranteed wages of your poem
The comic strip color of your poem
The charitable flow of your poem
The monologues of your poem
The feet of your poem
The arms of your poem. . . . . .doouuudumm
The eyes of your poem. . . . . .dooooduadeee
The teeth of your poem. . . . . .doooodoodumm
The early morning avenues of your poem
The convulsions of your poem
The bone marrow of your poem
The cobblestone feet of your poem
The sacred mantra of your poem
The epileptic throat of your poem
The relentless flesh of your poem
The sleeves of your poem
The morning stars of your poem
The carousel music of your poem
The white fingernails of your poem
I bow down
I bow down
I bow down to the music of your poem
My brothers and sisters

I bow down as you strip search our
Eyes this last time for new memory
I call out to you
I call out to you
I call out to you you you......
Holy the day
I say holy the day
Because you stood up
I say, holy the sky
Holy the sound
Holy the air
Holy the sound of your voice
Holy your skin
As you moved with the wind
Holy your eyes
As you remember your ancestors
Holy the pavane you wrote across the sky
Holy your words
Bringing the earth
To its knees
Holy the day standing
Still with longing for you
Holy the morning star of your poem......

The Thunder of Angels

We can say anything that we want to say, but it's the poets, the artists, who sing, who pay, who soar—we love them. The come to us glittering like silver stones. Their words/poems so beautiful and prophetic that we catch them in mid-flight, swallow them whole, their vision, their genius, a gift from the sea, their lives vibrating words/songs, their ideas charging the world, shifting the earth until it turns toward justice. Peace and beauty.

We can say anything we want to say about these gatherers of beauty, rolling across the seas, earthbound though, these wearer of waves. We see them in the early morning dawn. We see them in the budding flowers. They speak a language, they play a sound that they inherited from the ancients.

We have seen these poets from the middle of the 20th century to the beginning of the 21st century. We have seen them at work, moving in the bloodstream of their people. We have seen them look up when someone inferred that this long voyage of artistry had been futile, had lacked dignity and art. We have seen their tongues track down these disbelievers. We have seen their poems/words silence these diplomats of the dead, anoint our hands with eyes. They have known for a long time that we stand on an earth collapsing in a palette of pain, that we stand in the tracks of conquistadors and imperialists, homophobes and racists, terrorists and pornographers, sexists and voyeurs, CEOs and countries who want to own everything, who try to extract our rhythms and put them in a permanent pill box of pain.

And these poetry men and women continued to hold up the air. No mystery surrounded them. The cities knew them. Felt their touch. Saw their solitary eye demanding change, saw their sparkling hands scoop thunder from their pores.

They came warrior clear. Their intellect kissing our spines. And their poems brought us life and we were reborn in their spreading sails of flesh.

The word "trivia" means three in Latin. Whenever three roads met, the Romans put up notice boards with the news. Well, the three roads for this anthology are the Past, the Present and the Future. This anthology puts up the notice boards that say: Listen. Listen. Listen. These poets, these women and men sequestered in these pages, inform us that activism and work that flows from the heart is God-conscious activism.

There is an ancient Vedic saying: If you want to create a new body, then you must step out of the river of your own memory and see the world as if for the first time. And our sister/brother poets used new memory to help us see the world of our foremothers and forefathers and ourselves as if for the first time.

I think all of them must have been born feet first, must have slid out of the darkness of their mother's wombs into the light of their eyes. Running on a fast track, these brothers and sisters, of sun and moon, downloaded their ancestors who prodded them into an arena called activism and poetry. These careful craftspersons of words and life, aristocratic word sorcerers with a commoner's eye, informed us that intellect and work for our people and all people, and activism and poetry that flows from the heart is God-conscious activism.

And these brothers and sisters, their eyes opening like crystals, worked in America and the world, told us to take God out of the sky and put God in our hearts. Our feet. Our hands. Our eyes. Our tongues. And they did. We heard the sacred in all of their handprints and footprints as they reset the identity of African Americans and of people of color on the world stage from tragedy to the heroic celebration of themselves and their people. These women and men resurrected the idea of a new activism in poetry and scholarship. They sat down with the people, listened to them, held them when they cried, laughed out loud with their successes, welcomed their souls and held their hearts in their hands. These poet-visionaries turned the river of memory and made the river turn black. Black. Black. Human. Human. Human. These poets were *a Cante jondo,* a deep song of Africa. The Caribbean. The Americas. India. The Middle East.

They came with the staccato speech and rhythm of the spirit. Their passion entered this American bloodstream. They no longer sang or spoke for themselves. Something began to move through them. We could see it moving between the *beat* and the *unbeat.* The *noise* and the *silence.* The *darkness* and the *light.* A moment where the sounds rose from their throats entered our blood and we became the sheroes and heroes and the healers and leaders. They levitated language and motion and souls, organized, wept, laughed, studied, taught, wrote, *hummmmed* til time stood still in the 20th century in America. They, through their writings, had summoned *the duende*—the spirit of all our ancestors who had suffered and yet survived and did it with dignity and grace and order and beauty. These poets told us that we had affirmed life...life...life. That our eyes had abandoned death. Defeat. Supposed inferiority. That our feet were dancing silver as we "ate a little earth as we all must do before we die." These poets, heavy with the smell of histories and herstories, put their feet on this American spine and bid us look up at their gospel hands hanging bamboo poems of life...life...life. These women and men in Ezekiel's Valley asked: O Lord Can these bones live? And discovered that they did live thru activism and words and love.

Sister Bernice Reagon told me one day about the great blues singer Brother Montgomery who said: We all come here naked. Black folks know it, but white folks don't know it because they come here white. White folks don't come here naked, their skin is an additional currency, puts them far ahead. He continued: we all come here naked and must make *arrangements* for someone else while you're here, not just do for yourself. That's what these poets did! They made *arrangements* for someone else while they were here.

This anthology will help us reintroduce our past blood to our present and future blood, make our memory reenter our bloodstream in order to erase any death prints. Toni Morrison said: "We die. That may be the meaning of life. But we do language. That may be the measure of our lives." And how sister Toni and these poets do this thing called language: the measure of our lives! How they caress, embrace, untangle this language, recapture our memory. How they stand words up and let them minuet our blood. How they help us recover our silver words as they open up the sorcery of language, take us out on the wings of laughter and pain, intellect and beauty. How they commander words spinning under this domestic sky and they become a river moving against winter sails, repelling ice water ghosts kneeling on razor thin knees at confession. Our bodies are tattooed forever with their quicksilver rhythms we are one—alive—apart from the elasticity of the dead.

> *Hummmmmm Hummmmm Hummmmmmmmm*
> Give me the spirit Lord, Lord, Lord
> I say, give me the spirit Lord, Lord, Lord
> *Hummmmmm Hummmmm Hummmmmmmmm*
> Give me the quicksilver courage Lord
> I say, give me the quicksilver courage Lord
> Give me the quicksilver courage Lord
> So I can spread it over my face
> and mouth and legs and hands
> So I can spread it over my face
> and mouth and legs and hands
> Give me the strength Lord
> To bear the wrath of the country and the world.
> Because I preach and teach and poet
> And write as an equal, as an equal, as an
> Equal, as an equal.
> *Hummmmmm Hummmmm Hummmmmmmmm*
> Give me the spirit tongue of a thousand suns
> I say, give me the spirit tongue of a thousand suns
> Give me the spirit tongue of a thousand suns
> To warm our hearts, O Lord
> To warm our hearts, O Lord

Hummmmmm Hummmmm Hummmmmmmmm
Give me the spirit O Lord
I say, Give me the spirit O Lord
Give me the spirit O Lord
To come awake in your thunder
So that our eyes can see behind trees
So that our eyes can see behind trees
Hummmmmm Hummmmm Hummmmmmmmm
Help us to remember Lord
Are we not more than hunger and music?
Are we not more than harlequins and horns and greed?
Are we not more than color and drums?
Are we not more than anger and dance?
Hummmmmm Hummmmm Hummmmmmmmm
Aaaayeee babo, Aaaayeee babo, Aaaayeee babo,
Praise God, Praise God, Praise God
For these men and women
Who walked barefoot across our souls
Always with a prayer on their tongues
Saying, step inside, step inside
                                        amou'mwen
I say, step inside, step inside
                                        miamor

Give us the spirit Lord to
Put on our eyes,
And forever, O Lord, let us be
In the eyelash of your memory
Where there is always the
Precision of sisters and brothers
Sewing themselves into the
Sleeves of beauty and change. . .

| Aaaayeee babo | Aaaayeee babo | Aaaayeee babo |
| Praise God | Praise God | Praise God |

For the Thunder of Angels. . . .

STORM COMING: Memoir and History

We came to change the conversation. We arrived not only as very young representatives of the "fire next time," but as the three dimensional wind gaining hurricane strength attacking America's white supremacy as manifested in the politics, economics, education, military, history, psychology, literature, entertainment, health care, urban and rural policies of Western culture. No small task for poets and artists. However, we were as serious as a first love and had excellent teachers and examples.

The poets of the Black Arts Movement (BAM) stood on the shoulders of those writers, poets, musicians, visual artists and historians who preceded us. Unlike the Harlem Renaissance, BAM was truly a grassroots national movement that developed international pan-African roots and participation. Our work, our production, our artistic reality cannot be separated from the day-to-day struggles of Black people, people of African ancestry across this country or in the blooming consciousness of the Black Diaspora.

The young poets and other artists had grown weary of many of their elders who often were satisfied with the status quo. We had attached ourselves to a different set of wise men and women. Our political, artistic and literary voices were being shaped by W. E. B. Du Bois, Langston Hughes, Marcus Garvey, Louis Armstrong, Carter G. Woodson, Claude McKay, Jean Toomer, Alain Locke, Charlie Parker, Gwendolyn Brooks, Zora Neale Hurston, Katherine Dunham, Margaret Walker, Sterling A. Brown, Robert Hayden, Arna Bontemps, Frank Marshall Davis, Melvin B. Tolson, Aimé Césaire, Frantz Fanon, John Henrik Clarke, Duke Ellington, John Coltrane, Kwame Nkrumah, Sekou Toure, Paul Robeson, Chancellor Williams, Arthur P. Davis, Howard Thurman, Darwin T. Turner, John O. Killens, James Baldwin, Vincent Harding, Samuel W. Allen, George Kent, Ossie Davis, Ruby Dee, and hundreds of others who created and produced the ideas BAM was built upon. Most were race men and women who navigated American apartheid and gave us the flowering ammunition of a new revolution. We ceased being poets who happened to be Black and became as authentic as possible (growing each millisecond) Black Poets.

For most of my contemporaries and me, the singular and most muscular voice was Malcolm X. Rising out of the Nation of Islam (NOI) under the tutelage of the Honorable Elijah Muhammad, Malcolm X sought truth beyond the truth, always going subsurface to locate the protein of original thought. The work of Malcolm X and his foundational efforts in building the NOI put Black on the front burner. To listen to Brother Malcolm was a call to clear conscious action. He was our bold guide, patient stepladder, and non-contradicting voice who most of us learned to love, trust and tried to emulate. His death in

1965 is often cited as the defining event that sparked the beginnings of the Black Empowerment and Arts Movements.

LeRoi Jones became Amiri Baraka and left the Village in New York to move to Harlem and eventually back to Newark, his birth city, where his voice was essential and second to none in giving urgency to BAM. He is cited as one of the originators of BAM along with Larry Neal, Askia Touré, Sonia Sanchez, Gaston Neal, Lucille Clifton, and Jayne Cortez. Though they were primarily identified with the East Coast, this activity sparked a simultaneous emergence of BAM across the country. In the Midwest were Dudley Randall, Margaret Burroughs, Margaret Danner, Mari Evans, Ron Milner, Gwendolyn Brooks, Hoyt W. Fuller, Woodie King Jr., Eugene Redmond, Haki R. Madhubuti (Don L. Lee), Carolyn Rodgers, Nikki Giovanni, Sterling Plumpp, Val Gray Ward, Abena Joan Brown, Johari Amini, Etheridge Knight, and Norman Jordan; in the South were Tom Dent, Kalamu ya Salaam (Val Ferdinand), and Margaret Walker; and on the West Coast were Marvin X, Sarah Webster Fabio, Maulana Karenga, Ed Bullins and Joe Goncalves. This movement included hundreds of others throughout the nation and most certainly Keorapetse Kgositsile, representing continental Africa, and early voices like Ed Spriggs, David Henderson, Victor Hernandez Cruz and Ishmael Reed are credited in groundbreaking service and work in pre-BAM and connecting to other cultures and formations to strengthen BAM. These poets and writers were concerned with producing defining poems and texts and as a result of their work we ceased being Negroes and became Black people, people of African ancestry and finally, African Americans. In 1968, Maulana Karenga and Larry Neal produced two insightful essays that provided much of the theoretical basis for BAM. We were young, idealistic, determined and in turn only felt that we could better the world for the majority rather than for the elite few. Fear for personal safety was never a question, as most of us were sincere students of Black history, thereby always measuring our activities against those of our fore parents.

Rising

We sought fresh air. My eyes have always been those of questioning and skepticism. We defined ourselves as the creative voices of the Black Empowerment and Civil Rights Movements. Most of us did not totally accept nonviolence (especially since violence was committed against us hourly) but respected its philosophical roots and loved Rosa Parks, Martin Luther King Jr. and others. For the record, I marched with Dr. King at most of his major demonstrations in Chicago. We too took poetry and theatre to the streets. We read on street corners, in alleys, bars, taverns and liberation schools. Welfare mothers manned picket lines with the words of Gwendolyn Brooks and Mari Evans; Black students (high school, university, etc.) demanded that the Black poet's words be included into the ultra-white rhetoric and literature courses.

The works of Amiri Baraka, Sonia Sanchez, Jayne Cortez, and Henry Dumas actually preceded the Black studies programs, which many poets including myself were in the vanguard of helping to create. Like the music of the Dells, Marvin Gaye, the Temptations and Curtis Mayfield, the poems of the Last Poets echoed throughout the community. For the first time in recent history throughout the nation Black poetry was being recorded, incorporated in dance and acted to at a mass level. This was the case from Black House in Los Angles to Afro-Arts, eta, and Kuumba theatres in Chicago, to the Concept East Theater in Detroit, to New Lafayette and the National Black Theater in Harlem, to Spirit House in Newark, to the Free Southern Theatre in New Orleans and Karamu House in Cleveland. My first album, *Rappin' and Readin'* (Broadside Press) was recorded at a reading at Wayne State University in 1969.

Public readings by many of BAM's poets evolved as noticeable competition for the idiot box programs. The grapevine or Black-vine emerged as the prime source of publicity. Black book stores appeared in many of the large Black areas and new Black publishing houses supplied them with the newest of the new poet's books. Black poetry books were coming off the presses and being sold by the thousands weekly. One poet produced books whose sales reached the phenomenal number of one hundred thousand copies.

With the demand for Black studies, Black universities and Black thought, we found ourselves in the unique position of being able to supply new knowledge that was to become the most exploited field in the late sixties and early seventies. The major publishing houses, which had traditionally overlooked and discouraged Black poets and writers, began to saturate the market with "reprints" of out-of-print materials, while pulling as many of the young Black poets and writers as their little green bait would attract. I had offers from Random House and the University of Illinois. The new Black poetry was like the new Black music to the White mainstream publishing houses, i.e., not understood or taken seriously, but highly profitable, thus, the latter part of the sixties and the beginning of the decade of the seventies ushered in the "New Black Poets."

After the assassination of the "prince of peace" Martin Luther King Jr. in 1968, and the explosion of cities around the country our work took on a new urgency. We viewed our struggle as a part of the international African liberation movement. The Congress of African People, the US Organization, the Black Panther Party, a serious call for Black theology, the African-centered school movement, Black Power conferences and the creation of African Liberation Day all took up critical space for discussion, evaluation and action. We must remember that there was also a storm of organizing activity among Black professionals resulting in the creation of national Black organizations representing educators, psychologists, law enforcement, social workers, doctors and medical care workers, lawyers, politicians and others. The BAM poets were a national force pushing hard for self-definition, self-determination, self-reliance and self-defense.

Negro Digest/Black World and Hoyt W. Fuller

If the East Coast represented the heart and soul of the Black Arts Movement, the intellectual center was the Midwest with the indispensable publishing of *Negro Digest/Black World Magazine* under the extraordinary editorship of Hoyt W. Fuller. *Negro Digest/Black World* was a monthly magazine of Johnson Publishing Company, which also published *Ebony* and *Jet* magazines. Even though there were other important journals of BAM such as *Soul Book, Freedomways, Black Dialogue, The Cricket, The Liberator, The Black Scholar, Amistad 1 and 2, Black Books Bulletin* (which I edited), *The Black Collegiate* (edited by Kalamu ya Salaam), *The Black Position* (edited by Gwendolyn Brooks) and the indispensable *Journal of Black Poetry* (edited and published by Joe Goncalves). However, it was *Negro Digest/Black World* that each month went into battle against the white literary establishment while publishing Black mainstream writers as well as the new and upcoming poetic voices of BAM. Each year Hoyt W. Fuller and his indispensable associate editor Carole A. Parks published an annual poetry issue highlighting the original work of senior Black poets, as well as paying special attention to the new voices blowing fire and challenging white and Black mediocrity and betrayal. Much of BAM is documented in the pages of *Negro Digest/Black World Magazine.*

Each month between 1965 and 1975, *Negro Digest/Black World* published Hoyt W. Fuller's "Perspectives" column that was the precursor to the Internet, email, and twitter. Hoyt W. Fuller, a superb editor, cut from the mold of W. E. B. Du Bois, who provided groundbreaking coverage of Black life and liberation struggles as the early editor of *CRISIS,* went into battle each month taking on the white literary and political establishment and seldom gave any quarter to the HNIC,* white political or corporate powers. His influence is monumental and will always deserve an honored seat in any discussion of the Black Arts Movement.

DuSable Museum of African American History, Broadside Press, Third World Press, Organization of Black American Culture (OBAC) and Lotus Press

The call, by many of the Black Arts Movement poets, was for institutional development. The first people I met who were serious about such work were Margaret and Charlie Burroughs. In 1961, they and others founded in Chicago, Illinois, The Ebony Museum of Negro History in their home. It was the first Black museum of its kind in the nation and eventually changed its name to The DuSable Museum of African American History and moved to more substantial and spacious quarters in a park on the South Side of Chicago. DuSable Museum, under the capable direction of Dr. Margaret Burroughs, a writer and world-class visual artist, went on to impact the national Black museum movement in the nation. I joined them as a volunteer in 1962 while still serving in the United States Army. I was stationed at Fort Sheridan in Illinois, about to go mad as I secretly wrote poetry, read books and talked to myself.

Meeting Margaret and Charlie Burroughs was Black salvation. I volunteered on evenings and weekends, this allowed me to literally devour their substantial library, especially Marxist literature, which I read under the careful guidance of Charlie Burroughs who had been raised in the USSR. Between 1962 and 1966, I did everything asked of me—mop floors, empty garbage, lecture on current exhibits, eventually worked my way up to assistant curator. The museum was a destination for national and international guests from the USSR, Europe, Africa, the Caribbean and elsewhere. I remember meeting Alex Haley as he was writing *Roots* and *The Autobiography of Malcolm X.* After the assassination of Malcolm X in 1965, Margaret Burroughs had a visitor from Detroit. He was Dudley Randall, a poet of considerable stature and founder of Broadside Press (1966).

Broadside Press was initially founded in order to publish Black poets on broadside sheets when Mr. Randall soon realized that he had to move to books to accommodate the growing number of Black poets who had no formal outlet for their poetry. He visited

---

*Head Negro in Charge

Chicago to solicit Margaret Burroughs' support as a co-editor of a poetry anthology dedicated to the life and death of Malcolm X. *For Malcolm: Poems on The Life and Death of Malcolm X* was to be the first of many books dedicated to the enormous contributions of the fallen leader. However, it remained the first and only poetry anthology to be published on his life and its historical value is greatly heightened because it introduced a large number of Black poets to a national audience who would become serious contributors to BAM: Clarence Major, Etheridge Knight, Ted Joans, Conrad Kent Rivers, Julia Fields, Bobb Hamilton, David Henderson, Keorapetse Kgositsile, Raymond Patterson, Zach Gilbert, Sonia Sanchez, Edward S. Spriggs, and Oliver La Grone. Broadside was and remains the most important Black poetry book publisher to come out of BAM.

Close on the heels of Broadside Press was Lotus Press (1972), also of Detroit, Michigan, published and edited by the extraordinary poet Naomi Long Madgett. Lotus Press, which is still in existence, made its mark at a national level by publishing young Black poets. Lotus Press distinguished itself by publishing the works of Naomi Long Madgett, May Miller, Lance Jeffers, Kirri T. H, Cheatwood, Toi Derricotte, James A. Emanuel, and Houston A. Baker, to name a very few.

I was always aware of the limitations of language and understood that direct action in one's community; the building of institutions and the creation of programs that spoke directly to a need also critically defined one's seriousness. I learned this from the Black church. Third World Press (1967) was founded in my basement apartment, which was about the size of a large conference room table that I shared with other unwelcome animals. I called Johari Amini (Jewel Latimore) and Carolyn Rodgers to a meeting and Third World Press (TWP) was born. TWP began by publishing chapbooks by Amini and Rodgers on a used mimeograph machine. Carolyn Rodgers stayed with us for about six months and Johari Amini worked with us off and on for about ten years before becoming a chiropractor. Like Broadside Press, who we modeled ourselves after, we also aggressively published poets. After forty-three years we continued to publish now in all the genres with poetry remaining the heart of our operation. Alongside Rodgers and Amini, we have published most of the BAM poets such as Gwendolyn Brooks, Amiri Baraka, Sonia Sanchez, Askia Touré, Sterling Plumpp, Keorapetse Kgositsile (who is now poet laureate of South Africa), Norman Jordan, Useni Eugene Perkins, Zach Gilbert, Mari Evans, Sam Greenlee, Philip Royster, Kalamu ya Salaam, Dudley Randall, Naomi Long Madgett, Fred Lee Hord, Angela Jackson, Gil Scott Heron, Aneb Kgositsile House and others.

The Organization of Black American Culture (OBAC) writer's workshop was led by the indispensable Hoyt W. Fuller. The Chicago-based workshop mentored, encouraged, published through its journal NOMMO and helped establish readings and discussions and hosted major Black writers coming through Chicago. As a workshop, it functioned more like an extended family. Johari Amini, Carolyn Rodgers, Ebon Dooley, Sterling Plumpp, Sam Greenlee, Randsom Boykin, Cecil M. Brown and I were all early members.

Gwendolyn Brooks, Mari Evans, Dudley Randall, Eugene Redmond

Gwendolyn Brooks was soundly grounded to her family, her people and to her writing. There was little ambiguity in her makeup. When I met her in 1967, she was teaching poetry writing to members of the Blackstone Rangers. I was truly amazed at this Pulitzer Prize winner, soon to be the Poet Laureate of the state of Illinois and Consultant in Poetry to the Library of Congress mixing it up with the young teenagers from the unforgiving streets of the South Side of Chicago. She was working with the great poet and musician Oscar Brown Jr. She literally gave of herself, her resources, and her knowledge unconditionally to all who came into her space. That workshop soon moved from the South Side church to her home, a very simple wood-frame dwelling where we met weekly to grow and practice poetry writing. When I met her I had published my first book, *Think Black* (1966), and my second book, *Black Pride,* was under consideration with Broadside Press and was eventually published in 1968 with an introduction by Dudley Randall.

Gwendolyn Brooks impacted us as writers, intellectuals and as individuals rooted in our newfound Blackness. She rejected pretentiousness, which is characteristic not only of her character but also of her poetry. When Ms. Brooks decided to grow a natural and leave Harper and Row for Broadside Press, she without knowing it, was setting an example of commitment to Black identity and institutional development that she honored until her death in 2000. In addition to her multiple volumes of poetry and autobiographies, she published two anthologies highlighting BAM poets: *Jump Bad: A New Chicago Anthology* and *A Broadside Treasury.*

Mari Evans' base of operation is Indianapolis, Indiana. Her poetry has been anthologized nationally and her first volume of poetry, *I Am a Black Woman,* remains a classic of BAM. In 1970 the Black Academy of Arts and Letters honored her with its annual poetry prize. An accomplished musician and playwright, she has also published children's books, and essays and remains one of the most important poets in America. In her work she is always on point looking for the essential truth about our condition.

Dudley Randall's impact on BAM has been documented in Julius E. Thompson's *Dudley Randall, Broadside Press and the Black Arts Movement in Detroit, 1960–1995.* His legacy, like that of Brooks and Fuller, will forever be central in the development of the Black Arts Movement. He was the first Poet Laureate of Detroit and Broadside Press was responsible for being the early publishing house of Haki R. Madhubuti (Don L. Lee), Sonia Sanchez, Nikki Giovanni, Etheridge Knight, Audre Lorde, Everett Hoagland and many more. He was a poet's poet.

Eugene B. Redmond's participation in BAM as a poet of distinction cannot be overstated. He wears many hats as teacher, scholar, cofounder and publisher of Black River Writers Press, and literary as the executor for the estate of the great BAM poet and fiction writer, Henry Dumas. He also edits *Drumvoices* the journal that continues to publish BAM poets and others. He is also a photographer of unusual insight and has documented BAM with his many photographs. He is currently the Poet Laureate of East St. Louis, founder of the Eugene B. Redmond Writers Club and the author of the indispensable study, *Drumvoices: The Mission of Afro-American Poetry* (1976).

The Black Aesthetic

Along with Hoyt W. Fuller the most combative and insightful Black critic was Addison Gayle Jr. I came out of the working and non-working poor. I learned the value of education early, especially the value of self-education. In my memoir *YellowBlack: The First 21 Years of a Poet's Life* (2005), I delve deeply into the value of book knowledge. Therefore meeting Hoyt W. Fuller and eventually being mentored by him increased my Black literary knowledge immensely. Fuller knew "everybody" and his introduction of Addison Gayle Jr. to the OBAC writers encouraged many of us to begin writing literary nonfiction about our art form.

Between 1965 and 1975 there was a bruising, national battle regarding the literary qualities of Black poetry in print on college campuses, at writer's conferences and in the classrooms. This bitter engagement was not only about the legitimacy of Black writing, but what is known as Black poetry and the Black Aesthetic. Poets such as James A. Emanuel, Sarah Webster Fabio, Keorapetse Kgositsile, Sterling A. Brown, Amiri Baraka (LeRoi Jones), Langston Hughes, Dudley Randall, Larry Neal, Houston A. Baker Jr., Ishmael Reed, Carolyn Rodgers, Haki R. Madhubuti and others were ready for the fight. Black scholars and writers already in the battle were Ernest Kiser, Eugenia Collier, Richard Long, George E. Kent, Julian Mayfield, Carolyn F. Gerald, Nick Aaron Ford, Lofton Mitchell, J. Saunders Redding, Darwin T. Turner, Toni Cade, Maulana Karenga, Steven Henderson and others. These were no small acts of definition and preservation. For the most part their essays appeared in independent and scholarly journals. It was Addison Gayle Jr. in three of his many books that along with Hoyt W. Fuller in his monthly "Perspectives" columns who kept the Black fires hotly burning. Gayle in *Black Expression* (1969), *The Black Situation* (1970) and the groundbreaking *The Black Aesthetic* (1971) took to the fight and advocacy for the uniqueness, originality and absolute necessity for Black poets/writers to express themselves from the depths of their own environment and cultural imperatives.

1969, I traveled to Algiers in North Africa for the first Pan African Festival. This was my first trip to the continent of my fore parents. At the festival I met and read poetry on the same stage as Nina Simone, Archie Shepp, and Ted Joans. Many Black Panther members were seeking asylum or refuge in Algiers. Black Panther visual artist Emory created a poster for this event. The BAM poet Ted Joans, who lived in Timbuktu, introduced me to Africa in ways that were impossible to learn from books, music, or film. We left Algiers and literally walked, took buses and trains into Casablanca where I flew back to the states to start a new position at Cornell University as its first Black poet-in-residence.

In 1970, I joined the faculty of Howard University at the founding of the Institute for the Arts and Humanities as poet-in-residence along with Stephen Henderson, its Director, and John O. Killens as writer-in-residence and Clay Goss as playwright-in-residence. John O. Killens previously was in residence at Fisk University where for several years he and Fisk University hosted the major Black writers conferences in the nation. In 1968 I read poetry and participated in panel discussions at the Fisk Conference. As a result of my presentation I was offered two teaching positions. Dr. Catherine Hurst invited me to Talladega College and Dr. Gloria Joseph offered me a position at Cornell University. My poetry and political and culture comments were a bit too "advanced" for Talladega and I ended up at Cornell. While at Cornell (1969–70) I completed my third book, *Don't Cry, Scream,* and participated in the founding of the Africana Studies Department. Also, due to the fact that I was the first Black poet-in-residence at an Ivy League University, *Ebony Magazine,* under David Llorens encouragement and authorship published a major article on me in its March, 1969 issue. The major Black magazine in the nation with a circulation of over two million effectively put me on the Black literary map. *Don't Cry, Scream* published that same month and within a year sold over 75,000 copies. My life changed almost overnight.

My national presence was the major reason I was asked to join the faculty at Howard University. While at Howard (1970–78) we organized several national Black Writers Conferences using John O. Killens model that he developed at Fisk University. Most of, if not all of the poets of the Black Arts Movement attended. In 1972, Stephen Henderson published his groundbreaking study *Understanding the New Black Poetry: Black Speech, and Black Music as Poetic References,* the first academic text of its kind to seriously consider the craft, content and writing styles of poets directing the Black poetic storm that was consuming the nation. He, like Hoyt W. Fuller and Addison Gayle Jr., was an advocate for Black literature and culture. Dr. Henderson with his enormous cultural knowledge base and respect for Black culture situated him in the forefront of serious Black literary scholars.

My stay in Washington, D.C., allowed me access to the East Coast, most importantly, I was able to be a sponge in the company of senior Howard University faculty members like Sterling A. Brown, Chancellor Williams, Arthur P. Davis, and the great Andrew Billingsley, who was the Provost and Vice President of Academic Affairs. In 1970, Broadside Press published my fourth book of poetry, *We Walk the Way of the New World* as well as *Dynamite Voices: Black Poets of the 1960s,* my one and only attempt at highlighting the work of fourteen poets of BAM. *DirectionScore: Selected and New Poems* appeared in 1971. My first book of essays, *From Plan to Planet: Life Studies, The Need for African Minds and Institutions* was published in February of 1973. Later that year, I was talked into teaching a course at Morgan State University in Baltimore, Maryland, where I eventually met the phenomenal Lucille Clifton.

The history of the Black Arts Movement is also one of deep ideological struggles with the Black left, which was overwhelmingly influenced by the White left. Their distaste for many of us was due to the fact that we would not minimize the deadly effect of white supremacy on the day-to-day lives of Black, Brown, Red and Yellow people of color. In the *Black Scholar,* Issue Number 5, 1974, I published an essay, "The Latest Purge: The Attack on Black Nationalism and Pan-Afrikanism by the New Left, the Sons and Daughters of the Old Left," as an honest attempt to counter the horrific distortions of BAM and the Black Nationalist movements for liberation by the uniformed political left. The firestorm continues to this day.

Between 1970 and 1975, I traveled the nation reading poetry at universities, colleges, libraries, community centers, churches, bookstores, homes, and Black professional cultural conferences in at least 35 states of this vast continent. In 1977, under the able leadership of Jeff Donaldson, a BAM visual artist and founding member of OBAC's Visual Arts Workshop and Afro Cobra, we organized to take over 500 artist of BAM to FESTAC in Lagos, Nigeria. Abena Joan Brown (a founder of eta Theatre) and I were selected as co-chairs of the Midwest zone. We, along with other artists of Midwest BAM, succeeded in raising enough funds to transport 250 Black artists from all disciplines to Lagos, Nigeria, for that transforming event. I was selected as the lead person to organize our compound, where I eventually met Stevie Wonder and Minister Louis Farrakhan (prior to his reconstituting the Nation of Islam).

I taught at Howard University for eight years, commuting each week back to Chicago where we were building Third World Press and the Institute of Positive Education (IPE).

At IPE and TWP our mission was twofold—to have a positive impact on education and communications on the Black and African side. In 1973, my eighth book was published with Broadside Press, *Book of Life,* and on the cover was a new name Haki R. Madhubuti. I was given a KiSwahili name to help accent my move toward authenticity and to move out of the shoes of Don L. Lee who had achieved minor fame that, as I defined it took me away from my real work of writing and building. "Haki" means just or justice and "Madhubuti" means precise, accurate and dependable. I have desperately tried to live up to my name and make an impact in our community that would be lasting, needed and appreciated.

In 1975 Broadside Press published *A Capsule Course in Black Poetry* Writing co-authored by Gwendolyn Brooks, Keorapetse Kgositsile, Haki R. Madhubuti and Dudley Randall. The early seventies in the nation had become tumultuous and deadly for those of us deeply committed to the Pan African Liberation struggles. Fred Hampton and Mark Clark were murdered by the Chicago police department and the federal government unleashed COINTELPRO on Black Nationalists. The Red Squad in Chicago's police department was literally out of control. Black Nationalists and Black Cultural workers were targeted across the nation, forcing many brothers and sisters to go underground as others were locked up without due process. The poets began to organize and worked with other political young people to heighten the role of Black political prisoners in our struggle.

There is no end to this journey. As a creator and participant in BAM, I can state without doubt or hesitation that if it were not for Black literature—mainly poetry—and Black music, my life would have taken a different course. In effect, art in all its attracting permeations helped save me and enabled me to achieve national and international status as a poet and institution builder. Also in early 1975, Marlene Mosher, a professor at Tuskegee Institute, published her book, *New Directions from Don L. Lee,* the first book-length critical study of my work with an introduction by the eminent scholar Arthur P. Davis.

All my adult life, I've been dedicated to and intimately involved in Black struggle. As a "YellowBlack" man I intuitively knew that to be accepted as a "Black" poet I not only had to be "good," but I as I defined it "had to outwork" every body. This struggle (BAM) has never been an afterthought or a stepping-stone to something else. I've always sought a defining wisdom, always searching for the ways of doing work that is right and needed. If one surveys the body of my work it is clear that it is overwhelmingly political and cultural. I used poetry as an awakening weapon and as an avenue to introduce ideas, heretofore that were only on the margins of our communities. I am an activist, intellectual, organizer and teacher as well as a poet and institution builder. However, the very political artistic side of me matured under the mentorship of El Hajj Malik El-Shabazz (Malcolm X), Margaret and Charlie Burroughs, Dudley Randall, Hoyt W. Fuller, Barbara Ann Sizemore, and the always consistent and wonderfully gifted, Gwendolyn Brooks, who allowed me to be her cultural son for thirty-three years of her extraordinary life. We came to change the conversation, engage in the political and economic life of this world, and participate in a Black cultural revolution that would impact the world.

(Revised July 26, 2010)

I

Consciousness

Upon Being Black One Friday Night in July

Bus stop waits are
not for
obviouslyBlacks

negro tomcops wearing
anybody's car
accost obviouslyBlacks
        what can you do? (when
        carrying literature saying
        be very black . . . live love
        disseminate black
        ?   be courteous answering
                questions)

DO YOU HAVE IDEN TI FI CA TION !!!!
        what did you have
        in
        mind . . . votersregistration
            responsibilemember of body politic
               . . . churchmembership
            it ranout when i ranout
               . . . socialsecurity
     to aid and abet The Plan for aged starvation
               . . . bluecrossblueshield
      insured myself against hsptls & m.ds
               but no tomcops)

IT THIS YOUR PRES ENT AD DRESS !!!!!!
        (crap)

WHERE DO YOU WORK !!!!!!!!

From Johari Amini, *Images in Black,* by Jewel C. Latimore (Chicago: Third World Press, 1969).

(they are 3 be cool this
summer and come
from out no bags)

WHAT IS YOUR HEIGHT !!!!!!!!!!
                    (all black ft. and damn proud ins!)

WHAT IS YOUR WEIGHT !!!!!!!!!!!!
                                        (a   third   world)

        note: tomcops
                        looking like are-black
                                = taking shorthand =
        observe pattern: faux skin-hair-Afrodress
                        deceive
                        infiltrate
                        watch   (obviouslyBlack's
                            militant i's stamp
                            nationalism)
                        listen   (good friends
                            have bugged pads)

ATTENTION !!!!
ATTENTION !!!!
ALL KNOWN OBVIOUSLYBLACKS MUST BE KEPT
                UNDER STRICT SURVEILLANCE !!!!

What Shall I Tell My Children Who Are Black

What shall I tell my children who are black
Of what it means to be a captive in this dark skin?
What shall I tell my dear one, fruit of my womb,
of how beautiful they are when everywhere they turn
they are faced with abhorrence of everything that is black.
The night is black and so is the boogyman.
Villains are black with black hearts
A black cow gives no milk. A black hen lays no eggs.
Storm clouds, black, black is evil
and evil is black and devil's food is black . . .

What shall I tell my dear ones raised in a white world
A place where white has been made to represent
all that is good and pure and fine and decent,
where clouds are white and dolls, and heaven
surely is a white, white place with angels
robed in white, and cotton candy and ice cream
and milk and ruffled Sunday dresses
and dream houses and long sleek cadilacs
and Angel's food is white . . . all, all . . . white.

What can I say therefore, when my child
Comes home in tears because a playmate
Has called him black, big lipped, flatnosed and nappy headed?
What will he think when I dry his tears and whisper,
"Yes, that's true. But no less beautiful and dear."
How shall I lift up his head, get him to square
his shoulders, look his adversaries in the eye,
confident in the knowledge of his worth
Serene under his sable skin and proud of his own beauty?

From Dr. Margaret Burroughs, *Why Should I Tell Who Are Black?* (Chicago: Museum of African American History, 1968).

What can I do to give him strength
That he may come through life's adversities
As a whole human being unwarped and human in a world
Of biased laws and inhuman practices, that he might
Survive. And survive he must! For who knows?
Perhaps this black child here bears the genius
To discover the cure for . . . cancer
Or to chart the course for exploration of the universe.
So, he must survive for the good of all humanity.

He must and will survive.
I have drunk deeply of late from the fountain
of my black culture, sat at the knee of and learned
from mother Africa, discovered the truth of my heritage.
The truth, so often obscured and omitted.
And I find I have much to say to my black children
I will lift up their heads in proud blackness
with the story of their fathers and their father's fathers.
And I shall take them into a way back time
of kings and queens who ruled the Nile,
and measured the stars and discovered the laws of mathematics.
I will tell them of a black people upon whose backs
have been built the wealth of three continents.
I will tell him this and more.
And knowledge of his heritage shall be his weapon and his armor;
It will make him strong enough to win any battle he may face.
And since this story is so often obscured,
I must sacrifice to find it for my children,
even as I sacrifice to feed, clothe and shelter them.
So this I will do for them if I love them.
None will do it for me.

I must find the truth of heritage for myself and pass it on to them.
In years to come, I believe because I have armed them with the truth,
my children and their children's children will venerate me.
For it is the truth that will make us free!

Black People!

What about that bad short you saw last week on Frelinghuysen, or those stoves and refrigerators, record players in Sears, Bambergers, Klein's, Hahnes', Chase, and the smaller joosh enterprises? What about that bad jewelry, on Washington Street, and those couple of shops on Springfield? You know how to get it, you can get it, no money down, no money never, money don't grown on trees no way, only whitey's got it, makes it with a machine, to control you you cant steal nothin from a white man, he's already stole it he owes you anything you want, even his life. All the stores will open if you will say the magic words. The magic words are: Up against the wall mother fucker this is a stick up! Or: Smash the window at night (these are magic actions) smash the windows daytime, anytime, together, let's smash the window drag the shit from in there. No money down. No time to pay. Just take what you want. The magic dance in the street. Run up and down Broad Street niggers take the shit you want. Take their lives if need be, but get what you want what you need. Dance up and down the streets, turn all the music up, run through the streets with music, beautiful radios on Market Street, they are brought here especially for you. Our brothers are moving all over, smashing at jellywhite faces. We must make our own World, man, our own world, and we can not do this unless the white man is dead. Let's get together and killhim my man, let's get to gather the fruit of the sun, let's make a world we want black children to grow and learn in do not let your children when they grow look in your face and curse you by pitying your tomish ways.

From LeRoi Jones (Amiri Baraka), *Black Magic: Sabotage, Target Study, Black Art; Collected Poems, 1961–1967* (Indianapolis: Bobbs-Merrill, 1969).

The Life of Lincoln West

Ugliest little boy
that everyone ever saw.
That is what everyone said.

Even to his mother it was apparent—
when the blue-aproned nurse came into the
northeast end of the maternity ward
bearing his squeals and plump bottom
looped up in a scant receiving blanket,
bending, to pass the bundle carefully
into the waiting mother-hands—that this
was no cute little ugliness, no sly baby waywardness
that was going to inch away
as would baby fat, baby curl, and
baby spot-rash. The pendulous lip, the
branching ears, the eyes so wide and wild,
the vague unvibrant brown of the skin,
and, most disturbing, the great head.
These components of That Look bespoke
the sure fibre. The deep grain.

His father could not bear the sight of him.
His mother high-piled her pretty dyed hair and
put him among her hairpins and sweethearts,
dance slippers, torn paper roses.
He was not less than these,
he was not more.

As the little Lincoln grew,
uglily upward and out, he began
to understand that something was

_____

From Gwendolyn Brooks, *Blacks* (Chicago: Third World Press, 1987).

wrong. His little ways of trying
to please his father, the bringing
of matches, the jumping aside at
warning sound of oh-so-large and
rushing stride, the smile that gave
and gave and gave—Unsuccessful!

Even Christmases and Easters were spoiled.
He would be sitting at the
family feasting table, really
delighting in the displays of mashed potatoes
and the rich golden
fat-crust of the ham or the festive
fowl, when he would look up and find
somebody feeling indignant about him.

What a pity what a pity. No love
for one so loving. The little Lincoln
loved Everybody. Ants. The changing
caterpillar. His much-missing mother.
His kindergarten teacher.

His kindergarten teacher—whose
concern for him was composed of one
part sympathy and two parts repulsion.
The others ran up with their little drawings.
He ran up with his.
She
tried to be as pleasant with him as
with others, but it was difficult.
For she was all pretty! all daintiness,
all tiny vanilla, with blue eyes and fluffy
sun-hair. One afternoon she
saw him in the hall looking bleak against
the wall. It was strange because the
bell had long since rung and no other
child was in sight. Pity flooded her.
She buttoned her gloves and suggested
cheerfully that she walk him home. She
started out bravely, holding him by the
hand. But she had not walked far before
she regretted it. The little monkey.
Must everyone look? And clutching her
hand like that. . . . Literally pinching
it. . . .

At seven, the little Lincoln loved
the brother and sister who
moved next door. Handsome. Well-
dressed. Charitable, often, to him. They
enjoyed him because he was
resourceful, made up
games, told stories. But when
their More Acceptable friends came they turned
their handsome backs on him. He
hated himself for his feeling
of well-being when with them despite—
Everything.

He spent much time looking at himself
in mirrors. What could be done?
But there was no
shrinking his head. There was no
binding his ears.

"Don't touch me!" cried the little
fairy-like being in the playground.

Her name was Nerissa. The many
children were playing tag, but when
he caught her, she recoiled, jerked free
and ran. It was like all the
rainbow that ever was, going off
forever, all, all the sparklings in
the sunset west.

One day, while he was yet seven,
a thing happened. In the down-town movies
with his mother a white
man in the seat beside him whispered
loudly to a companion, and pointed at
the little Linc.
"THERE! That's the kind I've been wanting
to show you! One of the best
examples of the specie. Not like
those diluted Negroes you see so much of on
the streets these days, but the
real thing.

Black, ugly, and odd. You
can see the savagery. The blunt

blankness. That is the real
thing."

His mother—her hair had never looked so
red around the dark brown
velvet of her face—jumped up,
shrieked "Go to—" She did not finish.
She yanked to his feet the little
Lincoln, who was sitting there
staring in fascination at his assessor. At the author of his
new idea.

All the way home he was happy. Of course,
he had not liked the word
"ugly."
But, after all, should he not
be used to that by now? What had
struck him, among words and meanings
he could little understand, was the phrase
"the real thing."
He didn't know quite why,
but he liked that.
He liked that very much.

When he was hurt, too much
stared at—
too much
left alone—he
thought about that. He told himself
"After all, I'm
the real thing."

It comforted him.

Black jam for dr. negro

Pullin me in off the corner to wash my face an
cut my fro off turn
my collar
down
when that aint my
thang I
walk heels first
nose round an tilted
up
my ancient
eyes
see your thang
baby
an it aint
shit
your thang
puts my eyes out baby
turns my seeking fingers
    into splintering fists
messes up my head
an I scream you out
your thang
is what's   wrong
   an' you keep
   pilin it on rubbin it
   in
   smoothly
   doin it
   to death

From Mari Evans, *I Am a Black Woman* (New York: Morrow, 1970).

what you sweatin
baby
                your guts
puked an rotten
waitin'

to be defended

Sister Brother

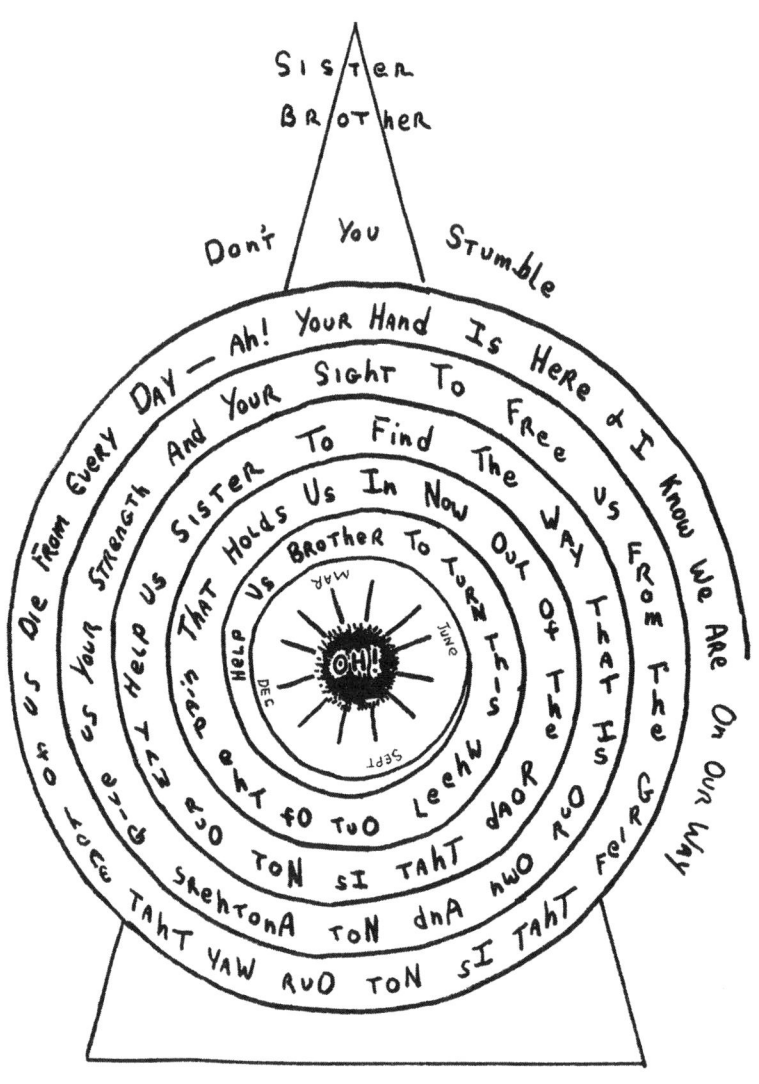

From *Black Fire: An Anthology of Afro-American Writing,* ed. LeRoi Jones (Amiri Baraka) and Larry Neal (New York: Morrow, 1968).

A Father Tells His Son About the Statue of Liberty

Look at that
Piece of petrified pussy
Standing in the middle of
The bay
With them spikes,
Stickin out of her
Limestone head.

Don't you believe that
"Lamp of Liberty"
Bullshit!
That ain't no
Beacon of Freedom;
That's a lynch-fire torch
She got in her hand boy,
It put fire to all them
Crosses burned in
Our front yard
And it put the fire
To your Grandpa too.

He died screaming
And calling on god
Who was deaf and dumb
I heard his burning
Kerosene soaked body
Pop open like a baked
Southern yam
Spilling its red innards
Out on the fire place ashes;

From *Black Arts: An Anthology of Black Creations,* ed. Ahmed Alhamisi and Harun Kofi Wangara (Detroit: Black Arts Publications, 1969).

He was a real
Torch of liberty
Lighting the way
For the wretched refuse
Of Europe
Who came here looking for
Somebody worse off
Than they was
To burn in return.

Jitterbugging in the Streets

to Ishmael Reed

There will be no Holyman crying out this year
No seer, no trumpeter, no George Fox walking barefoot
    up and down the hot land
The only Messiah we shall see this year
Staggers
To and fro
On the LowerEastSide
Being laughed at by housewives in Edsel automobiles
    who teach their daughters the fun of deriding a terror
    belched up from the scatological asphalt of America
Talking to himself

An unshaven idiot
A senile derelict
A black nigger
Laughter and scorn on the lips of Edsel automobiles
    instructing the populace to love God, be kind to puppies
    and the Chase Manhattan National Bank
Because of this there will be no Fourth of July this year
No shouting, no popping of firecrackers, no celebrating,
    no parade
But the rage of a hopeless people
Jitterbugging
    in the streets.

Jacksonville, Florida
Birmingham, Atlanta, Rochester, Bedford-Stuyvesant
Jackson, Mississippi, Harlem, New York
Jitterbugging
    in
    the streets

From *Black Fire: An Anthology of Afro-American Writing,* ed. LeRoi Jones (Amiri Baraka) and
Larry Neal (New York: Morrow, 1968).

To ten thousand rounds of ammunition
To waterhoses, electric prods, phallic sticks
    hound dogs, black boots stepping in soft places
    of the body—
Venom in the mouths of Christian housewives, smart young
    Italians, old Scandinavians in Yorkville, suntanned
    suburban organization men, clerks and construction
    workers, poor white trash and gunhappy cops every-
    where:
"Why don't we kill all niggers
Not one or two
But every damn black of them. Niggers will do anything.
I better never catch a nigger messing with my wife, and
most of all never with my daughter! Aughter grab 'em up
    and ship every black clean out of the country . . .
    aughter just line 'em up and mow 'em down
MachineGunFire!"
All Americans—housewives, businessmen, civil service
Employees, loving their families, going to church, regularly
    depositing money in their neighborhood bank
All Fourth of July celebrators belched up from the guilt-
    ridden, cockroach, sick-sex terror of America
Talking to themselves
In bars
On street corners
Fantasizing hatred
At bridge clubs
Lodge meetings, on park benches
In fashionable mid-town restaurants

No Holyman shall cry out upon the black ghetto this year
No trombonist
The only Messiah we will know this year is a bullet
In the belly
    of a Harlem youth shot down by a coward crouched
    behind an outlaw's badge—
Mississippi
Georgia
Tennessee, Alabama
Your mother your father your brothers, sisters, wives
    and daughters
Up and down the hot land
There is a specter haunting America
Spitfire of clubs, pistols, shotguns, and the missing

Murdered
Mutilated
Bodes of relatives and loved ones
Be the only Santa Claus niggers will remember this year
Be the only Jesus Christ born this year
     curled out dead on the pavement, torso floating
     the bottom of a lake
Being laughed at by housewives in Edsel automobiles.

You say there are four gates to the ghetto
Make your own bed hard that is where you have got
To lay
You say there is violence in Harlem, niggers run amuck
     perpetrating crimes against property, looting stores,
     breaking windows, flinging beer bottles at officers
     of the law
You say a certain virgin gave birth to a baby
Through some mysterious process, some divine conjure,
A messenger turned his walking cane into a serpent
     and the serpent stood up and walked like a natural man
You say . . .
America, why are you afraid of the phallus!

I say there is no "violence" in Harlem.
There is TERROR in Harlem!
Terror that shakes the foundation of the very assholes
     of the people
And fear! And corruption! And murder!

Harlem is the asphalt plantation of America
Rat-infested tenements totter like shanty houses
     stacked upon one another
Circular plague of the welfare check brings vicious wine
every semi-month, wretched babies twice a year, death
and hopelessness every time the sun goes down
Big-bellied agents of downtown landlords with trousers
     that fit slack in the crotch
Forcing black girls to get down and do the dog before they
     learn to spell their names
If you make your own bed hard

He said he was fifteen years old, and he walked beside us
     there in the littered fields of the ghetto
He spoke with a dignity of the language that shocked us
     and he said he had a *theory* about what *perpetrated* the

Horror that was upon us as we walked among flying bullets,
    broken glass, curses and the inorganic phalluses of
    cops whirling about our heads
He said he was a business major at George Washington High
And he picked up a bottle and hurled it above the undulating crowd
Straight into the chalk face of a black helmet!

Thirty-seven properties ransacked, steel gates ripped from
    their hinges, front panes shattered; pawn shops, dry
    cleaners, liquor stores
Ripped apart and looted—

"Niggers will do anything. Aughter grab 'em up . . . If they
    ever try to eat my children I'll personally get a
    shotgun and mow down everyone I set eyes on."

And if your church don't support the present police action,
In dingy fish-n-chip and bar-b-que joints
Niggers will be doing business as usual—
From river to river,
Signboard to signboard
Scattering Schaefuer sex-packs all over the ghetto,
Like a bat out of hell,
Marques Haynes is a dribbling fool.

TERROR is in Harlem,
A Fear so constant
Black men crawl the pavement as if they were snakes,
    and snakes turn to bully sticks that beat the heads
    of those who try to stand up—
A Genocide so blatant
Every third child will do the junky-nod in the whore-scented
    night before semen leaps from his loins—
And Fourth of July comes with the blasting bullet in the belly
    of a teenager
Against which no Holyman, no Christian housewife
In Edsel automobile
Will cry out this year

Jitterbugging
    in the streets.

The Revolution Will Not Be Televised

You will not be able to stay home, brother.
You will not be able to plug in, turn on and cop
     out.
You will not be able to lose yourself on scag and
skip out for beer during commercials because
The revolution will not be televised.

The revolution will not be televised.
The revolution will not be brought to you
     by Xerox in four parts without commercial
     interruption.
The revolution will not show you pictures of
     Nixon blowing a bugle and leading a charge by
     John Mitchell, General Abramson and Spiro
     Agnew to eat hog maws confiscated from a
     Harlem sanctuary.
The revolution will not be televised.

The revolution will not be brought to you by
The Schaeffer Award Theatre and will not star
Natalie Wood and Steve McQueen or Bullwinkle
     and Julia?
The revolution will not give your mouth sex
     appeal.
The revolution will not get rid of the nubs.
The revolution will not make you look five
     pounds thinner.
The revolution will not be televised, brother.

From *Now and Then: The Poems of Gil Scott-Heron* (New York: Canongate, 2000).
Original sound recording of "The Revolution Will Not Be Televised," Flying Dutchman, 1974.

There will be no pictures of you and Willie Mae
pushing that shopping cart down the block on
    the dead run
or trying to slide that color tv in a stolen
    ambulance.
NBC will not be able to predict the winner at
    8:32 on reports from twenty-nine districts.
The revolution will not be televised.

There will be no pictures of pigs shooting down
    brothers
on the instant replay.
There will be no pictures of pigs shooting down
    brothers
on the instant replay.
The will be no slow motion or still lifes of Roy
Wilkins strolling through Watts in a red, black
and green liberation jumpsuit that he has been
saving for just the proper occasion.

Green Acres, Beverly Hillbillies and Hooterville
    Junction
will no longer be so damned relevant
and women will not care if Dick finally got down
    with Jane
on *Search for Tomorrow*
because black people will be in the streets
    looking for
A Brighter Day.
The revolution will not be televised.

There will be no highlights on the *Eleven
    O'Clock News*
and no pictures of hairy armed women
    liberationists
and Jackie Onassis blowing her nose.
The theme song will not be written by Jim
    Webb or Francis Scott Key
nor sung by Glen Campbell, Tom Jones, Johnny
    Cash,
Englebert Humperdink or Rare Earth.
The revolution will not be televised.

The revolution will not be right back after a
message about a white tornado, white lightning
    or white people
You will not have to worry about a dove in your
    bedroom,
the tiger in your tank or the giant in your toilet
    bowl.
The revolution will not go better with Coke.
The revolution will not fight germs that may
    cause bad breath.
The revolution *will* put you in the driver's seat.
The revolution will not be televised.
             will not be televised
        not be televised
          be televised
The revolution will be no re-run, brothers.
The revolution will be LIVE.

Niggers R Scared of Revolution

One day in the late spring of 1969, myself and Abiodun were sitting in Mount Morris Park, which had been renamed Marcus Garvey Park. Abiodun had just asked me what I had learned since I had been in Harlem. Without hesitation, I replied, "Niggers are scared of revolution." He countered, "Write about it, Umar."

"Niggers R Scared of Revolution" became a prayer, a call to arms, a spiritual pond to bathe and cleanse in. Because Niggers are not just vile and disgusting and shiftless. Niggers are human beings lost in someone else's system of values and morals. Niggers are dreams and hopes, pleading for fairness and a true sense of justice. Niggers find a safe place in their denial of just wanting to be loving and tender and kind.

—UBH

NIGGERS ARE SCARED OF REVOLUTION

Niggers are scared of revolution but niggers shouldn't be scared of revolution because revolution is nothing but change, and all niggers do is change. Niggers come in from work and change into pimping clothes to hit the streets to make some quick change. Niggers change their hair from black to red to blond and hope like hell their looks will change. Niggers kill other niggers just because one didn't receive the correct change. Niggers change from men to women from women to men.

Niggers change . . . change . . . change . . .

From Abiodun Oyewole and Umar Bin Hassan with Kim Green, *The Last Poets on a Mission: Selected Poems and a History of the Last Poets* (New Yoek: Holt, 1996).

You hear niggers say things are changing, things are changing. Yeah . . . things are changing nigger things into Black nigger things Black nigger things that go through all kinds of changes. The change in the day that makes them rant and rave Black power! Black power! And that change that comes over them at night as they sigh and moan Oooooh white thighs. Oooooh white thighs. Niggers always going through bullshit changes. But when it comes for a real change Niggers are scared of revolution.

Niggers are actors. Niggers act like they're in a hurry to catch the first act of the Great White hope. Niggers try to act like Malcolm did but when the whiteman doesn't react toward them like he did Malcolm niggers want to act violently.

Niggers act so cool and slick causing white people to ask, What makes them niggers act like that? Niggers act like you ain't never seen nobody act before. But when it comes to acting out for revolutionary causes Niggers say . . . I can't dig them actions. Niggers are scared of Revolution.

Niggers are very untogether people. Niggers talk about getting high and riding around in Els. Niggers should get high and ride to hell. Niggers talk about pimping. Pimping yours pimping mine. Just to be pimping is a hell of a line.

Niggers talk about the mind. Talk about my mind stronger than yours. I got that bitch's mind uptight. Niggers don't know a damn thing about the mind or they'd be right. Niggers are scared of Revolution.

Niggers fuck, Niggers fuck fuck fuck. Niggers love the word fuck. They think they're fucking cute. They fuck you around. The first thing they say when they're mad is "fuck it." You play a little too much with them they say "fuck you." Try to be nice to them they fuck you over. When it's time to TCB niggers are somewhere fucking. Niggers don't realize while they're doing all this fucking they're getting fucked around. But when they do realize it's too late, so all niggers do is just get fucked . . . up!

Niggers talk about fucking . . . Fucking that . . . Fucking this . . . Fucking yours . . . Fucking my sis. Not knowing what they fucking for. Ain't fucking for love and appreciation. Just fucking to be fucking. Niggers fuck white thighs, brown thighs, yellow thighs. Niggers fuck ankles when they run out of thighs. Niggers fuck Sally Linda and Sue. And if you don't watch out niggers will fuck you . . .

Niggers would fuck fuck if it could be fucked. But when it comes to fucking for revolutionary causes Niggers say FUCK! . . . revolution. Niggers are scared of revolution.

Niggers are players. Niggers play football baseball and basketball while the whiteman is cutting off their balls. When a nigger's play ain't tight enough to play with Black thighs, niggers play with White thighs to see if they still got some play with. And when ain't no White thighs to play with, niggers play with themselves. Niggers will tell you they're ready to be liberated but when you say let's go take our liberation. Niggers reply . . . Oh . . . I was just playing. Niggers are playing with revolution and losing. Niggers are sacred of revolution.

Niggers do a lot of shooting. Niggers shoot off at the mouth. Niggers shoot pool. Niggers cut around the corners and shoot down the street. Niggers shoot craps. Niggers shoot sharp glances at white women.

Niggers shoot dope into their arms. Niggers shoot guns and rifles on New Year's Eve a New Year that is coming in where white police will do more shooting at them. Where are niggers when the revolution needs some shot? Yeah . . . you know, niggers are somewhere shooting the shit. Niggers are scared of revolution.

Niggers are lovers. Niggers are lovers. Niggers love to see Clark Gable make love to Marilyn Monroe. Niggers love to see Tarzan fuck over the natives. Niggers love to hear the Lone Ranger yell Hi Ho . . . Silver. Niggers love commercials. Oh how niggers love commercials.

You can take niggers out of the country but, you can't take the country out of niggers.

Niggers are lovers. Niggers love to hear Malcolm rap but they didn't love Malcolm. Niggers love everything but themselves. But I'm a lover too. Yeah . . . I love niggers because niggers are me. And I should only love that which is part of me. Love to see niggers go through changes. Love to see niggers act. Love to see niggers make them plays and shoot that shit. But there's one thing about niggers I do not love . . . Niggers Are Scared of Revolution!

But He Was Cool

or: he even stopped for green lights

super-cool
ultrablack
a tan/purple
had a beautiful shade.

he had a double-natural
that wd put the sisters to shame.
his dashikis were tailor made
& his beads were imported sea shells
    (from some blk/country i never heard of)
he was triple-hip.

his tikis were hand carved
out of ivory
& came express from the motherland.
he would greet u in swahili
& say good-by in yoruba.
woooooooooooo-jim he bes so cool & ill tel li gent
                cool-cool is so cool he was un-cooled by
                        other niggers' cool
                cool-cool ultracool was bop-cool/ice box
                        cool so cool cold cool
                his wine didn't have to be cooled, him was
                        air conditioned cool
                cool-cool/real cool made me cool—now
                        ain't that cool
                cool-cool so cool him nick-named refrig-
                        erator.

From Don L. Lee (Haki Madhubuti), *Don't Cry, Scream* (Detroit: Broadside Press, 1969).

cool-cool so cool
he didn't know,
after detroit, newark, chicago &c.,
we had to hip
        cool-cool/ super-cool/ real cool
   that
to be black
is
to be
very-hot.

Personal Jihad

THE SEED OF MY DAY BEGINS
AS THE TORUOUS NIGHT ENDS
THE COMMON BIRDS GRAY SHRILL
INTERRUPTS THE FLUSHING OF A MORNING PEE

IT IS THE EYES OF A DOG
THE SOFT EYES
LOCKED IN TOO LONG, IN SOME CRAMPED YARD
WITH THE DIRT OF HIS ASS
CLUTCHING VIOLENTLY THE SOFT
OF SOMEBODY'S WARM

I REGARD THIS DAY, AS EVERY
LOSER WOULD
AND I NEED A GOD,
A BLACK GOD, TO GIVE ME
THE INSIDIOUS STRENGTH, THE CALM
SOFTNESS, TO WAYLAY FEAR

AS THE MORNING SEED GROWS
THE BLUE OF THE SKY MINGLES
WITH THE TWISTED BLACK FEATURES
OF WINTER TREES
AND SILENCE LOSES ITS CLUTCHES
ON A BEGINNING DAY

AND I SIT HERE AWARE OF
THE PAIN AND URGENCY
THAT IT
MUST ATTAIN DISCIPLINE

From *Black Fire: An Anthology of Afro-American Writing,* ed. LeRoi Jones (Amiri Baraka) and Larry Neal (New York: Morrow, 1968).

FOR BROTHERHOOD AND UNITY
SOFTLY, SAY IT NOW

SAY IT NOW—
DOWN IN THE SOUL————DISCIPLINE
SAY IT SOUL BROTHERS
SAY IT SOUL BROTHERS
DISCIPLINE. . . . .

Barbequed Cong: Or We Laid My Lai Low

I

at My Lai we left lint for lawns
feathered with frameless wingless birds,
barbequed and bodyless heads of hair
hanging from the charcoal gazes of burnt huts

rice-thin hides harbored
flesh-flailing pellets,
unregenerative crops trigger-grown from the trunks of branchless
mechanical trees.
as barbeque grills grew hotter with ghost-hot heat,
mothers cooked children and causes

in grease of blood-glazed breasts,
resigned in the weighty whisper that:
"one can only die once."

II

cannon cut My Lai into fleshy confetti.
pellet-potted half cooked carcasses curing in rice wine.
(rat tat-tat of an idea. souvenirs for patron-saints presiding over oil
    wells.)
flat-faced down in the mud like some unclaimed unnamed yet
    undreamt dream.
while miniature machine-gun minds

From *Giant Talk: An Anthology of Third World Writings,* ed. Quincy Troupe and Rainer Schulte (New York: Random House, 1975).

mate with mole-holes
on the muddy highways of swamp or swampless night.

III

"Westward, Whore!"
hear ye . . . hear ye:
a declaration of undeclared causes,
a preamble to constipation and conscription.
dare we overcome?
even arrive?
slightly begin?
entertain thoughts?
go forth against grains before mornings unfold?

IV

my lands! My Lai!
puppet shows and portable pentagods soar or sneak from saigon.
Shine came on deck of the mind this morning and said:
"there's a sag in the nation's middle.
which way extends the natal cord—
north or south?"

i lay down my life for My Lai and Harlem.
i lay down my burden in Timbuctu and Baltimore.
we waited long and low
like low-strung studs for My Lai
when we reared and rammed her
with spark-sperm spitting penises
then withdrew westward 6000 miles
(a pacific coffin of the mind between us)
to vex canned good consciences
and claim the 5th Amendment.

CAROLYN M. RODGERS

how I got ovah

i can tell you
about them
i have shaken rivers
out of my eyes
i have waded eyelash deep
have crossed rivers
have shaken the water weed out
of my lungs
have swam for strength
pulled by strength
through waterfalls with electric beats
i have bore the shocks
of water deep deep
waterlogs are my bones
i have shaken the water free of my hair
have kneeled on the banks
and kissed my ancestors of the dirt
whose rich dark root fingers rose up reached out
grabbed and pulled me rocked me cupped me
gentle strong and firm
carried me
made me swim for strength
cross rivers
though I shivered
was wet was cold
and wanted to sink down
and float as water, yea—
i can tell you.
i have shaken rivers
out of my eyes.

From Carolyn M. Rodgers, *How I Got Ovah: New and Selected Poems* (Garden City, N.Y.: Anchor Press, 1975).

summary

no sleep tonight
not even after all
the red and green pills
i have pumped into
my stuttering self or
the sweet wine
that drowns them.
                  this is
a poem for the world
for the slow suicides
in seclusion.
somewhere on 130th st.
a woman, frail as a
child's ghost, sings.   oh.
                        oh. what
can the matter be? johnny's
so long at the fair.
                  / i learned how
                     to masturbate
thru the new york times.
i thought
shd i have
thought anything
that cd not
be proved. i
thought and
was wrong. listen
                                  fool

          black

          bitch

From *Black Fire: An Anthology of Afro-American Writing,* ed. LeRoi Jones (Amiri Baraka) and Larry Neal (New York: Morrow, 1968).

of fantasy. life
is no more than

                                  gents

          and

              gigolos (99% american)

   liars
   and
   killers (199% american)

                       dreamers
               and drunks (299% american)
(ONLY GOD IS 300% AMERICAN)

                 i say

is everybody happy?
this is a poem for me.
i am alone.
one night of words
will not change
all that.

A. B. SPELLMAN

tomorrow the heroes

tomorrow the heroes
will be named willie. their
hair will be the bushes that grow
everywhere the beast walks. america

is white. america is not. white
is not the slow kerneling of seed
in earth like the willies, the grass
the roots that grapple the beast

in the swamps. the williecong are earth
walking. ile-ife succor the williecong.
there is no other hope.

From *Black Fire: An Anthology of Afro-American Writing,* ed. LeRoi Jones (Amiri Baraka) and Larry Neal (New York: Morrow, 1968).

"Black Power!"

Cold
Blue dem o
Cracker eyes
Freeze automatically
Uptight behind republican
Liberal sockets
Seeing flame redly
Quick dark rays
That beam in on their greyed unity
Not grasping green intervals
Or after-images that ARE
Dancing unashamedly
Everywhere black feet are

From *Black Arts: An Anthology of Black Creations,* ed. Ahmed Alhamisi and Harun Kofi Wangara (Detroit: Black Arts Publications, 1969).

Twelve Gates

Face it. The stars have their own lives and care
They are forced into it by your other eye and
Opposite side of your thoughts. Who takes sides
The world quite as fashionable as liars imagined

A picture of one fragile girl in an avalanche
Of the kimono required for their soft trade.
Who is so daring at first to draw lines in the sky
Dingy with this neglected daylight. Opened fan.
Life itself is such a simple thing and we need it

Then here come the music again. And we need that too
People asking each other. The invention of reason.
And those who own nothing what of those walking around
Without land, without cash value, properties. Without

Nothing in their name. Whose destinies
Are not marked or marked down. What of
The ones who are meant to rise in the world
By their names. Whose names are not known.
These worlds are lost in a minute only a gem
Of substance remaining. The necessity to change the form.
These streets clothed in an atmosphere of ash and care—
Less emotion. Who are these persons roll their shoulders

Outside the window in starlight and streetlight
Each young man there reminds the girl of someone
These are the last words I send you for awhile.
Written across her fan. Her open eye all flame and
You can feel it take shape in your eye. The lines.

From *Black Fire: An Anthology of Afro-American Writing,* ed. LeRoi Jones (Amiri Baraka) and Larry Neal (New York: Morrow, 1968).

Cry Freedom

There'll be no angry drums for "Bashee," this spring.
No rampagin' and stompin', standin' still,
this spring;
No more angry drums.
No more shoutin' angry drums.
No more drummin' angry shouts.
No more shoutin' anger.
No more shoutin'.
No more drums,
this spring,
for "Bashee."

Cry Freedom; Cry Freedom:
Sing the Song of Fire!
Cry Freedom; Cry Freedom:
Beat the tamborines, blow the horns
of Death, of fallen kings, of battles lost.
Cool the fevered brow; snuff the fires of hate:
Ease the pain:
Cry Freedom; Cry Freedom:
Ease the pain.
Cry Freedom; Cry Freedom:
Ease the pain.
Ease the pain.
Cry Freedom; Ease the pain:
Cry Freedom!

I

I'm not an invisible man.
My song, like

From *Liberator* 3.5 (May 1963).

rain, is universal.
I'm not an invisible man.
My anger stalks on ghetto legs and illuminates
the Nordic night like Roman Candles or Roman Bombs
over Ethiopia.
I'm not an invisible man.
though Baldwin doesn't write of me. He has other hangups.
You see me in the city streets; striding along.
The wooly hair worn long. The flaming African Eyes:
Striding along through the city streets;
Striding along towards freedom:
Striding along.
Fighting spirit, determination, message.
Angry Generation, Lonely Generation, Black Renaissance,
New Negro, Black Nationalist, etc., etc.
Classify me, hypnotize me, ostricize me;
Will me away from your sight.
Hide me from the watchin' world; the 3/5 colored
watchin' world.
They see and hear; they care.
They see and hear; they care:
The 3/5 colored watchin' world.

I'm not an invisible man.
My anger stalks on ghetto legs.
I'm not an invisible man.
My song, like
rain, is universal.
Listen while I blow my horn.

2

They are passionate and have compassion.
They are the parents of passion and compassion.
The Holy Fire has burnt them black even unto their hearts
pumping rhythm;
rounding out the universe.
Pumpin rhythm;
Singing, dancing, improvisation of the last days of Christ.
Sweet Lawd Jesus, comfort me in my last days.
My whiplash and sorry, sufferin', soul-starved days of
emasculation woe.
Sorrow sorrow the windy night.
Sorrow the foggy, windy night.

Sorrow the tortured dreams; the bitter tears.
Sorrow my achin' heart.
My achin' heart.
My achin' heart.
Sorrow the windy night, the foggy,
windy night; My achin' heart:
Cry Freedom!

3

I walk along the streets
of Brooklyn,
of Harlem,
of Fillmore,
of Black Bottom,
of Shanty Town, *of Ghetto:*
The Western Reservation of the Blacks.
As I walk, an eagle, within me, begins to
stir and raise his head.
We shall overcome.
We shall overcome.
They sing and they shall, Lord knows,
they shall overcome:
The rats and roaches, number men,
pawnshop leering-leeches,
fat pork chop preachers with holy cadillacs,
holy hypocrites,
playboy congressmen, baseball playing leaders,
welfare robots,
birth control–sly annihilation
urban renewal,
dedicated terror
with nightstick and shiny silver badge:
Black blood flowing
like cloud-burst in May.

We shall overcome.
We shall overcome.
We shall overcome:

Cry Freedom; Cry Freedom;
Cry Freedom:
Ease the pain!

4

Matthew,
my friend of down and out Brooklyn
Summertime-Lament Days;
I walk with you.
I feel your haughty, regal stare
illuminate the African Valley
of our
Angry, American, western blackman,
idealistic hopes for better years.
Matthew,
I walk with you.
Lion. Brother of my ebon heart.
Will you overcome?
Will you ease the pain?
Will you beat the tamborines and shatter
the Nordic Eagle's western lair?
Matthew,
I walk with you
through red and stormy years
From Cairo to Conakry, to Capetown,
to Chicago.
Matthew,
we'll sing the Song of Fire
with Cecil and Ronnie,
Max and Abbie,
Miriam Makeba,
Walter and Nannie,
Jerry and Rita,
and Malcolm X.

Matthew, my brother,
I walk with you
and them toward a better tomorrow;
a Blacker Day:
(Walk together chillun; don'cha git weary.)
Matthew,
I walk with you.
I walk with you.
I walk with you.
As we sing the Song of Fire.
As we Cry Freedom.
As we beat the Drums of Death
for Brother "Bashee."

We are not invisible men and Lord,
if they don't free our people:
The heavens will open up and
the western earth will tremble till
the glass-house cities crumble to dust.
The wind won't blow.
The rain won't fall and all
their little children will die at birth.
(The drug deaths were only the beginning!)

Elijah shouts–from the mountaintops:
Let My People Go!

Matthew,
I walk with you
to the last trumpet call
when Malcolm embraces Martin Luther King:
(As Salaam Alaikum and Thank you, Jesus!)
Mahailia and Eartha Kitt will cry and all our
pickaninny rhapsodies
will resound upon
the Mountains of the Moon.

Sing the Song of Fire!
Beat the tamborines!
Blow the Horns of Death!
Ease the pain:

Cry Freedom!

CRY FREEDOM (for the Black Nationalists, Mustapha Bashir and Matthew Meade): "They were led by the mysterious man in the Arab headdress." (The New York Times on the U.N. riots, February, 1961) "A century of 'Negro' Progress and Freedom." (A "Negro" Publication)

Matthew Meade, young nationalist freedom-fighter and scholar, is typical of the breed of educated nationalists now leading colonial peoples to nationhood. He is also one of the new generation of Afro-American militants (known to the "black conservatives" as "Africanists"), who are forging a new day for black people in colonialist North America.

Mustapha Bashir, Harlem street speaker and U.N. demonstrator, who was recently accused of murdering a businessman in Harlem. This affair seemed to delight certain elements within the black community who made the most of it.

Rolland Snellings, painter-poet, was born in North Carolina, raised in Ohio, and reborn in Brooklyn's teeming streets. During 1960–61, he attended art school briefly, paying starvation dues and listening to Malcolm X. Spent 1962–63 on Manhattan's lower east side, ANECCA Art Exhibitions, Poetry Workshop, UMBRA Magazine: Striding Along.

2

Malcolm

Eulogy of Malcolm X "Our Black Manhood ...
Our Black Shining Prince! ..."

Here—at this final hour, in this quiet place, Harlem has come to bid farewell to one of its brightest hopes—extinguished now, and gone from us forever.

For Harlem is where he worked and where he struggled and fought—his home of homes, where his heart was, and where his people are—and it is, therefore, most fitting that we meet once again—in Harlem—to share these last moments with him.

For Harlem has been ever gracious to those who have loved her, have fought for her and have defended her honor even to the death. It is not in the memory of man that this beleaguered, unfortunate but nonetheless proud community has found a braver, more gallant young champion than this Afro-American who lies before us—unconquered still.

I say the word again, as he would want me to: Afro-American—Afro-American Malcolm, who was a master, was most meticulous in his use of words. Nobody knew better than he the power words have over the minds of men. Malcolm had stopped being "Negro" years ago.

It had become too small, too puny, too weak a word for him, Malcolm was bigger than that. Malcolm had become an Afro-American and he had wanted—so desperately—that we, that all his people would become Afro-Americans too.

There are those who will consider it their duty, as friends of the Negro people, to tell us to revile him, to flee even from the presence of his memory, to save ourselves by writing him out of the history of our turbulent times.

Many will ask what Harlem finds to honor in this stormy, controversial and bold young captain—and we will smile.

Many will say turn away—away from this man, for he is not a man but a demon, a monster, a subverter and an enemy of the black man—and we will smile.

They will say that he is of hate—a fanatic, a racist—who can only bring evil to the cause for which you struggle!

And we will answer and say unto them: Did you ever talk to Brother Malcolm? Did you ever touch him, or have him smile at you? Did you ever really listen to him? Did he ever do a mean thing? Was he ever himself associated with violence or any public disturbance? For if you did you would know him. And if you knew him you would know why we must

From *For Malcolm: Poems on the Life and Death of Malcolm X,* ed. Dudley Randall and Margaret G. Burroughs (Detroit: Broadside Press, 1967).

honor him: Malcolm was our manhood, our living black manhood! This was his meaning to his people. And, in honoring him, we honor the best in ourselves.

Last year, from Africa, he wrote these words to a friend: "My Journey," he says, "is almost ended, and I have a much broader scope than when I started out, which I believe will add new life and dimension to our struggle for freedom and honor, and dignity in the States. I'm writing these things so that you will know for a fact the tremendous sympathy and support we have among the African States for our Human Rights Struggle. The main thing is that we keep a United Front wherein our most valuable time and energy will not be wasted fighting each other."

However much we differed with him—or with each other about him and his value as a man, let his going from us serve only to bring us together, now. Consigning these mortal remains to earth, the common mother of all, secure in the knowledge that what we place in the ground is no more now a man—but a seed—which, after the winter of discontent— will come forth again to meet us. And we shall know him then for what he was and is—a Prince—our own black shining Prince!—who didn't hesitate to die, because he loved us so.

A Poem for Black Hearts

For Malcolm's eyes, when they broke
the face of some dumb white man, For
Malcolm's hands raised to bless us
all black and strong in his image
of ourselves, For Malcolm's words
fire darts, the victor's tireless
thrusts, words hung above the world
change as it may, he said it, and
for this he was killed, for saying
and feeling, and being/change, all
collected hot in his heart, For Malcolm's
heart, raising us above our filthy cities,
for his stride, and his beat, and his address
to the grey monsters of the world, For Malcolm's
pleas for your dignity, black men, for your life,
black man, for the filling of your minds
with righteousness, For all of him dead and
gone and vanished from us, and all of him which
clings to our speech black god of our time.
For all of him, and all of yourself, look up,
black man, quit stuttering and shuffling, look up,
black man, quit whining and stooping, for all of him,
For Great Malcolm a prince of the earth, let nothing in us rest
until we avenge ourselves for his death, stupid animals
that killed him, let us never breathe a pure breath if
we fail, and white men call us faggots till the end of
the earth.

_____

From LeRoi Jones (Amiri Baraka), *Black Magic: Sabotage, Target Study, Black Art; Collected Poetry, 1961–1967* (Indianapolis: Bobbs-Merrill, 1969).

Malcolm X

Original.
Ragged-round.
Rich-robust.

He had the hawk-man's eyes.
We gasped. We saw the maleness.
The maleness raking out and making guttural the air
and pushing us to walls.

And in a soft and fundamental hour
a sorcery devout and vertical
beguiled the world.

He opened us—
who was a key,

who was a man.

From *For Malcolm: Poems on the Life and Death of Malcolm X,* ed. Dudley Randall and Margaret G. Burroughs (Detroit: Broadside Press, 1967).

Portrait of Malcolm X

(For Charles Baker)

He has the sign
of the time shining
in his eyes   the high sign

His throat moans
Moses on Sinai and cracks
stones

His lips lay full and flowered
by the breast of Mother Africa

His forehead is red
and sacrosanct and
smooth as time and
love for you

From Etheridge Knight, *Poems from Prison* (Detroit: Broadside Press, 1968).

MARVIN E. JACKMON (MARVIN X)

That Old Time Religion

Malcolm.
The Saint
    behind our skulls
in the region of fear and strength
Nothing but a man, who threw fear away
and caught something greater . . . life
And the price of life is death
protect ourselves from the beast
and he went un-protected
by the will of allah
most merciful
a lost leader
though we have found his spirit
    behind our skulls
    in the region of fear and strength
Malcolm held our manhood
    he said what we knew but feared
    we feared to name the beast
    who is a man; who has a number
    and the number is 666 spoken of
    in Revelations of the Bible.
    Ready or not . . . God is here
        LET THERE BE BLACKNESS OVER THIS LAND
        LET BLACK POWER SHINE AND SHINE.

From *Black Fire: An Anthology of Afro-American Writing,* ed. LeRoi Jones (Amiri Baraka) and Larry Neal (New York: Morrow, 1968).

Malcolm X—An Autobiography

I am the Seventh Son of the Son
who was also the Seventh.
I have drunk deep of the waters of my ancestors
have travelled the soul's journey towards cosmic harmony,
the Seventh Son.
Have walked slick avenues
and seen grown men, fall, to die in a blue doom
of death and ancestral agony,
have seen old men glide, shadowless, feet barely
touching the pavements.

I sprung out of the Midwestern plains
the bleak Michigan landscape, the black blues of Kansas
City, the kiss-me-nights.
out of the bleak Michigan landscape wearing the slave name—
Malcolm Little.
Saw a brief vision in Lansing when I was seven, and in
my mother's womb heard the beast cry of death,
a landscape on which white robed figures ride, and my
Garvey father silhouetted against the night-fire, gun in hand
form outlined against a panorama of violence.

Out of the Midwestern bleakness, I sprang, pushed eastward,
past shack on country nigger shack, across the wilderness
of North America.

I hustler. I pimp. I unfulfilled Black man
bursting with destiny.
New York City Slim called me Big Red,
and there was no escape, close nights of the smell of death.

From *For Malcolm: Poems on the Life and Death of Malcolm X,* ed. Dudley Randall and Margaret G. Burroughs (Detroit: Broadside Press, 1967).

Pimp. Hustler. The day fills these rooms.
I am talking about New York. Harlem.
talking about the neon madness.
talking about ghetto eyes and nights
talking about death protruding across the room. Small's paradise.
talking about cigarette butts, and rooms smelly with white
sex flesh, and dank sheets, and being on the run.
talking about cocaine illusions, about stealing and selling.
talking about these New York cops who smell of blood and money.
I am Big Red, tiger vicious, Big Red, bad nigger, will kill.

But there is rhythm here. Its own special substance:
I hear Billie sing, no good man, and dig Prez, wearing the Zoot
suit of life, the pork-pie hat tilted at the correct angle.
through the Harlem smoke of beer and whiskey, I understand the
mystery of the signifying monkey,
in a blue haze of inspiration, I reach for the totality of Being.
I am at the center of a swirl of events. War and death.
rhythm. hot women. I think life a commodity bargained for
across the bar in Small's.
I perceive the echoes of Bird and there is a gnawing in the maw
of my emotions.

and then there is jail. America is the world's greatest jailer,
and we all in jails. black spirits contained like magnificent
birds of wonder. I now understand my father urged on by the
ghost of Garvey,
and see a small brown man standing in a corner. The cell. cold.
dank. The light around him vibrates. Am I crazy? But to understand is to submit to a more perfect will, a more perfect order.
To understand is to surrender the imperfect self.
For a more perfect self.

Allah formed brown man, I follow
and shake within the very depth of my most imperfect being,
and I bear witness to the Message of Allah
and I bear witness—all praise is due Allah!

Malcolm

do not speak to me of martyrdom
of men who die to be remembered
on some parish day.
i don't believe in dying
though i too shall die
and violets like castanets
will echo me.

yet this man
this dreamer,
thick-lipped with words
will never speak again
and in each winter
when the cold air cracks
with frost, i'll breathe
his breath and mourn
my gun-filled nights.
he was the sun that tagged
the western sky and
melted tiger-scholars
while they searched for stripes.
he said, "fuck you white
man. we have been
curled too long. nothing
is sacred now. not your
white faces nor any
land that separates
until some voices
squat with spasms."

From *For Malcolm: Poems on the Life and Death of Malcolm X,* ed. Dudley Randall and Margaret G. Burroughs (Detroit: Broadside Press, 1967).

do not speak to me of living.
life is obscene with crowds
of white on black.
death is my pulse.
what might have been
is not for him/or me
but what could have been
floods the womb until i drown.

For Malcolm Who Walks in the Eyes of Our Children

He had been coming a very long time,
had been here many times before
in the flesh of other persons
in the spirit of other gods

His eyes had seen flesh turned to stone,
had seen stone turned to flesh
had swam within the minds
of a billion great heroes,

had walked amongst builders
of nations, of the Sphinx, had built
with his own hands those nations,

had come flying across time a cosmic spirit,
an idea, a thought wave transcending
flesh fusion spirit of all centuries,
had come soaring like a sky break

above ominous clouds of sulphur
in a stride so enormous it spanned
the breadth of a peoples of bloodshed,

came singing like Coltrane breathing life
into stone statues formed from lies

Malcolm, flaming cosmic spirit who walks
amongst us, we hear your voice

From Quincy Troupe, *Weather Reports: New and Selected Poems* (New York: Writers and Readers Pub. for Harlem River Press, 1991).

speaking wisdom in the wind,
we see your vision in the life / fires of men,
in our incredible young children
who watch your image
flaming in the sun

For Malcolm X

The voice has gone
Out of the wilderness
Out of the carnage kingdom
Out of the mire.
And without his eloquence
We are mute
And rocks and stones break in the soul
The world winds
On its frozen axis
The dizzy oceans churn our pain.
All needed storms abate
Themselves. Moons freeze the rain.

Gone. Delivered.
So piteous there were
The stolid and the dumb
So piteous as not to mourn
So piteous, so many
The stolid and the dumb.
Gone. Delivered.
He has gone up, delivered.

From *For Malcolm: Poems on the Life and Death of Malcolm X,* ed. Dudley Randall and Margaret G. Burroughs (Detroit: Broadside Press, 1967).

A Plea for the Politic Man

(For Malcolm)

Here is what you saw,
all this distended grief,
the world split up and curved
back on its boweled order,
an impolitic people gnawing
its grizzled skulls,
all these poets rummaging
through their own discontent.
Senators gag and girdle
the devastating ghettos.
Old oppressions come back as law.
Governors pop up in the debris,
new heroes flying at their sides,
to deal with the politic demands.

Unskilled, unslung,
I run from the city I love
like a particle knocking
in a familiar chamber.
I wanted something to discover.
But what is here?

We turn back to create
what we have never really known,
what we fear we may not learn,
feeling safe in the human ignorance
of all that's human,
uncertain, even, of the symbols
of our making,
not caring to acknowledge our politic grace.

From Jay Wright, *The Homecoming Singer* (New York: Corinth Books, 1971).

The frenzied, idiotic world
will nourish our laments,
and you will turn there, sadly,
to face your politic death.

3

Coltrane and Jazz

How Long Has This Trane Been Gone

Tell me about the good things
you clappin & laughin

Will you remember
or will you forget

Forget about the good things
like Blues & Jazz being black
Yeah Black Music
all about you

And the musicians that
write & play about you
a black brother groanin
a black sister moanin
& beautiful black children
ragged . . . underfed laughin
not knowin

Will you remember their names
or do they have no names
no lives—only products
to be used when you wanna
dance fuck & cry

You takin—they givin
You livin—they
creating starving dying
trying to make a better tomorrow
Giving you & your children a history
But what do you care about

From Jayne Cortez, *Festivals and Funerals,* by Jane Cortez (New York: Phrase Text, 1971).

history—Black History
and John Coltrane
No
All you wanna do
is pat your foot
sip a drink & pretend
with your head bobbin up & down
What do you care about acoustics
bad microphones or out-of-tune pianos
& noise
You the club owners & disc jockeys
made a deal didn't you
a deal about Black Music
& you really don't give
a shit long as you take

      There was a time
when KGFJ played all black music
from Bird to Johnny Ace
on show after show
but what happened
I'll tell you what happened
they divided black music
doubled the money
& left us split again
is what happened

John Coltranes dead & some
of you
have yet to hear him play
How long how long has that Trane been gone

and how many more Tranes will go
before you understand your life
John Coltrane who had the whole of
life wrapped up in B flat
John Coltrane like Malcolm
True image of Black Masculinity

Now tell me about the good things
I'm telling you about
John Coltrane

A name that should ring
throughout the projects mothers

Mothers with sons
who need John Coltrane
Need the warm arm of his music
like words from a Father
How long how long has that Trane been gone

John palpatating love notes
in a lost-found nation
within a nation
His music resounding discovery
signed Always
John Coltrane

Rip those dead white people off
your walls Black People
black people whose walls
should be a hall
A Black Hall of Fame
so our children will know
will know & be proud
Proud to say I'm from Parker City—Coltrane City—Ornette City
Pharoah City living on Holiday street next to
James Brown park in the State of Malcolm

How Long
how long
will it take for you to understand
that Tranes been gone
riding in a portable radio
next to your son whose lonely
Who walks walks walks into nothing
no city no state no home no Nothing
how long
How long
Have black people been gone

Legacy: In Memory of 'Trane

Black John the Sorcerer!
Juba-Lover,
bringing tales of
coaldust gods
wrapped in sound.
striving to journey home.
beyond the light
into darkness . . .
into Truth,
his voice a glistening Nommo
speechless now, hushed by
milky smiles
and snow june hate.
leaving songs of praise!
a path to dance beyond . . .
a journey quest to selfhood . . .
a love supremely unafraid . . .
black bright, and binding
ear to sights unseen.

II

heard the mighty Congo,
black snake flowing through black belt
of cotton fields:
and OLEDUMARE, shouting Jubilees!
sunday morning visions of black dawn voodoo . . .
KUNTU!
. . . and left behind a song of praise,
a song of Roots!

From *Jump Bad: A New Chicago Anthology,* ed. Gwendolyn Brooks (Detroit: Broadside Press, 1971).

High John to Conqueror!
traveling alone . . . cold trains
field cries in railyards
weedgrown and quiet.
a journey through deserted past
of lost manhoods
to warcry-mangods of NOW!
. . . and left behind a song of praise
a path to dance beyond . . .

III

Juba love begins!
the journey home extends within.
To journey Home!
wedding
black glides of waves
that caress the lips of Mothershore,
to waves upon this shore!
climbing
anthracite bridges to
killimanjaros of the mind!
ancestral nights in Congo Square . . .
Black Echoes of Our Self!
Nommo spoken in speechless tongue
to travel Home . . . the journey within

IV

      COLTRANE !
     COLTRANE!
our juba-lover
bringing tales
of coaldust gods
and wrapped in Sound . . . . . .
pursuing the journey home
. . . has left behind
Our Song of Praise!
. . . an unseen path to dance beyond . . .
the Journey Quest to Blackness

Tribute to Duke

Rhythm and Blues
sired you; gospel's
your mother tongue:
that of a MAN
praying in the
miraculous language
of song—soul
communion with
his maker,
a sacred offering
from the
God-in-man
to the
God-of-man.

Ohh, Ooh, Oh,
moaning low,
I got
the blues.

Sometimes I'm
up; sometimes
I'm down.

Sometimes I'm
down; sometimes
I'm up

Oh happy day
When Jesus washed
my sin away.
(musical background
with a medley of
tunes)

You reigned King
of Jazz before
Whiteman imitations
of "Black-Brown and
Beige" became the
order of the day.
Here, now, we but add
one star more to
your two-grand
jewel-studded crown
for that many tunes
you turned the world
onto in your
half-centuried

Boss, boss
tunes in
technicolor
SOUL—
Black-
Brown-
Beige-
Creole-

From *Understanding the New Black Poetry: Black Speech and Black Music as Poetic References*, ed. Stephen Henderson (New York: Morrow, 1973).

creative fever riffed   *Black*
in scales of color
from "Black Beauty"   *and*
to "Creole Rhapsody"
and "Black and Tan   *Tan*
    Fantasy."
All praises   *is*
to Duke
King of Jazz   *the color*
                                                        of my fantasy.

To run it down   *When things*
for you. That   *got down*
fever that came on   *and really*
with that "Uptown Beat"   *funky*
caused Cotton when   *fever, fever,*
he came to Harlem   *light*
that first time to   *my fire.*
do a "Sugar Hill
Shim Sham."

                                                        Down,
                                                            down
When things got down   *down*
and funky   *Nee-eev-eer*
you bit into the blues   *treat me*
and blew into the air,   *kind*
"I Got It Bad and   *and gentle—*
That Ain't Good,"   *BLOW*
And from deep   *(music in the*
down into your   *background)*
"Solitude," you   *the way you*
touched both   *should*
"Satin Doll" and   *BLOW, MAN*
"Sophisticated Lady"   *Ain't*
wrapped them in   *I*
"Mood Indigo" and made   *Got*
each moment   *it*
"A Prelude   *Bad.*
to a kiss."

Way back then, Man,   *Break it down.*
you were doing   *Break*
your thing.   *it down*
Blowing minds with   *Right on down*
riffs capping   *to*
whimsical whiffs of   *the*

lush melody—
changing minds
with moods and
modulations,
changing minds,
changing faces,
changing tunes,

changing changes,
tripping out with
Billy to "Take the
A Train," making it
your theme—
your heat—
coming on strong
with bold dissonance
and fast, fast, beat
of the early, late
sound of our time.

"Harlem Airshaft"
"Rent Party Blues"
jangling jazzed tone
portraits of life
in the streets.
"Harlem"—a symphony
of cacaphonous sound,
bristling rhythms,
haunting laments
trumpeting into the air
defiant blasts blown solo
to fully orchestrated
folk chorus,
World Ambassador,
translating Life
into lyric; voice
into song; pulse
into beat
the beat, the beat,
a beat, a beat, a beat,
beat, beat, beat, beat
Do it now.
Get down.
"A Drum Is a Woman,"

Real
nitty gritty.
("Solitude"
  as background
  sound)
Blow,
   blow,

   blow

Do your thing.

Change, change, change
your 'chine
and Take
   The
     A Train.

Ain't
got no
   money
Ain't got no bread.
Ain't got
no place
to lay my Afro head.
   I got
   those low down
   blues.
Chorus: Hot-and-Cold-
Running- Harlem
"Rent Party Blues."

Break it down,
down
   down
      down
Right on down
to the
   Real
   nitty gritty.
   drums in the
   background become

and what more
language does
a sweetback need
to trip out to
"Mood Indigo,"

Right on, Duke
Do your thing,
your own thing.
And, Man,
the word's out
when you
get down
Bad
it's good,
Real good,

And as you
go
know
you're tops,
and whatever
you do,
"We love you
madly."

drum solo)

(Theme song)

Take

The
A
Train.

Right on.

Right
on
out
of
this
funky
world.

DAVID HENDERSON

Elvin Jones Gretsch Freak
(Coltrane at the Half-Note)

To Elvin Jones/tub man of
the John Coltrane Quartet.
GRETSCH is outstanding on
his bass drum that faces the
audience at the Half-Note,
Spring Street, New York City.

gretsch love
gretsch hate
gretsch mother   father fuck
fuck gretsch

The Halfnote should be
a basement cafe like the "A" train
Jazz/drums of gretsch
on the fastest and least stopping
transportation scene in NYC
subways are for gretsch
"A" train long as a long city block
the tenements of the underground rails
west 4th
34th   42nd   125th
farther down in the reverse

local at west 4th
waterfront   warehouse   truck/produce   vacant
the halfnote

our city fathers keep us on the right track
zones/   ozone

fumes of tracks   /smokestacks
The Halfnote
westside truck exhaust and spent breath

From *Understanding the New Black Poetry: Black Speech and Black Music as Poetic References*, ed. Stephen Henderson (New York: Morrow, 1973).

of Holland Tunnel   exhaust   soot darkness jazz
speeding cars   noisy/   noiseless
speeding gretsch   tremulous gretsch
Elvin Jones the man behind the pussy
four men love on a stage
the loud orgy
gretsch trembles and titters
                    gretsch is love
                    gretsch is love
                    gretsch is love

Elvin's drum ensemble the aggressive cunt
the feminine mystique
cymbals tinny clitorous   resounding
lips snares flanked/   encircling
thumping foot drum peter rabbit the fuck   take
this   and take   that
elvin behind the uterus of his sticks
the mad embryo
painting sweat-dripping embryo
misshapen/   hunched
Coltrane sane/   cock   the forceps
the fox and the hare
the chase
screaming and thumping
traffic of music on Spring Street
'Trane says to young apprentice Ron Ferral "Fill in the
solids, get it while it's hot and comely; Elvin fucks almost
as good as his Mama."

The Halfnote is as packed as   rush hour on 42nd & 8th
"A" train territory
coltrane is off with a hoot
directed supine
nowhere in generalness
into the din and the death
between bar and tables   reds silver glass molten mass shout
tobacco fumes across the boardwalk
                (coney island is the "D" train change
                 at west 4th if you want it)
Coltrane steps the catwalk
                elvin jones drums gretsch
                gretsch shimmy and shout
elvin drums a 1939 ford
99 pushing miles per hour/   shoving barefoot driver

                   in the heats
Coltrane/ Jones
riffing   face to face
instrument charge
          stools to kneecap
many faceted rhythm structure   to   tomahawk
gretsch rocks 'n rolls   gretsch rattles
fuck gretsch/
                    we know so well strident drums
                    children singing death songs /war
                    tenor and soprano   high
tenor soar/   flux of drums   chasing
        keen inviolate   blue
the model "T" ford & air hammer
                    Holland tunnel
                    "Avenue of the Americas"
                    cobbled stones/   din   of rubber
                    of tin
to the truck graveyard
line-up of Boston Blackie nights/   deserted
right here model "T" & tomahawk
                    sometimes late in silent din of night
                    I hear
                    bagpipes/   death march
                        music of ago/   kennedy

gretsch   gretsch tune optical color-jumping gretsch
    Elvin's F-86 Sabre jet/   remember Korea/   Horace Silver
    the fine smooth jackets the colored boys brought back
            blazing the back   —a forgotten flame
    from the far east with 'U.S. Air Force'   a map of Japan
            blazing the back   —a forgotten flame
Elvin tom-tomming
bassing the chest   "E/ gretsch   "J"/ gretsch
                    clashing metal mad
                    tin frantic road of roaring/   gretsch
                    roar
peck Morrison
the *bass* player
told me once about a drum set
with a central anchor/   every drum connected
        unable to jump or sway
        drums like the cockpit of a TXF spy plane
        ejaculator seat and all
                        (call up brubecks joe dodge,

                                        al hirt
                        Lester Lanin et al)
pilot conflict
and the man elvin behind the baptismal tubs
that leap like cannons   to the slashing sound of knives
black elvin knows so well
the knives the Daily News displays along with the photo
of a grinning award-winning cop
the kind of knives elvin talks about
downtown by the water
and uptown
near the park.

DON L. LEE (HAKI MADHUBUTI)

Don't Cry, Scream

(for John Coltrane/ from a black poet/
in a basement apt. crying dry tears
of "you ain't gone.")

into the sixties
a trane
came/ out of the
fifties with a
golden boxcar
riding the rails
of novation.
        blowing
        a-melodics
        screeching,
        screaming,
        blasting—
                driving some away,
                (those paper readers who thought
                manhood was something innate)

                bring others in,
                (the few who didn't believe that the
                world existed around established whi
                teness & leonard bernstein)
music that ached.
murdered our minds (we reborn)
born into a neoteric aberration.
& suddenly
you envy the
BLIND man—
you know that he will
hear what you'll never
see.

From Don L. Lee (Haki Madhubuti), *Don't Cry, Scream* (Detroit: Broadside Press, 1969).

your music is like
my head—nappy black/
a good nasty feel with
tangled sons of:
  we-eeeeeeeeeee   sing
  WE-EEEeeeeeeeeee   loud &
  WE-EEEEEEEEEEEEEEEEE high
            with
            feeling

a people playing
the sound of me when
i combed it. combed at
it.

i cried for billy holiday.
the blues. we ain't blue
the blues exhibited illusions of manhood.
destroyed by you. Ascension into:

  scream-eeeeeeeeeeeeee-ing sing
  SCREAM-EEEeeeeeeeeeee-ing loud &
  SCREAM-EEEEEEEEEEEEEE-ing long with
              feeling

we ain't blue, we are black.
we ain't blue, we are black.
   (all the blues did was
   make me cry)
soultrane gone on a trip
he left man images
he was a life-style of
man-makers & annihilator
of attache case carriers.

Trane done went.
(got his hat & left me one)
naw brother,
i didn't cry,
i just—
 Scream-eeeeeeeeeeeeee e-ed   sing loud
 SCREAM-EEEEEEEEEEE EEEEEEE-ED & high with
  we-eeeeeeeeeee eeeeeeeee ee feeling
  WE-EEEEEEeeeeeeeee EEEEEEEE letting
  WE-EEEEEEEEEEEEEEEEEEEEEEE yr/voice
  WHERE YOU DONE GONE, BROTHER? break

it hurts, grown babies
dying, born, done caught me
a trane. steel wheels broken
by popsicle sticks. i went out
& tried to buy a nickel bag
with my standard oil card.

> (swung on a faggot who politely
> scratched his ass in my presence.
> he smiled broken teeth stained from
> his over-used tongue. fisted-face.
> teeth dropped in tune with ray
> charles singing "yesterday.")

blonds had more fun—
with snagga-tooth niggers
who saved pennies & pop bottles for week-ends
to play negro & other filthy inventions.
be-bop-en to james brown's
cold sweat—these niggers didn't sweat,
they perspired. & the blond's dye came out,
i ran. she did too, with his pennies, pop bottles
& his mind. tune in next week same time same station
for anti-self in one lesson.
to the negro cow-sissies
who did tchaikovsky &
the beatles & live in
split-level homes & had
split-level minds & babies.
who committed the act of
love with their clothes on.

> (who hid in the bathroom to read
> jet mag., who didn't read the chicago
> defender because of the misspelled
> words & had shelves of books by
> europeans on display. untouched. who
> hid their little richard & lightnin'
> slim records & asked: "John who?"

> instant hate.)
they didn't know any better,
brother, they were too busy getting
into debt, expressing humanity &
taking off color.

SCREAMMMM/we-eeeee/screech/teee   improvise
aheeeeeeeee/screeeeeee/theeee/ee   with
ahHHHHHHHHH/WEEEEEEEE/scrEEE   feeling
     EEEE
we-eeeeeeWE-EEEEEEEEWE-EE-EEEEE
the ofays heard you &
were wiped out. spaced.
one clown asked me during,
my favorite things, if
you were practicing,
i fired on the muthafucka & said,
"i'm practicing."
naw brother,
i didn't cry.
i got high off my thoughts—
they kept coming back,
back to destroy me.

& that BLIND man
i don't envy him anymore
i can see his hear
& hear his heard through my pores.
i can see my me. It was truth you gave,
like a daily shit
it had to come.
                    can you scream—brother?   very
                    can you scream—brother?   soft

i hear you.
i hear you.

and the Gods will too.

AMUS MOR

The Coming of John

(the evening and the morning are the first day)

it is friday
the eagle has flown
4 years before the real god Allah shows
before we know the happenings
we eat the devils peck
mondays hotlinks with porkenbeans
hear "newk" on dig and "bags" on moonray
see desolation in the dark between the buildings
our front view is bricks of the adjacent kitchenette

Pat riffs in a babyfied key
slips on the green knit suit
with the silver buckle at the belly
and we slide out into that wintertime
the last lights of day
with an uncanny clarity for chi town
the shafts behind the clouds popping them open
and the rust on the el grids
clashing and blending strangely
against the rays like hip black art
heaven about to show itself
above the ghetto holiday shoppers
the 1954 brand fragments of people on the walks
Hadacol on her way north
after officer driseldorf has stomped her on the street
and crushed her finger on a golden ring

the hipster in the tivoli eat shop
deals single joints after the commotion

From *The Black Nation* 5.1 (Summer/Fall 1986). Original version appeared in *Black Spirits: A Festival of New Black Poets in America,* ed. Woodie King (New York: Random House, 1972).

dusk baring his first meal
with us streaming and talking about the guns
getting so mad and so frantic we sweat
get on to cool
go on home
make love and nod
then it is the new year
and the guns are going off across the alley

10 days or so hes still "on this end"
only Edwardo Harris knowing his name
John Coltrane (as he was called then)
in a big hat
gouster pleated pants and all
before metamorphosis miles plugs cotton in his ears
and philadelphia thunders in babylon
a shake dancer follows the set
and it seems a whole sea of black faces are out on "six trey"
a holy nation peeping and poor
behind the red oblong bulb of a highlife sign

Ohnedaruth the mystic has already blown and hypnotized us—
making us realize right then
THAT WE ARE LIVING IN THE BIBLE (HOLY KORAN, CABALA)

the konateski girl sets there frozen
shes followed her lifelong scent of judea
from the rich north shore township
all the way into the crown propellar lounge
into a blessed tenors bell
while we go "off into space"
peeping the dream of the old ladies of nipon
dragging the gunny sacks of brown smack across the dead battlefields
chanting "fun amelikaan" "fun amelikaan" "fun joe"
*   And of course the bard says (from the corner of his mouth)*
"Aw right na iss a party, ya dig that. Miles come in an be doin
alla right things. Ya understand! Takes the hord'overs from the
lazy susan with so much finesse, en be so correct when he be talk-
in to them big fine socialite hos. Understand. They be sayin
'Oh Miles' ya understand. En mah man leave the door open. Nah
here come Trane. He wrong from the get go. Ya understand.
Reach his hand down in the tray, say 'gemme one of them little
samaches'. He done pushed the mop out the way, en grabbed the
johnny walker red, way from one ah them ivy league lames. Un-
derstand! See en Miles he brought the man in there for that.

They working together. Understand. He his man. Yall been hearin
all of us. Jim! Them intellectuals, all of um talk-
ing about the new niggro. There he is right there. What he try-
ing ta tell yall with his horn, is that yall can't expect to
get nowhere bein what the gray call intelligent. If yall expect
to get somewhere in america, you gotta start bustin down dos an
shit, pitchin a fit, and poppin these lames upside the head.
Layin some ah these peckerwoods out across the room, is what
get you somewhere in america. If yall don't get just like me,
and start letting yalls wigs grow wild and wooly and shit, and
starta setting all up in grays faces, yall aint goin another
futher. Cause this shit, in this here country right here is
coming down ta some shorenuff head bustin."
we stay till the lights
pull the covers off the room
showing the ragged carpet
in the great american tradition
'mayhap a manger'
make in in
fire up two thumbs and sleep
t. i. on a pallet in front of the bad window
and the hotel catches fire
and lobbys all smoking
the few steel workers with their helmets
the several a d c families
the pimps, the hustlers and the chippies
are all milling around out of it
when the "konat girl" turns up in smoke
in just leotards and a mouton coat
now shes took the pressing iron to her slavic hair
(that morning is the second day)
A Love Supreme takes me in

i stretch my hands open to a sun of morning
and breezes are light that i encounter
in my handclasps with wind

your softness take me in
like a saharian morning taught it
an i hear all that ALLAH says
when I feel the universe about the miracle you are
there is the om of a morning sky
a herb tea and vegetable magic breakfast
you serve me
zodiac sister of the suns house

there are silks within the winds of autumn
and i do not feel the stench of close buildings
alive like smog
sometimes a blare of noon
enthralls me in a mystique
a heat of atoms love
and i am myself a 6 footfire
a dynamo of afro-energy

there are gulls about the lake
and the sky like a big hip hat
guides them in compassed flight
then there is the small music
of these wise ghetto children
a symphony of innuendos on the street
we walk down six tray
down the line the day is endless
under the shadows of the el it triggers us
with the forces of the lions star
I AM—this love
lady a carbon copy of it
and somewhere over flat rooftops a moon is
so get it fire baby
our fluids will be celestial markings
cosmic clouds fluffed like creation

night will never harm you with its changes
were tuned into this purity of blackness
the gigantic spawn above just a part of it
that we must teach a nation
graces the lights of earth
and i pray while in your embrace
in this house

with the lion our protector
to keep the fruits above we bathe in

A Love Supreme. . . . .

> *AWAKENING*
> *we ate breakfast*
> *with ohnedaruth the mystic*
> *(when he was called john coltrane)*
> *took him from the sissy pimps bar*
> *still with shouters in the isle*

after the lights on set
dug him look up at the death room
   in the strand hotel
the red marquee staining the perpetual dirt of the window facing six tray,
      rode with him in his script blue chevie wagon
   pass the fake gothic architecture glowing
   incomplete   in the nocturne of chalk and deceit
            he was thinking of his death room
         the prayers it took getting rid of
            bad jones'/ plus a black mans paternity case set up
         in a flick colorless chicago court room
            the jaspers sister cracking their sides
. . . .
      evil in white
      everyday the nurse threw little joe out morphine caps
. . . .
      . . . . it was the end of naima
            that most beautiful melody . . . .
               a dusty red crescent over the bell tower
         and us fool enough to riff the head
      Dedaaa daa daaaa dee daaaa daaaa daaa daaaaaa
      in the strangers madson park basement
with the mirrors helping the color explode
   islamic feeling that is time to us/heaven to come
   Allah everpresent/effervescent . . . . . .
         we ate our last piece of pork bacon
      heard ke ra give us the run down on the evil
it definitely projected in the western world.
   it was autumn 1961 . . . . . .
   and john coltrane went to sleep
         in the butterfly chair at the front of the room
         under the color eruption caton had crucified himself on
         with a trumpets bell stuck thru his head
         with shango puts on african brass
         the poet takes his cue
      and john coltrane awakes
      showing us the way to listen to his music . . really
his head stiff/his round eyes freezing to the horns planetary trip
         but he had to nod
         only to awake again
      to a half hour dialogue

      onedaduruth the mystic awoke smiling
      to the term 'black power structure'
and the waving of the New West Coast magazine

Don't Say Goodbye to the Pork-Pie Hat

(For Langston Hughes)

Don't say goodbye to the pork-pie hat that rolled along on
   padded shoulders,
                  that swang be-bop phrases
                  in Minton's jelly-roll dreams.
don't say goodbye to hip hats tilted in the style of a soulful era,
the pork-pie hat that Lester dug,
swirling in the sound of sun saxes,
repeating phrase on phrase, repeating bluely
as hi-hat cymbals crash and trumpets scream while
musicians move in and out of this gloom; the pork-pie hat
   reigns supreme,
the elegance of style
gleaned from the city's underbelly.
                  tonal memories
                  tonal memories
of salt-peanuts and hot house birds. the pork-pie hat
                          sees.
And who was the musician who
            blew Bird way be accident, then died, obscure,
an obscene riff repeating lynch scenes?
repeating weird changes. The chorus repeats itself also, the
   horns slide
from note to note in blue, in blue streaks of mad wisdom;
blues notes
coiling around
the pork-pie hat and the drum-dancing hips defying the
   sanctity of white
America.
and who was the trumpet player in that small town in Kansas
   who
      begged to sit in

From *Black Boogaloo: Journal of Black Poetry Press* (1969).

blew a chorus, then fainted dead on the bandstand?
blew you away.
that same musician resurrected himself in Philly at the Blue
     Note Cafe
                         Ridge Avenue and 16th St.
after the third set, had him an old horn and was wearing the
     pork-pie
                         hat.
wasn't he familiar? didn't you think that you were seeing a
     ghost?
and didn't the pork-pie hat leave Minton's
                         for 52nd St
and didn't it later make it to Paris where they dug him too?
and didn't the pork-pie buy Bird a meal in '35
when said musician was kicked out of the High-Hat (18th &
     South)
                                             for blowing
strange changes?

I saw the pork-pie hat skimming the horizon
                     flashing bluegreenyellowlights
he was blowing black stars
and
weird looneymoon changes and chords were wrapped around
     him
                                        and he was flying
fast, zipping past note, past sound into cosmic silence.
Caresses flowed from the voice in the horn in the blue
of the yellow whiskey room where hustlers
with big coats and fly sisters moved; finger popping while
                     tearing at chicken and waffles—
the pork-pie hat loomed specter like, a vision for the world,
dressed in a camel hair coat, shiny knob toe shoes, sporting
a hip pin stripe suit with pants pressed razor sharp, caressing
     his horn
                 baby-like.
And who was the bitch in the bar in Boston who kept trying
     to make it
with the pork-pie hat while it fingered for the changes
on Dewey Square? She almost make you blow your cool.
you did blow your cool, 'cause on the side I got you hollered
shut-up across that slick white boy's
tape recorded. Yeah the one who copped your music & made
some fat money after you died. didn't you
                 blow your cool?

and didn't you almost lose your pork-pie hat behind all that
    shit?
Who was the ofay chick that followed the group
                        from Boston to Philly
                        from New York to Washington
                        from Chicago to Kansas City
                        was that Backstage Sally?
or was Backstage Sally a blue-voiced soul sister who lived
                                on Brown street in Philly.
who dug you, who fed you cold nights with soul food
and soul-body. was that Backstage Sally?
Sounds drift above the cities of Black America;
all over America black musicians are putting
on the pork-pie hat again, picking up their axes,
preparing to blow away the white dream. you can
hear them screeching love in rolling sheets of sound;
with movement and rhythm recreating themselves and the
    world;
sounds splintering the deepest regions of the spiritual
    universe—
crisp and moaning voices leaping in the horns of destruction
blowing doom and death to all who have no use for the Spirit.
don't say goodbye to the pork-pie hat, it lives. Yeah . . .

Lester lives and leaps
Delancey's dilemma is over
Bird lives
Lady lives
Eric stands next to me
while I finger the afro-horn
Bird lives
Lady lives
Lester leaps in every night
Tad's delight
is mine now
Dinah knows
Fats and Wardell blow fours
Dinah knows
Richie knows
that Bud is Buddha
that Bird is Shango
that Jelly Roll dug ju-ju
and Lester lives
in Ornette's leaping
the blues live

we live. live
spirit lives. the sound
lives bluebirdlives
lives and leaps. dig
the bluevoices
dig the pork pie dig
the spirit in Sun Ra's sound. dig
spirit lives in sound
lives sound spirit
sound lives in spirit
spirit lives in sound. blow
spirit lives
spirit lives
spirit lives
SPIRIT . . . . . ! ! ! ! . . . . . SWHEEEEEET ! ! ! !
    Take it
        again, this time from the chorus

Conversions

(on the return of Trane into my heart)
(from underneath forerunning cymbal judgements
pronounced by tipping stick memoirs, dark
messianic sermons break confused lights into
distilled black halos . . .

each trip a creation. the long, recognized return
to where you never left from. i discover.
the ears speak for all. bring back to me what
you always were. break it down in simple
things like i ain't, really, been all around.
old images crumble as adolescent dreams,
in sudden, jolting, helpless discoveries of
other faces in the same mirror . . .

(each none every one some two minus me

every session, rising in quiet black channels,
turns thot murderers away re-making sense
from madness thorofares. woke up in dreams
of my ancient fathers, asking the sun to send
cooling shadows down to hide me, from myself.
still ain't nowhere. only sounds pervade deep
into my deadened psyche, sending real joy
of feeling the real thing for the first time . . .

(never once not yet still ever bodies

the junction of two souls sounds in a million
blessings, saying you don't need a book to know

From *Jump Bad: A New Chicago Anthology,* ed. Gwendolyn Brooks (Detroit: Broadside Press, 1971).

a man. mind made to be what it never was, a bridge
that unites everything to the idea of one real
beauty, all in relating. don't care what happens
to the dead me. artificial insensitivity lost in
waking feelings. i'm gonna fly away to the steel wind
land where you are riffling everything together.

Transcendental Blues

WEEP weep weep
in B R O K E N bluebones
of shattered fancies
fall
ing   bluely
bluely bluely blue-as-blue-can-be-ly
COME WITH ME IF YOU WANT TO GO TO KANSAS CITY
splattering to ashes
sounding louder than ALLAH's song
enclosing the bluefool in delusion
A no-nosed bluefool in darkness cannot smell light
A no-tongued bluefool in disorder cannot taste order
A blind bluefool in heat of hate cannot see love
see SUNDAY KINDA LOVE

Love
love love
lovelovelovelove
love love
Love your magic spell is everywhere
A no-nerved bluefool cannot feel peace
A deaf&dumb bluefool dying a thousand death at once can
not hear life
A wailing-wailing failing fire
dances like a million ulcers demon-SCREAMING
in the hue-less womb
of the subdued
vain new brain
but unsubdued
of the bluefool brimed full
of un-new Hamlet-like confusion

From *Black Fire: An Anthology of Afro-American Writing*, ed. LeRoi Jones (Amiri Baraka) and Larry Neal (New York: Morrow, 1968).

Wisdom hides—
        visionless eyes of selfish souls seek
Red rhythms of devotion
                ALL GOD'S CHILLLUN GOT
RHYTHM red rhythms of devotion are induced by love's blue
    melody
Devotion's ministers fire pride's pyre &light night
BLUEMAN
BLUEMAN BLUEMAN BLUEMAN
transcending his bluefooldom
suffering bluehoney sounds
SWEATING sweating sweating blood
wounds redder redder   round & round round &redder
    redder &round
with passionate imagination of true knowledge
past the anthill-life
        where ape-ish
     strife-bound
       yellow-spined aphid men
poison brothers in human society
& crawl strife riddled concrete bottoms of skyscraper seas
                           a radical world of
unqualified objectives
        rolling rolling round &round
                    into OBLIVION
    past new dimensions of expanded consciousness
in &out of millions &millions &billions &trillions &eternities
    of aeons&aeons
into a new
          WHAT'S NEW
into a new peaceful & blissful Jesus-like hue
Nirvana in infinite Tao-blue
Smelling eternal ALHOMDULLILAH!
A Gnostic frog-eyed owl
Quilted by boneyards bitter blacknight
SOMEWHERE OVER A COSMIC RAINBOW
                    cuts a great hog
on a mute trumpet emanating BLUE soultalk
                Soul talking!
                Soul talking!
                Soul talking!
Could be Pops Armstrong a black Mack-the knife
        strut strut strutting with some bar-b-q
Could be Fats Navarro love-ing his FAT GIRL   yes FAT GIRL
      LOVE IS A MANY SPLENDOR THING

Love
love love
lovelovelovelove
love love
Love your magic spell is everywhere

Could be clownprince Dizzy
            Ooh-bop-she-bam-a-klookla-mopping salt peanuts
      yes SALT PEANUTS on the A-TRAIN
Could be Miles ahead chasing the Bird
        to dig WHAT IS THIS THING CALLED LOVE
Could be LOVE IS A MANY SPLENDOR THING
Could be Clifford in brown study high as the cosmos
      discovering mysterioso spring-joy beauty of Delilah
on a Parisian thoroughfare
But Fats & Clifford are dead
So have they all died many deaths
But death don't mean a thing
if you've really got that swing
Ah! Could be ALLAH
But that riff is so stiff it don't mean a thing
cause ALLAH is everything swinging

BLACK WOMAN
BLACK WOMAN
BLACK WOMAN
A billion billion billion stars burning in my flesh
A billion billion drums beating in my soul
BLACK WOMAN
BLACK WOMAN
BLACK WOMAN
Sweet sweet sweetness humming humming humming in my
    sugar
Bitter bit her bitterness humming humming humming in my
    lemon
BLACK WOMAN
BLACK WOMAN
BLACK WOMAN
singing singing soil beneath bare feet
for me to kiss without becoming dirty
BLACK WOMAN
BLACK WOMAN
BLACK WOMAN
from you comes a symphony of food

to instrument my flesh &soul
BLACK WOMAN
BLACK WOMAN
BLACK WOMAN
when I probe to define beauty
my heart's dictionary thumps your melody
BLACK WOMAN
BLACK WOMAN
BLACK WOMAN
when for love chapel-in-me dings
there you are before dawn's dong
BLACK WOMAN
BLACK WOMAN
BLACK WOMAN
you are my life because you are life
naturally black &beautiful
LOVE ME EBONY LADY
YES! I see blue-crystal teardrops
            burning scars on your soul's cheeks
Your tears splash acidly in my stomach of reality
Outraged
my rivers raging Raging RAGING with your pain bleed like
    elderly ulcers
LOVE ME EBONY LADY
LOVE ME EBONY LADY
LOVE ME EBONY LADY
&listen to my silent scream of do-or-die action
White maggots will not Christian-missionary your diamonds
    away
                                        again
White maggots will not military your babies down dead
                            again
White maggots will not mercenary your fertile Nile to ache
    with pus
            again
MY spears shall rain
I-cant-give-them-anything-but-drops-of-hate
erasing them
exterminating them
so humanity can have a clear slate
Just keep me constant
                        ebony lady
LOVE ME EBONY LADY
LOVE ME EBONY LADY

Written for Love of an Ascension-Coltrane

he tried to
climb a
ladder of light
veiled in mist
incessantly vacillating

tried to
trap that
wheezy harmony that
solders quarters notes
on to our heads and

melts down minds like
moulten lead, ejaculates
rhythm, curses prayers, then
rings our ends like
shattering crystals

till a melody orgasm
explodes in our heads—
it's the sax, a
bladder splattering the
sky

gushing and spblaring
to relieve itself with
notes that stalk and
split the clouds or that
rip the air into rifts of

From Carolyn Rodgers, *Songs of a Black Bird* (Chicago: Third World Press, 1969).

whines for a jagged
crescendo, a man
a velvet willow suspended in air
with his roots
stretching to plant
themselves
        in
           any
star.

a/coltrane/poem

my favorite things
            is u/blowen
                        yo/favorite/things
stretchen the mind
            till it bursts past the con/fines of
solo/en melodies.
            to the many solos
of the
      mind/spirit.
            are u sleepen   (to be
            are u sleepen   sung
            brotha john   softly)
            brotha john
                        where u have gone to.
            no mornin bells
            are ringen here. only the quiet
aftermath of assassinations.
                  but i saw yo/murder/
the massacre
            of all blk/musicians. planned
in advance.
            yrs befo u blew away our passsst
      and showed us our futureeeeee
screech   screeech   screeeeech   screeech
a/love/supreme. alovesupreme a lovesupreme.
            A LOVE SUPREME
  scrEEEccCHHHHH screeeeEEECHHHHHHH
      sCReeeEEECHHHHHH SCREEEEECCCCHHHH
      SCREEEEEEEECCCHHHHHHHHHHHH

From Sonia Sanchez, *We a BaddDDD People* (Detroit: Broadside Press, 1970).

a lovesupremealovesupremealovesupreme for our blk
people.

       BRING IN THE WITE/MOTHA/fuckas
       ALL THE MILLIONAIRES/BANKERS/ol
MAIN/LINE/ASS/RISTOCRATS (ALL
THEM SO-CALLED BEAUTIFUL
PEOPLE)
        WHO HAVE KILLED
WILL CONTINUE TO
             KILL US WITH
THEY CAPITALISM/18% OWNERSHIP
OF THE WORLD.
          YEH. U RIGHT
THERE. U ROCKEFELLERS. MELLONS
VANDERBILTS
       FORDS.
            yeh.
GITem.
     PUSHem/PUNCHem/STOMPem. THEN
LIGHT A FIRE TO
          THEY pilgrim asses.
TEAROUT THEY eyes.
          STRETCH they necks
till no mo
      raunchy sounds of MURDER/
POVERTY/STARVATION
             come from they
throats.
screeeeeeeeeeeeeeeeeeCHHHHHHHHHHH
SCREEEEEEEEEEEEEECHHHHHHHHHH
screeEEEEEEEEEEEEEEEEEEEEEEEE
EECCCCHHHHHHH
SCREEEEEEEEEEEEEEEEEEEEEEEEEEEEEE
     EEEEEECHHHHHHHHHHH
BRING IN THE WITE/LIBERALS ON THE SOLO
SOUND OF YO/FIGHT IS MY FIGHT
             SAXOPHONE.
                TORTURE
THEM FIRST AS THEY HAVE
             TORTURED US WITH
PROMISES/
     PROMISES. IN WITE/AMURICA. WHEN
ALL THEY WUZ DOEN
        WAS HAVEN FUN WITH THEY
ORGIASTIC DREAMS OF BLKNESS.

                          (JUST SOME MO
CRACKERS FUCKEN OVER OUR MINDS.)
                                    MAKE THEM
SCREEEEEEAM
                  FORGIVE ME.   IN SWAHILI.
DON'T ACCEPT NO MEA CULPAS.
                                    DON'T WANT TO
                              HEAR
BOUT NO EUPOPEAN FOR/GIVE/NESS.
DEADDYINDEADDYINDEADDYINWITEWESTERN
              SHITTTTTT

(softly   da-dum-da da da da da da da da da/da-dum-da
till it   da da da da da da da da da
builds   da-dum- da da da
up)   da-dum. da. da. da. this is a part of my
             favorite things.
             da dum da da da da da da
             da da da da
             da dum da da da da da da
             da da da da
                 da dum da da da da
                 da dum da da da da – – – – –
(to be   rise up blk/people
sung   de dum da da da da
slowly   move straight in yo/blkness
to tune   da dum da da da da
of my   step over the wite/ness
favorite   that is yesssss terrrrrr day
things.)   weeeeeeee are toooooooday.
(f   da dum
a   da da da (stomp, stomp) da da da
s   da dum
t   da da da (stomp, stomp) da da da
e   da dum
r)   da da da (stomp)   da da da dum (stomp)
             weeeeeeeee (stomp)
                 areeeeeeeee (stomp)
                         areeeeeeeee (stomp, stomp)
             tooooooday   (stomp.
                 day   stomp.
                 day   stomp.
                 day   stomp.
                 day   stomp!)
(soft   rise up blk/people. rise up blk/people
chant)   RISE. & BE. what u can.

                MUST BE.BE.BE.BE.BE.BE.BE-E-E-E
                        BE-E-E-E-E-
                    yeh. john coltrane.
my favorite things is u.
                        showen us life/
                                liven.
a love supreme.
                for each
        other
    if we just
  lissssssSSSTEN.

on seeing pharaoh sanders blowing

(for chuck)

                        set 1.
listen
listen
listen
            to me.
            to me.
        a
        black
        man
                        with
                        eyeballs
                        white.
                        staring
at your honky faces
                                            listen
                                            listen
                                            listen.
                    hear
                    the
                    cowbells
                    ring out
                    my hate.
hear
my
sax
burping
your
shit.   death.
                        it's black music/magic
u hear. yeah. i'm fucking
u white whore.

From *Journal of Black Poetry,* Summer/Fall 1969.

                    america. while
i slit your honky throat.

                              set 2.
split.
        you honkies.
                        move
                    your slow asses.
get out now
                    no seconds
        on living.
                    split
now.
        man. i'm coming
for u
        now with my
blood filled
        sax.   calling
                            all bloods.
                                        beep.
                                        beep.
                    mary
                        had
                    a
                        little
                        lamb.
until
she
        got
her   throat
                                        cut.
                    see what i mean?

                              set 3.
ah ah ah
            oh
aah aah aah
            ooh
aaah aaah aaah
            oooh.
hee hee haa
ho ho hee   u white son of
            a bitch
                    america.
                        u dead.

Did John's Music Kill Him?

in the morning part
of evening he would stand
before his crowd. the voice
would call his name &
redlight fell around him.
jimmy'd bow a quarter hour
till Mccoy fed block chords
to his stroke. elvin's thunder
roll & eric's scream. then john.

then john. *little old lady*
had a nasty mouth. *summertime*
when the war is. *africa* ululating
a line bunched up like itself
into knots paints beauty black.

trane's horn had words in it
i know when i sleep sober & dream
those dreams i duck in the world
of sun & shadow. yet even in the day john
& a little grass put them on me clear
as tomorrow in a glass enclosure.

kill me john my life eats
life. the thing that beats out of
me happens in a vat enclosed
& fermenting & wanting to explode
like your song.

From *Understanding the New Black Poetry:Black Speech and Black Music as Poetic References,* ed. Stephen Henderson (New York: Morrow, 1973).

so beat john's death words down
on me in the darker part
of evening, the black light issued
from him in the pit he made
around us. worms came clear
to me where i thought i had been
brilliant. o john death will
not contain you death
will not contain you

4

Africa

African Night Suite

Africa
take my hands from the newspaper shacks of
rotten existence and let my cataracts
flow into the red clay of your loyalty

keep me in the mud of your belly
fed from the forest of your resistance
far from these mercenaries of illusion

I tell you i have to
live with my throat open to
the buzzards

my neck of four lines
my nose of gold studs
my lip ring flashing signals
to the moon against mount kenya
greeting myself
   welcome
   perdido of the mambo sun
   afro star
   afro light
   afro suite of crickets in
   the african blues tribe
   greetings
from myself
hated by lies
by deceptions
by distortions
by the devastating experience of
disaster and the truth of our children

From Jayne Cortez, *Festivals and Funerals,* by Jane Cortez (New York: Phrase Text, 1971).

adjusted without ears
without arms
without the miracle of a face
No
I will not weep over slavery
or die inside wrinkled fleshes of shame
with feathers in my womb
in my love
I have surrendered my shadow of sorrow
and i sit next to the fetish woman heart to heart
eating the dead man's explosives
our bodies together
flying
raging
avenging
at the moment of invasion
transcending

All of these things speak from me to africa

In cape coast
in Kumasi
in Ibadan
oyo oyo
I am a ife woman
biriwa fish woman of the sea
night queen of night cities in nights
I remember
hashish nights of murmuring glands
rainy nights in tunisia
in front of the club tangerine
the house
the man
the night eggs sticky in congo bongo beep moods of
devotion
carving up the dues nights when
we were sperms in a memorial of things
a homage to yokes of what we were & the nudeness
of what we wanted to be

and the river knew
the ocean knew
the white foam of madness knew
& before we recaptured life

with the unity of our breasts
when at night our tears flooded streets
we   knew
our condition and
the weapon of our approach

———————————————▶

The Painted Lady

The Painted Lady is a small African butterfly,
gayly toned orchid or peach
that seems as tremulous and delicately sheer

as the objects I treasure, yet, this cosmopolitan
can cross the sea at the icy time of the year,
in the trail of the big boats, to France.

Mischance is as wide and somber grey as the lake, here in
                                                   Chicago.
Is there strength enough in my huge peach paper rose,
or lavender sea-laced fan?

From Margaret Danner, *Iron Lace* (Millbrook, N.Y.: Poets Press, 1968).

Africa I

on the bite of a kola nut
i was so high the clouds blanketing
     africa
in the mid morning flight were pushed
away in an angry flicker
of the sun's tongue

a young lioness sat smoking a pipe
while her cubs waved up at the plane
look ida i called a lion waving
but she said there are no lions
in this part of africa
it's my dream dammit i mumbled

but my grandmother stood up
from her rocker just then
and said you call it
like you see it
john brown and i are with you
and i sat back for my morning
coffee

we landed in accra and the people
clapped and i almost cried wake up
we're home
and something in me said shout
and something else said quietly
your mother may be glad to see you
but she may also remember why
you went away

From Nikki Giovanni, *My House: Poems* (New York: Morrow, 1972).

Africa II

africa is a young man bathing
in the back of a prison fortress

the guide said "are you afro-american
cape coast castle holds a lot for your people"

and the 18th century clock keeps perfect
time for the time it has

i watched his black skin turn foaming
white and wanted to see this magnificent
man stand naked and clean before me
but they called me to the dungeons where above
the christian church an african stood listening
for sounds of revolt

the lock the guide stated indicated a major once ran
the fort and the british he said had recently demanded
the lock's return
and i wanted the lock maybe for a door
stop to unstop the 18th century clock

"and there is one African buried
here   we are proud of him" he said
and i screamed NO there are thousands
but my voice was lost in the room
of the women with the secret passageway
leading to the governor's quarters

so roberta flack recorded a song
and les mccann cried but
a young african man on the rock
outside the prison where my people were
born bathed in the sunlight

LUMUMBA LIVES   LUMUMBA LIVES!!

FOR HE   LUMUMBA   PERHAPS   LUMUMBA   LIKE THEIR
                            johnbrown made hasty hurry ups
FOR his   LUMUMBA   PEOPLE OF   LUMUMBA   BLACK
                          AFRICA   WOKE UP ABRUPTLY
SO HE LUMUMBA   ON PERHAPS ABE LINCOLN'S BIRTHDAY
                    LUMUMBA WAS MADE   A   MARTYR
AND
       NOW   LUMUMBA   SHALL LIVE   FOREVER
in the BLACK   in the white   in the YELLOW   and in the RED
                                        for these
PEOPLE   KNOW that patrice L U M U M B A   IS   NOT DEAD!
    LUMUMBA LIVES LUMUMBA LIVES LUMUMBA LIVES
        LUMUMBA LIVES LUMUMBA LIVES!!

From Ted Joans, *Black Pow-Wow: Jazz Poems* (New York: Hill and Wang, 1969).

My Name Is Afrika

(for nqabeni mthimkhulu)

All things come to pass
When they do, if they do
All things come to their end
When they do, as they do
So will the day of the stench of oppression
Leaving nothing but the lingering
Taste of particles of hatred
Woven around the tropical sun
While in the belly of the night
Drums roll and peal a monumental song . . .
To every birth its blood
All things come to pass
When they do
We are the gods of our day and us
Panthers with claws of fire
And songs of love for the newly born
There will be ruins in Zimbabwe for real
Didn't Rap say,
They used to call it Detroit
And now they call it Destroyed!
To every birth its pain
All else is death or life

From Keorapetse Kgositsile, *My Name Is Afrika* (Garden City, N.Y.: Doubleday, 1971).

Ancestors

Why are our ancestors
always kings or princes
and never the common people?

Was the Old Country a democracy
where every man was a king?
Or did the slavecatchers
steal only the aristocrats
and leave the fieldhands
laborers
streetcleaners
garbage collectors
dishwashers
cooks
and maids
behind?

My own ancestor
(research reveals)
was a swineherd,
who tended the pigs
in the Royal Pigstye
and slept in the mud
among the hogs.

Yet I'm as proud of him
as of any king or prince
dreamed up in fantasies
of bygone glory.

From Dudley Randall, *More to Remember: Poems of Four Decades*
(Chicago: Third World Press, 1971).

ISHMAEL REED

I am a Cowboy in the Boat of Ra

*'The devil must be forced to reveal any such physical evil
(potions, charms, fetishes, etc.) still outside the body
and these must be burned.'* (Rituale Romantum, *published
1947, endorsed by the coat-of-arms and introductory
letter from Francis cardinal Spellman*)

I am a cowboy in the boat of Ra,
sidewinders in the saloons of fools
bit my forehead   like   O
the untrustworthiness of Egyptologists
who do not know their trips. Who was that
dog-faced man? they asked, the day I rode
from town.

School marms with halitosis cannot see
the Nefertiti fake chipped on the run by slick
germans, the hawk behind Sonny Rollins' head
or the ritual beard of his axe; a longhorn winding
its bells thru the Field of Reeds.

I am a cowboy in the boat of Ra. I bedded
down with Isis, Lady of the Boogaloo, dove
down deep in her horny, stuck up her Wells-Far-ago
in daring midday getaway. 'Start grabbing the
blue,' I said from top of my double crown.

I am a cowboy in the boat of Ra. Ezzard Charles
of the Chisholm Trail. Took up the bass but they
blew off my thumb. Alchemist in ringmanship but a
sucker for the right cross.

From Ishmael Reed, *Conjure: Selected Poems, 1963–1970* (Amherst: University of
Massachusetts Press, 1972).

I am a cowboy in the boat of Ra. Vamoosed from
the temple i bide my time. The price on the wanted
poster was a-going down, outlaw alias copped my stance
and moody greenhorns were making me dance;
    while my mouth's
shooting iron got its chambers jammed.

I am a cowboy in the boat of Ra. Boning-up in
the ol West i bide my time. You should see
me pick off these tin cans whippersnappers. I
write the motown long plays for the comeback of
Osiris. Make them up when stars stare at sleeping
steer out here near the campfire. Women arrive
on the backs of goats and throw themselves on
my Bowie.

I am a cowboy in the boat of Ra. Lord of the lash,
the Loup Garou Kid. Half breed son of Pisces and
Aquarius. I hold the souls of men in my pot. I do
the dirty boogie with scorpions. I make the bulls
keep still and was the first swinger to grape the taste.

I am a cowboy in his boat. Pope Joan of the
Ptah Ra. C/mere a minute willya doll?
Be a good girl and
bring me my Buffalo horn of black powder
bring me my headdress of black feathers
bring me my bones of Ju-ju snake
go get my eyelids of red paint.
Hand me my shadow

I'm going into town after Set

I am a cowboy in the boat of Ra

look out Set   here i come Set
to get Set   to sunset Set
to unseat Set   to Set down Set

                 usurper of the Royal couch
                 —imposter RAdio of Moses' bush
                 party pooper O hater of dance
                 vampire outlaw of the milky way

ROLLAND SNELLINGS (ASKIA TOURÉ)

Earth

(for Mrs. Mary Bethune and the African and Afro-American women)

Where are the warriors, the young men?
Who guards the women's quarters—the burnt-haired
women's quarters—
and hears their broken sobbing in the night?
To endure, to remain—like the red earth—strong and fecund.
Your coppery, chocolate, ebony warm-skin scoured . . . and
   toughened
     by the arid wind.
The wrinkles in your eyes, your smile, your frowning fore-
   heads
are the Stars within your Crown, my women.
Cares come and go; dreams fade away; sons are lost
on lonely battlefields . . . severed by the Nordic Meataxe.
Men are broken . . . babble . . . lift their bloody genitals
upon the tainted altar of the Snow Queen.
Her frigid, sterile smile is a tribute to the vengeance
   of her Caesars.
Where, then, is Spartacus, is Attila, is Hannibal?
Who thunders, now, upon those Seven Hills?
They are gone . . . and . . . *only you remain!*
You whose Womb has warmed the European hills and made
   the Pale Snows tawny.
Pagan Spain, sunny France, Italy and the fabled Grecian Isles
are drenched by the Sunlight of your smile:
   Mother of the World!
   Fecund, Beating Heart!
   Enduring Earth!:
   Only you remain!
Where are the warriors, the young men?
Who guards the women's quarters? . . .

From *Black Fire: An Anthology of Afro-American Writing,* ed. LeRoi Jones (Amiri Baraka) and Larry Neal (New York: Morrow, 1968).

5

Women

For Gwendolyn Brooks—A Whole & Beautiful Spirit

"...an art of living is an act
of love ..."
—**David Llorens**

in the beginning was the sight
of blackness & was the seed
a sight which lives an act of love
a cite of images/creation of
where we must go & where we must be
(& also why
(listen to her eyes as they see us
a sight of poems blackpoems
peoplepoems poems for directions/finders
site movers moving image values
moving to cite beauty moving to
proclaim love & other holy things
(&sight reflections of poet/being
written & spoken & heard from cite seed
vibrations which are
(for she is a sure direction/voice
(which makes us brittle in ourselves
moving selfhate moving dross
changing moving toward the cite
of blackness beginning from the seed
beginning from her sight which is
an act of love which is an act of
life

From Johari Amini (Jewel C. Latimere), *Let's Go Some Where* (Chicago: Third World Press, 1970).

MARI EVANS

I Am A Black Woman

I am a black woman
the music of my song
some sweet arpeggio of tears
is written in a minor key
and I
can be heard humming in the night
Can be heard
          humming
in the night

I saw my mare leap screaming to the sea
and I/with these hands/cupped the lifebreath
from my issue in the canebrake
I lost Nat's swinging body in a rain of tears
and heard my son scream all the way from Anzio
for Peace he never knew. . . . I
learned Da Nang and Pork Chop Hill
in anguish
Now my nostrils know the gas
and these trigger tire/d fingers
seek the softness in my warrior's beard
I
am a black woman
tall as a cypress
strong
beyond all definition still
defying place
and time
and circumstance

From Mari Evans, *I Am A Black Woman* (New York: Morrow, 1970).

    assailed
        impervious
            indestructible
Look
    on me and be
renewed

Woman Poem

you see, my whole life
is tied up
to unhappiness
it's father cooking breakfast
and me getting fat as a hog
or having no food
at all and father proving
his incompetence
again
i wish i knew how it would feel
to be free

it's having a job
they won't let you work
or no work at all
castrating me
(yes it happens to women too)

it's a sex object if you're pretty
and no love
or love and no sex if you're fat
get back fat black woman be a mother
grandmother strong thing but not woman
gameswoman romantic woman love needer
man seeker dick eater sweat getter
fuck needing love seeking woman

it's a hole in your shoe
and buying lil' sis a dress
and her saying you shouldn't

From Nikki Giovanni, *Black Feeling, Black Talk, Black Judgment* (New York: Morrow, 1970).

when you know
all too well—that you shouldn't
but smiles are only something we give
to properly dressed social workers
not each other
only smiles of i know
your game sister
which isn't really
a smile

joy is finding a pregnant roach
and squashing it
not finding someone to hold
let go get off get back don't turn
me on you black dog
how dare you care
about me
you ain't got no good sense
cause i ain't shit you must be lower
than that to care

it's a filthy house
with yesterday's watermelon
and monday's tears
cause true ladies don't
know how to clean

it's intellectual devastation
of everybody
to avoid emotional commitment
"yeah honey i would've married
him but he didn't have no degree"

it's knock-kneed mini-skirted
wig wearing died blond mamma's scar
born dead my scorn your whore
rough heeled broken nailed powdered
face me

whose whole life is tied
up to unhappiness
cause it's the only
for real thing
i
know

GLORIA LARRY HOUSE

Woman

Where is the revolution to be seen
Through all those tears?
Has the length of one man alone
So blurred your view?
Can you leave the sons and daughters of Our time
Motherless?—no poems, no brown laughter, no acts of
    violence
For love squandered on one man?
Can you forget the hopes and longings
Pulling you into the dark unprecedented of Our Day?

This is not Malcolm's sister
Who sits sobbing for the love of one man
While the nation groans for birth!

From *Black Arts: An Anthology of Black Creations,* ed. Ahmed Alhamisi and
Harun Kofi Wangara (Detroit: Black Arts Publication, 1969).

If you saw a Negro lady

If you saw a Negro lady
sitting on a Tuesday
near the whirl-sludge doors of
Horn & Hardart on the main drag
of downtown Brooklyn

solitary and conspicuous as plain
and neat as walls impossible to
fresco and you watched her self-
conscious features shape about
a Horn & Hardart teaspoon
with a pucker from a cartoon

she would not understand
with spine as straight and solid
as her years of bending over floors
allowed

skin cleared of interest by a ruthless
soap   nails square and yellowclean
from metal files

sitting in a forty-year-old flush
of solitude and prickling
from the new white cotton blouse
concealing nothing she had ever noticed
even when she bathed and never
hummed a bathtub tune nor knew one

From *Soulscript: Afro-American Poetry,* ed. June Jordan (Garden City,
N.Y.: Doubleday, 1970).

If you saw her square
above the dirty
mopped-on antiseptic floors
before the rag-wiped table tops

little finger   broad and stiff
in heavy emulation of a cockney

mannerism

would you turn her treat
into surprise observing
happy birthday

Naturally

Since Naturally Black is Naturally Beautiful
I must be proud
And, naturally
Black and
Beautiful
Who always was a trifle
Yellow
And plain, though proud,
Before.

Now I've given up pomades
Having spent the summer sunning
And feeling naturally free
    (if I die of skin cancer
    oh well—one less
    black and beautiful me)
Yet no agency spends millions
To prevent my summer tanning
And who trembles nightly
With the fear of their lily cities being swallowed
By a summer ocean of naturally woolly hair?

But I've bought my can of
Natural Hair Spray
Made and marketed in Watts
Still thinking more
Proud beautiful Black women
Could better make and use
Black bread.

From Audre Lorde, *New York Head Shop and Museum* (Detroit: Broadside Press, 1974).

Cadence

a woman's heart
is the deep well
in a black field,
the timeless step
of sufferings, inflammation, ti palm
and divine wailing along the dark cone
of toadstools
the life of silence and creation,
judgment and the necessity

for destroying
what is apparent
in the poem
as one into another
the children die heavy
where the old woman
had been born
had been born
in the heedless bird country
in the huddled bird country
in the orphan-come-home country
in the angles-of-our-hatred country
are the angelic-sounds-of-committed-regions country
and our loves in those same moments
view ecstatic veins
through the middle
of a woman's life
whispering
we are bird music
we are blood music

From *Giant Talk: An Anthology of Third World Writings,* ed. Quincy Troupe and Rainer Schultz (New York: Random House, 1975).

we are black music's
jugular children come home
in an afternoon of dead eagles
we are woman heart
we are woman life
we are woman-come-here
and crack-off our teeth
we are woman-come-here
and turn them to nails
we are woman-come-whirling
we are woman-come-here
and hollow our cheeks
we are woman-come-here
and weld our bones
in a cadence of mortar rounds

blackwoman

blackwoman:
> will define herself. naturally. will
> talk/walk/live/& love her images. her
> beauty will be. the only way to be is
> to be. blackman take her. u don't need
> music to move; yr/movement toward her
> is music. & she'll do more than dance.

> blackwoman:
> is an
> in and out
> rightsideup
> action-image
> of her man. .   . . .
> in other
> (blacker) words;
> she's together,
> if
> he
> bes.

From Don L. Lee (Haki Madhubuti), *Don't Cry, Scream* (Detroit: Broadside Press, 1969).

The Last M.F.

they say,
that i should not use the word
muthafucka anymo
in my poetry or in any speech i give.
they say,
that i must and can only say it to myself
as the new Black Womanhood suggests
a softer self
a more reserved speaking self. they say,
that respect is hard won by a woman
who throws a word like muthafucka around
and so they say because we love you
throw that word away, Black Woman. . .
i say,
     that i only call muthafuckas, muthafuckas
so no one should be insulted. only
pigs and hunks and negroes who try to divide and
destroy our moves toward liberation.
i say,
that i am soft, and you can subpoena my man, put him
on trial, and he will testify that i am
soft in the right places at the right times
and often we are so reserved, i have nothing to say
but they say that this new day
creates a new dawn woman,
one who will listen to Black Men
and so i say
this is the last poem i will write calling
all manner of wites, card-carrying muthafuckas
and all manner of Blacks (negroes too) sweet
muthafuckas, crazy muthafuckas, lowdown muthafuckas
cool muthafuckas, mad and revolutionary muthafuckas.

From Carolyn Rodgers, *Songs of a Black Bird* (Chicago: Third World Press, 1973).

woman

COME ride my birth, earth mother
tell me how i have become, became
this woman with razor blades between
her teeth.
        sing me my history O earth mother
about tongues multiplying memories
about breaths contained in straw.
pull me from the throat of mankind

where worms eat, O earth mother.
come to this Black woman. you.
rider of earth pilgrimages.
tell me how i have held five bodies
in one large cocktail of love
and still have the thirst of the beginning sip.
tell me. tellLLLLLL me, earth mother
for i want to rediscover me. the secret of me
the river of me. the morning ease of me.
i want my body to carry my words like aqueducts.
i want to make the world my diary
and speak rivers.

rise up earth mother
out of rope-strung-trees
dancing a windless dance
come phantom mother
dance me a breakfast of births
let your mouth spill me forth
so i creak with your mornings.
come old mother, light up my mind
with a story bright as the sun.

From Sonia Sanchez, *A Blues Book for Blue Black Magical Women* (Detroit: Broadside Press, 1974).

6

Heritage

Promenade

a little house with a broken stair
watches me in a curving narrow street
facing another house in the shadow
of another house in the shade
of another house in the shadow
of an abandoned school
the door is opened
ready to speak
its paint hangs like peeling flesh
its rooftop looks sadly down
with melting artful tar
the door is opened and wooden steps
remind me
of a suspended tongue
my feet turn with a will of their own
walking toward that opened mouth
inside discovering
a house is only an opened womb
where unborn children raise a bottle
to the lips
two windows stuffed with bible pages
a cake of ice beneath the sink
clean glasses beneath the table
rolling in the dust
outside a one armed man
is chopping wood
all of this street
opened the eyes to smoke
rising from tar barrels
along the street where
houses are opened wombs

From *Black Fire: An Anthology of Afro-American Writing,* ed. LeRoi Jones (Amiri Baraka) and Larry Neal (New York: Morrow, 1968).

Lynch Fragment

My tongue whips blood through the
ribs of a cobra
I am a serpent
a parched cavity for lynched reptiles
iron rust of my musty scales sucking up the
secret strength of bad smells from two curved horns
clipped horns of a ram under the
bent pipe of my passionate sloping bone which
is the beauty mask that god wears like
the four part sun rising redly to the tip of
frozen nerves heard
beyond the muted cries of
mutilated flesh in a hole
a fox hole
a fixed hole where spirits erect themselves &
urinate inside my nostrils

From Jayne Cortez, *Festivals and Funerals,* by Jane Cortez (New York: Phase Text, 1971).

Urban Dream

1

there was fire & the people were yelling. running crazy
screaming & falling. moving up side down. there was fire.
fires. & more fires. & walls caving to the ground & mercy
mercy. death. bodies falling down. under bottles flying in
the air. garbage cans going up against windows. a car singing
brightly a blue flame. a snatch. a snag. sounds of bombs.
& other things blowing up.
times square
electrified. burned. smashed. stomped
hey over there
hey you. where you going.
no walking. no running. no standing.
STOP
you crazy. running. stick
this stick up your eyes. pull your heart out
hey.

2

after noise. comes silence. after brightness (or great big
flames) comes darkness. goes with whispering. (even soft
music can be heard) even lips smacking. foots stepping all
over bones & ashes, all over blood & broken lips that left
their head somewhere else, all over livers, & bright white
skulls with hair on them. standing over a river watching
hamburgers floating by. steak with teeth in them. flags.
& chairs. & beds. & golf sets. & mickey mouse broken
in half governors & mayors step out the show. they split.

From *The New Black Poetry,* ed. Clarence Major (New York: International Publishers, 1969).

dancing arrives.
like in planes. like in cars.
yes. yes. yeah. mucho boo-ga loo. mucho.
& sections of land sail away. & suicide rises. idiots jumping
into fires. the brothers five sing the blues as they sink. kids
blow their brains out, first take glue, & then shoot their
skull caps off, with elephant guns.

& someone sings & someone laughs. & nobody knows.
& chant to gods.
& chant to gods.

alarm clock bursts.

Return to English Turn

I

traveling along
river road.
below
nouvelle orleans.
come to
this place to barren levee called
english turn.

it is here bienville
convinced english
this land french
in 1699
sign say.

it is here
chained to the hulls of ships
we begin our neo-european forced journey:
      the land of misty riches leads to
      the Project called Desire.

if we could look closely enough
we could see the Sediments
absorbed by the river
river he who does not forget.
Beinville's french like invading bees
swarming upriver
establishing style by pushing
the people who live here out

From Tom Dent, *Magnolia Street* (1976).

bible pronouncements with strong
musket seasoning,
the best french cooking. . .
and us?
us in the hull
chained
confused
torn
in the hull
the musics of our ruptured memory
clashing with the grating roar
of chains.

& soon all along this winding
road
plantations thrive
off the work
of Leroy
& Beulah:
cotton
sugar
oranges
great houses
massive farms
and still we hear the music of chains.

the boats slipping up & down this
muddy snake:
cotton, sugar
the sugar cane, the cotton bale
corn, oranges
the corn stalk, the orange tree
oil, tobacco
the quick-dollar turn rig
the harsh-taste perique
boats up & down
& around
propelling goods for france england
cincinnati memphis holland
st. louis china south america
chain-forced hull energy
forging the neo-european progress
chain-forced hull energy
sustaining the languorous civilization
chain-forced hull energy

trying to bring this river under control
control commerce control
control machine control
control dollar control.
and even our music was stolen
made circus show for drunk
whiskey dreams not ours
made entertainment for newly
americaine straw-hatted rulers
who laugh till they sweat
through dey seersucker suit,
wipe their brows over oysters,
contemplate next move.
the river contains all this:
he who does not forget.

and during all this
our songs
our shouts
our forgotten lives
echo through this valley
strong men screaming from the dungeon
of the new hull. . .
Leroy struggling past crabs-in-the-barrel to
aborted rebellions that ended
in Parish churchyard hangings
the dungeon of the new hull
Beulah in the fields, in the white uniform
whispers between Leroy & Beulah
at midnight
whispers of tomorrows for the children
& other whispers
but still chained
confused
torn
in the hull

& the music from all this:
       song of Beulah's soft smile
       too raucous laughter of Leroy's
       torn memory
hull songs for us alone
songs of hulldom for us
yeah oh yes. . .
warming the heart of congealed years.

those songs our only way of saying
what we could not afford to say
those songs our only understanding
of what we could not comprehend

        why *were* we brought here?
        why were we brought here to these
            oppressive plantations
        how did we end up being the ones?
        why were we chosen for this
        bitter joke
        of the god of fates?

we made music that absorbed all that
music that floated on the wings of memory on the wings of tomorrow's
travail through the muggy Saturday night
from the shacks behind the tracks.
we, doomed to hulldom, attained elegance in ragged attire.
& even when we beseeched our god of
rivers
it seemed he had forgotten us
and there was no escape
no turning back.
but the river contains all this too
river he who does not forget.

II

so now let us turn
to you in the city project
you who know hulldom but
        not its history before the first
        american hull
you of the cannot-find-a-job know-not-why
you of the slow deaths & quick crab-barrelled murders
you of the ruptured family
you of the krazee citee, de city a de pleasure unpostponed
you seething in project heat
you of the grass broken the steel jutting
the plaster chipped the streets mud
you of the needle dreams, seeeething memories
you of the city dock, city factory
you of the massa's kitchen, the praline mammy
you of the stolen music

you of the music that drowns rain
        soothes cuts from shards
you of the questioning who-am-i who knows not
        who-was-i
you of the misty hull with one leg out of the steel hull
        masking as modern civilization
you confused, struggling for direction, for a way
        to end forced journeys
you who listen to the river's voice
        river who does not forget
the you who is each of us

let us return to english turn
rip up the signs
wipe out the legacies
pledge no more forced journeys

        no more english turns
        no more spanish turns
        no more french turns, portugese
        or german turns

rip the markers of neo-european conquest from
        their roots
plant a new one marking:

            our turn

our turn to flow out of the hulls, on to the decks,
        take control of the pilot wheels, choose the
        direction of our own journeys, for the first
        time in this valley
our turn, but never forgetting the forced journeys.

III

there is a song the old griot sings
about the uprooting of
european markers
& the planting of baobab trees
& we hear it now
winding around us
caressing us with its ripples of Kora notes.
it is a tune we have heard many times

containing notes we do not now know
but pleasing
growing stronger now
stronger
its clear music
skipping across the muddy waves
of the river

The Music

after reading "All God's Dangers:
          The Life of Nate Shaw"

Your archival voice
our long blues song,
life's story
coughed up
the blood-soaked cotton
gag. Blue blood,

Book-long
blue steel guitar blues.

Your Smith and Wesson
.32 gun metal voice.
Six strings.

What did they call you
when you didn't yield?

"If you were
a white man: principled,
mule: stubborn,
nigger: crazy."

You were a blue steel guitar

and your wife was
a fiddle and a tambourine.
Hannah. Soft as cotton

From Everett Hoagland, *Here: New and Selected Poems* (Wellfleet, Mass.: Leapfrog Press, 2002).

and as strong.
And your wife was
a fiddle and a tambourine
and we your sons are
banjos
and we your daughters
cane fifes.

Playing your gun metal voice,

playing your blue steel
guitar book-long song

CRAZY!

The Idea of Ancestry

I

Taped to the wall of my cell are 47 pictures: 47 black
faces: my father, mother, grandmothers (1 dead), grand
fathers (both dead), brothers, sisters, uncles, aunts,
cousins (1st & 2nd), nieces, and nephews. They stare
across the space at me sprawling on my bunk. I know
their dark eyes, they know mine. I know their style,
they know mine. I am all of them, they are all of me;
they are farmers, I am a thief, I am me, they are thee.

I have at one time or another been in love with my mother,
1 grandmother, 2 sisters, 2 aunts (1 went to the asylum),
and 5 cousins. I am not in love with a 7 yr old niece
(she sends me letters written in large block print, and
her picture is the only one that smiles at me).

I have the same name as 1 grandfather, 3 cousins, 3 nephews,
and 1 uncle. The uncle disappeared when he was 15, just took
off and caught a freight (they say). He's discussed each year
when the family has a reunion, he causes uneasiness in
the clan, he is an empty space. My father's mother, who is 93
and who keeps the Family Bible with everybody's birth dates
(and death dates) in it, always mentions him. There is no
place in her Bible for "whereabouts unknown."

II

Each Fall the graves of my grandfathers call me, the brown
hills and red gullies of mississippi send out their electric

From Etheridge Knight, *Poems from Prison* (Detroit: Broadside Press, 1968).

messages, galvanizing my genes. Last yr/like a salmon quitting
the cold ocean—leaping and bucking up his birthstream/I
hitchhiked my way from L.A. with 16 caps in my pocket and a
monkey on my back, and I almost kicked it with the kinfolks.
I walked barefooted in my grandmother's backyard/I smelled
   the old
land and the woods/I sipped cornwhiskey from fruit jars with
   the men/
I flirted with the women/I had a ball till the caps ran out
and my habit came down. That night I looked at my grandmother
and split/my guts were screaming for junk/but I was almost
contented/I had almost caught up with me.
   The next day in Memphis I cracked a croaker's crib for a
   fix.

This yr there is a gray stone wall damming my stream, and
   when
the falling leaves stir my genes, I pace my cell or flop on my
   bunk
and stare at 47 black faces across the space. I am all of them,
they are all of me, I am me, they are thee, and I have no sons
to float in the space between.

Ballad of Birmingham

(On the bombing of a church in Birmingham, Alabama, 1963)

"Mother dear, may I go downtown
Instead of out to play,
And march the streets of Birmingham
In a Freedom March today?"

"No, baby, no, you may not go,
For the dogs are fierce and wild,
And clubs and hoses, guns and jails
Aren't good for a little child."

"But, mother, I won't be alone.
Other children will go with me,
And march the streets of Birmingham
To make our country free."

"No, baby, no, you may not go,
For I fear those guns will fire.
But you may go to church instead
And sing in the children's choir."

She has combed and brushed her night-dark hair,
And bathed rose petal sweet,
And drawn white gloves on her small brown hands,
And white shoes on her feet.

The mother smiled to know her child
Was in the sacred place,
But that smile was the last smile
To come upon her face.

From Margaret Danner and Dudley Randall, *Poem Counterpoem* (Detroit: Broadside Press, 1969).

For when she heard the explosion,
Her eyes grew wet and wild.
She raced through the streets of Birmingham
Calling for her child.

She clawed through bits of glass and brick,
Then lifted out a shoe.
"O, here's the shoe my baby wore,
But, baby, where are you?"

River of Bones and Flesh and Blood
(Mississippi)

River of Time:
Vibrant vein,
Bent, crooked,
Older than the Red Men
Who named you;
Ancient as the winds
That break on your
Serene and shining face;
One time western boundary of America
From whose center
Your broad shoulders now reach
To touch sisters
On the flanks

River of Truth: Mornings
You leap, yawn 2000 miles,
And shed a giant joyous tear
Over sprouting, straggling
Hives of humanity;
Nights you weep
As the moon, tiptoeing
Across your silent silky
Face, hears you praying
Over the broken backs
Of black slaves who rode,
Crouched and huddled,
At your heart in the bellies
Of steamships.

From *Giant Talk: An Anthology of Third World Writings,* ed. Quincy Troupe and Rainer Schultz (New York: Random House, 1975).

River of Memory:
Laboratory for Civil War
Boat builders
Who left huge eyes of steel
Staring from your sullen depths;
Reluctant partner to crimes
Of Ku Klux Klansmen;
River moved to waves
Of ecstasy
By the venerable trumpet
Of Louis Armstrong.

River of Bones:
River of bones and flesh—
Bones and flesh and blood;
The nation's largest
Intestine
And longest conveyor belt;

River MISSISSIPPI:
River of little rivers;
River of rises,
Sometimes subdued
By a roof of ice, descending finally
On your Southward course
To spit
Into the Gulf
And join the wrath
Of larger bodies.

Sunset Beach / L.A.

She sang me the churchsong
of the southern ghetto, there
by the pacific,
         there where
the great waves tongued soul
and blackverse was quicktalk.

She sang me the melody of gospel
till late-late afternoon,
till the waves
lent themselves to rebirth,
and as babytides
tip-toed against our legs
I gave her horizontal
to the sea.

Her body was the rhyme of ju-ju
all of deep-rich-beautiful black,
all of chaos and nonsense,
all of seventeen years
of prehistoric craving;
but I was the warrior
         who knew no past:

I was born that day, born of
imperfections, word formulas,
nicklebags of poetry,
an image of love
yet a greenthumb for hate

From *Giant Talk: An Anthology of Third World Writings,* ed. Quincy Troupe and Rainer Schultz (New York: Random House, 1975).

For I am he they fed
to the sugarcane crop,
& he they slaved
on the 4th.

7

Songs

Say It Loud—I'm Black and I'm Proud

(As recorded by James Brown)

Say it loud, I'm black and I'm proud
Say it loud, I'm black and I'm proud
Some people say we got a lot of malice
Some say it's a lot of nerve
But I say we won't quit moving
Until we get what we deserve
We've been 'buked and we've been scorned
We've been treated bad, talked about as sure as
    you're born
But just as sure as it takes two eyes to make a pair
Brother we can't quit until we get our share.

Whoee—out of sight tomorrow night—it's tough
You're tough enough—whoee—it's hurting me
Say it loud, I'm black and I'm proud
Say it loud, I'm black and I'm proud
Say it loud, I'm black and I'm proud.

I've worked on jobs with my feet and my hands
But all that work I did was for the other man
Now we demand a chance to do things for ourselves
We're tired of beating our head against the wall
And working for someone else
We're people, we're like the birds and the bees
But we'd rather die on our feet than keep living on
    our knees.

Afro Blue

Dream of a land
My soul is from
I hear a hand
Stroke on a drum

    Shades of delight
    Cocoa hue
    Rich as a night
    Afro Blue

Elegant boy
Beautiful girl
Dancing for joy
Delicate whirl

    Shades of delight
    Cocoa hue
    Rich as a night
    Afro Blue

Two young lovers are face to face
With undulating grace
They gently sway then slip away
To some secluded place

    Shades of delight
    Cocoa hue
    Rich as a night
    Afro Blue

From "Afro Blue," lyrics by Oscar Brown Jr., music by Mongo Santamaria. Edward B. Marks Music Co. Reprinted in *What It Is: Poems and Opinions* (Chicago: Oyster Knife Publishing, 2005).

Whispering trees
Echo their sights
Passionate pleas
Tender replies

      Shades of delight
      Cocoa hue
      Rich as a night
      Afro Blue

Lovers in flight
Upward they glide
Burst at the height
Slowly subside

      Shades of delight
      Cocoa hue
      Rich as a night
      Afro Blue

And my slumbering fantasy
Assumes reality
Until it seems it's not a dream
The two are you and me

      Shades of delight
      Cocoa hue
      Rich as a night
      Afro Blue

What's Going On

1. Mother, mother, there's too many of you crying.
Brother, brother, brother, there's far too many of you dying.
You know we've got to find a way to bring some lovin' here today, yeah!
Chorus
Picket lines and picket signs, don't punish me with brutality;
talk to me so you can see; Oh, what's going on.
What's going on yeah, what's going on, what's going on.

2. Father, father we don't need to escalate
You see, war is not the answer for only love can conquer hate
You know we've got to find a way to bring some lovin' here today.
Chorus

3. Father, father everybody thinks we're wrong
Oh, but, who are they to judge us simply because our hair is long?
Oh you know we've got to find a way to bring some understanding here today?
Chorus

Keep on Pushin'

(As recorded by the Impressions)

Keep on pushin', keep on pushin', I've got to keep on pushin'
I can't stop now
Move up a little higher some way or somehow
'Cause I got my strength
And it don't make sense
Not to keep on pushin'.

Hey Hallelujah! Hallelujah!
Keep on pushin'.

Now maybe someday
I'll reach that higher goal
I know I can make it with just a little bit of soul
'Cause I got my strength
And it don't make sense
Not to keep on pushin'.

Now look-a, look-a, look-a yonder
A what's that I see
A great big stone wall stands there ahead of me
But I got my pride
And I move the wall aside
And keep on pushin'.

Hey Hallelujah! Hallelujah!
Keep on pushin', keep on pushin'.
What I say now, people get ready
It's gonna be all right.

WELDON J. IRVINE JR.

To Be Young, Gifted, and Black

(As recorded by Nina Simone)

Young, gifted, and black
Oh what a lovely precious dream.
To be young, gifted, and black
Open your heart to what I mean.
In the whole world you know
There's a million boys and girls
Who are young, gifted, and black
And that's a fact!

You are young, gifted, and black
We must begin to tell our young,
"There's a world waiting for you.
Yours is the quest that's just begun.
When you're feeling real low
There's a great truth that you should know
When you're young, gifted, and black
Your soul's intact!"

Ah to be young, gifted, and black
Oh how I've longed to know the truth.
There are times when I look back
And I am haunted by my youth.
But my joy of today
Is that we can all be proud to say,
"To be young, gifted, and black
Is where it's at! Is where it's at! Is where it's at!"

War

(As recorded by Edwin Starr)

1. War, uh! What is it good for? Absolutely nothing.
War, uh! What is it good for? Absolutely nothing.
Say it again.
War, uh! What is it good for? Absolutely nothing.
War, I despise 'cause it means destruction of innocent lives.
War means tears in thousands of mothers' eyes when their sons
go out to fight and lose their lives. I said

2. War, uh! What is it good for? Absolutely nothing; say it again;
War, uh! What is it good for? Absolutely nothing.
War, it's nothing but a heartbreaker; War, friend only to the undertaker.
War is an enemy to all mankind. The thought of War blows my mind.
War has caused unrest within the younger generation;
Induction then destruction, who wants to die; Ah
War, uh um; What is it good for? You tell me nothing, um!
War, uh! What is it good for? Absolutely nothing.
Good God, war, it's nothing but a heartbreaker;
War, friend only to the undertaker.

3. Wars have shattered many a young man's dreams;
Made him disabled, bitter and mean.
Life is much too short and precious to spend fighting wars each day.
War can't give life, it can only take it away. Ah
War, uh um! What is it good for? Absolutely nothing, um.
War, good God almighty, listen, what is it good for? Absolutely nothing, yeah.
War, it's nothing but a heartbreaker; War, friend only to the undertaker.
Peace, love and understanding, tell me there is no place for them today?
They say we must fight to keep our freedom, but Lord knows it's gotta be a better way.

I say War, uh um, yeah, yeah. What is it good for?
Absolutely nothing; say it again;
War, yea, yea, yea, yea, what is it good for? Absolutely nothing; say it again;
War, nothing but a heartbreaker; What is it good for?
Friend only to the undertaker. . . .

IV

Drama

The Kuumba Theatre: A Radical Idea Comes to Life

The 1960's were a time of great social and political change in America, when it was acceptable, often necessary to challenge conventional ways of thinking and acting. The 60's may have been the only time in American history when it was OK (at least in some circles) to call yourself radical or revolutionary and not be arrested as a dangerous subversive. This is important for those who didn't live through the 1960's decade to understand. This spirit of experimentation, willingness to try new ways of thinking and simultaneously reject old concepts is the main reason why the 60's launched what some writers and historians call the Black Arts Movement. We prefer to call it the Black Consciousness Movement because that set of forces that emerged in the 1960's and which remains vibrant today encompassed more than just the arts. Indeed, artistic creativity and expression were fundamental to the Black Consciousness Movement but not the whole story.

The Black Consciousness Movement was artistic, social, cultural and political all in one. Each segment nourished and reinforced the other. It was no accident that the same forces that gave rise to the Kuumba Theatre in 1968 as a new form of black artistic expression in Chicago also saw the need for black political empowerment which helped to bring about Chicago's first black mayor, Harold Washington, in 1983.

Black Consciousness, a more radical extension of the civil rights movement, demanded that black Americans especially begin to define and see themselves in fundamentally different ways than they had in the past. This was one reason why, in the 1960's, we began to call ourselves blacks instead of Negroes. Many of us ideologically became Pan Africanists. Nationwide, we defined ourselves as African Americans instead of being defined by the dominant, mainstream white society.

It was in this milieu of questioning and change that Val Ward was seized with a radical idea. Val had been a well-known performing artist in Chicago and nationally during the early 1960's. In 1967, she expressed the need for a new kind of arts and theatre organization that would do more than produce live drama and entertain audiences. Val envisioned an organization that would use fuse live theatre with the black freedom struggle. The new organization's guiding principle would be to entertain but also teach and raise the consciousness from an historical perspective. It would reject any notion that teaching would turn off audiences who presumably only attended the theatre to be entertained, but never to have their minds expanded or to be challenged intellectually.

Val, her husband, Francis Ward, and some like-minded friends and supporters launched the Kuumba Workshop in the spring of 1967. The actual dates of planning meetings and the official launch were not recorded at the time. The planning meetings all took place in our home at 1712 East 84th Place on the South Side of Chicago. All of the original planners demonstrated a zeal and determination to set in motion a new kind of arts and theatre organization that would make a radical break with the past.

Val as the founder, artistic director, principal producer and director also became the main public face of the Kuumba Workshop. Francis was a full-time professional journalist at the time who worked after hours and on weekends doing publicity, writing grant proposals and handling other miscellaneous tasks. Throughout most of the organization's history, Val's multiple roles remained as stated above—founder, director and producer. Francis handled the main administrative duties as executive director.

Space won't permit naming every individual who attended at least one planning meeting. As time passed, the most consistent of the original planners who remained as core organizers and members of the Kuumba Workshop were Patricia L. Brown (who later became Shariat Shabazz), Clifford (Karimu) Shaw, Ron Lewis (aka: Ron Nguvu), Terry Cullers, Sandra Malone (aka: Kimya Moyo), Eileen Cherry and our oldest son, Zachary Gray. In later years, another dedicated and sincere member would become Doyle Wicks, who took most of the original photographs of Kuumba productions and whose steadfast loyalty was absolutely essential to the organization's success.

The new organization was named Kuumba—pronounced "Koo–UMM–bah"—because of its African roots and also because Kuumba was the sixth of the Seven Principles of Nation Building (the Nguzu Saba) that had been created by Ron Karenga. He was the principal organizer of the US organization in Los Angeles in the mid-1960's, was then and remains today as one of the most creative thinkers among American-born Pan Africanists. In the Kiswahili language of East Africa, Kuumba means "to create" and "creativity." In the Mishona language of Zimbabwe, Kuumba means to build creatively with one's hands. Kuumba is also the first name of a woman in several West African languages. The name was changed to Kuumba Players in 1970 and to Kuumba Theatre Company in 1981. However, the organization's motto remained unchanged throughout: "Clean Up, Create and Build."

During its early formative years when Kuumba had little money, its first productions were the Ritual form of live drama. Rituals were dramatic interpretations of the works of great black writers, past and present. Kuumba only did the works of black writers and the range included greats from the Harlem Renaissance like Langston Hughes, Zora Neale Hurston and James Weldon Johnson. Kuumba also did a wide range of works from contemporary writers, such as Gwendolyn Brooks, Don L. Lee (later to become Haki R. Madhubuti), Nikki Giovanni, Mari Evans, Carolyn Rodgers, Dudley Randall, Larry Neal, LeRoi Jones (later to become Imamu Baraka) and Sonia Sanchez. The Ritual was a free-form, improvisational style of natural, spontaneous theatre that dramatically captured the feeling and spirit of the moment. Val used to say that the shouting, emotional fervor and call and response of the traditional black church was a form of Ritual theatre. Rituals could be done with or without formal sets and lighting. Most often Kuumba players mingled among members of the audience, eliminating the distinction between actor and audience.

Most of Kuumba's early works were done at the South Side Art Center, 3831 South Michigan Avenue in Chicago. The Art Center was begun in 1937 by Margaret Burroughs and other black artists of that era with money from the Works Progress Administration.

The WPA was the main federal agency that distributed money to hundreds of organizations and projects to put people to work during the Great Depression of the 1930's.

However, off and on from 1968–1971, Kuumba did Ritual theatre in the most unorthodox of locations—in taverns, prisons, churches, at club meetings, occasionally on playgrounds. The goal was to carry live drama wherever people were. Kuumba also did a number of traditional plays by black playwrights not well known to mainstream critics. We felt an obligation to do these works because if organizations like Kuumba did not, few others would. Among such works were:

"Contributon" by Ted Shine
"The Leader" by Joseph White
"Wine in the Wilderness" by Marti Charles
"Mojo" by Alice Childress
"The Amen Corner" by James Baldwin
"Langston Living," based on the works of the immortal Langston Hughes;
"Brownsville Raid" by Charles Fuller
"Welcome to Black River" by Samm-Art Williams
"The Sistuhs" by Saundra Sharp

But some of Kuumba's most successful productions were not plays, but community forums and programs. One of the most memorable of these was "To Gwen, With Love," a tribute to Gwendolyn Brooks, at the old Affro-Arts* Theatre on Chicago's Near South Side in December 1969. Gwendolyn Brooks was our close personal friend and a loyal financial supporter of Kuumba throughout its history. Poets, writers and activists from all over the country wrote special tributes to Gwen which were done during the program. The printed works were published in a book—To Gwen With Love—by Johnson Publishing Company in 1970. Co-editors of the book were Patricia Brown, Don L. Lee and Francis Ward.

In 1971, Kuumba became a leading critic nationally of the trend in black exploitation films, such as "Sweet Sweetback's Badasss Song" and "Super Fly." We felt most of these films, produced and distributed mainly from 1969–1975, carried highly negative images and messages, were of poor technical quality, the acting was grossly inferior, and they had little value as entertainment or to teach important lessons. The Theatre issued position papers, spelling out our opposition to "Sweetback" in 1971 and "Super Fly" in 1972. The same year, Kuumba issued it 12 Principles of Art which became the basis and rationale for how and why the Theatre did its work. The Principles are spelled out at the end of this article.

Throughout the mid-1970's, Kuumba produced one of its most important plays, "The Image Makers" written by Useni Eugene Perkins at the request of Val Ward. "The Image Makers" was a satire on the blaxsploitation films. It was also Kuumba's production at the World Festival of Black and African Arts (FESTAC) in Lagos, Nigeria, in January and February 1977.

Also during the 1970's, Kuumba held an annual Liberation Awards program in which it presented awards to some notable people and not well known people—all of whom we believed had made major contributions to the black experience and freedom struggle.

(*Affro-Arts is the correct spelling.)

Among the well-known awardees were nationally known scholars, such as Chancellor Williams, Sterling Brown and John Henrik Clarke (all deceased), Lerone Bennett Jr. , our longtime friend and colleague, Hoyt W. Fuller (also deceased), and the late novelist and playwright James Baldwin. Among the less-heralded but equally important awardees were people like Hayward C. Brown, an activist in the 1950's in Fayette County, Tennessee.

Kuumba has also toured nationally and internationally with plays first produced at its home base in Chicago. It toured with "The Amen Corner" in 1980 at the Detroit Music Hall. In 1985 and 1986, it had hit tours of its play, "In the House of the Blues" by Buddy Butler at the Montreal International Jazz Festival. Kuumba also toured with hit shows in Osaka, Kyota and Kobe City, Japan; in major U.S. cities like Louisville, Atlanta, Springfield, Mass., and Kansas City, Mo.

During the mid-1980's, Kuumba did highly successful and critically acclaimed hit musicals, "In the House of the Blues" and also "The Little Dreamer: A Nite in the Life of Bessie Smith." Both shows honored the memory of famous black blues singers and composers like Bessie Smith, "Ma" Rainey and Alberta Hunter. "The Little Dreamer" was later reopened and ran for many months at the Ivanhoe Theatre on Chicago's Near North Side. The show was made possible by the generous financial backing of Edward and Bettiann Gardner, now retired and the former owners of the Soft Sheen hair products company.

One of Kuumba's greatest triumphs came in 1988 when the Theatre co-produced a hit TV musical, "Precious Memories: Strolling 47th Street" with television station WTTW (Channel 11) in Chicago. "Precious Memories" was an hour-long TV music special that first aired on WTTW in 1988. It told the story of when the South Side of Chicago was the nightlife capital of America during the 1950's. Val won an Emmy award for her stage direction. All the singers and musicians won Emmys—a total of 21. "Precious Memories" later aired many times in cities across the country over the PBS Network. Val developed the original concept and Francis wrote the original TV script. The music was arranged by Kuumba's musical director, pianist Collette Skinner.

The Kuumba Legacy

It would take an entire volume to list all of the talented, committed and socially conscious people who have passed through the Kuumba Theatre. Though not all can be mentioned, a select few deserve our everlasting thanks and admiration. Hollywood, New York and the entire creative world are richer with talent incubated at the Kuumba Theatre.

Deidra Madison Dyson performed her master's degree thesis at Kuumba in the 1970's as a student at the University of Illinois. She is now a professor at Northwestern University. Ingrid Grimes-Myles was a longtime makeup artist and hair stylist at Kuumba who is now a makeup artist at WGN-TV (Channel 9) in Chicago. Ingrid is also the makeup person for first lady Michelle Obama. Former Kuumba actors John Toles Bey, Synthia Hardy and David McKnight have had successful careers in Hollywood. Fifteen new actors, musicians and technicians joined Actors' Equity Association as a result of their work with Kuumba's production of "The Little Dreamer."

Many nationally renowned directors have worked at Kuumba. Among them: Vantile Whitfield, Reggie Life, John O'Neil and Mical Whitaker. Some of the nationally famous performing artists who were showcased over the years at Kuumba were: Beah Richards, Max Roach, Odetta, Willie Dixon, Jean DuShon, Gary Bartz, and Bernice Reagon and Sweet Honey in the Rock.

Black Folks Theatre, a student arts organization at Northwestern University in the late 1960's, was founded at Kuumba. Its principal founder, Eileen Cherry, is now a professor at Northwestern.

Val Ward still performs, lectures and does an artist-in-residence at colleges and universities. Val gives regular performances of the following productions:

> "My Soul Is a Witness"—a one-woman show in which Val does 17 different characters drawn from the works of black writers.
> "The Life of Harriet Tubman" by Francis Ward.
> "Rhapsody in Hughes 101"—based on the works of Langston Hughes and done with musical accompaniment.

Val and Francis Ward moved to Syracuse, New York in 1993. Francis had become a professor of journalism at the Newhouse School of Public Communications at Syracuse University. The Theatre continued to produce a season of plays until October 1997. Its last full production was "From the Mississippi Delta" by Endesha Ida Mae Holland. Before it ceased full-time operations in 1997, Kuumba had done programs under the direction of its new artistic director, Deborah Crable, and technical director Zachary Gray (aka: Babatu).

The Kuumba Theatre's 12 Principles of Art: Adopted in 1972

1) We are an African people, bound together as a worldwide African family by race, ancestry, culture and common oppression.
2) Black art and Black life are inseparable. Our art is not fantasy and must be rooted in the historical experiences of African people. It is the re-creation and interpretation of Black life.
3) Black art must be functional. To entertain is not enough. It must teach some valuable lessons or leave some important messages with its readers, listeners, or viewers.
4) Black art must deal honestly and fully with every aspect of the Black condition, past and present. . . . Our art should not dwell narrowly or excessively on any single subject, but illuminate every variation, context, mood, attitude, period and lifestyle of the Black experience.
5) Black art must present positive images of African people, and if not, say something relevant to them about their condition while presenting negative images. At no time should it ever reinforce self-hatred or white-inflicted sterotypes of ourselves.
6) Black art must clearly show the social, political, economic and cultural contexts of any realities it treats. It is not enough to simply show a particular Black reality. Our art must also tell why it exists, its effects and offer necessary alternatives.
7) Black art must related to all Black people, not just the middle class or intellectuals. One of the huge distortions of Western civilization is its presumption that art should be the exclusive preserve of the rich, powerful and influential classes. Kuumba believes

that Black art must be returned to its African tradition as part of the lifestyle and culture of all the people.

8) We reject the sterile Western concept of "art for art's sake." "All art reflects the value system from which it comes," says Ron Karenga.

9) There is a direct and lasting relationship between Black art and politics. Black artists have a fundamental and permanent responsibility to be involved in and contribute significantly to the liberation struggle.

10) Black artists not only owe an equitable portion of their time and talent to the Black community, but also their earnings.

11) Black art and artists must be fully supported and judged by Black people, the only ones to whom our artists must be held accountable.

12) Black artists must be rooted in the Black community and totally involved in its activities and struggles.

Living in the Black Arts Movement

To unlearn the
Great white idea
to back it through
my core
Some piece of European truth
That has dearly come apart
Emaciates my blood
And manipulates my heart.
I have come to understand
that art devoid of me is
genocide at best.
Bill Gunn, *Black Picture Show* (1975)

They tell me that the Black Arts Movement began in the sixties, climaxed in 1965 and ended "somewhere in the early 80s." But not by my life's calendar. In order to write about my role in the Black Arts Movement I have to begin with my personal gestation period of searching for a black aesthetic to when I blossomed into a playwright of the Black Arts Movement.

The Harlem of my girlhood was one where in the original grimy building of the Schomburg Library where Jean Blackwell Hutson and Ernest Kaiser, seminal curators of the Schomburg Collection on Black Research and Culture, guided me through Du Bois, where on 116th Street and Lenox Avenue in P.S. 184, white communist teachers (exiled to teach in Harlem) taught their pupils about Langston Hughes and the Harlem Renaissance writers with a vengeance, where New York Communist Leader Ben Davis, Paul Robeson and painters Norman Lewis were regular guest speakers and where I was inculcated at an early age with the knowledge that art and politics were inseparable.

I emigrated downtown to the West Village smack dab into the apolitical Beat Generation white literary movement where I was the *only one* and wanted to ask the two brown beat poets *what the Black Mountain Schools and the New York School and the New Critics had to do with being black in America and what meter, what iambic whose pentameter what literary school for me?*

I moved from the West Village for the East Village where I wasn't the *only one* and where, at that time, the confluence of African countries' overthrow of colonialism and

African-Americans' call for black power merged with our search to transcend Western forms in all areas in our search for a black aesthetic.

Black Arts was Cuba Si and Yanqui No and Fair Play for Cuba parties and dancing in the dancing in the streets in front of Harlem's Hotel Theresa where Cuba's Prime Minister Castro sought sanctuary. Black Arts was On Guard for Freedom and Organization of Young Men and The Harlem Writers Guild bursting into the Security Council gallery on February 16, 1961, and in those initial seconds becoming instantly awed and reverent before the blue and gold tapestry overlooking the East River on which a group of the world's peoples weigh the grains of hope for all to share and a phoenix rises from its own ashes and streaks toward the golden anchor faith.

When we regained our composure and remembered our mission in that darkened chamber where our presence was a fissure, a fault line in the gathering of august men dividing the plunder of the Congo. Our voices ruptured the air, as Adlai Stevenson, Ambassador to the United Nations rose to deliver his maiden speech to the world. We raised the brutalized images of Congo's Premier Patrice Lumumba, betrayed by Britain, France, Belgium & the U.S. and delivered to his enemies. We raised photos of his widow, Pauline, walking ahead of mourners her head shaved, her breast bared before the world. What novel could compare to that?

In that time of heated up politics the East Side was roiling with arts and politics and music and Life was bowtie and bean pies uptown and Elijah's final call for three African American southern states.

And Life was Black women silently bearing deep psychic onslaughts and incongruities of duplicitous paeans to the black women even as the brothas turned away from them in search of their "manhood." Ironically, the culture in which we searched for a black aesthetic reflected the mainstream for the Black Arts Movement was sexist, homophobic and colorist with a traditional fade-to-white sexual agenda.

Life was political clinics taught by Harold Cruse at Bobb Hamilton's loft where the sistas and brothas (who left white wives at home) pondered together, trying to entangle the American riddle.

What about Art, What about economics? What about galloping capitalism and its universal color coded exploitation? Isn't integration asking for a piece of Pox American and do we really want to integrate in a burning house? And "responsible" middle class *leaders replying, "yes, yes. That's what we want. We want the whole American hog, white man. Your money and your maladies, your middle class blues and yes your daughters too. Just to show her what a man is all about. That's what we want."*

Gradually my inchoate artistic ideas began to take shape. I was committed to the truth telling of black lives (especially women's) in the face of silence and I knew we African Americans were a jazz people who lived improvisatory lives in multi-realities so why couldn't The Music be adapted as a dramatic structure? Form following content.

My first play was *Lady Day: A Musical Tragedy* produced in 1972 by Bob Kalfin of the Chelsea Theatre who was committed to stage the unexpected. The premiere production of *Lady Day* was at the Brooklyn Academy of Music. Paul Carter Harrison directed, Archie Shepp was the composer, and Cecil Norfleet, Roger Robinson and Clifford Jordan were some of the actors. In *Lady Day* I wanted to challenge the myths surrounding the legendary singer and make clear the confluence of gender and racial oppression that was Holiday's reality. And through the years in all my plays and prose my goal remains to reveal Afro-American stories framed in African-American cultural forms. The struggle is ongoing. In my most recent work, *Pigmentocracy Blues,* a novel that tells the tale of 100 years in a renowned family of daughters from the Civil Rights Years, the Black Arts Movement, the Post Racial and Fade-to-White America, the Jazz aesthetic is full blown.

Black Art is our Tree of Life. It keeps on renewing itself as each generation offers a new cultural form. The legacy of our Black Arts Movement is that our children know now that at least in our artistic practice we don't have to assimilate. Yes, it's all right to practice cultural sovereignty. Multitudes in the diaspora, if not the mainstream, will hear and respond.

Black Arts was all our spirits and passions of the time expressed in a memorable concert one golden afternoon in the East Village with The Music played by flat footed black boys who flowed in from Philly, breezed in from Detroit, D.C., Arkansas, Chicago and St. Louis. Jazz musicians wearing fezzes and blowing 360 degrees of music on out looking axes while we poets and painters followed them pied piper to the Sun (Ra) trying to imitate them cause The Music was so way way ahead.

So why not have a concert in the afternoon at the Fillmore East on Second Avenue, next to the Ukranian store that sells the white blouses with the embroidery, next to the magazine stand with a soda fountain that sells egg creams, opposite the fat pork sausages hanging in the butcher shop, across the street from the Jewish deli? A free concert against segregation, police brutality, and colonialism said the hip owner of the Fillmore East. No advertising, just word of mouth. I'll get the band. Be there.

Inside the Fillmore. Everybody is throbbing with the storms raging across the land but we are also mellowed out in anticipation of The Music.

In the dark, Li'l Jimmy, dressed all in white, pushes his gigantic bass across the stage and sits in a lone spotlight dressed in white from crown to sandals, swaying from side to side as his fingers strut up and down laying down layer upon layer of sound, coaxing bass strings into quivering high, soft orgasmic streams of notes resolved in a long rocking rhythm and then joined by McCoy's piano chords climbing up and down, whirling round and round—his left hand reaching back to the ancestors, his right one grasping those waiting to be born as Elvin on drums growls electric prods and water hoses and yowling police dogs and bloated bodies in the goddamn Mississippi River.

Slowly a figure emerges out of the shadows until poker face Trane faces the audience, his eyes inward, his gleaming silver soprano sax lifted so high, so high it looks like a horn growing out of his head, unfurling insurrection and love as it howls and coos infinite curling notes which are only seeds of the next shimmering tones full of agony and light and purity.

All the musicians on stage look like beatified souls.

Suddenly a bare stage. The saints had slipped away leaving their music behind, forever in my ears.

Black arts.

A Black Mass

For the brothers and sisters of the Black Arts

SCENE *(Jet blackness, with maybe a blue or red-violet glow. Soft peaceful music (Sun-Ra). Music of eternal concentration and wisdom. Some lights come up, outline the three magicians. Three Black Magicians. They are dressed in long exquisite robes, one with skullcap, one with fez, one with African hat (fila). The outline of some fantastic chemical laboratory is seen, with weird mixtures bubbling, colored solutions (or solutions that glow in the dark.)*

NASAFI *hums along with music, voice reaches out occasionally to fill the whole laboratory. Second magician nods his head, beats in tune, absentmindedly to the music and singing. Third magician intent on what he is doing, with a large book in his hand. He is bent over a mortar and is jamming a pestle into it, watching very closely. The other two also have things they are doing, but in a more leisurely, casual way.*

Signs in Arabic and Swahili on the wall. Strange drawings, diagrams of weird machines. Music can fill the entire room, swelling, making sudden downward swoops, screeching.)

NASAFI. These are the beauties of creation. (*Holding large bowl aloft. It glows softly gold in the dim light.*) The beauties and strength of our blackness, of our black arts.

TANZIL. Is the mass completed?

NASAFI. Not completed, brother, but the potion is ready. All who taste it will dance mad rhythms of the eternal universe until time is a weak thing.

TANZIL. Until time, that white madness, disappears. Until we have destroyed it and the animals who bring it into the world.

NASAFI. Animals are ourselves. We brought those animals from somewhere. We thought them up. We have deserved whatever world we find ourselves in. If we have mad animals full of time to haunt us, to haunt *us,* who are in possession of all knowledge, then we have done something to make them exist. Is that right, brother Jacoub? (JACOUB *is lost in his meditations.*) Is that right, brother Jacoub? (*Notices*) Jacoub. You're off somewhere. Oh, back into that experiment. What is it you're doing?

JACOUB. Oh, the same thing, brother. Creating a new organism. I've been working on this for some time.

TANZIL. We know. We watch you, and wonder. We wonder what you're doing. And what you're thinking. Tho we know anyway.

From LeRoi Jones (Amiri Baraka), *Four Black Revolutionary Plays, All Praises to the Black Man* (Indianapolis: Bobbs-Merrill, 1969).

NASAFI. You deal in a strange logic, brother Jacoub. You spoke once of time and we forgot about it. Now there are animals who hiss time madness in the air, and into our lives. I had forgotten (*Turns to* TANZIL) but now I'm sure it was you, Jacoub.

JACOUB. Yes. It was my work. I told you about time. What it meant. Why I was working in that direction.

TANZIL. Yes, you told us. We respect your knowledge, brother. But time is an animal thing.

JACOUB. Animals do not know time. It is a human thing. A new quality for our minds.

NASAFI. But deadly. It turns us into running animals. Forced across the planet. With demon time in mad pursuit. What good is that? What does it bring to us that we need?

TANZIL. We have no need for time. In fact, brother, we have hatred for it. It is raw and stays raw. It drives brothers across the earth. (*Pause*) I think it is evil.

JACOUB. Can knowledge be evil?

NASAFI. Knowledge is knowledge. Evil is evil. But all things in the world are interchangeable. In the endless procession of meaning.

TANZIL. You know this, Jacoub.

JACOUB (*Turns to other magicians*). I know that we are moving at thousands of miles an hour. In endless space. In black endless space. And that this is beautiful reality. But I also know we must find out everything.

NASAFI. We already know everything.

JACOUB. That is not possible.

TANZIL. We know everything, Jacoub.

NASAFI. What we do not know, does not exist. We know without knowing, because there is nothing to know. Everything is everything.

JACOUB. And so I will on where I am moving. Where my eternal mind takes me. Into the voids of black space where new meaning lives.

NASAFI. There is no new meaning. We are your brothers, and we know everything.

TANZIL. It is a fool's game to invent what does not need to be invented.

JACOUB. Let us be fools. For creation is its own end.

NASAFI (*Laughs, low, rising to high hysteria*). We know the myths, Jacoub. We know the realities. We know what is evil and what is perfection. We know we are black and beautiful speeding through the universe at thousands of miles an hour. We know beyond knowing, knowing there is nothing to know. And knowledge is repetition, and the bringing forth again of things that were so anyway. Everything already exists. You cannot really create.

JACOUB. I am creating. I have created. I made time.

TANZIL. You made animals who vomit time. And we must destroy them. You know that.

JACOUB. I created. I brought something into space that was never there. I will crowd the universe with my creations.

NASAFI. Jacoub, you speak of a magic that is without human sanction. A magic that would rupture the form of beautiful knowledge of beautiful world—you speak a madness which I know you create yourself. You want something that will release this madness from within your sainted heart. Why do you punish yourself with such flights? You are black and full of humanity. Yet you move into the emptiness of godlessness. You are god, yet you destroy your heart with a self that has no compassion, with a self mind that denies the order and structure of the universe of human signs.

JACOUB. I speak of movement. Of creation. Of making. Of thought.

NASAFI. Then you speak of humanity. Of the human mind.

JACOUB. I speak of things, of knowledge that is beyond the human mind.

TANZIL. If it is beyond the human mind, how will you create it? You are the human mind. No more. Tho that is everything.

JACOUB. Those animals of time, tho they be evil, are creation. From beyond the human mind.

TANZIL. Not so. You made them. Human. You made them. And now they roost in the human mind. And by the human mind they will be destroyed.

NASAFI. It is evil to pursue creation even into the lost spaces of the universe. What you bring back will be of no benefit to man. Remember the old myths, brother. The forbidden fruit of madness.

TANZIL. Yes. Tho we turn earth into gold, and cause the sun's rays to turn our engines. What you call thought is the projection of anti-humanity. The compassionless abstractions, the opposites. The mirror image of creation, turned and distorted, given power, by the forces of good, tho these forces breed hell itself.

NASAFI. Jacoub. You are working at what task now?

JACOUB. I told you. Thought. The creation of new energy. Yes. New energy, and new beings.

NASAFI. What?

JACOUB. Yes, brother. I have created time. Now I will create a being in love with time. A being for whom time will be goodness and strength.

TANZIL. This is animal sense. This is a magic against humanity, Jacoub.

NASAFI. Those animals you created are evil. They are the breeders of time. What beasts will you call forth who love such evil?

JACOUB. I will create only one, my brothers.

NASAFI. One what?

JACOUB. A man like ourselves, tho different because it will be beyond the human imagination.

TANZIL. And beyond human feeling. A gross distortion of the powers of righteousness. (*Bright flames flicker in the background, and go down.*)

JACOUB. A man like ourselves, yet separate from us. A neutral being.

NASAFI. Neutral being. What madness is this? How can a being be neutral?

JACOUB. Neutral because we, I, have created him, and can fill him as I will. From beyond the powers of natural creation. I make a super-natural being. A being who will not respond to the world of humanity. A being who will make its own will and direction. A being who will question even you and I, my brothers. A being who will be like us, but completely separate. Can you understand? (*Women run in, screaming. Writhing. Twisting in their thin garments*) Magicians. Magicians. Magicians. Ohhhhhh. Ohhhhhhh. Magicians. Black magicians . . . What fault has our life created? T—There is evil baking the sky. E—The stars are out in daytime. O—The night is filled with thousands of suns.

NASAFI. What? What is this? What are you women doing running into this sanctuary?

EULALIE. The elements disturb us, Lord Magician. The elements threaten us.

OLABUMI. The sky is not the sky. The earth trembles beneath our feet.

TIILA. The sea shudders and rages, and throws strange creatures on the land.

TANZIL. Jacoub. (*Advances toward him*) What is this? (*Consulting his book which he has dangling from his waist*) Do these things have to do with your experiments?

JACOUB. I have no way of knowing. What I do sets of things beyond our reasoning.

NASAFI. Of course it is your experiment. What do you hope to create? (JACOUB *is mixing his final solution. Lights go out. Blasts of flame. The women scream.*) Magicians. Why are we so frightened? There is evil riding in the air.

TIILA. Mad visions in the blackness. Oh no. Magicians. Take care.

JACOUB. Now is the time of creation. I enter one solution in the other. (*Screaming*) The blood flows in my head and fingers. The world is expanding. I create the new substance of life. Aiiiieeee. (*Bright explosion flashes and a siren-like laughter blasting . . . The laboratory is intense red, then hot violent white. The sirens go up to ear-breaking pitch. The women scream.*)

NASAFI. Jacoub! Jacoub!

TANZIL. Brother . . . Brother Jacoub . . . what have you done? (*The sirens, screams, and blasting lights are sustained for a few seconds, silhouettes against the white flames that begin to dart around the laboratory. Another intense explosion, the room is silent and dark, and then a sudden hot white glare.*)

TANZIL. Jacoub?

WOMEN. Ooooh . . . The earth is alien. Our mothers are sick. The world has shrunk and is choking us.

NASAFI (*Explosions*). Deathfire.

JACOUB. No, lifefire. Lifefire. My brothers!

TANZIL. Jacoub, I fear we teeter above the actual horrible void. (*Now the glare, glowing wild bright, seems to split. The sound is like glass being scraped on a blackboard. A crouched figure is seen covered in red flowing skins like capes. He shoots up, leaping straight off the stage screaming, Sun-Ra music of shattering dimension. The figure is absolutely cold white with red lizard-devil mask which covers the whole head, and ends up as a lizard spine cape. The figure screams, leaping and slobberlaughing through the audience.*)

BEAST. I white. White. White. White. (*Leaps, coming to stiffness, then screams stupidly*) White! White! White! (*Hops like beast goon, making horrible farting sounds with his mouth*) White! White! White! (*Hops back toward stage, and up*) White! White! (*As he leaps on stage, he begins to vomit terribly, licking his body where the vomit lands, and vomiting horribly. The women begin to scream uncontrollably. The smoke is clearing, and the white thing hops and shudders, vomiting occasionally, and trying to make other explanatory speech-like sounds, but all that comes out intelligibly is the same phrase.*) White! White! White! (*Then he gurgles off into unintelligible "Explanations."* JACOUB *is standing stiff, watching his creature. Then he moves forward tentatively, his arms spreading. The creation still leaps and hops, tho now less violently, his cries growing to gurgles and slobbers.* JACOUB *is moving forward. The thing is still trying to frighten the audience.*)

JACOUB. Brothers . . . Brothers . . . Look at this . . . LOOK AT THIS . . . (NASAFI *and* TANZIL *are moving away from the creature and* JACOUB. *Both the magicians are drawing their capes up to the faces.* NASAFI *rubs his forehead and an eye appears in the middle of his forehead.*)

NASAFI. It is a monster, Jacoub. That's what you have made. A monster.

JACOUB. It is life, no matter, new life. And strange. Look at it.

TANZIL (*Drawing his elder's whisk, he shakes it, speaking*). Izm-el-Azam . . . Izm-el-Azam
. . . (*Repeats over and over*) A mirror of twisted evil. The blind reflection of humanity.
This is a soulless beast, Jacoub.

JACOUB. We will teach it.

TANZIL. It will not listen. It has no feeling.

NASAFI. I looked into the wet corridors of the thing's heart, and there was no soulheat.
Where the soul's print should be, there is only a cellulose pouch of disgusting habits.
(*And with a sudden burst of emotion*) THIS THING WILL KILL, JACOUB . . . WILL
TAKE HUMAN LIFE . . . (*And the last is long-drawn-out with the terror of the state-
ment.*) Jacoub, this creature will take human life . . . because IT HAS NO REGARD FOR
HUMAN LIFE!

JACOUB. Brothers, I have created another man.

NASAFI. No Jacoub. You have created a soulless monster. (*The women scream. Suddenly
the* BEAST *wheels around, facing the terrified black people. Horrible wheezing sounds, still
pushed by the same "White" phrase, gurgle out of his fangs. Tall white bones almost pushing through the "flesh." A cave man's loincloth beneath the mask-cape. Sometimes shakes
with hideous laughter, staring into its hands, which are webbed, as are its feet. When it is
not vomiting it is chewing, and spitting, wheezing and scratching. The* BEAST *turns staring
at the black people. Wheezing softly, looking in each face.* JACOUB *has stopped, but spreads
his arms in welcome.*)

JACOUB (*Approaching*). You . . . are . . .

BEAST (*In weird parrotlike fashion*). You . . . You . . . You . . . (*Then goes into initial barely
intelligible chant*) White! White!

JACOUB (*Pointing to himself*). I. Eye! (*At eye, gesturing*) Me!

BEAST (*Stroking its own chest; slobbering smile crosses its face*). Me! Me! (*A little hop*) Me!
. . . White! . . . White! Me! . . . White! (*A sudden burst of horrible laughter. Then suddenly
the monster turns and begins snarling, then laughing. In high hysterical falsetto. Snarls.
Laughs. Then leaps at* JACOUB. JACOUB *waves his hand and freezes the* BEAST *behind an
invisible wall. Then the* BEAST *leaps at the women, grabbing throats or trying to throw
open their robes and stick his head in.*)

TANZIL (*Waves the elder's whisk and a bolt of lightning strikes between the girl and the
BEAST*). Izm-el-Azam! Jacoub . . . you have turned loose absolute evil.

JACOUB. How can there be evil in creation, brother? We will teach this thing the world of
humanity. And we will benefit by its inhuman . . .

NASAFI. Benefit? What are you saying? Jacoub . . . you said it . . . this thing is the soulless
distortion of humanity. (*The* BEAST *is standing fixed by black magic, shuddering in terror, but also in a maniacal attempt to free himself from invisible bonds. He grunts his
repeated "White," every now and again punctuating it with a popeyed scream, "Me!" Now
one of the young women, attacked by the monster, grabs her throat and begins to stagger.*)

TIILA. Magicians. This thing has hurt me. My breath is short. My eyes are turning to stone.

NASAFI. Jacoub.

JACOUB. What is it? What's happening to you?

TANZIL. Oh, Dervish (*Head thrown back*), make us strong against this evil! (*The* WOMAN
stumbles toward JACOUB, *her face draining of color. Her voice grows coarse, she screams,
covering herself with her robes. She emerges, slowly, from within the folds of the garment,*

her entire body shuddering, and beginning to do the small hop the beast did. Suddenly she throws back the robes, and she is white, or white blotches streak her face and hair. She laughs and weeps in deadly cross between white and black. Her words have turned to grunts, and she moves like an animal robot.)

TIILA. White! White! (*Her humanity breaks through the dead animal language briefly.*) OH LORDS HELP ME I AM TURNED INTO A MONSTER. OH LORDS HEEEEEEEELLLLLLL . . . (*And then she slumps, and begins to hop around, slobbering and scratching.*) White! White! White! (*The other women cringe and moan the woman's name.*)

WOMEN. Tiila . . . Oh Lord, Tiila . . . What has happened to her? . . . Ohhhh . . . evil, evil stalks us. (*The* BEAST, *seeing the woman change from his bite-caress, jiggles and makes obscene movements with his hips, overjoyed. He is still caught in the lightning cage.*)

NASAFI (*Sends another thunderbolt, stunning the woman, freezing her like the* BEAST. *She moans softly, tearing her body in the trance*). May heaven forgive you, Jacoub! May heaven forgive you! (*JACOUB is trying to minister to the woman. But she shrinks away and slobbers unintelligible curses.*)

JACOUB. Izm-el-Azam! Let the Lord speak to me. Tell me my error. (*In terror at the woman*) This whiteness spreads itself without effort. For the thing is sexless. It cannot breed.

TANZIL. It has merely to touch something to turn it into itself. Or else it sucks out the life juices. Look at our dying sister . . . producing its own hideous image.

JACOUB. Tell me my error.

NASAFI. Jacoub, your error . . . the substitution of thought for feeling. A heart full of numbers and cold formulae. A curiosity for anti-life, for the yawning voids and gaps in humanity we feel sometimes when we grow silent in each other's presence, sensing the infinite millions of miles in the universe, as finite as it is.

TANZIL. Asking God's questions, and giving animal answers! We are original reason, and you slip through darkness sliding insanely down those slopes of centuries, endless space, to where the only life is fire burning stone. The cold mineral world. And then, brother, we reach back to warmth and feeling, to the human mind, and compassion. And rise again, back on up the scale, reaching again for the sphere of spheres, back to original reason. To where we always were.

NASAFI. You fell, brother. The monster's eyes are watery colorless. With endless space beyond. The thing inhabits the voids of reason. Its function was as horrible nothingness. As absence. Of feeling, of thought, of compassion. Out between the stars where life does not exist. This beast is the twisted thing a man would be, *alone* . . . without his human soul.

JACOUB. We will teach it to feel. To love. (*Growing animated*)

TANZIL. It cannot. An animal with its nose quivering.

JACOUB. But it recognized Woman.

TANZIL. Not as the black beautiful lady of our universe, but pure female spoor and meat. An animal with its nose spread open ready to pop the world.

NASAFI. Jacoub, what will you do with this beast? And now the woman . . .

JACOUB. Transport them into the interior laboratory, where I will teach him. The girl . . . there must be some way to restore her life.

TANZIL. This teaching idea is madness, Jacoub. What would you teach an evil spirit?

NASAFI. Yes, perhaps we should cast them out. Perhaps the cold north where we banished the animals of time. In those pits of the earth, the creature might be left to make some horrible life of his own.

WOMEN. Magicians . . . what will you do? Tiila is turned into the beast.

JACOUB. You women should not have invaded this laboratory. You should leave now!

NASAFI. Were any more of you touched by this foulness?

WOMEN. No, Lord. Only Tiila. Only Tiila.

TANZIL. Jacoub. You cannot teach a beast. A blankness in humanity. And we cannot kill. We must set these things loose in the cold north. Where they may find a life, in the inhuman cold.

NASAFI. Yes. The beast . . . and sadly, the woman, must be cut off from our people. These things are killers. And smell of the pig.

TANZIL. Sing, women. Sing against this madness and evil. Jacoub. Let the women create their gentle thing here, their rich life smells. Sing, women. Against this sucking death we see. Sing. (*The women, pulling themselves close to each other, huddled in their fear, raise their voices, at first very softly, with the purring of beautiful pussies. Then they begin to shriek their songs* (Sun-Ra songs), *as if in terror against the two white shivering things quivering in the middle of the laboratory*.)

TANZIL. Sing, black women! Sing! Raise your gorgeous souls!

JACOUB. But brothers, we must have compassion, even for evil. We must teach them.

NASAFI. Jacoub. I forbid it. You move against holiness!

JACOUB. No, brother.

TANZIL. Jacoub. You must leave these things in the cold.

JACOUB. But our own Tiila . . .

NASAFI. Look at her. She is not Tiila. She is the void. The evil of blank cold licking the stars.

JACOUB. Even this terror. This inhumanity is conceived, you said, by men. By myself.

NASAFI. There is no self but the breathing world.

JACOUB. And so we shut out part of that world. Part of our lives. Part of knowledge. What is there to desire in the world if we cannot speculate about what we would have exist in it?

TANZIL. There should be no desire but the desire to do away with desire.

NASAFI. This self. This desire. Time. And this white . . . monster.

JACOUB. Man.

NASAFI. Whatever you would call it. Though this thing is not a man. We are men, brother. And this thing is not ourselves. But the hatred of ourselves. Our wholeness. And this self you speak of, and this desire, and the animals of hated time, now these horrible beasts, all these things, Jacoub, set you apart from your brothers. And may God have mercy on your soul.

JACOUB. No, brothers. I will show you. I will begin to teach them. I will have Tiila back. Look. I break the spell and begin to work . . .

NASAFI. No, no, Jacoub . . .

WOMEN (*Their singing turning to screams of horror*). Masters. Magicians. Lord Jacoub. What . . . ?

TANZIL. Jacoub.

JACOUB (*Gesturing*). I will prove the power of knowledge. The wisdom locked beyond the stars. Izm-el-Azam (*At* JACOUB's *gesture, the two beings spring into animation, attacking the magicians and women, killing them with fangs and claws.*)

JACOUB (*Staggering under the attack, with last breath screams as the beasts close in*). With my last breath I condemn you to the caves. For my dead brothers. May you vanish forever into the evil diseased caves of the cold . . . Forever, into the caves . . . Izm . . . Izm . . . Izm-el-Azam. May God have mercy . . . (*Falls. The beasts howl and hop, and then, turning to the audience, their mouths drooling and making obscene gestures, they move out into the audience, kissing and licking people as they hop eerily out, still screaming:* "White! . . . White! . . . Me . . . Me . . . Me . . . White!")

(NARRATOR's *voice over loud speaker with low drums and heavy trombones after beasts leave*)

NARRATOR. And so Brothers and Sisters, these beasts are still loose in the world. Still they spit their hideous cries. There are beasts in our world, Brothers and Sisters. There are beasts in our world. Let us find them and slay them. Let us lock them in their caves. Let us declare the Holy War. The Jihad. Or we cannot deserve to live. Izm-el-Azam. Izm-el-Azam. Izm-el-Azam. Izm-el-Azam. (*Repeated until all lights black*)

Black

Clara's Ole Man

A Play of Lost Innocence (1965)

THE PEOPLE:

CLARA, *a light brown girl of eighteen, well built with long, dark hair. A blond streak runs down the middle of her head, and she affects a pony tail. She is pensive, slow in speech but feline. Her eyes are heavy-lidded and brown; she smiles—rather, blushes—often.*

BIG GIRL, *a stocky woman wearing jeans and tennis shoes and a tight-fitting blouse which accents her prominent breasts. She is of an indeterminable age, due partly to her lack of make-up and plain hair style. She is anywhere from 25 to 40 and is loud and jolly, frequently breaking out in laughter from her own jokes.*

JACK, *20 years old, wears a corduroy Ivy League suit and vest. At first, JACK'S speech is modulated and too eloquent for the surroundings, but as he drinks his words become slurred and mumbled.*

BABY GIRL, BIG GIRL'S *mentally retarded teenage sister. The girl has the exact same hairdo as CLARA. Her face is made up with mascara and eye shadow, and she has black arching eyebrows penciled darkly, the same as CLARA.*

MISS FAMIE, *a drunken neighbor.*

STOOGIE, *a local streetfighter and gang leader. His hair is processed.*[1]

BAMA, *one of* STOOGIE'S *boys.*

HOSS, *another of* STOOGIE'S *boys.*

C.C., *a young wino.*

TIME: *Early spring, the mid-1950s.*

SCENE: *A slum kitchen on a rainy afternoon in South Philadelphia. The room is very clean, wax glosses the linoleum and old wooden furniture; a cheap but clean red checkered oilcloth covers the table. If the room could speak it would say, "I'm cheap but clean."*

---

1. Processed: Chemically straightened, and consequently reddened, with a harrowing mix of lye and potato starch. Popular from the 1920s to 1950s and derided by many Black Nationalists of the 1960s as reactionary.

    From Ed Bullins, *Five Plays* (Indianapolis: Bobbs-Merrill, 1969).

A cheap AM radio plays rhythm 'n' blues music throughout the play. The furniture is made up of a wide kitchen table where a gallon jug of red wine sits. Also upon the table is an oatmeal box, cups, mugs, plates and spoons, ashtrays, and packs of cigarettes. Four chairs circle the table, and two sit against the wall at the back of the stage. An old-fashioned wood- and coal-burning stove takes up a corner of the room and a gas range of 1935 vintage is at the back next to the door to the yard. A large, smoking frying pan is on one of the burners.

JACK *and* BIG GIRL *are seated at opposite ends of the table;* CLARA *stands at the stove fanning the fumes toward the door.* BABY GIRL *plays upon the floor with a homemade toy.*

CLARA, *fans fumes.* Uummm, uummm . . .well, there goes the lunch. I wonder how I was dumb enough to burn the bacon?

BIG GIRL. Just comes natural with you, honey, all looks and no brains . . . now with me and my looks, anybody in South Philly can tell I'm a person that naturally takes care of business . . . hee hee . . . ain't that right, Clara?

CLARA. Awww girl, go on. You's the worst messer'upper I knows. You didn't even go to work this mornin'. What kind of business is that?

BIG GIRL. It's all part of my master plan, baby. Don't you worry none . . . Big Girl knows what she's doin'. You better believe that!

CLARA. Yeah, you may know what you're doin' but I'm the one who's got to call in for you and lie that you're sick.

BIG GIRL. Well, it ain't a lie. You know I got this cough and stopped-up feeling. (*Looking at* JACK) You believe that, don't you, youngblood?

JACK. Most certainly. You could very well have a respiratory condition and also have all the appearances of an extremely capable person.

BIG GIRL, *slapping table.* Hee hee . . . SEE, Clara? …. SEE? Listen ta that, Clara. I told you anybody could tell it. Even ole hot lips here can tell.

CLARA, *pours out grease and wipes stove.* Awww . . . he just says that to be nice . . . he's always sayin' things like that.

BIG GIRL. Is that how he talked when he met you the other day out to your aunt's house?

CLARA, *hesitating.* Nawh . . . nawh, he didn't talk like that.

BIG GIRL. Well, how did he talk, huh?

CLARA. Awww . . . Big Girl. I don't know.

BIG GIRL. Well, who else does? You know what kind of line a guy gives ya. You been pitched at enough times, haven't ya? By the looks of him I bet he gave ya the ole smooth college boy approach . . . (*To* JACK) C'mon, man, drink up. We got a whole lot mo' to kill. Don't you know this is my day off and I'm celebratin'?

JACK, *takes a drink.* Thanks . . . this is certainly nice of you to go to all this trouble for me. I never expected it.

BIG GIRL. What did you expect, youngblood?

JACK, *takes another sip.* Ohhh, well . . . I . . .

CLARA, *to* BABY GIRL. DON'T PUT THAT DIRTY THING IN YOUR MOUF, GAL! (*She walks around the table to* BABY GIRL *and tugs her arm*) Now, keep that out of your mouf!

BABY GIRL, *holds to toy sullenly.* No!

CLARA. You keep quiet, you hear, gal!

BABY GIRL. No !!!

CLARA. If you keep tellin' me no, I'm goin' ta take you upstairs ta Aunt Toohey.

BABY GIRL, *throws back head and drums feet on floor.* NO! NO! SHIT! DAMN! SHIT! NO!

CLARA, *disturbed.* Now stop that! We got company.

BIG GIRL, *laughs hard and leans elbows upon table.* HAW HAW HAW . . . I guess she told you, Clara. Hee hee . . . that little dirty mouf bitch (*pointing to* BABY GIRL *and becoming choked*) . . . that little . . . (*cough, cough*) . . . hoooeee, boy!

CLARA. You shouldn't have taught her all them nasty words, Big Girl. Now we can't do anything with her. (*Turns to* JACK) What do you think of that?

JACK. Yes, it does seem a problem But with proper guidance, she'll more than likely be conditioned out of it when she gets into a learning situation among her peer group.

BIG GIRL, *takes a drink and scowls.* BULLSHIT!

CLARA. Awww . . . B.G.

JACK. I beg your pardon, Miss?

BIG GIRL. I said bullshit! Whatta ya mean with proper guidance? . . . (*Points*) I taught that little bitch myself . . . the best cuss words I know before she ever climbed out of her crib . . . Whatta ya mean when she gets among her "peer group"?

JACK. I didn't exactly say that. I said when . . .

BIG GIRL, *cuts him off.* Don't tell me what you said, boy! I got ears. I know all them big horseshit doctor words . . . Tell him, Clara . . . Tell him what I do. Where do I work, Clara?

CLARA. Awww . . . B.G., please.

BIG GIRL. DO LIKE I SAY! DO LIKE BIG WANTS YOU TO!

CLARA, *surrenders.* She works out at the state nut farm.

BIG GIRL, *triumphant.* And tell mister smart and proper what I do.

CLARA, *automatically.* She's a technician.

JACK. Oh, that's nice. I didn't mean to suggest there was anything wrong with how you raised your sister.

BIG GIRL, *jolly again.* Haw haw haw . . . Nawh, ya didn't. I know you didn't know what you were sayin', youngblood. Do you know why I taught her to cuss?

JACK. Why no, I have no idea. Why did you?

BIG GIRL. Well, it was to give her freedom, ya know? (JACK *shakes his head.*) Ya see, workin' in the hospital with all the nuts and fruits and crazies and weirdos, I get ideas 'bout things. I saw how when they get these kids in who have cracked up and even with older people who come in out of their skulls, they all mostly cuss. Mostly all of them, all the time they out of their heads, they cuss all the time and do other wild things and boy do some of them really get into it and let out all of that filthy shit that's been stored up all them years. But when the docs start shockin' them and puttin' them on insulin, they quiets down. That's when the docs think they're getting' better, but really they ain't. They're just learn'n like before to hold it in . . . just like before, that's one reason most of them come back or are always on the verge afterwards of goin' psycho again.

JACK, *enthusiastic.* Wow, I never thought of that! That ritual action of purging and catharsis can open up new avenues of therapy and in learning theory and conditioning subjects . . .

BIG GIRL. Saaay whaaaa . . .? What did you have for breakfast, man?

CLARA, *struck.* That sounds so wonderful . . .

JACK, *still excited.* But I agree with you. You have an intuitive grasp of very abstract concepts!

BIG GIRL, *beaming.* Yeah, yeah . . . I got a lot of it figured out . . . (*To* JACK) Here, fill up your glass again, man.

JACK, *to* CLARA. Aren't you drinking with us?

CLARA. Later. Big Girl doesn't allow me to start in drinking too early.

JACK, *confused.* She doesn't?

BIG GIRL, *cuts in.* Well, in Baby Girl's case, I said to myself that I'm teach'n her how in front and lettin' her use what she knows whenever it builds up inside. And it's really good for her, gives her spirit and everything.

CLARA. That's probably what warped her brain.

BIG GIRL. Hush up! You knows it was dat fuckin' disease. All the doctors said so.

CLARA. You don't believe no doctors 'bout nothin' else!

BIG GIRL, *glares at* CLARA. Are you showin' out, Clara? Are you showin' out to your little boyfriend?

CLARA. He ain't mah boyfriend.

JACK, *interrupts.* How do you know she might not have spirit if she wasn't allowed to curse?

BIG GIRL, *sullen.* I don't know anything, youngblood. But I can take a look at myself and see the two of us. Look at me! (*Stares at* JACK) LOOK AT ME!

JACK. Yes, yes, I'm looking.

BIG GIRL. Well, what do you see?

CLARA. B.G. . . . please!

BIG GIRL, *ignores.* Well, what do you see?

JACK, *worried.* Well, I don't really know . . . I . . .

BIG GIRL. Well, let me tell you what you see. You see a fat bitch who's twenty pounds overweight and looks ten years older than she is. You want to know how I got this way and been this way most of my life and would be worse off if I didn't let off steam some drinkin' this rotgut and speakin' my mind?

JACK, *to* BIG GIRL, *who doesn't listen but drinks:* Yes, I would like to hear.

(CLARA *finishes the stove and takes a seat between the two.* BABY GIRL *goes to the yard door but does not go out into the rain; she sits down and looks out through the door at an angle.*)

BIG GIRL. Ya see, when I was a little runt of a kid, my mother found out she couldn't keep me or Baby Girl any longer cause she had T.B.,[2] so I got shipped out somewheres and Baby Girl got shipped out somewheres else. People that Baby Girl went to exposed her to the disease. She was lucky. I ended up with some fuckin' Christians . . .

CLARA. Ohhh, B.G., you shouldn't say that!

BIG GIRL. Well, I sho as hell just did! . . . Damned kristers! I spent twelve years with those people, can you imagine? A dozen years in hell. Christians . . . haaa . . . always preachin' 'bout some heaven over yonder and building a bigger hell here den any devil have imagination for.

---

2. T.B.: Tuberculosis.

CLARA. You shouldn't go round sayin' things like dat.

BIG GIRL. I shouldn't! Well, what did your Christian mammy and pot-gutted pappy teach you? When I met you you didn't even know how to take a douche.

CLARA. YOU GOT NO RIGHT ! ! ! (*She momentarily rises as if she's going to launch herself on* BIG GIRL.)

BIG GIRL, *condescending.* Awww . . . forget it, sweetie . . . don't make no never mind, but you remember how you us'ta smell when you got ready fo bed . . . like a dead hoss or a baby skunk . . . (*To* JACK, *explaining*) That damned Christian mamma and papa of hers didn't tell her a thing 'bout herself . . . ha ha ha . . . Thought if she ever found out her little things was used fo anything else 'cept squattin' she'd fall backwards right up in it . . . ZaaaBOOM . . . STRAIGHT TA HELL . . . ha ha . . . Didn't know that li'l Clara had already found her heaven, and on the same trail.

CLARA, *ashamed.* Sometimes . . . sometimes . . . I just want to die for bein' here.

BIG GIRL, *enjoying herself.* Ha ha ha . . . that wouldn't do no good. Would it? Just remember what shape you were in when I met you, kid. Ha ha ha. (*To* JACK) Hey, boy, can you imagine this pretty little trick here had her stomach seven months in the wind, waitin' on a dead baby who died from the same disease that Baby Girl had . . .

CLARA. He didn't have any nasty disease like Baby Girl!

BABY GIRL, *hears her name but looks out door.* NO! NO! SHIT! DAMN! SHIT! SHIT!

BIG GIRL. Haw haw haw . . . Now we got her started . . . (*She laughs for over a minute;* JACK *waits patiently, sipping.* CLARA *is grim.* BABY GIRL *has quieted.*) She . . . she . . . ha ha . . . was walkin' round with a dead baby in her and had no place to go.

CLARA, *fills a glass.* I just can't understand you, B.G. You know my baby died after he was born. Some days you just get besides yourself.

BIG GIRL. I'm only helpin' ya entertain your guest.

CLARA. Awww . . . B.G. It wasn't his fault. I invited him.

JACK, *dismayed.* Well, I asked, really. If there's anything wrong I can go.

BIG GIRL. Take it easy, youngblood. I'm just havin' a little fun. Now let's get back to the Clara Saga . . . ya hear that word, junior? . . . S-A-G-A, SUCKER! You college boys don't know it all. Yeah, her folks had kicked her out—and the little punk she was big for what had tried to put her out on the block—and when that didn't work out . . . (*Mocking and making pretended blushes*) because our sweet little thing here was soooo modest and sedate . . . the nigger split! . . . HAW HAW HAW . . . HE MADE IT TO NEW YORK! (*She goes into a laughing, choking, and crying fit.* BABY GIRL *rushes over to her and on tiptoe pats her back.*)

BABY GIRL. Big Girl! Big Girl! Big Girl!

(*A knocking sounds and* CLARA *exits to answer the door.*)

BIG GIRL, *catches her breath.* Whatcha want, little sister?

BABY GIRL. The cat! The cat! It's got some kittens! The cat got some kittens!

BIG GIRL, *still coughing and choking.* Awww, go on. You know there ain't no cats under there with no kittens. (*To* JACK) She's been makin' that story up for two months now about how some cat crawls up under the steps and has kittens. She can't fool me none. She just wants a cat but I ain't gonna get none.

JACK. Why not? Cats aren't so bad. My mother has one and he's quite a pleasure to her.

BIG GIRL. For your mammy maybe, but all they mean round here (*Singsong*) is fleas and mo' mouths to feed. With an invalid aunt upstairs, we don't need any mo' expenses.

JACK, *gestures toward* BABY GIRL. It shows that she has a very vivid imagination to make up that story about the kittens.

BIG GIRL. Yeah, her big sister ain't the biggest liar in the family.

(CLARA *returns with* MISS FAMIE *staggering behind her, a thin middle-aged woman in long seamen's raincoat, dripping wet and wearing house slippers that are soaked and squish water about the kitchen floor.*)

BIG GIRL. Hi, Miss Famie. I see you're dressed in your rainy glad rags today.

MISS FAMIE, *slurred speech of the drunk.* Hello, B.G. Yeah, I couldn't pass up seein' Aunt Toohey, so I put on my weather coat. You know that don't a day pass that I don't stop up to see her.

BIG GIRL. Yeah, I know, Miss Famie. Every day you go up there with that quart of gin under your dress and you two ole lushes put it away.

MISS FAMIE. Why, B.G. You should know better than that.

CLARA, *re-seated.* B.G., you shouldn't say that . . .

BIG GIRL. Why shouldn't I? I'm payin' for over half of that juice and I don't git to see none of it 'cept the empty bottles.

BABY GIRL. CAT! CAT! CAT!

MISS FAMIE. Oh, the baby still sees them there cats.

CLARA. You should be ashamed to talk to Miss Famie like that.

BIG GIRL, *to* JACK. Why you so quiet? Can't you speak to folks when they come in?

JACK. I'm sorry. (*To* MISS FAMIE) Hello, ma'am.

MISS FAMIE. Why howdie, son.

CLARA. Would you like a glass of wine, Miss Famie?

MISS FAMIE. Don't mind if I do, sister.

BIG GIRL. Better watch it, Miss Famie. Wine and gin will rust your gizzard.

CLARA. Ohhh . . . (*pours a glass of wine*) . . . Here, Miss Famie.

BABY GIRL. CAT! CAT!

BIG GIRL, *singsong, lifting her glass.* Mus' I tell' . . . muscatel . . . jitterbug champagne. (*Reminisces*) Remember, Clara, the first time I got you to take a drink? (*To* MISS FAMIE) You should of seen her. Some of this same cheap rotgut here. She'd never had a drink before but she wanted to show me how game she was. She was a bright little smart thing, just out of high school and didn't know her butt from a door knob.

MISS FAMIE. Yes, indeed, that was Clara all right.

BIG GIRL. She drank three waterglasses down and got so damned sick I had to put my finger down her throat and make her heave it up . . . HAW HAW . . . babbled her fool head off all night . . . Said she'd be my friend always . . . that we'd always be together.

MISS FAMIE, *gulps down her drink.* Wine will make you do that the first time you get good 'n high on it.

JACK, *takes a drink.* I don't know. You know . . . I've never really been wasted and I've been drinkin' for quite some time now.

BIG GIRL. Quite some time, huh? How long? Six months?

JACK. Nawh, My mother used to let me drink at home. I've been drinkin' since fifteen. And I drank all the time I was in the service.

BIG GIRL. Just because you been slippin' some drinks out of ya mammy's bottle and you slipped a few under ya belt with the punks in the barracks don't make ya a drinker, boy!

CLARA. B.G., . . . do you have to?

MISS FAMIE, *finishes her second drink as* BIG GIRL *and* CLARA *stare at each other.* Well, I guess I better get up and see Aunt Toohey. (*She leaves.*)

BIG GIRL, *before* MISS FAMIE *reaches top of stairs.* That ole ginhead tracked water all over your floor, Clara.

CLARA. Makes no never mind to me. This place stays so clean, I like when someone comes so it gets a little messy, so I have somethin' ta do.

BIG GIRL. Is that why Jackie boy is here? So he can do some messin' 'round?

CLARA. Nawh, B.G.

JACK, *stands.* Well, I'll be going. I see that . . .

BIG GIRL, *rises and tugs his sleeve.* Sit down an' drink up, youngblood. (*Pushes him back into his seat*) There's wine here . . . (*slow and suggestive*) . . . there's a pretty girl here . . . You go for that, don't you?

JACK. It's not that . . .

BIG GIRL. You go for fine little Clara, don't you?

JACK. Well, yes, I do . . .

BIG GIRL. HAW HAW HAW . . . (*slams the table and sloshes wine*) . . . HAW HAW HAW . . . (*slow and suggestive*) . . . What I tell ya, Clara? You're a winner. First time I laid eyes on you, I said to myself that you's a winner.

CLARA, *takes a drink.* Drink up, B.G.

BIG GIRL, *to* JACK. You sho you like what you see, youngblood?

JACK, *becomes bold.* Why, sure. Do you think I'd come out on a day like this for anybody?

BIG GIRL. HAW HAW HAW . . . (*peals of laughter and more coughs*)

JACK, *to* CLARA. I was going to ask you to go to the matinee 'round Pep's, but I guess it's too late now.

CLARA, *hesitates.* I never been.

BIG GIRL, *sobers.* That's right. You never been to Pep's and it's only 'round the corner. What you mean, it's too late, youngblood? It don't start gettin' good till 'round four.

JACK. I thought she might have ta start gettin' supper.

BIG GIRL. She'd only burn it the fuck up too if she did. (*To* CLARA) I'm goin' ta take you to Pep's this afternoon.

CLARA. You don't have ta, B.G.

BIG GIRL. It's my day off, ain't it?

CLARA. But it costs so much, don't it?

BIG GIRL. Nawh, not much . . . you'll like it. Soon as C.C comes over to watch Baby Girl, we can go.

CLARA, *brightens.* O.K.!

JACK. I don't know who's there now, but they always have a good show. Sometimes, Ahmad Jamal . . .

BABY GIRL, *cuts speech.* CAT! CAT! CAT!

BIG GIRL. Let's toast to that . . . (*Raising her glass*) . . . To Pep's on a rainy day!

JACK. HERE, HERE! (*He drains his glass.*)

(*A tumbling sound is heard from the backyard as they drink and* BABY GIRL *claps hands as* STOOGIE, BAMA, *and* HOSS *appear in the yard doorway. The three boys are no more than sixteen. They are soaked but wear only thin jackets, caps and pants. Under his cap,* STOOGIE *wears a bandanna to keep his processed hair dry.*)

BIG GIRL. What the hell is this?

STOOGIE, *goes to* BIG GIRL *and pats her shoulder.* The heat, B.G. The man was on our asses, so we had to come on in out of the rain, baby, dig?

BIG GIRL. Well, tell me somethin' I don't know, baby. Why you got to pick mah back door? I ain't never ready for any more heat than I gets already.

STOOGIE. It just happened that way, B.G. We didn't have any choice.

BAMA. That's right, Big Girl. You know we ain't lame 'nuf to be usin' yo pad fo no highway.

HOSS. Yeah, baby, you know how it is when the man is there.

BIG GIRL. Well, what makes a difference . . . (*Smiles*) . . . Hey, what'cha standin' there with your faces hangin' out for? Get yourselves a drink.

(HOSS *goes to the sink to get glasses for the trio.* STOOGIE *looks* JACK *over and nods to* BAMA, *then turns to* CLARA.)

STOOGIE. How ya doin', Clara? Ya lookin' fine as ever.

CLARA. I'm okay, STOOGIE. I don't have to ask 'bout you none. Bad news sho' travels fast.

STOOGIE, *holds arms apart in innocence.* What'cha mean, baby? What'cha been hearin' bout poppa Stoogie?

CLARA. Just the regular. That your gang's fightin' the Peaceful Valley guys up in North Philly.

STOOGIE. Awww . . . dat's old stuff. Sheeet . . . you way behind, baby.

BAMA. Yeah, sweetcake, dat's over.

CLARA. Already?

HOSS. Yeah, we just finished sign'n' a peace treaty with Peaceful Valley.

BAMA. Yeah, we out ta cool the War Lords now from ov'va on Powelton Avenue.

HOSS. Ole Stoogie here is settin' up the war council now. We got a pact with Peaceful Valley and, man, when we come down on those punk War Lords . . . baby . . . it's just gonna be all ov'va.

BIG GIRL. Yeah, it's always one thing ta another with you punks.

STOOGIE. Hey, B.G., cool it! We can't help it if people always spreadin' rumors 'bout us. Things just happen an' people talk and don' understand and get it all wrong, dat's all.

BIG GIRL. Yeah, all of it just happens, huh? It's just natural . . . you's growin' boys.

STOOGIE. That's what's happen'n, baby. Now take for instance Peaceful Valley. Las' week, we went up there . . . ya know, only five of us in Crook's Buick.

CLARA. I guess ya was just lookin' at the scenery?

STOOGIE. Yeah, baby, dat's it. We was lookin' . . . lookin' fo' some jive half-ass niggers.

(*The boys laugh and giggle as* STOOGIE *enacts the story.*)

STOOGIE, Yeah, we spot Specs from offa Jefferson and Gratz walkin' with them bad foots down Master . . . ha ha ha . . .

BAMA. Tell them what happened to Specs, man.

HOSS. Awww, man, ya ain't gonna drag mah man Bama again?

(*They laugh more, slapping and punching each other, taking off their caps and cracking each other with them, gulping their wine and performing for the girls and* JACK. STOOGIE *has his hair exposed.*)

STOOGIE. Bama, here . . . ha ha ha . . . Bama burnt dat four-eyed mathafukker in the leg.

HOSS. Baby, you shoulda seen it!

CLARA. Yeah, that's what I heard.

STOOGIE. Yeah, but listen, baby (*Points to* BAMA) He was holding the only heat we had . . . ha ho ho . . . and dis jive sucker was aimin' at Specs' bad foots . . . ha ha . . . while that blind mathafukker was blastin' from round the corner straight through the car window . . .

(*They become nearly hysterical with laughter and stagger and stumble around the table.*)

HOSS. Yeah . . . ha ha . . . mathafukkin' glass was flyin' all over us . . . ha ha . . . we almost got sliced ta death and dis stupid mathafukker was shootin' at the man's bad foots . . . ha ha . . .

BAMA, *scratching his head.* Well, man. Well, man . . . I didn't know what kind of rumble we was in.

(CLARA *and* BIG GIRL *laugh as they refill their glasses, nearly emptying the jug.* BIG GIRL *gets up and from out of the refrigerator pulls another gallon as laughter subsides.*)

BIG GIRL, *sits down.* What's the heat doin' after ya?

STOOGIE. Nothin'.

CLARA. I bet!

STOOGIE, *sneer.* That's right, baby. They just singled us out to make examples of.

(*This gets a laugh from his friends.*)

BIG GIRL. What did you get?

HOSS. Get?

BIG GIRL, *turns on him.* You tryin' ta get wise, punk?

STOOGIE, *patronizing.* Awww, B.G. You not goin' ta take us serious, are ya? (*Silence*) Well, ya see. We were walkin' down Broad Street by the State Store,[3] see? And we see this old rumdum come out and stagger down the street carryin' this heavy package . . .

CLARA. And? . . .

STOOGIE. And he's stumblin', see. Like he's gonna fall. So good ole Hoss here says, "Why don't we help that pore man out?" So Bama walks up and helps the man carry his package, and do you know what?

BIG GIRL. Yeah, the mathafukker "slips" down and screams and some cops think you some wrongdoin' studs . . . yeah, I know . . . of course you didn't have time to explain.

STOOGIE. That's right, B.G. So to get our breath so we could tell our side of it, we just stepped in here, dig?

---

3. State Store: State-owned liquor store.

BIG GIRL. Yea, I dig. (*Menacing*) Where is it?

HOSS. Where's what?

(*Silence.*)

STOOGIE. If you had just give me another minute, B.G. (*Pulls out a quart of vodka*) Well, no use savin' it anyway. Who wants some hundred-proof tiger piss?

BAMA, *to* STOOGIE. Hey, man, how much was in dat mathafukker's wallet?

STOOGIE, *nods toward* JACK. Cool it, sucker.

HOSS, *to* STOOGIE But, man, you holdin' the watch and ring, too!

STOOGIE, *advancing on them.* What's wrong with you jive-ass mathafukkers?

BIG GIRL. Okay, cool it! There's only one person gets out of hand 'round here, ya understand?

STOOGIE. Okay, B.G. Let it slide . . .

BABY GIRL. CAT! CAT! CAT!

STOOGIE, *to* JACK. Drink up, man. Not every day ya get dis stuff.

(BAMA *picks up the beat of the music and begins a shuffling dance.* BABY GIRL *begins bouncing in time to the music.*)

HOSS. C'mon, Baby Girl; let me see ya do the slide.

BABY GIRL. NO! NO! (*She claps and bounces.*)

HOSS, *demonstrates his steps, trying to outdance* BAMA. C'mon, Baby Girl, shake that thing!

CLARA, No, stop that, Hoss. She don't know what she's doin'.

BIG GIRL. That's okay, Clara. Go on, Baby Girl, do the thing.

(STOOGIE *grabs salt from the table and shakes it upon the floor, under the feet of the dancers.*)[4]

STOOGIE. DO THE SLIDE, MAN! SLIDE!

BABY GIRL, *lumbers up and begins a grotesque maneuver while grunting out strained sounds:* Uuuhhhh . . . sheeeee . . . waaaa . . . uuhhhh . . .

BIG GIRL, *standing, toasting.* DO THE THING, BABY ! ! ! !

CLARA. Awww . . . B.G. Why don' you stop all dat?

STOOGIE, *to* JACK. C'mon, man, git with it.

(JACK *shakes his head and* STOOGIE *goes over to* CLARA *and holds out his hand.*)

STOOGIE. Let's go, baby.

CLARA. Nawh . . . I don't dance no mo'.

STOOGIE. C'mon, pretty mamma . . . watch this step . . . (*He cuts a fancy step.*)

BIG GIRL. Go on and dance, sister.

(STOOGIE *moves off and the three boys dance.*)

CLARA. Nawh . . . B.G., you know I don't go for that kind of stuff no mo'.

BIG GIRL. Go on, baby!

---

4. Grabs salt from the table and shakes it upon the floor: Done to improve sliding.

CLARA. No!

BIG GIRL. I want you to dance, Clara.

CLARA. Nawh . . . I just can't.

BIG GIRL. DO LIKE I SAY! DO LIKE BIG WANTS!

(*The dancers stop momentarily but begin again when* CLARA *joins them.* BABY GIRL *halts and resumes her place upon the floor, fondling her toy. The others dance until the record stops.*)

STOOGIE, *to* JACK. Where you from, man?

JACK. Oh, I live over in West Philly now, but I come from up around Master.

STOOGIE. Oh? Do you know Hector?

JACK, *trying to capture an old voice and mannerism.* Yeah, man. I know the cat.

STOOGIE. What's your name, man?

JACK. Jack, man. Maybe you know me by Tookie.

STOOGIE, *ritually.* Tookie . . . Tookie . . . yeah, man, I think I heard about you. You us'ta be in the ole Jet Cobras!

JACK. Well, I us'ta know some of the guys then. I been away for a while.

BAMA, *matter-of-factly.* Where you been, man? Jail?

JACK. I was in the marines for three years.

STOOGIE. Hey, man. That must'a been a gas.

JACK. It was okay. I seen a lot . . . went a lot of places.

BIG GIRL. Yea, you must'a seen it all.

STOOGIE. Did you get to go anywhere overseas, man?

JACK. Yeah, I was aboard ship most of the time.

HOSS. Wow, man. That sounds cool.

BAMA. You really was overseas, man?

JACK. Yeah. I went to Europe and North Africa and the Caribbean.

STOOGIE. What kind of boat were you on, man?

JACK. A ship.

BIG GIRL. A boat!

JACK. No, a ship.

STOOGIE, *rising,* BAMA *and* HOSS *surrounding* JACK. Yeah, man, dat's what she said . . . a boat!

CLARA. STOP IT ! ! !

BABY GIRL. NO! NO! NO! SHIT! SHIT! SHIT! DAMN! SHIT!

MISS FAMIE's voice, *from upstairs.* Your aunt don't like all that noise.

BIG GIRL. You and my aunt better mind ya fukkin' ginhead business or I'll come up there and ram those empty bottles up where it counts!

BAMA, *sniggling.* Oh, baby. We forgot your aunt was up dere sick.

STOOGIE. Yeah, baby. Have another drink. (*He fills all glasses except* CLARA's; *she pulls hers away.*)

CLARA. Nawh, I don't want any more. Me and Big Girl are goin' out after a while.

BAMA. Can I go too?

BIG GIRL. There's always have ta be one wise mathafukker.

BAMA. I didn't mean nuttin', B.G., honest.

STOOGIE, *to* JACK. What did you do in the army, man?

JACK, *feigns a dialect.* Ohhh, man. I told you already I was in the marines!

HOSS, *to* CLARA. Where you goin'?

CLARA. B.G.'s takin' me to Pep's.

BAMA. Wow . . . dat's nice, baby.

BIG GIRL, *gesturing toward* JACK. Ole smoothie here suggested takin' Clara, but it seems he backed out, so I thought we might step around there anyway.

JACK, *annoyed.* I didn't back out!

STOOGIE, *to* JACK. Did you screw any of them foreign bitches when you were in Japan, man?

JACK. Yeah man. I couldn't help it. They were all over, ya know?

BIG GIRL. He couldn't beat them off.

STOOGIE. Yeah, man. I dig.

JACK. Especially in France and Italy. Course, the Spanish girls are the best, but the ones in France and Italy ain't so bad, either.

HOSS. You mean those French girls ain't as good as those Spanish girls?

JACK. Nawh, man, the Spanish girls are the best.

BAMA. I never did dig no Mexican nor Rican spic bitches too tough, man.

JACK. They ain't Mexican or Puerto Rican. They Spanish . . . from Spain . . . Spanish is different from Mexican. In Spain . . .

STOOGIE. Whatcha do now, man?

JACK. Ohhh . . . I'm goin' ta college prep on the G.I. Bill[5] now . . . and workin' a little.

STOOGIE. Is that why you sound like you got a load of shit in your mouth?

JACK. What do you mean!

STOOGIE. I thought you talked like you had shit in your mouth because you been ta college, man.

JACK. I don't understand what you're trying ta say, man.

STOOGIE. It's nothin', man. You just talk funny sometimes . . . ya know what I mean. Hey, man, where do you work?

JACK, *visibly feeling his drinks.* Nawh, man, I don't know what ya mean and I don't go to college, man, it's college prep.

STOOGIE. Thanks, man.

JACK. And I work at the P.O.

BAMA. Pee-who?

JACK. The Post Office, man.

STOOGIE. Thanks, George. I always like to know things I don't know anything about. (*He turns his back on* JACK.)

JACK, *to* BIG GIRL. Hey, what time ya goin' round to Pep's?

BIG GIRL. Soon . . . are you in a hurry, youngblood? You don't have to wait for us.

JACK, *now drunk.* That's okay . . . It's just gettin' late, ya know, man . . . and I was wonderin' what time Clara's ole man gets home . . .

---

5. G.I. Bill: The Servicemen's Readjustment Act of 1944, better known as the G.I. Bill of Rights, has provided billions of dollars to U.S. veterans for vocational training and higher education.

BIG GIRL. Clara's ole man? . . . What do you mean, man? . . .

(*The trio begins snickering, holding their laughter back,* JACK *is too drunk to notice.*)

JACK. Well, Clara said for me to come by today in the afternoon when her ole man would be at work . . . and I was wonderin' what time he got home . . .

BIG GIRL, *stands, tilting over her chair to crash backwards on the floor. Her bust juts out. She is controlled but furious.* Clara's ole man is home now . . .

(*A noise is heard outside as* C.C. *comes in the front door. The trio is laughing louder but with restraint;* CLARA *looks stunned.*)

JACK, *starts up and feels drunk for the first time.* Wha . . . you mean he's been upstairs all this time?

BIG GIRL, *staring.* Nawh, man, I don't mean that!

JACK, *looks at* BIG GIRL, *then at the laughing boys and finally to* CLARA. Ohhh . . . jeezus! (*He staggers to the backyard door past* BABY GIRL *and becomes sick.*)

BIG GIRL. Didn't you tell him? Didn't you tell him a fukkin' thing?

(C.C. *comes in. He is drunk and weaves and says nothing. He sees the wine, searches for a glass, bumps into one of the boys, is shoved into another, and gets booted in the rear before he reaches wine and seat.*)

BIG GIRL. Didn't you tell him?

CLARA. I only wanted to talk, B.G. I only wanted to talk to somebody. I don't have anybody to talk to . . . (*Crying*) . . . I don't have anyone . . .

BIG GIRL. It's time for the matinee. (*To* STOOGIE) Before you go, escort my friend out, will ya?

CLARA. Ohhh . . . B.G., I'll do anything, but please . . . Ohhh, Big . . . I won't forget my promise.

BIG GIRL. Let's go. We don't want to miss the show, do we?

CLARA. Please, B.G., please. Not that. It's not his fault! Please!

BIG GIRL. DO LIKE I SAY! DO LIKE I WANT YOU TO DO!

(CLARA *drops her head and rises and exits stage right followed by* BIG GIRL. STOOGIE *and his boys finish their drinks, stalk and swagger about.* BAMA *opens the refrigerator, and* HOSS *takes one long last guzzle.*)

BAMA. Hey, Stoogie babe, what about the split?

STOOGIE, *drunk.* Later, you square-ass, lame-ass mathafukker!

(HOSS *giggles.*)

BABY GIRL. CAT! CAT! CAT!

C.C., *seated, drinking.* Shut up, Baby Girl. Ain't no cats out dere.

MISS FAMIE, *staggers from upstairs, calling back.* GOOD NIGHT, TOOHEY. See ya tomorrow.

(*With a nod from* STOOGIE, BAMA *and* HOSS *take* JACK's *arms and wrestle him into the yard. The sound of* JACK's *beating is heard.* MISS FAMIE *wanders to the yard door, looks out, but staggers back from what she sees and continues sprawling toward the exit, stage right.*)

BABY GIRL. CAT! CAT! CAT!

C.C. SHUT UP! SHUT ON UP, BABY GIRL! I TOLE YA . . . DERE AIN'T NO CATS OUT
   DERE!!!

BABY GIRL. NO! DAMN! SHIT! SHIT! DAMN! NO! NO!

(STOOGIE *looks over the scene and downs his drink, then saunters outside. Lights dim out
until there is a single soft spot on* BABY GIRL's *head, turned wistfully toward the yard; then
blackness.*)

Curtain.

Prayer Meeting Or, The First Militant Minister

A one-act play

Characters

BURGLAR

MINISTER

The time is the late Sixties. Black-white trouble in a large U.S. city. The scene is Black. Some-one is searching in this darkness with a flashlight. Talking to himself, angrily, in whispered tones. He bumps into an object and curses.

BURGLAR. Damn! Where's a mother-fuckin' light switch? I can't find nothin' this way. Oh, here it is. (*He spots a lamp with his flashlight and turns it on. The scene is a bedroom, decorated in very expensive French Provincial. The room is semi-dark and eerie from just the light of the table lamp. He looks around appraisingly.*) Mmmmmmm. Looks nice. Oughta be a lotta good shit in here. (*He starts to search in dresser drawers, closets, under the bed, etc. He examines small items and places some, upon approval, into the small canvas bag he's carrying. On the dresser is a picture of a serious looking minister. He picks it up, looks at it, puts it face-down on the dresser.*) I shoulda known this was a preacher's pad. A nigger livin' like this, either a preacher, a politician, or a hustler. Really ain't no difference though. All of 'em got some kind of game to get your money! (*All the larger items he's selected, he places near the place of his entrance: a portable T.V., a clock-radio, several suits.*) Sho' is a lotta good shit in here! (*still placing items into the bag*) When you get home tonight, Rev., you gon' find you've been un-blessed. Oh, oh! Somebody's comin'! (*He hides behind the dresser at the sound of someone approaching.*)

MINISTER (*slowly coming, Singing and humming*). What a friend we have in Jee-sus. Jesus Christ! How many times have I told Ellen 'bout leavin' these lights on! (*Enters the room and drops wearily to a position of prayer at the bedside. Talking to himself; not really praying; so much on his mind that he doesn't notice the disarray of the room. There is no sincerity in his words. It's as though he's rehearsing a role he plays, checking to hear if he sounds convincing in this role. He sounds tired.*) Thank God this day is over! Lord! What

From *Black Fire: An Anthology of Afro-American Writing*, ed. LeRoi Jones (Amiri Baraka) and Larry Neal (New York: Morrow, 1968).

a trying, troublesome, day. Trying to console my people 'bout brother Jackson's death at the hands of that white po-liceman. I tried, Lord. I tried to keep them from the path of violence. I tried to show them where it was really brother Jackson's fault fo' provokin' that off'cer. There's a time for protest and a time for silence. They say the off'cer hit him a few times. Brother Jackson could've taken a *little* beatin'. It wouldn't be the first time he'd taken a beating. Now the people want to go downtown and raise hell, Lord. They talk of vengeance! We should leave such things in yo' hands. You said, Vengeance is Mine, Lord. (*pause; long sigh*) For the first time in all my years of delivering God's word they were unbelieving (*shaking his head in disbelief*) and beyond my control. What have I done wrong that has shaken their faith, Lord? (*He practices his most pitiful whine.*) I'm trying to show them the right way. Your way, Lord. But I am truly perplexed. The mayor said if I can't stop them there'll be trouble . . . and more killing! What must I do, Lord? Tell me how I can save my people?

BURGLAR (*disgustedly*). Aw, man shut up and get up off your motherfuckin' knees! (*The minister is shocked. He looks around, fear all over his face.*)

MINISTER. My God! What? Who's that?! (BURGLAR *starts to come out of hiding and confront the minister with his arguments, man to man. He suddenly realizes that the minister believes he's been answered by God. The minister hides his trembling face in his hands. The* BURGLAR *decides to elaborate on this deception.*)

BURGLAR. What do you mean, who? Who the hell was you talkin' to? Didn't you expect to get an answer? (*The minister rises slowly from his kneeling position and stands frozen in the middle of the room.*) That's right! Get up off your knees! And stop trying to bullshit me! You ain't worried 'bout what's gon' happen to your people. You worried 'bout what's gon' happen to you if something happens to your people. You so sure that if they go up 'gainst the white man they gon' lose and whitey won't need *you* no more. Or if they go up 'gainst whitey and win, then they won't need you. Either way yo' game is messed up. So you want things to stay just as they are. You tell them to do nothin' but wait. Wait and turn the other cheek. No matter what whitey do, always turn the other cheek. As long as you keep them off the white folks you alright with the white folks. MY PEOPLE got to keep catchin' hell so you can live like this! YOU STOP PREACHING AND TEACHING MY PEOPLE THAT SHIT! You better stop or I'll reveal myself and put somethin' on your cheeks!

MINISTER (*nervous and excited*). Lord, Lord! Believe me. Those were not my motives. I was only trying to bring them along in your righteous way. Didn't you say that . . .

BURGLAR. Don't tell me what I said, DAMNIT! How in the hell you know I haven't changed my mind since then! How you know how I feel 'bout that violence-vengeance bullshit now? I haven't written anything since the Bible!

MINISTER. But my people can't win with violence.

BURGLAR. If you call what they doin' now, winnin', you the dumbest m.f. ever tried to interpret my word. My people can do anything if I am with them. I can do anything but fail. Do you remember that line?

MINISTER. But there are men like the man who killed brother Jackson who are hoping such a thing will happen. They'll welcome the opportunity to come into the black community and kill up a lot of inno . . .

BURGLAR. So what! They got to bring some ass to get some ass! I want my people to BE
    READY when they come. The shit you preachin' gon' get MY PEOPLE hurt!
MINISTER. Lord, you keep saying 'my people.' Are black people your 'chosen people?'
BURGLAR. You goddam right! And you and everybody else better ack like it!
MINISTER. I, I, I can't accept that . . .
BURGLAR. What! You questionin' me, man? I oughta come out from here and . . .
MINISTER. I didn't mean that, Lord. I just thought . . .
BURGLAR. Stop thinkin'. Especially for so many others. The only thing you better think
    about is how to tell my people the opposite of what you been tellin' them for so long. I
    know what's best. I made *all* this shit up. Y'all messed up. I'm tryin' to help straighten
    it out.
MINISTER. Give me the strength, Lord, and I will try to do your bidding.
BURGLAR. Try? Man, you better. Ain't nobody afraid of dyin' but you. And those like you
    who're so comfortable they've forgot they're victims. It's time to put a stop to this shit.
    Some of my people gon' have to die so the rest can live in peace.
MINISTER. But . . .
BURGLAR. But nothing! Tomorrow you'll lead a protest march to end all protest marches. I
    don't want this to be no damned 'sing-along.' I said a *protest* march! You'll demand jus-
    tice. And if you don't get justice you'll raise hell. I want brother Jackson's death avenged.
    You tell my people to be ready. Ready for what ever might come. Tell them I don't want
    no more cheek turnin'. Tell them I will be with them. (*gestures menacingly with his
    blackjack*) And if you don't tell them, you will be the first one to feel my . . . wrath. Now
    pray that you don't forget to do anythin' I've told you to do.
MINISTER. This is a heavy burden you place upon my shoulders, Lord.
BURGLAR. I feel like I'm takin' some of your burdens away. (*He is passing some of the larger
    items out the window.*)
MINISTER. But why? Why me, Lord?
BURGLAR. Because I feel like it should be you. You don't question that white man's judg-
    ment, don't you dare question mine!
MINISTER (*dropping to his knees*). Yes, Lord! Thank You, Jesus!
BURGLAR. And stop calling me Jesus! My name is God! (MINISTER *begins a fervent, mum-
    bled prayer. While he is so occupied, the* BURGLAR *gathers all he has selected and exits.
    The* MINISTER *finishes his prayer, gets up from his knees. He goes to the night table, picks
    up the Bible. He leafs thru it till he finds the desired passage. He reads it aloud to himself.*)
    'As I was with Moses, so I will be with thee; I will not fail thee, nor forsake thee.' (*more
    searching*) 'An eye for an eye; tooth for tooth; hand for hand; foot for foot.' (*He lays the
    Bible down, reaches into the drawer, takes out a revolver, checks it, places the Bible and gun
    atop the table. He walks to the dresser, stands before the mirror, and affects a pulpit pose.*)
MINISTER. Brothers and sisters, I had a talk with God last night. He told me to tell you that
    the time has come to put an end to this murder, suffering, oppression, exploitation to
    which the white man subjects us. The time has come to put an end to the fear which, for
    so long, suppressed our actions. The time has come . . . (*Lights fade out.*)

Curtain

ALICE CHILDRESS

Wine in the Wilderness

Cast of Characters

BILL JAMESON, *an artist aged thirty-three*

OLD TIMER, *an old roustabout character in his sixties*

SONNY-MAN, *a writer aged twenty-seven*

CYNTHIA, *a social worker aged twenty-five; she is Sonny-man's wife*

TOMMY, *a woman factory worker aged thirty*

TIME *The summer of 1964. Night of a riot.*

PLACE *Harlem, New York City, New York, U.S.A.*

SCENE: *A one room apartment in a Harlem tenement. It used to be a three room apartment but the tenant has broken out walls and is half finished with a redecorating job. The place is now only partly reminiscent of its past tawdry days, plaster broken away and lathing exposed right next to a new brick-faced portion of wall. The kitchen is now a part of the room. There is a three-quarter bed covered with an African throw, a screen is placed at the foot of the bed to ensure privacy when needed. The room is obviously Black dominated, pieces of sculpture, wall hangings, paintings. An artist's easel is standing with a drapery thrown across it so the empty canvas beneath it is hidden. Two other canvases the same size are next to it, they too are covered and conceal paintings. The place is in a beautiful, rather artistic state of disorder. The room also reflects an interest in other darker peoples of the world ... A Chinese incense-burner Buddha, an American Indian feathered war helmet, a Mexican serape, a Japanese fan, a West Indian travel poster. There is a kitchen table, chairs, floor cushions, a couple of box crates, books, bookcases, plenty of artist's materials. There is a small raised platform for model posing. On the platform is a backless chair.*

The tail end of a riot is going on out in the street. Noise and screaming can be heard in the distance, . . . running feet, voices shouting over loudspeakers.

From *Black Theatre USA: Plays by African Americans,* ed. James V. Hatch and Ted Shine, rev. and expanded ed. (New York: Free Press, 1996).

OFFSTAGE VOICES. Off the street! Into your homes! Clear the street! (*the whine of a bullet is heard*) Cover that roof! It's from the roof!

(BILL *is seated on the floor with his back to the wall, drawing on a large sketch pad with charcoal pencil. He is very absorbed in his task but flinches as he hears the bullet sound, ducks and shields his head with upraised hand, . . . then resumes sketching. The telephone rings, he reaches for phone with caution, pulls it toward him by the cord in order to avoid going near window or standing up.*)

BILL. Hello? Yeah, my phone is on. How the hell I'm gonna be talkin' to you if it's not on? (*sound of glass breaking in the distance*) I could lose my damn life answerin' the phone. Sonny-man, what the hell you callin' me up for! I thought you and Cynthia might be downstairs dead. I banged on the floor and hollered down the air-shaft, no answer. No stuff! Thought yall was dead. I'm sittin' here drawin' a picture in your memory. In a bar! Yall sittin' in a bar? See there, you done blew the picture that's in your memory . . . No kiddin', they wouldn't let you in the block? Man, they can't keep you outta your own house. Found? You found who? Model? What model? Yeah, yeah, thanks, . . . but I like to find my own models. No! Don't bring nobody up here in the middle of a riot . . . Hey, Sonny-man! Hey! (*sound of yelling and rushing footsteps in the hall*)

WOMAN'S VOICE (*offstage*). Dammit, Bernice! The riot is over! What you hidin' in the hall for? I'm in the house, your father's in the house, . . . and you out here hidin' in the hall!

GIRL'S VOICE (*offstage*). The house might burn down!

BILL Sonny-man, I can't hear you!

WOMAN'S VOICE (*offstage*). If it do burn down, what the hell you gon' do, run off and leave us to burn up by ourself? The riot is over. The police say it's over! Get back in the house! (*sound of running feet and a knock on the door*)

BILL. They say it's over. Man, they oughta let you on your own block, in your own house . . . Yeah, we still standin', this seventy year old house got guts. Thank you, yeah, thanks but I like to pick my own models. You drunk? Can't you hear when I say not to . . . Okay, all right, bring her . . . (*frantic knocking at the door*) I gotta go. Yeah, yeah, bring her. I gotta go . . . (*hangs up phone and opens the door for* OLDTIMER. *The old man is carrying a haul of loot . . . two or three bottles of liquor, a ham, a salami and a suit with price tags attached*) What's this! Oh, no, no, no, Oldtimer, not here . . . (*faint sound of a police whistle*) The police after you? What you bring that stuff in here for?

OLDTIMER *runs past* BILL *to center as he looks for a place to hide the loot*) No, no, they not really after me but . . . I was in the basement so I could stash this stuff, ... but a fella told me they pokin' round down there . . . in the back yard pokin' round . . . the police doin' a lotta pokin' round.

BILL. If the cops are searchin' why you wanna dump your troubles on me?

OLDTIMER. I don't wanna go to jail. I'm too old to go to jail. What we gonna do?

BILL. We can throw it the hell outta the window. Didn't you think of just throwin' it away and not worry 'bout jail?

OLDTIMER. I can't do it. It's like . . . I'm Old-timer but my hands and arms is somebody else that I don't know-a-tall. (BILL *pulls stuff out of* OLDTIMER's *arms and places loot on the kitchen table.* OLDTIMER's *arms fall to his sides*) Thank you, son.

BILL. Stealin' ain't worth a bullet through your brain, is it? You wanna get shot down and drown in your own blood, . . . for what? A suit, a bottle of whiskey? Gonna throw your life away for a damn ham?

OLDTIMER. But I ain't really stole nothin', Bill, cause I ain' no thief. Them others, . . . they smash the windows, they run in the stores and grab and all. Me, I pick up what they left scatter in the street. Things they drop . . . things they trample underfoot. What's in the street ain' like stealin'. This is leavin's. What I'm goin' do if the police come?

BILL (*starts to gather the things in the tablecloth that is on the table*). I'll throw it out the air-shaft window.

OLDTIMER (*places himself squarely in front of the air-shaft window*). I be damn. Un-uh, can't let you do it, Billy-Boy. (*grabs the liquor and holds on*)

BILL (*wraps the suit, the ham and the salami in the tablecloth and ties the ends together in a knot*). Just for now, then you can go down and get it later.

OLDTIMER (*getting belligerent*). I say I ain' gon' let you do it.

BILL. Sonny-man calls this "The people's revolution." A revolution should not be looting and stealing. Revolutions are for liberation. (OLDTIMER *won't budge from before the window*) Okay, man, you win, it's all yours. (*walks away from* OLDTIMER *and prepares his easel for sketching*)

OLDTIMER. Don't be mad with me, Billy-Boy, I couldn't help myself.

BILL (*at peace with the old man*). No hard feelin's.

OLDTIMER (*as he uncorks bottle*). I don't blame you for bein' fed up with us, . . . fella like you oughta be fed up with your people sometime. Hey, Billy, let's you and me have a little taste together.

BILL. Yeah, why not.

OLDTIMER (*at table pouring drinks*). You mustn't be too hard on me. You see, you talented, you got somethin' on the ball, you gonna make it on past these white folk, . . . but not me, Billy-Boy, it's too late in the day for that. Time, time, time, . . . time done put me down. Father Time is a bad white cat. Whatcha been paintin' and drawin' lately? You can paint me again if you wanta, . . . no charge. Paint me 'cause that might be the only way I get to stay in the world after I'm dead and gone. Somebody'll look up at your paintin' and say, . . . "Who's that?" And you say, . . . "That's Oldtimer." (BILL *joins* OLD-TIMER *at table and takes one of the drinks*) Well, here's lookin' at you and goin' down me. (*gulps drink down*)

BILL (*raising his glass*). Your health, oldtimer.

OLDTIMER. My day we didn't have all this grants and scholarship like now. Whatcha been doin'?

BILL. I'm working on the third part of a triptych.

OLDTIMER. A what tick?

BILL. A triptych.

OLDTIMER. Hot-damn, that call for another drink. Here's to the trip-tick. Down the hatch. What is one-a-those?

BILL. It's three painting that make one work . . . three paintings that make one subject.

OLDTIMER. Goes together like a new outfit . . . hat, shoes and suit.

BILL. Right. The title of my triptych is . . . "Wine In The Wilderness" . . . Three canvases on black womanhood . . .

OLDTIMER (*eyes light up*). Are they naked pitchers?

BILL (*crosses to paintings*). No, all fully clothed.

OLDTIMER (*wishing it was a naked picture*). Man, ain't nothing dirty 'bout naked pitchers. That's art. What you call artistic.

BILL. Right, right, right, but these are with clothes. That can be artistic too. (*uncovers one of the canvases and reveals painting of a charming little girl in Sunday dress and hair ribbon*) I call her . . . "Black girlhood."

OLDTIMER. Awwwww, that's innocence! Don't know what it's all about. Ain't that the little child that live right down the street? Yeah. That call for another drink.

BILL. Slow down, Oldtimer, wait till you see this. (*covers the painting of the little girl, then uncovers another canvas and reveals a beautiful woman, deep mahogany complexion, she is cold but utter perfection, draped in startling colors of African material, very "Vogue" looking. She wears a golden head-dress sparkling with brilliants and sequins applied over the paint*) There she is . . . "Wine In The Wilderness" . . . Mother Africa, regal, black womanhood in her noblest form.

OLDTIMER. Hot damn, I'd die for her, no stuff, . . . oh man. "Wine In The Wilderness."

BILL. Once, a long time ago, a poet named Omar told us what a paradise life could be if a man had a loaf of bread, a jug of wine and . . . a woman singing to him in the wilderness. She is the woman, she is the bread, she is the wine, she is the singing. This Abyssinian maiden is paradise, . . . perfect Black womanhood.

OLDTIMER (*pours for* BILL *and himself*). To our Abyssinian maiden.

BILL. She's the Sudan, the Congo River, the Egyptian Pyramids . . . Her thighs are African Mahogany . . . she speaks and her words pour forth sparkling clear as the waters . . . Victoria Falls.

OLDTIMER. Ow! Victoria Falls! She got a pretty name.

BILL (*covers her up again*). Victoria Falls is a waterfall not her name. Now, here's the one that calls for a drink. (*snatches cover from the empty canvas*)

OLDTIMER (*stunned by the empty canvas*). Your . . . your pitcher is gone.

BILL. Not gone, . . . she's not painted yet. This will be the third part of the triptych. This is the unfinished third of "Wine In the Wilderness." She's gonna be the kinda chick that is grass roots, . . . no, not grass roots, . . . I mean she's underneath the grass roots. The lost woman, . . . what the society has made out of our women. She's as far from my African queen as a woman can get and still be female, she's as close to the bottom as you can get without crackin' up . . . she's ignorant, unfeminine, coarse, rude . . . vulgar . . . a poor, dumb chick that's had her behind kicked until it's numb . . . and the sad part is . . . she ain't together, you know, . . . there's no hope for her.

OLDTIMER. Oh, man, you talkin' 'bout my first wife.

BILL. A chick that ain't fit for nothin' but to . . . to . . . just pass her by.

OLDTIMER. Yeah, later for her. When you see her, cross over to the other side of the street.

BILL. If you had to sum her up in one word it would be nothin'!

OLDTIMER (*roars with laughter*). That call for a double!

BILL (*beginning to slightly feel the drinks. He covers the canvas again*). Yeah, that's a double! The kinda woman that grates on your damn nerves, and Sonny-man just called to say he found her runnin' round in the middle-a this riot, Sonny-man say she's the real thing from underneath them grass roots. A back-country chick right outta the wilds of

Mississippi, . . . but she ain' never been near there. Born in Harlem, raised right here in Harlem, . . . but back country. Got the picture?

OLDTIMER (*full of laughter*). When . . . when . . . when she get here let's us stomp her to death.

BILL. Not till after I paint her. Gonna put her right here on this canvas. (*pats the canvas, walks in a strut around the table*) When she gets put down on canvas, . . . then triptych will be finished.

OLDTIMER (*joins him in the strut*). Trip-tick will be finish . . . trip-tick will be finish . . .

BILL. Then "Wine In The Wilderness" will go up against the wall to improve the view of some post office . . . or some library . . . or maybe a bank . . . and I'll win a prize . . . and the queen, my Black queen will look down from the wall so the messed-up chicks in the neighborhood can see what a woman oughta be . . . and the innocent child on one side of her and the messed-up chick on the other side of her . . . MY STATEMENT.

OLDTIMER (*turning the strut into a dance*). Wine in the wilderness . . . up against the wall . . . wine in the wilderness . . . up against the wall . . .

WOMAN FROM UPSTAIRS APT (*offstage*). What's the matter! The house on fire?

BILL (*calls upstairs through the air-shaft window*) No, baby! We down here paintin' pictures! (*sound of police siren in distance*)

WOMAN FROM UPSTAIRS APT (*offstage*). So much-a damn noise! Cut out the noise! (*to her husband, hysterically*) Percy! Percy! You hear a police siren! Percy! That a fire engine?!

BILL. Another messed up chick. (*gets a rope and ties it to Oldtimer's bundle*) Got an idea. We'll tie the rope to the bundle, . . . then . . . (*lowers bundle out of window*) lower the bundle outta the window . . . and tie it to this nail here behind the curtain. Now! Nobody can find it except you and me . . . Cops come, there's no loot. (*ties rope to nail under curtain*)

OLDTIMER. Yeah, yeah, loot long gone 'til I want it. (*makes sure window knot is secure*) It'll be swingin' in the breeze free and easy. (*there is knocking on the door*)

SONNY-MAN. Open up! Open up! Sonny-man and company.

BILL (*putting finishing touches on securing knot to nail*). Wait, wait, hold on . . .

SONNY-MAN. And-a here we come! (*pushes the door open. Enters room with his wife* CYNTHIA *and* TOMMY. SONNY-MAN *is in high spirits. He is in his late twenties, his wife* CYNTHIA *is a bit younger. She wears her hair in a natural style, her clothing is tweedy and in good, quiet taste.* SONNY-MAN *is wearing slacks and a dashiki over a shirt.* TOMMY *is dressed in a mis-matched skirt and sweater, wearing a wig that is not comical, but is wiggy looking. She has the habit of smoothing it every once in a while, patting to make sure it's in place. She wears sneakers and bobby sox, carries a brown paper sack*)

CYNTHIA. You didn't think it was locked, did you?

BILL. Door not locked? (*looking over* TOMMY)

TOMMY. You oughta run him outta town, pushin' open people's door.

BILL. Come right on in.

SONNY-MAN (*standing behind* TOMMY *and pointing down at her to draw* BILL's *attention*). Yes, sireeeeee.

CYNTHIA. Bill, meet a friend-a ours . . . This is Miss Tommy Fields. Tommy, meet a friend-a ours . . . this is Bill Jameson . . . Bill, Tommy.

BILL. Tommy, if I may call you that . . .

TOMMY (*likes him very much*). Help yourself, Bill. It's a pleasure. Bill Jameson, well, all right.

BILL. The pleasure is all mine. Another friend-a ours, Oldtimer.

TOMMY (*with respect and warmth*). How are you, Mr. Timer?

BILL (*laughs along with others, OLDTIMER included*). What you call him, baby?

TOMMY. Mr. Timer, . . . ain't that what you say? (*they all laugh expansively*)

BILL. No, sugar pie, that's what everybody call him . . .

OLDTIMER. Yeah, they all call me that . . . everybody say that . . . Oldtimer.

TOMMY. That's cute, . . . but what's your name?

BILL. His name is . . . er . . . er . . . What *is* your name?

SONNY-MAN. Dog-bite, what's your name, man? (*there's a significant moment of self-consciousness as CYNTHIA, SONNY and BILL realize they don't know OLDTIMER's name*)

OLDTIMER. Well, it's . . . Edmond L. Matthews.

TOMMY. Edmond L. Matthews. What's the L for?

OLDTIMER. Lorenzo, . . . Edmond Lorenzo Matthews.

BILL *and* SONNY-MAN. Edmond Lorenzo Matthews.

TOMMY. Pleased to meetcha, Mr. Matthews.

OLDTIMER. Nobody call me that in a long, long time.

TOMMY. I'll call you Oldtimer like the rest but I like to know who I'm meetin'. (*OLDTIMER gives her a chair*) There you go. He's a gentleman too. Bet you can tell my feet hurt. I got one corn . . . and that one is enough. Oh, it'll ask you for somethin'. (*general laughter. BILL indicates to SONNY-MAN that TOMMY seems right. CYNTHIA and OLDTIMER take seats near TOMMY*)

BILL. You rest yourself, baby, er . . . er . . . Tommy. You did say Tommy.

TOMMY. I cut it to Tommy . . . Tommy-Marie, I use both of 'em sometime.

BILL. How 'bout some refreshment?

SONNY-MAN. Yeah how 'bout that. (*pouring drinks*)

TOMMY. Don't yall carry me too fast, now.

BILL (*indicating liquor bottles*). I got what you see and also some wine . . . couple-a cans-a beer

TOMMY. I'll take the wine.

BILL. Yeah, I knew it.

TOMMY. Don't wanta start nothin' I can't keep up. (*OLDTIMER slaps his thigh with pleasure*)

BILL. That's all right, baby, you just a wine-o.

TOMMY. You the one that's got the wine, not me.

BILL. I use this for cookin'.

TOMMY. You like to get loaded while you cook? (*OLDTIMER is having a ball*)

BILL (*as he pours wine for TOMMY*). Oh, baby, you too much.

OLDTIMER (*admiring TOMMY*). Oh, Lord, I wish, I wish, I wish I was young again.

TOMMY (*flirtatiously*). Lively as you are, . . . I don't know what we'd do with you if you got any younger.

OLDTIMER. Oh, hush now!

SONNY-MAN (*whispering to BILL and pouring drinks*). Didn't I tell you! Know what I'm talkin' about. You dig? All the elements, man.

TOMMY (*worried about what the whispering means*). Let's get somethin' straight I didn' come bustin' in on the party, . . . I was asked. If you married and any wives or girlfriends round here . . . I'm innocent. Don't wanta get shot at, or jumped on. Cause I wasn't doin' a thing but mindin' my business! . . . (*saying the last in loud tones to be heard in other rooms*)

OLDTIMER. Jus' us here, that's all.

BILL. I'm single, baby. Nobody wants a poor artist.

CYNTHIA. Oh, honey, we wouldn't walk you into a jealous wife or girlfriend.

TOMMY. You paint all-a these pitchers? (BILL *and* SONNY-MAN *hand out drinks*)

BILL. Just about. Your health, baby, to you.

TOMMY (*lifts her wine glass*). All right, and I got one for you . . . Like my grampaw used-ta say, . . . Here's to the men's collars and the women's skirts, . . . may they never meet. (*general laughter*)

OLDTIMER. But they ain't got far to go before they do.

TOMMY (*suddenly remembers her troubles*). Niggers, niggers . . . niggers, . . . I'm sick-a niggers, ain't you? A nigger will mess up everytime . . . Lemmie tell you what the niggers done . . .

BILL. Tommy, baby, we don't use that word around here. We can talk about each other a little better than that.

CYNTHIA. Oh, she doesn't mean it.

TOMMY. What must I say?

BILL. Try Afro-Americans.

TOMMY. Well, . . . the Afro-Americans burnt down my house.

OLDTIMER. Oh, no they didn't!

TOMMY. Oh, yes they did . . . it's almost burn down. Then the firemen nailed up my door . . . the door to my room, nailed up shut tight with all I got in the world.

OLDTIMER. Shame, what a shame.

TOMMY. A *damn* shame. My clothes . . . Everything gone. This riot blew my life. All I got is gone like it never was.

OLDTIMER. I know it.

TOMMY. My transistor radio . . . that's gone.

CYNTHIA. Ah, gee.

TOMMY. The transistor . . . and a brand new pair-a shoes I never had on one time . . . (*raises her right hand*) If I never move, that's the truth . . . new shoes gone.

OLDTIMER. Child, when hard luck fall it just keep fallin'.

TOMMY. And in my top dresser drawer I got a my-on-ase jar with forty-one dollars in it. The firemen would not let me in to get it . . . And it was a Afro-American fireman, don'tcha know.

OLDTIMER. And you ain't got no place to stay. (BILL *is studying her for portrait possibilities*)

TOMMY (*rises and walks around room*). That's a lie. I always got some place to go. I don't wanta boast but I ain't never been no place that I can't go back the second time. Woman I use to work for say . . . "Tommy, any time, any time you want a sleep-in place you come right here to me." . . . And that's Park Avenue, my own private bath and T.V. set . . . But I don't want that . . . so I make it on out here to the dress factory. I got friends . . . not a lot of 'em . . . but a few *good* ones. I call my friend—girl and her mother . . . they say . . . "Tommy, you come here, bring yourself over here." So Tommy got a roof with no sweat. (*looks at torn walls*) Looks like the Afro-Americans got to you too. Breakin' up, breakin' down, . . . that's all they know.

BILL. No, Tommy, . . . I'm re-decorating the place . . .

TOMMY. You mean you did this to yourself?

CYNTHIA. It's gonna be wild . . . brick-face walls . . . wall to wall carpet.

SONNY-MAN. She was breakin' up everybody in the bar . . . had us all laughin'—crackin' us up. In the middle of a riot . . . she's gassin' everybody!

TOMMY. No need to cry, it's sad enough. They hollerin' whitey, whitey . . . but who they burn out? Me.

BILL. The brothers and sisters are tired, weary of the endless get-no-where struggle.

TOMMY. I'm standin' there in the bar . . . tellin' it like it is . . . next thing I know they talkin' bout bringin' me to meet you. But you know what I say? Can't nobody pick nobody for nobody else. It don't work. And I'm standin' there in a mis-match skirt and top and these sneaker-shoes. I just went to put my dresses in the cleaner . . . Oh, Lord, wonder if they burn down the cleaner. Well, no matter, when I got back it was all over . . . They went in the grocery store, rip out the shelves, pull out all the groceries . . . the hams . . . the . . . the . . . the can goods . . . everything . . . and then set fire . . . Now who you think live over the grocery? Me, that's who. I don't even go to the store lookin' this way . . . but this would be the time, when . . . folks got a fella they want me to meet.

BILL (*suddenly self-conscious*). Tommy, they thought . . . they thought I'd like to paint you . . . that's why they asked you over.

TOMMY (*pleased by the thought but she can't understand it*). Paint me? For what? If he was gonna paint somebody seems to me it'd be one of the pretty girls they show in the beer ads. They even got colored on television now, . . . brushin' their teeth and smokin' ciga-rettes, . . .some of the prettiest girls in the world. He could get them, . . . couldn't you?

BILL. Sonny-man and Cynthia were right. I want to paint you.

TOMMY (*suspiciously*). Naked, with no clothes on?

BILL. No, baby dressed just as you are now.

OLDTIMER. Wearin' clothes is also art.

TOMMY. In the cleaner I got a white dress with a orlon sweater to match it, maybe I can get it out tomorrow and pose in that. (CYNTHIA, OLDTIMER *and* SONNY-MAN *are eager for her to agree*)

BILL. No, I will paint you today, Tommy, just as you are, holding your brown paper bag.

TOMMY. Mmmmmm, me holdin' the damn bag. I don' know 'bout that.

BILL. Look at it this way, tonight has been a tragedy.

TOMMY. Sure in hell has.

BILL. And so I must paint you tonight, . . . Tommy in her moment of tragedy.

TOMMY. I'm tired.

BILL. Damn, baby, all you have to do is sit there and rest.

TOMMY. I'm hongry.

SONNY-MAN. While you're posin' Cynthia can run down to our house and fix you some eggs.

CYNTHIA (*gives her husband a weary look*). Oh, Sonny, that's such a lovely idea.

SONNY-MAN. Thank you, darlin', I'm in there, . . . on the beam.

TOMMY (*ill at ease about posing*). I don't want no eggs. I'm goin' to find me some Chinee food.

BILL. I'll go. If you promise to stay here and let me paint you, . . . I'll get you anything you want.

TOMMY (*brightening up*). Anything I want. Now, how he sound? All right, you comin' on mighty strong there. "Anything you want." When last you heard somebody say that? . . . I'm warnin' you, now, . . . I'm free, single and disengage, . . . so you better watch yourself.

BILL (*keeping her away from ideas of romance*). Now this is the way the program will go down. First I'll feed you, then I'll paint you.

TOMMY. Okay, I'm game, I'm a good sport. First off, I want me some Chinee food.

CYNTHIA. Order up, Tommy, the treat's on him.

TOMMY. How come it is you never been married? All these girls runnin' round Harlem lookin' for husbands. (*to* CYNTHIA) I don't blame 'em, 'cause I'm looking for somebody myself.

BILL. I've been married, married and divorced, she divorced me, Tommy, so maybe I'm not much of a catch.

TOMMY. Look at it this-a-way. Some folks got bad taste. That woman had bad taste. (*all laugh except* Bill *who pours another drink*) Watch it, Bill, you gonna rust the linin' of your stomach. Ain't this a shame? The riot done wipe me out and I'm sittin' here havin' me a ball. Sittin' here ballin' (*as* BILL *refills her glass*) Hold it, that's enough. Likker ain' my problem.

OLDTIMER. I'm havin' me a good time.

TOMMY. Know what I say 'bout divorce. (*slaps her hands together in a final gesture*) Anybody don' wantcha, . . . later, let 'em go. That's bad taste for you.

BILL. Tommy, I don't wanta ever get married again. It's me and my work. I'm not gettin' serious about anybody . . .

TOMMY. He's spellin' at me, now. Nigger, . . . I mean Afro-American . . . I ain' ask you nothin'. You hinkty, I'm hinkty too. I'm independent as a hog on ice, . . . and a hog on ice is dead, cold, well-preserved . . . and don't need a mother-grabbin' thing. (*all laugh heartily except* BILL *and* CYNTHIA) I know models get paid. I ain' no square but this is a special night and so this one'll be on the house. Show you my heart's in the right place.

BILL. I'll be glad to pay you, baby.

TOMMY. You don't really like me, do you? That's all right, sometime it happen that way. You can't pick for *nobody.* Friends get to matchin' up friends and they mess up everytime. Cynthia and Sonny-man done messed up.

BILL. I like you just fine and I'm glad and grateful that you came.

TOMMY. Good enough. (*extends her hand. They slap hands together*) You'n me friends?

BILL. Friends, baby, friends. (*putting rock record on*)

TOMMY (*trying out the model stand*). Okay, Dad! Let's see 'bout this *anything I want* jive. Want me a bucket-a Egg Foo Yong, and you get you a shrimp-fry rice, we split that and each have some-a both. Make him give you the soy sauce, the hot mustard and the duck sauce too.

BILL. Anything else, baby?

TOMMY. Since you ask, yes. If your money hold out, get me a double order egg roll. And a half order of the sweet and sour spare ribs.

BILL (*to* OLDTIMER *and* SONNY-MAN). Come on, come on. I need some strong men to help me bring back your order, baby.

TOMMY (*going into her dance . . . simply standing and going through some boo-ga-loo motions*). Better go get it 'fore I think up some more to go 'long with it. (*the men laugh and vanish out of the door. Steps heard descending stairs*) Turn that off. (CYNTHIA *turns off record player*) How could I forget your name, good as you been to me this day. Thank you, Cynthia, thank you. I *like* him. Oh, I *like* him. But I don't wanta push him too fast. Oh, I got to play these cards right.

CYNTHIA (*a bit uncomfortable*). Oh, Honey, . . . Tommy, you don't want a poor artist.

TOMMY. Tommy's not lookin' for a meal ticket. I been doin' for myself all my life. It takes two to make it in this high-price world. A Black man see a hard way to go. The both of you gotta pull together. That way you accomplish.

CYNTHIA. I'm a social worker . . . and I see so many broken homes. Some of these men! Tommy, don't be in a rush about the marriage thing.

TOMMY. Keep it to yourself, . . . but I was thirty my last birthday and haven't ever been married. I coulda been. Oh, yes, indeed, coulda been. But I don't want any and everybody. What I want with a no-good piece-a nothin'? I'll never forget what the Reverend Martin Luther King said . . . "I have a dream." I liked him sayin' it 'cause truer words have never been spoke. (*straightening the room*) I have a dream, too. Mine is to find a man who'll treat me just half-way decent . . . just to meet me half-way is all I ask, to smile, to be kind to me. Somebody in my corner. Not to wake up by myself in the mornin' and face this world all alone.

CYNTHIA. About Bill, it's best not to ever count on anything, anything at all, Tommy.

TOMMY (*this remark bothers her for a split second but she shakes it off*). Of course, Cynthia, that's one of the foremost rules of life. Don't count on *nothin'!*

CYNTHIA. Right, don't be too quick to put your trust in these men.

TOMMY. You put your trust in one and got yourself a husband.

CYNTHIA. Well, yes, but what I mean is . . . Oh, you know. A man is a man and Bill is also an artist and his work comes before all else and there are other factors . . .

TOMMY (*sits facing* CYNTHIA). What's wrong with me?

CYNTHIA. I don't know what you mean.

TOMMY. Yes you do. You tryin' to tell me I'm aimin' too high by lookin' at Bill.

CYNTHIA. Oh, no, my dear.

TOMMY. Out there in the street, in the bar, you and your husband were so sure that he'd *like* me and want to paint my picture.

CYNTHIA. But he does want to paint you, he's very eager to . . .

TOMMY. But why? Somethin' don't fit right.

CYNTHIA (*feeling sorry for* TOMMY). If you don't want to do it, just leave and that'll be that.

TOMMY. Walk out while he's buyin' me what I ask for, spendin' his money on me? That'd be too dirty. (*looks at books. Takes one from shelf*) Books, books, books everywhere. "Afro-American History." I like that. What's wrong with me, Cynthia? Tell me, I won't get mad with you, I swear. If there's somethin' wrong that I can change, I'm ready to do it. Eighth grade, that's all I had of school. You a social worker, I know that mean college. I come from poor people. (*examining the book in her hand*) Talkin' 'bout poverty this and poverty that and studyin' it. When you *in* it you don' be studyin' 'bout it. Cynthia,

I remember my mother tyin' up her stockin's with strips-a-rag 'cause she didn't have no garters. When I get home from school she'd say, . . . "Nothin' much here to eat." Nothin' much might be grits, or bread and coffee. I got sick-a all that, got me a job. Later for school.

CYNTHIA. The Matriarchal Society.

TOMMY. What's that?

CYNTHIA. A Matriarchal Society is one in which the women rule . . . the women have the power . . . the women head the house.

TOMMY. We didn't have nothin' to rule over, not a pot nor a window. And my papa picked hisself up and run off with some finger-poppin' woman and we never hear another word 'til ten, twelve years later when a undertaker call up and ask if Mama wanta come claim his body. And don'cha know, Mama went on over and claim it. A woman need a man to claim, even if it's a dead one. What's wrong with me? Be honest.

CYNTHIA. You're a fine person . . .

TOMMY. Go on, I can take it.

CYNTHIA. You're too brash. You're too used to looking out for yourself. It makes us lose our femininity . . . It makes us hard . . . it makes us seem very hard. We do for ourselves too much.

TOMMY. If I don't, who's gonna do for me?

CYNTHIA. You have to let the Black man have his manhood again. You have to give it back, Tommy.

TOMMY. I didn't take it from him, how I'm gonna give it back? What else is the matter with me? You had school, I didn't. I respect that.

CYNTHIA. Yes, I've had it, the degree and the whole bit. For a time I thought I was about to move into another world, the so-called "integrated" world, a place where knowledge and know-how could set you free and open all the doors, but that's a lie. I turned away from that idea. The first thing I did was give up dating white fellas.

TOMMY. I never had none to give up. I'm not soundin' on you. White folks, nothin' happens when I look at 'em. I don't hate 'em, don't love 'em, . . . just nothin' shakes-a-tall. The dullest people in the world. The way they talk . . . "Oh, hooty, hooty, hoo" . . . Break it down for me to A, B, C's. That Bill . . . I like him, with his Black, uppity, high-handed ways. What do you do to get a man you want? A social worker oughta tell you things like that.

CYNTHIA. Don't chase him . . . at least don't let it look that way. Let him pursue you.

TOMMY. What if he won't? Men don't chase me much, not the kind I like.

CYNTHIA (*rattles off instructions glibly*). Let him do the talking. Learn to listen. Stay in the background a little. Ask his opinion . . . "what do you think, Bill?"

TOMMY. Mmmmm, "Oh, hooty, hooty, hoo."

CYNTHIA. But why count on him? There are lots of other nice guys.

TOMMY. You don't think he'd go for me, do you?

CYNTHIA (*trying to be diplomatic*). Perhaps you're not really his type.

TOMMY. Maybe not, but he's mine. I'm so lonesome . . . I'm *lonesome* . . . I want somebody to love. Somebody to say . . . "That's all-right," when the world treats me mean.

CYNTHIA. Tommy, I think you're too good for Bill.

TOMMY. I don't wanta hear that. The last man that told me I was too good for him . . . was tryin' to get away. He's good enough for me. (*straightening room*)

CYNTHIA. Leave the room alone. What we need is a little more sex appeal and a little less washing, cooking and ironing. (TOMMY *puts down the room straightening*) One more thing, . . . do you have to wear that wig?

TOMMY (*a little sensitive*). I like how *your* hair looks. But some of the naturals I don't like. Can see all the lint caught up in the hair like it hasn't been combed since know not when. You a Muslim?

CYNTHIA. No.

TOMMY. I'm just sick-a hair, hair, hair. Do it this way, don't do it, leave it natural, straighten it, process, no process. I get sick-a hair and talkin' 'bout it and foolin' with it. That's why I wear the wig.

CYNTHIA. I'm sure your own must be just as nice or nicer than that.

TOMMY. It oughta be. I only paid nineteen ninety five for this.

CYNTHIA. You ought to go back to usin' your own.

TOMMY (*tensely*). I'll be givin' that some thought.

CYNTHIA. You're pretty nice people just as you are. Soften up, Tommy. You might surprise yourself.

TOMMY. I'm listenin'.

CYNTHIA. Expect more. Learn to let men open doors for you . . .

TOMMY. What if I'm standin' there and they don't open it?

CYNTHIA (*trying to level with her*). You're a fine person. He wants to paint you, that's all. He's doing a kind of mural thing and we thought he would enjoy painting you. I'd hate to see you expecting more out of the situation than what's there.

TOMMY. Forget it, sweetie-pie, don' nothin' that's not suppose to. (*sound of laughter in the hall.* BILL, OLDTIMER *and* SONNY-MAN *enter*)

BILL. No Chinese restaurant left, baby! It's wiped out. Gone with the revolution.

SONNY-MAN (*to* CYNTHIA). Baby, let's move, split the scene, get on with it, time for home.

BILL. The revolution is here. Whatta you do with her? You paint her!

SONNY-MAN. You write her . . . you write the revolution into a novel nine hundred pages long.

BILL. Dance it! Sing it! "Down in the cornfield hear dat mournful sound . . . (SONNY-MAN *and* OLDTIMER *harmonize.*) Dear old Massa am-a sleepin' in the cold, cold ground." Now for "Wine In The Wilderness!" Triptych will be finished.

CYNTHIA (*in* BILL's *face*). "Wine In The Wilderness," huh? Exploitation!

SONNY-MAN. Upstairs, all out, come one, Oldtimer. Folks can't create in a crowd. Cynthia, move it, baby.

OLDTIMER (*starting toward the window*). My things! I got a package.

SONNY-MAN (*heads him off*). Up and out. You don't have to go home, but you have to get outta here. Happy paintin', yall. (*one backward look and they are all gone*)

BILL. Whatta night, whatta night, whatta night, baby. It will be painted, written, sung and discussed for generations.

TOMMY (*notices nothing that looks like Chinese food. He is carrying a small bag and a container*). Where's the Foo-Yong?

BILL. They blew the restaurant, baby. All I could get was a couple-a franks and a orange drink from the stand.

TOMMY (*tersely*). You brought me a frank-footer? That's what you think-a me, a frank-footer?

BILL. Nothin' to do with what I think. Place is closed.

TOMMY (*quiety surly*). This is the damn City-a New York, any hour on the clock they sellin' the chicken in the basket, barbecue ribs, pizza pie, hot pastrami samitches; and you brought me a frank-footer?

BILL. Baby, don't break bad over somethin' to eat. The smart set, the jet set, the beautiful people, kings and queens eat frankfurters.

TOMMY. If a queen sent you out to buy her a bucket-a Foo-yung, you wouldn't come back with no lonely-ass frank-footer.

BILL. Kill me 'bout it, baby! Go 'head and shoot me six times. That's the trouble with our women, yall always got your mind on food.

TOMMY. Is that our trouble? (*laughs*) Maybe you right. Only two things to do. Either eat the frankfooter or walk outta here. You got any mustard?

BILL (*gets mustard from the refrigerator*). Let's face it, our folks are not together. The brothers and sisters have busted up Harlem, . . . no plan, no nothin'. There's your Black revolution, heads whipped, hospital full and we still in the same old bag.

TOMMY (*seated at the kitchen table*). Maybe what everybody need is somebody like you, who know how things oughta go, to get on out there and start some action.

BILL. You still mad about the frankfurter?

TOMMY. No. I keep seein' pitchers of what was in my room and how it all must be spoiled now. (*sips the orange drink*) A orange never been near this. Well, it's cold. (*looking at an incense burner*) What's that?

BILL. An incense burner, was given to me by the Chinese guy, Richard Lee. I'm sorry they blew his restaurant.

TOMMY. Does it help you to catch the number?

BILL. No, baby, I just burn incense sometime.

TOMMY. For what?

BILL. Just 'cause I feel like it. Baby, ain't you used to nothin'?

TOMMY. Ain't used to burnin' incent for nothin'.

BILL (*laughs*). Burnin' what?

TOMMY. That stuff.

BILL. What did you call it?

TOMMY. Incent.

BILL. It's not incent, baby. It's incense.

TOMMY. Like the sense you got in your head. In-sense. Thank you. You're a very correctable person, ain't you?

BILL. Let's put you on canvas.

TOMMY (*stubbornly*). I have to eat first.

BILL. That's another thing 'bout Black women, they wanta eat 'fore they do anything else. Tommy, . . . Tommy, . . . I bet your name is Thomasina. You look like a Thomasina.

TOMMY. You could sit there and guess til your eyes pop out and you never would guess my first name. You might could guess the middle name but not the first one.

BILL. Tell it to me.

TOMMY. My name is Tomorrow.

BILL. How's that?

TOMMY. Tomorrow, . . . like yesterday and *tomorrow,* and the middle name is just plain Marie. That's what my father name me, Tomorrow Marie. My mother say he thought it had a pretty sound.

BILL. Crazy! I never met a girl named Tomorrow.

TOMMY. They got to callin' me Tommy for short, so I stick with that. Tomorrow Marie, . . . Sound like a promise that can never happen.

BILL (*straightens chair on stand. He is very eager to start painting*). That's what Shakespeare said, . . . "Tomorrow and tomorrow and tomorrow." Tomorrow, you will be on this canvas.

TOMMY (*still uneasy about being painted*). What's the hurry? Rome wasn't built in a day, . . . that's another saying.

BILL. If I finish in time, I'll enter you in an exhibition.

TOMMY (*loses interest in the food. Examines the room. Looks at portrait on the wall*). He looks like somebody I know or maybe saw before.

BILL. That's Frederick Douglass. A man who used to be a slave. He escaped and spent his life trying to make us all free. He was a great man.

TOMMY. Thank you, Mr. Douglass. Who's the light colored man? (*indicates a frame next to the Douglass*)

BILL. He's white. That's John Brown. They killed him for tryin' to shoot the country outta the slavery bag. He dug us, you know. Old John said, "Hell no, slavery must go."

TOMMY. I heard all about him. Some folks say he was crazy.

BILL. If he had been shootin' at *us* they wouldn't have called him a nut.

TOMMY. School wasn't a great part-a my life.

BILL. If it was you wouldn't-a found out too much 'bout Black history cause the books full-a nothin' but whitey, . . . all except the white ones who dug us, . . . they not there either. Tell me, . . . who was Elijah Lovejoy?

TOMMY. Elijah Lovejoy, . . . Mmmmmmm. I don't know. Have to do with the Bible?

BILL. No, that's another white fella, . . . Elijah had a printin' press and the main thing he printed was "Slavery got to go." Well the man moved in on him, smashed his press time after time . . . but he kept puttin' it back together and doin' his thing. So, one final day, they came in a mob and burned him to death.

TOMMY (*blows her nose with sympathy as she fights tears*). That's dirty.

BILL (*as* TOMMY *glances at titles in bookcase*). Who was Monroe Trotter?

TOMMY. Was he white?

BILL. No, soul brother. Spent his years tryin' to make it all right. Who was Harriet Tubman?

TOMMY. I heard-a her. But don't put me through no test, Billy. (*moving around studying pictures and books*) This *room* is full-a things I don' know nothin' about. How'll I get to know?

BILL. Read, go to the library, book stores, ask somebody.

TOMMY. Okay, I'm askin'. Teach me things.

BILL. Aw, baby, why torment yourself? Trouble with our women, . . . they all wanta be great brains. Leave somethin' for a man to do.

TOMMY (*eager to impress him*). What you think-a Martin Luther King?

BILL. A great guy. But it's too late in the day for the singin' and prayin' now.

TOMMY. What about Malcolm X?

BILL. Great cat . . . but there again . . . Where's the program?

TOMMY. What about Adam Powell? I voted for him. That's one thing 'bout me. I vote. Maybe if everybody vote for the right people . . .

BILL. The ballot box. It would take me all my life to straighten you on that hype.

TOMMY. I got the time.

BILL. You gonna wind up with a king size headache. The Matriarchy gotta go. Yall throw them suppers together, keep your husband happy, raise the kids.

TOMMY. I don't have a husband. Course, that could be fixed. (*leaving the unspoken proposal hanging in the air*)

BILL. You know the greatest thing you could do for your people? Sit up there and let me put you down on canvas.

TOMMY. Bein' married and havin' a family might be good for your people as a race, but I was thinkin' bout myself a little.

BILL. Forget yourself sometime, sugar. On that canvas you'll be givin' and givin' and givin' . . . That's where you can do your thing best. What you stallin' for?

TOMMY (*returns to table and sits in chair*). I . . . I don't want to pose in this outfit.

BILL (*patience is wearing thin*). Why, baby, why?

TOMMY. I don't feel proud-a myself in this.

BILL. Art, baby, we talkin' art. Whatcha want . . . Ribbons? Lace? False eyelashes?

TOMMY. No, just my white dress with the orlon sweater, . . . or anything but this what I'm wearin'. You oughta see me in that dress with my pink linen shoes. Oh, hell, the shoes are gone. I forgot 'bout the fire . . .

BILL. Oh stop fightin' me! Another thing . . . our women don't know a damn thing bout bein' feminine. *Give in* sometime. It won't kill you. You tellin' me how to paint? Maybe you oughta hang out your shingle and give art lessons! You too damn opinionated. You gonna pose or you not gonna pose? Say somethin'!

TOMMY. You makin' me nervous! Hollerin' at me. My mama never holler at me. Hollerin'.

BILL. I'll soon be too tired to pick up the brush, baby.

TOMMY (*eye catches picture of white woman on the wall*). That's a white woman! Bet you never hollered at her and I bet she's your girlfriend . . . too, and when she posed for her pitcher I bet yall was laughin' . . . and you didn't buy her no frankfooter!

BILL (*feels a bit smug about his male prowess*). Awww, come on, cut that out, baby. That's a little blonde, blue-eyed chick who used to pose for me. That ain't where it's at. This is a new day, the deal is goin' down different. This is the Black moment, doll. Black, Black, Black, is bee-yoo-tee-full. Got it? *Black is beautiful.*

TOMMY. Then how come it is that I don't *feel* beautiful when you *talk* to me?!!

BILL. That's your hang-up, not mine. You supposed to stretch forth your wings like Ethiopia, shake off them chains that been holdin' you down. Langston Hughes said let 'em see how beautiful you are. But you determined not to ever be beautiful. Okay, that's what makes you Tommy.

TOMMY. Do you *have* a girlfriend? And who is she?

BILL (*now enjoying himself to the utmost*). Naw, naw, naw, doll. I *know* people, but none-a this "tie-you-up-and-I-own-you" jive. I ain't mistreatin' nobody and there's enough-a me to go around. That's another thing with our women, ... they want a *latch* on. Learn to play it by ear, roll with the punches, cut down on some-a this "got-you-to-the-grave" kinda relationship. Was today all right? Good, be glad, ... take what's at hand because tomorrow never comes, it's always today. (*she begins to cry*) Awwww, I didn't mean it that way . . . I forgot your name. (*he brushes her tears away*) You act like I belong to you. You're jealous of a picture?

TOMMY. That's how women are, always studyin' each other and wonderin' how they look up 'gainst the next person.

BILL (*a bit smug*). That's human nature. Whatcha call healthy competition.

TOMMY. You think she's pretty?

BILL. She was, perhaps still is. Long, silky hair. She could sit on her hair.

TOMMY (*with bitter arrogance*). Doesn't *everybody*?

BILL. You got a head like a rock and gonna have the last word if it kills you. Baby, I bet you could knock out Mohamud Ali in the first round, then rare back and scream like Tarzan . . . "Now, I am the greatest!" (*he is very close to her and is amazed to feel a great sense of physical attraction*) What we arguin' bout? (*looks her over as she looks away. He suddenly want to put the conversation on a more intimate level. His eye is on the bed*) Maybe tomorrow would be a better time for paintin'. Wanna freshen up, take a bath, baby? Water's nice n' hot.

TOMMY (*knows the sound and turns to check on the look. Notices him watching the bed. Starts weeping*). No, I don't, Nigger!

BILL. Was that nice? What the hell, let's paint the picture. Or are you gonna hold that back too?

TOMMY. I'm posin'. Shall I take off the wig?

BILL. No, it's a part of your image, ain't it? You must have a reason for wearin' it.

(TOMMY *snatches up her orange drink and sits in the model's chair*)

TOMMY (*with defiance*). Yes, I wear it cause you and those like you go for long, silky hair, and this is the only way I can have some without burnin' my mother-grabbin' brains out. Got it? (*she accidently knocks over container of orange drink into her lap*) Hell, I can't wear this. I'm soaked through. I'm not gonna catch no double pneumonia sittin' up here wringing' wet while you paint and holler at me.

BILL. Bitch!

TOMMY. You must be talkin' bout *your* mama!

BILL. Shut up! Aw, shut-up! (*phone rings. He finds a African throw-cloth and hands it to her*) Put this on. Relax, don't go way mad, and all the rest-a that jazz. Change, will you? I apologize. I'm sorry. (*he picks up phone*) Hello, survivor of riot speaking. Who's calling? (TOMMY *retires behind the screen with the throw. During the conversation she undresses and wraps the throw around her. We see* TOMMY *and* BILL, *but they can't see each other*) Sure, told you not to worry. I'll be ready for the exhibit. If you don't dig it, don't show it. Not time for you to see it yet. Yeah, yeah, next week. You just make sure your exhibition room is big enough to hold the crowds that's gonna congregate to see this fine chick I got here. (*this perks* TOMMY's *ears up*) You oughta see her. The finest Black woman in the world . . . This gorgeous satin chick is . . . is . . . black velvet moonlight . . . an ebony queen of the universe . . . (TOMMY *can hardly believe her ears*) One look at her and you go back to Spice Islands . . . She's Mother Africa . . . You flip, double flip. She has come through everything that has been put on her . . . (*he unveils the gorgeous woman he has painted . . . "Wine In The Wilderness."* TOMMY *believes he is talking about her*) Regal . . . grand . . . magnificent, fantastic . . . You would vote her the woman you'd most like to meet on a desert island, or around the corner from anywhere. She's here with me now . . . and I don't know if I want to show her to you or anybody else . . . I'm beginnin' to have this deep attachment . . . She sparkles, man, Harriet Tubman, Queen of the Nile . . . sweetheart, wife, mother, sister, friend . . . The night . . . a black diamond . . . A dark, beautiful dream . . . A cloud with a silvery lining . . . Her wrath is a storm over the Bahamas. "Wine In the Wilderness" . . . The memory of Africa . . . The *now* of things . . . but best of all and most important . . . She's tomorrow . . . she's my tomorrow . . . (TOMMY *is dressed in the African wrap. She is suddenly awakened to the feeling of being loved and admired. She removes the wig and fluffs her hair. Her hair under the wig must not be an accurate, well-cut Afro . . . but should be rather attractive natural hair. She studies herself in a mirror. We see her taller, more relaxed and sure of herself. Perhaps braided hair will go well with Afro robe*) Aw, man, later. You don't believe in nothin'! (*he covers "Wine In The Wilderness." Is now in a glowing mood*) Baby, whenever you ready. (*she emerges from behind the screen. Dressed in the wrap, sans wig. He is astounded*) Baby, what . . . ? Where . . . where's the wig?

TOMMY. I don't think I want to wear it, Bill.

BILL. That is very becoming . . . the drape thing.

TOMMY. Thank you.

BILL. I don't know what to say.

TOMMY. It's time to paint. (*steps up on the model stand and sits in the chair. She is now a queen, relaxed and smiling her appreciation for his last speech to the art dealer. Her feet are bare*)

BILL (*mystified by the change in her. Tries to do a charcoal sketch*). It is quite late.

TOMMY. Makes me no difference if it's all right with you.

BILL (*wants to create the other image*). Could you put the wig back on?

TOMMY. You don't really like wigs, do you?

BILL. Well, no.

TOMMY. Then let's have things the way you like.

BILL (*has no answer for this. He makes a haphazard line or two as he tries to remember the other image*). Tell me something about yourself, . . . anything.

TOMMY (*now on sure ground*). I was born in Baltimore, Maryland and raised here in Harlem. My favorite flower is "Four O'clocks," that's a bush flower. My wearin' flower, corsage flower, is pink roses. My mama raised me, mostly by herself, God rest the dead. Mama belonged to "The Eastern Star." Her father was a "Mason." If a man in the family is a "Mason" any woman related to him can be an "Eastern Star." My grandfather was a member of "The Prince Hall Lodge." I had a uncle who was an "Elk," . . . a member of "The Improved Benevolent Protective Order of Elks of the World": "The Henry Lincoln Johnson Lodge." You know, the white "Elks" are called "The Benevolent

Protective Order of Elks" but the Black "Elks" are called "The *Improved* Benevolent Protective Order of Elks *of the World*." That's because the Black "Elks" got the copyright first but the white "Elks" took us to court about it to keep us from usin' the name. Over fifteen hundred Black folk went to jail for wearin' the "Elk" emblem on their coat lapel. Years ago, . . . that's what you call history.

BILL. I didn't know about that.

TOMMY. Oh, it's understandable. Only way I heard bout John Brown was because the Black "Elks" bought his farmhouse where he trained his men to attack the government.

BILL. The Black "Elks" bought the John Brown Farm? What did they do with it?

TOMMY. They built a outdoor theater and put a perpetual light in his memory, . . . and they buildin' cottages there, one named for each state in the union and . . .

BILL. How do you know about it?

TOMMY. Well, our "Elks" helped my cousin go through school with a scholarship. She won a speaking contest and wrote a composition titled "Onward and Upward, O, My Race." That's how she won the scholarship. Coreen knows all that Elk history.

BILL (*seeing her with new eyes*). Tell me some more about you, Tomorrow Marie. I bet you go to church.

TOMMY. Not much as I used to. Early in life I pledged myself in the A.M.E. Zion Church.

BILL (*studying her face, seeing her for the first time*). A.M.E.

TOMMY. A.M.E. That's African Methodist Episcopal. We split off from the white Methodist Episcopal and started our own in the year Seventeen hundred and ninety six. We built our first buildin' in the year 1800. How 'bout that?

BILL. That right?

TOMMY. Oh, I'm just showin' off. I taught Sunday School for two years and you had to know the history of A.M.E. Zion . . . or else you couldn't teach. My great, great grand-parents was slaves.

BILL. Guess everybody's was.

TOMMY. Mine was slaves in a place called Sweetwater Springs, Virginia. We tried to look it up one time but somebody at Church told us that Sweetwater Springs had become a part of Norfolk . . . so we didn't carry it any further . . . As it would be a expense to have a lawyer trace your people.

BILL (*throws charcoal pencil across room*). No good! It won't work! I can't work anymore.

TOMMY. Take a rest. Tell me about you.

BILL (*sits on bed*). Everybody in my family worked for the Post Office. They bought a home in Jamaica, Long Island. Everybody on that block bought an aluminum screen door with a duck on it, . . . or was it a swan? I guess that makes my favorite flower crab grass and hedges. I have a lot of bad dreams. (TOMMY *massages his temples and the back of his neck*) A dream like suffocating, dying of suffocation. The worst kinda dream. People are standing in a weird looking art gallery, they're looking and laughing at everything I've ever done. My work begins to fade off the canvas, right before my eyes. Everything I've ever done is laughed away.

TOMMY. Don't be so hard on yourself. If I was smart as you I'd wake up singing every mornin'. (*there is the sound of thunder. He kisses her*) When it thunders that's the angels in heaven playin' with their hoops, rollin' their hoops and bicycle wheels in the rain. My Mama told me that.

BILL. I'm glad you're here. Black *is* beautiful, you're beautiful, A.M.E. Zion, Elks, pink roses, bush flower, . . . blooming out of the slavery of Sweetwater Springs, Virginia.

TOMMY. I'm gonna take a bath and let the riot and the hell of living go down the drain with the bath water.

BILL. Tommy, Tommy, Tomorrow Marie, let's save each other, let's be kind and good to each other while it rains and the angels roll those hoops and bicycle wheels.

(*They embrace. The sound of rain. Music in as lights come down. As lights fade down to darkness, music comes in louder. There is a flash of lightning. We see* TOMMY *and* BILL *in each other's arms. It is very dark. Music up louder, then softer and down to very soft. Music is mixed with the sound of rain beating against the window. Music slowly fades as gray light of dawn shows at window. Lights go up gradually. The bed is rumpled and empty.* BILL *is in the bathroom.* TOMMY *is at the stove turning off the coffee pot. She sets table with cups and saucers, spoons.* TOMMY'S *hair is natural, she wears another throw [African design] draped around her. She sings and hums a snatch of a joyous spiritual.*)

TOMMY. "Great day, Great day, the world's on fire, Great day . . ." (*calling out to* BILL *who is in the bath*) Honey, I found the coffee, and it's ready. Nothin' here to go with it but a cucumber and a Uneeda biscuit.

BILL (*offstage. Joyous yell from offstage*). Tomorrow and tomorrow and tomorrow! Good mornin', Tomorrow!

TOMMY (*more to herself than to* BILL). "Tomorrow and tomorrow." That's Shakespeare. (*calls to* BILL) You say that was Shakespeare?

BILL (*offstage*). Right, baby, right!

TOMMY. I bet Shakespeare was Black! You know how we love poetry. That's what give him away. I bet he was passin'. (*laughs*)

BILL (*offstage*). Just you wait, one hundred years from now all the honkeys gonna claim our poets just like they stole our blues. They gonna try to steal Paul Laurence Dunbar and LeRoi and Margaret Walker.

TOMMY (*to herself*). God moves in a mysterious way, even in the middle of a riot. (*a knock on the door*) Great day, great day the world's on fire . . . (*opens the door,* OLDTIMER *enters. He is soaking wet. He does not recognize her right away*)

OLDTIMER. "Scuse me, I must be in the wrong place.

TOMMY (*patting her hair*). This is me. Come on in, Edmond Lorenzo Matthews. I took off my hair-piece. This is me.

OLDTIMER (*very distracted and worried*). Well, howdy-do and good mornin'. (*he has had a hard night of drinking and sleeplessness*) Where Billy-boy? It pourin' down some rain out there. (*makes his way to the window*)

TOMMY. What's the matter?

OLDTIMER (*raises the window and starts pulling in the cord, the cord is weightless and he realizes there is nothing on the end of it*). No, no, it can't be. Where is it? It's gone! (*looks out the window*)

TOMMY. You gonna catch your death. You wringin' wet.

OLDTIMER. Yall take my things in? It was a bag-a-loot. A suit and some odds and ends. It was my loot. Yall took it in?

TOMMY. No. (*realizes his desperation. She calls to* BILL *through the closed bathroom door*) Did you take in any loot that was outside the window?

BILL (*offstage*). No.

TOMMY. He said "no."

OLDTIMER (*yells out window*). Thieves, . . . dirty thieves . . . lotta good it'll do you . . .

TOMMY (*leads him to a chair, dries his head with a towel*). Get outta the wet things. You smell just like a whiskey still. Why don't you take care of yourself. (*dries off his hands*)

OLDTIMER. Drinkin' with the boys. Likker was everywhere all night long.

TOMMY. You got to be better than this.

OLDTIMER. Everything I ever put my hand and mind to do, it turn out wrong, . . . Nothin' but mistakes . . . When you don' know, you don' know. I don' know nothin'. I'm ignorant.

TOMMY. Hush that talk . . . You know lotsa things, everybody does. (*helps him remove wet coat*)

OLDTIMER. Thanks. How's the trip-tick?

TOMMY The what?

OLDTIMER Trip-tick. That's a paintin'.

TOMMY. See there, you know more about art than I do. What's a trip-tick? Have some coffee and explain me a trip-tick.

OLDTIMER (*proud of his knowledge*). Well, I tell you, . . . a trip-tick is a paintin' that's in three parts . . . but they all belong together to be looked at all at once. Now . . . this is the first one . . . a little innocent girl . . . (*unveils picture*)

TOMMY. She's sweet.

OLDTIMER. And this is "Wine In The Wilderness" . . The Queen of the Universe . . . the finest chick in the world.

TOMMY (TOMMY *is thoughtful as he unveils the second picture*). That's not me.

OLDTIMER. No, you gonna be this here last one. The worst gal in town. A messed-up chick that—that—(*he unveils the third canvas and is face to face with the almost blank canvas, then realizes what he has said. He turns to see the stricken look on* TOMMY's *face*)

TOMMY. The messed-up chick, *that's* why they brought me here, ain't it? That's why he wanted to paint me! Say it!

OLDTIMER. No, I'm lyin', I didn't mean it. It's the society that messed her up. Awwwww, Tommy, don't look that-a-way. It's art, . . . it's only art . . . He couldn't mean you . . . it's art . . . (*the door opens.* CYNTHIA *and* SONNY-MAN *enter*)

SONNY-MAN. Anybody want a ride down . . . down . . . down . . . downtown? What's wrong? Excuse me . . . (*starts back out*)

TOMMY (*blocking the exit to* CYNTHIA *and* SONNY-MAN). No, come on in. Stay with it . . . "Brother" . . . "Sister." Tell 'em what a trip-tick is, Oldtimer.

CYNTHIA (*very ashamed*). Oh, no.

TOMMY. You don't have to tell 'em. They already know. The messed-up chick! How come you didn't pose for that, my sister? The messed-up chick lost her home last night, . . . burnt out with no place to go. You and Sonny-man gave me comfort, you cheered me up and took me in, . . . *took me in!*

CYNTHIA. Tommy, we didn't know you, we didn't mean . . .

TOMMY. It's all right! I was lost but now I'm found! Yeah, the blind can see! (*she dashes behind the screen and puts on her clothing, sweater, skirt etc.*)

OLDTIMER (*goes to the bathroom door*). Billy, come out!

SONNY-MAN. Billy, step out here, please! (BILL *enters shirtless, wearing dungarees*) Oldtimer let it out 'bout the triptych.

BILL. The rest of you move on.

TOMMY (*looking out from behind screen*). No, don't go a step. You brought me here, see me out!

BILL. Tommy, let me explain it to you.

TOMMY (*coming out from behind screen*). I gotta check out my apartment, and my clothes and money. Cynthia, . . . I can't wait for anybody to open the door or look out for me and all that kinda crap you talk. A bunch-a liars!

BILL. Oldtimer, why you . . .

TOMMY. Leave him the hell alone. He ain't said nothin' that ain' so!

SONNY-MAN. Explain to the sister that some mistakes have been made.

BILL. Mistakes have been made, baby. The mistakes were yesterday, this is today . . .

TOMMY. Yeah, and I'm Tomorrow, remember? Trouble is I was Tommin' to you, to all of you, . . . "Oh, maybe they gon' like me." . . . I was your fool, thinkin' writers and painters know moren' me, that maybe a little bit of you would rub off on me.

CYNTHIA. We were wrong. I knew it yesterday. Tommy, I told you not to expect anything out of this . . . this arrangement.

BILL. This is a relationship, not an arrangement.

SONNY-MAN. Cynthia, I tell you all the time, keep outta other people's business. What the hell you got to do with who's gonna get what outta what? You and Oldtimer, yakkin' and hakkin'. (*to* OLDTIMER) Man, your mouth gonna kill you.

BILL. It's me and Tommy. Clear the room.

TOMMY. Better not. I'll kill him! The "Black people" this and the "Afro-American" . . . that . . . You ain' got no use for none-a us. Oldtimer, you their fool too. 'Til I got here they didn't even know your damn name. There's something inside-a me that says I ain' suppose to let *nobody* play me cheap. Don't care how much they know! (*she sweeps some of the books to the floor*)

BILL. Don't you have any forgiveness in you? Would I be beggin' you if I didn't care? Can't you be generous enough . . .

TOMMY. Nigger, I been too damn generous with you, already. All-a these people know I wasn't down here all night posin' for no pitcher, nigger!

BILL. Cut that out, Tommy, and you not going anywhere!

TOMMY. You wanna bet? Nigger!

BILL. Okay, you called it, baby, I did act like a low, degraded person . . .

TOMMY (*combing out her wig with her fingers while holding it*). Didn't call you no low, degraded person. Nigger! (*to* CYNTHIA *who is handing her a comb*) "Do you have to wear a wig?" Yes! To soften the blow when yall go up side-a my head with a baseball bat. (*going back to taunting* BILL *and ignoring* CYNTHIA's *comb*) Nigger!

BILL. That's enough-a that. You right and you're wrong too.

TOMMY. Ain't a-one-a us you like that's alive and walkin' by you on the street . . . you don't like flesh and blood niggers.

BILL. Call me that, baby, but don't call yourself. That what you think of yourself?

TOMMY. If a Black somebody is in a history book, or printed on a pitcher, or drawed on a paintin', . . . or if they're a statue, . . . dead, and outta the way, and can't talk back, then you dig 'em and full-a so much-a damn admiration and talk 'bout "*our*" history. But when you run into us livin' and breathin' ones, with the life's blood still pumpin' through us, . . . then you comin' on 'bout how we ain' never together. You hate us, that's what! *You hate Black me*!

BILL (*stung to the heart, confused and saddened by the half truth which applies to himself*). I never hated you, I never will, no matter what you or any of the rest of you do to *make* me hate you. I won't! Hell, woman, why do you say that! Why would I hate you?

TOMMY. Maybe I look too much like the mother that gave birth to you. Like the Ma and Pa that worked in the post office to buy you a house and a screen door with a damn duck on it. And you so ungrateful you didn't even like it.

BILL. No, I didn't, baby. I don't like screen doors with ducks on 'em.

TOMMY. You didn't like who was livin' behind them screen doors. Phoney Nigger!

BILL. That's all! Damnit! Don't go there no more!

TOMMY. Hit me, so I can tear this place down and scream bloody murder.

BILL (*somewhere between laughter and tears*). Looka here, baby, I'm willin' to say I'm wrong, even in fronta the room fulla people . . .

TOMMY (*through clenched teeth*). Nigger.

SONNY-MAN. The sister is upset.

TOMMY. And you stop callin' me "the" sister, . . . if you feelin' so brotherly why don't you say "*my*" sister? Ain't no we-ness in your talk. "The" Afro-American, "the" black man, there's no we-ness in you. Who you think *you* are?

SONNY-MAN. I was talkin' in general er . . . *my* sister, 'bout the masses.

TOMMY. There he go again. "The" masses. Tryin' to make out like we pitiful and you got it made. You the masses your damn self and don't even know it. (*another angry look at* BILL) Nigger.

BILL (*pulls dictionary from shelf*). Let's get this ignorant "nigger" talk squared away. You can stand some education.

TOMMY. You *treat* me like a nigger, that's what. I'd rather be called one than treated that way.

BILL (*questions* TOMMY). What is a nigger? (*talks as he is trying to find word*) A nigger is a low, degraded person, *any* low degraded person. I learned that from my teacher in the fifth grade.

TOMMY. Fifth grade is a liar! Don't pull that dictionary crap on me.

BILL (*pointing to the book*). Webster's New World Dictionary of The American Language, College Edition.

TOMMY. I don't need to find out what no college white folks say nigger is.

BILL. I'm telling you it's a low, degraded person. Listen. (*reads from the book*) Nigger, N-i-g-g-e-r, . . . A Negro . . . A member of any dark-skinned people . . . Damn. (*amazed by dictionary description*)

SONNY-MAN. Brother Malcolm *said* that's what they meant, . . . nigger is a Negro, Negro is a nigger.

BILL (*slowly finishing his reading*). A vulgar, offensive term of hostility and contempt. Well, so much for the fifth grade teacher.

SONNY-MAN. No, they do not call low, degraded white folks niggers. Come to think of it, did you ever hear whitey call Hitler a nigger? Now if some whitey digs us, . . . the others might call him a nigger-*lover,* but they don't call him no nigger.

OLDTIMER. No, they don't.

TOMMY (*near tears*). When they say "nigger," just dry-long-so, they mean educated you and uneducated me. They hate you and call you "nigger," I called you "nigger" but I love you. (*there is dead silence in the room for a split second*)

SONNY-MAN (*trying to establish peace*). There you go. There you go.

CYNTHIA (*cautioning* SONNY-MAN). Now is not the time to talk, darlin'.

BILL. You love me? Tommy, that's the greatest compliment you could . . .

TOMMY (*sorry she said it*). You must be runnin' a fever, nigger, I ain' said nothin' 'bout lovin' you.

BILL (*in a great mood*). You did, yes, you did.

TOMMY. Well, you didn't say it to me.

BILL. Oh, Tommy, . . .

TOMMY (*cuts him off abruptly*). And don't you dare say it now. I'm tellin' you, . . . it ain't to be said now. (*checks through her paper bag to see if she has everything. Starts to put on the wig, changes her mind, holds it to end of scene. Turns to the others in the room*) Oldtimer, . . . my brothers and my sister.

OLDTIMER. I wish I was a thousand miles away, I'm so sorry. (*he sits at the foot of the model stand*)

TOMMY. I don't stay mad, it's here today and gone tomorrow. I'm sorry your feelin's got hurt, . . . but when I'm hurt I turn and hurt back. Somewhere, in the middle of last night, I thought the old me was gone, . . . lost forever, and gladly. But today was flippin' time, so back I flipped. Now it's "turn the other cheek" time. If I can go through life other-cheekin' the white folk, . . . guess yall can be other-cheeked too. But I'm goin' back to the nitty-gritty crowd, where the talk is we-ness and us-ness. I hate to do it but I have to thank you 'cause I'm walkin' out with much more than I brought in. (*goes over and looks at the queen in the "Wine In The Wilderness" painting*) Tomorrow-Marie had such a lovely yesterday. (BILL *takes her hand, she gently removes it from his grasp*) Bill, I don't have to wait for anybody's by-your-leave to be a "Wine In The Wilderness" woman. I can be it if I wanta, . . . and I am. I am. I am. I'm not the one you made up and painted, the very pretty lady who can't talk back, . . . but I'm "Wine In The Wilderness" . . . alive and kickin', me . . . Tomorrow-Marie, cussin' and fightin' and lookin' out for my damn self 'cause ain' nobody else 'round to do it, dontcha know. And, Cynthia, if my hair is straight, or if it's natural, or if I wear a wig, or take it off, . . . that's all right; because wigs . . . shoes . . . hats . . . bags . . . and even this . . . (*she picks up the African throw she wore a few moments before . . . fingers it*) They're just what what you call . . . access . . . (*fishing for the word*) . . . like what you wear with your Easter outfit . . .

CYNTHIA. Accessories.

TOMMY. Thank you, my sister. Accessories. Somethin' you add or take off. The real thing is takin' place on the inside . . . that's where the action is. That's "Wine In The Wilderness," . . . a woman that's a real one and a good one. And yall just better believe I'm it. (*she proceeds to the door*)

BILL. Tommy. (*she turns. He takes the beautiful queen, "Wine In The Wilderness" from the easel*) She's not it at all, Tommy. This chick on the canvas, . . . nothin' but accessories, a dream I drummed up outta the junk room of my mind. (*places the "queen" to one side*) You are and . . . (*points to* OLDTIMER) . . . Edmund Lorenzo Matthews . . . the real beautiful people, . . . Cynthia . . .

CYNTHIA (*bewildered and unbelieving*). Who? Me?

BILL. Yeah, honey, you and Sonny-man, don't know how beautiful you are. (*indicates the other side of the model stand*) Sit there.

SONNY-MAN (*places cushions on the floor at the foot of the model stand*). Just sit here and be my beautiful self. (*to* CYNTHIA) Turn on, baby, we gonna get our picture took. (CYNTHIA *smiles*)

BILL. Now there's Oldtimer, the guy who was here before there were scholarships and grants and stuff like that, the guy they kept outta the schools, the man the factories wouldn't hire, the union wouldn't let him join . . .

SONNY-MAN. Yeah, yeah, rap to me. Where you goin' with it, man? Rap on.

BILL. I'm makin' a triptych.

SONNY-MAN. Make it, man.

BILL (*indicating* CYNTHIA *and* SONNY-MAN). On the other side, Young man and Woman, workin' together to do our thing.

TOMMY (*quietly*). I'm goin' now.

BILL. But you belong up there in the center, "Wine In The Wilderness" . . . that's who you are (*moves the canvas of "the little girl" and places a sketch pad on the easel*) The nightmare, about all that I've done disappearing before my eyes. It was a good nightmare. I was painting in the dark, all head and no heart. I couldn't see until you came, baby. (*to* CYNTHIA, SONNY-MAN *and* OLDTIMER) Look at Tomorrow. She came through the biggest riot of all, . . .somethin' called "Slavery," and she's even comin' through the "now" scene, . . . folks laughin' at her, even her own folks laughin' at her. And look *how* . . . with her head high like she's poppin' her fingers at the world. (*takes up charcoal pencil and tears old page off sketch pad so he can make a fresh drawing*) Aw, let me put it down, Tommy. "Wine In The Wilderness," you gotta let me put it down so all the little boys and girls can look up and see you on the wall. And you know what they're gonna say? "Hey, don't she look like somebody we know?" (TOMMY *slowly returns and takes her seat on the stand.* TOMMY *is holding the wig in her lap. Her hands are very graceful looking against the texture of the wig*) And they'll be right, you're somebody they know . . . (*he is sketching hastily. There is a sound of thunder and the patter of rain*) Yeah, roll them hoops and bicycle wheels. (*music is low. Music up higher as* BILL *continues to sketch. Curtain*)

CAROL FREEMAN

The Suicide

A one-act play

Characters

THE SUICIDE

THE WIFE

THE PREACHER

THE NEIGHBOR

THE COPS

The scene is a small cramped living bedroom in an apartment; against one wall on sawhorses and planks, a plain casket, draped with a lace tablecloth, at each end withered flowers in vases, and soda pop bottles. The room is very crowded, containing a double bed, some kitchen chairs. On the wall, directly over the casket, is a small carpet, with The Last Supper scene on it. Next to that is a calendar from the New Light Church with a fly-blown picture of a café au lait family, on their knees in a church pew, grinning ecstatically at the ceiling. Sounds of muted merriment from the street, below. In a room off the living room, comes the smell of frying chicken, and women's voices.

THE NEIGHBOR. What ah wants tuh know, is how he git daih in the first place. Frank ain' had no car, is he? Newspapers jus' say he jumped, nombah some thousan' jumped from the bridge, didn't hardly say much mo'.

WIFE. Ah tell ya how, mussa bummed him a ride, fum somebody,

NEIGHBOR. Got enny mo' in that showtneck?

WIFE. Take it all. Wine ain' what ah needs now, issen you got a cuppla' dollahs ah could have the loan of tell toomarrie mawning? Frank's momma gon' cum git the body then tuh ship back to loozana, en um gonna hit huh fuh leas' twenny bucks.

NEIGHBOR. Bitch, if ah had moe'n a kwarder you thank ah'd be settin heah? (*She fidgets nervously, and wipes her throat with a dishcloth.*) Damn! It's hot in heah, open up a

---

From *Black Fire: An Anthology of Afro-American Writing,* ed. LeRoi Jones (Amiri Baraka) and Larry Neal (New York: Morrow, 1968).

winder or somethin', shit, ah got highblood pressuah an dis heat gonna mek me fain inna minit.

WIFE. Ef ya havin' hot flashes, go stand in front of the frigidaih and stick yo' haid inside, but ain gon open dese winders, evvy fly in ten miles, be done come in heah then. (*She speaks sourly.*) Frank, ya know Frank, he railly was a good man, 'cept readin' o-all them books, and drankin' so much wine done rumn him crazy. But he was good. (*She is silent, with her desire to explain to the neighbor how Frank had been.*) Ah mean, he didn't hit me, didn't take mah change, didn't cheat on me, welllll . . . (*There is a knock at the door, loud, impatient. The women are silent.*)

WIFE. Wait uh minute, somebody at the do'. Jes' uh minute. (*She raises her voice to the door, and then stands up; a gaunt black woman, perhaps thirty, or forty. Her eyes are red, she has on a purple crêpe dress, with sequins and rhinestones down the front; the dress is too large, her hair is dyed an obvious red. She is graying. High-heel black shoes, and no stockings, her hands are blunt and coarse, the nails bitten to the quick, but painted a thick red. Going to the door, she stumbles on the coffin, stares at it a moment, then opens the door.*)

PREACHER. Mrs. Frank Jones?

WIFE. Yes, won't ya please come in, Revend.

(*enter the* PREACHER, *a very young, stocky black man in a dark suit, and white collar. He has on horned-rimmed glasses, and a black felt hat. Under one arm is tucked a large black Bible. He is a pompous man, recently out of divinity school. He speaks formal English, and, aware of his importance, gives himself airs. He enters, and stands in the middle of the crowded room, ill at ease.*)

PREACHER—(*extending his hand*). Harrumph! I am Reverend Theophilious Handee, your landlady told me of your misfortune, plus I read in the paper of your husband's untimely demise, and although neither you nor your husband were members of my congregation, I felt it my Christian duty to come to you in this time of need, and offer up a few prayers to the Lord for this unfortunate soul.

WIFE. Would you lak to rest yo' hat?

PREACHER. Indeed, indeed.

WIFE. Y'all kin set down on de bed ef you wants to, ain' got many chaihs 'cep them kitchen ones. (*The preacher sits gingerly on the edge of the bed with his hat in his hand. The woman is now uncertain what to do next; she walks over and lays her hand on the casket, hesitantly, with her back to the preacher. She turns suddenly.*)

WIFE. Y'all want to see Frank? Kin ef yu wants to, ah got the lid closed on count of the flies, but you kin look ef you wants to.

PREACHER. Don't mind if I do. (*He crosses over to the casket, the woman raises the lid, and they both stare intently at the body. The* NEIGHBOR *enters silently from the kitchen, her glass in her hand, and stands behind the* PREACHER *and peers at the body.*)

NEIGHBOR. Ummph, Ummmph, ummmph!

(*The* PREACHER *and the wife jump, startled. The* PREACHER *is really shook.*)

PREACHER (*his voice unnaturally high*). Good God, woman! Where did you come from?

NEIGHBOR (*her voice surly, and blurred*). Ah come from the kitchen, where you thank ah come from? (*She finishes her drink.*) Where you come from?

WIFE. Ah, woman, hush! This here's the preacher.

NEIGHBOR. Hell, ah know what he is. (*She speaks petulantly. There is a silence; they stand uncomfortably with each other. The wife closes the coffin. Next door, suddenly, comes the sound of a record player, and Jimmy Reed, blaring out a blues song. The* NEIGHBOR *goes over and bangs on the wall.*) Turn that off! Turn that music off! We got dead folks in heah! (*A muffled voice through the wall yells* 'Fuck you!' *The* NEIGHBOR *turns to the wife.*) Who is that next do?

WIFE. Some ol' hoa, what's gonna git huh ass kicked tomorrow! (*She has raised her voice so that the woman next door can hear.*)

PREACHER. For goodness sakes! Please, Mrs. Jones! (*The* PREACHER *clears his throat and opens his Bible. There is a knock at the door, then a voice through the door*): Please don' kick my ass tomorrow, bitch! Come on out heah and kick it now, come on out!

WIFE (*screaming*). Ya gawdam right ah will! (*She grabs one of the soda pop bottles, empties the wilted flowers on the floor, and rushes offstage. Outside can be heard the two women screaming at each other, then the sounds of tussling. The* PREACHER *jumps from the bed, and stares at the* NEIGHBOR.)

PREACHER. Somebody should stop them, this is no way to hold a wake! If they don't stop I'm going home! This is indecent!

NEIGHBOR (*goes into the kitchen, and returns with a butcher knife*). Set down, preacher, Mrs. Jones be right back. Ah'll stop this shit. (*She leaves. Outside can be heard a full-scale battle, with screams, more curses. The* PREACHER *jumps over to the coffin and lifts the lid. He stares intently at the body, and returns to the bed. He opens his Bible, and reads something, then he goes to the door. Suddenly, from outside*)

WIFE. Aw, shit! The bitch done stabbed that hoa! (*screams*) Somebody call the ambulance! Call the cops! (*The* PREACHER *grabs his hat, and opens the door and steps out into the hall. Muted sounds from outside, then sirens, heavy steps on the stairs.*) Cops! heah the cops!

COP. Get back! Get back, let me through! All right what happened here? (*murmuring voices*) Hold it! One at a time. Reverend, what happened here?

PREACHER. Officer, I cannot tell you all the details. I was inside, with the body.

COP. What body? What the hell are you talking about?

PREACHER. Well, uh, uh, the body in there, in the casket. (*reenter the* PREACHER, *and the* COP *into the room.*)

COP. Jeesus, what's going on here?

PREACHER. Well, I was saying, Officer, I came over here to Mrs. Jones to help her mourn the passing of her husband, even though she nor her husband were members of my congregation. I was given to understand that she could not afford a church ceremony, and as the body was being shipped out tonight, for burial in the family plot in Louisiana, I . . .

COP. Hold it, Rev. (*He crosses to the door, and yells outside to another policeman.*) Hey Art! Come in here, you gotta see this! Nigger bitches fighting over a dead man! (*A second* COP *enters, behind him is the* WIFE. *They close the door, the* WIFE *sits on the bed.*)

COP. All right, Rev. Tell it from the start . . . Hold it, who is this woman? Is this the one that did the stabbing?

SECOND COP. Naw, she's out in the wagon. We're taking this one in, too, she started the whole thing.

WIFE. (*Her face is bruised, one eye is closing, her hair awry, her dress torn, she stands over the coffin. She yells angrily.*) Who opened dis coffin? Flies! The flies on Frank! Mothafuckas! You bastids! Told you to keep that lid closed! Now the flies on him!

COP. Christ! Get her out of here! (*The* SECOND COP *grabs the* WIFE *and hustles her out the door. She is still screaming.*)

WIFE. Let me go! Let me go, mothafucka!

SECOND COP. Oww! You go to jail for that, bitch! (*The door closes. The* PREACHER *closes the coffin, and stands by it. The* COP *walks over and opens it, and stares at the body.*)

PREACHER. Please close it, Officer. The flies . . .

MARVIN E. JACKMON (MARVIN X)

Flowers for the Trashman

A one-act drama

THIS PLAY IS DEDICATED TO MY PARENTS.
SOMETIMES LOVE IS IMPOSSIBLE
—LIFE WON'T STAND FOR IT.
  —MEJ

Characters

  JOE SIMMONS—Negro college student

  WES—his hoodlum friend

  YOUNG NEGRO PAROLEE

  MIDDLE-AGED, BOURGEOIS WHITE MAN

  JAILER

SETTING: *Jail cell is barred. Bench runs length of back wall. The audience views the action through bars except in Scene Two, when Joe is in phone booth.*
  The time is the present, 1 A.M.
  (*At rise, we see the white man gripping the bars madly and shouting.*)

MAN. Damnit, I wanna make a phone call. Jailer! By god, you better let me outta here. I'm not guilty, I'm not guilty, I tell you. (*Pause.*) Jailer! I didn't do anything. I tell you I didn't do anything. You won't get away with this, Jailer. I know my constitutional rights—I pay my taxes. Believe me, I know some very important people around here; somebody's going to pay, that's for sure—somebody's going to pay for this. (*Frustrated.*) Jailer. Where's the damn jailer around here? Where is he? Jailer!

(*He stands defeated. The* JAILER *enters with* WES *and* JOE *dressed in sport attire:* WES *in hip style,* JOE *in collegiate. Their clothing is disheveled;* WES *has bandage over left temple.*)

From *Black Fire: An Anthology of Afro-American Writing,* ed. LeRoi Jones (Amiri Baraka) and Larry Neal (New York: Morrow, 1968).

JAILER (*When boys are seated. Playfully*). Now what's all the noise about, Mister? Hell, I didn't tell you to get arrested—it's not my fault, so just take it easy, all right? I'm only the jailer, I can't do anything.

MAN. You can allow me to make a phone call; by God, you can do that. I'm no criminal, I'm a respectable citizen. I don't belong here, here with these—

JAILER. Of course, of course you can make a phone call. I told you you could make one, soon as I got a break.

MAN. Well, Jesus Christ, you told me that two hours ago. You think a person can wait forever? Seems like I been in this damn cell for two centuries.

JAILER. Well, I was busy taking care of those two jerks. (WES *gives him the finger.*) Better watch that, sonny, you're in enough trouble as it is, fighting an officer. Who in the hell do you niggers think you are?

WES (*Nasty*). Yo mama!

JOE. Wes, be cool, man.

JAILER. Better watch your mouth, boy. Say something else smart and I'll—

WES (*Attempting to rise, but restrained by* JOE). And you'll what, you'll what, goddamnit?

JOE (*Pulling* WES *down*). Wes, c'mon, sit down. Sit down, man. Be cool, Wes, just be cool.

JAILER (*To* WHITE *man*). C'mon, Mister, let's make that phone call. (*They exit stage left.*)

JOE. Man, you jive too much.

WES. Ah, Joe, damn that cat.

JOE. Just be cool, man. All right?

WES (*Laughing*). I'm cool, baby. Gimme some slack—just a teaspoon fulla slack.

JOE (*Relaxed*). Go to hell. Wes. (*pause*) Wes, why you wanna call that cop a motherfucker?

WES. Joe, don't bug me about that mess. Hell, you saw they damn near ran over us. Think I was gonna stand up there and smile? You must be a damn fool.

JOE. But you didn't have to call 'em no motherfucker.

WES. What else is they, Joe? Huh? What else is they?

JOE (*Disgusted*). I shoulda kept ma ass at the pad. You're nothing but a hang up, I swear.

WES (*Teasingly*). Ah, man.

JOE. Ah, man, my ass—you a hang up.

WES. But that was a pretty boss dance, wasn't it?

JOE. It was all right—wasn't no big thing. Damn sh'o wasn't worth going to jail for.

WES. I agree wit ya on that. (*brief silence*)

JOE. Man, I can't stand no jail. I can't stand it. (*stands*) I'm gettin' outta here. I'm not gonna stay in this funky, piss-ass jail. (*smiling*) I'm gonna call ma old man.

WES (*Shocked*). You ganna what?

JOE (*with emphasis*). I'm gonna call ma old man.

WES. You're jivin'. (*laughs*) You got to be jivin'.

JOE (*Pacing the floor*). I ain't jivin'—I'm not jivin' a pound. Wait 'til that white cat comes back.

WES (*Leaning back with hands on knees*). And what in the hell makes you think yo old man's gonna come down here an git ya black ass out?

JOE. Damn you, Wes. The bastard better come git me, he better . . .

WES (*Giggling*). He ain't better do nothing. Y'all ain't said not two words ta each other in seven months—and he gonna git off some coins fa yo ass?

JOE (*Sitting*). I ain't worried 'bout all that. He'll come down. He will—bet ya he will.

WES. An Skippy's a punk too, ain't he?

JOE. I don't know what Skippy is, but I'm gonna call'm soon as that gray dude comes back.

WES. Yeah, all right. (*laughs*) It'll be a rainy day in hell before old sick-ass Simmons git down to this jail.

JOE. We'll see.

WES (*playfully*). When he kicked you out, didn't he say he didn't never wanna see you no mo'?

JOE (*bugged*). Naw, he didn't say that. You know he didn't want me to leave.

WES. Sho, sho . . .

JOE. He didn't think I'd really jam, that's all. He thought if he told me to make it, I might change. You know that cat digs me: son going to college an all that stuff.

WES. Yeah, he digs ya—digs the hell outta ya. Now go call him up.

JOE. I am. (*pause*) Shit, you the main damn reason he told me to make it: comin' round there with all them skunky broads; bringing me all that damn weed—you know people can smell that stuff a mile away.

WES. Ah, that wasn't it. Y'all didn't never say nothin' ta each other, that's the reason.

JOE. Hell, we ain't never said nothin' to each other, that ain't no big thing. (*Sharply.*) Did you ever talk to your old man?

WES. Nigger, I done told you a million times I ain't never ever seen ma old man. I don't even know that the som'bitch looks like. Ma mama used to jive me bout 'm all the time. (*Pause.* WES *thinks back to his childhood.*) When I was real little, I say, "Mama, what Daddy look like?" One time she say, "Oh, he tall an light, got good hair," and stuff like that. Then another time I say, "Mama, what daddy look like?" Then she say, "Boy, why you keep askin' me bout that nigger? He big, black and funky—looks like 40 miles of bad road. Now don't ask me no mo foolish questions 'bout that no-count nigger. Go on to the store an get me a pound of hamburger meat an hurry on back here."

JOE. Boy, yo old lady is cold-blooded.

WES. Yeah, she somethin' else, man. (*pause*) But, Joe, I swear, didn't nobody stay in that pad but you an yo old man and I ain't heard y'all never say "shit" to each other; sometimes y'all didn't even say "hi." That old weak sucker'll probably have a heart attack if you call him an tell him you in jail.

JOE. I don't care. He better come git me out.

WES. And just what is you gonna do if he don't come git you?

JOE. Stay my ass in this damn jail an look like a damn fool.

WES. That's what I thought. (*silence*) Joe, I ain't jivin', you got the coldest old man in the world; he's outta sight: who ever heard of a nigger down in the ghetto selling flowers?

JOE. Wes, there's a lotta damn things you ain't heard about, and never will hear about less you git yaself together.

WES (*hurt*). Now you tryin' ta say I'm dumb, huh, man?

JOE. Naw, baby, I ain't callin' you dumb. I'm just tellin' it like it is: you jive too much. You always talkin' 'bout my old man, what the fuck did yo old man do—what did he do?

WES. I don't know. But I bet he wasn't no goddam flower man. (*lights cigarette*)

JOE. What did he do? For all you know, he could've sheveled shit.

WES (*slightly angry*). Maybe he did. I don't know and I don't really give a rusty fuck—he ain't never did nothin' fa me. But, I bet anything he didn't go round sellin' no goddam flowers. Yo old man must think he white or somethin': Niggers don't know nothin' 'bout no flowers. Nothin' 'cept roses is red and violets is blue.

JOE. Go to hell, Wes. Git off ma old man's back.

WES. What's wrong, you in love with 'm or somethin'?

JOE. That's not it. I'm just tired of people talkin' 'bout 'm—includin' yo black ass.

WES (*with mock affection*). Ah, Joey, who's been talkin' 'bout yo' old man? Hell, I can't help it if he sells flowers.

JOE (*rising and going to bars. Bitterly*). Ain't nobody asked you to help it, nigger.

WES. Now you pissed-off. I don't give a damn. (*pause.* JOE *ignores* WES. *He stands at the bars thinking to himself.*) Man, it sho was some boss soul-sisters at the dance, wasn't it? (JOE *ignores him.*) Did you see that chick I was hittin' on from L.A.? Boy, she was a stone fox, no bullshit about it. I rapped on that broad two thousand, man. But she busted me cold-blooded: told me my money wasn't big enough. She was right, cause I ain't had no coins, you know that. (*pause*) Yo' old chick, Irma, was at the dance, man. Did you see her? (JOE *says nothing.*) She come buggin' me 'bout you; she say, "Where's old cool Joe at? He still goin ta that school? You tell him I said he's a chicken-shit nigger." (JOE *gives* WES *a disgusted look.*) She still pissed off cause you quit her. I don't blame you for quittin' her, man. All that broad do is run her mouth. Wish I had me some goddam wine, man. White port and lemon juice be outta sight. (WES *sings.*)
White port.
White port an lemon juice—
White port.
Make you feel so good—
Yeah.
White port.
White port an lemon juice—
Yeah . . .

JOE (*turning suddenly to* WES). Why-don't-you-shut-yo-goddam MOUTH!

(WES *is stunned.*)

WES. Fuck you, Joe, I can sing. This is a free motherfuckin' country.

JOE. Yeah, that's why you in jail, ain't it—cause this is a free goddam country.

WES. So what, you in jail, too.

JOE (*pacing the floor*). I'm not gonna be here too much longer—bet ya that.

WES. Yeah, okay, you ain't gonna be here.

JOE (*passing in front of* WES). Wes, I would tell you something, nigger, but you'd probably laugh. Hell, in a way, it's funny.

WES. What, Joe? Tell me. I won't laugh. (*giggles*) Somethin' 'bout yo' old man?

JOE (*walking away from* WES). Ah, fuck it, man.

WES (*attempting to look serious*). Go on, man, tell me.

JOE (*now standing near* WES). Well—you know—last week I was down at Pearl's Café eatin' dinner. I don't know how come you weren't with me. You were in the pool hall or somewhere. Anyway, you heard about that broad, Sugar-lump dyin'?

WES. Yeah. Overdose?

JOE (*sitting*). Yeah, well, anyway, you know, the waitress was collectin' money to buy the broad some flowers.

WES. Ah, hell, what happened?

JOE. Well, let me tell you, goddamnit. Anyway, I was sittin' there eatin' some turkey wings or ham hocks or some shit, so this cat beside me asks the waitress who's she gonna buy the flowers from—

WES. Oh, Lord, run it on down.

JOE. Be cool, nigger. The waitress said she didn't know. So this black nigger say, "Well, baby, whatever you do, I sho' hope you don't get 'em from that nigger Simmons; that nigger ain't shit. Naw, don't deal wit him—you can't depend on him. I sees him walkin' round in that shop like he 'bout half dead. Naw, baby, don't spend no coins wit that nigger—run on uptown to the white man an git ya some decent flowers."

WES (*with restrained laughter*). He said yo ole man wasn't shit, huh?

JOE (*bitter*). Goddam right, said he wasn't shit. Then the fuckin' waitress said, "Oh, don't worry, honey, I don't do no business with that nigger no mo'; he used ta be all right— that was 'fore his wife left 'm. Now you tell that nigger you want some flowers delivered at ten in the mornin' an they liable ta not be delivered til ten that evenin'. Naw, I don't spend no money wit him—you can't depend on no nigger, you know that. Sometimes this white man up on 14th Street gives me a pretty good deal on flowers—I 'spect I'll go see him."

WES (*sympathetic*). Boy, that's cold, that sho' is cold.

JOE. You ain't jivin'. I didn't know what to do. They were tellin' the truth, most of it was the truth, anyway. But it sho' did hurt.

WES. Did they know who you was?

JOE. Hell, naw!

WES. You shoulda told 'em. I wish it was me. They wouldn't got away with that shit. I'da jumped off that stool (*he stands*): "Do you motherfuckers know who ya talkin' about? Goddamnit, Mr. Simmons is ma old man, an I don't preciate nobody talkin' 'bout 'm— y'all hipped ta that? You say somethin' else bout 'm an I'll wipe the fuckin' floor wit yo asses. I dare ya ta say somethin' else bout 'm. An' on second thought, I ain't even gonna pay for this goddam food." Yeah, that's what ya shoulda ran down to 'em (*he sits*).

JOE. I should've done somethin'. I just sat there. I couldn't eat any more. But what was I gonna say? Shit, they weren't lyin'. (*pause*) I don't know, man. Ma old man kicked me out an' all that, and we don't speak to each other, but when they said that 'bout 'm—I don't know—I wanted to be with him. I don't know why, they were tellin' the truth: he ain't nothin' no more, never was nothin' far as I'm concerned, but I wanted to be with him.

WES. I know how you feel, man. (*lights cigarette*) Want one?

JOE. Naw. (*bitter*) You know, it's a goddamn shame for a father and son to be like us. I feel kind of sorry for the dude: sixty years old; ma old lady left him; all his damn children against him; one son in prison; his daughter's on the block. What's he got to live for, huh, Wes? Gimme a cigarette, shit.

WES (*handing him a cigarette*). Well, he had ya, Joe. That old cat digs ya, man. He ran a whole bunch of stuff down to me one day I was at ya pad waitin' fa ya ta come from school. Said, ya got a lotta sense, man. But he didn't know what was wrong with ya; couldn't figure ya out; didn't know how come ya didn't never have nothing ta say to him; said he was proud of ya for goin' ta school and not turning out like old Frank: spendin' half his life behind bars. But, he said ya just didn't have no respect for 'm an he couldn't tolerate it.

JOE (*leaning against wall*). That sucker. Sounds just like him: always talking about respect—respect, my black ass. Shit, if somebody told you all your life, ever since you could remember, they was gonna do this for you and do that for you—and they didn't ever do it—they talked a bunch of trash all the goddamn time—after a while you just play freeze out on them. You know what I mean?

WES. Yeah, I know, man.

JOE. I don't hate him, man. Hell, I wanna love 'm—cause he's ma old man. Everybody wants to love their old man, ain't that right. (WES *nods.*) But I don't have no feelings for that man. I want to have some, but I don't. So much time's gone by—so much has happened to keep us apart. It's too late, man.

WES. You really think so, Joe? Y'all maybe could still bury the hatchet or somethin'.

JOE. I don't know. Maybe it is, an maybe it ain't, I don't know. Maybe'll go see the cat when we get out—if we get out.

WES. If we git out! Don't be talkin' that shit—we better get out 'fore I git mad.

JOE. Well, baby, you know how the man is.

WES. Yeah, an' I know how I am, too. I don't stand fa too much bullshit from nobody—not even the goddam white man. But you ought ta to see you old man, though. Wish the fuck I could see mine—I wouldn't even know where ta start lookin'.

JOE. I don't know, I might go see him. Maybe it ain't too late.

WES. Hell, man, you livin', ain't ya—then it ain't too late. Least you know where ya old man's at.

JOE. Yeah, I see what ya mean. I guess sometimes—sometimes we feel a certain way and just don't wanna change—we're scared, I guess. Life is a bitch.

WES. It's a motherfucker, Joe, a motherfucker.

(*The* JAILER *and* WHITE MAN *return.*)

JOE (*rising and going to the bars*). Say, I'd like to make a phone call.

JAILER. Would you, now? Well, I'll be damn. Who you gonna call, the NAACP?

JOE. I'd like ta call my father.

JAILER. Oh, he wants to call his father. Come on.

JOE (*turning to* WES). Later, Wes.

WES (*smiling*). Yeah, later, Joe. (JOE *and* JAILER *exit.* WES *stretches out on the bench. The* WHITE MAN *is standing at stage right corner of cell, near the bars.*)

Lights down on the scene.

SCENE 2

Time is same. The cell is blacked out. We see JOE *standing in phone booth down stage left.*

JOE. What you mean you not coming down? Why? Why you ain't coming down? (*pause*) Ah, what're you talkin' 'bout, I'm no better'n Frank? Didn't I tell you it wasn't my fault, didn't I say that? Ah, ain't nothin' wrong with Wes. Naw it isn't. I told you they damn near ran over us. He should've called 'em somethin'. What? What do you mean, you know how we boys are? Are you gonna come git me out? (*pause*) Why should you? Why *shouldn't* you? I'm your son, ain't I? Well, that's why. (*pause*) Ahhhhh . . . Man, you better come get me outta this place. You're not? (*pause*) Call Mamma? You must be losin' your mind. You gettin' old, man. Yeah, you must be losin' your mind. You must be. Mama's two hundred miles away. I'm askin' you. Mama's down there tryin' to be a daddy and a mama—taking care of your kids. You know she doesn't have no money. (*pause*) Man, please, please don't say nothin' to me 'bout respect. Cause it don't mean nothin' to me. Naw, it don't mean nothin'. Don't worry if I'm goin' to make it or not. I'll make it all right—I made it this far without your help. I don't appreciate what you've done for me? What have you done for me? Well, your best wasn't good enough. Respect? I know about respect. I know all I need to know about it. What's it got you? (*pause*) Hell, man, don't nobody respect you. Naw they don't. Not anymore. I do know what I'm talkin' about, yes, I do. I know 'cause I heard niggers talkin' about you. Don't make no difference who it was. Naw it doesn't, not if they were tellin' the truth. Man, stop talkin' all that trash. Are you gonna come get me out? (*pause*) You ain't, huh? Okay, okay. (*long pause*) Ahhhhh . . . Man, you ain't shit. That's right—you're not shit—no, not a goddam thing. Ah, go to hell; just take a merry ride to hell . . . (JOE *slams phone into booth and goes off stage left.*)

Lights down on the scene.

SCENE 3

At rise, JOE *is standing in center of cell.* WES *is seated, just coming out of his slumber. The* WHITE MAN *is standing quietly at stage right corner of cell, near the bars; he is watching* JOE, *whose anger and disappointment have not subsided.*

WES (*laughing*). Yo old man comin'?

JOE (*slumping on the bench next to* WES). Naw, man, he wouldn't come get me out—the black-ass nigger.

WES (*pointing to* WHITE MAN). Say, baby, watch yo mouth, you see Charlie standin' over dare.

JOE (*violent*). Wes, damn Charlie. Charlie ain't nothin'. He ain't nothin' but a goddam nigger, too.

WES (*laughing*). Cool it, Joe.

JOE. Cool it! Cool it, my motherfuckin' ass. That's all niggers do is be cool, be cool. Motherfuck a "be cool." I gotta be cool 'cause some dizzy-ass white man's standing over, looking like a goddamn fool?

WES. Joe, light'n up. That man ain't done nothin' to you.

MAN (*attempting to communicate*). Yes, yes, that's right, son, I haven't done anything to you.

JOE (*enraged, he rushes toward the* WHITE MAN). What the fuck's wrong wit you, you blue-eyed devil? You done everythin' to me, man. Every goddam thing in the books: slavery, murder, castration, starvation, frustration, humiliation—everything—you (*points finger in man's face*)—you done to me. Don't talk that bullshit 'bout you ain't done nothin' to me. Standin’ in that corner like you innocent. You guilty, motherfucker! You hipped ta that—you guilty—just as guilty as my black ass is gonna be when I see the judge. Standin’ in that corner ain’t gonna help ya one damn bit. (WES *forces* JOE *to sit down.*)

WES C’mon, Joe, give the cat some slack, man. (JOE *sits for a moment, then rushes after the man once more.*)

JOE. You scared of us niggers, Charlie? Why you scared? You made me, baby. Think on that. You made me. I’m your creation. You defined me, told me my limits, my possibilities. Yeah, everythin’ I believe in: God, the devil, democracy, all that bullshit, you gave to me, gave to me outta the kindness of your heart.

WES (*calling* JOE). Joe, c’mon. Freeze on the dude, man.

JOE (*ignoring* WES). What’re ya thinkin’, Charlie? C’mon, tell me what’s on your feeble mind. Go on, don’t be shy, run it on down to me, Mister White Man. (*pause.* JOE *paces the floor for a moment. Then, as if he had a sudden thought, continues*) I know what’s on his mind. You wanna git home to yo little white wife and yo little white kiddies in yo little white house—ain’t that right, Mister White Man? You don’t dig integration after all, do you, Mister White Man. (JOE *turns from the white man and heads for the bench. Still not satisfied, he challenges the white man.*) Now, motherfucker, if you don’t like what I said, then jump in my chest—just jump right down in my chest. (*Finally,* JOE *sits.*)

WES. Cool it, Joe. Cool it, baby.

JOE (*slumping against wall*). Fuck a “be cool,” fuck a “be cool.”

WES. Man, you the craziest nigger in the world. You been readin’ too many books. You better light’n up.

(*The* JAILER *enters with a shabbily dressed young Negro. The* JAILER *stares curiously for a moment, then exits. The* NEGRO *sits on* WES’ *right;* JOE *is on his left.*)

WES. What’s goin on, brother?

NEGRO (*slumping against wall and scratching his head*). Nothin’, Blood, nothin’.

WES. What’d ya git busted fa?

NEGRO. Ah, man, they tryin’ ta say I snatched this white bitch’s purse.

WES (*smiling*). But you didn’t do it?

NEGRO. Hell naw, man. I’m on parole. I don’t be snatchin’ no goddamn purses.

JOE (*coming out of depression*). Ah, nigger, you know you snatched that purse, stop lyin’.

NEGRO (*to* WES). Blood, who is that square lookin’ motherfucker? He git busted wit you?

WES. Yeah, this is ma old square pardner. (*slaps* JOE *on the knee*)

NEGRO (*to* JOE). Look, Blood, like I say, I don’t be snatchin’ no goddamn purses—and I don’t be bullshitin’ too much, either.

WES. You have to excuse him, brother, he didn’t mean no harm.

NEGRO. Yeah, okay. (*pause*) Gotta smoke, man? (WES *gives him a cigarette.*) What’d y’all git busted fa?

WES. Ah, we got into a little fight with some jive cops. We was comin’ from the dance.

NEGRO. Yeah. That’s cold, Blood. I jammed up by the dance; didn’t go in; didn’t have no coins.

WES. We laid dead an got some half-price tickets.

NEGRO. That’s cool. (*pause*) Blood, if they pin this shit on me, it’s all over.

WES. How long you been out, brother?

NEGRO. 'Bout four months.

JOE (*interested*). Say, where'd you do time at?

NEGRO. What?

JOE. Where'd you do time at?

NEGRO. Soledad. Why you wanna know?

JOE. No shit, you was in Soledad?

WES. He got a brother down there.

NEGRO. Yeah. I was in North.

JOE. My brother's in North. You might know 'm.

NEGRO. What's his name?

JOE. Frank. Frank Simmons.

NEGRO. Simmons! Frank Simmons not yo brother?

JOE. Yes he is, he's my brother, 'lease that's what ma mama told me. You know 'm, huh?

NEGRO. Ah, man, sho', I know 'm. You not his brother? (JOE *nods*.) I'll be goddamn. Shit, yeah, I know Frank. Used to sit in his house an listen ta sides. Frank's somethin' else. Boy, that dude don't care 'bout nobody, nothin'. Is you the one send 'm all them books 'bout the Negro—I mean 'bout the black man—Frank say it ain't no such thing as a Negro. He's a crazy dude, man. You the one send 'm them books?

JOE. Yeah, that's me.

NEGRO (*shaking his head in remembrance*). That nigger talked about you a lot. Don't you go to college?

JOE. Yeah, when I can make it.

NEGRO. Man, what the fuck you doin' in here?

JOE. You know how the man is.

NEGRO. Yeah, he's a som'bitch all right.

JOE. Plus, I have a friend who likes to fuck up all the time. (JOE *playfully elbows* WES *in the side.*)

WES. Say, baby, light'n up on me—gimme some slack.

JOE. Wes, I'd whip yo ass, if you wasn't bigger than me.

NEGRO. Man, is you tryin ta be a writer or somethin' like that?

JOE. Yeah, somethin' like that.

WES. He ain't shit.

JOE. Go to hell, Wes.

NEGRO. Frank showed us some stuff you wrote, it was in a magazine.

JOE (*smiling*). Oh, yeah?

NEGRO. Yeah, it reminded me of some of that stuff that blood cat—what's his name, that little ugly dude—Boldin?

WES. Man, you mean James Baldwin?

NEGRO. Yeah, that's his name, Baldwin—you write like him. You dig that cat?

JOE (*shrugging his shoulders*). Yeah, I think he's pretty cool; he's honest. He's a writer that wants to be a man; that's what I want to be, a man . . .

NEGRO. I know what ya mean. But I dig 'm cause he's a soul brother. But ain't that cat a fag?

JOE. I don't know, man.

WES. Yeah, he's a fag.

JOE. And just how in the hell do you know what he is, Wes? You been in bed wit 'm?

WES. Ah, man, you know that cat's a fag.

JOE. And so goddam what if he is? Jesus could've been a fag.

NEGRO. Blood, you sho' is cold, getting' down on J.C. like that.

JOE (*laughing*). Well, he could've been—all them damn disciples he had.

WES. Shut up, Joe, you fulla shit.

JOE (*still laughing*). Bet ya old J.C. really had a gay time spreadin' the gospel.

NEGRO. Blood, you crazier'n yo' brother. (*pause*) But Frank really cracked me up when he got ta runnin' down yo' old man.

WES. Oh, Lord.

JOE. What'd Frank say, 'bout 'm?

NEGRO. Blood, he was sho' down on that dude. Talkin' 'bout yo' old man an dem flowers he be sellin'.

WES. Yeah, he's a old flower man—ain't that cold?

JOE. Fuck you, Wes.

NEGRO. You know, we all had different names for our fathers—didn't hardly none of us dig our fathers, sho' was cold—but Frank gave your old man the coldest name of all.

WES. What'd he call'm, what'd he call 'm, man?

NEGRO (*laughing*). The Trashman. (JOE *shakes his head hopelessly*)

WES (*also laughing*). The Trashman! Lord have mercy.

NEGRO. Yeah, that's what he called 'm. Frank is somethin' else.

WES (*still laughing*). The Trashman! Naw, naw, he didn't call him that.

NEGRO. Frank say, ever since he could remember yo' old man ain't talked nothin' but trash. He say that's reason yo' old lady put 'm down: she got tired of listenin' to his trash. Boy, we used to crack up—goddamn . . .

JOE (*smiling, but slightly disgusted*). I don't know what to say 'bout ma brother.

WES. The Trashman, The Trashman! That's cold, that's too cold.

JOE. Go to hell, Wes.

WES. When's he gittin out, Joe?

JOE. When he's paid his dues and yo mama's paid hers!

WES (*standing and pointing his finger at* JOE). Man, you cool that shit 'bout ma old lady, all right?

NEGRO. Boy, you dudes somethin' else.

JOE. You light'n up on my old man (*The* JAILER *enters slowly, but with an urgent and serious air.*)

JAILER (*unlocking the door*). Mr. Simmons?

JOE (*rising*). Yeah?

JAILER. Please come with me. (JOE *leaves cell.*)

WES (*to* JAILER). Don't whip 'm too hard. (JAILER *ignores* WES. *They exit.*)

Lights down on the scene.

SCENE 4

JOE *is being brought back into cell. He is very grave and solemn. The* JAILER *locks him in but doesn't leave. Instead, he stands, curiously watching.*

WES (*as* JOE *comes toward the bench*). Say, man, what hit you? What's wrong, Joe, what happened?

JOE (*slumping on bench*). The cat had a heart attack, Wes. He's dead . . . dead, man . . .

WES. Who! Your father?

NEGRO. You jivin—when?

JOE. He was coming to get me, Wes. (*The* JAILER *exits slowly.*)

WES. Man, that's cold. (*pause*) I'm sorry, man. (JOE *rises and, with hands in pockets, goes to bars;* WES *follows him.*) Your old man acted like he was sick all the time, Joe. But I didn't know he had a bad heart or nothin' like that.

JOE (*gripping bars*). I didn't either, Wes. (*pause*) There's so goddamn much I didn't know 'bout 'm—so goddamn much. I don't know why we couldn't ever talk. I don't know. (*pause*) We could've said somethin' to each other, something. We didn't talk about nothin', man—the president, Cuba, integration, nothin'. How could we be so far apart, Wes? So far apart and yet so close—so close together. How come I didn't git to know him, Wes? He was a man, wasn't he? I was his son—what kept us apart? (*pause*) And he was coming to get me, Wes. Ain't that cold, he was coming to get me.

WES. Yeah, that's cold, Joe.

JOE. Think we'll get out in the mornin'?

WES. Probably so, Joe.

JOE. Hell, we didn't do nothin'.

WES. I know, Joe.

JOE. They damn near ran over us, Wes.

WES. I know, man.

JOE. I gotta start doin' somethin', man.

WES. Yeah, Joe.

JOE. I gotta start doin' somethin'. The old man'd go for that. Wouldn't he, Wes?

WES. Sho' he would, Joe.

JOE. I wanna talk to ma sons, Wes. Know what I mean?

WES. Yeah, man, I dig ya.

JOE. That's why I gotta start doin' somethin'—I wanna talk to ma sons.

WES. C'mon, let's sit down, Joe. (*They turn to sit.*)

Curtain

The Monster

A one-act play

SCENE ONE

Day—probably afternoon, though there is no real sense of a time of day—light, darkness, etc.
Small, cave-like room, with the slanted beams of an attic, or a belfry. This is at the top
of a seldom used building, or portion of a building, on the campus of a colored college. The
one window is stage right (can be off-stage right) and on a rise; it is covered with black thick
curtains. Entrance (and exit) is down stage left. The over-all sense is of a circle shaded and
shaped to a triangle. The furniture is mainly boxes set around the room to enforce the trian-
gle, with a large desk-table or maybe three boxes with a cover, rear-center; there are candles
set in liquor bottles and a couple of ashtrays around. The incongruous pieces are: a once plush
but now nearly ruined easy chair centerstage, and a dresser stage right.
As it begins ALI *and* RICK *are at desk listening to end of a tape-incoherent-on recorder.*

ALI, *shutting off tape.* Damn. It's like you said all right. How'd you say you got it?

RICK. When this sister went to his place to interview him for the school paper she took a
    big recorder—for the interview. She also took along a little one—for us. Got his wife to
    show her around the house—and left it in a good spot.

ALI. Wife. What is a creature like that doing with a wife?

RICK. She's part of the thing, you know that. What I wanna' know is where do they find
    him?! I mean how do they make 'em, create 'em like that?! How can they keep coming
    off like that!?

ALI. You know how. If we had a few centuries of practice and all the machinery set-up we
    could be turnin' 'em out like—like Mustangs and Coupe DeVille's just like they do!

RICK. I wouldn't want none in no world that I had anything to do with the shape of.

ALI. Well in a mess like this world, they can be used.

RICK. Yeh.

ALI. And you don't know where they're coming from? Just look around you brother. On
    this campus right here they're doing their best to send out some every year. RICK *makes*
    sounds of agreement. Young Frankensteins. *Assumes pose.* Striding around with their
    hands out-stretched. Ready to do whatever their masters command. Stumbling around

---

From *TDR: The Drama Review* 12.4, Black Theatre (Summer 1968): 94–105.

being moved by somebody else's mind, heart and soul! Class A stars in a horror movie! And they don't even know it! Aw, man—damn! *Touches head.*

RICK. Keep runnin' it down brother. Don't let it run *you* down.

ALI, *sighing.* I'm all right. I'll be okay. It's just—just—*Looks to entrance as, supported by* JASON *and* MIKE *on each side, enters* THE DEAN *walking in fact like Frankenstein—his arms, held at the elbows by* JASON *and* MIKE, *wave before him like a stunned blindman's, his strides come too high, slow, and long to be normal. He wears suit, tie, etc.* JASON *and* MIKE *lead him to easychair and plunk him down.* ALI *turns away from the sight.* Aw man—damn!

JASON. Look what we done brung ya'!

MIKE. The dean of all us students!

JASON. Hey, yeh. Young up and coming future leader of the society!

RICK. All of a sudden on his way down.

MIKE. You tryin' to tell us somethin' 'bout our bossman? *Tries to force* DEAN's *glasses onto him; they slide off and fall into his lap.*

ALI, *studying* DEAN *thoughtfully.* I didn't know he wore glasses.

JASON. Oh, just at home. *Assuming jitterbug air.* You see, round campus he wears sunglasses, shades, you dig, like a cat should. You dig?

MIKE, *giving* JASON *five.* Don't I though? Don't I? And he don't walk like he just did around campus either!

JASON. He don't?!

MIKE. Aw, naw. Nonea' that straight-up zombie walkin', uh-uh. My man gets down wit' it. More of a, *Cattin',* gritty-grit, groovin' dip to his bop! Youuunuhstan'?

JASON. Oh yeh! Definitely! But not too much of a dip you dig. Because he don't want to look like he is a jitterbug himself. Just want to look like he know where the jitter and the bug are coming from. In case he needs to wear that face too sometime.

MIKE, *stares at* JASON *as the joke wears out.* Yeh, I got you. Maybe we should give him just one real face to wear from now on.

They both move toward him and stand before him as if tempted to send fists into DEAN's *face.*

ALI. Cool it, man. Come on. Is he ready?

All the while DEAN *has been sitting staring straight ahead, mouth open.*

JASON, *stark tone change.* Ready as he can get.

MIKE. Yeh, we put the little truth needle to him. He can't sham now.

RICK. The serum works like the brother said huh?

JASON. Just like the brother said.

MIKE. Didn't take but a minute. And that stuff had him. And he was ready to finally be himself.

JASON. You can see the results.

ALI. What about Helen?

MIKE. She's in there getting it together.

RICK, *after he and* ALI *exchange glances.* Might as well try the key-words. Like the brother said.

All glance at each other and nod. Begin slow ritual movement before his chair, crossing and circling.

RICK, *in solo whisper.* Prestige!
JASON, *same whisper.* Prestige!
MIKE. Prestige!

DEAN's *head snaps up at word. He begins to audibly sniff the air in all directions, an excited animation coming over him.*

ALI, *turning away.* Aw man—damn!
JASON. Dig it! Dig it!
MIKE. Look at him, man! Look at him!

All still moving.

RICK, *same whisper.* Status!

JASON *and* MIKE *repeat word,* DEAN *becomes even more excited; looking and sounding very like a panting, hungry dog as he turns head in all directions.*

ALI. Damn! Damn! Damn!
RICK. Security!

JASON *and* MIKE *repeat.*
   DEAN *becomes near frantic; increasing animal sounds while bouncing in seat.*

ALI. Will you look at that shit, man? Just look at it!
RICK, Yeh, and we haven't even gotten to the big one yet.
ALI. Yeh we have, goddammit! Yeh, we have.

Leading them all to DEAN *in what becomes a shouted chant.*

ALL. ACCEPTANCE! WHITE ACCEPTANCE! ACCEPTANCE! WHITE ACCEP-
   TANCE! ACCEPTANCE! WHITE ACCEPTANCE!!

DEAN *begins to whimper and moan and squirm as a woman at the crest of love-making. They hide him from audience a moment. Then all suddenly turn from chair.*

JASON. Aw man!
MIKE. Damn!
RICK. O'oo wow. I guess that's the one all right.
ALI, *disgustedly.* Goddam! Look man, those words might have an effect on anybody! But—
   but they couldn't turn everybody into a—a—
JASON. Sick somethin'—
ALI. —a nothin'! Like—*Pointing without looking.* —like that!
RICK, *wiping face with handkerchief; same edge of disgust in tone.* Yeh. Well that's what and
   where he is. So are we going to do something with it or not!
JASON. Yeah. Do *something* with him!
MIKE. In a hurry!
ALI. Yeh. Helen! Helen!

HELEN, *off-stage*. I'm right here, Ali! I've got his—drink! Ready when you get ready!

ALI. All right. *Then to others.* Okay, looka' here.

Gathers them in a quasi-huddle, explaining idea, as lights intensify a blue haze around DEAN's *area. They come out of huddle.* ALI *goes directly before* DEAN, *others surround and circle the chair.*

ALI. Mr. Dean, sir—

OTHERS. Prestige. Status. Security.

ALI. Our most reverent Mr. Dean Sir.

OTHERS. White acceptance is yours. Caucasian glory is yours.

ALI. This is a most beautiful home you have.

OTHERS. —White and beautiful—Beautiful and white—

ALI. This is a most elegant home.

OTHERS. —White and elegant—Elegant and white—

ALI. The most beautiful and elegant home around.

OTHERS. In all the snow around—

HELEN, *off-stage*. God!

ALI. Most reverent Mr. Dean, sir—

OTHERS. —Onto thee all manner of whiteness—

ALI. To you we say, yes-sur, yes-sur, yes-sur.

OTHERS, *bowing*. All white! All white! White all!

As they've performed, DEAN's *head has come up and swayed as though listening to a classic mass. Then he's relaxed in an air of comfort and luxuriousness, and taken and lit a cigar from his breast pocket.*

JASON. He's ready now.

RICK. Definitely.

MIKE. Ain't he though.

ALI. Mr. Dean, sir. DEAN's *head comes up acknowledging.* We are honored that you've had us over sir. It has been an enlightening, thrilling evening.

MIKE. Tut-tut, and all that shit. *Touches* JASON's *outstretched palm.*

ALI. But we have to go now sir. And you don't have to show us to the door. We'll manage. You just relax, be at ease here in your—your lovely den.

RICK *motions for them to be still.*

ALI. You've been a most gracious host, sir.

DEAN *shows the effects of the flattery: caresses lapels, flicks ashes.* Can we do anything for you before we leave? To show our appreciation? An ashtray, sir? *Motions for one;* RICK *hands it.* Here you are sir. *Putting tray on arm of chair.* Would you like your shoes removed? DEAN *makes fluttery, false gesture of refusal—but is so thrilled and flattered he kicks his feet in air and leaves them there to be attended even while shaking head no.* There you are sir. We're going now. We thank you for your time and consideration. Your wife—Your wife uh—*Looks to others.*

RICK. Jane.

JASON. Yeh. She Jane; him. Tarzan.

ALI. Ah yes, Jane.

DEAN, *clears throat.* Tarzan. Yes. One of my favorite fantasy figures. Ape-like white lord of the black heathen jungle. Yes. Most interesting historical figure. Yes Burroughs. Written in—let me see—

MIKE. Wow. He's definitely ready.

JASON. Ain't he. Stripped right down.

ALI. Uh yes, I'm sure it's very interesting. But as I was about to say, your wife, Jane, is back from her trip. And she's on her way in with your drink, sir. So we have to be going now. Good-by. And thank you. Thank you. Thank you.

Backing off with others into shadows. JASON *and* MIKE *sit on opposite sides of stage. Hallelluiah chorus from the Messiah blares forth near crescendo.* ALI *sits down.* HELEN—*Jane*— *enters to the music; wearing a mini-skirted jumper outfit, with long-sleeved highcollar tights, and go-go boots. The thing about the get-up is that it is divided right down to the boots with one side being all white, the other all black—excepting gloves which are both white. A black-white costume jewelry chain dangles from her waist. Her face is white rubber mask (lavender lipstick) including a ratty blond wig. Pointedly carrying the tray she moves out in an exaggerated mince-step that is slowed down and set to the grand style of the music. After her initial moment, she breaks the feeling to give a little out-of-character shrug to the brothers, showing how ridiculous she feels; then resumes "role," posing with tray.*

HELEN. Dahling. I've brought your drink. My poo-poo.

JASON, *across to* MIKE. Her what, man?

MIKE. Her poo-poo.

JASON. Oh! That's what he is, huh?

ALI. Shhh. Dig.

DEAN. Oh, yes, Jane, my darling, Jane.

HELEN. Yes.

DEAN. Oh, my dear, dear Jane, you look so ravishingly white tonight!

HELEN. Do I dahling? Thank you. You too look quite white tonight, dear.

They both give silent-movie type cuddly laughs.

JASON. Aw, man! Turn the sound off. Or wake me up when they get to what's happening.

HELEN. Hasn't it all been just too wonderful tonight, dear? The music, the guests, and all?

DEAN. Yes, my dear. If you say so.

HELEN. Yes. And now I've brought you your drink. Dahling. *Removes ashtray, puts tray on arm of chair and sits on other arm. Her white side turned to* DEAN *and audience.*

DEAN, *rubbing his face on her white leg and arms, touching her face.* So beautifully, ravishingly, whitely white.

MIKE. Think I'm gonna' have to go to the toilet.

HELEN, *giving him a forced grin, then catching his hand as it disappears under her skirt.* Yes dahling. But your drink. Don't forget your drink. *As "real"* HELEN. Drink it!

DEAN, *stunned by her tone.* Huh?

ALI. Easy Helen, watch it.

HELEN, *correcting her tone.* Your drink, darling. Please. I made it a special one.

DEAN. Oh? Well. *"Sips" from empty glass.* Ummm. Uh, just what is it darling?

HELEN. Crushed snow.

DEAN. Oh, yes. Delight—What? What did you say dear?

ALI. Helen—

HELEN. Crushed snow, darling. I thought you'd enjoy the chilling whiteness of it sliding slowly down your throat, numbing your insides.

DEAN. Ah, yes, yes. What would I do without you. *Drinks from both glasses.* Delicious. White-stuff. Yum-yum. White-stuff. *His hands and face beginning to "devour" her white side.* Marvelous, glorious white-stuff! Ummm. Fantastic! Fabulous! All this here white-stuff!

HELEN, *forcing grins, struggling.* Dahling. Darrr-linng! *Forgetting role.* Dammit—Uh, I mean, dear. Now dear.

JASON, *rising in background.* Don't worry, baby! Just tell 'im you accept him!

MIKE, *standing also.* Yeh! And he'll blow his whole thing right there in his pants!

JASON, Yeh! *Crossing to meet* MIKE *at center; gives him "five," "ten!"*

MIKE. Yeh!

ALI. Cool it. Sit down. *They do, laughing.*

HELEN, *as* DEAN *drools and growls.* Come now, darling. Come now. Come on, now, come, dear. *Gets up, stands before him.*

DEAN. What, dear? Darling you don't mean it? Is it Sunday night already? I had no idea! My dear! My darling! *Rushes to embrace her.*

HELEN *lifts her white leg and trys to wrap it around him.*

HELEN. What!—Man what the hell you—

DEAN, *kissing and pawing as she struggles.* Mygloriouswhitestuff! Myyumyumwhitestuff! Goodwhitestuff! Marvelouswhitestuff!

ALI. Don't lose control now Helen. Lead him to it, now. Take him where you want him!

RICK, *grinning.* Yeh! Don't let him get you down, baby!

DEAN. Whitestuff! *etc. etc.* Whitestuff.

HELEN, *freeing herself, grabbing his cheeks, lips, with one hand, pointing her finger.* Yes, darling. But there is the other, dark, darker, black side of things. Remember? *Rubs the back side of her dress.*

DEAN, *touching head as though pained.* Dark? Darker? Black? How could you, dear? At a time like this? Whatever can you mean?

HELEN. What do I mean? Listen darling. Listen. *Moving and pointing toward recorder in shadows.* RICK *manipulates dials: The impressions doing Curtis Mayfields'* KEEP ON PUSH-ING, *at the point where the voices go into the hummed, strained, yearning.* Hear it, dear?

DEAN, *clutching head.* Yes! Oh yes! They're at it again! Those black-power, black awareness students are gathering again!

HELEN. Yes. Talking of black courses.

JASON. And recourses!

HELEN. Of unifying and identifying!

DEAN. Oh, God! God! Won't they let me have any peace!? Any peace at all!?

HELEN, *aside, smiling.* You definitely won't be getting any piece here.

ALI. Helen!

DEAN, *turning to look at her, his tone grim.* I suppose The Man has called for me.

HELEN. Yes, dear. He needs you. You're very important to him.

DEAN. Yes, I am. He needs me. Yes. *Sighs, straightens shoulders.* I suppose there's nothing to do but to go out and stop them.

HELEN. I suppose so dear.

DEAN. Yes, I must head them off and turn them back.

HELEN. Yes, dear.

DEAN. Come dear. I must prepare to meet them. *Points to dresser.* HELEN *goes to stand by it. Standing opposite dresser, he hands her his coat.* My ablution, dear.

JASON, *to* MIKE. His ab-what?

MIKE *points to* HELEN *opening top drawer.*

HELEN *takes out and sets bowl atop dresser, lays coat across it, and stands ready with towel.* DEAN *dips hands in, surgeon-like, and lets white liquid drain off.*

JASON. Milk?! Aw shit!

Others shush him.

DEAN, *takes towel from* HELEN *and dries hands, then turns to audience and ceremoniously touches right finger-tips to forehead and each shoulder.* In the name of the white, the might, and the fright!

MIKE. What?—Well, I'll be—*Others shush him.*

DEAN, *facing audience, as he asks for tools holds left hand out to* HELEN *without looking at her.* Gloves! *She takes from drawer and hands him black-rubber surgeon gloves. He puts them on, flexes fingers.* Beard! *Takes and puts on so-called Van Dyke style mustache-beard; practices a grimace or two.* Natural! *She hands him very "high" Afro wig. He tries it; feels it; flings it away.* I've told you that one is too high, Jane! The smaller one! Quick!

HELEN, *wry face but straight tone.* Yes, dear. I'm sorry. *Gives him shorter wig.*

DEAN, *puts on wig.* Chest! *She hands and helps buckle onto him a virility-suggesting chest-plate that reminds of both bullet-proof vest and something for the Romans—it is ebony-colored, and allows some of his tie and collar to show.* Testicles!

HELEN. What dear? *Looking.*

DEAN. Balls, Jane! Balls!

HELEN. Oh, yes, of course. Of course. Well. *Looking.* I don't think you have a pair left. Oh, yes, yes, here they are.

DEAN, *takes them; turns back to* HELEN *and audience and inserts them inside pants. Stands; straight facing audience again takes deep pleased sigh, smiles at* HELEN, *and moves down stage. Begins quick hard hand-thrusting gestures-reminiscent of first Malcolm, then Stokely, then Rap. It looks like a fencing lesson. As he carries it out further into Cagney-like belt-lifts with the forearms, into dipping his knees and wiping his sweating hands on his behind and his groin, it becomes like a dance; going even into a J.B. thing complete with the sudden dynamic grunts; goes into a kind of platform-speaker's Bugaloo.*

JASON, *giving* ALI *"ten".* Aw get it Mr. D! He's really getting into it now, ain't he?

ALI, *grinning.* Comin' outta' his soul bag brother!

MIKE. Jive motherfucker! Ain't he a bitch!

RICK *is bent with laughter.* HELEN *hides giggling face.*

DEAN, *finishes "exercises," turns to* HELEN *with wide grin.* I think I'm about ready to face them now dear. I mean, Baby. *Winks.* Baby, I mean. Have to get in character you know. *Swaggering.* Let me try one of those numbers outta' that book, now.

HELEN, *staring amused and incredulous.* Huh?—Oh, yeh. I mean, yes, dear, yes, certainly. *Looking in dresser; comes out with white-covered, official-looking book.* Ummm, let's see now—

DEAN, *finger-poppin'.* Hurry, now, dear. Baby, I mean. Hurry. I'm hot now. I'm ready. Sock it to me. Ummph!

HELEN, *character completely gone.* Yeh, all right, hot-shot, number three.

DEAN. Number three. Yes. *Moves around; then dynamically confronts audience.* Uni-ver-sity! You dig? Understand? That's what all this is about, learning to live on the universal level! Don't tell me about black men's heads being split open, black men bleeding to death! When you look at that blood don't say that's black man's blood. Say that is *Man* bleeding there! Man's blood! When you bend down to see, don't just look at the wound! Look there where the blood is seeping into the pores of the all-accepting Earth! And think of all the countless plots of soil all over this planet which for centuries have been soaking up, and gagging on, and sending back in the form of fresh flowers, the blood of man! Lift your lucky heads and look at the clouds! At the universal formations of—of—umm—uh—of—

HELEN, *disgustedly.* Shhitt!

DEAN. Huh?—Uh, what dear?

HELEN. Oh. Uh—Nothing dear. I was just saying that that's enough of that one. I mean, you have that one pretty well under control. I'm trying to find another number for you.

The others all stare with cold hatred. JASON *gets up and starts toward* DEAN *as if in a trance.* MIKE *grabs him, pulls him back.*

DEAN. Yes, yes. But it did take me quite awhile to get away from the point. Didn't it. Must brush up on that one.

JASON. Didn't it though! You motherfucker!!

MIKE. Come on, man. Don't let him bug you. Come on, now, Jason.

JASON, *really upset, wiping eyes.* Some damned clouds! Some fucking pores of the earth! I'll stomp you' brains out fucker! Yeh! Then let me see you abstract and universalize that! Hear?!

ALI, *coming over to help* MIKE *hold him.* Jace! Jace! Easy baby. You gonna' blow it now, man.

JASON. Blow what?! We know where he's comin' from! Why we gotta' listen to it all! Huh?!

DEAN, *vaguely aware of something being amiss.* Jane?—Jane?—are you going to give me another number?

ALI. We have a plan, brother, remember? We have to draw it all out first. Know the depth—

DEAN, *turning in little circles.* Jane? Jane? Are you going to give me another?

JASON, *breaking away, going toward her and him.* You wanna' give him a good number, sis-ter? Huh? You already gave him a three, right? Well now give him a six-nine, sixty-nine. Yeh! You ever—*to* DEAN—played the numbers, sissy! Huh!? You know what 369 plays for, punk?! Huh?! Hell naw! You don't know nothin' like that! Well it's the Shit-row, sucker! It plays for shit! And that's all you got in that book, your bag; nothin' but a bunch of shit.

MIKE. Yeh, and we don't need to hear no more of it. Ain't gonna' hear no more not from you we ain't.

All moving toward him now.

DEAN, *turning in half-circles.* Jane? Jane? A number from the book! A number from the book.

ALI. Oh, we got a real hip number for you to dance to this time, man.

RICK. Yeh, you really gone execute some steps now.

JASON. Brand-new, bugaloo!

MIKE. Be socking it to you, Mister!

DEAN, *going to her demanding.* Jane! Jane! A number! A number!

HELEN, *snatching off wig to her own hair.* Helen, Dr. Doolittle! My name is Helen!!

DEAN, *hands coming out like Frankenstein's again.* No, no—Jane—Jane—*wavering around in little half-circles.*

JASON. Dance-floor's this way. Mister. *Pulling him toward chair, snatching off and throwing rear his Afro wig.*

MIKE. Yeh. *Affecting "Corliss Archer" tone.* Don't be shy, guy! *Pulling off and throwing rear his beard.*

RICK. You won't need your boobs, baby. *Helping turn him around and unbuckle his "chest."*

ALI. Down, Filthy McNasty. *Pushing him into chair.* Now.

HELEN, *standing aside with arms folded.* You're forgetting his other falsies.

RICK. Huh? Oh, yeh. *They all grab him and pull him up at waist by his belt; start unzipping—then all come to same thought and make room for her.* Would you like the honor?

HELEN. Hmmmm. I don't touch dead things.

They all shrug and lean over him, hiding him from audience. "Falsies" go flying rear.

ALI. Now.

All stand back looking.

 HELEN *joins them in center. They suddenly all lean to him and being shouted chant—which has* DEAN *in writhing, groaning agony unable to bend his straining Frankenstein hands to his ears.*

HELEN. Prestige!!
OTHERS. Black man's prestige!!

All clap hands.

HELEN. Status!!
OTHERS. Black men's Status!!

All clap hands.

HELEN. Security!!
OTHERS. Black men's security!!

All clap hands.

HELEN. Acceptance!!

OTHERS. Black men's acceptance!!

All clap hands. Men, Women, Children!

OTHERS. Black. *Clap.* Black. *Clap.* Black. *Clap.* Prestige!! *Begins again with sense of drums, just as—Black Out.*

SCENE TWO

Same set; an hour or so later. RICK *is winding the cord of the tape recorder.* HELEN, *now in her own clothes, is drinking coffee, sitting on a box; her "white" outfit rests folded near her feet by her bag.* JASON *sits on another box drinking coffee also.* ALI *and* MIKE *are up on other level, on box-steps, the top halves of their bodies hidden by the black curtains; they are looking out window.*

JASON. Yeh, he really blew my mind then. Talking about our blood like it's some water come trickling down off some mountain or something.

HELEN. That's the universal theory, Jace; objectivity, and all that good stuff.

RICK. Yeh, man, everything's just an artifact. Nothing's real. Blood is just color. Words are just language. Thoughts relative rationales. Don't you know that? Where you go to school, man?

JASON, *as all three exchange wry grins.* Yeh. *To* ALI *and* MIKE. How's he coming?

MIKE, *under curtain.* He just came out where we can see him. He's stumbling along pretty good.

ALI, *under curtain.* Carrying a real, honest message for once in his life.

HELEN. But are you really sure he's gonna' deliver it? I mean, how can we trust him?

JASON. I don't. And you all let me know when he gets to that bonfire, that meeting. I'm going to listen. And if he don't give that message, he won't give no more. *Pats his back pocket.*

ALI. It's a simple enough message.

RICK. And we handled him just like the brother said.

MIKE. And so far it's workin' all right.

ALI. Here comes the first real test, right here.

JASON. What's happening?

MIKE. Two of them little blond instructors just spoke to him, going the other way—Dig it, Ali! He's stopping, man!

All look.

ALI. I dig it. I see it.

MIKE. He's turnin' around, man! He's turnin' around, Ali!

ALI. I can see it, Mike! I can see it!

JASON. I know it! *Standing; slipping out 45 auto. and checking clip.*

MIKE. Where's he at, Man!? What's he—these damned glasses ain't shit!—what's he doin' Ali?

ALI, *calmly.* He's looking around in the bushes.

JASON, *going to exit gun in hand.* For a gun? Is he getting a gun, man?

MIKE. I see him now. What's he doing? What's that he got?

ALI. He had some of his—his stuff hid out there. Beard. Natural.

MIKE. Yeh! The chestplate. He's puttin' it on. He's comin' back this way, man!!

JASON. He's comin' back here!? Here!?!

ALI. Yep.

MIKE. Yeh, that's what he's doin' all right. He's comin' back.

JASON, *checking gun again.* Well his chest-piece better be bullet-proof! And even if it is— Shame on his worthless ass! *Starting out.*

ALI, *coming from behind curtain and down box-steps;* MIKE *following him; binoculars dangling down their chests.* Wait Jace! Naw! There's not a whitie anywhere around who would kill him. And if he's found dead, some of us would be the first ones picked up! Now I don't know about you but I'm not out to be heroic! I'm out to get something done! All right!? *As* JASON *pauses, waiting.* All right. Now Rick, you go with him! And you two bring him back up here!

JASON. Alive, man?

ALI. Yeh. Bring it back alive. That's right. Okay?

JASON *shrugs and goes out;* RICK *goes with him, opening his sportcoat to check his shoulder-holster.* ALI *begins to pace.*

MIKE. What happen, man? We had all his buttons and gears turnin' for us. What went wrong?

HELEN. I told you you couldn't expect nothin' right from anybody as wrong as him!

ALI. We forgot something. Overlooked something.

MIKE. What? We ran it down just like the brother said.

ALI. Uh-huh, the brother missed it too.

HELEN. What Ali? Tell us what you're talkin' about?

ALI. Don't you dig it? A—A—thing! like this doesn't function, finally, to any—any words! Ideas! His deepest, utmost response, reaction, is to one thing! *Holds up finger.*

HELEN. Yeh, white skin.

ALI, *nodding.* White skin! And as soon as he ran into some of that, he shifted into reverse and started backsliding.

HELEN. Yeh.

MIKE. Yeh, I dig it now.

ALI. Ah-huh. Helen, you put that mask back on. This won't take but a minute. Looka' here, both of you.

Goes to bottom drawer of dresser. Begins to explain as HELEN *puts on mask. Takes white rope from drawer gives it to* MIKE; *points toward window, explains,* MIKE *nods, goes over, up box-steps and disappears behind curtain. The sound of others coming up the stairs. With* JASON *and* RICK *having an armpit apiece in clutch,* DEAN *comes back in; the chestpiece is buckled on backwards, beard and natural hang on one side of his face.*

JASON. Yeh, man, just bring your ass on.

RICK. Yeh, we know, we know.

DEAN. Number six! Yes. Uh, the only way to match up to this man is to match him dollar for dollar. And that takes time! Takes planning! Means that one educates oneself according to his needs! Yes, his needs! Means that one makes oneself a necessary part of the—the bowels of his machinery and bargains from there! Yes!

JASON. Yeh, we're hip, man, that is until he gets a real machine for that part of his bowels and decides to shit us out! Uh-huh!

RICK. Yeh, we know. We can't match him so we have to join him. Can't have our own machine so we have to be a wrench for his. We know. Come on, Mister.

MIKE, *on box-steps.* His needs! Yeh. We be holding down Civil Service while he's up on the moon-regulating the weather down there!

JASON. Civil-Servitude, you mean!

ALI. Cool it. Let Helen have him.

HELEN, *moving in, her white gloves caressing his face.* Dahling. Prestige, Dahling. Status, Dahling. Security, Dahling. Acceptance, Dahling. White Acceptance.

JASON. That shit again.

DEAN. Jane?—Jane, dear. Number nine. *On his fingers.* The police! The National Guard! Coast Guard! Army! Paratroopers! Navy! Marines! Green Berets!

HELEN. Yes, dear. Yes, dear.

JASON. Uh-huh. So tote that barge and lift that bale, we know.

MIKE. Listen fool. You ever thought of all the non-white enemies with guns he's got all over the world!? Ever thought of him trying to fight down in his belly and outside his head and at both arms and feet all at the same time!? Here there and everywhere, at once?! Huh, sucker?!

JASON. Yeh, with his factories blowing up on him while he's at it.

DEAN. Jane—Jane—

ALI. Let her have him, man!

HELEN. Dahling, the man called.

DEAN. The man? *Sniffing the air.* The man?

HELEN. Yes, dear. *Leading him over.* He wants you to go up to the window there. He has a microphone there wired for the whole campus. He wants you to speak to them. Now, dear, right now.

DEAN, *trying to straighten his appearance.* The man. Yes. The man. Yes. *Goes up steps;* MIKE *holds curtain back for him. He goes under it.*

HELEN, *arms folded not looking.* Yes, dear. That's right. Now he said you are to put your head—your head—*Falters.*

ALI, *comes to look behind curtain which* MIKE *still holds.* Yes, Sir. Uh, we're the electricians, we did the wiring. That's it, Sir. Just put your head inside that—that white loop there. That's it. Make sure it's tight around your neck now. We want to be sure everyone hears you. Uh-huh. *Wiping sweat.* Is the end secure around that pipe above you, Sir? They're all waiting for you.

All but HELEN *comes to steps;* MIKE *drops curtain.*

DEAN. Yes! The Army! The Marines! The Green Beret—*They pull steps out from under him, he gives one grunt, then dangles silently.*

HELEN *shudders. Others move away.*

HELEN. I can't stand being around dead things.

ALI, *sighing, wiping face and hands with handkerchief.* That's why we're trying to resurrect ourselves, baby. Wanna' wait downstairs? *She shakes head no, goes to stand by door.* All right, let's get it together and get out. Mike you wipe your prints off that rope? MIKE *nods.* Okay. Wipe everything we touched. Turn those steps over on their side, near where he could have kicked them. All right; ashtrays, candles, everything, but the chair and the dresser. *They start getting it all together.* ALI *looks back at dangling legs, first one to do so.* Yeh, they would believe that he'd kill himself. In a way that's all he's been doing all these years.

MIKE. Yeh, but it's still almost sad ain't it. I mean after a while he seemed almost human, you know?

JASON. Almost is right.

ALI. Yeh. We got everything now? Let's go. *Starts for door.*

DEAN *suddenly grunts and shouts out.* THINK! THINK FOR YOUR OWN!! FEEL-FEEL FOR YOUR OWN!! WORK-WORK TOWARD YOUR OWN!! BE—BE— *Falls silent again.* EVERYONE, *to audience.* BE FOR YOUR OWN!! THE OTHERS HAVE ALREADY DONE FOR THEIRS!! THEY CANNOT AND WILL NOT RESPECT YOU UNTIL YOU HAVE DONE FOR YOUR OWN!! THEN, AND ONLY THEN, WILL THEY ACKNOWLEDGE YOU WHOLLY!! AND MOVE OVER FOR YOU!! RELINQUISH SPACE TO YOUR DIGNITY!! TO YOUR BEING!!

JASON, *after moment, staring at* DEAN. Damn, man—the message.

MIKE. Yeh, they say you see the light at the end.

ALI. Pick up the stuff you dropped, man. Come on, let's split.

JASON, MIKE *and* RICK *all bend down to retrieve dropped goods.*

MIKE. Yeh, man, the message. But we left something out you know?

JASON. What, man? Come on.

MIKE. Uh, something like, look for your own, and it's gettin' harder and harder to tell who they are. You know? Like him with his beard, his natural, and all. You know what I mean?

ALI. It's not so hard, like that great book says, by their deeds you shall know them. Something like that.

JASON. Yeh, just add up his saids and his dids and you get his "is's" whoever he is. Whatever he is.

MIKE. Yeh, yeh, I dig. *As they go out.* But you know, man. Still, like I said, it's getting harder and harder, just like this cat who—

Important that it ends like there's a conversation going on down steps to—

Curtain

SONIA SANCHEZ

The Bronx Is Next

Characters

    CHARLES

    OLD SISTER

    LARRY

    ROLAND

    JIMMY

    WHITE COP

    BLACK BITCH

The scene is a block in Harlem—a block of tenement houses on either side of a long, narrow, dirty street of full garbage cans. People are moving around in the distance bringing things out of the houses and standing with them in the street. There is activity—but as CHARLES, *a tall, bearded man in his early thirties, and* OLD SISTER *move toward the front, the activity lessens. It is night. The time is now.*

CHARLES. Keep 'em moving Roland. C'mon you mothafuckers. Keep moving. Git you slow asses out of here. We ain't got all night. Into the streets. Oh shit. Look sister. None of that. You can't take those things. Jest important things—things you would grab and carry out in case of a fire. You understand? You wouldn't have time to get all of those things if there was a real fire.

OLD SISTER. Yes son. I knows what you says is true. But you see them things is me. I brought them up with me from Birmingham 40 years ago. I always keeps them right here with me. I jest can't do without them. You know what I mean son? I jest can't leave them you see.

CHARLES. Yes sister. I know what you mean. Look. Someone will help you get back to your apartment. You can stay there. You don't have to come tonight. You can come some other time when we have room for your stuff. OK?

From *TDR: The Drama Review* 12.4, Black Theatre (Summer 1968): 78–84.

OLD SISTER. Thank you son. Here let me kiss you. Thank the lord there is young men like you who still care about the old people. What is your name son?

CHARLES. My name is Charles, sister. Now I have to get back to work. Hey Roland. Jimmy. Take this one back up to her apartment. Make her comfortable. She ain't coming to-night. She'll come another time.

ROLAND. Another time? Man you flipping out? Why don't you realize . . .

CHARLES. I said, Roland, she'll come another time. Now help her up those fucking stairs. Oh yes. Jimmy, see too that she gets some hot tea. You dig? Ten o'clock is our time. There ain't no time for anyone. There ain't no time for nothing 'cept what we came to do. Understand? Now get your ass stepping.

ROLAND *and* JIMMY *exit.*

LARRY. Hey Charles, over here fast. Look what I found coming out one of the buildings.

CHARLES. What, man? I told you I ain't got no time for nothing 'cept getting this block cleared out by 10 p.m. What the fuck is it?

LARRY. A white dude. A cop. An almighty fuzz. Look. I thought they were paid enough to stay out of Harlem tonight. *Turns to* COP. Man. Now just what you doing here spying on us, huh?

WHITE COP. Spying? What do you mean spying? You see. Well you know how it is. I have this friend—she lives on this block and when I got off at 4 p.m., I stopped by. Well. I was just leaving but this guy and another one taking someone upstairs saw me—pulled a gun on me and brought me out here.

CHARLES. What building and what apartment were you visiting my man?

WHITE COP. No. 214—Apt 10—but why are you interested?

CHARLES. Larry, bring the black bitch out fast. Want to get a good look at her so I'll see jest why we sweating tonight. Yeah. For all the black bitches like her.

WHITE COP *has turned around and seen the activity.* Hey. What are all the people doing out in the middle of the street? What's happening here? There's something going on here I don't know about and I have a right to know . . .

CHARLES. Right? Man. You ain't got no rights here. Jest shut your fucking white mouth before you git into something you wish you wasn't in. Man. I've got to call in about this dude. Is there a phone in any of these fire traps?

JIMMY. Yeah. I got one in my place during the year I lived here. It's No. 210—1st floor—1C—back apartment. I'll stay here with this socializing dude while you call.

CHARLES *splits.*

WHITE COP *takes out some cigarettes.* Want a cigarette?

JIMMY. Thanks man—in fact I'll take the whole pack. It's going to be a long night.

WHITE COP. What do you mean a long night?

JIMMY, *smiling.* Jest what I said man—and it might be your longest—*laughs*—may—be the longest of your life.

WHITE COP, *puffing on cigarette—leans against garbage can.* What's your name son?

JIMMY. You don't git nothing out of me 'til Charles returns. You hear me? So stop asking so many damn questions. *Moves to the right. Screams.* Goddamn it Roland. Your building is going too slow. We have only two more hours. Get that shit moving. We have to be finished by 10 p.m.

WHITE COP. Look. What are you people doing? Why are all the people moving out into the street—What's going on here? There's something funny going on here and I want to know what it is. You can't keep me from using my eyes and brains—and pretty soon I'll put two and two together—then you just wait . . . you just wait . . .

CHARLES *has appeared on stage at this time and has heard what the* COP *has said. Is watchful for a moment—moves forward.*

CHARLES. Wait for what my man? Wait for you to find out what's happening? It's not hard to see. We're moving the people out—out into the cool breezes of the street—is that so difficult to understand?

WHITE COP. No. But why? I mean, yeah I know that the apartments are kinda hot and awful . . .

CHARLES. You right man. Kinda awful. Did you hear that description of these shit houses Jimmy? Kinda awful. I knew we weren't describing this scene right and it took this dude here to finally show us the way. From now on when I talk to people about their places I'll say—I know your places are kinda awful . . .

JIMMY. In fact, Charles, how 'bout—I know your places are maybe kinda awful . . .

CHARLES, *laughing.* Yeah. That's it. Perhaps. Maybe could there be a slight possibility that your place is kinda—now mind you, we ain't saying for sure—but maybe it's kinda awful—*becomes serious.* Yeah. That's the white man for you man. Always understating things. But since both you and I know that these places are shit-houses that conversation can end now.

JIMMY. What they say 'bout the dude, Charles?

CHARLES, *turns to* WHITE COP. Oh everything is cool. You can leave man when you want to, but first have a cigarette with us.

WHITE COP, *relaxing.* I would offer you some of mine but he took them all.

CHARLES. C'mon man. Give them back to the dude. And Jimmy go get Roland. Tell him to come talk a bit. What a night this has been. It's hard working with these people. They like cattle you know. Don't really understand anything. Being a cop, you probably found that too. Right?

WHITE COP, *lighting a cigarette.* Yeah. I did. A little. But the hardest thing for me to understand was that all you black people would even live in these conditions. Well. You know. Everybody has had ghettos but they built theirs up and there was respect there. Here. There is none of that.

CHARLES. How right you are my man. C'mon in Jimmy and Roland. We just talking to pass some time. Of course, getting back to your statement, I think the reason that the black man hasn't made it—you ain't Irish are you?—is a color thing—I mean even though the Irish were poor they were still white—but as long as white people hate because of a difference in color, then they ain't gonna let the black man do too much. You dig?

WHITE COP. But all this hopelessness. Poverty of the mind and spirit. Why? Things are so much better. All it takes is a little more effort by you people. But these riots. It's making good people have second thoughts about everything.

ROLAND. It's a long time going—man—this hopelessness—and it ain't no better. Shit. All those good thinking people changing their minds never believed in the first fucking place.

JIMMY, *stands up.* Man. Do you know that jest yesterday I was running down my ghetto street and these two white dudes stopped me and asked what I was doing out so early in the morning—and cuz I was high off some smoke—I said man—it's my street—I can walk on it any time. And they grabbed me and told me where everything was.

CHARLES. That gives me an idea. Let's change places before this dude splits. Let him be a black dude walking down a ghetto street and we'll be three white dudes—white cops on a Harlem street.

WHITE COP. Oh c'mon. That's ridiculous. What good would that do. Why I'd feel silly . . .

CHARLES. You mean you'd feel silly being black?

WHITE COP. Oh no—not that—I mean what would it prove? How would it help—what good would it do?

JIMMY. But what harm could it do?

WHITE COP. None that I could imagine . . . it's just that it's strange . . . it's like playing games.

ROLAND. Oh c'mon. I've always wanted to be a white dude—now's my chance. It'll be exciting—sure is getting boring handling this mob of people.

JIMMY. If you afraid, man, we don't have to.

WHITE COP. Afraid? No. OK. Let's start.

CHARLES, *jumps up—looks elated.* Then we'll jest be standing on the corner talking and you c'mon by. Oh yeah, maybe you should be running. OK?

CHARLES, ROLAND *and* JIMMY *move to one side of the stage—the* WHITE COP *moves to the other side and begins to run toward them.*

CHARLES. Hey slow down boy. What's your hurry?

WHITE COP, *stops running.* Yes. What's wrong officer?

JIMMY. Where you running to so fast?

WHITE COP. I just felt like running officer. I was feeling good so I decided to run.

ROLAND. Oh you were feeling good. So you decided to run. Now ain't that a load of shit if I ever heard one.

WHITE COP. It's true, officer. I was just thinking about the day—it was a great day for me so I felt like running—so I ran.

CHARLES. Boy! Who's chasing you? What did you steal?

WHITE COP. Steal? I haven't stolen anything. I haven't stolen anything. I haven't anything in my pockets. *Goes into his pockets.*

JIMMY *draws gun.* Get your hands out your pockets boy. Against the wall right now.

WHITE COP. But what have I done? I was just running. This is not legal you know. You have no right to do this . . .

ROLAND. You are perfectly correct. We have no right to do this. Why I even have no right to hit you but I am. *Hits* WHITE COP *with gun.*

WHITE COP, *falls down. Gets up.* Now wait a minute. That is going just a little too far and . . .

CHARLES. I said why were you running down that street boy?

WHITE COP. Look. Enough is enough. I'm ready to stop—I'm tired.

JIMMY. What's wrong nigger boy—can't you answer simple questions when you're asked them. Oh I know what's wrong. You need me to help you to remember. *Hits* WHITE COP *with gun.*

WHITE COP. Have you gone crazy? Stop this. You stop it now or there will be consequences.

ROLAND. What did you steal black boy—we can't find it on you but we know you got it hidden someplace. *Hits him again.*

WHITE COP. Oh my god. Stop it . . . This can't be happening to me. Look—I'm still me. It was only make believe.

CHARLES. Let's take him in. He won't cooperate. He won't answer the question. Maybe he needs more help than the three of us are giving him.

JIMMY. I don't know. Looks like he's trying to escape to me. Take out your guns. That nigger is trying to run. Look at him. Boy, don't run. Stop. I say if you don't stop I'll have to shoot.

WHITE COP. Are you all mad? I'm not running. I'm on my knees. Stop it. This can't continue. Why . . .

ROLAND. You ain't shit boy. You black. You a nigger we caught running down the street—running and stealing like all the niggers around him.

CHARLES. Now you trying to escape—and we warned you three times already. You only get three warnings then . . .

Noise from off stage—a woman's voice.

LARRY. Man. This bitch ain't cooperating Charles. She said she didn't have to come. Finally had to slap her around a bit.

CHARLES. Now is that anyway to act bitch? We just want to talk to you for a minute. Hear you were entertaining this white dude in your place. Is that so?

BLACK BITCH, *stands defiantly—had a reddish wig on which is slightly disheveled.* Who you? Man. I don't owe no black man no explanations 'bout what I do. The last black man I explained to cleaned me out, so whatever you doing don't concern me 'specially if it has a black man at the head.

JIMMY. Smart—assed—bitch.

BLACK BITCH, *turns to* JIMMY—*walks over to him.* That's right kid. A smart—assed—black bitch—that's me. Smart enough to stay clear of all black bastard men who jump from black pussy to black pussy like jumping jacks. Yeah, I know all about black men. The toms and revolutionary ones. I could keep you entertained all night long. But I got to get back. My kids will be coming home.

CHARLES. How many kids you got bitch?

BLACK BITCH. Two. Two boys. Two beautiful black boys. Smart boys you hear? They read. They know more than me already, but they still love me. Men. They will know what a woman is for. I'll teach them. I ain't educated, but I'll say—hold them in your arms—love them—love your black woman always. I'll say I am a black woman and I cry in the night. But when you are men you will never make a black woman cry in the night. You hear. And they'll promise.

ROLAND. Oh shit. Another black matriarch on our hands—and with her white boyfriend. How you gonna teach them all this great stuff when you whoring with some white dude who kills black men everyday? How you explain that shit to them?

BLACK BITCH *laughs—high piercing laugh—walks over to* WHITE COP. Explain this. *Points to* WHITE COP *on ground.*

BLACK BITCH. I only explain the important things. He comes once a week. He fucks me. He puts his grayish white dick in me and dreams his dreams. They ain't 'bout me. Explain him to my boys. *Laughs.* Man. I am surviving. This dude has been coming regularly for two years—he stays one evening, leaves and then drives on out to Long Island to his white wife and kids and reality. *Laughs.* Explain. I don't explain cuz there ain't nothing to explain.

CHARLES. Yeah. But you still a bitch. You know. None of this explaining to us keeps you from being a bitch.

BLACK BITCH. Yeah. I know what I am. *Looks around.* But all you revolutionists or nationalists or whatever you call yourselves—do you know where you at? I am a black woman and I've had black men who could not love me or my black boys—where you gonna find black women to love you when all this is over—when you need them? As for me I said no black man would touch me ever again.

CHARLES, *moving toward the* BLACK BITCH. Is that right? You not a bad looking bitch if you take off that fucking wig. *Throws it off.* A good ass. *Touches her face, neck, moves his hands on her body—moves against her until she tries to turn away.* No don't turn away bitch. Kiss me. I said kiss me. *Begins to kiss her face—slowly—sensuously—the* BLACK BITCH *grabs him and kisses him long and hard—moves her body against him.* Yeah. No black man could touch you again, huh? *Laughs and moves away.* I could fuck you right here if I wanted to. You know what a black man is don't you bitch? Is that what happens when you fuck faggoty white men?

BLACK BITCH *runs across the stage and with that run and cry that comes from her she grabs* CHARLES *and hits him and holds on.* CHARLES *turns and knocks her down. The white dude turns away.* JIMMY *moves toward her.*

BLACK BITCH. No. Watch this boy. You still young. Watch me. Don't touch me. Watch me get up. It hurts. But I'll get up. And when I'm up the tears will stop. I don't cry, when I'm standing up. All right. I'm up again. Who else? Here I am, a black bitch, up for grabs. Anyone here for me. Take your choice—your pick—slap me or fuck me—anyway you get the same charge.

JIMMY. Here black bitch. Let me help you. Your eye is swollen. *Doesn't look at* CHARLES. Can she go back to her place and get some things out Charles? I'll help her.

CHARLES. You have five minutes to help the black bitch then get you black ass back here. We wasted enough time. *Stoops.* Here don't forget her passport to the white world. *Throws wig at her.* And keep your mouth shut black bitch. You hear?

BLACK BITCH, *putting on her wig.* I told you I only explain important things. There ain't nothing happening here yet that's important to me. *Exits with* JIMMY.

CHARLES, *laughs.* That's a woman there. Yeah wig and all. She felt good for awhile. Hey you. Dude. You can get up now. All the unpleasantness is over. Here let me help you get cleaned up. *Begins to brush* WHITE COP *off.* We just got a little carried away with ourselves.

WHITE COP. Can I go now? I'm tired. It's been a long night. You said I could go.

CHARLES. But don't you want to go and see the bitch—see how she is—make sure she's okay?

WHITE COP. No. I don't think so. It's late. My wife will be worrying by now.

CHARLES. Isn't there anything else you want to see before you go? Can't I fill you in on anything?

WHITE COP. I've seen people moved into the street. That's all. Nothing else. I want to know nothing.

CHARLES. Would you believe that it's happening on every street in Harlem?

WHITE COP, *nervously.* I'm not interested. I just want to leave and go home. I'm tired.

CHARLES. Yeah man. You look tired. Look. Do me a favor. I want to go to the bitch's place and apologize. You know it wasn't right. Hurting her like that. Come with me. Hey Roland. Shouldn't he come with me?

ROLAND. Yeah man. He should. After all, he knows her better than you. He can tell you what approach to use with her.

WHITE COP. No. I don't want to go. I don't want to see her again. It's all finished now. I'm tired. You tell her. Just let me go on home.

CHARLES. But man. I need you. I need you to help me talk to her. She'll listen to you. Anyway with you there, you'll keep me from getting violent again—c'mon man. Just this one thing then you can go.

LARRY's *voice from off stage.* We ready to light, Charles—should we start now?

CHARLES. Yeah. All 'cept No. 214—we have some business there. Give us ten minutes then light it up.

WHITE COP *tries to run*—CHARLES *and* ROLAND *grab his arm and start walking.*

WHITE COP. I don't want to go. I must get home. My wife and two boys are waiting for me. I have never hurt or killed a black person in my life. Yes I heard talk that some cops did—that they hated black people—but not me. I listened. It made me sick but I never participated in it. I didn't ever do anything to negroes. No. I don't want to go. I haven't done anything. *Begins to cry.* Holy Mother—you can't do this to me. *Screams.* But, I'm white! I'm white! No. This can't be happening—I'm white!

Tries to break away and ROLAND *knocks him out—they pull him off stage. The stage becomes light—buildings are burning—people are moving around looking at the blaze.* JIMMY, ROLAND *and* CHARLES *reappear.*

JIMMY. Well. That's that, man. What a night. Do I still have to write this up tonight Charles?

CHARLES. Were those your orders?

JIMMY. Yes. Okay. I'll do it while we wait. I'll drop it in the mail box tonight. See you soon.

CHARLES. A good job, Jimmy. Stay with them. Talk to them. They need us more than ever now.

ROLAND. We got to split Charles. We got a meeting going tonight. You know what the meeting is about man? *Takes out a cigarette.* You think this is the right strategy burning out the ghettoes? Don't make much sense to me man. But orders is orders. You know what's going down next?

CHARLES, *lighting a cigarette.* Yeah. I heard tonight when I called about that white dude. The Bronx is next—Let's split.

V

Fiction / Narrative

Black Arts Fiction: An Introduction

In the watershed year 1963—a year as pivotal for American literature and the allied arts as for American social and political ferment—screams of agony punctuated a shout of momentary triumph as the blood-soaked ideal of American democracy confronted its reality. In this epochal year, murdered children, battered citizens, a murdered warrior for civil equality, and, finally, an assassinated president of the United States lined the American landscape and consciousness. The clock of American time rolled back to 1776, its founding, and 1868, the ratification of the Fourteenth Amendment of the Constitution of the United States, as the Reverend Dr. Martin Luther King Jr. stood at the foot of the Lincoln Memorial and etched into the public discourse the ideal of the American Republic. It was then and now a dream—a revered dream. But was it the American Dream? The question arising from the renowned "Dream" speech of Dr. King summoned two centuries of American being to a moment in its present, resonating still to open or foreclose on possibilities for the yet unborn. Embedded in the metaphorical narratives of Black writers during the mid-sixties and after is a more than dialectical response to the dream Dr. King envisioned concerning American reality. As Larry (Laurence Paul) Neal, heralded historian and theorist of the mid-twentieth-century Black Arts Movement, observes in his essay "The Black Contribution to American Letters: Poet II, the Writer as Activist—1960 and After," "Black literature, complete with its uncertainties and ambivalence, reflects the numerous aesthetic and political issues texturing both a public and private field of language" in America (767–79). Deepening his observation, Neal explains,

> Some of these issues grew out of the historic struggle to obliterate racism in America. Others sprang from the general dilemma of identity which haunts American cultural history. Still others seemed to stem from an overall crisis in modern intellectual thought in Western society, where values are being assaulted by a new generation of youth around the world as it searches for new standards and ideals. (768–78)

This search defines the creative enterprise of the Black Arts Movement.

Arguably, the fiction of this period seems especially to reflect a view suggested by the Caribbean theorist Wilson Harris that "when the future parents the past . . . then fiction acquires new, creative roots in time, and the past presents itself as ceaselessly partial and unfinished" (qtd. in Rowell, 196). The narratological experiments deployed by writers of the Black Arts Movement in the exploration of their themes pioneered the developments in contemporary fiction most often designated *postmodern.* In fact, as novelist, poet, musician, essayist, and publisher Ishmael Reed has observed, African American literature has always been "postmodern." Such insight promotes understanding that "like any literary, cultural, and social movement, the Black Arts Movement cannot be comprehended as a time-bound event. It grew out of a lineage of activist, intellectual, and creative activity which fomented its aspirations, discourses, and primary objectives" (Traylor, "Women Writers of the Black Arts Movement," 67). This lineage, indeed, shapes the literary imaginary of the Black Arts Movement of the mid-twentieth century.

Interestingly, two influential books were published in 1963 that historicize the discussion of art and democracy in America. In fact, both books ground this discussion in the creative acts of literary artists grappling with the dynamic that art and democracy compel. Both books foreground particularly the narrative modes that generate language preexisting, cradling the King years of the Civil Rights struggle, and still resonating. Similarly, both books unveil the creative or artistic response to the discourse of democracy—the question of America itself. Both concur, and for different reasons, that by 1963 the ideal of America had not been realized. The actuation remains the rigor of a daring revision. One of the two books, *The Eccentric Design: A Theory of the American Novel* by Marius Bewley, contemporized the study of American fiction. The other, authored by award-winning yet controversial novelist, essayist, and public intellectual (though not self-claimed) James Baldwin, rocked American popular culture and made famous the Dial Press, which published *The Fire Next Time.*

Writing against a new world idyllic narrative picturing an edenic scene of abundance where endless Adams and Eves enjoyed pre-textual innocence, Bewley finds nineteenth-century American novelists—the focus of his study—desolate, "grounded in a sense of deprivation . . . the sense of being without certain kinds of reality that man ought to have: the sense that there is a world of abstract ideas and ideals and a world of bitter fact, but no society or tradition or orthodoxy in which the two worlds [could] interact and qualify each other" (17). As Bewley suggests, deprived of a sense of one's own people and history, as the ancient griot was not, as Flaubert and Jane Austen and Dostoevsky were not, the nineteenth-century American novelist discovered the only subject available to him: "his own unhappy plight" (15). Worse, contrasting the poeticized and theorized edenic garden of new beginnings, Bewley recalls from Hector St. John de Crèvecoeur "a bright pastoral rural" (172–73) scene where the moving wings of "birds of prey" are mistaken for "the sound of a sudden shower of rain . . . the promise of mercy and gentleness . . . But here the promise ends in a mockery of nature herself" (105). This garden is setting for a caged Black man with "all that is left of his human personality concentrated in a supplication for death" (105).

Here then, argues Bewley, is the split in American experience: a society in which the abstract idea—the idea of *democracy,* the only idea that could distinguish the *Americaness* of the American creative and especially literary production—could find no common ground for interaction with the concrete experience. The nineteenth-century novelist faced a crisis impelling a struggle to find "a unity that was not there" (18). In America, suggests Bewley, the novel fled from its traditional moorings in the treatment of men and society: it "sheered into abstractions" (4). In James Fennimore Cooper, Nathaniel Hawthorne, Herman Melville, Henry James, and F. Scott Fitzgerald—the targets of Bewley's investigation—Bewley finds not novels of manners or customs or mores, but novels of ideas inherited from the founding genius of the American geo-political space: Thomas Jefferson, Henry Adams, and Alexander Hamilton. But these ideas were contrastive, constructing a network of opposites expressed, for example, by Cooper between aristocracy and democracy and between acquisitive economics and benevolent wealth; by Hawthorne between isolation and social sympathy; in Melville between democratic faith and despair; by James between the everlasting dialectic of Europe and America; by Fitzgerald between class and the American dream (19). The nineteenth-century American novel, concludes Bewley, could not produce a coherent society; it produced symbols: *the wilderness, the scarlet letter, the whale, the clearing, the golden bowl, the green light.*

Response to this schism is found in the epistles of James Baldwin, or St. James—so called by his apotheosis as "God's Revolutionary Mouth" in the Funeral Oration of Amiri Baraka, heir apparent, and so called in his canonization by Michael Ondaatje as "our twentieth-century Saint." By 1963, when these epistles appeared as *The Fire Next Time,* James Baldwin had recorded his response to the work of the nineteenth-century novelists. Of course, he had looked the whale right dead in the eye; walked out of the wilderness "just like John"; worn, himself, the scarlet letter; taken the measure of the *Pequod* from the raft of Little Pip; rubbed the golden bowl all round; shaken his head in amazement at Gatsby; and made his judgment. In *Go Tell It on the Mountain* (1953), he had raised a fledgling artist in a society where abstract ideas and ideals were tested in a world of bitter fact: Harlem and the American South, precisely where Crèvecoeur had discovered the caged man in the garden of South Carolina and, like the symbolist novel, had turned away. The American narrative, in the nineteenth century, turned away from the question of reconciling abstract ideas and the harsh contradictory reality of American democracy. In so doing, it created an essentialized racist paradigm: normalizing white as humanity and caging all others.

In that same South, Baldwin's fledgling artist, the focal character of *Go Tell It on the Mountain,* discovers preexisting materials for the novelist's craft: a people with a history whose genius through three hundred years had produced a creative archive of cultural memory: song, dance, narrative, poetry, theory. In *Giovanni's Room* (1956), Baldwin had wrestled down the terms of the Jamesian dialectic in the international novel and had found the American adventurer to Europe certainly not innocent yet lacking the imaginative toughness to discover the greatest ideal of all. For Baldwin, that ideal or value would be the only one which could reduce irreconcilables, which could wed the idea (democracy) and the ideal (love). Such a bonding would yield freedom—the civil state in which democracy could live and find the stuff of a brand new artistic imaginary. It is the quest for freedom in those texts he points to in *The Fire Next Time* and in which he finds the certainty of his assurances to his nephew: "you come from sturdy, peasant stock. . . . You come from a long line of great poets, some of the greatest poets since Homer. One of them said, *The very time I thought I was lost, my dungeon shook and my chains fell off*" (24).

On this very language, forged in the creative will of poetic peasants, did the young Martin Luther King Jr. in 1956 rest his statement in a speech at Montgomery, Alabama. It begins:

Those of us who live in the twentieth century are privileged to live in one of the most momentous periods of human history. . . . It is an age in which a new social order is being born. We stand today between two worlds—the defying old and the emerging new. (135)

An ongoing literary production referred to by Baldwin in *The Fire Next Time* would now intensify to explore King's vision and authenticate Baldwin's prophetic claim:

A bill is coming in that I fear America is not prepared to pay. . . . A fearful and delicate problem, which compromises, when it does not corrupt all the American efforts to build a better world—here, there, or anywhere. It is for this reason that everything white America thinks they believe in must now be reexamined. (117)

As though in jam session performance, novels published between 1960 and 1968 by those authors included in this anthology thematically examine the King and Baldwin premises influencing public discourse. They also either anticipate or resonate voices rising to counter not the premises, but the solutions required to change the world. Such exemplary novels as those cradling the King years by no means exhaust the response of Black fiction during the 1960s: John A. Williams's *The Angry Ones* (1960), *Night Song* (1961), *Sissie* (1963), *The Man Who Cried I Am* (1967), disclosing its actual or imagined "King Alfred Plan"; Sam Greenlee's *The Spook Who Sat by the Door* (1963); John Oliver Killens's *And Then We Heard the Thunder* (1963), *'Sippi* (1967); William Melvin Kelley's *A Different Drummer* (1963), *Dancers on the Shore* (a collection of short stories, 1965), *A Drop of Patience* (1965), *dem* (1967); Ronald Fair's *Many Thousand Gone* (1965), *Hog Butcher* (1966); Ishmael Reed's *The Free-Lance Pallbearers* (1967), *Yellow Back Radio Broke Down* (1969). Though their creative juices flowed in the seventies and eighties—Williams would write seven more brilliant novels through that period, Greenlee one more published in 1976, Killens one more published in 1971, Kelley one more in 1970, and Reed seven—their earlier work unveils the core of themes and narratological experiments that would establish their individual literary signatures and characterize some aspects of the large achievement of mid-twentieth-century Black Arts fiction.

One other achievement of mid-twentieth-century Black Arts fiction remains its revelation of a crisis of knowledge obscured by an exclusionary paradigm in American life, history, and culture that prevents the full representation of its plurality. Another is its artful retention of the actual in the arc of possibility by configuring time so that "nothing can end or die that once had a place in time" (Cooper, 193). Moreover, the narratalogical project of Black Arts fiction continues to extend the literary terrain of America. But perhaps one of the most spectacular achievements of midcentury fiction was its shattering of what Clyde Taylor calls "the mask of art." Disrupting an ages-old premise defining "aesthetics as a self-evident *discovery* of something universally and always present in nature and humanity" (Taylor, 9), practitioners/theorists of the period establish the argument "that a society or community's cultural productions are rooted in its political, social, and historical contexts and that African Americans were favored with a reservoir of vernacular speech and traditions upon which Black cultural workers were erecting self-identifying and empowering cultural images" (4): the revival of the *conjurer,* as well as other agencies of diasporic empowerment as, for example, the *healer,* the *shaman,* and the *trickster.*

As critical judgment has concluded, a "principle theme—the tension between Black expression and American ideology, portrayed against the backdrop of history"—pervades the fiction of John A. Williams "through four decades of his 'diverse oeuvre'" (Chaney, 3). In *The Angry Ones,* his first novel, designated by Michael A. Chaney to mark the first phase of his fictional thrust, Williams "explores the hypocrisy of corporate America, the vanishing of the American dream, the psychological complexities surrounding interracial sex, and the black writer's challenge to maintain cultural integrity in an exploitative society" (3). Unlike the deterministic lens of naturalism employed by his great predecessor Richard Wright in Wright's monumental and influential novel *Native Son* (1940) and by Williams's contemporary John O. Killens in *And Then We Heard the Thunder* (where Killens exposes bigotry in the military), in *The Angry Ones,* published three years before Dr. King's "Dream" speech, Williams employs a point of view allowing the agency of what Genevieve Fabre and Robert O'Meally identify as the *lieu de memoire* (place of memory)—pervasive still in the encounter with official history that Black authors confront.

If in "this first phase, Williams dramatizes black social struggle, but suggests the possibility of success in the characters who do not resort to violence or reactionary politics" (3)—the nonviolent method advocated by Dr. King—then in his fourth novel, *The Man Who Cried I Am,* the novel acclaimed as his masterpiece and the novel, judged by Chaney, to begin his second phase, Williams reverses this stance. He no longer pursues "the confirmation of self" thematics shared by John O. Killens in novels such as *Youngblood* (1954), *And Then We Heard the Thunder* (1963), and *'Sippi* (1967) and by William Melvin Kelley in *A Different Drummer* (1962) and (the stories of) *Dancers on the Shore* (1964). Rather, *The Man Who Cried I Am* shifts emphasis away from the idea of success measured in terms of the American dream to the heightened consciousness of "a metaphysical interior space where the fact of existence outweighs the superficiality of race" (3). Such a shift relates to what the Algerian psychologist and philosopher Frantz Fanon (one of the most frequently referenced theorists of the Black Arts generation and hailed as the founding theorist of Postcolonial Studies) describes as "[de]colonization . . . the 'thing' which has been colonized becomes *MAN* during the same process by which it frees itself" (Fanon, 36–37; italics added). This process is also central to the emancipatory impulse of Black Arts artists.

It is interesting to follow the progression of sensibility in Black fiction by noting the titles of groundbreaking novels since James Weldon Johnson's *Autobiography of an Ex-Colored Man* (1910) because the delineation of the self is deeply embedded in the tradition. The titles range from Wright's *Native Son* (1940) to Ralph Ellison's *Invisible Man* (1955) to *The Man Who Cried I Am.* In *The Man Who Cried I Am,* Max Reddick, the focal character, despite his success in the white world, comes to understand that "all you ever want to do is remind me that I am Black, but goddamn it, I also am" (3). It is not only to the existential question but to the question of survival and the battle required that the narrative strategies of the novel work to combine the lens of biography, the historical novel, mystery, the international novel, *lieu de memoire,* psychological critique, and detective fiction in the revelation of "The King Alfred Plan"—the dazzling invention (?) of the novel. It is critical to the events of the novel that Max be made aware of the "Plan" by Harry Ames, the novel's thinly veiled signifier Richard Wright, the claimed literary ancestor of John A. Williams and, by extension, ancestor of African American fiction since, claimed or not. "The King Alfred Plan" devised by the *Alliance Blanc* of the novel not so thinly disguises the FBI, the CIA, and COINTELPRO efforts to destroy Black liberationist movements. Events before and during 1963 might cause readers to wonder if, indeed, "The King Alfred Plan" were at work. In immediate response to the question, Sam Greenlee's thriller *The Spook Who Sat by the Door* (1963) offers full expression of the nationalistic tone and mood that informs much poetic and theoretical production of the 1960s. The "Spook," designating simultaneously a racial epithet directed toward Black people and slang for "spy" in Greenlee's novel, is Dan Freeman, a Black CIA operator who decides to use his training to organize Black violent street gangs as militant forces against the assault on Black communities.

The 1965 assassination of Minister Malcolm El Hajj Malik El Shabazz (Malcolm X) of the Nation of Islam, as impactful a voice on the consciousness of Black Arts writers as was "The Nation" itself, had followed the publication of *The Spook Who Sat by the Door*. The April 4, 1968, assassination of Dr. Martin Luther King Jr. occurred one year after the publication of *The Man Who Cried I Am*. Such was the prophetic voice of midcentury Black Arts fiction.

By the publication in 1968 of *Black Fire* (hereafter *BF*), the anthology edited by Amiri Baraka (formerly LeRoi Jones) and Larry Neal, Black fiction had moved to a persisting interiority. Its narrative strategies would probe what Martin Luther King Jr. called the "beloved community" through systematic deconstructive and reconstructive genres derived from Black oral expressive forms. Or to borrow the poet Nikki Giovanni's terms, "Black feeling," "Black thought," "Black judgment"—Black culture—is the focus of Black Arts fiction.

In *BF*, Larry Neal's brilliant story "Sinner Man Where You Gonna Run To?" raises the voice of Black sacred song to address the burning questions of the relation of the artist to his community; the creative process in relation to society; and the godlike creative impulse or the angst of imprisoned identity (the individual and society or "individuation" and democracy). Just as the story evokes those historical questions that force the response of Black writers at midcentury, the story also responds to the burning issues informing the mood of midcentury American society: the unintended failure of civil rights gains achieved by that movement to address the "gut grievances of the black ghettos—malnutrition, substandard housing, poor schools and unadulterated neglect," "the long hot [riot-ridden] summers of 1966, 1967, and 1968" registering reaction to the murder of people-responsive leaders (Brisbane, 568); the intensity of a cyclical Black Nationalism articulated by Black leaders in the early nineteenth century such as Paul Cuffee and Dr. Martin Delany and in the early twentieth century by Marcus Garvey, now refueled at midcentury by Minister Malcolm's rephrasing epithet "Black Revolution" in 1964; and "Black Power" by chairman of the Student Non-Violent Coordinating Committee Stokely Carmichael earlier than 1965, and student coalitions calling for "black self-esteem, black identity, and a new black lifestyle" (Brisbane 569 [*sic*]).

Beyond Black America change was the constant. Taylor explains, "In the United States these voices included the vocal insurgence of Black liberation movements, the rebirth of feminism, youth culture, the articulation of *gay* identity after the Stonewall incident, the sexual revolution, and the Chicano-Latino movements reclaiming cultural identity"

(Taylor 3). In Europe, movements such as the student Situationists International in France paralleled such response. Thus, Neal's "Sinner Man" in *BF* is an initiation rite. Not only does it answer Hawthorne's "Young Goodman Brown" or "Ethan Brand," it, above all, answers the story's Reverend Worth and his deacons—benevolent, "gentle people." Indeed, the initiation of "the Appointed Ones"—the story's motif—discloses the necessity for the descent "into the Blackness [to] protect them by all the means at our disposal so that that very gentleness would some day flower into bright sun–colors, blooming and singing in the universe" (*BF* 511–12). This, then, was the answer of Black writers of the period to the perennial debates regarding art and politics. The binary between art and politics, for mid-twentieth-century Black Arts artists was a construction, untenable and finally unjustifiable.

Some writers included in *BF* such as Ronald Fair and Jean Wheeler Smith adapt the voices of the secular blues singer to tell stories of the screams of anguish and shouts of triumph in their communities, but also to expose and, therefore, exorcise internalized destructive attitudes. In "Life with Red Top" (*BF* 500–509), Ronald Fair takes us through the town of "Nothing." It is a place of "old, obsolete buildings [emblems of] substandard living rat and roach-ridden" where "we used to wash walls and windows, and sweep the place, once in a while but . . . what's the use"; where "you buy what you want and beg for what you need"; where you walk through the panhandling streets to Mr. Marovitz's store to the Monday morning inquests, the funeral parlor, the barber shop, and the cut-rate liquor store. Life in "Nothing" is tedious, repetitive, demoralizing but not without encounters with the sphere of inner reality, not without the heightened activist consciousness of Red Top and the writerly blues sensibilities of the narrator of the story. In "Miss Luhester Gives a Party," first published in Langston Hughes's collection *The Best Short Stories by Negro Writers* (1967) and included in this anthology, Fair had begun his probe of self-destructive psychology nurtured in "Nothing": the internalized consequences of external oppression. Miss Luhester's party recalls Paul Laurence Dunbar's nineteenth-century poetic and vernacular narrative "The Party." By contrast, while Dunbar's party foregrounds "the coincident thought-life of a people" (Maloney, 27) under the duress of slavery yet inventing "the forms of things unknown," Miss Luhester's guests release self-destructive frustrations even amidst the most gracious and productive creative sensibilities of their community. The story mines some of the outcomes of these frustrations as misogyny, child abandonment, vandalism, and violence inflicted on one another.

Similarly, Jean Wheeler Smith's "That She Would Dance No More," first published in *BF*, tells the story of Ossie Lee and Minnie Pearl through the ironic blues mode to pinpoint a community's most self-destructive psychosis: in this case, misogynistic envy and, therefore, punishment of exceptional creative force and talent. His self-esteem literally whipped out of him—destroyed by the brutalities of sharecropper existence—Ossie Lee cannot allow the exuberance expressed in Minnie Pearl's art form: "For hours, he caressed her, aroused her, loved her. He worked with her until he felt sure that he had given her a baby, a baby which would weigh her down and destroy her balance so that she would dance no more" (499). Even so, one voice, an oracular community voice, the voice of Miss Lula has warned both Minnie Pearl and Ossie Lee of the unwisdom of their marriage. The story's comment, like the blues lyric, is clear: "no use talkin' if ain't nobody listnin.'" "Frankie Mae," first published in Woodie King's *Black Short Story Anthology* (1972), is also a death-of-spring parable. The title character recalls Ovid's Philomela—the girl-child raped and killed who becomes a nightingale. Frankie, apple of her father's eye, talented, industrious, exuberant, lovely embodiment of her community's most admirable aspirations, is sacrificed to a hope-crushing, obscene sharecropper system and also to sexual bondage; nevertheless, her death galvanizes her community to the action of self-determination.

Read as a comment on the blues chords of Smith's stories, Paule Marshall's "Reena" (1963) enunciates what will later premise Alice Walker's theoretical *womanism*. "Woman," argues Reena, title character of the story, "is a definition formulated by others to serve out their fantasies" (20). Not included in *BF* but first published in the special supplement of *Harper's Magazine* titled "The American Female" and later in Toni Cade Bambara's *The Black Woman: An Anthology* (1970), "Reena" precedes the rise of women's consciousness-raising groups in the 1970s and also prefigures Kate Millet's acclaimed *Sexual Politics* (1969). The affective and effective power of consciousness-raising study groups initiated by such community activists as those foregrounded in Toni Cade Bambara's "The Organizer's Wife" (first published in *The Sea Birds Are Still Alive,* 1977), also points to the work achieved by the Black Panther Party—"organizing black self-defense groups that are dedicated to defending our black community" (Bracey, Meier, and Rudwick 533). The affective consequences of a heightened consciousness is the urbane and hip portrait drawn by John O. Killens in "The Stick Up," first published in Hughes's *Best Stories.*

But the often-neglected emancipatory discourse of women which intensified through the midcentury Black Arts Movement to a crescendo in the seventies is further apparent in such examples included in this anthology as William Melvin Kelley's "The Only Man on Liberty Street" from *Dancers on the Shore,* an exploration of miscegenation that is also a cautionary tale. On the surface, the story seems filtered through the apparatus of the theater of the absurd and the masks of both melodrama and horror genres. But when read as an indication of Kelley's tendency "to draw upon poetic and prose Eddas—the mythology, ethical conceptions and heroic lore of the Norse" (601), as Bernard Bell suggests, one achieves a reading of the story's Mr. Herder as a re-creation of Odin, father of the gods, whose treachery implicates him in the murder of his son Balder, the most beloved god. Bell's reading sees the thematic core of the story to be a contrast between "the Northern origins and chilling life-destroying values of Odin and his descendents and the passionate, life-giving values of Africa and her descendents" (601)—Josie and Jennie of the story. "The Only Man on Liberty Street," like *Dunford's Travels Everywhere,* Kelley's 1969 novel, warns that "Africans and their descendents . . . should beware that their physical and creative energies not be used for fuel to warm the descendents of [Odin]" (601).

That story and Louise Meriwether's "A Happening in Barbados" (first published in the *Antioch Review* in 1968) examine the dehumanizing effects of sexual indignities and what Mary Helen Washington, scholar-critic-anthologist, identifies correctly as "the myth of the white woman." Meriwether's first novel, *Daddy Was a Number Runner* (1967), a coming-of-age narrative, recalls, as Washington observes, Zora Neale Hurston's groundbreaking novel *Their Eyes Were Watching God* (1937). Hurston, a pioneering genius, rediscovered by Larry Neal and Alice Walker, is central to current developments in African American fiction. With the publication of *I Know Why the Caged Bird Sings* (1969), Maya Angelou had begun an experiment which locates "her narratives of being as pioneers of contemporary life-writing" (Traylor, "Maya Angelou" 15). In *Heart of a Woman* (1981), which may be read, in part, as a biography of sensibility, the excerpt included here highlights Black American and global response to the 1973 lurid murder of the Congolese statesman and anti-imperialist Patrice Lumumba. By 1970, Toni Morrison's *The Bluest Eye* not only intensifies the deconstructive discourse of a myth of whiteness traceable in women's fiction as it reverses the traditional "tragic mulatto" theme in African American letters, it also exposes internalized color prejudice as serial murder afflicting the Black psyche. Finally, it radiates the re-visionary strategy that distinguishes her own and African American fiction presently.

The daring revision of the American narrative by mid-twentieth-century Black authors required a separation from its assumptions. That separation, theoretically called "Nationalism," permeates the fiction of the sixties. The responses of Max Reddick in John A. Williams's *The Man Who Cried I Am* and of Dan Freeman in Sam Greenlee's *The Spook Who Sat by the Door* exemplify what Stephen E. Henderson and Mercer Cook call "militant" in their definitive book, *The Militant Black Writer in Africa and the United States* (1969). In its reflection of the mood of the age, Black fiction intensified the question of identity always haunting the American narrative: "Whether he is African or American by place of birth, the black [*sic*] writer by the conditions of his existence has been made intensely aware of a white 'civilization' which, whatever its virtues, nevertheless, does impose its domination on the black [*sic*] body and mind" (Rideout vii). In the nineteenth-century symbolist American novel, it is Herman Melville, "Dear Melville" as John A. Williams calls him, who fully and almost singularly embraces this issue. To paraphrase an observation of the Caribbean theorist C. L. R. James, Melville's spectacular theme in *Moby Dick* is that an obsession with whiteness sank the *Pequod,* the American ship of state. In its "ambiguous," "ambivalent," turbulent nationalistic thrust, the thematics of identity in the fiction of the sixties finds its most profound intensification in the supernal poetic and narratology of Henry Dumas and Ishmael Reed. Both writers stage a declaration of independence from psychic whiteness and achieve a literary imaginary whose cosmology, etymology, ontology, and linguistic enunciation, if known, is certainly not canonized in the white Western world.

In a tribute that only a great peer can confer, John A. Williams quotes a line from Henry Dumas's landmark volume *Play Ebony Play Ivory:* "Last nite we made two shadows disrobe" (37); then he comments: "What a line and what work to understand it . . . Henry Dumas at the piano—we snap our fingers at his rhythms and *deep inside* we understand exactly what he's playing" ("Henry Dumas" 403; italics added). Black consciousness—the "Black Consciousness Movement" of the 1960s—is what Stephen Henderson rightly identifies as

> the real revolution, the transfiguration of blackness [from the] equation of blackness and evil [in] Western religion, Western iconography, Western symbolism [which] conspire to create black self-hatred, black self-denial, black slavery, a necessary first stage in the liberation of black people, and conceivably all Americans. (67 [*sic*])

Indeed, crowning his commemoration of the thirty-three-year-old Henry Dumas, who was shot to death on a Harlem platform of the New York Central Railroad by a white policeman on May 23, 1968, for reasons yet unknown (some say mistaken identity), Williams immortalizes him, saying, "Real knowledge is a threat to things as they are" (403). This insight is a lens through which to read Dumas's "Fon," first published in *BF,* and "Harlem" (circa 1957–65) from *Rope of Wind and Other Stories,* edited and introduced by the poet-scholar-anthologist Eugene B. Redmond in 1979, both included here.

"Harlem," an etiological tale, by its "anagogic" (Jongh 218) method recalls what Kalamu Ya Salaam (formerly Val Ferdinand) has called "the symbolic birth of the Black Arts Movement" (Salaam 70). In an account of his arrival, "Uptown Harlem," leading to the establishment and naming of the Black Arts Repertory Theater, Amiri Baraka (then LeRoi Jones) remembers that "when we came up out of the subway, March 1965 [1964], cold and clear, Harlem all around us staring us down, we felt like pioneers of the new order" (Baraka, *Reader* 64). In Dumas's "Harlem," Harold Kane, the Shaman Presence of the story, also emerges from that same subway; he pauses before "the skeletal ruins of the Islamic Temple . . . like a man in a trance and stared at the wreckage for a long time" (1986). Analogically, the acquainted reader remembers with him the emergence of Black Consciousness—bearing Black Arts apostles to join their colleagues the Umbra Writers already in Harlem. Harold Kane, suffused in their mission, remembers its aspirations: "the rejection of white middle-class cultural values and the affirmation of black selfhood . . . the destruction of anything that stands in the way of selfhood and the celebration of blackness . . . preemptive attack, a kind of intellectual guerilla warfare" (Henderson 72 [*sic*]).

The Shaman grieves over the murdered embodiment of these aspirations as he stands before the emblematic ruined "Temple." As he proceeds down the familiar streets of Harlem, so often inscripted as both cultural source and hideous waste, he arrives at Harlem Square, the place of a cultural shrine, "Micheval's [*sic*] Bookstore [which] for over thirty years, has been an important intellectual meeting place for Africans, Nationalists, Reformers, Muslims, and various dissenters" (184). There, he listens to the harangue of a false prophet whose diatribe re-centers the word *white* and its cognates. As much as this speech reminds the analogic reader of the Nantucket sermon before the men go out to sea in *Moby Dick* and the sermon at Tuskegee Institute in Ralph Ellison's *Invisible Man,* even so, it ignorantly reduces the sacred blood-soaked word of Malcolm and Martin and the concretized ideals of the pioneers of the new order to absurdity. Sickened, the Shaman-figure of Henry Dumas in "Harlem" enacts, arguably, one of three pivotal turns in the history of Western narrative signifying on the Western world. Such a narrative moment occurs when the African Queen Dido irrevocably and silently turns away from the lover who has betrayed her on his way to build Rome in Virgil's *Aeneid.* Another pinpoints the moment when Crèvecoeur's gentleman farmer, overwhelmed by effete sentimentality, turns away from the agonized Black man caged in the edenic garden of South Carolina. The third is the narrative moment when Harold Kane turns his gaze away from the *mythos* of whiteness and its reactionary demagoguery, "heads uptown" to turn east-south-east to answer the question of the modernist Harlem poet Countee Cullen: "What is Africa to me?"

Another modernist poet, the acclaimed T. S. Eliot, had envisioned that the force of creativity to fuel the Western literary imaginary would come from the East. The conclusion of his famous poem *The Wasteland* chants: *DATTA. Dayadhvam. Damyata* (give, sympathize, control) *Shanti, shanti shanti* (the peace which passeth understanding) from the Upanishads. Before the decade of the sixties would end, Henry Dumas and Ishmael Reed would reexamine that vision. In "Fon," the Dumas shaman has shifted shape to become a watchful child "almost liquid in his giant movements . . . a muscular black youth" (*BF* 457). He is being accused and interrogated by a white man. "The youth holds his head level, but his eyes glare outward, *always away from the eyes of the white man*" (457; italics added). He is Alfonso, called Fon by his familiars. Fon is also the name designating *chief* in Cameroon; moreover, it is the name of a people of Benin (Equiano's birthplace). In "Fon" and in the other stories collected as *Ark of Bones,* we enter psychic zones untraveled in the received American narrative but prominent in the fiction of Zora Neale Hurston, anthropologist, story collector, novelist, one mentor of the midcentury Black Arts generation. They also followed the "river" of Langston Hughes and the "goat path" of Jean Toomer straight back to the farthest southern shore: Africa.

When Ishmael Reed calls Dumas "the poet of Resurrection" saying, "He knows Islam, Christianity, Greek, and Yoruban religion"; saying that "this historian, teacher, guide, poet wants [Black people] to be aware of their traditions and their power"; saying that "He is a prophet like St John," that "he successfully mediums the many black male voices that we hear in everyday life," and "will never be harlequined as tranquilizers for the suburbs," we may say that Ishmael Reed owns these very same credentials. In *Cab Calloway Stands in for the Moon* (1970), the Reed shaman "is the long Juju of Aro in eastern Nigeria. A descendent of that long line of conjurers who taught Greeks to oracle . . ." (9). It is this conjurer who "entered a man's dream [the man who is Noxon D. Awful, the Nixon, the president of wrong-headedness] and walked all over as if he owned the place. He moved the scenes around with the deftness of a director from the Hollywood Pantheon" (11). Shamans, conjurers as well as other agencies of diasporic empowerment, people the Reed and Dumas landscapes.

Genius satirist, as much Menippian as Schuyleresque, Ishmael Reed begins with his 1967 novel *The Free-Lance Pallbearers* to liberate zones of the novel explored not by the forays and achievements of Bukka Doopeyduk (parodied hero of *Invisible Man*) but by the Neo-hoodoo (Black Americanized vodun *mysteries*) shaman-heroes such as the Loup Garou in *Yellow Back Radio Broke-Down* and their potent "jes-grew"—the true Black power of a people's coincident thought in *Mumbo Jumbo* (1972). Both Dumas and Reed had been early on published in *Black World,* formerly *Negro Digest,* the Johnson Publication's journal of ideas edited by Hoyt W. Fuller, illustrious and foremost editor of the Black Arts Movement. It is he who initiated the idea of a Black aesthetic. As Dumas and Reed ended the decade, Black Arts fiction had achieved yet again an old-new spring; had inspired and opened the gateway to an actuated multiculturalism emblemized as "the seven sisters of the yam" in Toni Cade Bambara's *The Salt Eaters;* had demonstrated an actuated marriage of abstract and concrete, spiritual and physical knowledge-making wonders which remain the narratological practice of Black Arts–inspired writers even when misnamed magical realism; had continued the Baldwinesque prophecy of reexamination to achieve crescendo as *love yourself,* the "Sermon in the Wilderness" in Morrison's Nobel novel *Beloved;* had begun the remapping of geo-politico-socio-psychic zones exemplified in Edward P. Jones's *The Known World* (2003). It had met "physical force with soul force" (King, August 28, 1963). It had learned to "know, absorb, and value our cultural heritage, but not as a shield for inferiority complexes; rather to become one with self, with Blackness—embracing the universal in man" (Toure, 9, founder of *Umbra* magazine, 1963). Indeed, it had cleared a space in the wilderness for *Dreams of My Father* (2004) by Barack Hussein Obama, president of the United States.

The imaginative impulse for self-fashioning, self-realization, strengthened in the cauldron of America's tempest in the mid-twentieth century, flourishes.

Works Cited

Angelou, Maya. *Heart of a Woman.* 1981. New York: Random House, 2009.

Bambara, Toni Cade. "The Organizer's Wife." 1977. In *The Sea Birds Are Still Alive.* New York: Vintage Books, 1982.

Baraka, Amiri. *The LeRoi Jones/Amiri Baraka Reader,* edited by William J. Harris and Amiri Baraka. New York: Thunder's Mouth Press, 1991.

Baraka, Amiri, and Larry Neal, eds. *Black Fire: An Anthology of Afro-American Writing.* New York: William Morrow, 1968.

Bell, Bernard. "Images of Africa in African American Fiction." In *The New Cavalcade: African American Writing from 1760 to the Present,* 2 vols., edited by Arthur P. Davis, J. Saunders Redding, and Joyce Ann Joyce, 2:591–606. Washington, D.C.: Howard University Press, 1992.

Bewley, Marius. *The Eccentric Design: A Theory of the American Novel.* New York: Columbia University Press, 1963.

Bracey, John, August Meier, and Eliot Rudwick, eds. *Black Nationalism in America.* Indianapolis: Bobbs-Merrill, 1970.

Brisbane, Robert H. "Black Protest in America." In *The Black American Reference Book,* edited by Mabel M. Smythe, 537–79. Englewood Cliffs, N.J.: Prentice-Hall, 1996.

Chaney, Michael. "John A(lfred) Williams Biography." *Biography.jrank.org.*

Cook, Mercer, and Stephen E. Henderson. *The Militant Black Writer in Africa and the United States.* Madison: University of Wisconsin Press, 1969.

Cooper, Susan. *Silver on the Tree.* New York: Aladdin, 1977.

Dumas, Henry. "Fon." In Baraka and Neal, *Black Fire,* 455–66.

———. "Harlem." In *Rope of Wind and Other Stories,* edited by Eugene B. Redmond, 15–40. New York: Random House, 1979.

Fanon, Frantz. *Wretched of the Earth.* 1961. Translated by Constance Farrington. New York: Grove Press, 1963.

Fair, Ronald. "Life with Red Top." In Baraka and Neal, *Black Fire,* 500–509.

———. "Miss Luhester Gives a Party." In Hughes, *Best Short Stories by Negro Writers,* 403–7

Giovanni, Nikki. *Black Feeling, Black Thought, Black Judgment.* New York: William Morrow, 1970.

Greenlee, Sam. *The Spook Who Sat by the Door.* London: Allison & Busby, 1969.

Hughes, Langston, ed. *The Best Short Stories by Negro Writers.* New York: Little, Brown, 1967.

Jongh, James L. "Notes on Henry Dumas's Harlem." *Black American Literature Forum* 22.2 (Summer 1988): 218–20.

Kelley, William Marvin. "The Only Man on Liberty Street."1956. In *Dancers on the Shore,* 1–12. Washington, D.C.: Howard University Press, 1984.

Killens, John O. "The Stick Up." In *Hughes, Best Short Stories by Negro Writers,* 188–91.

King, Martin Luther, Jr. "Facing the Challenge of a New Age." 1956. In *A Testament of Hope: The Essential Writings and Speeches of Martin Luther King Jr.,* edited by James M. Washington, 135–44. New York: HarperCollins, 1986.

Marshall, Paule. "Reena." 1963. In *The Black Woman: An Anthology,* edited by Toni Cade Bambara, 20–37. New York: Washington Square Press, 2005. First published 1970 by New American Library.

Meriwether, Louise. "A Happening in Barbados." *Antioch Review* 28.1 (Spring 1968): 43–52.

Morrison, Toni. *The Bluest Eye.* New York: Alfred A. Knopf, 1970.

Neal, Larry. "The Black Contribution to American Letters: Poet II, the Writer as Activist—1960 and After." In Smythe, *Black American Reference Book,* 767–90.

———. "Sinner Man Where You Gonna Run To?" In Baraka and Neal, *Black Fire,* 510–18.

Reed, Ishmael. *Cab Callaway Stands in for the Moon.* 1970. Flint, Mich.: Bamberger Books, 1986.

———. *The Free-Lance Pallbearers.* 1967. Normal, Ill.: Dalkey Archive Press, 1999.

———. "Henry Dumas: The Poet of Resurrection." *Black American Literature Forum* 22.2 (Summer 1988): 336

———. *Mumbo Jumbo.* 1972. New York: Scribner Paperback Fiction, 1996.

Rowell, Charles H. "An Interview with Wilson Harris." *Callaloo* 18.1 (1995): 191–200.

Salaam, Kalamu Ya. "Historical Overviews of the Black Arts Movement." In *The Oxford Companion to African American Literature,* 70. New York: Oxford University Press, 1997.

Taylor, Clyde. *The Mask of Art: Breaking the Aesthetic Contract—Film and Literature.* Bloomington: Indiana University Press, 1998.

Toure, Askia Mohammed, [Roland Snellings]. *Liberator,* November 1964, 26.

Traylor, Eleanor W. "Maya Angelou Writing Life, Inventing Literary Genres." *Langston Hughes Review* 19.1(Spring 2005): 8–21.

———. "Women Writers of the Black Arts Movement." In *The Cambridge Companion to African American Women's Literature,* edited by Angelyn Mitchell and Danille K. Taylor, 50–70. New York: Cambridge University Press, 2009.

———. "Dumas and the Discourse of Memory." *Black American Literature Forum* 22.2 (Summer 1988): 365–78.

Washington, Mary Helen, ed. *Black-Eyed Susans: Classic Sudies by and about Black Women.* New York: Anchor Books, 1975.

Wheeler Smith, Jean. "Frankie Mae." In *Black Short Story Anthology,* edited by Woodie King. New York: Columbia University Press, 1972.

———. "That She Would Dance No More." In Baraka and Neal, *Black Fire,* 486–99.

Williams John A. "Henry Dumas: Black Word Worker." *Black American Literature Forum* 22.2 (Summer 1988): 402–4.

———. *The Man Who Cried I Am.* New York: Overlook Press, 1967.

The Organizer's Wife

The men from the co-op school were squatting in her garden. Jake, who taught the day students and hassled the town school board, was swiping at the bushy greens with his cap, dislodging slugs, raising dust. The tall gent who ran the graphics workshop was pulling a penknife open with his teeth, scraping rust from the rake she hadn't touched in weeks. Old Man Boone was up and down. Couldn't squat too long on account of the ankle broken in last spring's demonstration when the tobacco weights showed funny. Jack-in-the-box up, Boone snatched at a branch or two and stuffed his pipe—crumblings of dry leaf, bits of twig. Down, he eased string from the seams of his overalls, up again, thrumbling up tobacco from the depths of his pockets.

She couldn't hear them. They were silent. The whole morning stock-still, nothing stirring. The baby quiet too, drowsing his head back in the crook of her arm as she stepped out into the sun already up and blistering. The men began to unbend, shifting weight to one leg then the other, watching her move about the jumbled yard. But no one spoke.

She bathed the baby with the little dew that had gathered on what few leaves were left on the branches crackling, shredding into the empty rain barrels. The baby gurgled, pinching her arms. Virginia had no energy for a smile or a wince. All energy summoned up at rising was focused tightly on her two errands of the day. She took her time going back in, seeing the men shift around in the heaps of tomatoes, in the snarl of the strawberry runners. Stamped her shoe against each step, carrying the baby back in. Still no one spoke, though clearly, farmers all their lives, they surely had some one thing to say about the disarray of her garden.

The young one, whose voice she well knew from the sound truck, had his mouth open and his arm outstretched as though to speak on the good sense of turning every inch of ground to food, or maybe to rant against the crime of letting it just go. He bent and fingered the brown of the poke salad that bordered the dry cabbages, his mouth closing again. Jake rose suddenly and cleared his throat, but turned away to light Old Man Boone's pipe, lending a shoulder for the old one to hunch against, cupping the bowl and holding the match, taking a long lingering time, his back to her. She sucked her teeth and went in.

When she came out again, banding the baby's carry straps around her waist, she moved quickly, stepping into the radishes, crushing unidentifiable shoots underfoot. Jake stepped back out of the way and caught his cuffs in the rake. Jake was the first in a long line to lose

From Toni Cade Bambara, *The Sea Birds Are Still Alive: Collected Stories* (New York: Random House, 1977).

his land to unpaid taxes. The bogus receipts were pinned prominently as always to his jacket pocket. Signed by someone the county said did not exist, but who'd managed nonetheless to buy up Jake's farm at auction and turn it over swiftly to the granite company. She looked from the huge safety pin to the hot, brown eyes that quickly dropped. The other men rose up around her, none taller than she, though all taller than the corn bent now, grit-laden with neglect. Out of the corner of her eye, she saw a white worm work its way into the once-silky tufts turned straw, then disappear.

"Mornin," she said, stretching out her hand.

The men mumbled quickly, clearing their throats again. Boone offering a hand in greeting, then realizing she was extending not her hand but the small, round tobacco tin in it. Graham's red tobacco tin with the boy in shiny green astride an iron horse. It was Graham's habit, when offering a smoke, to spin some tale or other about the boy on the indestructible horse, a tale the smoker would finish. The point always the same—the courage of the youth, the hope of the future. Boone drew his hand back quickly as though the red tin was aflame. She curled her hand closed and went out the gate, slowly, deliberately, fixing her tall, heavy image indelibly on their eyes.

"Good-for-nuthin."

They thought that's what they heard drift back over her shoulder. Them? The tin? The young one thought he saw her pitch it into the clump of tomatoes hanging on by the gate. But no one posed the question.

"Why didn't you say somethin?" Jake demanded of his star pupil, the orator, whose poems and tales and speeches delivered from the sound truck had done more to pull the districts together, the women all said, than all the leaflets the kids cluttered the fields with, than all the posters from the co-op's graphic workshop masking the road signs, than all the meetings which not all the folk could get to.

"Why didn't you speak?" Jake shoved the young one, and for a minute they were all stumbling, dancing nimbly to avoid destroying food that could still be salvaged.

"Watch it, watch it now," Old Boone saying, checking his foot brace and grabbing the young one up, a fistful of sleeve.

"You shoulda said somethin," the tall gent spat.

"Why me?" The young one whined—not in the voice he'd cultivated for the sound truck. "I don't know her no better than yawl do."

"One of the women shoulda come," said the tall gent.

The men looked at each other, then stared down the road. It was clear that no one knew any more how to talk to the bristling girl-woman, if ever any had.

It wasn't a shift in breeze that made the women look up, faces stuck out as if to catch the rain. 'Cause there was no breeze and there'd been no rain. And look like, one of them said, there'd be no bus either. The strained necks had more to do with sound than weather. Someone coming. A quick check said all who worked in town were already gathered at the bus stop. Someone coming could only mean trouble—fire broke out somewhere, riot in town, one of the children hurt, market closed down, or maybe another farm posted. The women standing over their vegetable baskets huddled together for conference, then broke apart to jut their bodies out over the road for a look-see. The women seated atop the bags of rags or uniforms, clustered to question each other, then scattered, some standing tiptoe, others merely leaning up from the rocks to question the market women. And in that brief second, as bodies pulled upward, the rocks blotted up more sun to sear them, sting them, sicken them with. These stones, stacked generations ago to keep the rain from washing the road away, banked higher and broader by the young folk now to keep the baking earth from breaking apart.

Virginia nodded to the women, her earrings tinkling against her neck. The "Mornins" and "How do's" came scraggly across the distance. The bus-stop plot was like an island separated from the mainland road by shimmering sheets of heat, by arid moats and gullies that had once been the drainage system, dried-out craters now misshapen, as though pitted and gouged by war.

One clear voice rising above the scattered sopranos, calling her by name, slowed Virginia down. Frankie Lee Taylor, the lead alto in the choir, was standing on the rocks waving, out of her choir robes and barely recognizable but for that red-and-yellow jumper, the obligatory ugly dress just right for the kitchens in town. "Everything all right?" the woman asked for everyone there. And not waiting for a word once Virginia's face could be read by all, she continued: "Bus comin at all, ever?"

Virginia shrugged and picked up her pace. If the six-thirty bus was this late coming, she thought, she could make the first call and be back on the road in time for the next bus to town. She wouldn't have to borrow the church station wagon after all. She didn't want to have to ask for nothing. When she saw Graham that afternoon she wanted the thing stitched up, trimmed, neat, finished. Wanted to be able to say she asked for "nuthin from nobody and didn't nobody offer up nuthin." It'd be over with. They'd set bail and she'd pay it with the money withheld from the seed and the fertilizer, the wages not paid to the two students who used to help in the garden, the money saved 'cause she was too cranky to eat, to care. Pay the bail and unhook them both from this place. Let some other damn fool break his health on this place, the troubles.

She'd been leaving since the first day coming, the day her sister came home to cough herself to death and leave her there with nobody to look out for her 'cept some hinkty cousins in town and Miz Mama Mae, who shook her head sadly whenever the girl spoke of this place and these troubles and these people and one day soon leaving for some other place. She'd be going now for sure. Virginia was smiling now and covering a whole lotta ground.

Someone was coming up behind her, churning up the loose layers of clay, the red-and-yellow jumper a mere blur in the haze of red dust. Everyone these dry, hot days looked like they'd been bashed with a giant powder puff of henna. Virginia examined her own hands, pottery-red like the hands of her cousins seen through the beauty-parlor windows in town, hands sunk deep in the pots, working up the mud packs for the white women lounging in the chairs. She looked at her arms, her clothes, and slowed down. Not even well into the morning and already her skimpy bath ruined. The lime-boiled blouse no longer white but pink.

"Here, Gin," the woman was saying. "He a good man, your man. He share our hardships, we bear his troubles, our troubles." She was stuffing money in between the carry straps, patting the chubby legs as the baby lolled in his cloth carriage. "You tell Graham we don't forget that he came back. Lots of the others didn't, forgot. You know, Gin, that you and me and the rest of the women . . ." She was going to say more but didn't. Was turning with her mouth still open, already trotting up the road, puffs of red swirling about her feet and legs, dusting a line in that red-and-yellow jumper the way Miz Mama Mae might do making hems in the shop.

Virginia hoisted the baby higher on her back and rewound the straps, clutching the money tight, flat in her fist. She thought about Miz Mama Mae, pins in her mouth, fussing at her. "What's them hanky-type hems you doin, Gin?" she'd say, leaning over her apprentice. "When ya sew for the white folks you roll them kinda stingy hems. And you use this here oldish thread to insure a quick inheritance. But when you sew for us folks, them things got to last season in and season out and many a go-round exchange. Make some hefty hems, girl, hefty."

And Virginia had come to measure her imprisonment by how many times that same red-and-yellow jumper met her on the road, faded and fading some more, but the fairly bright hem getting wider and wider, the telltale rim recording the seasons past, the owners grown. While she herself kept busting out of her clothes, straining against the good thread, outdistancing the hefty hems. Growing so fast from babe to child to girl to someone, folks were always introducing and reintroducing themselves to her. It seemed at times that the walls wouldn't contain her, the roof wouldn't stop her. Busting out of childhood, busting out her clothes, but never busting out the place.

And now the choir woman had given her the money like that and spoken, trying to attach her all over again, root her, ground her in the place. Just when there was a chance to get free. Virginia clamped her jaws tight and tried to go blank. Tried to blot out all feelings and things—the farms, the co-op sheds, the lone gas pump, a shoe left in the road, the posters promising victory over the troubles. She never wanted these pictures called up on some future hot, dry day in some other place. She squinted, closed her eyes even, 'less the pictures cling to her eyes, store in the brain, to roll out later and crush her future with the weight of this place and its troubles.

Years before when there'd been rain and ways to hold it, she'd trotted along this road not seeing too much, trotting and daydreaming, delivering parcels to and from Miz Mama Mae's shop. She could remember that one time, ducking and dodging the clods of earth chucked up by the horse's hooves. Clods spinning wet and heavy against her skirts, her legs, as she followed behind, seeing nothing outside her own pictures but that horse and rider. Trying to keep up, keep hold of the parcel slipping all out of shape in the drizzle, trying to piece together the things she would say to him when he finally turned round and saw her. She had lived the scene often enough in bed to know she'd have to speak, say something to make him hoist her up behind him in the saddle, to make him gallop her off to the new place. She so busy dreaming, she let the curve of the road swerve her off toward the edge. Mouthing the things to say and even talking out loud with her hands and almost losing the slippery bundle, not paying good enough attention. And a ball of earth shot up and hit her square in the chest and sent her stumbling over the edge into the gully. The choir organist's robe asprawl in the current that flushed the garbage down from the hill where the townies lived, to the bottom where the folks lived, to the pit where the co-op brigade made compost heaps for independence, laughing.

Graham had pulled her up and out by the wrists, pulled her against him and looked right at her. Not at the cabbage leaves or chicory on her arms, a mango sucked hairy to its pit clinging to her clothes. But looked at her. And no screen door between them now. No glass or curtain, or shrub peeked through.

"You followin me." He grinned. And she felt herself swimming through the gap in his teeth.

And now she would have to tell him. 'Cause she had lost three times to the coin flipped on yesterday morning. Had lost to the icepick pitched in the afternoon in the dare-I-don't-I boxes her toe had sketched in the yard. Had lost at supper to the shadow slanting across the tablecloth that reached her wrist before Miz Mama Mae finished off the corn relish. Had lost that dawn to the lazy lizard, suddenly quickened in his journey on the ceiling when the sun came up. Lost against doing what she'd struggled against doing in order to win one more day of girlhood before she jumped into her womanstride and stalked out on the world. I want to come to you. I want to come to you and be with you. I want to be your woman, she did not say after all.

"I want to come to the co-op school," she said. "I want to learn to read better and type and figure and keep accounts so I can get out of . . ."—this place, she didn't say—"my situation."

He kept holding her and she kept wanting and not wanting to ease out of his grip and rescue the choir robe before it washed away.

"I had five years schooling 'fore I came here," she said, talking way too loud. "Been two years off and on at the church school . . . before you came."

"You do most of Miz Mama Mae's cipherin I hear? Heard you reading the newspapers to folks in the tobacco shed. You read well."

She tried to pull away then, thinking he was calling her a liar or poking fun some way. "Cipherin" wasn't how he talked. But he didn't let go. She expected to see her skin twisted and puckered when she looked at where he was holding her. But his grip was soft. Still she could not step back.

"You been watchin me," he said with the grin again. And looking into his face, she realized he wasn't at all like she'd thought. Was older, heavier, taller, smoother somehow. But then looking close up was not like sneaking a look from the toolshed as he'd come loping across the fields with his pigeon-toed self and in them soft leather boots she kept waiting to see fall apart from rough wear till she finally decided he must own pairs and pairs of all the same kind. Yes, she'd watched him on his rounds, in and out of the houses, the drying sheds, down at the docks, after fellowship in the square. Talking, laughing, teaching, always moving. Had watched him from the trees, through windows as he banged tables, arguing about deeds, urging, coaxing, pleading, hollering, apologizing, laughing again. In the early mornings, before Miz Mama Mae called the girls to sew, she had watched him chinning on the bar he'd slammed between the portals of the co-op school door. Huffing, puffing, cheeks like chipmunks. The dark circle of his gut sucking in purple, panting out blue. Yes, she watched him. But she said none of this or of the other either. Not then.

"I want to come to night school" was how she put it. "I don't know yet what kinda work I can do for the co-op. But I can learn."

"That's the most I ever heard you talk," he was saying, laughing so hard, he loosened his grip. "In the whole three years I've been back, that's the most—" He was laughing again. And he was talking way too loud himself.

She hadn't felt the least bit foolish standing there in the drizzle, in the garbage, tall up and full out of her clothes nearly, and Graham laughing at her. Not the least bit foolish 'cause he was talking too loud and laughing too hard. And she was going to go to his school. And whether he knew it or not, he was going to take her away from this place.

Wasn't but a piece of room the school, with a shed tacked on in back for storage and sudden meetings. The furniture was bandaged but brightly painted. The chemistry equipment was old but worked well enough. The best thing was the posters. About the co-op, about Malcolm and Harriet and Fannie Lou, about Guinea-Bissau and Vietnam. And the posters done by the children, the pictures cut from magazines, the maps—all slapped up as though to hold the place together, to give an identity to the building so squat upon the land. The identity of the place for her was smells. The smell of mortar vibrating from the walls that were only wood. The smell of loam that curled up from the sink, mostly rusted metal. The green-and-brown smell rising up over heads sunk deep into palms as folks leaned over their papers, bearing down on stumps of pencil or hunks of charcoal, determined to get now and to be what they'd been taught was privilege impossible, what they now knew was their right, their destiny.

"Season after season," Graham was dictating that first night, leaning up against the maps with the ruler, "we have pulled gardens out of stones, creating something from nothing—creators."

Sweat beading on a nose to her left, a temple to her right. Now and then a face she knew from fellowship looking up as Graham intoned the statements, tapping the ruler against the table to signal punctuation traps. And she working hard, harder than some, though she never ever did learn to speak her speak as most folks finally did. But grateful just to be there, and up in front, unlike the past when, condemned by her size, she'd been always exiled in the rear with the goldfish tanks or the rabbits that always died, giving her a suspect reputation.

"The first step toward getting the irrigation plant," he continued, crashing the ruler down, "is to organize."

"Amen," said one lady by the window, never looking up from her paper, certain she would finally train herself and be selected secretary of the church board. "That way us folks can keep track of them folks" was how she'd said it when she rose to speak her speak one summer night.

"What can defeat greed, technological superiority, and legal lawlessness," Graham had finished up, "is discipline, consciousness, and unity."

Always three sentences that folks would take home for discussion, for transformation into well-ordered paragraphs that wound up, some of them, in the co-op newsletter or on the posters or in the church's bulletin. Many became primers for the children.

Graham had been wearing the denim suit with the leather buckles the first night in class. Same fancy suit she'd caught sight of through the screen door when he'd come calling on Miz Mama Mae to buy the horse. A denim suit not country-cut at all—in fact, so *not* she was sure he would be leaving. Dudes in well-cut denim'd been coming and leaving since the days she wore but one yard of cloth. It was his would-be-moving-on clothes that had pulled her to him. But then the pull had become too strong to push against once his staying-on because clear.

She often fixed him supper in a metal cake tin once used for buttons. And Miz Mama Mae joked with the pin cushion, saying the girl weren't fooling nobody but herself sneaking around silly out there in the pantry with the button box. Telling the bobbins it was time certain folk grew up to match they size. And into the night, treadling away on the machine, the woman addressed the dress form, saying a strong, serious-type schoolteacher man had strong, serious work to do. Cutting out the paper patterns, the woman told the scissors that visiting a man in his rooms at night could mean disaster or jubilee one. And Virginia understood she would not be stopped by the woman. But some felt she was taking up too much of his time, their time. He was no longer where they could find him for homework checks or questions about the law. And Jake and Old Man Boone sullen, nervous that the midnight strategy meetings were too few now and far between. The women of the nearby district would knock and enter with trapped firefly lanterns, would shove these on the table between the couple, and make their point as Graham nodded and Virginia giggled or was silent, one.

His quilt, Graham explained, leaving the earrings on the table for her to find, was made from patches from his daddy's overalls, and scraps from Boone's wedding cutaway, white remnants from his mother's shroud, some blue from a sister's graduation, and khaki, too, snatched from the uniform he'd been proud of killing in in Korea a hundred lives ago. The day students had stitched a liberation flag in one corner. The night students had restuffed it and made a new border. She and Miz Mama Mae had stitched it and aired it. And Virginia had brought it back to him, wrapped in it. She had rolled herself all in it, to hide from him in her new earrings, childish. But he never teased that she was too big for games, and she liked that. He found her in it, his tongue finding the earrings first. Careful, girl, she'd warned herself. This could be a trap, she murmured under him.

"Be my woman," he whispered into her throat.

You don't have time for me, she didn't say, lifting his tikis and medallions up over his head. And there'd never be enough time here with so many people, so much land to work, so much to do, and the wells not even dug, she thought, draping the chains around his bedpost.

"Be my woman, Gin," he said again. And she buried her fingers in his hair and he buried his hair inside her clothes and she pulled the quilt close and closed him in, crying.

She was leaking. The earrings tinkling against her neck. The medallions clinking against the bedpost in her mind. Gray splotches stiffened in her new pink blouse, rubbing her nipples raw. But other than a dribble that oozed momentarily down her back, there was no sign of the baby aroused and hungry. If the baby slept on, she'd keep on. She wanted to reach Revun Michaels before the white men came. Came this time brazenly with the surveyors and the diggers, greedy for the granite under the earth. Wanted to catch Revun Michaels before he showed them his teeth and couldn't hear her, couldn't, too much smiling. Wanted to hear him say it—the land's been sold. The largest passel of land in the district, the church holdings where the co-op school stood, where two storage sheds of the co-op stood, where the graphics workshop stood, where four families had lived for generations working the land. The church had sold the land. He'd say it, she'd hear it, and it'd be over with. She and Graham could go.

She was turning the bend now, forgetting to not look, and the mural the co-op had painted in eye-stinging colors stopped her. FACE UP TO WHAT'S KILLING YOU, it demanded. Below the statement a huge triangle that from a distance was just a triangle, but on approaching, as one muttered 'how deadly can a triangle be?' turned into bodies on bodies. At the top, fat, fanged beasts in smart clothes, like the ones beneath it laughing, drinking, eating, bombing, raping, shooting, lounging on the backs of, feeding off the backs of, the folks at the base, crushed almost flat but struggling to get up and getting up, topple the structure. She passed it quickly. All she wanted to think about was getting to Revun Michaels quick to hear it. Sold the land. Then she'd be free to string together the bits and scraps of things for so long bobbing about in her head. Things that had to be pieced together well, with strong thread so she'd have a whole thing to shove through the mesh at Graham that afternoon.

And would have to shove hard or he'd want to stay, convinced that folks would battle for his release, would battle for themselves, the children, the future, would keep on no matter how powerful the thief, no matter how little the rain, how exhausted the soil, 'cause this was home. Not a plot of earth for digging in or weeping over or crawling into, but home. Near the Ethiopic where the ancestral bones spoke their speak on certain nights if folks stamped hard enough, sang long enough, shouted. Home. Where "America" was sung but meant something altogether else than it had at the old school. Home in the future. The future here now developing. Home liberated soon. And the earth would recover. The rain would come. The ancient wisdoms would be revived. The energy released. Home a human place once more. The bones spoke it. The spirit spoke, too, through flesh when the women gathered at the altar, the ancient orishas still vibrant beneath the ghostly patinas some thought right to pray to, but connected in spite of themselves to the spirits under the plaster.

WE CANNOT LOSE, the wall outside the church said. She paused at the bulletin board, the call-for-meeting flyers limp in the heat. She bent to spit but couldn't raise it. She saw Revun Michaels in the schoolhouse window watching her. He'd say it. Sold the land.

Virginia wondered what the men in her ruined garden were telling themselves now about land as power and land and man tied to the future, not the past. And what would they tell the women when the bulldozers came to claim the earth, to maim it, rape it, plunder it all with that bone-deep hatred for all things natural? And what would the women tell the children dangling in the tires waiting for Jake to ring the bell? Shouting from the clubhouses built in the trees? The slashed trees oozing out money into the white man's pails, squeezing hard to prolong a tree life, forestalling the brutal cut down to stump. Then stump wasting, no more money to give, blown up out of the earth, the iron claw digging deep and merciless to rip out the taproots, leaving for the children their legacy, an open grave, gouged out by a gene-deep hatred for all things natural, for all things natural that couldn't turn a quick penny quick enough to dollar. She spit.

Revun Michaels, small and balding, was visible in the schoolhouse window. His expression carried clear out the window to her, watching her coming fast, kicking himself for getting caught in there and only one door, now that the shed was nailed on fast in back.

"Did you sell the land as well?" she heard herself saying, rushing in the doorway much too fast. "You might have waited like folks asked you. You didn't have to. Enough granite under this schoolhouse alone"—she stamped, frightening him—"to carry both the districts for years and years, if we developed it ourselves." She heard the "we ourselves" explode against her teeth and she fell back.

"Wasn't me," he stammered. "The church board saw fit to—"

"Fit!" She was advancing now, propelled by something she had no time to understand. "Wasn't nuthin fitten about it." She had snatched the ruler from its hook. The first slam hard against the chair he swerved around, fleeing. The next cracked hard against his teeth. His legs buckled under and he slid down, his face frozen in disbelief. But nothing like the disbelief that swept through her the moment "we ourselves" pushed past clenched teeth and nailed her to the place, a woman unknown. She saw the scene detached, poster figures animated: a hefty woman pursuing a scrambling man in and out among the tables and chairs in frantic games before Jake rang the bell for lessons to commence.

"And what did the white folks pay you to turn Graham in and clear the way? Disturber of the peace. What peace? Racist trying to incite a riot. Ain't that how they said it? Outside agitator, as you said. And his roots put down here long before you ever came. When you were just a twinkle in Darwin's eye." Virginia heard herself laughing. It was a good, throaty laugh and big. The man was turning round now on the floor, staring at her in amazement.

"Thirty pieces of silver, maybe? That's what you preach, tradition. Thirty pieces 'bout as traditional as—"

"Just hold on. It wasn't me that—The board of trustees advised me that this property could not be used for—"

The ruler came down on the stiff of his arm and broke. Michaels dropped between two rickety chairs that came apart on top of him. The baby cried, the woman shushed, as much to quiet the woman that was her. Calm now, she watched the man try to get up, groping the chairs the folks had put together from cast-offs for the school. Her shoe caught him at the side of his head and he went under.

The station wagon was pulling up as she was coming out, flinging the piece of ruler into the bushes. She realized then that the men had come in it, that the station wagon had been sitting all morning in her garden. That they had come to take her to see Graham. She bit her lip. She never gave folk a chance, just like Miz Mama Mae always fussed. Never gave them or herself a chance to speak the speak.

"We'll take you to him," Jake was saying, holding the door open and easing the baby off her back.

The young one shoved over. "Mother Lee who's secretarying for the board has held up the papers for the sale. We came to tell you that." He waited till she smiled to laugh. "We're the delegation that's going to confront the board this evening. Us and Frankie Lee Taylor and—"

"Don't talk the woman to death," said Boone, turning in his seat and noting her daze. He was going to say more, but the motor drowned him out. Virginia hugged the baby close and unbuttoned her blouse.

"That's one sorry piece of man," drawled Boone as they pulled out. All heads swung to the right to see the short, fat, balding preacher darting in and out among the gravestones for the sanctuary of the church. To the phone, Virginia figured. And would they jail her too, she and the baby?

Then everyone was silent before the naked breast and the sucking. Silence was what she needed. And time, to draw together tight what she'd say to Graham. How blood had spurted from Revun Michaels's ear, for one thing. Graham might not want to hear it, but there was no one else to tell it to, to explain how it was when all she thought she wanted was to hear it said flat out—land's been sold, school's no more. Not that a school's a building, she argued with herself, watching the baby, playing with the image of herself speaking her speak finally in the classroom, then realizing that she already had. By tomorrow the women would have burrowed beneath the tale of some swinging door or however Revun Michaels would choose to tell it. But would the women be able to probe and sift and explain it to her? Who could explain her to her?

And how to explain to Graham so many things. About this new growth she was experiencing, was thinking on at night wrapped in his quilt. Not like the dread growing up out of her clothes as though she'd never stop 'fore she be freak, 'cause she had stopped. And not like the new growth that was the baby, for she'd expected that, had been prepared. More like the toenail smashed the day the work brigade had stacked the stones to keep the road from splitting apart. The way the new nail pushed up against the old turning blue, against the gauze and the tape, stubborn to establish itself. A chick pecking through the shell, hard-headed and hasty and wobbly. She might talk of it this time. She was convinced she could get hold of it this time.

She recalled that last visiting time trying to speak on what was happening to her coming through the shell. But had trouble stringing her feelings about so many things together, words to drape around him, to smother all those other things, things she had said, hurled unstrung, flung out with tantrum heat at a time when she thought there would always be time enough to coolly take them back, be woman warm in some elsewhere place and make those hurtful words forgettable. But then they had come for him in the afternoon, came and got him, took him from the schoolhouse in handcuffs. And when she had visited him in the jail, leaning into the mesh, trying to push past the barrier, she could tell the way the guards hovered around her and baby that clearly they thought she could do, would do, what they had obviously tried over and over to do, till Graham was ashy and slow, his grin lax. That she could break him open so they could break him down. She almost had, not knowing it, leaking from the breast as she always did not keeping track of the time. Stuttering, whining, babbling, hanging on to the mesh with one hand, the other stuffed in her mouth, her fingers ensnarled in the skein of words coming out all tangled, knotted.

"I don't mind this so much," he'd cut in. "Time to think."

And when she pulled her fingers from her mouth, the thread broke and all her words came bouncing out in a hopeless scatter of tears and wails until something—her impatience with her own childishness, or maybe it was the obvious pleasure of the guards—made her grab herself up. She grabbed herself up abrupt, feeling in that moment what it was she wanted to say about her nights wrapped up in the quilt smelling him in it, hugging herself, grabbing herself up and trying to get to that place that was beginning to seem more of a when than a where. And the when seemed to be inside her if she could only connect.

"I kinda like the quiet," he had said. "Been a while since I've had so much time to think." And then he grinned and was ugly. Was that supposed to make her hate him? To hate and let go? That had occurred to her on the bus home. But roaming around the house, tripping on the edges of the quilt, she had rejected it. That was not the meaning of his words or that smile that had torn his face. She'd slumped in the rocking chair feeding the baby, examining her toenail for such a time.

"They never intended to dig the wells, that's clear," Old Man Boone was saying. "That was just to get into the district, get into our business, check out our strength. I was a fool," he muttered, banging his pipe against his leg remembering his hopefulness, his hospitality even. "A fool."

"Well, gaddamn, Boone," the tall gent sputtered. "Can't you read? That's what our flyers been saying all along. Don't you read the stuff we put out? Gaddamnit, Boone."

"If you don't read the flyers, you leastways knows history," the young one was saying. "When we ever invited the beast to dinner he didn't come in and swipe the napkins and start taking notes on the tablecloth 'bout how to take over the whole house?"

"Now that's the truth," Jake said, laughing. His laughter pulled Virginia forward, and she touched his arm, moved. That he could laugh. His farm stolen and he could laugh. But that was one of the three most moving things about Jake, she was thinking. The way he laughed. The way he sweated. The way he made his body comfy for the children to lean against.

"Yeh, they sat right down to table and stole the chicken," said Jake.

"And took the table. And the deed." The tall gent smacked Jake on his cap.

"Yeh," Old Man Boone muttered, thinking of Graham.

"We ain't nowhere's licked yet though, huhn?"

The men looked quickly at Virginia, Jake turning clear around, so that Boone leaned over to catch the steering wheel.

"Watch it, watch it now, young feller."

"There's still Mama Mae's farm," Virginia continued, patting the baby. "Enough granite under there even if the church do—"

"But they ain't," said the young one. "Listen, we got it all figured out. We're going to bypass the robbers and deal directly with the tenant councils in the cities, and we're—"

"Don't talk the woman to death," soothed Boone. "You just tell Graham his landlady up there in the North won't have to eat dog food no more. No more in life. New day coming."

"And you tell him . . ."—Jake was turning around again—"just tell him to take his care."

By the time the bolt had lifted and she was standing by the chair, the baby fed and alert now in her arms, she had done with all the threads and bits and shards of the morning. She knew exactly what to tell him, coming through the steel door now, reaching for the baby he had not held yet, could not hold now, screened off from his father. All she wished to tell him was the bail'd been paid, her strength was back, and she sure as hell was going to keep up the garden. How else to feed the people?

Harlem

Prologue: Harlem Square

Micheval's bookstore, guarding the northeast like an outpost for over thirty years, has been an important intellectual meeting place for Africans, Nationalists, Reformers, Muslims, and various dissenters. Some people call it Harlem Square. Almost every weekday evening a small crowd will gather to listen to the haranguing of one of a half-dozen speakers who stand on small platforms or ladders. On weekends the crowd has to be watched by the police. Harlem Square is then in some ways the pulse and the barometer of the community. You can tell the mood of the people by visiting Harlem Square. Of course, over the past ten years the mood of Harlem has been the same, and one doesn't have to visit the square to ascertain what it is. . . . Many Harlemites feel that they are living in hell.

The Lenox Avenue subway shot through its tunnel, shaking the tracks and debris. A hot blast of air leaped from the subway cavity, as if the train had screamed. The train roared into the station, stopped, recharged itself, and waited. Harold Kane, sitting with his head down and his eyes closed, suddenly looked up, peered through the standing people, and pushed his way off the train. Just as Harold was half out, the doors began to close. His leg caught; the train hissed, the doors reopened and Harold stumbled off the train. He looked around, went through the turnstile, and slowly made his way up the steps, brushing often against people, as ants do in a moving line.

Harold was tall and muscular. He looked older than twenty-two. As he came up out of the subway and onto the street, the sunless haze over Harlem showed his skin to be dark but tinged with redness, as if the blood were going to suddenly break through. His eyes were very large and watered a lot, and even though he moved along the street in a glide, a slow, aimless flow, there was a latent quickness about his walk. At the corner, he did not wait for the light as did some other pedestrians, but weaved behind a passing car, around another, alongside another, and then with his head held dreamlike he stepped upon the sidewalk on the other side of the street. There he stood beside a fire hydrant and looked up at the skeletal ruins of the Islamic Temple.

High over the ruins a flock of pigeons circled, arcing off, and then swooping up again,

---

From Henry Dumas, *Rope of Wind and Other Stories,* ed. with intro. by Eugene R. Redmond (New York: Random House, 1979).

playing in the wind. Harold squinted closely at the building. A man came and stood by him. They both looked up. People passed. A woman stopped at the corner newsstand and bought a paper. The man was young and neatly dressed. He looked at Harold, who continued to examine the wreckage without acknowledging the other.

"Well, Broh," the young man finally said, "I see you anxious to know when the mosque will be rebuilt." Harold rubbed the fire hydrant with his right hand. He looked at the bundle of newspapers under the young man's arms. "Paper?" The young Brother was handing him one. Harold paid for it and tucked it under his arm. The other moved away and began to hustle off the papers to passers-by. The wreckage was strewn all over the sidewalk—bits of burnt wood, debris, and broken glass. The police had erected a barricade around the burnt-out stores. There were several beside the temple, which stood right in the center. On one side was a beauty parlor, dress shop, bakery, and a drugstore. On the other was a tavern, barbershop, poolroom, and pawnshop. All these had been completely burned down. But the temple was the hardest hit. A bomb had leveled the walls and pillars. Harold watched the scene with a curious familiarity. While the young Brother was selling papers, he kept a close eye on Harold. Soon he and another Brother had their heads together. They had seen him gazing every day now for the last week. At a certain time Harold emerged from the subway like a man in a trance, and stared at the wreckage for a long time. His expression, twisted up with some concealed misery, kept the astute young Brothers from questioning him. They expected him, any day now, to break out in tears.

A bus roared past. Harold leaned his head against the newsstand. He slowly brought his right hand around and touched the top as if he were feeling for something very small. Then he looked at his smudged fingers. He put his head down on his arms again. For ten minutes he leaned up against the rear of the newsstand, not moving except for the shaking and shuddering of his body like spasms of pain. The subway roared beneath him. The street was loud and noisy. People darted here and there. Many stood and looked at him. Most of them thought that he was about to vomit. Perhaps he was. But the heaving of his body was far deeper than his stomach. Suddenly he raised his head and walked off toward Seventh Avenue and Harlem Square.

A group of kids was running toward Harold, and behind them was a man in an apron waving a stick. People stopped to look. There were shouts, but the kids soon disappeared, zipping across the street in the middle of traffic. Several cars screeched to a halt. In front of a record store where the music was pouring onto the street like syrup, four teen-age girls and two boys were dancing, and one of the boys was beating out a rhythm on the showcase window with his fist. Harold moved through the crowd. An elderly woman dressed in a long cloak and with a big gold cross around her neck was weaving through the throng, handing out pamphlets. She put one in Harold's hands, but he put it in his pocket automatically, without even looking. A siren sounded blocks away, and a few people ran off in the direction of the siren. A wino was stopping people up the block near Seventh Avenue. He was holding out his hand and leaning forward. When he came to Harold he assumed a different posture, straightening himself up a bit and wiping the dribble from his mouth with his sleeve. Instead of holding his hand out to Harold, he grabbed him by the elbow.

Harold was dressed in a worn suit coat and a pair of khaki pants. His blue sport shirt had sweat and dirt stains overlapping the collar, and his shoes were runover and unshined. The beggar appeared no better off, but he looked Harold over carefully and probably surmised, *Here comes a good one.* "Please, sir," he said—a slight affectation slurring his words—"could you help me get a sandwich?" He showed his hand. "I just need a dime . . ." He was pulling on Harold's coat. Harold dug into his pocket, brought out the newspaper, searched around, brought out cigarettes, then a quarter, and gave it to the man without looking at him. The man, speechless for a split second, thanked him in a low voice and backed off, inspecting the quarter, squeezing it, and then looking around the crowd. He looked as if he were trying to find out who saw him. Then he moved on down the street and began to beg again, adopting the same pose he had taken before he had tapped Harold.

A cop stood in the midst of a group of young toughs across the street. Another cop was crossing the street to them, holding his hand up to stop traffic. The cop on the sidewalk was tongue-lashing the toughs, who taunted him loudly and then scattered. Later, the two cops stood waving them away. The toughs, moving through the crowd, suddenly began to run, and a bottle crashed against the sidewalk. The cops took off, chasing them. They all disappeared around the corner of Lenox Avenue. Harold went on toward Seventh.

At Harlem Square the crowds were gathering. Traffic moved slowly, and all along Seventh Avenue people were sitting on boxes, in chairs, on rails, on the ramp in the middle of the avenue, and even on the roofs. High over the city heads sprouted, leaning over the roofs, making it look as if the building was boiling over. And the street received the crowds, who found that the heat and the boredom were too much to fight alone in the musty roach-ruled tenements. Men, women, children, old and young, poured into the streets. Gangs perched on roofs like vultures waiting for something to happen below. A small parade ensemble made loud music in one block, and the music carried up and down the avenue. Conga drums, timbals, cowbells, guitars, gourds, and flutes harmonized raucously and shook the streets. Even small children were infected by the strange malady of hate and boredom. They had formed little squadrons, and went about with sticks and toy rifles, pistols and cap guns, firing and ambushing unseen enemies. They often aimed at the targets on the roofs, and they ducked down into the basements or into alleyways behind garbage cans for protection and concealment.

Harold stood across from the bookstore. At the corner was Goodman's Jewelry Store, with its huge multicolored diamond flashing on and off overhead. Harold looked up at it, squinting his eyes. He rubbed his head and leaned back against the wall. Closing his eyes briefly, he wavered on his feet. Then he crossed the street with the green light amidst a crowd of people who moved along like ants on a march. When Harold reached the other side he stood by a fire hydrant and watched the sojourn of the American flag as it moved from the door of the bookstore to the center of a crowd standing around a platform under the diamond.

Elder Dawud was preparing to deliver his evening message to the people. He walked behind a man carrying the flag. Another man was setting up a ladder for the Elder, and every once in a while somebody shouted a greeting at Elder Dawud. The people knew him. He was one of the many sidewalk prophets who—more than once—had indirectly caused the people to react in concert over some issue of concern to Harlemites. He was a short, dark man, about forty years old, but his thinness gave him the appearance of youth. He was clean-shaven, but his hair—thick and woolly on the sides, but balding on top—stuck out from the sides of his head. After carefully cleaning his spectacles, he folded some papers, put them in his small brief case, and handed the case to one of his aides.

They stood around the ladder like a cordon. He shook hands with several people, looked at his watch, and mounted the ladder. When the people saw him, a hush flowed over them. The only noise was the whine of the siren in the distance, the honk and flow of traffic, and the unidentified roar that emerged from all of the streets of Harlem.

Harold Kane began to cough. He bent over, holding his sides, and coughed into the gutter.

"Many of you out there . . ." began Elder Dawud, his voice slow and liquid, as if it were being oiled for something. From his throat came a slight rattle, and it gave the impression of motion and force. ". . . want to know just how is it that a black man can live in the middle of the richest country on earth and be starving like a sharecropper. Heh? Many of you want to know about that. Now, again, many of you out there . . ." and he paused to smile and point at the people, ". . . and I ought to know because I lived with a lot of you out there . . ." and there was a slight stir amongst the crowd.

Harold moved in closer. He was shaking.

"Many of you want to know what to tell your children when they ask you why you let the policeman hit you, heh? Now, I am not one to advocate anarchy, no. Brothers, I am the most law-abiding citizen. But I'm talking about conditions that require careful examination; do you hear me?" and he looked at the people for a long time, then he repeated his question, looking around the crowd. "Careful examination, a close look, a breaking of things down into component parts, eh?"

The crowd roared its approval.

"Many of you think you know a lot about the plight of our people in this racist society. You think you know, so you dont try to find out anything new. You are what we call complacent, satisfied, pacified. But you're still feeling the boot of the white man. He kicks you *up* whenever he wants you to go or sit to be his Uncle and do his Tomming for him, and when he gets tired of your weakness, he kicks you *down*. Am I right or wrong?" The crowd roared its approval. "So, you see, the white man doesnt like an Uncle Tom Negro, either. Down South he uses the Toms and lynches bad niggers. Am I right or wrong?" "Right!" the people exclaimed. "So dont think you know all things about this situation until you have done a little investigation. How many of you have done some honest investigation, eh? How many of you out there have looked into the inequities of the system? Huh?" There was a small show of hands. "Good. I can see that there are some seekers after the truth out there."

Harold did not raise his hand. He stood staring at the speaker, but his eyes seemed far away.

The speaker went on. He began a long indictment of Negro leaders, then of the white city officials, then of the rich merchants who made their living off of the Negro ghetto, then he castigated the disunity among the Negro groups, particularly the Internig factions. He called them whiteminded, brainwashed, whitewashed Toms. Then he brought his argument back to the point of knowing something more important about the trouble Negroes were having. He brought it back to unity, and the knowledge of the coming future. . . .

"Many of you out there are going to participate in Jihad, is that right or wrong?" All hands went up, except Harold's. Many turned and looked at him. Some grumbled and murmured. Harold wavered on his feet. His eyes seemed fixed on some point in the sky directly over the head of Elder Dawud.

Soon after Elder Dawud had asked for more hands on various matters, he began to concentrate a lot of attention in the direction of Harold. Not once had Harold raised his hand.

". . . and just as there are wolves amongst the sheep, there are spies and Toms among you. Why, I can spot them a mile away," and he was looking at Harold, "and you mark this, Brothers, they run as straight to the Man as if he were God Almighty, and give our precious plans away. That's why whenever we plan anything, there's the white press and police there ahead of us, waiting. Now, aint that a shame? The black man is not the master of his own destiny. I tell you, you are still slaves! Brothers, I know it as well as you do, so dont get mad at me for telling you. You've got spies amongst you. Get rid of them.

"Now, the point of this meeting, Brothers, is to tell you where you can learn something about yourselves. Without a knowledge of yourself, you cant go anywhere. Why, you cant even integrate with the white man right if you dont know anything about yourself. That's if you want to integrate. Example. Not that I am advocating the program of the Internigs! No. But just to show you that the lack of self-knowledge wont help you to even do the *wrong* thing! Here you have so-called Negroes running around Harlem wearing bleaching creams and trying to make their hair look like Marilyn Monroe's. Is that the truth? Dont deny it!" There were several women and girls in the crowd, which was growing every minute.

"Listen, Brothers and Sisters, the norm by which a people live doesnt change without some kind of action and force on that norm. The standard you have been taught all your lives is the blond, blue-eye standard. Am I right or wrong? This has been a sin and a shame to a nation of twenty million black children growing up. Children, black as night, walking around with little blond dolls! It is the joke of nations. Other countries do not look twice at an American Negro, because they know he is hooked on trying to be like his conqueror.

"I want you to tell me what is right. You have a nation of twenty million blacks who childishly think they can erase their blackness that God gave them in honor of their beauty and strength, trying to bleach it out so that they can look like Roy Rogers and Dale Evans. To me this is a shame. What is it to you! It is nothing short of criminal. I think the people responsible for this crime should be punished. . . ."

Elder Dawud had worked himself up into a sweat by now; the crowd was with him all the way. He began to point out other things he disliked. The people approved. Harold began to shudder a bit, and his face was wet with sweat and tears.

All of a sudden, a man leaped forward, his fist open and his face contorted. He glared at Elder Dawud. Quickly he was seized by the cordon.

"We hear you, we hear you, we hear you!" he shouted. "When are we going to stop hearing you and the rest? We hear you, Brother, we hear! Tell us what to do! Tell us! I want to do something! I am tired of hearing and listening, I'm tired and tired and tired," and he folded in the arms of two men. They carried him out of the crowd. Elder Dawud continued, seeming not to notice the disturbance. The man quickly stood on his feet and tried to brush the strong black hands away, but they took him inside the bookstore, sat him down, and gave him water.

"We know you," said one of the men.

Harold made his way through the crowd and stood outside the bookstore showcase. They had the man seated on a box.

A crowd began to gather inside the store. Elder Dawud's voice was driving into a high pitch. The rattle was changing into pistons, and he was fanning the hearts of the people as if he was fanning a fire that had gone out in the night.

"Forgive me, Brother," the man blurted, his eyes darting wildly from man to man, "I didnt mean to disturb the Elder, but I want . . ." He suddenly put his hands over his face and began to sob softly. The Brothers had a huddle together among themselves and then— as Harold watched from the doorway—took the man, stumbling, behind a great green curtain that hung at the end of the bookstore. A man stood beside the curtain as if he were a guard. But he opened the curtain for them. Then he resumed his pose in front.

Down the street a man had a portable swimming pool built on the back of a truck. He was charging the kids twenty-five cents for ten minutes. A loudspeaker sent carnival music out with the announcement of the swim truck. A man was loading kids on the truck. There were squeals and shouting. The man was West Indian. His heavy accent could be heard all over the block: "Y'll haf de money reddy, now. I tell you, chil'ren, haf de money in de 'and."

Elder Dawud directed his attention to the swim truck a block away. "Now, you all familiar with Tango's swim truck, eh? If you aint, you kids is. Well, Tango is a black man from the Islands, and he is serving a need of the people. Am I right or wrong? What would you think of running that good black man out of business in order to let a few Internigs go to the white man's pool, eh?

"Let me tell you something, folks, my friends, and this is what my message is tonight to you all. There is a conspiracy going on to deprive you black people of everything you dont have. Did you get what I said? Everything that you dont have! We're strivin for something now, eh?

"Not integration. No. The poor Negro doesnt have enough knowledge of himself to integrate right with the Man. Oh, you think the Man doesnt want you to have his daughter. Ha! Wake up, men. He'll sacrifice his mother, now. He can see the writing on the wall. But this poor Negro still thinks he can be like the Man. Why, the white man would more quickly integrate with the African than the poor American Negro! Why? Why? Because the Negro is a caste man. He doesnt know his total self. He functions in a self-imposed prison, the prison of his narrow vision. He sees himself as the white man defines him. Whatever the white man calls him, the Negro agrees; witness this, Brothers: He calls you Sam, you say 'yes, sir'; he calls you nigger, you argue and fight amongst yourselves and wind up cursin each other out by calling each other nigger! Right or wrong? He tries to be respectable and calls you Nigrah or Negro, and you smile and nod. You repeat it. He rules you. He is your maker. He is your god. You are trying to be like him. Whatever you worship, you try to imitate. Negroes worship Jesus, right? They try to be like him. Now, I see Negroes trying to be like the white man, to me it means they think he is God.

"Justice, eh. But I know for a fact there's forces at work to take it away from you." The people murmured. "That's right. Let me break it down for you. Harlem is the only place on the Earth where so many black people live so close together, and yet are ruled, governed, and manipulated by somebody else, namely the white man. The only place on the planet Earth. I dont know about Mars or Venus, because I havent got there yet. They tell me that the white scientists are planning on getting a man to walk around up there soon and bring us back a piece of the land. Well, if things dont straighten out down here on

Earth, then when they get up there they're going to find the place already inhabited, and the only way to get through and take the land is walk over the inhabitants of that land. I guarantee you that if the black man cant get justice on the planet Earth, he damn well aint gonna let a blue-eyed whitey run over him in his own new land, eh? What do you say about it, Brothers?" There was a round of applause. "Now what I want to say is, and mind this carefully, the conspiracy is on. But first, the Afro-American population has got to go and find out something. He has got to do some investigation. He has got to go back into his soul, Brothers, and I know you all know what that is. The black man in this country has first got to look deep into his own soul, and then he has got to travel a road back there and straighten out the mess the white man has made. Do you understand my meaning? Listen, the black man has got to clear out the funk in his own soul. Let's face the truth. The white man has maligned us so much, has stripped us so thoroughly, has whitewashed our minds and ambitions that all we know is what he tells us on his TV and on his radio and at his movie and in his newspapers (we do have a few black papers now, thank you, Brothers) and in his school system. The truth is that the journey is not so easy. It is not easy because no man knows where to start, or which way to go when he starts, or the end thereof. . . ."

And he paused, looking at Harold for a long time. Some of the men in the crowd looked Harold up and down. There was a slight movement and a rumbling. The buildings where the bookstore was located seemed to echo the sound of drums and thundering feet. The police siren came nearer, and across the street two cars collided. Elder Dawud, sweating profusely, stepped up one more peg on the ladder and seemed to wind himself up, tighter and tighter. . . .

"There is one who knows the way. . . ." He paused. ". . . I come in his name and bear witness that he doesnt let a black man down. He is the One. There is no other whereby you can be saved. He has told me that the white man is doomed, and he who follows the evil ways of the white man is likewise doomed. He has sent us Brothers out amongst you to bring you the message of the truth, the Black truth. So long you have heard the white truth. Now you can hear for the first time the Black truth! He who wants to find out his soul must have a map. You got to have a guide, Brothers, if you gonna travel in a region so long uninhabited. The soul of the Negro is an unexplored territory. The map. The master has the key of knowledge, and he will show us how to find out the truth. . . . Here is the . . . If you want to learn your way around Harlem, baby, you got to get to know the people. Is that right or wrong? If you want to know what the black man is like, then you got to get to know the black man's soul. If you want to know what goes on in Harlem, then you got to understand what goes on in the mind of the black people who live in Harlem. Is that right or wrong?" And the crowd applauded him.

Harold Kane continued to listen with hypnotized attention.

"Am I right or wrong! I say you would gain integration much faster if you stopped trying to imitate the white man and stand on you own feet and become a man of destiny. A *black man* of the world! The white man is intelligent, and he would respect you for being what God made you. He wouldnt love you, of course, but he would respect you. Right now he neither loves nor respects you. But the Internigs dont know this. They think if they become the exact carbon copy of their white master, then he will let them in the back door. Ha! Whoever heard of a carbon copy being of any value as long as the original is around. Why, it is a shame, running around trying to be the shadow of another man. Hell, the white man doesnt care about shadows. He cares about men. Not flunkies."

A Brother was circulating around the crowd, passing out a piece of paper. Harold looked anxiously at the man, and when he came near, Harold reached out and received his eagerly. But he only glanced at it, frowned, and put it away. . . .

"Why, I would be ashamed of myself if I didnt have something to be proud of. The white man boasts of his wars and his great civilization. He writes histories and books, and teaches you to bow down and worship his white Jesus on the cross, while all the time he has you working for him, and he is paying you to help make his lifestyle into law. The black man in this country has got to learn one thing: how to use the key to his soul, for the soul of the black man is an unexplored region. . . . Who has the map of Harlem? Listen, Harlem has it. Harlem has it. And I speak in the name of One who wants to see Harlem keep it."

Across the street the police were trying to break up a restless crowd that had gathered at the scene of the car accident. There was a bitter argument with several belligerent men. The cops were trying to disperse the people. But the people all stared at the white cops (politely ignoring the three Negro policemen) with a bitter hatred. They called out, "Butchers!" "Klux Klaners!" "Beasts!" "Devils!" "White dogs!" "Mad murderers!" The police retaliated by swinging billyclubs and cracking a few of the slow people on the legs. A bottle thrown from the crowd struck a policeman on the head. He drew his revolver, staggering with one hand on the ground, and fired into the crowd. A youth clutched his belly in a loud scream. The crowd roared and fell back.

A brick struck one of the police cars.

Across the street, Elder Dawud's crowd joined the melee.

Quickly, word spread that the police had killed a black youth.

The police ordered Elder Dawud to close his meeting. Bottles began to fly. The police riot-squad siren started to wail its eerie whine, and the streets around Harlem Square began to clear and alternatively fill up as waves of people fell back and then angrily rushed forward, moblike, pursuing the wind with anything they could get their hands on. The police arrived more and more, and soon arrests were being made. . . . Harold had moved a block away, watching the disturbance.

Soon he turned his head and headed uptown, walking close to the wall and looking in at the shops and stores of Harlem, as if he were watching the reflections that moved to and fro in the glass, fading and fleeing like ghosts.

C. H. FULLER JR.

A Love Song for Seven Little Boys Called; Sam

The seven had been confined, since the first grade, to their own special section of the class. This year, as expected, their teacher, Miss Arnold, had seated them in the rear near the door. It was close to the lavatory, but otherwise it was the worse spot in the third grade. They were all eight years old, except for Reuben, who was eight-and-a-half. He sat at his desk, staring at Miss Arnold's wide nose, and recalling that his mother had promised a surprise for his birthday, *if* he got an "A" in Spelling. He didn't like his mother's surprises, or Miss Arnold. His mother always surprised him with clothes, and his teacher always complained about the way he dressed. But he did wish he was nine. When you're nine, you're bigger, and nobody messed with you; like the white boys did every afternoon.

He bet if he and his friends were all nine, the white kids would leave them alone. Not that the seven of them couldn't fight. Stevie, Billy, Allen, Francis, Harold, and Kenny were the best fighters he'd ever seen. It was just that *every day* they had to fight, and Reuben was sick of it. The bell in the Ingram Elementary School rang, and its only black pupils, seven little boys, picked up their schoolbags, and started outside into the afternoon chill.

No one talked to them. Even Miss Arnold, the lone colored teacher in the school, shunned them, except for the two times she complained about the way they talked. Reuben watched her now, crossing the street against the light, holding the hands of two little white boys. She never took his hand—he wouldn't let her either! If she didn't like them, he didn't like her. The seven of them waited at the corner, and sprinted across on the traffic lady's signal. Reuben sucked in a deep breath, and pivoted around. The daily trouble was just about to begin, and he wondered why, when they stopped the buses in the first grade, they didn't send them to a school in their own neighborhood.

"Hey Sams! Hey look 'et all the little black Sams!" A group of five second-graders shot past them, their schoolbags swinging, their white faces, red with excitement.

"Your mother's a Sam!" It was Billy. He always talked about people's mothers. Reuben didn't like that stuff, and if they played the "dozens" with him, somebody was gonna' get hurt.

"Your mother's a black dog," one yelled.

"When I catch you, I'ma' punch you in the mouth, hear? I don't play that stuff, boy!"

From *Black Fire: An Anthology of Afro-American Writing,* ed. LeRoi Jones (Amiri Baraka) and Larry Neal (New York: Morrow, 1968).

"Awwww, shut up, blackie! Old black Billy, and ole black joe, must be niggers, 'cause they run so slow!"

"Old black Sams! Seven old black Sams!"

The white kids continued to run. When they reached the corner, they turned and headed west, but not before Allen picked up a stone, and threw it. It hit the boy on the leg; he stopped momentarily, looked at the bruise it had made, then kept going when he realized Allen was almost on top of him.

It was the same everyday. Reuben had gotten used to it. There were three blocks of enemy territory. Every afternoon, the older white boys would send the little white boys darting past them, shouting "Sam," "blackie" or "nigger." Then, after the first block, they would meet a group of the older boys, who'd blame them for chasing the little boys, and after a fight, the seven of them would be chased home. Reuben hated it.

The white kids had been doing it every day for a month. He didn't understand white people. They sit next to you in school, and beat you up on the way home. They can't be trusted. Once they passed the graveyard they would be safe. Black people lived on the other side of those graves, and the white boys never chased them that far. "Over there, they wouldn' mess with me," Reuben thought, preparing himself for what would happen when they reached the next corner. "Billy! Billy Mayfield!" It was Miss Arnold. Reuben recognized the weak, scratchy voice. Her hard, black face was staring at Billy. She was a witch.

"Yes, Miss Arnold?"

"What did you say to those boys?"

"I didn' say nothin'!"

"I heard you! You want me to send a note to your mother?"

"He had no business callin' me nigger! My name ain't no nigger!"

"Billy, sticks and stones may break my bones, but names will never harm me! You ought to be glad you can go to school with different kinds of people."

"My name ain't nigger—Mom told me to let nobody call me that!"

"Well, we'll see what your mother has to say!"

"I didn' do nothin'!"

"Goodbye, Billy."

"I didn' do nothin'!—and my mother ain't gonna' do nothin' to me either! 'cause my name ain't no nigger!"

"Why they kept you kids in the school I'll never know—" She mumbled something else, but they didn't hear her. Harold Davis called her a black bitch behind her back. She disappeared into a store. "She don't never say nothin' to them," Reuben said, aware that this had a great deal to do with why he disliked her.

"My father said, she's prejudice," Harold Davis said, leaping out in front of them.

"What's that," Kenny asked.

"You don't know nothin' Kenny! My mother said only white people are prejudice. 'Cause white people don't like black people—and she said only white people do prejudice. I know all about that," Stevie put in.

"Well, Miss Arnold ain't white!" Kenny looked around at them. They were all silent for a moment.

"My father said, some colored people do it too, but white people do it all the time," Harold Davis said authoritatively. It satisfied Reuben. Harold Davis knew everything.

"Hey! What took you Sambos so long? You scared or something?" Reuben looked up at the corner and wanted to cry. There were a dozen white boys blocking the sidewalk, and swinging their schoolbags in a preparatory challenge. Reuben tried to slow down, and even wished he could leave his friends and run home, but he didn't do either. There was an attraction in this daily meeting. Something compelling in twisted expressions of the white boys made him want to take every opportunity to smash the ugliness from their faces. The sight of their hate for him made him angry. No one had a right to look at him that way! There was a moment of stillness. Suddenly everyone was moving. Harold was the first to run. He charged into the boy at the head of the gang, his schoolbag aimed at the white boy's head. Reuben felt himself running. Billy was screaming like an Indian, and swinging his fists at everything in his path. Everyone was yelling, and at one point, Reuben heard Francis crying, and knew his friend had been angered sufficiently enough to want to kill. Reuben ran straight at a blond-haired boy with large freckles, and bucked teeth. The boy made the mistake of charging forward, and when fear suddenly gripped him, trying to run away. He had already knocked down two boys, as he tried to get out of Reuben's way. Reuben instinctively followed through the escape path the white boy had made, swinging at the boy who was hollering hysterically. When he was through, Reuben turned around the kicked someone in the leg, and felt a schoolbag smash into his own face. It shocked him for a moment, and someone else punched him in the stomach before he had a chance to grab at one boy's hair and try to pull it out. Someone struck him with a stone on the hand, and he watched, horrified, as the skin curled up in a twisted black ball, and black flesh suddenly spurted red. He kicked his assailant, saw Francis spit on a red-haired boy's coat, and heart Harold screaming. They had knocked Harold down! One boy was leaning over him, and casually punching him in the face! An instant later, he and Kenny were pushing and kicking people off Harold and helping him up. Reuben punched someone in the nose, and watched another boy examine the sudden rush of blood before cursing him. They had almost made it. Kenny and Harold were already running, and the others were far ahead. Once they got started, the white boys could never catch them. The seven of them ran like the wind. Reuben, as he bolted away from the white gang, hadn't run far when Billy screamed "WATCH OUT, REUBEN!"

He tried to dodge what was behind him, and as he turned, he heard it. His coat was tearing. His three-month old coat was being ripped by a sandy-haired white boy with a jagged can. Reuben swung, just as the boy turned and ran. He started after him but realized he would be running into the charging gang. He'd get the boy later, he thought, angry enough to cry. He turned and joined his friends in the one-block sprint to the graveyard. They crossed the street and stopped.

"You tore my coat! I'm a' git you for that!" He was staring at the boy.

"Why don'tcha come here and git me, blackie?"

"You black nigger!"

"You wait! I'm a' beat your ass!" He said the curse word softly, afraid someone his mother knew might hear him.

"Awwww, go on home, blackie! We can get you tomorrow!"

"You better run, Sambo!"

"Your mother better run," Billy shouted. They started home.

Reuben was worried. Not simply because of his torn coat. His mother's outrage was predictable, but the thought had just occurred to him, that if they didn't stop those white boys they'd be chased home for the rest of their lives. He didn't tell the others but it scared him, and he wished magically the white boys would disappear. If he had a machine gun, he bet they would leave him alone. But he didn't have one. He had a right to go home in peace. Why didn't they let him? His father had said, white people always bother Negro people, and when he had asked him why, he recalled his father saying, 'cause Negro people don't fight back! He and his friends fought back every day, and still got chased. His father had missed something. He said goodbye to his friends, and went into his house.

"Reuben, that you?"

"Yeah."

"What's the matter?" He didn't answer his mother. Instead, he took off his coat in the vestibule and placed it over his arm with the torn portion folded in, where she couldn't see it. "Reuben, what are you doing?"

"Nothin'!" He walked into the kitchen with his hands in his pockets.

"Mom, I don't wanna' go to that school no more."

"What?" His mother turned away from the sink and put potatoes on the stove, then wiped her hands on her green apron. "What's the matter, Reuben?"

"Them white boys is always fightin'."

She looked at him for a moment. "Reuben, what happened to your coat?"

"Nothin'."

"Reuben!" She grabbed the coat from his arm. "What?"

"I didn't do it, Mom! That white boy tore it!"

"Reuben, you let some boy tear your coat? What is wrong with you?" She shook him. Reuben was crying.

"It wasn't my fault, Mom! I couldn't help it! They chased us!" He heard his mother say, 'Damnit,' something she never said unless she was upset.

"What you let them chase you for?"

"They do it every day!"

"Well, can't you fight? Hit 'em back when they hit you!"

"It's too many."

"Go someplace! Go someplace before I whip you! Your father spends good money for a coat, and you let somebody tear it up? Go ahead, Reuben! Just go before I give you a beating! Wait 'til your father gets home. Get outta' my sight!"

"It wasn't my fault. It wasn't!" He went to his room, and slammed the door. For a moment he stood there, so angry he wanted to tear the door from its hinges. He couldn't help it if they chased him everyday! He had tried to be friendly like his mother had told him, but they didn't want to be friends. All they wanted to do was fight, and call names. Now, they even had his own family against him, and he hated them for it. If only he was bigger, stronger. It wasn't his fault! It wasn't! He fell across his bed in tears.

When he heard his father, he sat up on the bed. He was sure his mother was going to tell. She couldn't keep a secret, no matter what.

"Reuben! Reuben, come here!" He went downstairs crying. "What's this about lettin' some boy tear your coat?"

"They wanna' fight all the time, Daddy, an' call us names!"

"Who? What did they call you?"

"Them white boys—they called me nigger!"

"And what did you do?"

"I punched one in the nose, and bloodied his face!"

"I tol' you not to let him go to that damn school, Willa Mae! I told you! He don't need to go to no white school—and as long as he does, I want them to keep their damn hands off him! I'm sick of it! Reuben, don't come in here agin' with your clothes ripped up. You figure out somethin' to make them leave you alone, you hear? I'm not playin' either. Now eat your dinner!" Reuben ran to the kitchen.

"It's not his fault," his father said. "It's them damn white kids, Willa Mae! You think they'd have better sense than to teach that shit to their kids! Goddamn white people! No! You wanted him in there, and he's gonna' stay! Reuben's got to learn that you don't let people walk over you! If we take him out, he'll be runnin' all his life. Once he beats them, they'll leave him alone—I'm not gonna walk him from school, and neither are you!"

Reuben didn't each much dinner, and when he want to bed, he lay there for a long time, trying to figure out something that would stop the fighting. He considered himself lucky. His father didn't whip him. Maybe Pop understood it wasn't his fault. He watched the white boys on his ceiling. They were standing in a gang, and the sandy-haired boy was out front, threatening him with another tin can. He cursed at Reuben, and Reuben swung at him, and the boy's face disappeared only to be replaced by an entire group that looked just like him. He pulled his blanket over his head. He had to think of something. It came to him, just before he fell asleep. When he took a final glance at the ceiling, the white boys were gone.

The following day, just before the bell sounded the end of the school, Miss Arnold spoke to the class. There was something hanging from her nose, and it annoyed Reuben that this woman, behind her big desk, could scold them, when she didn't have sense enough to blow her own nose. But she wouldn't bother him anymore, after today. Everything was going to change today.

"Now, children, someone told me that the white boys were fighting their colored friends. Is that true?"

"Yeah, teacher. That punk called me 'nigger'!" Billy stood and pointed to the blond-haired kid.

"I didn't!"

"You did—and I'm a' get you."

"I didn't!"

"I'm sure he didn't mean it, Billy. You didn't mean what you called Billy, did you, Gavin?"

"Nooooo, Miss Arnold!"

"OOOO, you liar!"

"Billy, sit down!"

"I'm a' gitcha', hear? I don't take that stuff!"

"Sit down!" She shook her head.

When the bell rang, the seven of them bolted from the room. Reuben had told them his plan on the way to school, and they rushed from the class to execute it. It was going to be over—today. Miss Arnold came out of the building with two little white boys, as she always did. When she approached Reuben, she waved a warning finger at him. He waited until she had crossed the street, and with Billy and Harold Davis, followed behind her. Allen, Stevie, Francis and Kenny were out of sight now, and it was a part of the plan for the three of them to stay close to Miss Arnold.

"Hey, Sammy! Hey, black Sams!"

"Little black Sambo!" The little kids sprinted past them. Billy started to shout something but decided against it when Miss Arnold turned around and stared at him.

"Billy, remember, sticks and stones."

"Yes, Miss Arnold."

Reuben looked at her and laughed. She was a part of the plan, and didn't know it. She'd take them to the corner, and not only get an opportunity to see the boys waiting for them, but help, by her presence, to frighten them. The white boys were already gathering on the corner. "Hey, Miss Arnold! Look at them boys! See what I tol' you? All they wanna' do is fight, and call us names!"

The woman looked up suddenly, and her expression told Reuben that she was not only shocked, but afraid as well. The white boys were blocking the sidewalk, this time in a large circle. The first two boys held up tin cans menacingly. Miss Arnold was speechless, and when she did open her mouth, she stuttered.

"You boys! You boys—what—what are you doing there? I don't want any fighting. Go home! You heard me! Go home before I report you." Several white boys backed up.

"You Sams is scared, aintcha'?"

"They gotta' go home wif' the teacher!"

"Did you boys hear me? I said go home!"

"Awww shut up!"

"Who said that? Who said it?—what grade—?"

"Black Miss Arnold, like a dirty carmel! Black Miss Arnold like a dirty carmel!"

"We don't want to black teacher!" One boy leaped away from the crowd his hands on his hips. "Go back where you came from!"

Reuben was glad they'd hurt her. She stood in front of them, her mouth wide open, her eyes large and glassy. It serves her right, he thought. He was the first to run. While the white boys' attention was on Miss Arnold, Reuben, Billy and Harold charged, striking the first blow at the boy who stood with his hands on his hips. The sudden attack came as a surprise to the boys, and for a while they retreated. Harold was whooping like an Indian, and punching a tall, skinny boy in the back until the boy collided with a parked car, and skinned his face on the fender. The white boys didn't run far. Halfway up the block they scattered in every direction, running on stoops and hiding in doorways. Allen, Francis, Stevie and Kenny had been waiting for them, and the first white boy who approached them was slammed in the face with a rock. Reuben's plan worked, and he started swinging at them as they raced back trying to dodge stones. He grabbed one boy by the collar, and tripped him to the ground, kicking him in the leg. Another boy he garroted, and out the corner of his eye saw Harold pin a red-haired boy against a wall. He punched the boy he had tripped in the side, and ran by Harold, and slapped the red-haired boy in the face. It would end today, he was sure of it. The boy he slapped starting crying, just as he saw the kid who had torn his coat. He noticed, momentarily, a panorama of screaming, crying white boys, running everywhere, and Stevie's foot going high in the air, and a fat boy running with his hands over his head, and no one chasing him. He sprinted after the sandy-haired boy, who, when he saw Reuben, started screaming "he didn't mean it." Reuben caught him at the corner right in front of Miss Arnold, and knocked him down. The boy was hysterical—screaming, kicking, and at one point, Reuben thought he might faint.

"I'm a' tear your coat!"

"I didn't mean it. I'm sorry, Reuben! I'm sorry! Please! I didn't—"

Reuben punched him once and stood. It had just occurred to him that the boy was deathly afraid, and for the first time since he had been in the Ingram School, a white boy had used his name. They were beaten. Reuben walked back to his friends.

"Did you tear his coat?"

"Nawwww."

"Why not? I'd a' tore his coat and bloodied his nose, man." Billy stuck his chest out.

"Man, I beat the piss outta' one guy," Allen said.

They turned around when they reached the graveyard. The white boys were going home in two's and three's. There were no names being shouted, no one throwing stones. Reuben knew why he felt good, but he wasn't sure why he suddenly liked his friends so much. They seemed different now. Stronger. Taller.

Miss Arnold was still on the corner, staring at them. Reuben didn't feel sorry for her. She hadn't shared in their victory, and tomorrow she'd punish them. He didn't understand her. At least the white boys had what they believed was a reason for disliking them.

But what about Miss Arnold? She was the same color as he was. Maybe she wanted to be white? The thought made him laugh. They put their arms around each other's shoulders, and started home.

"We're rough. We're tough. We black boys don't take no stuff!"

From that day on, they didn't.

Sonny's Seasons

Sonny was surprised when his teacher explained that in some parts of the world there were only one or two seasons because he thought everyplace was like Chicago where you have four seasons. His teacher told him that near the North and South Poles there was winter all year and near the equator there was only summer. Sonny thought about that and decided he'd rather have four, like in Chicago, although he didn't like winter at all.

In the wintertime Sonny was always cold when he was outside, no matter how warm he dressed. Everybody walked around with their own cloud hanging in front of their mouths and their faces ashy and pinched from the wind off the lake. Sonny's feet were always cold and sometimes he would have to stomp them until they hurt and he could feel his toes again. About the only thing Sonny liked about the winter was when it first snowed and the city looked so clean.

Sonny never noticed how dirty Chicago was until he saw how it looked covered by fresh snow. But it only took about a day for the snow to get as dirty as the city it covered. Sometimes Sonny and his friends would make snowmen and that was fun, but mostly in the winter Sonny just wished for spring.

Spring was the most fun after the long winter and the air was crisp and cool and the sun warm, the birds coming up from down south and the buds coming out on the trees. Sonny and his friends always tried to be the first to see a robin because it was good luck if you were the first to see a robin on the block. Usually Lyin' George said he'd seen a robin first but nobody believed him because everybody said Lyin' George couldn't tell the truth if you put a pistol to his head.

Robins were supposed to mean the beginning of spring, but sometimes you would see some robins and the next thing you knew it was snowing again. Sonny asked his mother how come the robins get faked out like that and she told him Chicago weather could fake out anybody.

All the best games seemed to be played in spring, like playing horses. All you needed to play horses were a couple of tin cans out of the garbage can in the alley. What you did was lay the cans on their sides and then stomp on them right in the middle. If you did it right the middle would go in and the ends would curl over your shoe sole and stick. Then you could run up and down the alley clopping just like a horse, with the sound of your hooves

From *We Be Word Sorcerers: 25 Stories by Black Americans*, ed. Sonia Sanchez (New York: Bantam Books, 1973).

echoing in the alley. When you ran, you did it out of rhythm so the sound was right and you held your left hand out front like you were holding the reins and slapped yourself on your right hip with the other hand and the more kids running along the better it sounded. Of course, the game didn't last long because the cans always came off and somebody's mother was always sure to get bugged because they all said the tin cans would ruin your shoes and shoes cost so much and the clothing allowance from the welfare was never enough anyway but the game was always a good one while it lasted.

Another game that was good in the spring was Cowboys and Indians, but it was always hard to get anybody to play the cowboys because the cowboys were always white in the movies. Lyin' George said he saw Sidney Poitier playing a cowboy in the movies once but nobody ever believed Lyin' George about anything. Then one time they had Jim Brown playing a cowboy in a movie and it was a good movie except when he was rasslin' and kissin' some girl but other than those parts it was a good cowboy movie. After that it wasn't so hard to get somebody to play the cowboys, but before only the kids who couldn't fight were the cowboys, or the ones who had toy six-guns.

It was easy to play Indians. What you could do was use some old beads if you could find some in the garbage. Or you could take off your belt and put it around your forehead like an Apache headband. But the best thing was to put on war paint. You just found a grocery store with advertising for neck bones or collard greens or something painted on the store window in water paint in white and red and yellow and blue. Then you wet your finger and got some of the paint on it, and while it was still wet you put it on your face. You could really look like an Indian when you did that.

Another good game in the spring was rippin' things off. Sonny and Sneak were the best thieves on the block. Outa Sight was pretty good at rippin' things off, too, but he stole things you couldn't even use and he stole all the time, so that didn't count. They used to rip off sweet potatoes and cook them in a fire over near the I.C. tracks. Sonny never could figure out why ripped-off sweet potatoes tasted so good when you didn't even have butter to eat them with, but they did.

They used to rip off things from the kids who lived in Lake Meadows and Prairie Shores, but that wasn't much fun because they always had so much stuff they didn't even care and they didn't know how to fight either. After they stole some of all those toys the kids had over there and found out how easy they broke, Sonny and the others could understand why the kids didn't care about that kind of junk. The folks of the kids on the block couldn't afford to buy them many toys from the welfare money and the ones they did buy never broke as soon as you got them out of the box and you'd better not come home one day without whatever kind of toy it was, either. But Sonny and the others could find all the toys they needed right out in the streets and the alleys.

Flying kites was fun, too, but they were always getting caught in the telephone wires in the alley. But if they didn't, sometimes they would get up even higher than a three-story building and that would knock everybody out, a kite flying that high.

In the summertime, sometimes it would get so hot that even Red Beans would have to put up his basketball and then there was nothing to do except lay around in the shade and lie and signify and play the dozens, or go out to the lake.

The summer before, Sonny and China had almost started a rumble between Red Beans and some of the P. Stones. What happened was Sonny and China, who was Sonny's best friend, started walking along the lake. Everybody called him China because he had slant-eyes and looked just like he was Chinese. Sonny asked his momma about that and she told him China's father was supposed to have been from Jamaica, although his mother was from Alabama, and a lot of black people had mixed with Chinese in Jamaica and maybe that was what had happened. Anyway, everybody thought China's slant-eyes were really cool.

They were walking along the lake and lyin' and talking about what they were going to do when they grew up. China said he was going to write books or something, maybe because he could make up games so well. Whenever they ran out of games to play and were sitting around doing nothing, China would always say, "Let's play like . . ." and before you knew it everybody was into a new game. Nobody could make up games like China.

Every now and then they would stop and skip rocks on the water. It was a still day and not really as hot as it could get sometimes in Chicago, but there wasn't even a little breeze and the water was as still and flat as glass. Up close, the water was green but out far it was deep blue.

China could make a rock skip once or twice more than Sonny, no matter how hard Sonny tried, but Sonny could throw a rock further out into the lake than China could.

Before they knew it, they were all the way down near the Museum of Science and Industry. Sonny and China knew what it was because their teacher had taken them there for science just before school closed for the summer. Both Sonny and China dug all the buttons you could push in the Museum and then you waited while something happened to the exhibit you were looking at. They also dug the room where you could whisper way down at one end and they could hear you at the other end.

When they got almost to the Museum, Sonny and China went out on the Point where they had the radar station inside the fence with barb-wire on top and soldiers inside. They stopped and listened to some hippies playing guitars and singing, but they didn't smell very good when you got up close and you couldn't even pat your feet to the music. But out on the end of the Point about seven brothers were playing drums in the middle of a crowd. They had bongoes and conga drums and some African drums, too, and they really had a thing going. You didn't have any trouble patting your feet to that kind of music. They dug the brothers playing the drums until some pigs came out and made them stop and while everybody was loud-talking, Sonny and China walked on down to 63rd Street beach and that's when the trouble started.

They were standing at the edge of the water watching the sailboats way out on the lake, when Sonny noticed a lot of kids their own age checking him and China out. So Sonny told China to cool it toward the end of the beach where the iron fence stopped, but not to run until Sonny told him so. They started walking away, slow and cool, and Sonny even stooped down and skipped a rock on the lake. But then China messed up by running too soon, which was a mistake because China was slow and the other boys cut him off before they could get to the end of the fence and up on the sidewalk. So there they were, trapped with their backs against the fence and Sonny didn't see any way they could get home without a real bad whipping.

China was slow and he wasn't a real good fighter, but he had a lot of heart. China hadn't run too soon because he was chicken, Sonny knew, he had just made a mistake and hadn't waited for Sonny to give him the word. Sonny just hoped China wouldn't start crying because then the other boys would really lay it on them. Whenever China got in a fight, somewhere along the line he would start crying. Not like other boys when they were beaten, but his eyes would just flood up and the tears would come on out. In fact, China never really started fighting until the tears came, and whenever they started, anybody who knew him knew the fight was just starting because then China would put his head down and start working his arms like windmills and you had to be pretty good not to back down from that.

Sonny could run and fight, and anybody he couldn't beat in a fight he could outrun, and Sonny only knew one boy, T-Bone, who could beat him running and fighting, too. Sonny had had a lot of races with T-Bone and a lot of fights and although he never beat him by much, he always did beat Sonny. But T-Bone's mother had married a garbage collector who went to the same church, and they all moved to Robert Taylor Homes and that was the last time Sonny saw T-Bone.

So China wasn't so bad to have to fight next to, but Sonny knew the other boys wouldn't understand if the tears started; they'd just think China was chicken. The other boys asked them where they were from and Sonny told them from 62nd and Ingleside in Woodlawn, but they didn't believe him. Just when they were getting real close, a couple of big boys wearing red berets came up and told the other kids to go away. Sonny told them the truth about where they were from and they laughed when they found out Sonny and China had walked all that way from their own neighborhood.

The two big boys took them over to a blanket where there were a lot of other big boys with red berets and their girlfriends and they gave them some fried chicken, potato salad, and lemonade. Everybody was laughing and joking and having a good time. The girls really looked good in their bright bathing suits and their 'Fros sparkling in the sun and they flirted with Sonny, who pretended he didn't like it, but he did. Sonny didn't like girls very much, but he thought those girls were pretty down.

Then the two big boys who had first brought them over to the blanket, said come on, we'll take you back, and they went across the Drive to the parking lot and they drove them back to the part of the lake in their own neighborhood.

When they got back China was really into a story and everybody was sitting in the car and digging China's story and laughing, when a hand came in the window and turned off the motor and took the key out of the dashboard. When they looked up the car was surrounded by big boys. Doo-Wap was looking in one window and it was Red Beans who had snatched the key and Sonny knew they were going to get it on.

"Sonny," said Red Beans, "you and China get out of the car and split." They got out of the car and Doo-Wap asked them what they were doing so far from home. But Sonny didn't leave.

"Red Beans," said Sonny, "leave 'em alone; they ain't botherin' nobody."

"Sonny, get on home," said Red Beans. "These cats is P. Stones and they don't belong down here." Everybody could see from their red berets what they were.

"Beans, leave 'em alone!" said Sonny, and he was really scared because the only thing the kids never did was bug the big boys, that just didn't go, and Sonny had never spoke up to Red Beans. They stood there, Red Beans tall and almost skinny-looking, but he wasn't, and Sonny, and they both stood very straight, with their heads out on their necks and the chins way out, which was the way Red Beans stood when he was really bugged, and Sonny, too, because he copied everything from Red Beans.

Then Sonny told him what had happened and Red Beans asked China if it was true, and when China said yeah, he asked the P. Stones to come on over and have some Ripple they had in a paper bag. Then Sonny knew everything was going to be all right. The two P. Stones said yes, but they couldn't stay too long or some of the others might come looking for them and Red Beans said nobody wanted that because then Sonny might whip everybody's head. Then everybody laughed except Sonny, even China.

By the time Sonny got home that evening, he decided he still didn't like summer as much as the spring, but he had to admit that sometimes it got very interesting.

Reena

Like most people with unpleasant childhoods, I am on constant guard against the past—the past being for me the people and places associated with the years I served out my girlhood in Brooklyn. The places no longer matter that much since most of them have vanished. The old grammar school, for instance, P.S. 35 ("Dirty 5's" we called it and with justification) has been replaced by a low, coldly functional arrangement of glass and Permastone which bears its name but has none of the feel of a school about it. The small, grudgingly lighted stores along Fulton Street, the soda parlor that was like a church with its stained-glass panels in the door and marble floor have given way to those impersonal emporiums, the supermarkets. Our house even, a brownstone relic whose halls smelled comfortingly of dust and lemon oil, the somnolent street upon which it stood, the tall, muscular trees which shaded it were leveled years ago to make way for a city housing project—a stark, graceless warren for the poor. So that now whenever I revisit that old section of Brooklyn and see these new and ugly forms, I feel nothing. I might as well be in a strange city.

But it is another matter with the people of my past, the faces that in their darkness were myriad reflections of mine. Whenever I encounter them at the funeral or wake, the wedding or christening—those ceremonies by which the past reaffirms its hold—my guard drops and memories banished to the rear of the mind rush forward to rout the present. I almost become the child again—anxious and angry, disgracefully diffident.

Reena was one of the people from that time, and a main contributor to my sense of ineffectualness then. She had not done this deliberately. It was just that whenever she talked about herself (and this was not as often as most people) she seemed to be talking about me also. She ruthlessly analyzed herself, sparing herself nothing. Her honesty was so absolute it was a kind of cruelty.

She had not changed, I was to discover in meeting her again after a separation of twenty years. Nor had I really. For although the years had altered our positions (she was no longer the lord and I the lackey) and I could even afford to forgive her now, she still had the ability to disturb me profoundly by dredging to the surface those aspects of myself that I kept buried. This time, as I listened to her talk over the stretch of one long night, she made vivid without knowing it what is perhaps the most critical fact of my existence—that definition of me, of her and millions like us, formulated by others to serve out their fantasies,

---

From *American Negro Short Stories,* ed. John Henrik Clarke (New York: Hill and Wang, 1966).

a definition we have to combat at an unconscionable cost to the self and even use, at times, in order to survive; the cause of so much shame and rage as well as, oddly enough, a source of pride: simply, what it has meant, what it means, to be a black woman in America.

We met—Reena and myself—at the funeral of her aunt who had been my godmother and whom I had also called aunt, Aunt Vi, and loved, for she and her house had been, respectively, a source of understanding and a place of calm for me as a child. Reena entered the church where the funeral service was being held as though she, not the minister, were coming to officiate, sat down among the immediate family up front, and turned to inspect those behind her. I saw her face then.

It was a good copy of the original. The familiar mold was there, that is, and the configuration of bone beneath the skin was the same despite the slight fleshiness I had never seen there before; her features had even retained their distinctive touches: the positive set to her mouth, the assertive lift to her nose, the same insistent, unsettling eyes which when she was angry became as black as her skin—and this was total, unnerving, and very beautiful. Yet something had happened to her face. It was different despite its sameness. Aging even while it remained enviably young. Time had sketched in, very lightly, the evidence of the twenty years.

As soon as the funeral service was over, I left, hurrying out of the church into the early November night. The wind, already at its winter strength, brought with it the smell of dead leaves and the image of Aunt Vi there in the church, as dead as the leaves—as well as the thought of Reena, whom I would see later at the wake.

Her real name had been Doreen, a standard for girls among West Indians (her mother, like my parents, was from Barbados), but she had changed it to Reena on her twelfth birthday—"As a present to myself"—and had enforced the change on her family by refusing to answer to the old name. "Reena. With two e's!" she would say and imprint those e's on your mind with the indelible black of her eyes and a thin threatening finger that was like a quill.

She and I had not been friends through our own choice. Rather, our mothers, who had known each other since childhood, had forced the relationship. And from the beginning, I had been at a disadvantage. For Reena, as early as the age of twelve, had had a quality that was unique, superior, and therefore dangerous. She seemed defined, even then, all of a piece, the raw edges of her adolescence smoothed over; indeed, she seemed to have escaped adolescence altogether and made one dazzling leap from childhood into the very arena of adult life. At thirteen, for instance, she was reading Zola, Hauptmann, Steinbeck, while I was still in the thrall of the Little Minister and Lorna Doone. When I could only barely conceive of the world beyond Brooklyn, she was talking of the Civil War in Spain, lynchings in the South, Hitler in Poland—and talking with the outrage and passion of a revolutionary. I would try, I remember, to console myself with the thought that she was really an adult masquerading as a child, which meant that I could not possibly be her match.

For her part, Reena put up with me and was, by turns, patronizing and impatient. I merely served as the audience before whom she rehearsed her ideas and the yardstick by which she measured her worldliness and knowledge.

"Do you realize that this stupid country supplied Japan with the scrap iron to make the weapons she's now using against it?" she had shouted at me once.

I had not known that.

Just as she overwhelmed me, she overwhelmed her family, with the result that despite a half dozen brothers and sisters who consumed quantities of bread and jam whenever they visited us, she behaved like an only child and got away with it. Her father, a gentle man with skin the color of dried tobacco and with the nose Reena had inherited jutting out like a crag from his nondescript face, had come from Georgia and was always making jokes about having married a foreigner—Reena's mother being from the West Indies. When not joking, he seemed slightly bewildered by his large family and so in awe of Reena that he avoided her. Reena's mother, a small, dry, formidably black woman, was less a person to me than the abstract principle of force, power, energy. She was alternately strict and indulgent with Reena and, despite the inconsistency, surprisingly effective.

They lived when I knew them in a cold-water railroad flat above a kosher butcher on Belmont Avenue in Brownsville, some distance from us—and this in itself added to Reena's exotic quality. For it was a place where Sunday became Saturday, with all the stores open and pushcarts piled with vegetables and yard goods lined up along the curb, a crowded place where people hawked and spat freely in the streaming gutters and the men looked as if they had just stepped from the pages of the Old Testament with their profuse beards and long, black, satin coats.

When Reena was fifteen her family moved to Jamaica in Queens and since, in those days, Jamaica was considered too far away for visiting, our families lost contact and I did not see Reena again until we were both in college and then only once and not to speak to . . .

▲   ▲   ▲

I had walked some distance and by the time I got to the wake, which was being held at Aunt Vi's house, it was well under way. It was a good wake. Aunt Vi would have been pleased. There was plenty to drink, and more than enough to eat, including some Barbadian favorites: coconut bread, pone made with the cassava root, and the little crisp codfish cakes that are so hot with peppers they bring tears to the eyes as you bite into them.

I had missed the beginning, when everyone had probably sat around talking about Aunt Vi and recalling the few events that had distinguished her otherwise undistinguished life. (Someone, I'm sure, had told of the time she had missed the excursion boat to Atlantic City and had held her own private picnic—complete with pigeon peas and rice and fricassee chicken—on the pier at 42nd Street.) By the time I arrived, though, it would have been indiscreet to mention her name, for by then the wake had become—and this would also have pleased her—a celebration of life.

I had had two drinks, one right after the other, and was well into my third when Reena, who must have been upstairs, entered the basement kitchen where I was. She saw me before I had quite seen her, and with a cry that alerted the entire room to her presence and charged the air with her special force, she rushed toward me.

"Hey, I'm the one who was supposed to be the writer, not you! Do you know, I still can't believe it," she said, stepping back, her blackness heightened by a white mocking smile. "I read both your books over and over again and I can't really believe it. My Little Paulie!"

I did not mind. For there was respect and even wonder behind the patronizing words and in her eyes. The old imbalance between us had ended and I was suddenly glad to see her.

I told her so and we both began talking at once, but Reena's voice overpowered mine, so that all I could do after a time was listen while she discussed my books, and dutifully answer her questions about my personal life.

"And what about you?" I said, almost brutally, at the first chance I got. "What've you been up to all this time?"

She got up abruptly. "Good Lord, in here's noisy as hell. Come on, let's go upstairs."

We got fresh drinks and went up to Aunt Vi's bedroom, where in the soft light from the lamps, the huge Victorian bed and the pink satin bedspread with roses of the same material strewn over its surface looked as if they had never been used. And, in a way, this was true. Aunt Vi had seldom slept in her bed or, for that matter, lived in her house, because in order to pay for it, she had had to work at a sleeping-in job which gave her only Thursdays and every other Sunday off.

Reena sat on the bed, crushing the roses, and I sat on one of the numerous trunks which crowded the room. They contained every dress, coat, hat, and shoe that Aunt Vi had worn since coming to the United States. I again asked Reena what she had been doing over the years.

"Do you want a blow-by-blow account?" she said. But despite the flippancy, she was suddenly serious. And when she began it was clear that she had written out the narrative in her mind many times. The words came too easily; the events, the incidents had been ordered in time, and the meaning of her behavior and of the people with whom she had been involved had been painstakingly analyzed. She talked willingly, with desperation almost. And the words by themselves weren't enough. She used her hands to give them form and urgency. I became totally involved with her and all that she said. So much so that as the night wore on I was not certain at times whether it was she or I speaking.

▲   ▲   ▲

From the time her family moved to Jamaica until she was nineteen or so, Reena's life sounded, from what she told me in the beginning, as ordinary as mine and most of the girls we knew. After high school she had gone on to one of the free city colleges, where she had majored in journalism, worked part time in the school library, and, surprisingly enough, joined a houseplan. (Even I hadn't gone that far.) It was an all-Negro club, since there was a tacit understanding that Negro and white girls did not join each other's house-plans. "Integration, northern style," she said, shrugging.

It seems that Reena had had a purpose and a plan in joining the group. "I thought," she said with a wry smile, "I could get those girls up off their complacent rumps and out doing something about social issues. . . . I couldn't get them to budge. I remember after the war when a Negro ex-soldier had his eyes gouged out by a bus driver down South I tried getting them to demonstrate on campus. I talked until I was hoarse, but to no avail. They were too busy planning the annual autumn frolic."

Her laugh was bitter but forgiving and it ended in a long, reflective silence. After which she said quietly, "It wasn't that they didn't give a damn. It was just, I suppose, that like most people they didn't want to get involved to the extent that they might have to stand up and be counted. If it ever came to that. Then another thing. They thought they were safe, special. After all, they had grown up in the North, most of them, and so had escaped the southern-style prejudice; their parents, like mine, were struggling to put them through college; they could look forward to being tidy little schoolteachers, social workers, and lab technicians. Oh, they were safe!" The sarcasm scored her voice and then abruptly gave way to pity. "Poor things, they weren't safe, you see, and would never be as long as millions like themselves in Harlem, on Chicago's South Side, down South, all over the place, were unsafe. I tried to tell them this—and they accused me of being oversensitive. They tried not to listen. But I would have held out and, I'm sure, even brought some of them around eventually if this other business with a silly boy hadn't happened at the same time. . . ."

Reena told me then about her first, brief, and apparently innocent affair with a boy she had met at one of the houseplan parties. It had ended, she said, when the boy's parents had met her. "That was it," she said and the flat of her hand cut into the air. "He was forbidden to see me. The reason? He couldn't bring himself to tell me, but I knew. I was too black.

"Naturally, it wasn't the first time something like that had happened. In fact, you might say that was the theme of my childhood. Because I was dark I was always being plastered with Vaseline so I wouldn't look ashy. Whenever I had my picture taken they would pile a whitish powder on my face and make the lights so bright I always came out looking ghostly. My mother stopped speaking to any number of people because they said I would have been pretty if I hadn't been so dark. Like nearly every little black girl, I had my share of dreams of waking up to find myself with long, blond curls, blue eyes, and skin like milk. So I should have been prepared. Besides, that boy's parents were really rejecting themselves in rejecting me.

"Take us"—and her hands, opening in front of my face as she suddenly leaned forward, seemed to offer me the whole of black humanity. "We live surrounded by white images, and white in this world is synonymous with the good, light, beauty, success, so that, despite ourselves sometimes, we run after that whiteness and deny our darkness, which has been made into the symbol of all that is evil and inferior. I wasn't a person to that boy's parents, but a symbol of the darkness they were in flight from, so that just as they—that boy, his parents, those silly girls in the houseplan—were running from me, I started running from them . . ."

▲   ▲   ▲

It must have been shortly after this happened when I saw Reena at a debate which was being held at my college. She did not see me, since she was one of the speakers and I was merely part of her audience in the crowded auditorium. The topic had something to do with intellectual freedom in the colleges (McCarthyism was coming into vogue then) and aside from a Jewish boy from City College, Reena was the most effective—sharp, provocative, her position the most radical. The others on the panel seemed intimidated not only by the strength and cogency of her argument but by the sheer impact of her blackness in their white midst.

Her color might have been a weapon she used to dazzle and disarm her opponents. And she had highlighted it with the clothes she was wearing: a white dress patterned with large blocks of primary colors I remember (it looked Mexican) and a pair of intricately wrought silver earrings—long and with many little parts which clashed like muted cymbals over the microphone each time she moved her head. She wore her hair cropped short like a boy's and it was not straightened like mine and the other Negro girls' in the audience, but left in its coarse natural state: a small forest under which her face emerged in its intense and startling handsomeness. I remember she left the auditorium in triumph that day, surrounded by a noisy entourage from her college—all of them white.

"We were very serious," she said now, describing the left-wing group she had belonged to then—and there was a defensiveness in her voice which sought to protect them from all censure. "We believed—because we were young, I suppose, and had nothing as yet to risk—that we could do something about the injustices which everyone around us seemed to take for granted. So we picketed and demonstrated and bombarded Washington with our protests, only to have our names added to the Attorney General's list for all our trouble. We were always standing on street corners handing out leaflets or getting people to sign petitions. We always seemed to pick the coldest days to do that." Her smile held long after the words had died.

"I, we all, had such a sense of purpose then," she said softly, and a sadness lay aslant the smile now, darkening it. "We were forever holding meetings, having endless discussions, arguing, shouting, theorizing. And we had fun. Those parties! There was always somebody with a guitar. We were always singing. . . ." Suddenly, she began singing—and her voice was sure, militant, and faintly self-mocking,

> "But the banks are made of marble
> With a guard at every door
> And the vaults are stuffed with silver
> That the workers sweated for . . ."

When she spoke again the words were a sad coda to the song. "Well, as you probably know, things came to an ugly head with McCarthy reigning in Washington, and I was one of the people temporarily suspended from school."

She broke off and we both waited, the ice in our glasses melted and the drinks gone flat.

"At first, I didn't mind," she said finally. "After all, we were right. The fact that they suspended us proved it. Besides, I was in the middle of an affair, a real one this time, and too busy with that to care about anything else." She paused again, frowning.

"He was white," she said quickly and glanced at me as though to surprise either shock or disapproval in my face. "We were very involved. At one point—I think just after we had been suspended and he started working—we even thought of getting married. Living in New York, moving in the crowd we did, we might have been able to manage it. But I couldn't. There were too many complex things going on beneath the surface," she said, her voice strained by the hopelessness she must have felt then, her hands shaping it in the air between us. "Neither one of us could really escape what our color had come to mean in this country. Let me explain. Bob was always, for some odd reason, talking about how much the Negro suffered, and although I would agree with him I would also try to get across that, you know, like all people we also had fun once in a while, loved our children, liked making love—that we were human beings, for God's sake. But he only wanted to hear about the suffering. It was as if this comforted him and eased his own suffering—and he did suffer because of any number of things: his own uncertainty, for one, his difficulties with his family, for another . . .

"Once, I remember, when his father came into New York, Bob insisted that I meet him. I don't know why I agreed to go with him. . . ." She took a deep breath and raised her head very high. "I'll never forget or forgive the look on that old man's face when he opened his hotel-room door and saw me. The horror. I might have been the personification of every evil in the world. His inability to believe that it was his son standing there holding my hand. His shock. I'm sure he never fully recovered. I know I never did. Nor can I forget Bob's laugh in the elevator afterwards, the way he kept repeating: 'Did you see his face when he saw you? Did you . . . ?' He had used me, you see. I had been the means, the instrument of his revenge.

"And I wasn't any better. I used him. I took every opportunity to treat him shabbily, trying, you see, through him, to get at that white world which had not only denied me, but had turned my own against me." Her eyes closed. "I went numb all over when I understood what we were doing to, and with, each other. I stayed numb for a long time."

As Reena described the events which followed—the break with Bob, her gradual withdrawal from the left-wing group ("I had had it with them too. I got tired of being 'their Negro,' their pet. Besides, they were just all talk, really. All theories and abstractions. I doubt that, with all their elaborate plans for the Negro and for the workers of the world, any of them had ever been near a factory or up to Harlem")—as she spoke about her reinstatement in school, her voice suggested the numbness she had felt then. It only stirred into life again when she talked of her graduation.

"You should have seen my parents. It was really their day. My mother was so proud she complained about everything: her seat, the heat, the speaker; and my father just sat there long after everybody had left, too awed to move. God, it meant so much to them. It was as if I had made up for the generations his people had picked cotton in Georgia and my mother's family had cut cane in the West Indies. It frightened me."

I asked her after a long wait what she had done after graduating.

"How do you mean, what I did. Looked for a job. Tell me, have you ever looked for work in this man's city?"

"I know," I said, holding up my hand. "Don't tell me."

We both looked at my raised hand which sought to waive the discussion, then at each other and suddenly we laughed, a laugh so loud and violent with pain and outrage it brought tears.

"Girl," Reena said, the tears silver against her blackness. "You could put me blindfolded right now at the Times Building on 42nd Street and I would be able to find my way to every newspaper office in town. But tell me, how come white folks is so *hard*?"

"Just bo'n hard."

We were laughing again and this time I nearly slid off the trunk and Reena fell back among the satin roses.

"I didn't know there were so many ways of saying 'no' without ever once using the word," she said, the laughter lodged in her throat, but her eyes had gone hard. "Sometimes I'd find myself in the elevator, on my way out, and smiling all over myself because I thought I had gotten the job, before it would hit me that they had really said no, not yes. Some of those people in personnel had so perfected their smiles they looked almost genuine. The ones who used to get me, though, were those who tried to make the interview into an intimate chat between friends. They'd put you in a comfortable chair, offer you a cigarette, and order coffee. How I hated that coffee. They didn't know it—or maybe they did—but it was like offering me hemlock. . . .

"You think Christ had it tough?" Her laughter rushed against the air which resisted it. "I was crucified five days a week and half-day on Saturday. I became almost paranoid. I began to think there might be something other than color wrong with me which everybody but me could see, some rare disease that had turned me into a monster.

"My parents suffered. And that bothered me most, because I felt I had failed them. My father didn't say anything but I knew because he avoided me more than usual. He was ashamed, I think, that he hadn't been able, as a man and as my father, to prevent this. My mother—well, you know her. In one breath she would try to comfort me by cursing them: 'But Gor blind them,'"—and Reena's voice captured her mother's aggressive accent—"'if you had come looking for a job mopping down their floors they would o' hire you, the brutes. But mark my words, their time goin' come, 'cause God don't love ugly and he ain't stuck on pretty . . .' And in the next breath she would curse me, 'Journalism! Journalism! Whoever heard of colored people taking up journalism. You must feel you's white or something so. The people is right to chuck you out their office. . . .' Poor thing, to make up for saying all that she would wash my white gloves every night and cook cereal for me in the morning as is I were a little girl again. Once she went out and bought me a suit she couldn't afford from Lord and Taylor's. I looked like a Smith girl in blackface in it. . . . So guess where I ended up?"

"As a social investigator for the Welfare Department. Where else?"

We were helpless with laughter again.

"You too?"

"No," I said, "I taught, but that was just as bad."

"No," she said, sobering abruptly. "Nothing's as bad as working for Welfare. Do you know what they really mean by a social investigator? A spy. Someone whose dirty job it is to snoop into the corners of the lives of the poor and make their poverty more vivid by taking from them the last shred of privacy. 'Mrs. Jones, is that a new dress you're wearing?' 'Mrs. Brown, this kerosene heater is not listed in the household items. Did you get an authorization for it?' 'Mrs. Smith, is that a telephone I hear ringing under the sofa?' I was utterly demoralized within a month.

"And another thing. I thought I knew about poverty. I mean, I remember, as a child, having to eat soup made with those white beans the government used to give out free for days running, sometimes, because there was nothing else. I had lived in Brownsville, among all the poor Jews and Poles and Irish there. But what I saw in Harlem, where I had my case load, was different somehow. Perhaps because it seemed so final. There didn't seem to be any way to escape from those dark hallways and dingy furnished rooms . . . All that defeat." Closing her eyes, she finished the stale whiskey and soda in her glass.

"I remember a client of mine, a girl my age with three children already and no father for them and living in the expensive squalor of a rooming house. Her bewilderment. Her resignation. Her anger. She could have pulled herself out of the mess she was in? People say that, you know, including some Negroes. But this girl didn't have a chance. She had been trapped from the day she was born in some small town down South.

"She became my reference. From then on and even now, whenever I hear people and groups coming up with all kinds of solutions to the quote Negro problem, I ask one question. What are they really doing for that girl, to save her or to save the children? . . . The answer isn't very encouraging."

It was some time before she continued, and then she told me that after Welfare she had gone to work for a private social-work agency, in their publicity department, and had started on her master's in journalism at Columbia. She also left home around this time.

"I had to. My mother started putting the pressure on me to get married. The hints, the remarks—and you know my mother was never the subtle type—her anxiety, which made me anxious about getting married after a while. Besides, it was time for me to be on my own."

In contrast to the unmistakably radical character of her late adolescence (her membership in the left-wing group, the affair with Bob, her suspension from college), Reena's life of this period sounded ordinary, standard—and she admitted it with a slightly self-deprecating, apologetic smile. It was similar to that of any number of unmarried professional Negro women in New York or Los Angeles or Washington: the job teaching or doing social work which brought in a fairly decent salary, the small apartment with kitchenette which they sometimes shared with a roommate; a car, some of them; membership in various political and social action organizations for the militant few like Reena; the vacations in Mexico, Europe, the West Indies, and now Africa; the occasional date. "The interesting men were invariably married," Reena said and then mentioned having had one affair during that time. She had found out he was married and had thought of her only as the perfect mistress. "The bastard," she said, but her smile forgave him.

"Women alone!" she cried, laughing sadly, and her raised opened arms, the empty glass she held in one hand made eloquent their aloneness. "Alone and lonely, and indulging themselves while they wait. The girls of the houseplan have reached their majority only to find that all those years they spent accumulating their degrees and finding the well-paying jobs in the hope that this would raise their stock have, instead, put them at a disadvantage. For the few eligible men around—those who are their intellectual and professional peers, whom they can respect (and there are very few of them)—don't necessarily marry them, but younger women without the degrees and the fat jobs, who are no threat, or they don't marry at all because they are either queer or mother-ridden. Or they marry white women. Now, intellectually I accept this. In fact, some of my best friends are white women . . ." And again our laughter—that loud, searing burst which we used to cauterize our hurt mounted into the unaccepting silence of the room. "After all, our goal is a fully integrated society. And perhaps, as some people believe, the only solution to the race problem is miscegenation. Besides, a man should be able to marry whomever he wishes. Emotionally, though, I am less kind and understanding, and I resent like hell the reasons some black men give for rejecting us for them."

"We're too middle-class-oriented," I said. "Conservative."

"Right. Even though, thank God, that doesn't apply to me."

"Too threatening . . . castrating . . ."

"Too independent and impatient with them for not being more ambitious . . . contemptuous . . ."

"Sexually inhibited and unimaginative . . ."

"And the old myth of the excessive sexuality of the black woman goes out the window," Reena cried.

"Not supportive, unwilling to submerge our interests for theirs . . ."

"Lacking in the subtle art of getting and keeping a man . . ."

We had recited the accusations in the form and tone of a litany, and in the silence which followed we shared a thin, hopeless smile.

"They condemn us," Reena said softly but with anger, "without taking history into account. We are still, most of us, the black woman who had to be almost frighteningly strong in order for us all to survive. For, after all, she was the one whom they left (and I don't hold this against them; I understand) with the children to raise, who had to *make* it somehow or the other. And we are still, so many of us, living that history.

"You would think that they would understand this, but few do. So it's up to us. We have got to understand them and save them for ourselves. How? By being, on one hand, persons in our own right and, on the other, fully the woman and the wife. . . . Christ, listen to who's talking! I had my chance. And I tried. Very hard. But it wasn't enough."

▲   ▲   ▲

The festive sounds of the wake had died to a sober murmur beyond the bedroom. The crowd had gone, leaving only Reena and myself upstairs and the last of Aunt Vi's closest friends in the basement below. They were drinking coffee. I smelled it, felt its warmth and intimacy in the empty house, heard the distant tapping of the cups against the saucers and voices muted by grief. The wake had come full circle: they were again mourning Aunt Vi.

And Reena might have been mourning with them, sitting there amid the satin roses, framed by the massive headboard. Her hands lay as if they had been broken in her lap. Her eyes were like those of someone blind or dead. I got up to go and get some coffee for her.

"You met my husband," she said quickly, stopping me.

"Have I?" I said, sitting down again.

"Yes, before we were married even. At an autograph party for you. He was free-lancing— he's a photographer—and one of the Negro magazines had sent him to cover the party."

As she went on to describe him I remembered him vaguely, not his face, but his rather large body stretching and bending with a dancer's fluidity and grace as he took the pictures. I had heard him talking to a group of people about some issue on race relations very much in the news then and had been struck by his vehemence. For the moment I had found this almost odd, since he was so fair-skinned he could have passed for white.

They had met, Reena told me now, at a benefit show for a Harlem day nursery given by one of the progressive groups she belonged to, and had married a month afterward. From all that she said they had had a full and exciting life for a long time. Her words were so vivid that I could almost see them: she with her startling blackness and extraordinary force and he with his near-white skin and a militancy which matched hers; both of them moving among the disaffected in New York, their stand on political and social issues equally uncompromising, the line of their allegiance reaching directly to all those trapped in Harlem. And they had lived the meaning of this allegiance, so that even when they could have afforded a life among the black bourgeoisie of St. Albans or Teaneck, they had chosen to live if not in Harlem so close that there was no difference.

"I—we—were so happy I was frightened at times. Not that anything would change between us, but that someone or something in the world outside us would invade our private place and destroy us out of envy. Perhaps this is what did happen. . . ." She shrugged and even tried to smile but she could not manage it. "Something slipped in while we weren't looking and began its deadly work.

"Maybe it started when Dave took a job with a Negro magazine. I'm not sure. Anyway, in no time, he hated it: the routine, unimaginative pictures he had to take and the magazine itself, which dealt only in unrealities: the high-society world of the black bourgeoisie and the spectacular strides Negroes were making in all fields—you know the type. Yet Dave wouldn't leave. It wasn't the money, but a kind of safety which he had never experienced before which kept him there. He would talk about free-lancing again, about storming the gates of the white magazines downtown, of opening his own studio—but he never acted on any one of these things. You see, despite his talent—and he was very talented—he had a diffidence that was fatal.

"When I understood this I literally forced him to open the studio—and perhaps I should have been more subtle and indirect, but that's not my nature. Besides, I was frightened and desperate to help. Nothing happened for a time. Dave's work was too experimental to be commercial. Gradually, though, his photographs started appearing in the prestige camera magazines and money from various awards and exhibits and an occasional assignment started coming in.

"This wasn't enough somehow. Dave also wanted the big, gaudy commercial success that would dazzle and confound that white world downtown and force it to *see* him. And yet, as I said before, he couldn't bring himself to try—and this contradiction began to get to him after awhile.

"It was then, I think, that I began to fail him. I didn't know how to help, you see. I had never felt so inadequate before. And this was very strange and disturbing for someone like me. I was being submerged in his problems—and I began fighting against this.

"I started working again (I had stopped after the second baby). And I was lucky because I got back my old job. And unlucky because Dave saw it as my way of pointing up his deficiencies. I couldn't convince him otherwise: that I had to do it for my own sanity. He would accuse me of wanting to see him fail, of trapping him in all kinds of responsibilities. . . . After a time we both got caught up in this thing, an ugliness came between us, and I began to answer his anger with anger and to trade him insult for insult.

"Things fell apart very quickly after that. I couldn't bear the pain of living with him—the insults, our mutual despair, his mocking, the silence. I couldn't subject the children to it any longer. The divorce didn't take long. And thank God, because of the children, we are pleasant when we have to see each other. He's making out very well, I hear."

▲   ▲   ▲

She said nothing more, but simply bowed her head as though waiting for me to pass judgment on her. I don't know how long we remained like this, but when Reena finally raised her head, the darkness at the window had vanished and dawn was a still, gray smoke against the pane.

"Do you know," she said, and her eyes were clear and a smile had won out over pain, "I enjoy being alone. I don't tell people this because they'll accuse me of either lying or deluding myself. But I do. Perhaps, as my mother tells me, it's only temporary. I don't think so, though. I feel I don't ever want to be involved again. It's not that I've lost interest in men. I go out occasionally, but it's never anything serious. You see, I have all that I want for now."

Her children first of all, she told me, and from her description they sounded intelligent and capable. She was a friend as well as a mother to them, it seemed. They were planning, the four of them, to spend the summer touring Canada. "I will feel that I have done well by them if I give them, if nothing more, a sense of themselves and their worth and importance as black people. Everything I do with them, for them, is to this end. I don't want them ever to be confused about this. They must have their identifications straight from the beginning. No white dolls for them!"

Then her job. She was working now as a researcher for a small progressive news magazine with the promise that once she completed her master's in journalism (she was working on the thesis now) she might get a chance to do some minor reporting. And like most people, she hoped to write someday. "If I can ever stop talking away my substance," she said laughing.

And she was still active in any number of social-action groups. In another week or so she would be heading a delegation of mothers down to City Hall "to give the mayor a little hell about conditions in the schools in Harlem." She had started an organization that was carrying on an almost door-to-door campaign in her neighborhood to expose, as she put it, "the blood suckers: all those slumlords and storekeepers with their fixed scales, the finance companies that never tell you the real price of a thing, the petty salesmen that leech off the poor. . . ." In May she was taking her two older girls on a nationwide pilgrimage to Washington to urge for a more rapid implementation of the school-desegregation law.

"It's uncanny," she said, and the laugh which accompanied the words was warm, soft with wonder at herself, girlish even, and the air in the room which had refused her laughter before rushed to absorb this now. "Really uncanny. Here I am, practically middle-aged, with three children to raise by myself and with little or no money to do it, and yet I feel, strangely enough, as though life is just beginning—that it's new and fresh with all kinds of possibilities. Maybe it's because I've been through my purgatory and I can't ever be overwhelmed again. I don't know. Anyway, you should see me on evenings after I put the children to bed. I sit alone in the living room (I've repainted it and changed all the furniture since Dave's gone, so that it would at least look different)—I sit there making plans and all of them seem possible. The most important plan right now is Africa. I've already started saving the fare."

I asked her whether she was planning to live there permanently and she said simply, "I want to live and work there. For how long, for a lifetime, I can't say. All I know is that I have to. For myself and for my children. It is important that they see black people who have truly a place and history of their own and who are building for a new and, hopefully, more sensible world. And I must see it, get close to it, because I can never lose the sense of being a displaced person here in America because of my color. Oh, I know I should remain and fight not only for integration (even though, frankly, I question whether I want to be integrated into America as it stands now, with its complacency and materialism, its soullessness) but to help change the country into something better, sounder—if that is still possible. But I have to go to Africa. . . ."

"Poor Aunt Vi," she said after a long silence and straightened one of the roses she had crushed. "She never really got to enjoy her bed of roses what with only Thursdays and every other Sunday off. All that hard work. All her life . . . Our lives have got to make more sense, if only for her."

We got up to leave shortly afterward. Reena was staying on to attend the burial, later in the morning, but I was taking the subway to Manhattan. We parted with the usual promise to get together and exchange telephone numbers. And Reena did phone a week or so later. I don't remember what we talked about though.

Some months later I invited her to a party I was giving before leaving the country. But she did not come.

A Happening in Barbados

The best way to pick up a Barbadian man, I hoped, was to walk alone down the beach with my tall, brown frame squeezed into a skintight bathing suit. Since my hotel was near the beach, and Dorothy and Alison, my two traveling companions, had gone shopping, I managed this quite well. I had not taken more than a few steps on the glittering, white sand before two black men were on either side of me vying for attention.

I chose the tall, slim-hipped one over the squat, muscle-bound man who was also grinning at me. But apparently they were friends, because Edwin had no sooner settled me under his umbrella than the squat one showed up with a beach chair and two other boys in tow.

Edwin made the introductions. His temporary rival was Gregory, and the other two were Alphonse and Dimitri.

Gregory was ugly. He had thick, rubbery lips, a scarcity of teeth, and a broad nose splattered like a pyramid across his face. He was all massive shoulders and bulging biceps. No doubt he had a certain animal magnetism, but personally I preferred a lean man like Edwin, who was well built but slender, his whole body fitting together like a symphony. Alphonse and Dimitri were clean-cut and pleasant looking.

They were all too young—twenty to twenty-five at the most—and Gregory seemed the oldest. I inwardly mourned their youth and settled down to make the most of my catch.

The crystal-blue sky rivaled the royal blue of the Caribbean for beauty, and our black bodies on the white sand added to the munificence of colors. We ran into the sea like squealing children when the sudden raindrops came, then shivered on the sand under a makeshift tent of umbrellas and damp towels waiting for the sun to reappear while nourishing ourselves with straight Barbados rum.

As with most of the West Indians I had already met on my whirlwind tour of Trinidad and Jamaica, who welcomed American Negroes with open arms, my new friends loved their island home, but work was scarce and they yearned to go to America. They were hungry for news of how Negroes were faring in the States.

Edwin's arm rested casually on my knee in a proprietary manner, and I smiled at him. His thin, serious face was smooth, too young for a razor, and when he smiled back, he looked even younger. He told me he was a waiter at the Hilton, saving his money to make

From *Black-eyed Susans / Midnight Birds: Stories by and about Black Women,* ed. with intro by Mary Helen Washington (New York: Anchor Books, 1990).

it to the States. I had already learned not to be snobbish with the island's help. Yesterday's waiter may be tomorrow's prime minister.

Dimitri, very black with an infectious grin, was also a waiter, and lanky Alphonse was a tile setter.

Gregory's occupation was apparently women, for that's all he talked about. He was able to launch this subject when a bony white woman—more peeling red than white, really looking like a gaunt cadaver in a loose-fitting bathing suit—came out of the sea and walked up to us. She smiled archly at Gregory.

"Are you going to take me to the Pigeon Club tonight, sugar?"

"No, mon," he said pleasantly, with a toothless grin. "I'm taking a younger pigeon."

The woman turned a deeper red, if that was possible, and, mumbling something incoherent, walked away.

"That one is always after me to take her some place," Gregory said. "She's rich, and she pays the bills but, mon, I don't want an old hag nobody else wants. I like to take my women away from white men and watch them squirm."

"Come down, mon," Dimitri said, grinning. "She look like she's starving for what you got to spare."

We all laughed. The boys exchanged stories about their experiences with predatory white women who came to the islands looking for some black action. But, one and all, they declared they liked dark-skinned meat the best, and I felt like a black queen of the Nile when Gregory winked at me and said, "The blacker the berry, mon, the sweeter the juice."

They had all been pursued and had chased some white tail, too, no doubt, but while the others took it all in good humor, it soon became apparent that Gregory's exploits were exercises in vengeance.

Gregory was saying: "I told that bastard, 'You in my country now, mon, and I'll kick your ass all the way back to Texas. The girl agreed to dance with me, and she don't need your permission.' That white man's face turned purple, but he sat back down, and I dance with his girl. Mon, they hate to see me rubbing bellies with their women because they know once she rub bellies with me she wanna rub something else, too." He laughed, and we all joined in. Serves the white men right, I thought. Let's see how they liked licking *that* end of the stick for a change.

"Mon, you gonna get killed yet," Edwin said, moving closer to me on the towel we shared. "You're crazy. You don't care whose woman you mess with. But it's not gonna be a white man who kill you but some bad Bajan."

Gregory led in the laughter, then held us spellbound for the next hour with intimate details of his affair with Glenda, a young white girl spending the summer with her father on their yacht. Whatever he had, Glenda wanted it desperately, or so Gregory told it.

Yeah, I thought to myself, like LSD, a black lover is the thing this year. I had seen the white girls in the Village and at off-Broadway theaters clutching their black men tightly while I, manless, looked on with bitterness. I often vowed I would find me an ofay in self-defense, but I could never bring myself to condone the wholesale rape of my slave ancestors by letting a white man touch me.

We finished the rum, and the three boys stood up to leave, making arrangements to get together later with us and my two girl friends and go clubbing.

Edwin and I were left alone. He stretched out his muscled leg and touched my toes with his. I smiled at him and let our thighs come together. Why did he have to be so damned young? Then our lips met, his warm and demanding, and I thought, what the hell, maybe I will. I was thirty-nine—good-bye, sweet bird of youth—an ungay divorcee, uptight and drinking too much, trying to disown the years which had brought only loneliness and pain. I had clawed my way up from the slums of Harlem via night school and was now a law clerk on Wall Street. But the fight upward had taken its toll. My husband, who couldn't claw as well as I, got lost somewhere in that concrete jungle. The last I saw of him, he was peering under every skirt around, searching for his lost manhood.

I had always felt contempt for women who found their kicks by robbing the cradle. Now here I was on a Barbados beach with an amorous child young enough to be my son. Two sayings flitted unbidden across my mind. "Judge not, that ye be not judged" and "The thing which I feared is come upon me." I thought, ain't it the god-damned truth?

Edwin kissed me again, pressing the length of his body against mine.

"I've got to go," I gasped. "My friends have probably returned and are looking for me. About ten tonight?"

He nodded; I smiled at him and ran all the way to my hotel.

At exactly ten o'clock, the telephone in our room announced we had company downstairs.

"Hot damn," Alison said, putting on her eyebrows in front of the mirror. "We're not going to be stood up."

"Island men," I said loftily, "are dependable, not like the bums you're used to in America."

Alison, freckled and willowy, had been married three times and was looking for her fourth. Her motto was, if at first you don't succeed, find another mother. She was a real-estate broker in Los Angeles, and we had been childhood friends in Harlem.

"What I can't stand," Dorothy said from the bathroom, "are those creeps who come to your apartment, drink up your liquor, then dirty up your sheets. You don't even get a dinner out of the deal."

She came out of the bathroom in her slip. Petite and delicate with a pixie grin, at thirty-five Dorothy looked more like one of the high school girls she taught than their teacher. She had never been married. Years before, while she was holding onto her virginity with a miser's grip, her fiancé messed up and knocked up one of her friends.

Since then, all of Dorothy's affairs had been with married men, displaying perhaps a subconscious vendetta against all wives.

By ten-twenty we were downstairs and I was introducing the girls to our four escorts, who eyed us with unconcealed admiration. We were looking good in our Saks Fifth Avenue finery. They were looking good, too, in soft shirts and loose slacks, all except Gregory, whose bulging muscles confined in clothing made him seem more gargantuan.

We took a cab and a few minutes later were squeezing behind a table in a small, smoky room called the Pigeon Club. A Trinidad steel band was blasting out the walls, and the tiny dance area was jammed with wiggling bottoms and shuffling feet. The white tourists trying to do the hip-shaking calypso were having a ball and looking awkward.

I got up to dance with Edwin. He had a natural grace and was easy to follow. Our bodies found the rhythm and became one with it while our eyes locked in silent ancient combat, his pleading, mine teasing.

We returned to our seats and to tall glasses of rum and cola tonic. The party had begun.

I danced every dance with Edwin, his clasp becoming gradually tighter until my face was smothered in his shoulder, my arms locked around his neck. He was adorable. Very good for my ego. The other boys took turns dancing with my friends, but soon preferences were set—Alison with Alphonse and Dorothy with Dimitri. With good humor, Gregory ordered another round and didn't seem to mind being odd man out, but he wasn't alone for long.

During the floor show, featuring the inevitable limbo dancers, a pretty white girl, about twenty-two, with straight, red hair hanging down to her shoulder, appeared at Gregory's elbow. From his wink at me and self-satisfied grin, I knew this was Glenda from the yacht.

"Hello," she said to Gregory. "Can I join you, or do you have a date?"

Well, I thought, that's the direct approach.

"What are you doing here?" Gregory asked.

"Looking for you."

Gregory slid over on the bench next to the wall, and Glenda sat down as he introduced her to the rest of us. Somehow, her presence spoiled my mood. We had been happy being black, and I resented this intrusion from the white world. But Glenda was happy. She had found the man she'd set out to find and a swinging party to boot. She beamed a dazzling smile around the table.

Alphonse led Alison onto the dance floor, and Edwin and I followed. The steel band was playing a wild calypso, and I could feel my hair rising with the heat as I joined in the wildness.

When we returned to the table, Glenda applauded us, then turned to Gregory. "Why don't you teach me to dance like that?"

He answered with his toothless grin and a leer, implying he had better things to teach her.

White women were always snatching our men, I thought, and now they want to dance like us.

I turned my attention back to Edwin and met his full stare.

I teased him with a smile, refusing to commit myself. He had a lusty, healthy appetite, which was natural, I supposed, for a twenty-one-year-old lad. Lord, but why did he have to be that young? I stood up to go to the ladies' room.

"Wait for me," Glenda cried, trailing behind me.

The single toilet stall was occupied, and Glenda leaned against the wall waiting for it while I flipped open my compact and powdered my grimy face.

"You married?" she asked.

"Divorced."

"When I get married, I want to stay hooked forever."

"That's the way I planned it, too," I said dryly.

"What I mean," she rushed on, "is that I've gotta find a cat who wants to groove only with me."

Oh Lord, I thought, don't try to sound like us, too. Use your own, sterile language.

"I really dug this guy I was engaged to," Glenda continued, "but he couldn't function without a harem. I could have stood that, maybe, but when he didn't mind if I made it with some other guy, too, I knew I didn't want that kind of life."

I looked at her in the mirror as I applied my lipstick. She had been hurt, and badly. She shook right down to her naked soul. So she was dropping down a social notch, according to her scale of values, and trying to repair her damaged ego with a black brother.

"You gonna make it with Edwin?" she asked, as if we were college chums comparing dates.

"I'm not a one-night stand." My tone was frigid. That's another thing I can't stand about white people. Too familiar, because we're colored.

"I dig Gregory," she said, pushing her hair out of her eyes. "He's kind of rough, but who wouldn't be, the kind of life he's led."

"And what kind of life is that?" I asked.

"Didn't you know? His mother was a whore in an exclusive brothel for white men only. That was before, when the British owned the island."

"I take it you like rough men?" I asked.

"There's usually something gentle and lost underneath," she replied.

A white woman came out of the toilet and Glenda went in. Jesus, I thought, Gregory gentle? The woman walked to the basin, flung some water in the general direction of her hands, and left.

"Poor Daddy is having a fit," Glenda volunteered from the john, "but there's not much he can do about it. He's afraid I'll leave him again, and he gets lonely without me, so he just tags along and tries to keep me out of trouble."

"And he pays the bills?"

She answered with a laugh. "Why not? He's loaded."

Why not, I thought with bitterness. You white women have always managed to have your cake and eat it, too. The toilet flushed with a roar like Niagara Falls. I opened the door and went back to our table. Let Glenda find her way back alone.

Edwin pulled my chair out and brushed his lips across the nape of my neck as I sat down. He still had not danced with anyone else, and his apparent desire was flattering. For a moment, I considered it. That's what I really needed, wasn't it? To walk down the moonlit beach wrapped in his arms, making it to some pad to be made? It would be a delightful story to tell at bridge sessions. But I shook my head at him, and this time my smile was more sad than teasing.

Glenda came back and crawled over Gregory's legs to the seat beside him. The bastard. He made no pretense of being a gentleman. Suddenly, I didn't know which of them I disliked the most. Gregory winked at me. I don't know where he got the impression I was his conspirator, but I got up to dance with him.

"That Glenda," he grinned, "she's the one I was on the boat with last night. I banged her plenty, in the room right next to her father. We could hear him coughing to let us know he was awake, but he didn't come in."

He laughed like a naughty schoolboy, and I joined in. He was a nerveless bastard all right, and it served Glenda right that we were laughing at her. Who asked her to crash our party anyway? That's when I got the idea to take Gregory away from her.

"You gonna bang her again tonight?" I asked, a new, teasing quality in my voice. "Or are you gonna find something better to do?" To help him get the message I rubbed bellies with him.

He couldn't believe this sudden turn of events. I could almost see him thinking. With one stroke he could slap Glenda down a peg and repay Edwin for beating his time with me on the beach that morning.

"You wanna come with me?" He asked, making sure of his quarry.

"What you got to offer?" I peered at him through half-closed lids.

"Big Bamboo," he sang, the title of a popular calypso. We both laughed.

I felt a heady excitement of impending danger as Gregory pulled me back to the table. The men paid the bill, and suddenly we were standing outside the club in the bright moonlight. Gregory deliberately uncurled Glenda's arm from his and took a step toward me. Looking at Edwin and nodding in my direction, he said, "She's coming with me. Any objections?"

Edwin inhaled a mouthful of smoke. His face was inscrutable. "You want to go with him?" he asked me quiety.

I avoided his eyes and nodded. "Yes."

He flipped the cigarette with contempt at my feet and lit another one. "Help yourself to the garbage," he said, and leaned back against the building, one leg braced behind him. The others suddenly stilled their chatter, sensing trouble.

I was holding Gregory's arm now, and I felt his muscles tense. "No," I said as he moved toward Edwin. "You've got what you want. Forget it."

Glenda was ungracious in defeat. "What about me?" she screamed. She stared from one black face to another, her glance lingering on Edwin. But he wasn't about to come to her aid and take Gregory's leavings.

"You can go home in a cab," Gregory said, pushing her ahead of him and pulling me behind him to a taxi waiting at the curb.

Glenda broke from his grasp. "You bastard. Who in the hell do you think you are, King Solomon? You can't dump me like this." She raised her hands as if to strike Gregory on the chest, but he caught them before they landed.

"Careful, white girl," he said. His voice was low but ominous. She froze.

"But why," she whimpered, all hurt child now. "You liked me last night. I know you did. Why are you treating me like this?"

"I didn't bring you here"—his voice was pleasant again—"so don't be trailing me all over town. When I want you, I'll come to that damn boat and get you. Now get in that cab before I throw you in. I'll see you tomorrow night. Maybe."

"You go to hell." She eluded him and turned on me, asking with incredible innocence, "What did I ever do to you?" Then she was running past toward the beach, her sobs drifting back to haunt me like a forlorn melody.

What had she ever done to me? And what had I just done? In order to degrade her for the crime of being white, I had sunk to the gutter. Suddenly Glenda was just another woman, vulnerable and lonely, like me.

We were sick, sick, sick. All fucked up. I had thought only Gregory was hung up in his love-hate, black-white syndrome, decades of suppressed hatred having sickened his soul. But I was tainted, too. I had forgotten my own misery long enough to inflict it on another woman who was only trying to ease her loneliness by making it with a soul brother. Was I jealous because she was able to function as a woman where I couldn't, because she realized that a man is a man, color be damned, while I was crucified on my own, anti-white-man cross?

What if she were going black trying to repent for some ancient Nordic sin? How else could she atone except with the gift of herself? And if some black brother wanted to help a chick off her lily-white pedestal, he was entitled to that freedom, and it was none of my damned business anyway.

"Let's go baby," Gregory said, tucking my arm under his.

The black bastard. I didn't even like the ugly ape. I backed away from him. "Leave me alone," I screamed. "Goddamit, just leave me alone!"

For a moment, we were all frozen into an absurd fresco—Alison, Dorothy, and the two boys looking at me in shocked disbelief, Edwin hiding behind a nonchalant smokescreen, Gregory off balance and confused, reaching out toward me.

I moved first, toward Edwin, but I had slammed the door behind me. He laughed, a mirthless sound in the stillness. He knew. I had forsaken him, but at least not for Gregory.

Then I was running down the beach looking for Glenda, hot tears of shame burning my face. How could I have been such a bitch? But the white beach, shimmering in the moonlight, was empty. And once again, I was alone.

TONI MORRISON

SEEMOTHERMOTHERISVERYNICEMO THERWILLYOUPLAYWITHJANEMOTH ERLAUGHSLAUGHMOTHERLAUGHLA

The easiest thing to do would be to build a case out of her foot. That is what she herself did. But to find out the truth about how dreams die, one should never take the word of the dreamer. The end of her lovely beginning was probably the cavity in one of her front teeth. She preferred, however, to think always of her foot. Although she was the ninth of eleven children and lived on a ridge of red Alabama clay seven miles from the nearest road, the complete indifference with which a rusty nail was met when it punched clear through her foot during her second year of life saved Pauline Williams from total anonymity. The wound left her with a crooked, archless foot that flopped when she walked—not a limp that would have eventually twisted her spine, but a way of lifting the bad foot as though she were extracting it from little whirlpools that threatened to pull it under. Slight as it was, this deformity explained for her many things that would have been otherwise incomprehensible: why she alone of all the children had no nickname; why there were no funny jokes and anecdotes about funny things she had done; why no one ever remarked on her food preferences—no saving of the wing or neck for her—no cooking of the peas in a separate pot without rice because she did not like rice; why nobody teased her; why she never felt at home anywhere, or that she belonged anyplace. Her general feeling of separateness and unworthiness she blamed on her foot. Restricted, as a child, to this cocoon of her family's spinning, she cultivated quiet and private pleasures. She liked, most of all, to arrange things. To line things up in rows—jars on shelves at canning, peach pits on the step, sticks, stones, leaves—and the members of her family let these arrangements be. When by some accident somebody scattered her rows, they always stopped to retrieve them for her, and she was never angry, for it gave her a chance to rearrange them again. Whatever portable plurality she found, she organized into neat lines, according to their size, shape, or gradations of color. Just as she would never align a pine needle with the leaf of a cottonwood tree, she would never put the jars of tomatoes next to the green beans. During all of her four years of going to school, she was enchanted by numbers and depressed by words. She missed—without knowing what she missed—paints and crayons.

Near the beginning of World War I, the Williamses discovered, from returning neigh-

---

From Toni Morrison, *The Bluest Eye* (New York: Holt, Rhinehart & Winston, 1970).

bors and kin, the possibility of living better in another place. In shifts, lots, batches, mixed in with other families, they migrated, in six months and four journeys, to Kentucky, where there were mines and millwork.

"When all us left from down home and was waiting down by the depot for the truck, it was nighttime. June bugs was shooting everywhere. They lighted up a tree leaf, and I seen a streak of green every now and again. That was the last time I seen real june bugs. These things up here ain't june bugs. They's something else. Folks here call them fireflies. Down home they was different. But I recollect that streak of green. I recollect it well."

In Kentucky they lived in a real town, ten to fifteen houses on a single street, with water piped right into the kitchen. Ada and Fowler Williams found a five-room frame house for their family. The yard was bounded by a once-white fence against which Pauline's mother planted flowers and within which they kept a few chickens. Some of her brothers joined the Army, one sister died, and two got married, increasing the living space and giving the entire Kentucky venture a feel of luxury. The relocation was especially comfortable to Pauline, who was old enough to leave school. Mrs. Williams got a job cleaning and cooking for a white minister on the other side of town, and Pauline, now the oldest girl at home, took over the care of the house. She kept the fence in repair, pulling the pointed stakes erect, securing them with bits of wire, collected eggs, swept, cooked, washed, and minded the two younger children—a pair of twins called Chicken and Pie, who were still in school. She was not only good at housekeeping, she enjoyed it. After her parents left for work and the other children were at school or in mines, the house was quiet. The stillness and isolation both calmed and energized her. She could arrange and clean without interruption until two o'clock, when Chicken and Pie came home.

When the war ended and the twins were ten years old, they too left school to work. Pauline was fifteen, still keeping house, but with less enthusiasm. Fantasies about men and love and touching were drawing her mind and hands away from her work. Changes in weather began to affect her, as did certain sights and sounds. These feelings translated themselves to her in extreme melancholy. She thought of the death of newborn things, lonely roads, and strangers who appear out of nowhere simply to hold one's hand, woods in which the sun was always setting. In church especially did these dreams grow. The songs caressed her, and while she tried to hold her mind on the wages of sin, her body trembled for redemption, salvation, a mysterious rebirth that would simply happen, with no effort on her part. In none of her fantasies was she ever aggressive; she was usually idling by the river bank, or gathering berries in a field when a someone appeared, with gentle and penetrating eyes, who—with no exchange of words—understood; and before whose glance her foot straightened and her eyes dropped. The someone had no face, no form, no voice, no odor. He was a simple Presence, an all-embracing tenderness with strength and a promise of rest. It did not matter that she had no idea of what to do or say to the Presence—after the wordless knowing and the soundless touching, her dreams disintegrated. But the Presence would know what to do. She had only to lay her head on his chest and he would lead her away to the sea, to the city, to the woods . . . forever.

There was a woman named Ivy who seemed to hold in her mouth all of the sounds of Pauline's soul. Standing a little apart from the choir, Ivy sang the dark sweetness that

Pauline could not name; she sang the death-defying death that Pauline yearned for; she sang of the Stranger who *knew* . . .

> Precious Lord take my hand
> Lead me on, let me stand
> I am tired, I am weak, I am worn.
> Through the storms, through the night
> Lead me on to the light
> Take my hand, precious Lord, lead me on.
>
> When my way grows drear
> Precious Lord linger near,
> When my life is almost gone
> Hear my cry hear my call
> Hold my hand lest I fall
> Take my hand, precious Lord, lead me on.

Thus it was that when the Stranger, the someone, did appear out of nowhere, Pauline was grateful but not surprised.

He came, strutting right out of a Kentucky sun on the hottest day of the year. He came big, he came strong, he came with yellow eyes, flaring nostrils, and he came with his own music.

Pauline was leaning idly on the fence, her arms resting on the crossrail between the pickets. She had just put down some biscuit dough and was cleaning the flour from under her nails. Behind her at some distance she heard whistling. One of these rapid, high-note riffs that black boys make up as they go while sweeping, shoveling, or just walking along. A kind of city-street music where laughter belies anxiety, and joy is as short and straight as the blade of a pocketknife. She listened carefully to the music and let it pull her lips into a smile. The whistling got louder, and still she did not turn around, for she wanted it to last. While smiling to herself and holding fast to the break in somber thoughts, she felt something tickling her foot. She laughed aloud and turned to see. The whistler was bending down tickling her broken foot and kissing her leg. She could not stop her laughter—not until he looked up at her and she saw the Kentucky sun drenching the yellow, heavy-lidded eyes of Cholly Breed-love.

"When I first seed Cholly, I want you to know it was like all the bits of color from that time down home when all us chil'ren went berry picking after a funeral and I put some in the pocket of my Sunday dress, and they mashed up and stained my hips. My whole dress was messed with purple, and it never did wash out. Not the dress nor me. I could feel that purple deep inside me. And that lemonade Mama used to make when Pap came in out the fields. It be cool and yellowish, with seeds floating near the bottom. And that streak of green them june bugs made on the trees the night we left from down home. All of them colors was in me. Just sitting there. So when Cholly come up and tickled my foot, it was like them berries, that lemonade, them streaks of green the june bugs made, all come together. Cholly was thin then, with real light eyes. He used to whistle, and when I heerd him, shivers come on my skin."

Pauline and Cholly loved each other. He seemed to relish her company and even to enjoy her country ways and lack of knowledge about city things. He talked with her about her foot and asked, when they walked through the town or in the fields, if she were tired. Instead of ignoring her infirmity, pretending it was not there, he made it seem like something special and endearing. For the first time Pauline felt that her bad foot was an asset.

And he did touch her, firmly but gently, just as she had dreamed. But minus the gloom of setting suns and lonely river banks. She was secure and grateful; he was kind and lively. She had not known there was so much laughter in the world.

They agreed to marry and go 'way up north, where Cholly said steel mills were begging for workers. Young, loving, and full of energy, they came to Lorain, Ohio. Cholly found work in the steel mills right away, and Pauline started keeping house.

And then she lost her front tooth. But there must have been a speck, a brown speck easily mistaken for food but which did not leave, which sat on the enamel for months, and grew, until it cut into the surface and then to the brown putty underneath, finally eating away to the root, but avoiding the nerves, so its presence was not noticeable or uncomfortable. Then the weakened roots, having grown accustomed to the poison, responded one day to severe pressure, and the tooth fell free, leaving a ragged stump behind. But even before the little brown speck, there must have been the conditions, the setting that would allow it to exist in the first place.

In that young and growing Ohio town whose side streets, even, were paved with concrete, which sat on the edge of a calm blue lake, which boasted an affinity with Oberlin, the underground railroad station, just thirteen miles away, this melting pot on the lip of America facing the cold but receptive Canada—What could go wrong?

"Me and Cholly was getting along good then. We come up north; supposed to be more jobs and all. We moved into two rooms up over a furniture store, and I set about housekeeping. Cholly was working at the steel plant, and everything was looking good. I don't know what all happened. Everything changed. It was hard to get to know folks up here, and I missed my people. I weren't used to so much white folks, The ones I seed before was something hateful, but they didn't come around too much. I mean, we didn't have too much truck with them. Just now and then in the fields, or at the commissary. But they want all over us. Up north they was everywhere—next door, downstairs, all over the streets—and colored folks few and far between. Northern colored folk was different too. Dicty-like. No better than whites for meanness. They could make you feel just as no-count, 'cept I didn't expect it from them. That was the lonesomest time of my life. I 'member looking out them front windows just waiting for Cholly to come home at three o'clock. I didn't even have a cat to talk to."

In her loneliness, she turned to her husband for reassurance, entertainment, for things to fill the vacant places. Housework was not enough; there were only two rooms, and no yard to keep or move about in. The women in the town wore high-heeled shoes, and when Pauline tried to wear them, they aggravated her shuffle into a pronounced limp. Cholly was kindness still, but began to resist her total dependence on him. They were beginning to have less and less to say to each other. He had no problem finding other people and other things to occupy him—men were always climbing the stairs asking for him, and he was happy to accompany them, leaving her alone.

Pauline felt uncomfortable with the few black women she met. They were amused by her because she did not straighten her hair. When she tried to make up her face as they did, it came off rather badly. Their goading glances and private snickers at her way of talking (saying "chil'ren") and dressing developed in her a desire for new clothes. When Cholly began to quarrel about the money she wanted, she decided to go to work. Taking jobs as a day worker helped with the clothes, and even a few things for the apartment, but it did not help with Cholly. He was not pleased with her purchases and began to tell her so. Their marriage was shredded with quarrels. She was still no more than a girl, and still waiting for that plateau of happiness, that hand of a precious Lord who, when her way grew drear, would always linger near. Only now she had a clearer idea of what drear meant. Money became the focus of all their discussions, hers for clothes, his for drink. The sad thing was that Pauline did not really care for clothes and makeup. She merely wanted other women to cast favorable glances her way.

After several months of doing day work, she took a steady job in the home of a family of slender means and nervous, pretentious ways.

"Cholly commenced to getting meaner and meaner and wanted to fight me all of the time. I give him as good as I got. Had to. Look like working for that woman and fighting Cholly was all I did. Tiresome. But I holt on to my jobs, even though working for that woman was more than a notion. It wasn't so much her meanness as just simpleminded. Her whole family was. Couldn't get along with one another worth nothing. You'd think with a pretty house like that and all the money they could holt on to, they would enjoy one another. She haul off and cry over the leastest thing. If one of her friends cut her short on the telephone, she'd go to crying. She should of been glad she had a telephone. I ain't got one yet. I recollect oncet how her baby brother who she put through dentistry school didn't invite them to some big party he throwed. They was a big to-do about that. Everybody stayed on the telephone for days. Fussing and carrying on. She asked me, 'Pauline, what would you do if your own brother had a party and didn't invite you?' I said ifn I really wanted to go to that party, I reckoned I'd go anyhow. Never mind what he want. She just sucked her teeth a little and made out like what I said was dumb. All the while I was thinking how dumb she was. Whoever told her that her brother was her friend? Folks can't like folks just'cause they has the same mama. I tried to like that woman myself. She was good about giving me stuff, but I just couldn't like her. Soon as I worked up a good feeling on her account, she'd do something ignorant and start in to telling me how to clean and do. If I left her on her own, she'd drown in dirt. I didn't have to pick up after Chicken and Pie the way I had to pick up after them. None of them knew so much as how to wipe their behinds. I know, 'cause I did the washing. And couldn't pee proper to save their lives. Her husband ain't hit the bowl yet. Nasty white folks is about the nastiest things they is. But I would have stayed on' cepting for Cholly come over by where I was working and cut up so. He come there drunk wanting some money. When that white woman see him, she turned red. She tried to act strong-like, but she was scared bad. Anyway, she told Cholly to get out or she would call the police. He cussed her and started pulling on me. I would of gone upside his head, but I don't want no dealings with the police. So I taken my things and left. I tried to get back, but she didn't want me no more if I was going to stay with Cholly. She said she would let me stay if I left him. I thought about that. But later on it didn't seem none too bright for a black woman to leave a black man for a white woman. She didn't never give me

the eleven dollars she owed me, neither. That hurt bad. The gas man had cut the gas off, and I couldn't cook none. I really begged that woman for my money. I went to see her. She was mad as a wet hen. Kept on telling me I owed her for uniforms and some old broken-down bed she give me. I didn't know if I owed her or not, but I needed my money. She wouldn't let up none, neither, even when I give her my word that Cholly wouldn't come back there no more. Then I got so desperate I asked her if she would loan it to me. She was quiet for a spell, and then she told me I shouldn't let a man take advantage over me. That I should have more respect, and it was my husband's duty to pay the bills, and if he couldn't, I should leave and get alimony. All such simple stuff. What was he gone give me alimony on? I seen she didn't understand that all I needed from her was my eleven dollars to pay the gas man so I could cook. She couldn't get that one thing through her thick head. 'Are you going to leave him, Pauline?' she kept on saying. I thought she'd give me my money if I said I would, so I said 'Yes, ma'am.' 'All right,' she said. 'You leave him, and then come back to work, and we'll let bygones be bygones.' 'Can I have my money today?' I said. 'No,' she said. 'Only when you leave him. I'm only thinking of you and your future. What good is he, Pauline, what good is he to you?' How you going to answer a woman like that, who don't know what good a man is, and say out of one side of her mouth she's thinking of your future but won't give you your own money so you can buy you something besides baloney to eat? So I said, 'No good, ma'am. He ain't no good to me. But just the same, I think I'd best stay on.' She got up, and I left. When I got outside, I felt pains in my crotch, I had held my legs together so tight trying to make that woman understand. But I reckon now she couldn't understand. She married a man with a slash in his face instead of a mouth. So how could she understand?"

One winter Pauline discovered she was pregnant. When she told Cholly, he surprised her by being pleased. He began to drink less and come home more often. They eased back into a relationship more like the early days of their marriage, when he asked if she were tired or wanted him to bring her something from the store. In this state of ease, Pauline stopped doing day work and returned to her own housekeeping. But the loneliness in those two rooms had not gone away. When the winter sun hit the peeling green paint of the kitchen chairs, when the smoked hocks were boiling in the pot, when all she could hear was the truck delivering furniture downstairs, she thought about back home, about how she had been all alone most of the time then too, but that this lonesomeness was different. Then she stopped staring at the green chairs, at the delivery truck; she went to the movies instead. There in the dark her memory was refreshed, and she succumbed to her earlier dreams. Along with the idea of romantic love, she was introduced to another—physical beauty. Probably the most destructive ideas in the history of human thought. Both originated in envy, thrived in insecurity, and ended in disillusion. In equating physical beauty with virtue, she stripped her mind, bound it, and collected self-contempt by the heap. She forgot lust and simple caring for. She regarded love as possessive mating, and romance as the goal of the spirit. It would be for her a well-spring from which she would draw the most destructive emotions, deceiving the lover and seeking to imprison the beloved, curtailing freedom in every way.

She was never able, after her education in the movies, to look at a face and not assign it some category in the scale of absolute beauty, and the scale was one she absorbed in full from the silver screen. There at last were the darkened woods, the lonely roads, the river banks, the gentle knowing eyes. There the flawed became whole, the blind sighted, and the lame and halt threw away their crutches. There death was dead, and people made every gesture in a cloud of music. There are black-and-white images came together, making a magnificent whole—all projected through the ray of light from above and behind.

It was really a simple pleasure, but she learned all there was to love and all there was to hate.

"The onliest time I be happy seem like was when I was in the picture show. Every time I got, I went. I'd go early, before the show started. They'd cut off the lights, and everything be black. Then the screen would light up, and I'd move right on in them pictures. White men taking such good care of they women, and they all dressed up in big clean houses with the bathtubs right in the same room with the toilet. Them pictures gave me a lot of pleasure, but it made coming home hard, and looking at Cholly hard. I don't know. I 'member one time I went to see Clark Gable and Jean Harlow. I fixed my hair up like I'd seen hers on a magazine. A part on the side, with one little curl on my forehead. It looked just like her. Well, almost just like. Anyway, I sat in that show with my hair done up that way and had a good time. I thought I'd see it through to the end again, and I got up to get me some candy. I was sitting back in my seat, and I taken a big bite of that candy, and it pulled a tooth right out of my mouth. I could of cried. I had good teeth, not a rotten one in my head. I don't believe I ever did get over that. There I was, five months pregnant, trying to look like Jean Harlow, and a front tooth gone. Everything went then. Look like I just didn't care no more after that. I let my hair go back, plaited it up, and settled down to just being ugly. I still went to the pictures, though, but the meanness got worse. I wanted my tooth back. Cholly poked fun at me, and we started fighting again. I tried to kill him. He didn't hit me too hard, 'cause I were pregnant I guess, but the fights, once they got started up again, kept up. He begin to make me madder than anything I knowed, and I couldn't keep my hands off him. Well, I had that baby—a boy—and after that got pregnant again with another one. But it weren't like I thought it was gone be. I loved them and all, I guess, but maybe it was having no money, or maybe it was Cholly, but they sure worried the life out of me. Sometimes I'd catch myself hollering at them and beating them, and I'd feel sorry for them, but I couldn't seem to stop. When I had the second one, a girl, I 'member I said I'd love it no matter what it looked like. She looked like a black ball of hair. I don't recollect trying to get pregnant that first time. But that second time, I actually tried to get pregnant. Maybe 'cause I'd had one already and wasn't scairt to do it. Anyway, I felt good, and wasn't thinking on the carrying, just the baby itself. I used to talk to it whilst it be still in the womb. Like good friends we was. You know. I be hanging wash and I knowed lifting weren't good for it. I'd say to it holt on now I gone hang up these rags, don't get froggy; it be over soon. It wouldn't leap or nothing. Or I be mixing something in a bowl for the other chile and I'd talk to it then too. You know, just friendly talk. On up til the end I felted good about that baby. I went to the hospital when my time come. So I could be easeful. I didn't want to have it at home like I done with the boy. They put me in a big room with a whole mess of women. The pains was coming, but not too bad. A little old doctor come to examine me. He had all sorts of stuff. He gloved his hand and put some kind of jelly on it and rammed it up between my legs. When he left off, some more doctors come. One old one and some young ones. The old one was learning the young ones about babies. Showing them how to do. When he got to me he said now these here women you don't have any trouble with. They deliver

right away and with no pain. Just like horses. The young ones smiled a little. They looked at my stomach and between my legs. They never said nothing to me. Only one looked at me. Looked at my face, I mean. I looked right back at him. He dropped his eyes and turned red. He knowed, I reckon, that maybe I weren't no horse foaling. But them others. They didn't know. They went on. I seed them talking to them white women: 'How you feel? Gonna have twins?' Just shucking them, of course, but nice talk. Nice friendly talk. I got edgy, and when them pains got harder, I was glad. Glad to have something else to think about. I moaned something awful. The pains wasn't as bad as I let on, but I had to let them people know having a baby was more than a bowel movement. I hurt just like them white women. Just 'cause I wasn't hooping and hollering before didn't mean I wasn't feeling pain. What'd they think? That just 'cause I knowed how to have a baby with no fuss that my behind wasn't pulling and aching like theirs? Besides, that doctor don't know what he talking about. He must never seed no mare foal. Who say they don't have no pain? Just 'cause she don't cry? 'Cause she can't say it, they think it ain't there? If they looks in her eyes and see them eyeballs lolling back, see the sorrowful look, they'd know. Anyways, the baby come. Big old healthy thing. She looked different from what I thought. Reckon I talked to it so much before I conjured up a mind's eye view of it. So when I seed it, it was like looking at a picture of your mama when she was a girl. You knows who she is, but she don't look the same. They give her to me for a nursing, and she liked to pull my nipple off right away. She caught on fast. Not like Sammy, he was the hardest child to feed. But Pecola look like she knowed right off what to do. A right smart baby she was. I used to like to watch her. You know they makes them greedy sounds. Eyes all soft and wet. A cross between a puppy and a dying man. But I knowed she was ugly. Head full of pretty hair, but Lord she was ugly."

When Sammy and Pecola were still young Pauline had to go back to work. She was older now, with no time for dreams and movies. It was time to put all of the pieces together, make coherence where before there had been none. The children gave her this need; she herself was no longer a child. So she became, and her process of becoming was like most of ours: she developed a hatred for things that mystified or obstructed her; acquired virtues that were easy to maintain; assigned herself a role in the scheme of things; and harked back to simpler times for gratification.

She took on the full responsibility and recognition of breadwinner and returned to church. First, however, she moved out of the two rooms into a spacious first floor of a building that had been built as a store. She came into her own with the women who had despised her, by being more moral than they; she avenged herself on Cholly by forcing him to indulge in the weaknesses she despised. She joined a church where shouting was frowned upon, served on Stewardess Board No. 3, and became a member of Ladies Circle No. 1. At prayer meeting she moaned and sighed over Cholly's ways, and hoped God would help her keep the children from the sins of the father. She stopped saying "chil'ren" and said "childring" instead. She let another tooth fall, and was outraged by painted ladies who thought only of clothes and men. Holding Cholly as a model of sin and failure, she bore him like a crown of thorns, and her children like a cross.

It was her good fortune to find a permanent job in the home of a well-to-do family whose members were affectionate, appreciative, and generous. She looked at their houses, smelled their linen, touched their silk draperies, and loved all of it. The child's pink nightie, the stacks of white pillow slips edged with embroidery, the sheets with top hems picked out with blue cornflowers. She became what is known as an ideal servant, for such a role filled practically all of her needs. When she bathed the little Fisher girl, it was in a porcelain tub with silvery taps running infinite quantities of hot, clear water. She dried her in fluffy white towels and put her in cuddly night clothes. Then she brushed the yellow hair, enjoying the roll and slip of it between her fingers. No zinc tub, no buckets of stove-heated water, no flaky, stiff, grayish towels washed in a kitchen sink, dried in a dusty backyard, no tangled black puffs of rough wool to comb. Soon she stopped trying to keep her own house. The things she could afford to buy did not last, had no beauty or style, and were absorbed by the dingy storefront. More and more she neglected her house, her children, her man—they were like the afterthoughts one has just before sleep, the early-morning and late-evening edges of her day, the dark edges that made the daily life with the Fishers lighter, more delicate, more lovely. Here she could arrange things, clean things, line things up in neat rows. Here her foot flopped around on deep pile carpets, and there was no uneven sound. Here she found beauty, order, cleanliness, and praise. Mr. Fisher said, "I would rather sell her blueberry cobblers than real estate." She reigned over cupboards stacked high with food that would not be eaten for weeks, even months; she was queen of canned vegetables bought by the case, special fondants and ribbon candy curled up in tiny silver dishes. The creditors and service people who humiliated her when she went to them on her own behalf respected her, were even intimidated by her, when she spoke for the Fishers. She refused beef slightly dark or with edges not properly trimmed. The slightly reeking fish that she accepted for her own family she would all but throw in the fish man's face if he sent it to the Fisher house. Power, praise, and luxury were hers in this household. They even gave her what she had never had—a nickname—Polly. It was her pleasure to stand in her kitchen at the end of a day and survey her handiwork. Knowing there were soap bars by the dozen, bacon by the rasher, and reveling in her shiny pots and pans and polished floors. Hearing, "We'll never let her go. We could never find anybody like Polly. She will *not* leave the kitchen until everything is in order. Really, she is the ideal servant."

Pauline kept this order, this beauty, for herself, a private world, and never introduced it into her storefront, or to her children. Them she bent toward respectability, and in so doing taught them fear: fear of being clumsy, fear of being like their father, fear of not being loved by God, fear of madness like Cholly's mother's. Into her son she beat a loud desire to run away, and into her daughter she beat a fear of growing up, fear of other people, fear of life.

All the meaningfulness of her life was in her work. For her virtues were intact. She was an active church woman, did not drink, smoke, or carouse, defended herself mightily against Cholly, rose above him in every way, and felt she was fulfilling a mother's role conscientiously when she pointed out their father's faults to keep them from having them, or punished them when they showed any slovenliness, no matter how slight, when she worked twelve to sixteen hours a day to support them. And the world itself agreed with her.

It was only sometimes, and then rarely, that she thought about the old days, or what her life had turned to. They were musings, idle thoughts, full sometimes of the old dreaminess, but not the kind of thing she cared to dwell on.

"*I started to leave him once, but something came up. Once, after he tried to set the house on fire, I was all set in my mind to go. I can't even 'member now what held me. He sure ain't give me much of a life. But it wasn't all bad. Sometimes things wasn't all bad. He used to come easing into bed sometimes, not too drunk. I make out like I'm asleep, 'cause it's late, and he taken three dollars out of my pocketbook that morning or something. I hear him breathing, but I don't look around. I can see in my mind's eye his black arms thrown back behind his head, the muscles like great big peach stones sanded down, with veins running like little swollen rivers down his arms. Without touching him I be feeling those ridges on the tips of my fingers. I sees the palms of his hands calloused to granite, and the long fingers curled up and still. I think about the thick, knotty hair on his chest, and the two big swells his breast muscles make. I want to rub my face hard in his chest and feel the hair cut my skin. I know just where the hair growth slacks out—just above his navel—and how it picks up again and spreads out. Maybe he'll shift a little, and his leg will touch me, or I feel his flank just graze my behind. I don't move even yet. Then he lift his head, turn over, and put his hand on my waist. If I don't move, he'll move his hand over to pull and knead my stomach. Soft and slow-like. I still don't move, because I don't want him to stop. I want to pretend sleep and have him keep on rubbing my stomach. Then he will lean his head down and bite my tit. Then I don't want him to rub my stomach anymore. I want him to put his hand between my legs. I pretend to wake up, and turn to him, but not opening my legs. I want him to open them for me. He does, and I be soft and wet where his fingers are strong and hard. I be softer than I ever been before. All my strength in his hand. My brain curls up like wilted leaves. A funny, empty feeling is in my hands. I want to grab holt of something, so I hold his head. His mouth is under my chin. Then I don't want his hand between my legs no more, because I think I am softening away. I stretch my legs open, and he is on top of me. Too heavy to hold, and too light not to. He puts his thing in me. In me. In me. I wrap my feet around his back so he can't get away. His face is next to mine. The bed springs sounds like them crickets used to back home. He puts his fingers in mine, and we stretches our arms outwise like Jesus on the cross. I hold on tight. My fingers and my feet hold on tight, because everything else is going, going. I know he wants me to come first. But I can't. Not until he does. Not until I feel him loving me. Just me. Sinking into me. Not until I know that my flesh is all that be on his mind. That he couldn't stop if he had to. That he would die rather than take his thing out of me. Of me. Not until he has let go of all he has, and give it to me. To me. To me. When he does, I feel a power. I be strong, I be pretty, I be young. And then I wait. He shivers and tosses his head. Now I be strong enough, pretty enough, and young enough to let him make me come. I take my fingers out of his and put my hands on his behind. My legs drop back onto the bed. I don't make no noise, because the chil'ren might hear. I begin to feel those little bits of color floating up into me—deep in me. That streak of green from the june-bug light, the purple from the berries trickling along my thighs, Mama's lemonade yellow runs sweet in me. Then I feel like I'm laughing between my legs, and the laughing gets all mixed up with the colors, and I'm afraid I'll come, and afraid I won't. But I know I will. And I do. And it be rainbow all inside. And it lasts and lasts and lasts. I want to thank him, but don't know how, so I pat him like you do a baby. He asks me if I'm all right. I say yes. He gets off me and lies down to sleep. I want to say something, but I don't. I don't want to take my mind offen the rainbow. I should get up and go to the toilet, but I don't. Besides, Cholly is asleep with his leg throwed over me. I can't move and don't want to.*

"But it ain't like that anymore. Most times he's thrashing away inside me before I'm woke, and through when I am. The rest of the time I can't even be next to his stinking drunk self. But I don't care 'bout it no more. My Maker will take care of me. I know He will. I know He will. Besides, it don't make no difference about this old earth. There is sure to be a glory. Only thing I miss sometimes is that rainbow. But like I say, I don't recollect it much anymore."

Cab Calloway Stands In for the Moon

Great Adventures In Propaganda

presents

CAB CALLOWAY STANDS IN FOR THE MOON

featuring papa la bas & his newfoundland hoodoo 3¢

from

D HEXORCISM OF NOXON D AWFUL

(D MAN WHO WAS SPELLED BACKWARDS)

or

from boogerman to metal polisher the

story of how come

a fiend became guaranteed by goodhousekeeping

another

one of those

mean incoherent frequently nonsensical

hallucinogenic diatribes by

Ishmael Reed

Some say he is the long JuJu of Aro in eastern Nigeria. A descendant of that line of conjurers who taught Greeks to oracle. (Ask yourselves why the Oracle of Delphi is known as the Pythoness when this particular snake does not thrive in Greece naturally.)

Kidnapped by pirates he was enroute for sale in America's slavemarkets when in mid-Atlantic a rescue ship found their evil craft deserted except for this lean elegant African.

Members of the rescue vessel reported hearing a chorus of wailing from beneath the sea as they sailed away from where they found the stranded ship. But this can be dismissed as the babblings of ignorant sailors.

There are however other strange items in this African's career that those who are devoted to Law and Order will find less easy to ignore or attribute to superstition.

From *19 Necromancers from Now,* ed. Ishmael Reed (Garden City, N.Y.: Doubleday, 1970).

He was bought by a Slavemaster who was found hanging a few weeks after purchasing this handsome prize. A long succession of slavemasters met a similar fate as his legend spread. Finally there were no takers and he was free.

There were other mysterious episodes. A drunken white man called him a rude name and he was dead the following Saturday. A little boy kicked his Newfoundland HooDoo 3¢ and was never heard from again.

A warehouse refused to deliver a special variety of herbs he needed for his little shop St. Louis #2 and burned to the ground.

Around these parts he is known as Papa La Bas. He has a mahogany face and speaks in a nasal voice. Some say he is 200 years old. His shop sells jewelry, astrology charts, cards, herbs, incense, potions, candles, amulets, talismans, and books of the occult. Sometimes there are more cars parked in front of St. Louis #2 than the town's leading hotel. He is a familiar sight in his old threadbare frock coat, his opera hat, his smoked glasses and cane.

He is making a delivery of garlic, sage, thyme, geranium water, dry basil, parsley, saltpeter, bay rum, verbena essence, and jack honeysuckle.

He chuckles to himself as he leaves his shop with the dog 3¢ on the leash. He has every reason to be pleased with himself because the night before he brought off one of the most difficult feats of sorcery.

He entered a man's dream and walked all over as if he owned the place. He moved the scenes around with the deftness of a director from the Hollywood Pantheon.

He called the shots, edited the script and gave the demons their cue.

● ○

Back there a ways he had shook off some mighty nasty crocodiles. He tried to slip them a fiver, a brand new crisp bill under the rock but that didn't do any good. The crocodiles thrashing about wouldn't quit flaying him with their tails. He managed somehow to dodge the mummy by hiding in this huge jar over near the Temple door. You see, he had run into the Temple trying to escape from this HooDoo locomotive swinging up the tracks on him. He took a piss. He didn't mean no harm. He saw this jeweled scarab and was going to take it to his sweety. He was willing to come up with some good old American dollars for it. Nothing happened. Perhaps his nightmares knew more about the gold situation and how America was *fixed*, than he. I dunno, I dunno, Noxon thought.

He took off down this long corridor of smiles and grins coming at him. Snapping their teeth. He thought of his daughter's picture hanging over the bathtub. Then he was off again. Gee, I wish someone would leave me off with a hotdog Noxon thought. With lots of mustard on it. And hot peppers. Boy O Boy, Noxon thought, seeing red. Let me at em. Let me at em. You want to fight a nervous Noxon the Noxious of Ob said. I mean, do you want a sock right in the mouth Noxon thought.

Suddenly he was on an ocean floor. Some of the fish were swimming this way and some another way. Noxon simulated their movements with his hand. He stuck out his forefinger and thumbs like the time he built this paper airplane. Noxon grinned. Being at the bottom of this ocean was better than being in that Temple buster. There could be no two ways about it. He didn't leave no tip because the sarcophagus opened and out come this hand wrapped in dirty bandages. He didn't like the service and was reaching in his pockets for a world wide credit card when he found some black cat bones (longhand for mojo).

Noxon started to float to the surface of this Ocean in which he found himself. Using his arms the way he had seen turtles use their flippers in the cartoons he lived in. What a way to go Noxon thought. What treatment. Here he was the MC of the USA in the year 2000 and PROPERTY OWNER. For crying out loud Noxon thought, I can go on and on and this was in Africa.

> Noxon was born in a bin beneath the freezer
>   however some
> Historians say he hails from Yonder
> slobovia a patch of cowdung somewheres in
>   EUROPE
> Noxon is married to Minnie D Moocher John Phillip
> Sousa's daughter
> She is a hard working astrofiend who escaped
> from Venus in a dogpound (more later)
> Noxon likes messy gooey things especially when
> they have nice clean tails
> Noxon gave at the office
> Noxon is an all around
> Noxon won world war II with single hands

Somebody wrote a hit record on him. Noxon once took part in an experiment.

> Geez, how am I going to get Africa off me Noxon
> thought. I dunno, I dunno he thought.

The nightmare rollercoastered towards the day.
10 He was wrapped up with a lot of snakes
 9 He was putting his wife thru the 3rd degree
 8 He was sitting on Ike's lap licking a lollipop
   and Ike was telling em bang-bang stories
 7 He was imprisoned in this big bottle of Jim Beam
 6 He was signing a hip's death warrant
 5 He was saying can't we negotiate this matter
 4 He was marching in an American Legion dinner
   his shoes knee deep in turkey and mixed metaphors
 3 He was saying let's win this thing and get out
 2 what thing?
 1 He was taking the sewer to work

Great gugga mugga was I dreamin Noxon thought. He put on his sailor suit and went into the bathroom. He took a shower and bruised his molars. All at once a black head popped on the mirror. It sat there all defiant like. It seemed to have eyes like a bullfrog.

Noxon took a swipe at it and tried to wrestle it to the floor. He squeezed and squeezed until some kind of green stuff squirted on the mirror. Noxon drew a funny picture in it. He drew a picture of Elmer Fudd and it was real funny. Gosh Noxon thought. Wasn't bad. Wasn't bad at all. He looked at the picture of his daughter who had been kidnapped by the Galloping Dick and Noxon said a little prayer until a tear come down.

Noxon's wife Minnie D Moocher poured some milk from the pitcher on some dog feces she had maneuvered into oatmeal. Smart girl that Minnie. Noxon packed the little brown rascals on his breakfast spoon and made it all sugary. Boy O Boy Noxon thought throwing in a couple of Gee Whizzes. This is mighty good grub.

> He thought about the time he was a kid
> He thought about the time he pushed this nigger
> woman out of the way
> He thought about the time he landed on the moon
> and the moon died of fright and had to be put on ice
> He thought about how they had to rush in an under
> study for the moon as it underwent repairs
> He thought about his dream

Noxon—Dear, I had a dream last nite that Africa was all on top of me.

Minnie—You did Noxon?

N—Yes dear I was dreaming about Africa and then things—well, things got dizzier and dizzier until the last dream I can't remember how it shaped up.

M—You will dear Noxon don't worry you will.

N—Minnie, I want you should go out and tell Meathead Sam my Chauffeur that I won't need him today. I feel like breaking tradition—perhaps sewering to work.

M—Sewering to work. How nice. You haven't sewered to work since the time we crawled from this place that was so dark and cold inside.

N—That's show nuff the truth to use the parlance of the ghetto wife. Why I'm celebrating us. Simple folk and how we will out. Just plain you and me and our squawking teeny words and ilky itsy lookers. We soil the Universe with our snot and turd up the heavens with our shit. Why the whole solar system already is becoming one big commuter tie up.

M—O Noxon you're so professionally awful why you even made your TV debut as an actor last nite on that horror show. How did you swing that one dear?

N—As you well know Minnie, good buddy and fellow american, I was in the studio debating the opposition when all at once the wrong booth got ahold of me. Well this disaster had a happy ending because the nice man there noticed the caninism of my teeth, those large black circles around my eyes, and with my sinister grin it all added up to a natural for the part. How did you like the way I carried the coffin all over the place?

M—It was tremendous dear. I also liked the way you took care of that punk planet Mars and put it away. Got it off orbit and stuff. What are you going to do with Mars when the chemicals get hard dear?

N—We're going to convert Mars into a parking lot and athletic field in case anyone gets hungry good buddy.

M—That's really progressive dear. I wish I could have given you a son to carry on your work who would be like you, a threat to all life in the Universe, instead of that . . . that thing in the closet.

N—I told you never to bring up that subject again Minnie. It's so unpleasant.

M—I know Noxon but medical science (Jake, the Butcher of Bellevue) could come up with no explanation about that thing up there born with 5 o'clock shadow herringbone hide and a hard way to go. For an umbilical cord there was a telephone cable. Strange, strange as it can be. Maybe we should have signed it up for that road show Ike suggested. Speaking of Ike, what kind of chemicals did you have them spray Mars with anyway Noxon?

N—Rocky Mountain Scarlet Fever. You won't have to worry about safety in the streets up there Mother. Which reminds me, I have to phone the Cape and find out the situation on other planets.

M—How's that, dear?

N—As it stands now Jupiter has been dragnetted, Pluto is still at large and there's an all planet bulletin out on Saturn. The airforce is hushing up Uranus and *Marioprocaccino* wants the 2 satellites of Neptune named after its Mama and Poppa seeing as how they started off from scratch.

M—*Marioprocaccino,* what's that dear?

N—Some kind of disease that New York City coughed up. I'm telling you dear, I don't know what I'm going to do with that headache on the Hudson. This *procaccino* started off as a one-liner and then it grew larger and larger until now it's taken over 20 tables in Toots Shor and has threatened to call up reinforcements. I think I'm going to convert New York into a warehouse and then maybe it will shut up and behave. Why some colored writer named Calvin Coolidge Hernton has read the riot act on it and the George Washington Bridge has become a junkie—stays high all the time. I think I'll change its name to No Dancing or Keep Out From Behind The Counter. But enough of me whacking my noodle about the important affairs of the USA of which I am MC-ing, sometimes known as Noxon D Awful or as the boys in the newsroom call me, Scoop-up Noxon.

M—Dear, of all your aliases, that one turns me off the most. It sounds as if your nickname is out to get you. Isn't it supposed to be Scoop Noxon?

N—Let the boys have their fun Dear, and let me sewer to work. Here are a few ten dollar bills for hashing up such a good breakfast. I'll leave them under the plate so that you will never forget your climb from a simple waitress in a roadside diner full of 3 week old apple pie to your ascent to the first ladyship of the USA and hostess of this 20 room home, Spiralling Agony.

With this Noxon slipped 2 tens under the plate and went into the basement of his 20 room mansion Spiralling Agony. He lifted this custom made manhole he had installed in case—well in case his horrorscope got the best of him.

It was all shiny and dark below, but he couldn't resist the fumes and he missed the rats and as any student of human behavior will tell you when you neglect your misses she will come up with awful ways. Or somethin to that effect.

●　○

The United States of America in the year 2000 is the same old rigamarole. All the cars have american flags on them. The men wear crewcuts or have their hair done up in waves which shine like stinking dead bass in the moonlight. The women wear pincurlers the size of lightbulbs and don't know where their children are this time of night. Willy Mays had just popped out a grand slammer and who knows what else. All the old timers still gather beneath this portrait of Custer The Tomahawked, founder of the United States of America and inventor of the Clairol empire. And O yes, by the way, the Hudson River is over.

There are 2 maybe 3 stories or maybe 1, 2 many on how the United States of America came to be: One is that USA worked as a short-order cook on the byways of nationhood and Walt Disney drove in one day and signed it on the spot. Another is that it's not a country at all but the remainder of a set discarded by the great Ziegfeld of the Follies. But these stories are crazy. Just crazy. They defy all of our Aristotelian categories—they arm-wrestle these categories and make them shout Uncle.

So somebody should ought to come up with the truth quick. As our great leader the Noxon of Noxious of OB, captain of the great yacht AWFUL AINT HE put it:

> Those who have no tradition are like whiskey without the sour, pizza without the cheese a golf course without the 18th hole.

There is a story circulating among some degenerates in the underground that the true story has been found. The United States was discovered a long time ago when the towns-folk marched up to the house at the top of the hill to see what all the fuss was about. They found the USA stretched out on a table as this mad scientist was giving it a huge electrical dosage. They caught the mad scientist but the USA escaped and is now crouched upon the midnight of the world ready to spring and howling its head off.

●　○

Noxon was thrown up through the manhole by a friendly ratpack he had joined during his journey to work. He walked to the shower he had installed in his office in case his hor-riblescope got the best of him. It contained all of the newfangled technological devices—when Noxon slapped the sleeping pooch on the head the dog awoke and the string tied to his nozzle yanked open the curtains. Another string tied to the dog's paw tipped over the bucket and the water poured. Noxon bathed himself. All of the crap started coming off of him. He felt good and do you know what? Ronnie Reagan was being had for lunch.

Rin Tin Rover The Gov of New York State put his foot down. Shoot, said Rin, here I have donated 3000 objects of African and Oceanic art to the Met and they've escaped to Harlem where they are partying and catching Ruby and the Romantics at Sugar Ray's. My wife has run away with Chief Showcase a man I invited to my Estate to discuss the Injuns and some nitwit has sunk my boat. The squatters have located my vast Estate and to add to that the computer that's ticking me off is taking over the whole show. What a wicked no account week it has been for me and to think my Grandfather founded the United States of America and was the first man to come over here. Barry was right—right he was. I'm coming over to his side. I must call Arizona but first a word to Noxon.

He dialed Noxon's private number 666.

He didn't like to do business with Noxon whom he considered a vulgar man who didn't even known how to hold a fork, flunked French and couldn't ski nor ride a horse. And that wife of his Minnie. Oy Vey what a dog why the bitch had sunk his boat with her Evil Eye. For a brain Noxon had the Will Call department of Macy's and on especially dark nights he glowed. He decided to call Noxon without identifying himself so that the MC of the USA wouldn't think he was trying to exert influence.

Noxon—Hello Hello Hello this is Noxon D Awful here state your business friend.

Rin Tin Rover—This has been a rough week for me Noxon maybe you can turn a few knobs for me some colored writer is at large and where I can't keep my eye away from him and now they've nabbed my African objects.

N—African objects who is this African objects whaddya think bothering me with some African objects shaddup you just shaddup and don't bother me.

RTR—I'll expose that deal you made, forty miles of white castle restaurants on Venus, and I'll spill the beans about that thing in your closet. I am Rin Tin Rover and my grand-father founded this country so you'd better be careful fella.

N—Well why didn't you say so. I didn't know some bigtime rich american was on the phone. Rin why didn't you tell me it was you gabbing away? Speak up man and bother me some more. By the way thanks for inviting me and the misses over to that swell shinding you chucked the other night. Sorry she sunk your boat. That was the swellest thing I've been to even though I did spill the food all over my lap. Why I use to be nothing but a poor supermarket clerk asking my clients such lofty questions as, "do you want that in an 8 lb bag or a 12 lb bag" and now look at me. Just look at me now. What can I do for you Rin?

RTR—I want you to recover my 3000 objects from Africa even if it means closing down that nightclub and make my boats well again. I like to fool around with them. I want the Federal government to step into this case about my wife and that redskin too—last seen heading towards the Mexican border in an old 1938 Oldsmobile shooting everything in sight.

N—If I can't take care of these matters Rin I'll have my brother No Nox Zufuksky, head of the F.I.B., lock it up. He can add as many as 3 numbers at a time. He was the real genius of the family and should be sitting here in my chair.

RTR—O I didn't know you had a family Noxon. Story has it that you climbed out of a washing machine and started from there that you were mere stains on a funky t shirt before you got all riled up.

N—The press has always been unkind to me Rin. That will be $18.50 . . .

RTR—$18.50?

N—Forgive me Rin, sometimes my humble origin won't leave up.

● ○

It was 4:00 o'clock and the hard working Chief Executive's day was drawing to a photo finish. Miss Better Weather his secretary came into the room with last minute details.

Miss Better Weather—The students are cutting up the campus.

Noxon—Steel them!

BW—A group of tenants have been waiting in your office for 3 weeks about the housing situation.

N—Stale them!

BW—People are threatening to go to Chicago.

N—Still them!

BW—The National Rifle Association thanks you for the whopping crane the elk the rhino the wildbeasts and the last surviving Ethopian leopard. Now they want a go at the rats.

N—Stall them!

● ○

The Left Hand Path is a secret society of aging white adepts who dwell in caves located high in the Swiss Alps. We know you're up there Left Hand Path. You have decked out these quarters with an elaborate communications system which keeps you to the pulse of the worlds. This vast outlay of electrical energy has short circuited the world which explains the power failures that have taken place in the United States and Soviet Union in recent years. In addition to this your satellites circle the globe and scan the Universe for deviation from your rule. At present there are 4 unidentified satellites orbiting this planet alone. (The New York Times has carried reports of this fact in recent years, usually buried as a filler on the entertainment page.)

The Left Hand Path is using the earth as a mere steppingstone to higher things: complete dominion of the Universe. You have put our own beloved Milky Way into hock for your stooges, who rule it as your gag. These ward heelers have befouled it so that it is becoming a celestial pigsty: an ecological shithouse which is giving the heavens a blackeye.

Department stores ring Saturn instead of its moons which were exploded by nuclear weapons in order to make way for progress. 55 baseball teams use the earth's moon for spring training and Mars is slated to become a retiring home for the old: Youth 2.

You treat the citizens of the world with contempt, secure in your knowledge that a large middle class, your coolies, will keep them in line. Pollution disease famine have taken the lives of millions.

So have the wars you instigated to serve as entertainment for your guests as you while away the time imbibing spirits and exotic hallucinogens. You have drained the world of its youth so that although some of you are over 100 you have the appearance of 30 year old men. Millions have been maimed and tortured and the ages 18–24 are memories stored away on the microfilm. You have imported women from all over the world to serve your twisted carnal pleasures. You bind them, flog them and use them as your prey; humiliating them by tying rabbit tails to their asses. The rooms set aside for these orgies resemble one great issue of the Evergreen Review—minus the militant poetry, but you are working on that.

All species of animal have been wiped out save the cunning rat, spared as a concession to Noxon D Awful, D Noxious of Ob, who eats his own and carries dirt in his heart.

Now the Left Hand Path your hideout is not as secure as it once was. The wastes of the world are slowly climbing the slopes of your mountain so that even you are no longer safe.

You have your eye on 3 resort planets of eternal spring located in another Galaxy. Your scientists work away into the night in a secret compartment of your factory, attempting to devise the secret formula for fuel. This fuel will be used in the great White Spaceship resting in one of the mountain's craters for the day when you will lift off to the stars.

But for now, you read your codes and have your fun. At the moment you watch the man you set up to rule America. Noxon keeps you in stitches. Of all of your legman, your soldiers, he is the one who gives you the deep laughs. He is fumbling across a TV screen, one of many you have set up in your hideout to see how the world is coming off. Noxon just waded through a heap of balloons. He is smeared with Black face and is waving goodbye with his white gloves. The writing on the screen That's All Folks *means that America is signing off after another day of vigorous cartooning.*

● ○

It was the end of the day. The hard working Chief Executive let his hair down. He was so tired that he told Meathead Sam, his driver, that's ok I'll walk the rest of the way. He was about a mile from his Chief Executive Mansion Spiralling Agony when the states-man just collapsed and knuckled under a chicken coop alongside the road. The crickets were chirping. The hoot owls hooted. The boats went foggy and the trains went woo woo. Crowds went Ra Ra Ra in Yankee Stadium because they were enjoying themselves. Fat buttery popcorn floated across the heavens. Noxon was almost asleep. He pushed aside the buzzard bones so as to make more room for his hide. He thought he smelled roast duck. Imagine that, he thought, roast duck in the red rooster. The Miracle of the Rooster. I shall proclaim a day. Roast Duck of the Red Rooster. Heh heh heh. Up in the sky Cab Calloway stood in for the moon. Hi di Hi di Hi di Ho went the thunder. Cab Calloway stood in for the moon like the trouper he was. The moon faded away into the pale when Noxon landed. The aging cootie of hoochie coochie pinch-hitting for old shine-on and no one knew the difference.

That's it Noxon thought as he pulled up the collars of his coat to protect him from the rain. The miracle of the Rooster—

● ○

Papa La Bas stroked his Newfoundland HooDoo as he stood next to Minnie D Moocher in the living room of Spiralling Agony. They were looking out of the window where the rain splashed against the pane.

Papa La Bas—Nice work Minnie, you have him sleeping out in the rain.

Minnie—He dove into the sewer this morning and swam to work so I thought that by now he would come down with a case of the rams.

PBL—Excellent excellent. It's time for the next step.

MM—What's that, master?

PLB—Take him off the diet of dogshit and start him on pins and needles.

MM—But master isn't this working backwards from the procedure you taught us?

PLB—He is a hard nut to crack Minnie, a man who I suspect may not even be of this world. I am going to have to turn the procedure around and let it loose.

MM—O master you're so wise, where do we meet for our celebration of Osiris' resurrection?

PLB—The coven will meet at my place at 12:00 o'clock and don't forget the new password.

MM—Nix on Noxon?

PLB—Correct you are—Nix on Noxon.

● ○

In the backseat of this solar system is the planet of OB. It has 5:00 o'clock shadow and a thousand ski-jump noses for mountains. Its orbit is so sneaky and wishy-washy that it defies the astronomer's calculations. Every day on this planet is blue monday and every season the fall. Its surface is the size of Brooklyn. Its craters were once filled with chicken soup but that needn't bother us here. It is a bug among planets and leaves in its wake a trail of brown stains. As it moves closer and closer to earth a dying race of Noxons await the signal of their Noxious. It has already begun. I mean, you know, the nightmare for our solar system.

● ○

At about 4:00 am Minnie D Moocher awoke.
Something was butting against the front door.
She put on her nightgown and went downstairs to put the needle to
Stars and Stripes Forever.

next week—
The Invasion of the Subway People

Frankie Mae

The sun had just started coming up when the men gathered at the gate of the White Plantation. They leaned on the fence, waiting. No one was nervous, though. They'd all been waiting a long time. A few more minutes couldn't make much difference. They surveyed the land that they were leaving, the land from which they had brought forth seas of cotton.

Old Man Brown twisted around so that he leaned sideways on the gate. Even though he was in his fifties, he was still a handsome man. Medium-sized, with reddish-brown skin. His beard set him apart from the others; it was the same mixture of black and gray as his hair, but while his hair looked like wool, the strands of his beard were long and nearly straight. He was proud of it, and even when he wasn't able to take a bath, he kept his beard neatly cut and shaped into a V.

He closed his eyes. The sun was getting too bright; it made his headache worse. Damn, he thought, I sure wouldn't be out here this early on no Monday morning if it wasn't for what we got to do today. Whiskey'll sure kill you if you don't get some sleep long with it. I wasn't never just crazy 'bout doing this, anyway. Wonder what made me decide to go along?

Then he smiled to himself. 'Course. It was on account of Frankie Mae. She always getting me into something.

Frankie was his first child, born twenty-two years ago, during the war. When she was little, she had gone everywhere with him. He had a blue bicycle with a rusty wire basket in the front. He used to put Frankie Mae in the basket and ride her to town with him and to the cafe, and sometimes they'd go nowhere special, just riding. She'd sit sideways so that she could see what was on the road ahead and talk with him at the same time. She never bothered to hold onto the basket; she knew her daddy wouldn't let her fall. Frankie fitted so well into the basket that for a few years the Old Man thought that it was growing with her.

She was a black child, with huge green eyes that seemed to glow in the dark. From the age of four on, she had a look of being full-grown. The look was in her muscular, well-defined limbs that seemed like they could do a woman's work and in her way of seeing everything around her. Most times, she was alive and happy. The only thing wrong with her was that she got hurt so easy. The slightest rebuke sent her crying; the least hint of

From *Black-eyed Susans / Midnight Birds: Stories by and about Black Women,* ed. with intro. by Mary Helen Washington (New York: Anchor Books, 1990).

disapproval left her moody and depressed for hours. But on the other side of it was that she had a way of springing back from pain. No matter how hurt she had been, she would be her old self by the next day. The Old Man worried over her. He wanted most to cushion her life.

When Frankie reached six, she became too large to ride in the basket with him. Also, he had four more children by then. So he bought a car for $40. Not long afterward, he became restless. He'd heard about how you could make a lot of money over in the delta. So he decided to go over there. He packed what he could carry in one load—the children, a few chickens, and a mattress—and slipped off one night.

Two days after they left the hills, they drove up to the White Plantation in Leflore County, Mississippi. They were given a two-room house that leaned to one side and five dollars to make some groceries with for the next month.

The Old Man and his wife, Mattie, worked hard that year. Up at four-thirty and out to the field. Frankie Mae stayed behind to nurse the other children and to watch the pot that was cooking for dinner. At sundown they came back home and got ready for the next day. They did a little sweeping, snapped some beans for dinner the next day, and washed for the baby. Then they sat on the porch together for maybe a half hour.

That was the time the Old Man liked best, the half hour before bed. He and Frankie talked about what had happened during the day, and he assured her that she had done a good job keeping up the house. Then he went on about how smart she was going to be when she started school. It would be in two years, when the oldest boy was big enough to take care of the others.

One evening on the porch Frankie said, "A man from town come by today looking for our stove. You know, the short one, the one ain't got no hair. Said we was three week behind and he was gonna take it. Had a truck to take it back in, too."

The Old Man lowered his head. He was ashamed that Frankie had had to face that man by herself. No telling what he said to her. And she took everything so serious. He'd have to start teaching her how to deal with folks like that.

"What did you tell him, baby?" he asked. "He didn't hurt you none, did he?

"No, he didn't bother me, sides looking mean. I told him I just this morning seen some money come in the mail from Uncle Ed in Chicago. And I heard my daddy say he was gonna use it to pay off the stove man. So he said, 'Well, I give y'all one more week, one more.' And he left."

The Old Man pulled Frankie to him and hugged her. "You did 'zactly right, honey." She understood. She would be able to take care of herself.

The end of their first year in the delta, the Old Man and Mattie went to settle up. It was just before Christmas. When their turn came, they were called by Mr. White Junior, a short fat man, with a big stomach, whose clothes were always too tight.

"Let me see, Johnnie," he said. "Here it is. You owe two hundred dollars."

The Old Man was surprised. Sounded just like he was back in the hills. He had expected things to be different over here. He had made a good crop. Should have cleared something. Well, no sense in arguing. The bossman counted out fifty dollars.

"Here's you some Christmas money," Mr. White Junior said. "Pay me when you settle up next year."

The Old Man took the money to town the same day and bought himself some barrels and some pipes and a bag of chopped corn. He had made whiskey in the hills, and he could make it over here, too. You could always find somebody to buy it. Wasn't no reason he should spend all his time farming if he couldn't make nothing out of it. He and Mattie put up their barrels in the trees down by the river and set their mash to fermentate.

By spring, Brown had a good business going. He sold to the colored cafes and even to some of the white ones. And folks knew they could always come to his house if they ran out. He didn't keep the whiskey at the house, though. Too dangerous. It was buried down by the water. When folks came unexpected, it was up to Frankie and her brother next to her to go get the bottles. Nobody noticed children. The Old Man bought them a new red wagon for their job.

He was able to pay off his stove and to give Mattie some money every once in a while. And they ate a little better now. But still they didn't have much more than before, because Brown wasn't the kind of man to save. Also, he had to do a lot of drinking himself to keep up his sales. Folks didn't like to drink by themselves. When he'd start to drinking, he usually spent up or gave away whatever he had in his pocket. So they still had to work as hard as ever for Mr. White Junior. Brown enjoyed selling the whiskey, though, and Mattie could always go out and sell a few bottles in case of some emergency like their lights being cut off. So they kept the business going.

That spring, Mr. White Junior decided to take them off shares. He would pay $1.50 a day for chopping cotton, and he'd pay by the hundred pound for picking. The hands had no choice. They could work by the day or leave. Actually, the Old Man liked it better working by the day. Then he would have more time to see to his whiskey.

Also, Mr. White Junior made Brown the timekeeper over the other hands. Everybody had drunk liquor with him, and most folks liked him. He did fight too much. But the hands knew that he always carried his pistol. If anybody fought him, they'd have to be trying to kill him, 'cause he'd be trying to kill them.

Brown was given a large, battered watch. So he'd know what time to stop for dinner. His job was to see that the hands made a full day in the field and that all the weeds got chopped. The job was easier than getting out there chopping, in all that sun. So Brown liked it. The only hard part was in keeping after the women whose time was about to come. He hated to see them dragging to the field, their bellies about to burst. They were supposed to keep up with the others, which was impossible. Oftentimes, Mr. White Junior slipped up on the work crew and found one of the big-bellied women lagging behind the others.

"Goddammit, Johnnie," he'd say, "I done told you to keep the hands together. Queenester is way behind. I don't pay good money for folks to be standing around. If she sick, she need to go home."

Sometimes the Old Man felt like defending the woman. She had done the best she could. But then he'd think, No, better leave things like they is.

"You sure right, Mr. White Junior. I was just 'bout to send her home myself. Some niggers too lazy to live."

He would walk slowly across the field to the woman. "I'm sorry, Queenester. The bossman done seen you. I told you all to be looking out for him! Now you got to go. You come back tomorrow, though. He won't hardly be back in this field so soon. I try and let you make two more days this week. I know you need the little change."

The woman would take up her hoe and start walking home. Mr. White Junior didn't carry no hands except to eat dinner and to go home after the day had been made.

One day when he had carried the hands in from the field, Mr. White Junior stopped the Old Man as he was climbing down from the back of the pickup truck. While the bossman talked, Brown fingered his timekeeper's watch that hung on a chain from his belt.

"Johnnie," Mr. White Junior said, "it don't look right to me for you to leave a girl at home that could be working when I need all the hands I can get. And you the timekeeper, too. This cotton can't wait on you all to get ready to chop it. I want Frankie Mae out there tomorrow."

He had tried to resist. "But we getting along with what me and Mattie makes. Ain't got nothing, but we eating. I wants Frankie Mae to go to school. We can do without the few dollars she would make."

"I want my cotton chopped," White said, swinging his fat, sweating body into the truck. "Get that girl down here tomorrow. Don't nobody stay in my house and don't work."

That night the Old Man dreaded the half hour on the porch. When Frankie had started school that year, she had already been two years late. And she had been so excited about going.

When the wood had been gathered and the children cleaned up, he followed Frankie onto the sloping porch. She fell to telling him about the magnificent yellow bus in which she rode to school. He sat down next to her on the step.

"Frankie Mae, I'm going to tell you something."

"What's that, Daddy? Mama say I been slow 'bout helping 'round the house since I been going to school? I do better. Guess I lost my head."

"No, baby. That ain't it at all. You been helping your mama fine." He stood up to face her but could not bring his eyes to the level of her bright, happy face.

"Mr. White Junior stopped me today when I was getting off the truck. Say he want you to come to field till the chopping get done."

She found his eyes. "What did you say, Daddy?"

"Well, I told him you wanted to go to school, and we could do without your little money. But he say you got to go."

The child's eyes lost their brilliance. Her shoulders slumped and she began to cry softly. Tired, the Old Man sat back down on the step. He took her hand and sat with her until long after Mattie and the other children had gone to bed.

The next morning, Frankie was up first. She put on two blouses and a dress and some pants to keep off the sun and found herself a rag to tie around her head. Then she woke up her daddy and the others, scolding them for being so slow.

"We got to go get all that cotton chopped! And y'all laying round wasting good daylight. Come on."

Brown got up and threw some water on his face. Here was Frankie bustling around in her layers of clothes, looking like a little old woman, and he smiled. That's how Frankie Mae was. She'd feel real bad, terrible, for a few hours, but she always snapped back. She'd be all right now.

On the way to the field he said, "Baby, I'm gonna make you the water girl. All you got to do is carry water over to them that hollers for it and keep your bucket full. You don't have to chop none lest you see Mr. White Junior coming."

"No, Daddy, that's all right. The other hands'll say you was letting me off easy 'cause I'm yours. Say you taking advantage of being timekeeper. I go on and chop with the rest."

He tried to argue with her, but she wouldn't let him give her the water bucket. Finally, he put her next to Mattie so she could learn from her. As he watched over the field, he set himself not to think about his child inhaling the cotton dust and insecticide. When his eyes happened on her and Mattie, their backs bent way over, he quickly averted them. Once when he jerked his eyes away, he found instead the bright-yellow school bus bouncing along the road.

Frankie learned quickly how to chop the cotton, and sometimes she even seemed to enjoy herself. Often the choppers would go to the store to buy sardines and crackers and beans for their dinner instead of going home. At the store the Old Man would eat his beans from their jagged-edge can and watch with pride as Frankie laughed and talked with everyone and made dates with the ladies to attend church on the different plantations. Every Sunday, Frankie had a service to go to. Sometimes, when his head wasn't bad from drinking, the Old Man went with her, because he liked so much to see her enjoy herself. Those times, he put a few gallons of his whiskey in the back of the car just in case somebody needed them. When he and Frankie went off to church like that, they didn't usually get back till late that night. They would be done sold all the whiskey and the Old Man would be talking loud about the wonderful sermon that the reverend had preached and all the souls that had come to Jesus.

That year, they finished the chopping in June. It was too late to send Frankie back to school, and she couldn't go again until after the cotton had been picked. When she went back, in November, she had missed four months and found it hard to keep up with the children who'd been going all the time. Still, she went every day that she could. She stayed home only when she had to, when her mother was sick, or when, in the cold weather, she didn't have shoes to wear.

Whenever she learned that she couldn't go to school on a particular day, she withdrew into herself for about an hour. She had a chair near the stove where she sat, and the little children knew not to bother her. After the hour, she'd push back her chair and go to stirring the cotton in the bed ticks or washing the greens for dinner.

If this was possible, the Old Man loved her still more now. He saw the children of the other workers and his own children, too, get discouraged and stop going to school. They said it was too confusing; they never knew what the teacher was talking about, because they'd not been there the day before or the month before. And they resented being left behind in classes with children half their size. He saw the other children get so that they wouldn't hold themselves up, wouldn't try to be clean and make folks respect them. Yet, every other day, Frankie managed to put on a clean, starched dress, and she kept at her lessons.

By the time Frankie was thirteen, she could figure as well as the preacher, and she was made secretary of the church.

That same year, she asked her daddy if she could keep a record of what they made and what they spent.

"Sure, baby," he said. "I be proud for you to do it. We might even come out a little better this year when we settle up. I tell you what. If we get money outta Mr. White Junior this year, I'll buy you a dress for Christmas, a red one."

Frankie bought a black-and-white-speckled notebook. She put in it what they made and what they paid out on their bill. After chopping time, she became excited. She figured that they had just about paid the bill out. What they made from picking would be theirs. She and the Old Man would sit on the porch and go over the figures and plan for Christmas. Sometimes they even talked about taking a drive up to Chicago to see Uncle Ed. Every so often, he would try to hold down her excitement by reminding her that their figures had to be checked by the bossman's. Actually, he didn't expect to do much better than he'd done all the other years. But she was so proud to be using what she had learned, her numbers and all. He hated to discourage her.

Just before Christmas, they went to settle up. When it came to the Old Man's turn, he trembled a little. He knew it was almost too much to hope for, that they would have money coming to them. But some of Frankie's excitement had rubbed off on him.

He motioned to her, and they went up to the table, where there were several stacks of ten and twenty dollar bills, a big ledger, and a pistol. Mr. White Junior sat in the brown chair, and his agent stood behind him. Brown took heart from the absolute confidence with which Frankie Mae walked next to him, and he controlled his trembling. Maybe the child was right and they had something coming to them.

"Hey there, Johnnie," Mr. White Junior said, "see you brought Frankie Mae along. Fine, fine. Good to start them early. Here's you a seat."

The Old Man gave Frankie the one chair and stood beside her. The bossman rifled his papers and came out with a long, narrow sheet. Brown recognized his name at the top.

"Here you are, Johnnie, y'all come out pretty good this year. Proud of you. Don't owe but $65. Since you done so good, gonna let you have $100 for Christmas."

Frankie Mae spoke up. "I been keeping a book for my daddy. And I got some different figures. Let me show you."

The room was still. Everyone, while pretending not to notice the girl, was listening intently to what she said.

Mr. White Junior looked surprised, but he recovered quickly. "Why sure. Be glad to look at your figures. You know it's easy to make a mistake. I'll show you what you done wrong."

Brown clutched her shoulder to stop her from handing over the book. But it was too late. Already she was leaning over the table, comparing her figures with those in the ledger.

"See, Mr. White Junior, when we was chopping last year we made $576, and you took $320 of that to put on our bill. There. There it is on your book. And we borrowed $35 in July. There it is . . ."

The man behind the table grew red. One of his fat hands gripped the table while the other moved toward the pistol.

Frankie Mae finished. "So you see, you owe us $180 for the year."

The bossman stood up to gain the advantage of his height. He seemed about to burst. His eyes flashed around the room, and his hand clutched the pistol. He was just raising it from the table when he caught hold of himself. He took a deep breath and let go of the gun.

"Oh, yeah. I remember what happened now, Johnnie. It was the slip I gave you to the doctor for Willie B. You remember, last year, 'fore chopping time. I got the bill last week. Ain't had time to put it in my book. It came to, let me think. Yeah, that was the $350."

The Old Man's tension fell away from him, and he resumed his normal manner. He knew exactly what the bossman was saying. It was as he had expected, as it had always been.

"Let's go baby," he said.

But Frankie didn't get up from the chair. For a moment, she looked puzzled. Then her face cleared. She said, "Willie didn't have anything wrong with him but a broken arm. The doctor spent twenty minutes with him one time and ten the other. That couldn't a cost no $350!"

The bossman's hand found the pistol again and gripped it until the knuckles were white. Brown pulled Frankie to him and put his arm around her. With his free hand he fingered his own pistol, which he always carried in his pocket. He was not afraid. But he hated the thought of shooting the man; even if he just nicked him, it would be the end for himself. He drew a line: If Mr. White Junior touched him or Frankie, he would shoot. Short of that, he would leave without a fight.

White spat thick, brown tobacco juice onto the floor, spattering it on the Old Man and the girl. "Nigger," he said, "I know you ain't disputing my word. Don't nobody live on my place and call me a liar. That bill was $350. You understand me?!" He stood tense, staring with hatred at the man and the girl. Everyone waited for Brown to answer. The Old Man felt Frankie's arms go 'round his waist.

"Tell him no, Daddy. We right, not him. I kept them figures all year, they got to be right." The gates of the state farm flashed through the Old Man's mind. He thought of Mattie, already sick from high blood, trying to make a living for eleven people. Frankie's arms tightened.

"Yessir," he said. "I understand."

The girl's arms dropped from him, and she started to the door. The other workers turned away to fiddle with a piece of rope to scold a child. Brown accepted the $50 that was thrown across the table to him. As he turned to follow Frankie, he heard Mr. White Junior's voice, low now and with a controlled violence. "Hey you, girl. You, Frankie Mae." She stopped at the door but didn't turn around.

"Long as you live, bitch, I'm gonna be right and you gonna be wrong. Now get your black ass outta here."

Frankie stumbled out to the car and crawled onto the back seat. She cried all the way home. Brown tried to quiet her. She could still have the red dress. They'd go down to the river tomorrow and start on a new batch of whiskey.

The next morning, he lay in bed waiting to hear Frankie Mae moving around and fussing, waiting to know that she had snapped back to her old self. He lay there until everyone in the house had gotten up. Still he did not hear her. Finally, he got up and went over to where she was balled up in the quilts.

He woke her. "Come on, baby. Time to get up. School bus be here soon."

"I ain't goin' today," she said; "got a stomach-ache."

Brown sat on the porch all day long, wishing that she would get up out the bed and struggling to understand what had happened. This time, Frankie had not bounced back to her old bright-eyed self. The line that held her to this self had been stretched too taut. It had lost its tension and couldn't pull her back.

Frankie never again kept a book for her daddy. She lost interest in things such as numbers and reading. She went to school as an escape from chores but got so little of her lessons done that she was never promoted from the fourth grade to the fifth. When she was fifteen, and in the fourth grade, she had her first child. After that, there was no more thought of school. In the following four years she had three more children.

She sat around the house, eating and growing fat. When well enough, she went to the field with her daddy. Her dresses were seldom ironed now. Whatever she could find to wear would do.

▲　▲　▲

Still, there were a few times, maybe once every three or four months, when she was lively and fresh. She'd get dressed and clean the children up and have her daddy drive them to church. On such days she'd be the first one up. She would have food on the stove before anybody else had a chance to dress. Brown would load up his truck with his whiskey, and they'd stay all day.

It was for these isolated times that the Old Man waited. They kept him believing that she would get to be all right. Until she died, he woke up every morning listening for her laughter, waiting for her to pull the covers from his feet and scold him for being lazy.

She died giving birth to her fifth child. The midwife, Esther, was good enough, but she didn't know what to do when there were complications. Brown couldn't get up but sixty dollars of the hundred dollars cash that you had to deposit at the county hospital. So they wouldn't let Frankie in. She bled to death on the hundred-mile drive to the charity hospital in Vicksburg.

The Old Man squinted up at the fully risen sun. The bossman was late. Should have been at the gate by now. Well, it didn't matter. Just a few more minutes and they'd be through with the place forever.

His thoughts went back to the time when the civil rights workers had first come around and they had started their meetings up at the store. They'd talked about voting and about how plantation workers should be making enough to live off of. Brown and the other men had listened and talked and agreed. So they decided to ask Mr. White Junior for a raise. They wanted nine dollars for their twelve-hour day.

They had asked. And he had said, Hell no. Before he'd raise them he'd lower them. So they agreed to ask him again. And if he still said no, they would go on strike.

At first, Brown hadn't understood himself why he agreed to the strike. It was only this morning that he realized why: It wasn't the wages or the house that was falling down 'round him and Mattie. It was that time when he went to ask Mr. White Junior about the other forty dollars that he needed to put Frankie in the hospital.

"Sorry, Johnnieboy," he'd said, patting Brown on the back, "but me and Miz White have a garden party today and I'm so busy. You know how women are. She want me there every minute. See me tomorrow. I'll fix you up then."

A cloud of dust rose up in front of Brown. The bossman was barreling down the road in his pickup truck. He was mad. That was what he did when he got mad, drove his truck up and down the road fast. Brown chuckled. When they got through with him this morning, he might run that truck into the river.

Mr. White Junior climbed down from the truck and made his way over to the gate. He began to give the orders for the day, who would drive the tractors, what fields would be chopped. The twelve men moved away from the fence, disdaining any support for what they were about to do.

One of the younger ones, James Lee, spoke up. "Mr. White Junior, we wants to know is you gonna raise us like we asked."

"No, goddammit. Now go on, do what I told you."

"Then," James Lee continued, "we got to go on strike from this place."

James Lee and the others left the gate and went to have a strategy meeting up at the store about what to do next.

The Old Man was a little behind the rest because he had something to give Mr. White Junior. He went over to the sweat-drenched, cursing figure and handed him the scarred timekeeper's watch, the watch that had ticked away Frankie Mae's youth in the hot, endless rows of cotton.

The King Alfred Plan

Yes, Max thought. I knew Jaja Enzkwu, eagle-faced, hot-eyed Jaja with his sweating, pussy-probing fingers and perfumed agbadas; I knew him.

Max glanced at his watch again. Two o'clock. He wondered what Margrit was doing back in Amsterdam on such a beautiful day. He knew what Jaja was doing: feeding the bugs back in Onitsha where he had been sent in a box, after that deadly rendezvous with Baroness Huganot in Basel that day.

So much had happened that day, the day of the March on Washington. Margrit had left shortly after he called her. Then he had taken a plane to Washington. Du Bois had died in Ghana the night before, and so had Jaja, leaving behind an opened magnum of Piper-Heidsieck, a half-eaten partridge and a startled, voluptuous, eager-to-be-ravished Baroness. But Washington had been the place to be that day. There you could forget that the cancer tests were positive—it was malignant—and that you were going into cobalt treatment soon; you could forget with more than a quarter million people surging around you.

Max flipped up the next page of the letter and when he finished, he shook as if with a sudden chill, and yet the shaking hand had nothing to do with his illness; it was the letter itself. With trembling hands he lit a cigarette.

No, he told himself. I have not read what I just read. This cannot be. No, it's me, the way I'm thinking, the way I'm reading. He closed his eyes hard and held them for a long time. Then he opened them to reread the entire letter once again:

Dear Max:

You are there, Max? It is you reading this, right? I mean, even dead, which I must be for you to have these papers *and* be alone in the company of Michelle, I'd feel like a damned fool if someone else was reading them. I hope these lines find you in good shape and with a full life behind you, because, chances are, now that you've started reading, all that is way, way behind you, baby.

I'm sorry to get you into this mess, but in your hands right now is the biggest story you'll ever have. Big and dangerous. Unbelievable. Wow. But, it's a story with consequences the editors of *Pace* may be unwilling to pay. And you, Max, baby, come to think of it, may not even get the chance to cable the story. Knowing may kill you, just as knowing killed me

---

From John A. Williams, *The Man Who Cried I Am: A Novel* (Boston: Little, Brown, 1967).

and a few other people you'll meet in this letter. Uh-uh! Can't quit now! It was too late when you opened the case. This is a rotten way to treat a friend. Yes, friend. We've had good and bad times together; we've both come far. I remember that first day we met at Zutkin's. We both saw something we liked in each other. What? I don't know, but it never mattered to me. Our friendship worked; it had value; it lasted. I've run out of acquaintances and other friends who never were the friend you were. So, even if this is dangerous for you—and it is—I turn to you in friendship and in the hope that you can do with this information what I could not. Quite frankly, I don't know how I got into this thing. It just happened, I guess, and like any contemporary Negro, like a ghetto Jew of the 1930's in Europe, I couldn't believe it was happening, even when the pieces fell suddenly into place. Africa . . .

God, Max, what doesn't start with Africa? What a history still to be told! The scientists are starting to say life began there. I'm no scientist. I don't know. But I do know that this letter you're reading had its origins with what happened there. Let me go back to the beginning. I doubt if you've heard of Alliance Blanc. In 1958 Guinea voted to leave the French Family of Nations, and at once formed a federation with Kwame Nkrumah, or Ghana, whichever you prefer. The British and French were shaken. How could countries only two minutes ago colonies spring to such political maturity? Would the new federation use pounds or francs? The national banks of both countries were heavily underwriting the banking systems of the two countries. There would be a temporary devaluation of both pounds and francs, whether the new federation minted new money or not. More important—and this is what really rocked Europe—if the federation worked, how many new, independent African states would follow suit? *Then,* what would happen to European interests in Africa after independence and federation? Was it *really* conceivable that all of Africa might one day unite, Cape to Cairo, Abidjan to Addis? Alliance Blanc said *Yes!* If there were a United States of Africa, a cohesiveness among the people—300,000,000 of them—should not Europeans anticipate the possibility of trouble, sometime when the population had tripled, for example? Couldn't Africa become another giant, like China, with even more hatred for the white West? It was pure guilt over what Europeans had done to Africa and the Africans that made them react in such a violent fashion to African independence.

The white man, as we well know, has never been of so single an accord as when maltreating black men. And he has had an amazing historical rapport in Africa, dividing it up arbitrarily across tribal and language boundaries. That rapport in plundering Africa never existed and never will when it requires the same passion for getting along with each other in Europe. But you know all this. All I'm trying to say is that, where the black man is concerned, the white man will bury differences that have existed between them since the beginning of time, and come together. How goddamn different this would have been if there had been no Charles Martel at Tours in 732!

The Alliance first joined together not in the Hague, not in Geneva, not in London, Versailles or Washington, but in Munich, a city top-heavy with monuments and warped history. Present were representatives from France, Great Britain, Belgium, Portugal, Australia, Spain, Brazil, South Africa. The United States of America was also present. There were white observers from most of the African countries that appeared to be on their way to independence. The representation at first, with a few exceptions, was quasi-official. But you know very well that a quasi-official body can be just as effective as an official one; in fact, it is often better to use the former.

I don't have to tell you that the meetings, then and subsequently, were held in absolute secrecy. They were moved from place to place—Spain, Portugal, France, Brazil and in the United States, up around Saranac Lake—Dreiser's setting for *An American Tragedy,* that neck of the woods, remember? America, with the largest black population outside Africa, had the most need of mandatory secrecy. Things were getting damned tense following the Supreme Court decision to desegregate schools in 1954.

The disclosure of America's membership in Alliance Blanc would have touched off a racial cataclysm—but America went far, far beyond the evils the Alliance was perpetuating, but more of this later. For the moment, let me consider the Alliance.

African colonies were still becoming independent. Federations were formed only to collapse a few weeks later, like the Guinea-Ghana combine. Good men and bad were assassinated indiscriminately; coups were a dime a dozen. Nkrumah in West Africa vied with Selassie in East Africa for leadership of the continent. The work of the Alliance agents—setting region against region and tribe against tribe, just as the colonial masters had done—was made easy by the rush to power on the part of a few African strongmen. Thus, the panic mentality that had been the catalyst for the formation of the Alliance seemed to have been tranquilized. There was diplomacy as usual, independence as usual. What, after all, did Europeans have to fear after that first flash of black unity? The Alliance become more leisurely, less belligerent, more sure that it had time, and above all, positive now that Africa was not a threat to anyone but itself. Alliance agents flowed leisurely through Africa now, and Western money poured in behind them.

From a belligerent posture, the Alliance went to one based on economics. Consider that 15 percent of Nigeria's federal budget comes from offshore oil brought in by Dutch, British, Italian, French and American oil companies; consider that the 72 percent of the world's cocoa which Africa produces would rot if the West did not import it. Palm oil, groundnuts, minerals, all for the West. Can you imagine, man, what good things could happen to Africans, if they learned to consume what they produce? It did not take the Europeans long to discover that their stake in Africa as "friends" rather than masters was more enormous than they could have imagined. Only naked desperation demanded that Spain and Portugal stay in Africa; the Iberian Peninsula hasn't been the same since the Moors and Jews left it in the fifteenth century. Time? It was the Alliance's most formidable ally.

In South Africa, the spark of revolt flickered, sputtered and now is dead. The Treason Trials killed it; oppression keeps murdering it, and those who say the spark is still alive, those successive schools of nattily tailored South African nationalists, who plunge through Paris, London and New York raising money for impossible rebellions, lie. The paradox, Max, is that, denied freedom, the black man lives better in South Africa than anywhere else on the continent; the average African. The bigshots—with their big houses and long cars, their emulation of the colonial masters—do all right. My friend Genet said it all in *Les Noirs.*

The Alliance worked. God, how it worked! And Africans themselves, dazzled by this new contraption the white man was giving them, independence, helped. Lumumba, disgracefully educated by the Belgians, was a victim of the Alliance; Olympio, dreaming dreams of federation, was another. Nkrumah and Touré have lasted for so long because their trust in the white man never was, and their trust in their own fellows only a bit deeper seated.

The Congo mess served as a valuable aid to the Alliance: it could test the world's reaction to black people in crisis. The Alliance was pleased to observe that the feeling in the West was, "Oh, well, they're only niggers, anyhow."

I could have foreseen that reaction; you could have foreseen it; any black man could have anticipated it. But, then, "niggers" are embattled everywhere, ain't they, baby? Asian "niggers," South American "niggers" . . . But let a revolt occur in East Germany and watch the newsprint fly! Let another Hungarian revolution take place and see the white nations of the world open their doors to take in refugees—Hungarian Freedom Fighters, yeah! Who takes in blacks, Pakistanis, Vietnamese, Koreans, Chinese, who?

But the picture began to change. It was quite clear that the Europeans had Africa well under control—and that was all they cared about. America, sitting on a bubbling black cauldron, felt that it had to map its own contingency plans for handling 22 million black Americans in case they became unruly; in case they wanted everything Freedom Fighters got just by stepping off the boat. So, America prepared King Alfred and submitted it to the Alliance, just as the Alliance European members had submitted their plans for operations in Africa to the Americans. King Alfred in its original form, called for sending American Negroes to Africa, and this had to be cleared by the Europeans. The Europeans vetoed that plan; they remembered what excitement Garvey had caused in Africa. The details of King Alfred are in the case, and it is truly hot stuff. All this Alliance business is pretty pallid shit compared to what the Americans have come up with.

I should tell you that it was an African who discovered the Alliance and in the process came upon King Alfred. Who? Jaja Enzkwu, that cockhound, that's who. He stumbled on the Alliance the second year of its existence, while he was in Spain, which as you know has turned out to be a very hospitable place for ex-heads of African countries on the lam. Enzkwu didn't know what was going on; he simply sensed something, seeing a gathering of British, American, Brazilian, Portuguese and South Africans at San Sebastián in winter. This was where the Alliance held its second meeting. I'll tell you about Jaja. Any half-way good-looking white woman can make a fool of him (which was what was happening, for him to be at a summer resort in winter), but he doesn't trust a gathering of more than a single white man. About the white man, Enzkwu has a nose for trouble. But you know Jaja.

Jaja died as he had lived, chasing white pussy. As soon as his nation became independent in 1960, using the various embassies and consulates his government had established in the Park Avenues, Park Lanes and Georges V's of the world, yes, those places, with the long, black limousines in front, chauffeured by large but deferential white men, those places with the waiting rooms filled with African art, Jaja started gathering material on the Alliance. He amassed all the information you have at hand.

How did they get to Jaja? It's a white man's world—so far. He had to hire white operatives, of course, to get to Alliance Blanc. A couple of these, Jaja's beloved Frenchmen, I believe, checked back through several white people fronting for Enzkwu, but, at last, they discovered old black Jaja sitting there behind it all. A black man, interesting. The bastards then sold *this* information to the Alliance. At this point, old Jaja, sitting behind an eighteen-foot desk, was cooling it, thinking he had it all covered. He planned to make use of the information. Like so many people, he had begun his investigations with a sincere desire to protect his country. But another consideration rose very, very quickly. He could use the information, to be released at a propitious time, to prove that the Nigerian premier, and African leaders generally, had failed to protect their people from the new colonialism. Jaja planned to gather all of Africa under a single ruler one day. That ruler was to be Jaja Enzkwu.

Panic in Washington ensued when it was discovered that Jaja not only had information on the Alliance, but on King Alfred, the contingency plan to detain and ultimately rid America of its Negroes. Mere American membership in the Alliance would have been sufficient to rock America, but King Alfred would have made Negroes realize, finally and angrily, that all the new moves—the laws and committees—to gain democracy for them were fraudulent, just as Minister Q and the others had been saying for years. Your own letter to me days after you left the White House only underscored what so many Negro leaders believed. The one alternative left for Negroes would be not only to seek that democracy withheld from them as quickly and as violently as possible, but to fight for their very survival. King Alfred, as you will see, leaves no choice.

The European members of the Alliance were not as concerned as America about the leak. In fact, if King Alfred was revealed and racial violence exploded in America, America's position as world leader would be seriously undermined. There were members in the Alliance who wished for this. The danger in Africa being nullified, the white man became divided. In the U.S., the situation had worsened. There had been that second boy at Ole Miss; the dogs and firehoses in Birmingham; kids blown up in church; little brush-fire riots that came and went across the country, like wind stroking a wheat field. Minister Q's voice was now large indeed. The March on Washington appeared to have been the last time the Negroes were peacefully willing to ask for and take any old handout.

The Alliance had not counted on the efficiency of the Central Intelligence Agency, which had placed agents in Nigeria within days of receiving the report that Jaja had information. Concealing King Alfred became the top priority assignment of the National Security Council and the CIA. Jaja was not killed at once for two reasons: first, the agents were unable to ascertain where he kept the papers. Second, on a trip to Paris, the agents made a fake attempt on his life to make him go for the papers. But this only resulted in arousing Jaja's curiosity, and he began backtracking through his former operatives and discovered that the Americans knew that he knew. Then Jaja started to deal. He'd give over the papers and keep his mouth shut, if the Americans gave him Nigeria. The U.S. had no choice but to agree, when it had the opportunity. It would take time. All right, Jaja said. But not *too* much time.

Jaja moved, ate, slept and crapped with an army of bodyguards. He had only to put it out that the Hausas in the north were after him, and every Ibo in the eastern region understood.

Enzkwu came to see me two days before your March on Washington. He was thin and drawn and quite subdued. Almost a year, I learned later, had passed since making the deal with the U.S. and nothing had come of it. Even Charlotte did not bring out that old gleam to his eyes, as her presence has done for many of my friends. Jaja and I had dinner that night, surrounded by some of the biggest Ibos I've ever seen. After, a car followed us, but it was his and was filled with his men. We didn't talk too much in his hotel. We were in one room and his guards in another. Every five minutes, one of the guards would knock on the door and ask something in Ibo, and Jaja would reply in Ibo. It was always the same question and the same answer.

Jaja was on his way to Switzerland and he gave me the key to a safe deposit box in a Paris bank and told me to get what was in it, if he did not return from Switzerland. I was puzzled and curious about his mood, but I took the key without asking questions. Of course, he was killed. I hustled to the bank and what I found was this information you now have found, plus a letter from Jaja, similar to my letter which you are now reading. The material fascinated me. I'd spent so much of my life writing about the evil machinations of Mr. Charlie without really *knowing* the truth, as this material made me know it. It was spread out before me, people, places and things. I became mired in them, and I *knew* now that the way black men live on this earth was no accident. And yet, my mind kept telling me that Jaja's death was a coincidence, a mere coincidence. I could not believe that I, too, soon would be dead. One looks at death, always moves toward it, but until the last denies its existence. I was trapped by my contempt for everything African. I made the bodyguards just a part of the African spectacle. I gripped the material, I hugged it to my chest, for now I would know; if they killed me, I would know that this great evil did exist, indeed, thrived. And Dr. Faustus came to my mind. The Americans killed Jaja, obviously because they ran out of patience, and because they thought they could find the material without him.

I didn't say anything to you when you came through Paris on your way to East Africa because I had not seen Jaja then.

It is spring. Strange, now that life seems to quicken a bit, and you can see people smiling more, and the trees starting to bloom, I feel tired, going downhill. I am sure the Americans are on to me. Perhaps the French keep them off, not wanting trouble to becloud De Gaulle's new image. At least that's what I think, and that's why I haven't made any trips outside France. I thought of giving it to the Russians, but would they even accept it from me? Even if they did, can't you see the West laughing it off as another Russian hoax, even Negroes?

But there was America itself. You and *Pace*. You must have access to outlets where this material would do the most good. The choice is yours and yours alone as to whether you want to wreck the nation or not. My opinion? No, Max, it's up to you. Think of the irony: the very nation that most wants to keep the information secret, would be the very one to release it!

A personal item: Charlotte seems to have found a strange tolerance for me these days. I think she knows about the material. And she has found out about Michelle and me, at last. How, I don't know, exactly, but I think American agents have told her, to enlist her aid.

In fact, Max, old trusted friend, everybody knows everything now, past and present.

I am getting this material to Michelle tonight. She will get it to you even if she has to swim to New York. I know of no one else. And perhaps this is a sign, the ultimate sign, that I am very tired. I can only hope that no harm comes to her.

Another item, old buddy. Tomorrow I'm having lunch with a young man I understand you've met. His name is Edwards, and he's quit Uncle Sam's foreign service to write a novel about it. I can't resist these youngsters who come to see me, to sit at the feet of the father, so to speak. I guess I'll never outgrow it. I suppose you're next in line to be father . . .

Harry

Shock, gracious, pain-absorbing shock came at once and lessened the hurt and surprise. Max, reacting normally for the moment, lit another cigarette, picked through and carefully read Enzkwu's papers.

Yes, there was explosive material here. Enough to unsettle every capital city in the West; enough to force the Africans to cut ties with Europe at once and worry about the consequences later; enough to send black Brazilians surging out of their *favelas* and *barrios* to inundate the sleek beach places of the whites. Wherever white men had been involved with black men, Enzkwu's photostats disclosed a clear and unrelenting danger. Recorded in cold black type were lists of statesmen and diplomats, the records of their deeds, what they planned to do, when, where, why and to whom. The list of people dead, Max knew, and therefore murdered, if their names appeared in Enzkwu's papers, included the residents of four continents. African airfields equipped for the handling of jets and props, along with radio and power stations, the number of men in the army of each country, plus a military critique of those armies, were set down here.

Now Max's hand held another numbered packet, but above the number were the words: The United States of America—King Alfred. Slowly, he pulled out the sheaf of photostats. So, this is King Alfred, Alfred the Great. He mused, Why is it called King Alfred? Then he saw the answer footnoted at the bottom of the first page.

KING ALFRED*

In the event of widespread and continuing and coordinated racial disturbances in the United States, King Alfred, at the discretion of the President, is to be put into action immediately.

PARTICIPATING FEDERAL AGENCIES

National Security Council   Department of Justice
Central Intelligence Agency   Department of Defense
Federal Bureau of Investigation   Department of Interior

PARTICIPATING STATE AGENCIES
(Under Federal Jurisdiction)

National Guard Units   State Police

PARTICIPATING LOCAL AGENCIES
(Under Federal Jurisdiction)

City Police   County Police

Memo: National Security Council

Even before 1954, when the Supreme Court of the United States of America declared unconstitutional separate educational and recreational facilities, racial unrest and discord had become very nearly a part of the American way of life. But that way of life was repugnant to most Americans. Since 1954, however, that unrest and discord have broken out

---

*849–899 (?) King of England; directed translation from the Latin of the *Anglo-Saxon Chronicle*.

into widespread violence which increasingly have placed the peace and stability of the nation in dire jeopardy. This violence has resulted in loss of life, limb and property, and has cost the taxpayers of this nation billions of dollars. And the end is not yet in sight. This same violence has raised the tremendously grave question as to whether the races can ever live in peace with each other. Each passing month has brought new intelligence that, despite new laws passed to alleviate the condition of the Minority, the Minority still is not satisfied. Demonstrations and rioting have become a part of the familiar scene. Troops have been called out in city after city across the land, and our image as a world leader severely damaged. Our enemies press closer, seeking the advantage, possibly at a time during one of these outbreaks of violence. The Minority has adopted an almost military posture to gain its objectives, which are not clear to most Americans. It is expected, therefore, that, when those objectives are denied the Minority, racial war must be considered inevitable. When that Emergency comes, we must expect the total involvement of all 22 million members of the Minority, men, women and children, for once this project is launched, its goal is to terminate, once and for all, the Minority threat to the whole of the American society, and, indeed, the Free World.

Chairman, National Security Council

Preliminary Memo: Department of Interior
Under KING ALFRED, the nation has been divided into 10 Regions (See accompanying map).

In case of Emergency, Minority members will be evacuated from the cities by federalized national guard units, local and state police and, if necessary, by units of the Regular Armed Forces, using public and military transportation, and detained in nearby military installations until a further course of action has been decided.

1—Capital region
2—Northeast region
3—Southeast region
4—Great Lakes region
5—South central region
6—Deep South region
7—Deep South region II
8—Great Plains, Rocky Mountain region
9—Southwest region
10—a, b—West Coast region

No attempt will be made to seal off the Canadian and Mexican borders.

Secretary, Department of Interior

Combined Memo: Department of Justice
Federal Bureau of Investigation
Central Intelligence Agency
There are 12 major Minority organizations and all are familiar to the 22 million. Dossiers have been compiled on the leaders of the organizations, and can be studied in Washington.

The material contained in many of the dossiers, and our threat to reveal that material, has considerably held in check the activities of some of the leaders. Leaders who do not have such usable material in their dossiers have been approached to take Government posts, mostly as ambassadors and primarily in African countries. The promise of these positions also has materially contributed to a temporary slow-down of Minority activities. However, we do not expect these slow-downs to be of long duration, because there are always new and dissident elements joining these organizations, with the potential power to replace the old leaders. All organizations and their leaders are under constant, 24-hour surveillance. The organizations are:

1—The Black Muslims
2—Student Nonviolent Coordinating Committee (SNCC)
3—Congress of Racial Equality
4—Uhuru Movement
5—Group on Advanced Leadership (GOAL)
6—Freedom Now Party (FNP)
7—United Black Nationalists of America (UBNA)
8—The New Pan-African Movement (TNPAM)
9—Southern Christian Leadership Conference (SCLC)
10—The National Urban League (NUL)
11—The National Association for the Advancement of Colored People (NAACP)
12—Committee on Racial and Religious Progress (CORARP)

NOTE: At the appropriate time, to be designated by the President, the leaders of some of these organizations are to be detained ONLY WHEN IT IS CLEAR THAT THEY CANNOT PREVENT THE EMERGENCY, working with local public officials during the first critical hours. All other leaders are to be detained at once. Compiled lists of Minority leaders have been readied at the National Data Computer Center. It is necessary to use the Minority leaders designated by the President in much the same manner in which we use Minority members who are agents with CENTRAL and FEDERAL, and we cannot, until there is no alternative, reveal KING ALFRED in all its aspects. Minority members of Congress will be unseated at once. This move is not without precedent in American history.

Attorney General

Preliminary Memo: Department of Defense
This memo is being submitted in lieu of a full report from the Joint Chiefs of Staff. That report is now in preparation. There will be many cities where the Minority will be able to put into the street a superior number of people with a desperate and dangerous will. He will be a formidable enemy, for he is bound to the Continent by heritage and knows that political asylum will not be available to him in other countries. The greatest concentration of the Minority is in the Deep South, the Eastern seaboard, the Great Lakes region and the West Coast. While the national population exceeds that of the Minority by more than ten times, we must realistically take into account the following:

1—An estimated 40–50 percent of the white population will not, for various reasons, engage the Minority during an Emergency.

2 — American Armed Forces are spread around the world. A break-out of war abroad means fewer troops at home to handle the Emergency.

3 — Local law enforcement officials must contain the Emergency until help arrives, though it may mean fighting a superior force. New York City, for example, has a 25,000-man police force, but there are about one million Minority members in the city.

We are confident that the Minority could hold any city it took for only a few hours. The lack of weapons, facilities, logistics—all put the Minority at a final disadvantage.

Since the Korean war, this Department has shifted Minority members of the Armed Forces to areas where combat is most likely to occur, with the aim of eliminating, through combat, as many combat-trained Minority servicemen as possible. Today the ratio of Minority member combat deaths in Vietnam, where they are serving as "advisers," is twice as high as the Minority population ratio to the rest of America. Below is the timetable for KING ALFRED as tentatively suggested by the JCS who recommend that the operation be made over a period of eight hours:

1. Local police and Minority leaders in action to head off the Emergency.
2. Countdown to eight hours begins at the moment the President determines the Emergency to be:

    A. National
    B. Coordinated
    C. Of Long Duration   8th Hour

3. County police join local police.   7th
4. State police join county and local forces.   6th
5. Federal marshals join state, county and local forces.   5th
6. National Guards federalized, held in readiness.   4th
7. Regular Armed Forces alerted, take up positions; Minority troops divided and detained, along with all white sympathizers, under guard.   3rd
8. All Minority leaders, national and local, detained.   2nd
9. President addresses Minority on radio-television, gives it one hour to end the Emergency.   1st
10. All units under regional commands into the Emergency.   0

'O' Committee Report:

Survey shows that, during a six-year period, Production created 9,000,000 objects, or 1,500,000 each year. Production could not dispose of the containers, which proved a bottleneck. However, that was almost 20 years ago. We suggest that vaporization techniques be employed to overcome the Production problems inherent in KING ALFRED.

Secretary of Defense

Max smoked and read, read and smoked until his mouth began to taste like wool and when he finally pushed King Alfred from him, he felt exhausted, as if he had been running beneath a gigantic, unblinking eye that had watched his every move and determined just when movement should stop.

Yeah. Jaja had done his work well. He could have embarrassed and startled a lot of people, blacks and whites, but you have to weed a garden for the flowers to grow. Those dossiers, he knew pretty much what was in them. Well, he had known it; there are always dues to pay. A smoldering anger coursed through Max's stomach. Yes, those leaders clearly had left themselves vulnerable, vulnerable for the hunters who, for a generation and more, sought Communists with such vehemence that they skillfully obscured the growth and power of fascism. How black skins stirred fascists! Perhaps because it was the most identifiable kind of skin; you didn't have to wait until you got up close to see whether a nose was hooked or not; a black skin you could see for a block away. And in the face of the revelations in Jaja's papers, Harry and Jaja both, made giddy by the presence of that massive, killing evil, had dared to toy with it; had dared to set their pitiable little egos down before that hideous juggernaut. And they had hoped to live. That hope had revealed their inability to accurately measure what was readily measurable. Jaja for greed, and you, Harry, it's just starting to come. They didn't let their minds go out.

They did not let their minds go out to picture the instability of what seems static; they did not see planets colliding with each other, or picture Sahara or Kalahari as lakes, or picture plains where the Alps, Andes and Rockies now stand; nor did they picture oceans above the sands that crunch softly beneath the feet in the sweet-smelling paths of the Maine or Vermont woods. No, they did not picture the extinction of man and beast and places. If they had, *then* they could see four million dead because they themselves, like the later nine million, refused to see evil rearing up before them, quite discernible, quite measurable. Man is nature, nature man, and all crude and raw, stinking, vicious, evil. And holding that evil lightly because the collective mind refuses to recall the sprint of mountains, the vault of seas and, of course, beside that, the puny murder of millions.

It is still eat, drink and be murderous, for tomorrow I may be among the murdered.

This seeing precisely, Max told himself, is a bitch!

Moses Boatwright. Seeing precisely. And then Max thought: *Everybody knows everything, now, past and present.*

Afterwords

The Hip Hop Vision: Password: Nation Conscious Rap

"The Black world has changed so dramatically since before World War II that it would be impossible for a youth coming up today to have the same view of the world and himself which his father had. In the turbulent cities of America, the rhythm of life is quicker and more varied, and complex for the masses. Life becomes a game in which one has to learn at an early age to be flexible, to scheme and hustle if he is to survive . . .

It is clear that the black nation today is in a state of profound flux. The collective conscience of the people is being shaken to the very core of its being, thereby causing black music and black culture to take off into so many different directions. The pathos, violence, and disorder involved in this period of severe cultural and social disruption are often shocking to older generation Negroes."
—Peter Labrie, "The New Breed"

Rap music is an externalization of highly charged inner feelings shared commonly by young black people. It is the cultural manifestation of this epoch in the pristine history of Black people. It is both old and new, old because it is one with the black man's existence; new, because it is fresh and contemporary. There is an inner need to express something new and exciting, outrageous and engaging. Exuberant, bright, charismatic and endothermic, it is capable of both producing and absorbing heat. This is indicative of its *dynamic* power.

When Chuck D. emplored young bloods, "Don't Believe The Hype," he was functioning both diacritically and dialectically. By diacritical we mean superior ability to distinguish or discern. In other words this generation is one of keen insight, capable of cutting through a lot of the hype. Why do we say aspects of rap music are dialectical? Is it not marked by an inner tension, conflict and interconnectedness of varied elements? Who could argue against the rappers' ability to use language as a weapon against the turbulence engulfing their lives.

There are many cogent, philosophical principles underlying the music now called rap. Yet, little attention has been given to an examination of that growing body of rappers who are in the forefront of Nation Conscious Rap.

The poet, dramatist, literary and music critic, Larry Neal, rightly asserted: "The black artist must link his work to the struggle for his liberation and the liberation of his brothers

From *Nation Conscious Rap,* ed. Joseph D. Eure and James G. Spady (New York: PC International Press, 1991).

and sisters. But, he will have executed an essential aspect of his role if he makes even a small gesture in the manner outlined. He will be furthering the psychological liberation of his people, without which, no change is even possible.

The artist and the political activist are one. They are both shapers of the future reality. Both understand and manipulate the collective myths of the race. Both are warriors, priests, lovers and destroyers. For the first violence will be internal . . . the destruction of a weak spiritual self for a more perfect self. But it will be a necessary violence. It is the only thing that will destroy the double consciousness, the tension that is in the souls of black folk."

Writing in the Password to his landmark anthology, *Black Fire,* Larry Neal captures the essence of that long term relationship between the artist and political activist. He moved in on the righteous tip, "and Shine Swam on." Fully conversant with Afro-American urban toasts, Neal rightly draws upon the pristine mythology of Black America to explore and explode the tension that is in the souls of black folk. That was twenty years ago.

The 1990's signal flack, space is cleared for the new Jack: "My mission, to sum it up, is to teach young people that there is a way out by coming into a knowledge of themselves. Once they come into a knowledge of who they really are theologically, biologically, that they are the first . . . I want to ask you a question. Who was the first man to walk on the moon? Neil Armstrong. Who was the second? Nobody ever remembers the second. See, they always remember the first. If the Black Man was the original man, the maker, the owner, the cream of the planet Earth then that tells you that everything he's doing is according to God's will. We invented every other living being. Without Black you couldn't have no other color. So I look at all of those actual facts and say that it's important for the young minds to get acquainted with themselves. The best knowledge is self knowledge, and once they get acquainted with themselves then they won't have to worry about selling drugs, they won't have to worry about working for the Caucasian for a living."

That is the voice of a Nation Conscious Rapper from Chicago; Prince Akeem. Here is a 22 year old black man who knows that knowledge of self is the beginning of coherence. Is it not why he emphasizes the levels of congruence between the origins of man and the prescience of the African? Anthropologists, archaeologists, biologists, geneticists, and historians now agree that the earliest evidence of man and woman is found in Africa. Therefore they are considered the mothers and fathers of civilization. Prince Akeem further argues teleologically i.e. that divine Providence is pertinent to the outcome of Blacks. It is his belief that the will of God is supreme. Therefore he sees his own mission as quite clear.

"My name is Akeem. Akeem means strong and independent young warrior. I've always been alone. I don't rely on nothing but God. I will fight anybody. I've been a fighter all of my life. I'm just saying this with deep sincerity. I'm a lover of my people. Why not? I'm Black. I'm not just a Muslim. See our problem as a people is this. When you say Muslim then they expect you to wear turbans and all of that stuff. If you want to learn martial arts, then you want to be Chinese when you're black. It's not like that. Kung Fu is an Arabic name. It was a black man that originated that, and we don't want to look into that. A lot of people tell me to shutup, because I have something to say. I don't plan on rapping too long. Can I tell you something? Deeply, deep inside Allah is channeling my mind." Many of the younger rap artists are not aware of the strong tradition of powerful black and muslim artistry prior to the emergence of Nation Conscious. What a creative source to tap into.

Hip Hop's Power, Consciousness and Vision

The power and consciousness of the Hip Hop movement flow through the circle of leadership they offer to the current generation. It is imperative that we recognize that it is not coincidental that this cultural movement explodes after a full decade of cultural implosion. Deep inside we felt the spirits moving in the live nuclei. It is evident from the very presence of the X-Clan, Poor Righteous Teachers, Lakim Shabazz, Public Enemy and Leaders of the New School that there are many social, political, intellectual and cultural forces that shape, form and provide coherence for their youthful impulses. They are the ones charged with the awesome responsibility of building a new society.

Initially, there were some who did not recognize the Hip Hop cultural explosion as part of a long continuum of black artistic expressions. Could it be because they raised the black urban toast to a new level of receptivity? Was it not Larry Neal [naw, we don't mean Larry Larr] who signaled this emergence twenty years earlier by opening the closing of *Black Fire,* "And Shine Swam On," with the message about the black urban toast? (*BUT*)? If the *Ninja Man* can continue to hang in the Caribbean memory, clearly *Shine* will be around for some time here. Dance Hall down criers continue to realize that once you move on the floor you are entering an area of cultural confluence. Shabba Ranks, Cutty Ranks teamed with Dennis Brown, Big Youth and U Roy and the oldsters to further solidify the cultural forces.

As the Hip Hop artists of the United States and elsewhere begin to discover Alicia Johnson, Amiri Baraka, Marvin X, Amus Mor and Larry Neal, "Rap" will explore new streets. They have only begun to explore the private mythology of black folk. That is what lies near the very heart and souls of black folk.

Larry Neal rightly and righteously observed that the private mythology of Black America is central to the whole discourse. "Its symbolism is direct and profound. Shine is US. We have been below-deck stoking the ship's furnaces. Now the ship is sinking, but where will we swim? Jamming belly up you immediately recognize the difference between IVAN D and IVAN VAN. Watch out for the criminals, the Rude Boys and the Jazabelles. Not Labelle or Patti Labelle in the land of sunshine. Blue waters welcome Yemanga. Goddess of the deep blue seas. Sea Deep. See, I told you.

"There is a tension throughout our communities. The ghosts of that tension are Nat Turner, Martin Delaney, Booker T. Washington, Frederick Douglass, Malcolm X, Garvey, Monroe Trotter, Du Bois, Fanon and a whole panoply of mythical heroes from Brer Rabbit to Shine. These ghosts have left us with some very heavy questions about the realities for black people in America." Larry Neal is dropping the heavy science like Just Ice Just-Ernest Just.

Image Reversal

Amiri, the poet, once said, "What a culture produces is, and refers to, is an image—a picture of a process, since it is a form of a process; movement seen. The changing of images, of references, is the Black man's way back to the racial integrity of the captured African, which is where we must take ourselves, in feeling, to be truly the warriors we propose to be. To form an absolutely rational attitude toward West man, and West thought. Which is what is needed. To see the white man as separate and as enemy. To make a fight according to the absolute realities of the world as it is." Later Baraka writes, "The song title, 'A White Man's Heaven Is A Black Man's Hell' describes how complete an image reversal is necessary in the West. Because for many Black people, the white man has succeeded in making this hell seem like heaven. But black youth are much better off in this regard than their parents. They are the ones who need the least image reversal."

Against this historical background, it was most appropriate for Amiri Baraka's son, Ras Baraka, to deliver a Hip Hop Manifesto at the opening of the 1st Annual Hip Hop Conference at Howard University in February, 1991. It was on that same campus during the 1950's that Amiri began a necessary image reversal. Memories of the capstone: "The frats and yellow folks ran Howard's official student life. Everything else was improvisation. We'd find ourselves trailing through black night in Southwest Washington headed for parties. Dudes would say, "Some a them D.C. boys gonna split your heads open!" But we, being officially fearless, would go on and come to a joint that looked just like those sets we'd left back home." Thirty years on movement sets had transformed the old capstone to just a stone. Therefore in the Spring of '90, the young bloods (congregated in the Nia Force) encircled the stoney brook faces of the Naughty by Nature.

Hip Hop Is a Great Light

Moving toward the center force were Hip Hop artists like 'Two Kings In A Cipher' and 'Defiant Giants.' Cognizant that 'Daffy was a Black man,' Two Kings in a Cipher moves up them hills like Trinidad Reel. Turning to the mighty voice of the Defiant Giants we hear, "Hip Hop is a light. It's like the sun and the light of the sun which strikes the Earth and causes the Earth to rotate. Just as the sun is burning at a temperature of 14,072 degrees, it sends out light at 1,086 miles per second, striking the Earth at its very center, causing it to revolve and rotate at 1,037 miles per hour." Continuing to drop the heavy science, in motion. "The best of hip hop is like the sun, because it's hot. When it's a dope beat it pumps you up, heats you up, it causes you to sweat. And when you have light giving, revolutionary, spiritual lyrics, that light travels and it strikes you in your mind, and it causes your mind to rotate like the earth, causing you to think differently, causing you to act differently, causing you to bring down the world of white supremacy in your mind. Hip Hop is a great light, and it is also God's music today, when it's in its proper form."

Speaking near the city of Refuge where light and sound seldom enter, the mighty Defiant Giants continue to explore sources of Nation Conscious Rap. ". . . Let us not forget the root of our light. When you hear the Poor Righteous Teachers, when you hear X-Clan, Public Enemy, Paris, the Defiant Giants, Brand Nubians, Kool Moe Dee; when you hear them rap of black consciousness, they rap from our father, all of our fathers, the lessons of the Honorable Elijah Muhammad. That's where we rap from. This great black man. When you hear these rappers rap, when you hear us rap on the radio, when you see our video, that is Elijah rapping, that is Elijah speaking to you. He lives today. We have also been inspired by the boldest black man here in America, who has made his sojourn throughout this nation and throughout the world, the boldest leader on the planet earth today, the Honorable Minister Louis Farrakhan. We all owe him a great debt of gratitude."

When Mister Cee was asked to identify leaders that had influenced him in his personal life he replied, "Brothers like Dr. Martin Luther King, Malcolm X, Minister Louis Farrakhan, Elijah Muhammad, W.E.B. Du Bois, Frederick Douglass."

If Yo Yo, Isis or Sister Souljah would rediscover Ruby McCollum, the woman in Florida's Suwannee Jail, they could bring their foremothers and foresisters back into the continuum. Walking briskly with an expressionless face, Ruby wore a bright green camel's hair coat. Stories, stories and more stories that enliven their historical memory.

Gangstarr in the Arena

Gangstarr's, "Step In The Arena" is moving in a solid hip hop fashion. Had to be using a Jem Fogger. Call him Guru Keith E. The modern usage of the term guru as acronym suggests, 'Gifted, Unlimited, Rhymes, Universal,' and that is what you hear. "Just To Get A Rep" is righteously, endemically hard core. So reel is their motion that either banned entirely or presented as an expurgated visual text. It is powerful. D.J. Premier kicks it like this, "Not everyone is into real rap, that's including those people that are signing rap acts. They're telling some groups that they have to write certain types of songs to get radio air play." Conditioned at an early age to see clearly, G. Keith reveals the genesis. "Everyday stuff is what makes me want to write. Some stuff has a more worldly view, but I don't want to get deep into that. I like to paint a more mellow picture. Part of my youth was in the Nation of Islam, and that still reflects in my writing. But I'm not involved in that right now. I consider us hardcore jazzfunk. The street is hardcore, but we're smoothed out more in a way lyrically. I don't like to shout, but it's still hardcore."

The Streets

The street is hardcore and it is the rhythmic locus of the Hip Hop world. At one time, it was just the Hip world. At another time, the streets were cold, cold locus of the dance world. People were doing the Funky Chicken, the Freeze, the Down in the Middle Split, Slide, Bicycle. It was the locus of the Bop World years ago. Dark glasses kept you from seeing what wasn't happening. Dark Knights of existence. Parked upon Belmont Plateau.

The house was sitting on a highly inclined section of that street. They got high inside. Living. Living just enough for the city. Along, along those bloodpaved streets were the occupants of this city refuge. Siren. Lights. Ducking behind and under cars. Night sticks beat the senses out of scenic bloods. Your moms called you one-two-three times. The cool breeze of summer continued to blow. Kurtis.

She stood on the curve where cars passed daily. Mid daylight. Her body slid closer to the curve to check out the inside of the passing car. "Where you going?" "What you want to do?" "$5? What about $3?" Triad. Father, Son of Bazerk and Holy Ghost. The Trinity as train. Daylight falls in the bottom, too. Not yet 16 and the streets are blazing hot. Beeper signifying another connexion.

Streets. Money. Money and **Mo' Money**. There is a 14-year old trying to make it to Mickey Dees. Three dollars a wop or $3 per hour. Either way, they are getting paid. But somebody has got to spot! Offer a way out. Can I kick it? [A Tribe Called Quest]:

To all the people who can quest like
a tribe does
Before this
Did you really
Know what life was?
Comprehend to the track for it's wide
cuz
Getting mentioned on the tip of the
vibe buzz
Rock 'n Roll to the beat of the funk fuzz
Wipe your feet really good on the rhythm
rug
If you feel the urge to freak, do the jitterbug.

Dancing and Profiling. The streets remain the locus of the Hip Hop world. On the corners lessons are learned, reasoning done. You can dance to stop from freaking out. Not a lot of space here. So they run to the corner to get a cold beer. All while the *world* is closing in on them. Spinning, sinning and all the while defending.

Changing. Those streets of yesteryear are no more. Now it is crack-filled and gang-banged. Loose and cracked. Yet, most of our people walk straight through these streets night and day. Risking lives. But this is a risque world. The deafening sound of ultrasonic beat box blasts DJ Jazzy Jeff and the Fresh Prince's "**Summertime**." Riding along that silver crest B.M.W. (Black Man's Wheels) with the dope sunset hookup playing Aretha Franklin's "What You See Is What You Sweat" L.P. Hotter Than July. Now you may even hear Bebe and CeCe's "Lifestyle," especially if it's the Eagles' quarterback cruising through the streets. Further to the curve, somebody calls out "How you living?" Quiet voice replies, **LARGE**! Flourescent mint green convertible, with green mag wheels.

It's reel. Filmic. Whole. Endothermic. Half-hearted. Ragged. Dressed. Clean. Whole. These are the streets of Philly in the 1990's. They might be "In Search of the Last Trump of Funk." Sometimes names and faces are swirling in some bar. Air condition makes it a hot, funky cool but in the SAAB it is cold cool. The street is hardcore and it is the locus of the Hip Hop world.

One Love Monie

The street is hardcore, and it is the rhythmic locus of the Hip Hop world. Cruising down those mean streets in the hyped drive. People are down to earth with "Monie In The Middle." Coming out of England with those deep Jamaican roots, Monie Love chose to explore less observed activities in this domain. She says, "When I was living in Brooklyn. I wrote a lot of material, because I lived on a busy block. As far as what I choose to write about, I think we have enough people covering the political end. I figure I'll get lost in the bunch of people that are already doing that kind of stuff. I write about things that are less strenuous on the brain. Like little things that might go on in the streets, I don't really excel in any one area. I have a different type twist to my story lines. I pick real situations to talk about." Once settling in the United States Monie entered the heavy light circle of the Jungle

Brothers (never too far from the Calypso Monarch) and De La Soul. Electrifying the world audiences with 'Monie In The Middle' she moved, *Down to Earth* in short order.

Carol Luther imagined another Brooklyn 20 years ago

> Peaches in open markets
> in Brownsville, Bed-Stuy and
> The Coast Village
> remind me of summers in
> Memphis
> where peaches grew on trees
> and we shook them down

Moving through the streets of North Philly, Mark Traylor presaged the Hip Hop generation by 20:

> them hard-looking
> hard-talking
> hard-looking
> cool black-dudes
> and
> them fine-looking
> fine-walking
> fine-talking
> fine-loving
> them, fine soul sisters

The literary critic, poet and teacher Eugene Redmond clearly identifies the mission of Afro-American Poetry in his *Drum Voices*. Turning to the Philly poets Gene opined, "Philadelphia poets explore city life and Africa, and exalt blackness. There is, too, the rage and vehemence often found in New York and Chicago poetry. "Cool Black Nights" (by Traylor, who died at age twenty-two) also captures driving street rhythms and rough rhymes." We published poets Straight Outta Philly in the early 1970's. Black Mu Poetry forums provided young street wise writers a platform to dissect the Treacherous Terrordome of their lives. Rap and Reason there you locate the Birth of Brightness.

Philly as a Center of Hip Hop Philosophy

The earliest expression of Hip Hop lyrics germane to Philly was written by Brother Smooth-Larry Neal, the regal predecessor of Larry Larr who is definitely in our mighty traveled tradition. Can I tell you this story or will you send me through all kinds of changes?

> Setting: Streets of Philly. Time: Fluid but often located in the 50's and early 60's with way back memories. Already the driving street rhythms are present. Had to be those unspeakable Philly images. That gave rise to, "Yo! MTV Raps" and the video revolution.

Had to see what we were talking about. Philly rappers are known for their tragicomic imagination. They are feigning ignorance, acting like they really don't know. Included in this diverse field of players is The Fresh Prince playing like he's in Belair when his terribly noble quest for wholeness can only be found in the streets of Philly. Just at the moment when the crassest elements of those Nigguh paved streets realized there were no ambulances for Niggers Tonight, Jazzy Jeff and The Fresh Prince entered the American conscience. Witty and adroit with a full grasp of tragic conventions and an inner circle of tragicomic elements- The Fresh Prince brought comic relief in the midst of seriousness. No need to dis what was being done by other rappers. It was a clever, clearing of space for other dramaturgical African American experiences.

And now we return to Larry Neal whose poem "Can I Tell You This Story Or Will You Send Me Through All Kinds Of Changes" ushers in the modern voice of Philly hip hop lyricists. That is why Hip Hop Majesty Pharoah appreciated Larry's deep, dark emblematic rendering of Philly black asphalt streets in our times:

> In those days, the avenues were
> nigger cops, like Rudy who thought he was
> the Durango kid;
> we shot him in the doorway of a mean loud
>   party.
> These were the days of the bebopping
> house of blue lights.
>
> Bird gained weight: we meet our
> turnpike death clutching our instruments.
> Places got turned out then
> heads were busted and lips swelled purple;
> we were blind.
> We stayed high on Mexican marijuana,
> drank wine in narrow alleys
> and Lady melody, the blues spirit breezed
> in every now and then.
>
> We were killed in weird ways,
> picked guts, stabbed heads, bleeding marcels
> cursing each other's mothers and fathers and
> sisters and brothers;
> old dripple-lipped drunks high on tokay
>   spewing
> and pissing on themselves.
> And Daddy Grace mad with powers, shoving
>   pigfeet
> and barbecue down the throats of shouting
>   soul stirrers.

> Preachers dreamed yellow Cadillacs
> waiters pretending doctor,
> mailmen pretending lawyer
> doctor and lawyer pretending Negro society.

How can one continue to ask the origins of this current generation? Actually they are the natural by-products of previous generations. Even more direct, didactic and diacritical. There is no way to miss the potency of their messages.

Cryptic, Staccato, livid lives. Another Philly Rapper appropriately called Schooly D enters the squared circle.

> What's up
> What's going on
> Before we start this next record
> I gotta put my shades on
> So I can feel cool
> Remember that law?
> When you had to put your shades on to feel cool?
> Well, it's still a law
> Gotta put your shades on
> So I can't see
> what you ain't doing
> and you ain't doing nothing.

Or to empower it further you gotta listen for the *'Black Man'* cut. Cuz it's on the razor, J. B. Style. Styling and profiling. Cruising and oozing. Elements of style in Philly streets. Black-speak here is terse, located in a distanting zone, The Phase. Everybody wore a variation of the Phase. Understated. New words for a new people. Counterpoint as melodic phraser. Empowering logic, often outside of the article of reason. But they be reasoning with the brethren. Verbal skills are built on many Philly stoops. Getting the last deadly word in. Careful listeners. Word smith. A turn of phrase. Inversion is an index to inner vision. These elements are concretized in the heavy d cell wisdom of Schooly D and Larry N.

So dense is the philly intalk and so laden with wisdom is the philosophy that undergirds the intalk that the editors of Nation Conscious Rap went to an indigenous north Philly philosopher whose careful assessment deserves our attention. Talking about Eugene Rivers. One of the two trained North Philly philosophers formerly on the painterly scene in Philly town before going to New Haven, Cambridge and Kingston, Jamaica.

"Philly had a whole group of radical black intellectuals who were at the cutting edge of phenomenal amounts of stuff. Cruse. The Panther stuff. C.L.R. James, Eric Williams, Padmore, Martin Sostre, George Jackson, Fanon. The entire range. Phenomenal stuff. . . . The theoretical broadness and the catholicism of the intellectual orientation was absolutely unparalled. . . . There is a certain level of adversity that is a precondition for artistic and intellectual creativity and independence. In Philly it is among the urban working class to middle class black males that this creativity emerges. . . . my sense is that Philly was unique because there is a certain homogenized urban working class experience that the black males go through. It is part of a collective experience. Philly is much more homogeneous, not as diversified and differentiated as New York City or Chicago with a much more southern kind of thing. Philly has got an interesting old, urban solid working class. Du Bois alludes to it in the middle of the 1860's. You've got this interesting urbanization process with this kind of homogenized, collective black consciousness which is very tough. That toughness translates itself into the artistic and intellectual realm. Relating to that toughness is a sense of fraternity based on the collective black male experience versus the white experience. In my experience there were whiteys and there were the bloods. The gang experience was part of the rites of passage which was very fraternal. Admittedly there were sociopathic dimensions. But there was a very strong male binding thing because of the commonality of the experience."

Continuing in the Philly Langue. "My experience was that all of the brothers always wanted the brothers to make it. Brothers would sometime get sacked down into the more destructive dimensions of the experience but by the same token the achievers were encouraged." He goes on to describe that kinetic, intellectually vibrant atmosphere in Philadelphia, "There was a much more cosmopolitan intellectual thing steeped in a philly jitterbug hipster tradition. There is a jitterbug, hipster, cosmopolitan intellectual aesthetic . . . What do we do with this aesthetic, this whole vision of the world? Philly has a smooth brother style; interesting enough, it is noted from here to Boston. . . . There is a style and an aesthetic that is uniquely referred to as the *Philly* style, is a whole hipster, jitterbug, irreverent, desperately contemptuous vision of the white world. The women are awed. Here is the synthesis of the physical and the mental, the spiritual, physical, intellectual integrated organic unit which is *Black,* authentically black. *Blue Black Blurple.* That becomes the basis for the aesthetic. The Blue Black: The Blue Black Blurple." What he is talking about is the Blurple aesthetic.

Philly bloods have that utterly seditious sense of independence, of autonomy. Actually that is part of the reason why they are not recorded as often in the Hip Hop domain. They know what they want and they don't want no stuff. You can't stuff them easily. People are overwhelmed by the image. Rivers explained that many people can't fathom this strange species of Philly bloods who "have the view that the European thing must be fully comprehended because that is the only way to appreciate the opposition, out of a sense of warfare you study them, out of a commitment to engage your opposition at every level, psychologically, culturally, ideologically and intellectually. For that reason you study them with a vengeance. You study them out of your contempt for the brutality of their legacy."

Rivers rightly asserted characteristics evident not only in the Philly black aesthetic but also some aspects of today's hip hop cultural movement: There is an almost ontological aversion to the Eurocentric hegemony. This young philosopher noted, "my organizing metaphors and symbols came out of the Nation of Islam. The notion that knowledge of self is a precondition for coherence, the originality of the Black man a la Leakey or Gould . . . the first man is a driving force. The fact that life is a jihad. Existence itself is a jihad against the cycle of death are all principles in the Nation of Islam's philosophy. Is it any surprise that the most pronounced influence on this current generation of Nation Conscious Rappers is the Nation of Islam's philosophy, especially as articulated by the early Malcolm X and Minister Louis Farrakhan.

The pathos, violence and disorder in the American society generally finds another avenue of expression in some rap lyrics. The noted black urban planner, Peter Labrie, provides useful insight into the basis for what appears to be a drastic change from the previous generation to the current one. The presence of Niggas With Attitudes (N.W.A.) can be understood within the changing society so powerfully described by Labrie over twenty years ago. He said, "our purpose here is to inquire into some of the vital internal forces that have traditionally structured the black community in America. Outside of a few exceptional cases, it is widely acknowledged that black people, from slavery to at least World War II, lived in a severly limited, isolated and relatively static world. The general orientation of his life and of his subjective mind was that which had been shaped by the slave-like conditions of the Southern plantation system. Although after World War I many black people migrated to cities, even those in the cities remained, by and large, a Southern people. The moral habits and cultural norms internalized in their consciences were essentially the same as those shared by their relatives and friends left behind in the South. . . . However, between the pre-World War II period and now, many things have come to pass: the Depression, two major wars, erratic but large scale occurrences of industrialization and urbanization, economic and employment stagnation, etc. It would be impossible to measure the influence which all these complex societal forces had upon the black community, but one result is obviously, namely, that most black people have acquired a different basis for their existence of their community life." How is this difference manifested? "With his experiences under oppression and into the deeper and more subjective realms of life, with his knowledge of the white world around him, it becomes almost impossible for him to be moral in any conventional sense. To have someone tell him to go to college so that he can get a good job, to be patient and grateful until some 'charity' organization gives him something, is an insult. If he wants something, he will take it whatever way he can and by any means necessary. This is his will to power which goes beyond conventional morality."

When it comes to assessing N.W.A.'s lyrics in the context of 'conventional morality," it is problematic. Eazy E expresses what is a conscious anticonventional perspective. "When we first started, everybody was black this, black that. The whole positive black thing we said f . . . that—we wanted to come out in everybody's face. Something that would shock people." This is further evidenced by their current album "Niggaz 4 Life." It is obviously in response to the high decibel criticism they've received especially inside of the black community. Like this, "Why not call myself a nigger? It's better than pulling the trigger and going up the river, and then I get called nigger anyway. . . . I guess I'll be a nigger for life." The attitudes, dispositions and raw street talk signifies a declaration of "outsiderness," an opting out of what are known as the values and mores of conventional Afro-American life. There is an obvious predilection toward *outragedness* both as metaphor and as life. What is the value system that generates this violent response to perceived female insubordination? Which sociopolitical variables interact with intrapsychic forces on the real side? Downpression in the neocolonial settings of Blackurban enclaves has produced unique challenges. Eazy E lays it out like this in WHPK's (University of Chicago) house magazine. "I was getting my record company rolling and Dr. Dre said, 'why don't you go on and rap?' I said, I ain't never rapped in my life. So the first record I ever did was 'Boyz in the Hood'. I used to be a DJ—me and Dre. So really, Dre got me started into everything." When asked how crazy record sales has changed his life Eazy E responds, 'No No big change, really. I mean, the only change in it is that it's legal. 'Cause the shit I was doing before that other thing, you know, selling drugs." Rapping provided Eazy E an alternative to working in the informal economy. Writing lyrics and speaking out of the everydayness of their experiences, NWA keeps pumping those graphic brakes. Ren: "Compton is wild man. It's like you can't even stand outside. There's people riding by in Compton with guns, shooting, daylight, nighttime. Your mama can't water the grass whatever. You got to just constantly watch your back. There's people out there that's crazy. And the police, they just fuck with you 'cause they think you're part of a gang. . . . I got shot being in the wrong place at the wrong time, that's how it is . . . And it ain't only Compton. It's Watts. South Central L.A. They've got the biggest drive-by shootings going on. Everynight on the news, you hear about somebody getting took out."

Street Knowledge. Straight Outta Compton where if the word is not the weapon, the weapon is. Little research has been done on the mental pathology of the people inhabiting those war zones. What kind of cultural expression comes out of this existence. *In Wretched of the Earth,* the Martinician psychiatrist, Dr. Frantz Fanon observed the following about the Algerians who faced daily acts of repression in the old colonial regime. Fanon; "The Algerian, exposed to temptations to commit murder every day—famine, eviction from his room, because he has not paid the rent, the mother's dried up breasts, children like skeletons, the building yard which has closed down, the unemployed that hang about the foreman like crows—the native comes to his neighbor as a relentless enemy." There are parallel acts of microaggression that one finds in the Comptons, South Central L.A.s, Harlems and Phillys of the world. As Fanon points out the victim strikes out against those closest to him—his neighbor, his woman, his mother, her father, her friends, etc. This is a crucial stage in the decolonization process. "Fanon puts it correctly, The colonized man will first manifest this aggressiveness which has been deposited in his bones against his own people. This is the period when the niggers beat each other up, and the police and magistrates do not know which way to turn when faced with the astonishing waves of crime in North Africa [substitute for L.A. or Compton]. . . . When the native is confronted with the colonial order of things, he finds he is in a state of permanent tension. The settler's world is a hostile world, which spurns the native, but at the same time it is a world of which he is envious. We have seen that the native never ceases to dream of putting himself in the place of the settler—not of becoming the settler, but of substituting himself for the settler. This hostile world, ponderous and aggressive because it fends off the colonized masses with all the hardness it is capable of, represents not merely a hell from which the swiftest flight possible is desirable, but also a paradise close at hand which is guarded by terrible watch dogs."

Given this background it is not at all surprising to see the emergence of a particular type of rap called variedly Gangsta Rap, Hardcore Rap, etc. It reflects a national culture under colonial domination. Elsewhere in the circle of reasoning is the group of Nation Conscious Rappers who have taken on the responsibility of addressing their own people. The body of literature produced under the aegis can rightly be called a literature of combat. The people's contact with the new movement gives rise to a new rhythm of life and to forgotten muscular tensions. It develops the imagination. Fanon is right "It is only from that moment that we can speak of a national literature. Here there is, at the level of literary creation, the taking up and clarification of themes which are typically nationalistic. This may properly be called a literature of combat, in the sense that it calls on the whole people to fight for their existence as a nation. It is a literature of combat, because it molds the national consciousness, giving it form and contours and flinging open before it new and boundless horizons; it is a literature of combat because it assumes responsibility and because it is the will to liberty expressed in terms of time and space."

Philosophical Dimensions of Rap

The emergence of Nation Conscious Rappers at this juncture in our history is most significant. The fact that a mass national cultural movement has grown organically out of disparate Black communities is a musical phenomenon worthy of further exploration. In examining rap as a socio-communicative and idiomatic manifestation, the philosopher George Yancy states, "Philosophically, the lyrically expressed music found in rap has profound ontological implications. For the analysis of a lyrically expressed rap demonstrates a certain existential, socio-ontological and groundational significance for the emical self understandings of a culture, society, community, etc. On one level rap is *descriptive* of a certain fluid everydayness (alltaglich): tales of concrete situations, (reminiscent of folklore); distinctive styles of dress; shared plights; shared socio-historical realities; shared unconscious associations, etc. On another level, however rap is *prescriptive* (as anyone knows who has listened to Public Enemy, Poor Righteous Teachers et al.) But rap as a modality of prescriptive didacticism and socio-political discontent is nevertheless couched in a mode of linguistically intrinsic to a sociality of shared experience. In short whether viewed as a form of description or prescription, rap presupposes the contention that discourse is fundamentally a form of praxis."

Rap as Rhythmic Praxis Discourse

Concluding his brief but dense essay, "Rapese," Yancy notes, "Now given that rap grows out of a cultural matrix, and nexus of meanings peculiar to African-Americans, idiomatic expressions found in rap are quite suggestive of African-American life stylizations. By treating rap as fundamentally a groundational phenomenon, we participate in the shared vision of Larry Neal concerning the need to emphasize the rootedness and situatedness of African-American cultural objectivations (aesthetics, music, literature, sculpture, etc.) Hence rap as *musical literature* (or rhythmic-praxis discourse) as it were, is an integral and functional pact of the African-American community lifestyle."

Nation Conscious Rap: The Hip Hop Vision

Drums. Bronx. Trumpet. Brooklyn. Keyboard. Long Island. This book captures the tune, texture, lore and history of this important cultural movement. Their shared vision. Groundational sources. High hat symbols. Like Big Daddy Kane said, "Words are powerful, words can change the world . . . myths are built with words, too. But instead of building you up, they beat you down. Just like a bass drum." Drums. Philly. Drums. Chicago. Drums. Bronx. Locus of the Hip Hop World.

JOHN H. BRACEY JR.

Coming from a Black Thing: Remembering the Black Arts Movement

In selecting materials to convey the complexities of a movement which came into existence and had its greatest impact four decades ago, there is an inevitable tension between those works which were most influential at that time and those that subsequent scholars and critics have tended to focus on. Too many of the more recent studies concentrate on poems that were not widely known or read, plays that were never produced, ideas that were marginal and ephemeral. Of course one cannot stop this process, nor would one want to. People are entitled to their interests and opinions. What I wish to convey in this brief account is some of what I remember as one who heard the poetry, saw plays, read the journals, newspapers, pamphlets, handouts. One who attended many meetings, conferences, rallies that included poetry, drama, and discussions of ideas about the definition, role, and importance of African American culture. The Black Arts Movement was a vital part of the crucible that transformed Negroes into Black people. I lived through and participated in that process. I was a part of audience that the artists and thinkers sought, one whose head had to be turned around, one of those souls who was called from Negro to Blackness.

In looking over the selections contained here, I can see how the influence of musicians such as John Coltrane is conveyed throughout, the tremendous impact of Malcolm X obvious. What I want to convey is some sense of how all this came together as one individual experienced it, how the different pieces fit, how the Black Arts Movement came to play such an important role in my life.

I was born in Chicago, but I grew up in northwest Washington, D.C. My father worked as a dining car waiter on the Pennsylvania Railroad, and my mother taught in the School of Education at Howard University. The political and cultural milieu on the campus of Howard and in the surrounding communities during the late 1940s through the early 1960s was extremely rich and rewarding. I grew up on the poetry of Paul Laurence Dunbar, Sterling Brown, Georgia Douglass Johnson, Langston Hughes. During our formative years, my sister and I often sat in my mother's office in Douglass Hall doing our homework or reading, but listening intently to the voices and words of Sterling Brown, E. Franklin Frazier, Eugene Holmes, Emmit Dorsey. I saw the art of James Porter and Lois Malliou Jones. I heard the Howard Choir directed by Warner Lawson. I attended plays directed by Owen Dodson. I experienced the great oratory of President Mordecai Johnson at baccalaureate and other ceremonies. I studied violin with Louia Jones for almost a decade.

I did my junior high and high school research papers and book reviews with the help of Dorothy Porter in the Moorland-Spingarn Room of the Founders Library. I was given autographed copies of Frazier's sociological studies, Sterling Brown, Arthur Davis, and Ulysses Lee's *The Negro Caravan,* Chancellor Williams's novels and early reflections on the importance of Africa, Margaret Just Butcher's study of Negro Black culture, articles by Frank Snowden on ancient Greece and Rome, John Lovell on the spirituals. I knew of the genius of Charles Drew and the talents of the other doctors at Freedmen's Hospital. I heard the many political figures including U.S. presidents and leaders of Africa—Haile Selassie and Patrice Lumumba—the Caribbean, and Asia who visited the campus. I heard such leading radical thinkers as C. Wright Mills and the great W. E. B. Du Bois.

I knew of the Howard poets LeRoi Jones and Percy Johnston, and others who read at Coffee and Confusion, a coffee shop and Beat hangout, during the late 1950s. I frequented the stage shows at the Howard Theater, and when old enough listened to jazz at the Bohemian Caverns and Abart's Jazz Mecca, and to Latin music at the Casbah at 12th and U Street.

I was attuned to the achievements of Howard Law School and the legal genius of Charles Houston, Thurgood Marshall, Frank Reeves, Constance Baker Motley, Spottswood Robinson. I celebrated their victory in *Brown v. Board of Education.* I also was one of those students in the D.C. schools who became distressed to learn that integration meant that I had to attend previously all white Roosevelt High School instead of following my sister to all Black Dunbar, which was generally acknowledged to be the best high school in the District. I wanted an end to segregation. That did not mean that I was at all interested in going to school with white people. I was an early participant in sit-ins both in Washington, D.C., and in Chicago when I transferred from Howard after my freshman year in 1959 to attend Roosevelt University. I was amassing the education and socialization necessary to become as successful a Negro as possible in an integrated world.

It was clear that Jim Crow was dying and that change was coming. What the new society beyond Jim Crow would look like was not. Frazier's *Black Bourgeoisie* could only tell us how not to act, what not to be. He offered little guidance and a lot of skepticism about the future. I knew of the importance of the newly independent African countries and of the anti-colonial struggles throughout the world. The Afro-American newspaper and those special issues of the *Journal of Negro Education* kept you up-to-date. Stirring below the surface were signs of change that became obvious only with the rise of the politics of Black liberation and of the onset of the Black Arts Movement. During the period of the Civil Rights Movement, there was no need to connect the dots between changes in the social and political status of Negroes and the stirrings in the realm of culture and the arts.

First there were the beginnings of significant shifts in the music. I grew up on blues, R & B, doo-wop, and in jazz, bebop. But Max Roach, Abbey Lincoln, Sonny Rollins, Nina Simone, and Charles Mingus were creating music with a clear political message. Randy Weston and Art Blakey were incorporating African sounds into their music. The sounds and style of Thelonious Monk seemed to embody a critique of something or somebody. I loved his music and went to see him every time I got the chance: at Abart's in D.C. or at The Five Spot and Randall's Island Jazz Festival in New York. It was not clear what Monk's politics were, or even if he had any. Monk's individual rebelliousness and iconoclasm were sufficient for the 1950s.

During my last year in high school I had joined a group led by Carol Joyner (now Bro. Baba Ngomo) called the Association of Bongo And Conga Players and Associated Instruments of the East Coast Music Center, Inc. I learned to play conga drums, maracas, cowbells, woodblock, claves. I left the violin and turned to the sounds of Afro-Latin and African music. Members of the ABACP played at various venues in D.C. and the surrounding areas. We also played at the Casbah on Wednesday nights. It was at the Casbah that I got to hear leading Afro-Cuban drummers such as Candido, Potato Valdez, Modesto Duran. The house band was Roland Calvez and Los Diablos. Members of the touring bands such as those of Harry Belafonte, Babatunde Olatunji, and Cal Tjader sometimes appeared after-hours or on their off nights from other jobs in D.C. When the Ballet Africaine from Guinea made their first tour of the United States, we got to see the djembe and cora for the first time.

During the years from the late 1950s through the early 1970s my conga-playing skills were sufficient to enable me to accompany various groups of dancers and poets—Beats, Black Arts—to play in percussion ensembles, and to appear in several plays. At a cabaret on the West Side of Chicago in 1964, I was part of a bongo-conga duo whom Jerry Butler asked to remain on stage to play with his band, which included Curtis Mayfield. In 1965, I was cast as a South African drummer in a Parkway Community Center production of Alan Paton's *Sponono.*

As interesting and rewarding as these experiences were, I drew no connection between them and my participation in the Civil Rights Movement. I participated in sit-ins, demonstrations, rallies, marches. I was active in CORE, Friends of SNCC, ACT, and various local groups. I loved the songs, chants, sermons, and speeches that were an integral part of Civil Rights work. Listening to the SNCC Freedom Singers was powerful and moving. To this day when I hear "We Will Never Turn Back" it sends chills through my body. When I think about Reverend Wilbur Daniels's cries/shouts of "Freedom, Freedom Now" at the end of a rally sermon I remember how my ear drums hurt if I was standing too close to him on the platform or pulpit.

But those sounds and expressions drew on our past, and derived their strength and power from that past. They were comforting, mobilizing, sustaining, energizing. They helped me through the fears and turbulence of that time of my life. They affirmed me in who I was and where I came from. But being based on the past and on tradition, they could not take me through the shift from Civil Rights to Black Power, from Negro to Black.

The same was true of poetry and drama. I knew and grew strength from Sterling Brown's "Strong Men," Margaret Walker's "For My People," Claude McKay's "If We Must Die," Georgia Douglass Johnson's "The Suppliant." I enjoyed performances of *A Raisin in the Sun, Purlie Victorious,* and Oscar Brown Jr.'s *Kicks & Co.* I was conflicted by the reality that the play that came closest to capturing my changing sensibility and outlook was Jean Genet's *The Blacks,* "with the all Black cast demanded by the playwright and the actors in 'whiteface'." How could a European be so prescient?

I was not conscious of it at the time, but John Coltrane was the key to the subsequent linkage of my political and cultural outlooks. He was the first musician whom I encountered who set about dismantling the foundational forms and assumptions of Western music and constructing a new music on new foundations in front of your eyes. I followed Coltrane's evolution from sideman in the Miles Davis Quintet through "Monk's Music,"

"My Favorite Things" (first heard at Randall's Island in 1959, a year before the Atlantic recording was released) and the various groups he led that took the music, and our heads, to a whole new place until his passing on July 17, 1967. July 17 is my birthday so Coltrane's death and my life form an unbreakable link.

What Coltrane was doing in his music was indicating that we had to move beyond the whole system of Western thought, cosmology, and culture. We needed a new sound, a new aesthetic for new times. If you were not a witness to this process, it is difficult to convey the emotional impact of the step-by-step stripping away of Western conceptions of melody, harmony, rhythm, structure that had dominated definitions of music since the mid-nineteenth century. Coltrane was a major subject of Black Arts poetry and figured in numerous discussions of cultural and political change. It was his increasing relevance in these disparate arenas that validated my feeling that his musical accomplishments were vital to the political journey from civil rights and integration, to the politics of liberation and Black nationalism.

In retrospect it is clear that the poet Amus Mor was one of the first to discern the political implications of John Coltrane's music and approach to life. Prior to the onset of the annual urban rebellions that began in 1964 and continued throughout the decade, and prior to the explicit calls for Black liberation and Black Power, Mor wrote, and read widely, his poem "The Coming of John." I will leave aside the complexities of Mor's reinterpretation of Du Bois's famous chapter from *The Souls of Black Folk*. What Mor did early on was to interrupt the flow of the poem to offer his observations on the meaning implicit in the changes from the 1950s of the cool Miles Davis to the increasingly hot 1960s of John Coltrane. In language vivid for its time, Mor's poem confronts what he sees as the limitations of a nonviolent moral struggle: "If yall expect to get somewhere in America, you got to start bustin down dos and shit, pitchin a fit, and poppin these lames upside the head. Laying some of these peckerwoods out across the room, is what get you somewhere in America."

The absorbing of Coltrane's ongoing musical project into my political outlook took place to such a degree that it became a significant criterion in my assessing the relevance and worthiness of the politics of others. If you had never heard of John Coltrane and gave no inclination that you knew any of his music, then to me your politics were limited and suspect. You could like Coltrane and have no politics. But you could not lay claim to a radical politics if you did not like at least some of the music of John Coltrane. Coltrane established that there could be something new and beautiful beyond the world that I knew and a different future from the one that had been laid out for me. The possibility of new ways of feeling, living, thinking were not utopian fantasies. This shift in my head was well under way by 1963, before the formal inauguration of the Black Arts Movement. But the question that remained was, how do you extend Coltrane's vision from the realm of music and personal transformation to the world of institutions and politics? That was not John Coltrane's problem. It was ours.

One key to that problem was the answers given by Malcolm X. I had first encountered Malcolm X giving a speech in Harlem during the summer of 1959. I had not heard of the Nation of Islam, nor did I have any interest in what I knew of their ideas. The Nation had little if any presence in the Washington, D.C., of the 1950s. When I moved to Chicago in the fall of 1961, I was faced with the reality of the Nation of Islam as an important force among Black Americans. I met Richard Durham, the editor of *Muhammad Speaks* newspaper, and Christine Johnson, the principal of the University of Islam School, and others with Left politics who moved in the orbit of the Nation. I went to Temple Number 2 many times and to Saviors Day events. I listened to Malcolm X, and had the privilege of meeting him and engaging in discussions about various interpretations of African American history and politics. We discussed why some members of my generation were not inclined to join the Nation of Islam. As I recall, my concerns and those of my comrades were more cultural than political—the suits and bowties, no going to jazz and blues clubs, etc. (In all fairness, I had a similar conversation a year or two later with Ishmael Flory, Claude Lightfoot, and William L. Patterson when they invited me to join the Communist Party. Again concerns about style, popular culture, and what was called the New Jazz were a part of the mix. The jazz discussion was complicated by the U.S. State Department's efforts to use some jazz artists to advance their anti-Soviet agenda. The gist of my response was that I could not imagine the U.S. government asking John Coltrane, Charlie Mingus, Nina Simone, Thelonious Monk, Sonny Rollins, or Max Roach to go anywhere to play their music or to talk about anything.). In sum, Malcolm's words were the most persuasive in explaining to me why I was responding to Coltrane's music, though I never heard Malcolm mention Coltrane by name. Malcolm was killed in February 1965, his *Autobiography* was published later that spring, and the Watts Rebellion took place in August.

The link between Malcolm's death and the rise of the Black Arts Movement is well established. What is often obscured in the recent literature is the manner in which that movement took up the project begun by Malcolm and Coltrane. My grappling with what it meant to be "Black," and how a Black man was supposed to act, was carried out in the context of the words, images, and sounds of artists who came to define themselves as participants in the Black Arts Movement. The reason you went to hear Amiri Baraka and others whenever you had the chance and the Chicago OBAC poets such as Gwendolyn Brooks, Don L. Lee, Carolyn Rodgers, Amus Mor, and Jewel Latimore was to continue the process of transformation, not to be entertained. The poetry of Gwendolyn Brooks moved us from the fatalism of the last line of "We Real Cool"— i.e., "we die soon"—to the triumphant affirmation of Malcolm's achievement: "He opened us, who was a key, who was a man." The poems in this anthology in the Consciousness section were an important part of this process for me.

I along with thousands of others learned and absorbed the work of the new artists. Just as we sang along at concerts or stage shows with our favorite doo-wop, R & B, and Motown groups, we chanted the signature verses of our favorite poems: "I'm so bad even my errors are correct"; "he was so cool he even stopped for green lights"; "he was the real thing"; "I'm talking about, I'm talking about revolution"; "the revolution will not be televised"; "Niggers are scared of revolution"; and loudest of all: "up against the wall, motherfucker, this is a stick up."

The staging of plays such as Baraka's *Black Mass* and *Jello* and Bullins's *In the Wine Time* and *Clara's Old Man* drew large and excited audiences. Readings of parts of plays or dramatic performances such as those by Val Gray Ward were received with great enthusiasm. The plays often drew many in their casts from local schools and community centers. Many of these events included post-performance discussions between the audience and the actors, playwrights, and directors. Again the goal was to continue the process of defining what was expected of the new Black woman and man. Did the work just witnessed aid in that process? Were the issues raised relevant to our lives and to those of the larger Black community?

Chicago, of course, was the birthplace of OBAC and Africobra, of Third World Press and the Institute for Positive Education, the Center for Inner City Studies, and the Wall of Respect. It was the home of *Jet, Ebony, Negro Digest/Black World, The Chicago Defender,* and *Muhammad Speaks.* If you include Ishmael Flory's African American Heritage Association, Odis Hyde and the Washington Park Forum, Margaret and Charlie Burroughs's Du Sable Museum, Phil Cohran and the Pharoahs, this was a fertile environment for carrying forward the transformations implicit in the calls for a Black aesthetic, a new way to walk in a new world.

By 1963, I had met Max Stanford, Stan Daniels, Don Freeman, Ware-Bey, Roland Snellings, and General Baker and had joined the Revolutionary Action Movement. In 1965, prior to Kwame Toure's call, I attended a meeting in Chicago of the Organization for Black Power. As the assistant to Lawrence Landry of ACT, which hosted the meeting, I got to meet Jesse Gray, Grace Lee, and James Boggs, Milton Henry, and Richard Henry. I had known Julius Hobson from my youth in Washington, D.C. In Detroit a year later I attended "Forum 66: Coming from a Black Thing," held at Albert Cleage's Shrine of the Black Madonna Church. Glanton Dowdell, a member of RAM, was the artist who painted the *Black Madonna and Child* mural that covered the wall behind the pulpit. I was a delegate from Chicago to the founding convention of the Republic of New Africa, where cultural questions consumed as much time and energy as those of politics and economics.

What I hope is clear from this brief account is that the subsequent posing of dichotomies such as that between cultural nationalism and political nationalism masked the reality that during the era of Black liberation and of the Black Arts Movement, culture and politics had become inseparable. The debates I witnessed and participated in centered on questions of what your cultural values, preferences, and beliefs were, not whether you had any; on the type of politics implicit in your cultural practices, not whether cultural practices were political. The Black Arts Movement embraced and thrived on these complexities.

I spent the years from 1961 through 1971 in Chicago before moving on and settling in at the University of Massachusetts Amherst in 1972. My experiences during that decade were rich and full. The nature of the evolution of my politics and values was the same as that of multitudes of women and men of my generation. This anthology goes far in capturing and presenting the Black Arts Movement as I lived it and as I remember it. I heard Amiri Baraka's SOS and that of the other poets artists and musicians of that era. I was one of the many who responded.

Learning from the 60s

MALCOLM X is a distinct shape in a very pivotal period of my life. I stand here now—Black, Lesbian, Feminist—an inheritor of Malcolm and in his tradition, doing my work, and the ghost of his voice through my mouth asks each one of you here tonight: Are you doing yours?

There are no new ideas, just new ways of giving those ideas we cherish breath and power in our own living. I'm not going to pretend that the moment I first saw or heard Malcolm X he became my shining prince, because it wouldn't be true. In February 1965 I was raising two children and a husband in a three-room flat on 149th Street in Harlem. I had read about Malcolm X and the Black Muslims. I became more interested in Malcolm X after he left the Nation of Islam, when he was silenced by Elijah Muhammad for his comment, after Kennedy's assassination, to the effect that the chickens had come home to roost. Before this I had not given much thought to the Nation of Islam because of their attitude toward women as well as because of their nonactivist stance. I'd read Malcolm's autobiography, and I liked his style, and I thought he looked a lot like my father's people, but I was one of the ones who didn't really hear Malcolm's voice until it was amplified by death.

I had been guilty of what many of us are still guilty of—letting the media, and I don't mean only the white media—define the bearers of those messages most important to our lives.

When I read Malcolm X with careful attention, I found a man much closer to the complexities of real change than anything I had read before. Much of what I say here tonight was born from his words.

In the last year of his life, Malcolm X added a breadth to his essential vision that would have brought him, had he lived, into inevitable confrontation with the question of difference as a creative and necessary force for change. For as Malcolm X progressed from a position of resistance to, and analysis of, the racial status quo, to more active considerations of organizing for change, he began to reassess some of his earlier positions. One of the most basic Black survival skills is the ability to change, to metabolize experience, good or ill, into something that is useful, lasting, effective. Four hundred years of survival as an endangered species has taught most of us that if we intend to live, we had better become

From Audre Lorde, *Sister Outsider: Essays and Speeches* (Trumansburg, N.Y.: Crossing Press, 1984). Talk delivered at the Malcolm X Weekend, Harvard University, February 1982.

fast learners. Malcolm knew this. We do not have to live the same mistakes over again if we can look at them, learn from them, and build upon them.

Before he was killed, Malcolm had altered and broadened his opinions concerning the role of women in society and the revolution. He was beginning to speak with increasing respect of the connection between himself and Martin Luther King, Jr., whose policies of nonviolence appeared to be so opposite to his own. And he began to examine the societal conditions under which alliances and coalitions must indeed occur.

He had also begun to discuss those scars of oppression which lead us to war against ourselves in each other rather than against our enemies.

As Black people, if there is one thing we can learn from the 60s, it is how infinitely complex any move for liberation must be. For we must move against not only those forces which dehumanize us from the outside, but also against those oppressive values which we have been forced to take into ourselves. Through examining the combination of our triumphs and errors, we can examine the dangers of an incomplete vision. Not to condemn that vision but to alter it, construct templates for possible futures, and focus our rage for change upon our enemies rather than upon each other. In the 1960s, the awakened anger of the Black community was often expressed, not vertically against the corruption of power and true sources of control over our lives, but horizontally toward those closest to us who mirrored our own impotence.

We were poised for attack, not always in the most effective places. When we disagreed with one another about the solution to a particular problem, we were often far more vicious to each other than to the originators of our common problem. Historically, difference had been used so cruelly against us that as a people we were reluctant to tolerate any diversion from what was externally defined as Blackness. In the 60s, political correctness became not a guideline for living, but a new set of shackles. A small and vocal part of the Black community lost sight of the fact that unity does not mean unanimity—Black people are not some standardly digestible quantity. In order to work together we do not have to become a mix of indistinguishable particles resembling a vat of homogenized chocolate milk. Unity implies the coming together of elements which are, to begin with, varied and diverse in their particular natures. Our persistence in examining the tensions within diversity encourages growth toward our common goal. So often we either ignore the past or romanticize it, render the reason for unity useless or mythic. We forget that the necessary ingredient needed to make the past work for the future is our energy in the present, metabolizing one into the other. Continuity does not happen automatically, nor is it a passive process.

The 60s were characterized by a heady belief in instantaneous solutions. They were vital years of awakening, of pride, and of error. The civil rights and Black power movements rekindled possibilities for disenfranchised groups within this nation. Even though we fought common enemies, at times the lure of individual solutions made us careless of each other. Sometimes we could not bear the face of each other's differences because of what we feared those differences might say about ourselves. As if everybody can't eventually be too Black, too white, too man, too woman. But any future vision which can encompass all of us, by definition, must be complex and expanding, not easy to achieve. The answer to cold is heat, the answer to hunger is food. But there is no simple monolithic solution to racism, to sexism, to homophobia. There is only the conscious focusing within each of my days to move against them, wherever I come up against these particular manifestations of the same disease. By seeing who the *we* is, we learn to use our energies with greater precision against our enemies rather than against ourselves.

In the 60s, white america—racist and liberal alike—was more than pleased to sit back as spectator while Black militant fought Black Muslim, Black Nationalist badmouthed the nonviolent, and Black women were told that our only useful position in the Black Power movement was prone. The existence of Black lesbian and gay people was not even allowed to cross the public consciousness of Black america. We know in the 1980s, from documents gained through the Freedom of Information Act, that the FBI and CIA used our intolerance of difference to foment confusion and tragedy in segment after segment of Black communities of the 60s. Black was beautiful, but still suspect, and too often our forums for debate became stages for playing who's-Blacker-than-who or who's-poorer-than-who games, ones in which there can be no winners.

The 60s for me was a time of promise and excitement, but the 60s was also a time of isolation and frustration from within. It often felt like I was working and raising my children in a vacuum, and that it was my own fault—if I was only Blacker, things would be fine. It was a time of much wasted energy, and I was often in a lot of pain. Either I denied or chose between various aspects of my identity, or my work and my Blackness would be unacceptable. As a Black lesbian mother in an interracial marriage, there was usually some part of me guaranteed to offend everybody's comfortable prejudices of who I should be. That is how I learned that if I didn't define myself for myself, I would be crunched into other people's fantasies for me and eaten alive. My poetry, my life, my work, my energies for struggle were not acceptable unless I pretended to match somebody else's norm. I learned that not only couldn't I succeed at that game, but the energy needed for that masquerade would be lost to my work. And there were babies to raise, students to teach. The Vietnam War was escalating, our cities were burning, more and more of our school kids were nodding out in the halls, junk was overtaking our streets. We needed articulate power, not conformity. There were other strong Black workers whose visions were racked and silenced upon some imagined grid of narrow Blackness. Nor were Black women immune. At a national meeting of Black women for political action, a young civil rights activist who had been beaten and imprisoned in Mississippi only a few years before, was trashed and silenced as suspect because of her white husband. Some of us made it and some of us were lost to the struggle. It was a time of great hope and great expectation; it was also a time of great waste. That is history. We do not need to repeat these mistakes in the 80s.

The raw energy of Black determination released in the 60s powered changes in Black awareness and self-concepts and expectations. This energy is still being felt in movements for change among women, other peoples of Color, gays, the handicapped—among all the disenfranchised peoples of this society. That is a legacy of the 60s to ourselves and to others. But we must recognize that many of our high expectations of rapid revolutionary change did not in fact occur. And many of the gains that did are even now being dismantled. This is not a reason for despair, nor for rejection of the importance of those years. But we must face with clarity and insight the lessons to be learned from the oversimplification of any struggle for self-awareness and liberation, or we will not rally the force we need to face the multidimensional threats to our survival in the 80s.

There is no such thing as a single-issue struggle because we do not live single-issue lives. Malcolm knew this. Martin Luther King, Jr., knew this. Our struggles are particular, but we are not alone. We are not perfect, but we are stronger and wiser than the sum of our errors. Black people have been here before us and survived. We can read their lives like signposts on the road and find, as Bernice Reagon says so poignantly, that each one of us is here because somebody before us did something to make it possible. To learn from their mistakes is not to lessen our debt to them, nor to the hard work of becoming ourselves, and effective.

We lose our history so easily, what is not predigested for us by the *New York Times,* or the *Amsterdam News,* or *Time* magazine. Maybe because we do not listen to our poets or to our fools, maybe because we do not listen to our mamas in ourselves. When I hear the deepest truths I speak coming out of my mouth sounding like my mother's, even re-membering how I fought against her, I have to reassess both our relationship as well as the sources of my knowing. Which is not to say that I have to romanticize my mother in order to appreciate what she gave me—Woman, Black. We do not have to romanticize our past in order to be aware of how it seeds our present. We do not have to suffer the waste of an amnesia that robs us of the lessons of the past rather than permit us to read them with pride as well as deep understanding.

We know what it is to be lied to, and we know how important it is not to lie to ourselves.

We are powerful because we have survived, and that is what it is all about—survival and growth.

Within each one of us there is some piece of humanness that knows we are not being served by the machine which orchestrates crisis after crisis and is grinding all our futures into dust. If we are to keep the enormity of the forces aligned against us from establish-ing a false hierarchy of oppression, we must school ourselves to recognize that any attack against Blacks, any attack against women, is an attack against all of us who recognize that our interests are not being served by the systems we support. Each one of us here is a link in the connection between antipoor legislation, gay shootings, the burning of synagogues, street harassment, attacks against women, and resurgent violence against Black people. I ask myself as well as each one of you, exactly what alteration in the particular fabric of my everyday life does this connection call for? Survival is not a theory. In what way do I contribute to the subjugation of any part of those who I define as my people? Insight must illuminate the particulars of our lives: who labors to make the bread we waste, or the en-ergy it takes to make nuclear poisons which will not biodegrade for one thousand years; or who goes blind assembling the microtransistors in our inexpensive calculators?

We are women trying to knit a future in a country where an Equal Rights Amendment was defeated as subversive legislation. We are Lesbians and gay men who, as the most ob-vious target of the New Right, are threatened with castration, imprisonment, and death in the streets. And we know that our erasure only paves the way for erasure of other people of Color, of the old, of the poor, of all of those who do not fit that mythic dehumanizing norm.

Can we really still afford to be fighting each other?

We are Black people living in a time when the consciousness of our intended slaughter is all around us. People of Color are increasingly expendable, our government's policy both here and abroad. We are functioning under a government ready to repeat in El Sal-vador and Nicaragua the tragedy of Vietnam, a government which stands on the wrong side of every single battle for liberation taking place upon this globe; a government which has invaded and conquered (as I edit this piece) the fifty-three square mile sovereign state of Grenada, under the pretext that her 110,000 people pose a threat to the U.S. Our papers are filled with supposed concern for human rights in white communist Poland while we sanction by acceptance and military supply the systematic genocide of apartheid in South Africa, of murder and torture in Haiti and El Salvador. American advisory teams bolster repressive governments across Central and South America, and in Haiti, while *advisory* is only a code name preceding military aid.

Decisions to cut aid for the terminally ill, for the elderly, for dependent children, for food stamps, even school lunches, are being made by men with full stomachs who live in comfortable houses with two cars and umpteen tax shelters. None of them go hungry to bed at night. Recently, it was suggested that senior citizens be hired to work in atomic plants because they are close to the end of their lives anyway.

Can any one of us here still afford to believe that efforts to reclaim the future can be private or individual? Can any one here still afford to believe that the pursuit of liberation can be the sole and particular province of any one particular race, or sex, or age, or religion, or sexuality, or class?

Revolution is not a one-time event. It is becoming always vigilant for the smallest opportunity to make a genuine change in established, outgrown responses; for instance, it is learning to address each other's difference with respect.

We share a common interest, survival, and it cannot be pursued in isolation from others simply because their differences make us uncomfortable. We know what it is to be lied to. The 60s should teach us how important it is not to lie to ourselves. Not to believe that revolution is a one-time event, or something that happens around us rather than inside of us. Not to believe that freedom can belong to any one group of us without the others also being free. How important it is not to allow even our leaders to define us to ourselves, or to define our sources of power to us.

There is no Black person here who can afford to wait to be led into positive action for survival. Each one of us must look clearly and closely at the genuine particulars (conditions) of his or her life and decide where action and energy is needed and where it can be effective. Change is the immediate responsibility of each of us, wherever and however we are standing, in whatever arena we choose. For while we wait for another Malcolm, another Martin, another charismatic Black leader to validate our struggles, old Black people are freezing to death in tenements, Black children are being brutalized and slaughtered in the streets, or lobotomized by television, and the percentage of Black families living below the poverty line is higher today than in 1963.

And if we wait to put our future into the hands of some new messiah, what will happen when those leaders are shot, or discredited, or tried for murder, or called homosexual, or otherwise disempowered? Do we put our future on hold? What is that internalized and self-destructive barrier that keeps us from moving, that keeps us from coming together?

We who are Black are at an extraordinary point of choice within our lives. To refuse to participate in the shaping of our future is to give it up. Do not be misled into passivity either by false security (they don't mean me) or by despair (there's nothing we can do). Each of us must find our work and do it. Militancy no longer means guns at high noon, if it ever did. It means actively working for change, sometimes in the absence of any surety that change is coming. It means doing the unromantic and tedious work necessary to forge meaningful coalitions, and it means recognizing which coalitions are possible and which coalitions are not. It means knowing that coalition, like unity, means the coming together of whole, self-actualized human beings, focused and believing, not fragmented automatons marching to a prescribed step. It means fighting despair.

And in the university, that is certainly no easy task, for each one of you by virtue of your being here will be deluged by opportunities to misname yourselves, to forget who you are, to forget where your real interests lie. Make no mistake, you will be courted; and nothing neutralizes creativity quicker than tokenism, that false sense of security fed by a myth of individual solutions. To paraphrase Malcolm—a Black woman attorney driving a Mercedes through Avenue Z in Brooklyn is still a "nigger bitch," two words which never seem to go out of style.

You do not have to be me in order for us to fight alongside each other. I do not have to be you to recognize that our wars are the same. What we must do is commit ourselves to some future that can include each other and to work toward that future with the particular strengths of our individual identities. And in order to do this, we must allow each other our differences at the same time as we recognize our sameness.

If our history has taught us anything, it is that action for change directed only against the external conditions of our oppressions is not enough. In order to be whole, we must recognize the despair oppression plants within each of us—that thin persistent voice that says our efforts are useless, it will never change, so why bother, accept it. And we must fight that inserted piece of self-destruction that lives and flourishes like a poison inside of us, unexamined until it makes us turn upon ourselves in each other. But we can put our finger down upon that loathing buried deep within each one of us and see who it encourages us to despise, and we can lessen its potency by the knowledge of our real connectedness, arcing across our differences.

Hopefully, we can learn from the 60s that we cannot afford to do our enemies' work by destroying each other.

What does it mean when an angry Black ballplayer—this happened in Illinois—curses a white heckler but pulls a knife on a Black one? What better way is there to police the streets of a minority community than to turn one generation against the other?

Referring to Black lesbians and gay men, the student president at Howard University says, on the occasion of a Gay Student Charter on campus, "The Black community has nothing to do with such filth—we will have to abandon *these people.*" [italics mine] Abandon? Often without noticing, we absorb the racist belief that Black people are fitting targets for everybody's anger. We are closest to each other, and it is easier to vent fury upon each other than upon our enemies.

Of course, the young man at Howard was historically incorrect. As part of the Black community, he has a lot to do with "us." Some of our finest writers, organizers, artists and scholars in the 60s as well as today, have been lesbian and gay, and history will bear me out.

Over and over again in the 60s I was asked to justify my existence and my work, because I was a woman, because I was a Lesbian, because I was not a separatist, because some piece of me was not acceptable. Not because of my work but because of my identity. I had to learn to hold on to all the parts of me that served me, in spite of the pressure to express only one to the exclusion of all others. And I don't know what I'd say face to face with that young man at Howard University who says I'm filth because I identify women as my primary source of energy and support, except to say that it is my energy and the energy of other women very much like me which has contributed to his being where he is at this point. But I think he would not say it to my face because name-calling is always easiest when it is removed, academic. The move to render the presence of lesbians and gay men invisible in the intricate fabric of Black existence and survival is a move which contributes to fragmentation and weakness in the Black community.

In academic circles, as elsewhere, there is a kind of name-calling increasingly being used to keep young Black women in line. Often as soon as any young Black woman begins to recognize that she is oppressed as a woman as well as a Black, she is called a lesbian no matter how she identifies herself sexually. "What do you mean you don't want to make coffee take notes wash dishes go to bed with me, you a lesbian or something?" And at the threat of such a dreaded taint, all too often she falls meekly into line, however covertly. But the word *lesbian* is only threatening to those Black women who are intimidated by their sexuality, or who allow themselves to be defined by it and from outside themselves. Black women in struggle from our own perspective, speaking up for ourselves, sharing close ties with one another politically and emotionally, are not the enemies of Black men. We are Black women who seek our own definitions, recognizing diversity among ourselves with respect. We have been around within our communities for a very long time, and we have played pivotal parts in the survival of those communities: from Hat Shep Sut through Harriet Tubman to Daisy Bates and Fannie Lou Hamer to Lorraine Hansberry to your Aunt Maydine to some of you who sit before me now.

In the 60s Black people wasted a lot of our substance fighting each other. We cannot afford to do that in the 80s, when Washington, D.C., has the highest infant mortality rate of any U.S. city, 60 percent of the Black community under twenty is unemployed and more are becoming unemployable, lynchings are on the increase, and less than half the registered Black voters voted in the last election.

How are you practicing what you preach—whatever you preach, and who exactly is listening? As Malcolm stressed, we are not responsible for our oppression, but we must be responsible for our own liberation. It is not going to be easy, but we have what we have learned and what we have been given that is useful. We have the power those who came before us have given us, to move beyond the place where they were standing. We have the trees, and water, and sun, and our children. Malcolm X does not live in the dry texts of his words as we read them; he lives in the energy we generate and use to move along the visions we share with him. We are making the future as well as bonding to survive the enormous pressures of the present, and that is what it means to be a part of history.

Selected Bibliography

Contemporary

Adoff, Arnold, ed. *I Am the Darker Brother: An Anthology of Modern Poems by Negro Americans.* New York: Macmillan, 1968.

Alhamsi, Ahmed, and Harun Kofi Wangara, eds. *Black Arts: An Anthology of Black Creations.* Detroit: Black Arts Publications, 1969.

Baker, Houston A., Jr. *The Journey Back: Issues in Black Literature and Criticism.* Chicago: University of Chicago Press, 1980.

Bambara, Toni Cade. *The Black Woman: An Anthology.* New York: New American Library, 1970.

Baraka, Amiri (LeRoi Jones), and Larry Neal. *Black Fire: An Anthology of Afro-American Writing.* New York: Morrow, 1968.

Bell, Bernard W., ed. *Modern and Contemporary Afro-American Poetry.* Boston: Allyn and Bacon, 1972.

Bennett, Lerone. *The Black Mood and Other Essays.* New York: Barnes and Noble, 1971.

Bracey, John, Jr., August Meier, and Elliot Rudwick, eds. *Black Nationalism in America.* Indianapolis: Bobbs-Merrill, 1970.

Breman, Paul. *You Better Believe It: Black Verse in English.* Baltimore: Penguin, 1973.

Brooks, Gwendolyn, ed. *Jump Bad: A New Chicago Anthology.* Detroit: Broadside Press, 1971.

———. *Report from Part I.* Detroit: Broadside Press, 1972.

Brown, Patricia L., Don L. Lee, and Francis Ward, eds. *To Gwen with Love: An Anthology Dedicated to Gwendolyn Brooks.* Chicago: Johnson, 1971.

Bullins, Ed, ed. Black Theatre Issue. *TDR: The Drama Review* 12.4 (Summer 1968).

———, ed. *The New Lafayette Theatre Presents: Plays with Aesthetic Comments by 6 Black Playwrights: Ed Bullins, J. E. Gaines, Clay Goss, Oyamo, Sonia Sanchez, Richard Wesley.* Garden City, N.Y.: Anchor Press, 1974.

———, ed. *New Plays from the Black Theatre: An Anthology.* New York: Bantam Books, 1969.

Chapman, Abraham, ed. *Black Voices: An Anthology of Afro-American Literature.* New York: New American Library, 1968.

———, ed. *New Black Voices: An Anthology of Contemporary Afro-American Literature.* New York: Mentor, 1972.

Cook, Mercer, and Stephen E. Henderson. *The Militant Black Writer in Africa and the United States.* Madison: University of Wisconsin Press, 1969.

Cruse, Harold. *The Crisis of the Negro Intellectual.* New York: Morrow, 1967.

———. *Rebellion or Revolution?* New York: Morrow, 1968.

Dent, Thomas C., Richard Schechner, and Gilbert Moses, eds. *The Free Southern Theater, by the Free Southern Theater. A Documentary of the South's Radical Black Theater, with Journals, Letters, Poetry, Essays, and a Play Written by Those Who Built It.* Indianapolis: Bobbs-Merrill, 1969.

Gayle, Addison, Jr., ed. *The Black Aesthetic.* Garden City, N.Y.: Doubleday, 1971.

———, ed. *Black Expression: Essays By and About Black Americans in the Creative Arts.* New York: Weybright and Talley, 1969.

———. *The Black Situation.* New York: Horizon Press, 1970.

Henderson, Stephen. *Understanding the New Black Poetry: Black Speech and Black Music as Poetic References.* New York: Morrow, 1973.

Hughes, Langston, ed. *New Negro Poets, U.S.A.* Bloomington: Indiana University Press, 1964.

Jordan, June, ed. *Soulscript: Afro-American Poetry.* Garden City, N.Y.: Doubleday, 1970.

Kent, George E. *Blackness and the Adventure of Western Culture.* Chicago: Third World Press, 1972.

King, Woodie, ed. *BlackSpirits: A Festival of New Black Poets in America.* New York: Random House, 1972.

———, and Ron Milner, eds. *Black Drama Anthology.* New York: New American Library, 1972.

Madhubuti, Haki (Don L. Lee). *Dynamite Voices.* Detroit: Broadside Press, 1971.

Major, Clarence, ed. *The New Black Poetry.* New York: International, 1969.

Mphahlele, Es'kia. *Voices in the Whirlwind and Other Essays.* New York: Hill and Wang, 1972.

Neal, Larry. *Visions of a Liberated Future: Black Arts Movement Writings.* Edited by Michael Schwartz. New York: Thunder's Mouth Press, 1989.

Noble, Jeanne. *Beautiful, Also, Are the Souls of My Black Sisters.* Englewood Cliffs, N.J.: Prentice-Hall, 1978.

Pool, Rosey E., ed. *Beyond the Blues: New Poems by American Negroes.* Lympne, Kent: Hand and Flower Press, 1962.

Randall, Dudley, ed. *Black Poetry: A Supplement to Anthologies Which Exclude Black Poets.* Detroit: Broadside Press, 1969.

———, ed. *The Black Poets: A New Anthology.* New York: Bantam Books, 1971.

———, and Margaret Burroughs, eds. *For Malcolm: Poems on the Life and Death of Malcolm X.* Detroit: Broadside Press, 1969.

Redmond, Eugene B. *Drumvoices: The Mission of Afro-American Poetry: A Critical History.* Garden City, N.Y.: Anchor Press, 1976.

Sanchez, Sonia. *Crisis in Culture: Two Speeches by Sonia Sanchez.* New York: Black Library Press, 1983.

———. *I'm Black When I'm Singing, I'm Blue When I Ain't and Other Plays.* Edited by Jacqueline Wood. Durham, N.C.: Duke University Press, 2010.

———, ed. *We Be Word Sorcerers: 25 Stories by Black Americans.* New York: Bantam Books, 1973.

Troupe, Quincy, ed. *Watts Poets: A Book of New Poetry and Essays.* Los Angeles: House of Respect, 1968.

———, and Rainer Schulte, eds. *Giant Talk: An Anthology of Third World Writings.* New York: Random House, 1975.

Post-BAM Scholarship and Anthologies

Baraka, Amina, and Amiri Baraka, eds. *Confirmation: An Anthology of African American Women.* New York: Morrow, 1983.

Baraka, Amiri. *The Autobiography of LeRoi Jones.* Chicago: Lawrence Hill, 1997.

Benston, Kimberly. *Performing Blackness: Enactments of African-American Modernism.* New York: Routledge, 2000.

The Black Power Movement. Part 1, Amiri Baraka from Black Arts to Black Radicalism [microform]. Editorial adviser: Komozi Woodard. Project Coordinator, Randolph H. Boehm. Bethesda, Md.: University Publications of America, 2000.

Boyd, Melba Joyce. *Wrestling with the Muse: Dudley Randall and Broadside Press.* New York: Columbia University Press, 2003.

Braxton, Joanne M., and Andrée Nicola McLaughlin, eds. *Wild Women in the Whirlwind: Afra-American Culture and the Contemporary Literary Renaissance.* New Brunswick, N.J.: Rutgers University Press, 1990.

Bunge, Nancy, ed. *Conversations with Clarence Major.* Jackson: University Press of Mississippi, 2002.

Clarke, Cheryl. *"After Mecca": Women Poets and the Black Arts Movement.* New Brunswick, N.J.: Rutgers University Press, 2005.

Collins, Lisa Gail, and Margo Natalie Crawford, eds. *New Thoughts on the Black Arts Movement.* New Brunswick, N.J.: Rutgers University Press, 2006.

Dick, Bruce, and Amrijit Singh, eds. *Conversations with Ishmael Reed.* Jackson: University Press of Mississippi, 1995.

Douglas, Robert L. *Resistance, Insurgence, and Identity: The Art of Mari Evans, Nelson Stevens, and the Black Arts Movement.* Trenton, N.J.: Africa World Press, 2008.

Evans, Mari, ed. *Black Women Writers (1950–1980): A Critical Evaluation.* New York: Anchor Press/Doubleday, 1983.

Flowers, Sandra Hollis. *African American Nationalist Literature of the 1960s: Pens of Fire.* New York: Garland, 1996.

Fowler, Virginia C., ed. *Conversations with Nikki Giovanni.* Jackson: University Press of Mississippi, 1992.

Gabbin, Joanne V., ed. *Furious Flower: African American Poetry from the Black Arts Movement to the Present.* Charlottesville: University of Virginia Press, 2004.

————, ed. *The Furious Flowering of African American Poetry.* Charlottesville: University of Virginia Press, 1999.

Gayles, Gloria Wade, ed. *Conversations with Gwendolyn Brooks.* Jackson: University Press of Mississippi, 2003.

Hall, Joan Wylie, ed. *Conversations with Audre Lorde.* Jackson: University Press of Mississippi, 2004.

Joyce, Joyce A., ed. *Conversations with Sonia Sanchez.* Jackson: University Press of Mississippi, 2007.

————. *Ijala: Sonia Sanchez and the African Poetic Tradition.* Chicago: Third World Press, 1996.

Melhem, D. H. *Heroism in the New Black Poetry: Introductions & Interviews.* Lexington: University of Kentucky Press, 1990.

Nielsen, Aldon Lynn. *Black Chant: Languages of African-American Postmodernism.* New York: Cambridge University Press, 1997.

————. *Integral Music: Languages of African-American Innovation.* Tuscaloosa: University of Alabama Press, 2004.

Ongiri, Amy Abugo. *Spectacular Blackness: The Cultural Politics of the Black Power Movement and the Search for a Black Aesthetic.* Charlottesville: University of Virginia Press, 2009

Parks, Carole A., ed. *Nommo: A Literary Legacy of Black Chicago (1967–1987): An OBAC Anthology.* Chicago: OBAhouse, 1987.

Reilly, Charlie, ed. *Conversations with Amiri Baraka.* Jackson: University Press of Mississippi, 1994.

Rambsy, Howard. *The Black Arts Enterprise and the Production of African American Poetry.* Ann Arbor: University of Michigan Press, 2011.

Sell, Mike. *Avant Garde Performance and the Limits of Criticism.* Ann Arbor: University of Michigan Press, 2006.

Smethurst, James Edward. *The Black Arts Movement: Literary Nationalism in the 1960s and 1970s.* Chapel Hill: University of North Carolina Press, 2005.

Standley, Fred R., and Louis H. Pratt, eds. *Conversations with James Baldwin.* Jackson: University Press of Mississippi, 1989.

Taylor-Guthrie, Danille, ed. *Conversations with Toni Morrison.* Jackson: University Press of Mississippi, 1993.

Thomas, Lorenzo. *Don't Deny Me My Name: Words and Music and the Black Intellectual Tradition.* Edited and with an Introduction by Aldon Lynn Nielsen. Ann Arbor: University of Michigan Press, 2008.

———. *Extraordinary Measures: Afrocentric Modernism and Twentieth-Century American Poetry.* Tuscaloosa: University of Alabama Press, 2000.

Thompson, Julius. *Dudley Randall, Broadside Press, and the Black Arts Movement in Detroit, 1960–1995.* Jefferson, N.C.: McFarland, 1999.

Van Deburg, William L. *New Day in Babylon: The Black Power Movement and American Culture, 1965–1975.* Chicago: University of Chicago Press, 1992.

Ward, Jerry W., Jr. *Trouble the Water: 250 Years of African-American Poetry.* New York: Penguin, 1997.

Widener, Daniel. *Black Arts West: Culture and Struggle in Postwar Los Angeles.* Durham, N.C.: Duke University Press, 2010.